Brewer's Anthology
of England
and the English

Brewer's Anthology of England and the English

David Milsted

CASSELL&CO

My thanks to everybody who,
in many ways, has helped me
to make this book:

To Richard Milbank, who took
to the idea of it over coffee at my
kitchen table in March 1999, and
has seen me through to the end of it;
may *Ex pede Herculem* be one day
emblazoned on his escutcheon;

To Rosie Anderson, the most
sympathetic of editors;

To Ian Crofton, for services well
beyond the call of copy-editing;

To Vastiana Belfon, Sid Blanche,
Margaret Busby, Jonathon Green,
David Kifer, Frank Lynch,
Lewis Milsted, Philip Payton,
Jeremy Taylor, and Francis Wheen;

And to all the copyright holders for
their permission to quote extracts,
and whole poems, in this book.

THIS BOOK IS FOR ANNIE

and in memory of

RODERICK MILSTED (1905–85)

and

MARY MILSTED (1920–96)

Contents

'Speak for England'

This book was conceived and compiled as a 'parliament of voices', most of them English, some not, speaking across roughly fifteen hundred years, on the subject of England, the English and Englishness. Its working title – the words the Conservative MP Leo Amery called across the floor of the House of Commons to the Labour leader Arthur Henderson in the War Debate of September 1939 – appears above (and the story behind it on pages 183–84). It has been two years, on and off, in the making. I have enjoyed every minute of it.

First, a note about how this book came to be. It is not the product of a committee, nor of a team of researchers; I am not, in that sense, its 'editor'. It is a *personal* selection; its faults, its virtues, and its editorial opinions, are mine. Comments are welcome; please note, however, that this anthology complies with the two Golden Rules of all anthologies: (1) It includes material you think should have been left out; (2) It leaves out material you think should have been included. There are all sorts of explanations for this; all of them are valid. No anthology is ever complete.

Let us define and establish our terms. First, there is the matter of the 'British/English Dichotomy', as someone has no doubt called it, and how to avoid giving offence by getting stuck in it.

The original inhabitants of England were Britons – before, as Noël Coward somewhat inaccurately put it:

> those beastly Roman bowmen
> Ditched our local yeomen.

One of those beastly Romans, Tacitus, writing in AD 98, was witheringly dismissive of us:

> Who the first inhabitants of Britain were, whether natives or immigrants, remains obscure; one must remember we are dealing with barbarians.

George Mikes observed half a century ago that 'When people say England, they sometimes mean Great Britain, sometimes the United Kingdom, sometimes the British Isles – but never England.' That is certainly less true than it was, but it was only a few years ago that an Irish acquaintance, met on the Galway-to-Dublin bus, said, on learning that I lived in the Isle of Skye: 'Ah, yes, it's a lovely part of England, Scotland.'

I have taken what seems to me a commonsensical approach. When an American comments on 'the typical British stiff upper lip' he is clearly not referring to the Scots, Welsh or Irish; on the other hand, when Para Handy refers to himself as 'wan o' Britain's hardy sons' he certainly isn't claiming to be English. Using this rule – so simple as not to need defining further, yet so elegant as to be incapable of further definition – I have left out 'Rule, Britannia' but included 'England expects ...'. I hope that makes things quite clear and inoffensive. (Anyone who really wants to be offended may turn immediately to the short section entitled 'Other Bits of Britain'.)

Now, as to what I mean by 'the English' – and all the rest of it. I am almost certainly one of those 'Anglo-Saxons' whom a retiring Tory MP recently said were 'under threat of dilution' by immigrants. This might be a good place to put his mind at rest. I am, of course, as English as they come – meaning that I was born and raised in a small Sussex village and that I'm roughly 25% something else; Scots, in my case, through a Gaelic-speaking MacGregor grandmother (she was born in a house in Inverness in whose garden grows a tree planted in 1746, in memory of the fallen at Culloden). I have lived for fifteen years in Scotland, and a part of me rightly belongs there. My four sons were born in Scotland (three of them were born in Orkney, so if the Northern Isles ever decide to join Norway they'll have an extra allegiance to choose from).

My father was born in Allahabad. The house he grew up in overlooks the Ganges. When India became independent in 1947 he found himself obliged to produce grandparental birth certificates in order to prove his entitlement to a British passport. He qualified thanks to Roderick MacGregor – born, two years after the compulsory registration of births, in Skye. His father's family, for umpteen generations, had lived in the village of Milsted, in Kent; some of them still do. So, thanks to my father, my four sons could, if they wanted to and were good enough, play international football for one of three countries.

Since much of the old MacGregor territory was once settled by Vikings, I probably have the odd cell of Norse blood chugging around my system; and, according to recent DNA researches, I have a one-in-five chance of carrying the genes of at least one black ancestor – one black *English* ancestor, that is to say. Oh, and I have four Anglo-Nigerian second cousins, whose maternal grandfather is Manx.

My local football club, Yeovil Town, is nicknamed 'The Glovers' – thanks to all the Huguenot refugees who, driven out by Louis XIV of France, settled in these parts over three centuries ago. The small town I live in has a glove factory that dates from those times, and those people.

My two stepsons were born in Cambridgeshire, smack in the middle of the Danelaw, not far from where Hereward the Wake held out against William of

Normandy. (So far, so 'Anglo-Saxon' – or rather, so Anglo-Saxon-Jutish-Norse.) Their maternal grandfather was the result of a union between a Yorkshire Irishman and a Moravian-American. Their maternal grandmother's family hailed from the Border Country between Hexham and Berwick. On their father's side there is the usual quota of Scottish ancestry. They have two Anglo-Sierra Leonian cousins.

All in all, then, we are a pretty typical English family.

Now consider the family of Railton Beazer, described by Michael Wood in his book *In Search of England*. My paternal ancestors are lost in the Highland mist (Rob Roy is alleged to be among them), but Mr Beazer can trace his with accuracy back to a John Bezor of Little Sodbury, who emigrated to the colonies to seek his fortune (or perhaps it was just work) around 1720. Before that the trail gets fuzzier, although there are three Beasers recorded in Little Sodbury as being 'Fit for His Majesty's Services in the Wars' in 1608. The surname, Wood observes, is derived from the Norman French: Beausire. So it would seem that Railton Beazer can make that most blue-blooded of English claims: his family came over with the Conqueror. His bit of it left these shores in the early 18th century, and he himself came home in the 1950s – from Barbuda. As one might suspect, this Englishman is neither blond nor blue-eyed.

If all this appears to labour a point then it is, I think, a point worth labouring. One might think that Daniel Defoe's *True-Born Englishman* (deservedly quoted at length in the first chapter of this book) would be a sufficient response to people like that (mercifully) retiring MP; but then, Defoe does not – how shall we put it? – specifically mention people with non-pinko-grey skins. The point is not merely that the English are, and have been for well over a thousand years, arguably the most mongrel race on earth, but that 'being English' (and for that matter, nationality generally, but *especially* being English) is, and always has been, pre-eminently an attitude – perhaps 'habit' would be a better word – of mind; 'Englishness' is all that feeds that habit, and all that flows from it. It always has been and always will be. And the English – whether English by birth, by ancestry or by choice – are those who, to a greater or lesser degree, share in it. It has nothing to do with 'race'. To categorise the English as a 'race' is as absurd as to categorise library books by their size or the colour of their binding: what defines us is, in the words of the black American writer Shelby Steele, 'the content of our character'.

One could advance all sorts of powerful and irrefutable arguments against that expiring MP. All of them would be wasted. Extensive DNA sampling reveals the wonderful fact that a randomly sampled white English person will have, genetically speaking, more in common with a randomly sampled black African than with another person of the same so-called 'race'. But then, it's also true that the average human being has 80% of his or her genes in common with a potato. One is bound to conclude that some of us have more in common with the potato than others. All we can do is wait for such people to fade away – as, thankfully, they are doing, in England as much as (and probably more than) almost anywhere else.

Let us spare a thought for the 'Cricket Test'. For those of you who are happily too young to remember it, the Cricket Test was devised in the 1980s by the then chairman of the Conservative Party, Norman Tebbit. It was intended to gauge the 'loyalty' of English people with non-pinko-grey skins. It ran thus: 'When England are playing, which side do they cheer for?' The idea was that anyone who didn't always cheer for England (*England, England über alles*) Did Not Really Belong Here, And Ought To Consider Going Away. In that case, I for one don't really belong here. I support England when they play anyone, at anything – except when they are playing Scotland. Partly this is because (and you really can't get more English than this) Scotland – with a population one-seventh that of England's and, let's face it, no tradition either of cricket or of reliable goalkeeping – are the underdogs. And I do belong here; and so do all my non-pinko-grey second cousins and step-nieces and nephews, not to mention those of my Scottish-born sons who cheer for Scotland too. One wonders what Lord Tebbitt, as he now is, would have said to Alfred the Great: 'Angle or Saxon? Which side do you cheer for?' His day is done. We have moved on.

I am old enough to remember seeing signs in London windows that read: ROOM TO LET – NO COLOUREDS, NO IRISH, NO DOGS. In the last forty years we have shed a lot of shameful habits; we have grown up. Few would think of putting up a sign like that, these days – but what is much more to the point is that fewer and fewer of us would even fantasise about it. The Laws of England have made such racism illegal, and we have since been learning to drop the mental habit; it is no longer a part of Englishness, as the vast majority of us understand it. No candidate for the National Front or the equally repulsive British National Party has ever succeeded in being elected to the House of Commons, and none ever will. It is not so in many other countries. Is racism a thing of the past in England? Assuredly not – but it is becoming so, and one day will be.

So does this make England a Multi-Cultural Society? In my understanding of the term, no, it doesn't. To me, a 'multi-cultural society' is compartmentalised – even Balkanised – and not inclusive. England does not insist on 'melting-pot' assimilation, and never has, but the offer to join in is always there – and the large and growing number of inter-racial relationships in England shows the extent to which it is being taken up. England is an *Omni*-Cultural Society: diverse, variegated, equal-but-different, and still capable of drawing together, and pulling together, when the need arises; just as it always has been.

Surely, now, it is time for the English to stop being apologetic. It is time for the English to emerge from their 'state of denial'. We have for too long perfected the art of putting ourselves down; it is time for us, without boastfulness, humbly to acknowledge our virtues – and our history; that cultural baggage which, whether we want to or not, we all carry with us. If we do not know about it, we are impoverished, and the luggage becomes a burden rather than an asset.

One of my sons took his GCSEs last year. In History, he was examined in 'The Native Americans', 'Apartheid in South Africa', 'Medicine Through the Ages', and 'A Study of a Local Castle'. Only the last of these involved learning a modicum of the *story* of his country (of, indeed, *his* country). Of course he should know about these other things (some of his ancestors, as it happens, emigrated and intermarried with Native Americans, and some of his blood-relatives are of black African origin). He has a reasonable working knowledge of English History – the story of where he comes from and what he belongs to – but almost all of it has been gained at home. Is this a 'Good Thing'? I don't think so. You don't have to be Thomas Babington Macaulay to think that the story of the English is (warts and all) a story worth hearing. Of course we should learn about other cultures, other lands, other peoples and their histories – but we should learn all that *in addition* to learning about our own, not instead of it. An educated sense of national identity is a prerequisite of a civilised citizen; an ignorant, wilfully uninformed national identity is a gateway to barbarism.

When Martin Bell, the first Independent Member of Parliament to be elected since the abolition of the University constituencies in 1947, gave his victory speech in Tatton, Cheshire, in May 1997, he quoted G.K. Chesterton:

> Smile at us, pay us, pass us; but do not quite forget.
> For we are the people of England, that never have spoken yet.

Chesterton, it must be said, had many habits of mind that we, the English, now consider unacceptable: anti-Semitism, for one. But part of accepting, and respecting, one's past – and the people, our own ancestors, who lived in it – involves making allowances for the *mores* of past times, and not throwing the baby out with the bathwater. (Are you, dear reader, completely happy with everything you have ever said, or thought, or done, in your entire life? Of course you aren't. Does this mean you can't change, and still be the same person? Does this mean you are invalidated as a human being? Well, there you are then.)

The point is that all of us who live in England (and some of us who don't) *are* English, and that we have not spoken – out loud, and (with due but not outlandish acknowledgement of all our shortcomings) confidently – for some time. And we should. It helps us to be the better sort of people that we, deep down, believe ourselves to be. We are the people of England. We might as well get used to it. And we shouldn't be ashamed of ourselves because of it.

Am I proud to be English? Of course not: it's what I am, that's all. I might as well be proud to have blue eyes, or size 11 feet, and that would be silly.

Am I happy to be English? Yes.

Here's why.

DAVID MILSTED
david.milsted@virgin.net
Dorset, England

Questions of Identity

I FEEL ENGLISH, MY KIND OF ENGLISH.
Mike Phillips, quoted in Jonathon Green,
Them: Voices from the Immigrant Community in Contemporary Britain, 1990.

*'Who are the English?' is a question that has rarely bothered the English them-
selves; unlike, say, the USA, Britain does not insist that would-be 'new nation-
als' undergo a course of 'Englishism' or 'Britishisation' before being granted
citizenship. There was a great deal of excitement after the discovery of 'The First
Englishman' at Piltdown in Sussex, in 1912; but the first Englishman was proved
to have been cobbled together from odd bits of human and ape skull, and the DNA
profiling of Cheddar Man in 1997 was regarded as something interesting, rather
than as something of national (far less 'racial') significance.*

*The answer to the question would seem to be twofold: an English person is (a)
anyone who can trace his or her English ancestry back for 9,000-odd years, or
(b) anyone who lives here and feels like being English. (As some of the extracts in
the second part of this chapter show, not everyone who lives here does.) English
people are fully capable of being prejudiced, but they are seldom self-regarding –
and when they are, it is usually with self-deprecation. After the invention of
'Great Britain' in 1707, and of the 'United Kingdom' roughly a century later,
the English tended to take themselves for granted. Foreigners might say
'England', meaning 'Britain'; the English did the opposite. 'Made in England'
might apply to willow-pattern china, but not to people.*

*Three centuries after the Act of Union, England is beginning to re-emerge –
blinking, and more than a little bemused.*

A HOMOGENEOUS DIVERSITY

To go back to the very beginning:

A history teacher was 'overwhelmed' yesterday when scientists told him that he was a direct descendant of a hunter who lived in the Cheddar Gorge 9,000 years ago.

DNA from a tooth in the skull of Cheddar Man, the oldest complete skeleton found in Britain, matched a DNA sample from the mouth of Adrian Targett, 42, a teacher at Kings of Wessex School, Cheddar, Somerset. The matching gene can only be passed on through the female line and its discovery established that Mr Targett descended from Cheddar Man's mother.

He said yesterday: 'It is a very strange piece of news to receive. I'm not quite sure how I feel. . . . I was astonished when they said I was a descendant. I took part to make up the numbers. . . . Appropriately enough, I am a history teacher but I have to admit I know next to nothing about Cheddar Man. It is not my period. I suppose I should try to include him in my family tree – but going back 9,000 years could take some time. My family have been in these parts for a long time. On my father's side they were farm labourers. In archaeological terms it is very important that this has happened, I am just astonished it has happened to me. . . .'

Dr Bryan Sykes, who discovered the genetic match, said although the discovery was not surprising in scientific terms, it remained an intriguing piece of research. 'It is a fascinating demonstration of a direct link between ourselves and our pre-historic ancestors,' he said. 'We are revealing connections which go far beyond any written record.' . . .

Dr Sykes said the link undermined the theory that modern Europeans were largely descended from peoples who migrated from the East and brought farming techniques with them. 'Cheddar Man lived well before the advent of farming and this discovery shows a clear link between us and hunter-gatherers,' he said. . . .

Mr Targett's wife had the last word: 'Perhaps this explains why he likes his steaks rare,' she said.

Sean O'Neill, 'Cheddar Man is my long-lost relative', *Daily Telegraph*, 8 March 1997.

Few English people have as 'unsullied' an ancestry as Mr Targett, as Daniel Defoe explained:

> The Romans first with Julius Caesar came,
> Including all the nations of that name,
> Gauls, Greeks, and Lombards; and by computation,
> Auxiliaries or slaves of every nation.
> With Hengist, Saxons; Danes with Sueno came,
> In search of plunder, not in search of fame.
> Scots, Picts, and Irish from th' Hibernian shore:
> And conqu'ring William brought the Normans o're.
>   All these their barb'rous offspring left behind,
> The dregs of armies, they of all mankind;
> Blended with Britains who before were here,
> Of whom the Welsh ha' blessed the character.
>   From this amphibious ill-born mob began

That vain ill-natured thing, an Englishman.
The customs, surnames, languages, and manners,
Of all these nations are their own explainers:
Whose relics are so lasting and so strong,
They ha' left a shibboleth upon our tongue;
By which with easy search you may distinguish
Your Roman-Saxon-Danish-Norman English.
. . .

These are the heroes that despise the Dutch,
And rail at new-come foreigners so much;
Forgetting that themselves are all derived
From the most scoundrel race that ever lived.
A horrid medley of thieves and drones,
Who ransacked kingdoms, and dispeopled towns.
The Pict and painted Britain, treach'rous Scot,
By hunger, theft, and rapine, hither brought.
Norwegian pirates, buccaneering Danes,
Whose red-haired offspring everywhere remains.
Who joined with Norman-French, compound the breed
From whence your True-Born Englishmen proceed.
And lest by length of time it be pretended,
The climate may this modern breed ha' mended,
Wise Providence, to keep us where we are,
Mixes us daily with exceeding care:
We have been Europe's sink, the jakes where she
Voids all her offal out-cast progeny.
From our fifth Henry's time, the strolling bands
Of banished fugitives from neighb'ring lands,
Have here a certain sanctuary found.
. . .

Dutch, Walloons, Flemings, Irishmen, and Scots,
Vaudois and Valtolins, and Huguenots,
In good Queen Bess's charitable reign,
Supplied us with three hundred thousand men.
Religion, God we thank thee, sent them hither,
Priests, Protestants, the Devil and all together:
. . .

The offspring of this miscellaneous crowd,
Had not their new plantations long enjoyed,
But they grew Englishmen, and raised their votes
At foreign shoals of interloping Scots.
The royal branch from Pict-land did succeed,
With troops of Scots and scabs from North-by-Tweed.
The seven first years of his pacific reign,
Made him and half his nation Englishmen.
Scots from the northern frozen banks of Tay,

With packs and plods came whigging all away:
Thick as the locusts which in Egypt swarmed,
With pride and hungry hopes completely armed:
With native truth, diseases, and no money,
Plundered our Canaan of the milk and honey.
Here they grew quickly Lords and Gentlemen,
And all their race are True-Born Englishmen.
    The Civil Wars, the common purgative,
Which always use to make the nation thrive,
Made way for all that strolling congregation,
Which thronged in pious Ch[arle]s's restoration.
The royal refugee our breed restores,
With foreign courtiers, and with foreign whores:
And carefully repeopled us again,
Throughout his lazy, long, lascivious reign,
With such a blessed and True-Born English fry,
As much illustrates our nobility.
. . .
    French cooks, Scotch pedlars, and Italian whores,
Were all made Lords, or Lords' progenitors.
Beggars and bastards by his new creation,
Much multiplied the peerage of the nation;
Who will be all, e're one short age runs o're,
As True-Born Lords as those we had before.
    Then to recruit the Commons he prepares,
And heal the latent breaches of the wars:
The pious purpose better to advance,
He invites the banished Protestants of France:
Hither for God's sake and their own they fled,
Some for religion came, and some for bread:
Two hundred thousand pair of wooden shoes,
Who, God be thanked, had nothing left to lose;
To Heav'n's great praise did for religion fly,
To make us starve our poor in charity.
In every port they plant their fruitful train,
To get a race of True-Born Englishmen:
Whose children will, when riper years they see,
Be as ill-natured and as proud as we:
Call themselves English, foreigners despise,
Be surly like us all, and just as wise.
Thus from a mixture of all kinds began,
That het'rogeneous thing, an Englishman:
. . .
The Scot, Pict, Britain, Roman, Dane submit,
And with the English-Saxon all unite:
And these the mixture have so close pursued,

The very name and memory's subdued:
No Roman now, no Britain does remain;
Wales strove to separate, but strove in vain:
The silent nations undistinguished fall,
And Englishman's the common name for all.
Fate jumbled them together, God knows how;
Whate're they were, they're True-Born English now.
    The wonder which remains is at our pride,
To value that which all wise men deride.
For Englishmen to boast of generation,
Cancels their knowledge, and lampoons the nation.
A True-Born Englishman's a contradiction,
In speech an irony, in fact a fiction.
A banter made to be a test of fools,
Which those that use it justly ridicules.
A metaphor invented to express
A man akin to all the universe.
. . .

    But England, modern to the last degree.
Borrows or makes her own nobility,
And yet she boldly boasts of pedigree:
Repines that foreigners are put upon her,
And talks of her antiquity and honour . . . .

Daniel Defoe (1660–1731), from *The True-Born Englishman*, 1701.

The personification of England, the archetype of the English character, is John Bull, a figure created in 1712 by John Arbuthnot:

For the better understanding the following History, the reader ought to know, that Bull, in the main, was an honest plain-dealing fellow, cholerick, bold, and of a very unconstant Temper; … he was very apt to quarrel with his best Friends, especially if they pretended to govern him: If you flatter'd him, you might lead him like a child. John's Temper depended very much upon the Air; his spirits rose and fell with the Weatherglass. John was quick and understood his business very well; but no man alive was more careless in looking into his Accounts, or more cheated by Partners, Apprentices, and Servants. This was occasioned by his being a boon Companion, loving his Bottle and his Diversion; for, to say truth, no man kept a better House than John, nor spent his Money more generously.

John Arbuthnot (1667–1735), *The History of John Bull*, 1712, Part 1, chapter 5.

There is in the Englishman a combination of qualities, a modesty, an independence, a repose, combined with an absence of everything calculated to call a blush into the cheek of a young person, which one would seek in vain among the Nations of the Earth.

Charles Dickens (1812–70), Mr Podsnap in *Our Mutual Friend*, 1865.

By and large the Victorians were so convinced of the natural superiority of the English that they did not feel the need to make a song and dance about it. Gilbert and Sullivan were moved to make a satirical exception:

> ALL:
> He is an Englishman!
> BOATSWAIN:
> He is an Englishman!
> For he himself has said it,
> And it's greatly to his credit,
> That he is an Englishman!
> ALL:
> That he is an Englishman!
> BOAT:
> For he might have been a Roosian,
> A French, or Turk, or Proosian,
> Or perhaps Itali-an!
> ALL:
> Or perhaps Itali-an!
> BOAT:
> But in spite of all temptations
> To belong to other nations,
> He remains an Englishman!
> ALL:
> For in spite of all temptations,
> To belong to other nations,
> He is an Englishman –
> He is an Englishman!

W.S. Gilbert (1836–1911), *H.M.S. Pinafore*, 1878.

Ask any man what nationality he would prefer to be, and ninety-nine out of a hundred will tell you that they would prefer to be Englishmen.

Cecil Rhodes (1853–1902), in Gordon Le Sueur, *Cecil Rhodes*, 1913.

In 1902 Rhodes told an audience of schoolboys, 'Remember that you are an Englishman, and have consequently won first prize in the lottery of life.'

George Orwell was a patriot, a great lover of England, but not of the chauvinistic persuasion. In the darkest moments of the Second World War he struggled to find just what it was about England and the English …

When you come back to England from any foreign country, you have immediately the sensation of breathing a different air. Even in the first few minutes dozens of small things conspire to give you this feeling. The beer is bitterer, the coins are heavier, the grass is greener, the advertisements are more blatant. The crowds in the big towns, with their mild knobby faces, their bad teeth and gentle manners, are different from a European crowd. Then the vastness of England swallows you up, and you lose for a while your feeling that the whole nation has a single identifiable character. Are there really such things as nations? Are we not forty-six million individuals, all different? And the diversity of it, the chaos! The clatter of clogs in the Lancashire mill towns, the to-and-fro of the lorries on the Great North Road, the queues outside the Labour Exchanges, the rattle of pin-tables in the Soho pubs, the old maids biking to Holy Communion through the mists of the autumn morning – all these are not only fragments, but characteristic fragments, of the English scene. How can one make a pattern out of this muddle?

But talk to foreigners, read foreign books or newspapers, and you are brought back to the same thought. Yes, there is something distinctive and recognizable in English civilization. It is a culture as individual as that of Spain. It is somehow bound up with solid breakfasts and gloomy Sundays, smoky towns and winding roads, green fields and red pillar-boxes. It has a flavour of its own. Moreover it is continuous, it stretches into the future and the past, there is something in it that persists, as in a living creature. What can the England of 1940 have in common with the England of 1840? But then, what have you in common with the child of five whose photograph your mother keeps on the mantelpiece? Nothing, except that you happen to be the same person.

And above all, it is your civilization, it is you. However much you hate it or laugh at it, you will never be happy away from it for any length of time. The suet puddings and the red pillar-boxes have entered into your soul. Good or evil, it is yours, you belong to it, and this side the grave you will never get away from the marks that it has given you. . . .

We are a nation of flower-lovers, but also a nation of stamp-collectors, pigeon-fanciers, amateur carpenters, coupon-snippers, darts-players, crossword-puzzle fans. All the culture that is most truly native centres round things which even when they are communal are not official – the pub, the football match, the back garden, the fireside and the 'nice cup of tea'. The liberty of the individual is still believed in, almost as in the nineteenth century. But this has nothing to do with economic liberty, the right to exploit others for profit. It is the liberty to have a home of your own, to do what you like in your spare time, to choose your own amusements instead of having them chosen for you from above. The most hateful of all names in an English ear is Nosey Parker. It is obvious, of course, that even this purely private liberty is a lost cause. Like all other modern people, the English are in process of being numbered, labelled, conscripted, 'co-ordinated'. But the pull of their impulses is in the other direction, and the kind of regimentation that can be imposed on them will be modified in consequence. No party rallies, no Youth Movements, no coloured shirts, no Jew-baiting or 'spontaneous' demonstrations. No Gestapo either, in all probability. . . .

It is quite true that the so-called races of Britain feel themselves to be very different from one another. A Scotsman, for instance, does not thank you if you call him an Englishman. You can see the hesitation we feel on this point by the fact that we call our islands by no less than six different names, England, Britain, Great Britain, the British Isles, the United Kingdom and, in very exalted moments, Albion. Even the differences between north and south England loom large in our own eyes. But somehow these differences fade away the moment that any two Britons are confronted by a European. It is very rare to meet a foreigner, other than an American, who can distinguish between English and Scots or even English and Irish. To a Frenchman, the Breton and the Auvergnat seem very different beings, and the accent of Marseilles is a stock joke in Paris. Yet we speak of 'France' and 'the French', recognizing France as an entity, a single civilization, which in fact it is. So also with ourselves. Looked at from the outside, even the cockney and the Yorkshireman have a strong family resemblance. . . .

England is not the jewelled isle of Shakespeare's much-quoted message, nor is it the inferno depicted by Dr Goebbels. More than either it resembles a family, a rather stuffy Victorian family, with not many black sheep in it but with all its cupboards bursting with skeletons. It has rich relations who have to be kow-towed to and poor relations who are horribly sat upon, and there is a deep conspiracy of silence about the source of the family income. It is a family in which the young are generally thwarted and most of the power is in the hands of irresponsible uncles and bedridden aunts. Still, it is a family. It has its private language and its common memories, and at the approach of an enemy it closes its ranks. A family with the wrong members in control – that, perhaps, is as near as one can come to describing England in a phrase.

George Orwell (1903–50), *The Lion and the Unicorn*, 1941.

When people say England, they sometimes mean Great Britain, sometimes the United Kingdom, sometimes the British Isles – but never England.

George Mikes (1912–87), *How to be an Alien*, 1946.

When the CURTAIN rises, it is a typically English evening at home. Typical English MR SMITH, in his favourite armchair L of the fireplace, wearing English slippers, is smoking an English pipe and reading an English newspaper. He is wearing English spectacles and has a small grey English moustache. Typically English MRS SMITH is seated in the armchair L of the table, darning English socks. There is a long English silence. An English clock chimes three English chimes.

MRS SMITH: Goodness! Nine o'clock! This evening for supper we had soup, fish, cold ham and mashed potatoes and a good English salad, and we had English beer to drink. The children drank English water. We had a very good meal this evening. And that's because we are English, because we live in a suburb of London and because our name is Smith.

Eugene Ionesco (1912–94), *The Bald Prima Donna* ('La Cantatrice Chauve'), 1950, tr. Donald Watson. This play has been running continuously in Paris since its first performance on 11 May 1950 – a record that beats even that of *The Mousetrap*.

I have been blessed with God's two greatest gifts,
to be born English and heterosexual.

John Osborne (1929–94), quoted in John Mortimer, 'The Angry Young Man Who Stayed That Way', *New York Times*, 8 January 1995.

At the turn of the millennium, as the Welsh gained their Assembly, the Scots restored their Parliament and home rule returned to Northern Ireland, the question of the nature of English – as opposed to British – identity has re-emerged:

No one could expect a country's sense of itself to remain constant for ever. Naturally, it evolves with history. Nevertheless, it must share some common values or it will fall apart. In the past, the inclusion of most people into the common whole meant the exclusion of others. Blacks, women, homosexuals and Jews have all at different times been excluded. Today's challenge is to support ideals to which as many of the population as possible can subscribe. But the danger may not be that the British are too excluding of those who display divergent tastes and attitudes, but too inclusive. One aspect of national identity must be the assumption of shared standards. Those standards have become elusive, in an age in which it seems that virtually no manifestation of individuality, or even perversion, is too extreme to find general censure. ...

There was a time when people routinely stood to attention during the national anthem, wherever it was heard and whatever they were otherwise doing. By the 1960s, it had become the signal for filmgoers to start trooping out of the cinema when it was played at the end of the programme. Now, children are not taught its words. Again, this is all very different from America, where families regularly – and with apparent pride – join together in singing the American anthem at the close of football and baseball matches. What is true for Britain as a whole is doubly so of England. A sense of persecution gives zest to the self-expression of the other countries in the United Kingdom. The Welsh proudly wear leeks on St David's Day; the Scots celebrate St Andrew's Day and drink themselves patriotically stupid on Burns Night; the Irish variously sport shamrocks on St Patrick's Day or relive the Battle of the Boyne on 12 July. But nobody in England wears a red rose on St George's Day; many people do not even know when St George's Day is. Red nose day has a greater currency than red rose day.

Clive Aslet (1951–), *Anyone for England?*, 1997.

The myth that the English were the original inhabitants of this island is still, I suspect, believed by many English people, as a poll of the nearest bus queue or shopping mall would demonstrate. This belief sanctifies the status quo. The 'real' natives of Britain are the English. Anyone else is somehow a foreigner, a Taff, a Jock or Mick. So universal is this perception and so powerful that real foreigners, those from beyond the sea, themselves use 'British' and 'English' as interchangeable; most of their languages have some form of 'Anglo', Anglais, Inglese, Englisch, to describe the inhabitants of Great Britain, otherwise known on official forms as the United Kingdom, a bow towards the Ulster loyalists with the inclusion of Northern Ireland. I can't think of another state that has so many recognized versions of its name, in itself an indication of a confused identity, or that seems to need reinforcement by the highly centralized form of government of the last three centuries and the repeated affirmation of the national myths. Behind the mask of English phlegm, often seen as a form of arrogance, must lie a deep uncertainty about who we are. Recent moves towards devolution and the terror of absorption into a federal European state have only highlighted our insecurity and increased our dependence on the myth of olde England.

Maureen Duffy (1933–), *England: The Making of the Myth*, 2001.

A DIVERSE HOMOGENEITY

Towards the beginning of this chapter, Daniel Defoe remarked (in detail) on the very mixed origins of the English among wave after wave of immigrants, all of whom became absorbed and homogenised. Since his time, further peoples have come to settle in England, and it is their voices and experiences that make up much of this part of the chapter.

Ireland almost in as true a state of rebellion as America. – Admirals quarrelling in the West-Indies – and at home Admirals that do not choose to fight. – The British empire mouldering away in the West – annihilated in the North – Gibraltar going – and England fast asleep. . . . For my part, it's nothing to me as I am only a lodger – and hardly that.

Ignatius Sancho (1729–80), black English shopkeeper, musician and writer, letter, late 1770s.

In *The Prelude*, William Wordsworth recalled a visit to London in 1791, and celebrated its cosmopolitanism:

Now homeward through the thickening hubbub, where
See, among less distinguishable shapes,
The begging scavenger, with hat in hand;
The Italian, as he threads his way with care,
Steadying, far-seen, a frame of images
Upon his head; with basket at his breast
The Jew; the stately and slow-moving Turk,
With freight of slippers piled beneath his arm!

Enough; – the mighty concourse I surveyed
With no unthinking mind, well pleased to note
Among the crowd all specimens of man,
Through all the colours which the sun bestows
And every character of form and face:
The Swede, the Russian; from the genial south,
The Frenchman and the Spaniard; from remote
America the Hunter-Indian; Moors,
Malays, Lascars, the Tartar, the Chinese,
And Negro Ladies in white muslin gowns.

William Wordsworth (1770–1850), in *The Prelude*, 1850, Book VII.

Not all the English were as welcoming …

It is niggers this and niggers that,
And send the bastards back
But when Blissett or Chamberlain score for England,
It's wave the Union Jack.

Anonymous Wembley graffito, quoted in Woolnough, *Black Magic*, 1980.

Yes, it is wonderful to be British – until one comes to Britain.

Edward R. Braithwaite (1920–), Guyanese writer, *To Sir With Love*, 1959.

In England I was taken to be a foreigner. I was continually being asked where I was from. I would invariably say Nigeria; but it would have been equally accurate, in some ways more so, if I had said England. That I didn't was telling. By rejecting my Englishness, I was colluding in a subtle form of racism. I couldn't be English, I was assuring them, since I was clearly not white.

Adewale Maja-Pearce (1953–), British-born writer, critic and editor, *In My Father's Country: A Nigerian Journey*, 1987.

Labour say he's black. Tories say he's British.

Conservative Party election poster caption, 1983, beneath a photograph of a black man.

Intended to portray 'inclusiveness', the poster was not always received that way; Caryl Philips (1997) wrote: 'Implicit in the new Thatcherite concept of nationhood was the idea that one could not be both black and British'. The opposite view is equally tenable.

The following extracts are from Jonathon Green, *Them: Voices from the Immigrant Community in Contemporary Britain*, 1990:

The crucial issue in this country for both black and white people is what does it mean to be an English person? Am I English, having lived here since 1956? I was coming in from France the other day and I had forgotten to fill in a landing card – I still have a Guyanese passport. This girl in her 20s, working as an immigration officer, told me to fill it in. So I did. But it struck me that I had been living in this country considerably longer than she had been alive. And that goes for a number of my white colleagues, and the kids whom I am teaching. So I feel that they can't tell me what it means to be English. I've been English longer than they have. I feel English, my kind of English. I'm not an English person like Ken Livingstone or Prince Charles, I'm my own kind, the kind of English person who came here in 1956 and lived in bloody Islington and lived in London most of his life. With a different history and so on, but that's still what it means to be English too. That is the struggle, that is one of the things that we have to begin to understand. In the United States a black population like ours would be saying, 'We are Caribbean-Americans.' If we work by the same logic here we would be saying, 'We are black English people, this is the kind of English people we are; as such we are part of this state and this state should reform its identity to allow for that.' In fact what we do is this business of adopting or readopting Caribbean manners and dialects and music and so forth. Which seems to me a sort of cop-out, this never having had the confidence to make a claim on the identity of this nation. . . .

The crucial thing to me is the sense in which the black community is a bastard offspring of England. What interests me now is the sense in which blacks and whites in England, and especially in London, are coming to share a difficult identity, an identity which is difficult and which has to be constantly negotiated. Neither side is quite aware of what they are doing, even while they are engaged in the process. Most black people have more relationships with white people than they do with black people. When you go to work you're not working only with black people; you might even be the only black person there. So this theme interests me: the sense in which we are negotiating our identity in this country, what the country is, what the nation is, what we all are, without being conscious of it.

Mike Phillips

You can't become English, ever. One never becomes English, but one likes them. I don't feel British. I don't know what that means. I like England as a geographical entity. I like the way of life. I am sure that if I were in France I would have found all the good side of France as well. Or Italy. I think I'm pretty adaptable. Things haven't been as forbidding as England was in the spring of '34. One is quite welcome, as long as you know that you're not one of us. As long as one knows one's place.

Alla Weaver

I lived here since 1948. I don't feel English or German. Not even in between. And it doesn't worry me at all. As somebody said, if Mary were at the North Pole the North Pole would just become 'at Mary's.'

Mary Rose

I'm a Londoner. These streets are as much mine as anyone else's. I would hate ever to come back here and be a tourist. I want to leave, but I'll always be a Londoner. If I did leave, it would be to Tobago. I hate this thing where people come back, 'I used to live here, I used to have a place over there …' No way. I pay taxes. I've paid my fucking dues. There ain't nobody going to push me around out there. This is my country. I have the passport. I'm a Brit.

Wilf Walker

I belong, I have rights, and there's nobody going to take my rights away. You better believe it. I don't join things, I'm not a joiner. I belong. The National Front can't say to me: if you don't like it, then why don't you go home. They can't say that. I've defended this country, I've got a medal for being in Malaya. I've helped to make this country what it is.

Vincent Reid

I feel very British. I wouldn't swear by the Queen, and I wouldn't promise to be loyal to her personally, but if anything goes wrong or anyone attacks Britain in a way that would harm the national interest yes, I would fight for it. I did swear an oath when I was made a citizen but that doesn't make me a patriot. Millions do it. After all, what Mrs Thatcher is doing to Britain, selling most of it to America, is hardly patriotic. So definitions of loyalty and patriotism might differ; but if I saw anyone doing positive harm to the interests of Britain as a community I will fight to defend it. I don't need an oath for that, it is what comes naturally. I am not an alien, I am a part of this community; they might not like me, but that doesn't worry me one way or another: I am here and I am part of it.

Shreeram Vidyarthi

I see myself as precisely what I am: somebody of Pakistani/Indian origin – I don't really recognise Partition – who happens to be culturally English, and that is exactly what I am. I feel almost completely English. Although there is the very strong knowledge that I am not. I don't feel alien, but I do feel an outsider. I know that I'm not English, and would never, as some people do, make any decision for instance to change my name and pass, say, as East European. In an argument I will always bring up the point that I am not English, if it is relevant to the argument. Just before the '79 election, I met a chap from the Conservative research department. I was saying that I wasn't going to vote Tory. I agreed on the whole with the policies Mrs Thatcher was putting forward, and on the whole I agreed with her immigration policy, but there had been a very callous speech on race relations she had made quite recently, and the end product of that would be that some poor sod in the East End was going to be beaten up. So I said that was why I wouldn't vote for her. He said, 'But Anwar, you must understand about immigrants ...' and started telling me how they all stuck together, cheated the system, etc., etc. So I said, 'Excuse me, Adrian, I am one.' 'Ah,' he said, 'you're different.' I said, 'No, I'm not, and if I saw somebody being beaten up in the East End I would pile in and help him.'

Anwar Bati

I became a naturalized British subject after the war. I have a British passport but it is very difficult to say what 'feeling British' means. I was the child of Polish Jewish parents, born and educated in Berlin, and as an adolescent was uprooted and asked to start a new life in this country. Each period of my life has deeply influenced me. When I lecture abroad I might say, 'In England we do it this way'. I could not bring myself to say, 'We British do it this way.' My home is here and my friends are here.

Bianca Gordon

How British do I feel? I went to Paris on one of my early forays into Europe and hung out with black Parisians. They called me English. 'Hey Eeengleesh!' and I realised there and then that I couldn't escape England. I couldn't be French. Even though I stayed in Paris I would still be called English even by black people from the Caribbean. They think French, their desires, the way they do things, their culture is French. They see the English in me, not just the language, but what I wear, the songs I sing, the way I phrase things, the way I think. It's all 'Brittanique' and not 'à la France.' So yes, I do feel English. I do feel British in the sense that I use the language and the culture to communicate and live. But I don't feel English in a patriotic sense of waving our flag and so on. But especially in the face of non English-speaking peoples I feel English. I have Moroccans who come to my office and they look up to me to correct them, their language, their behaviour, to help them fit into an English standard of living. Like most Caribbeans I've been inculcated with English. Not just the language, but English the thing. I've lived here many more years than I did in the Caribbean. I'm not half way across the Atlantic, I'm here. I do want eventually to retire in the Caribbean, but that's nothing to do with the culture there, just the sun and the sand. And the anonymity. I won't be identified as a black man. That's a treasure, you're just another person walking down the street. There's nobody black in the Caribbean in that sense. Like you're not Jewish in Israel.

Desmond Gittens

A leading Tory MP called last night for a St George's Day 'write-in' campaign by the English to assert their identity in this year's census.

There is no separate box for the English in the ethnicity section of the census, though there is for the Irish. In Scotland, there is a 'tick box' for Scottish as an ethnic group and the Welsh have been targeted by a campaign encouraging them to write in their origins under 'any other white background'.

Last night, Gerald Howarth, Conservative MP for Aldershot, said the English should do the same.

Mr Howarth ... said he would write in 'Anglo-Scot' under 'any other white background'. He added: 'My family will write "English" and I urge every other Englishman and woman to do the same.' ...

A spokesman said it was open to anyone to use the space to describe their ethnic origin. 'When the form was tested, the English appeared happier to describe themselves as British,' he said. ...

Census confusion has reinforced the threat to the concept of a separate English identity highlighted by research published today. A study by Young and Rubicam, the advertisers, suggests that, while Scots and Welsh are considered to have distinctive national features, the English are often synonymous with more generally British attributes.

While the English were seen by many as independent, tolerant, and lovers of tradition, these characteristics were also ascribed to the British as a whole.

Asked which brands they most associated with England and the United Kingdom, respondents gave identical results, selecting the BBC, the RAF, the Royal Navy and Channel 4. ...

A different picture emerged when English, Scots and Welsh were asked what they thought of one another. Scots and the Welsh considered the British as a whole to be 'socially responsible' and 'restrained' but considered the English to be 'arrogant', 'independent', and 'unapproachable'.

Scots also associated England with Beefeater and Little Chef restaurants and with the Liberal Democrats.

Philip Johnston, report, *Daily Telegraph*, 23 April 2001.

'Dear Old,
Bloody Old England'

DEAR OLD, BLOODY OLD ENGLAND
OF TELEGRAPH POLES AND TIN,
SEEMINGLY SO INDIFFERENT
AND WITH SO LITTLE SOUL TO WIN.
John Betjeman (1906–84), from 'A Lincolnshire Church', in *Selected Poems*, 1948.

John Betjeman's line gives the title to a chapter looking at some perceptions of the best and worst of England and Englishness. A strong current of the English trait of nostalgia flows through both. Nothing causes so much English bile as the comparison between the way things are, and the way they were, and therefore ought to be; the most characteristic English patriotism is a deep loyalty to a Country of the Past. Much of what we celebrate and cherish is (and always has been) perceived as going, or already gone. The future never turns out as good as it was cracked up to be, the past was nearly always better, and the present is nothing more (and certainly nothing better) than the endlessly recurring process by which good things go irredeemably bad. Even when we capture and sing the joy of the moment it is often with the pang of imminent loss; conversely, when things go horribly wrong, we feel a duty to look on the bright side. Eric Idle, nailed to a cross in Monty Python's Life of Brian *and singing 'Always look on the bright side of life', is an Englishman in Bronze-Age Palestine. We reduce ecstasy to 'quite nice, really' and agony to 'mustn't grumble'. We are Laodiceans, neither hot nor cold, living in a state of complacent discontent, in which 'England! With all thy faults I love thee still' is indistinguishable from 'England! With all your virtues, I despair of you'. Dear old, bloody old England suits us, as we suit it.*

THE DEAR: ENGLISH PASTORAL

The possessive love the English bear for everything that is implied in the word 'country-side' – whether it is experienced, remembered or idealised – runs very deep. While much else that is 'typical' of England will be found elsewhere in this book, this section is unashamedly rural, dealing not with Nature (which is entire unto itself) but with a landscape and the ways of life that go with it; a landscape that has been created, and tended, and loved, by English people. Think with warmth and affection of England, and you yearn for what follows.

An early celebration of spring in the English countryside comes from Geoffrey Chaucer, in a passage vivid enough to be preserved in the original Middle English:

Whan that Aprille with his shoures soote
The droghte of March hath perced to the roote,
And bathed every veyne in swich licour
Of which vertu engendred is the flour;
Whan Zephirus eek with his sweete breeth
Inspired hath in every holt and heeth
The tendre croppes, and the yonge sonne
Hath in the Ram his halve cours yronne,
And smale foweles maken melodye,
That slepen al the nyght with open ye
(So priketh hem nature in hir corages);
Thanne longen folk to goon on pilgrimages ...

Geoffrey Chaucer (c.1343–1400), from the General Prologue
to the *Canterbury Tales*, begun about 1386.

Chaucer also gives this portrait of simple rural virtues:

There was a Plowman with him there, his brother
Many a load of dung one time or other
He must have carted through the morning dew.
He was an honest worker, good and true,
Living in peace and perfect charity,
And, as the gospel bade him, so did he,
Loving God best with all his heart and mind
And then his neighbour as himself, repined
At no misfortune, slacked for no content,
For steadily about his work he went
To thrash his corn, to dig or to manure
Or make a ditch; and he would help the poor
For love of Christ and never take a penny
If he could help it, and, as prompt as any,
He paid his tithes in full when they were due
On what he owned, and on his earnings too.

Geoffrey Chaucer (c.1343–1400), from the General Prologue
to the *Canterbury Tales*, translated by Nevill Coghill, 1951.

The English Arcadia is to be found under the greenwood tree, in the company of Robin Hood and his merry men – as celebrated in this anonymous 15th-century poem:

> In somer when the shawes be sheyne,
> And leves be large and long,
> Hit is full merry in feyre foreste
> To here the foulys song.
>
> To se the dere draw to the dale
> And leve the hilles hee,
> And shadow him in the leves grene
> Under the green-wode tree.
>
> Hit befell on Whitsontide
> Early in a May mornyng,
> The Sonne up faire can shyne,
> And the briddis mery can syng.
>
> 'This is a mery mornyng,' said Litulle Johne,
> 'Be Hym that dyed on tre;
> A more mery man than I am one
> Lyves not in Christiantè
>
> 'Pluk up thi hert, my dere mayster,'
> Litulle Johne can say,
> 'And thynk hit is a fulle fayre tyme
> In a mornynge of May.'

Anonymous, 15th century, 'May in the Green-Wood'.

In *As You Like It*, Shakespeare created an Arcadia in which the politics of his age were cleansed and healed; he set it in a Warwickshire landscape of his boyhood, the Forest of Arden:

> Now, my co-mates and brothers in exile,
> Hath not old custom made this life more sweet
> Than that of painted pomp? Are not these woods
> More free from peril than the envious court?
> Here feel we not the penalty of Adam;
> The seasons' difference, as the icy fang
> And churlish chiding of the winter's wind,
> Which, when it bites and blows upon my body
> Even till I shrink with cold, I smile and say
> 'This is no flattery; these are counsellors
> That feelingly persuade me what I am.'
> Sweet are the uses of adversity,
> Which, like the toad, ugly and venomous,
> Wears yet a precious jewel in his head;
> And this our life, exempt from public haunt,

Finds tongues in trees, books in the running brooks,
Sermons in stones, and good in everything.

William Shakespeare (1564–1616), *As You Like It*, 1599, II.i.

Under the greenwood tree
    Who loves to lie with me,
And turn his merry note
    Unto the sweet bird's throat,
Come hither, come hither, come hither.
    Here shall he see no enemy
But winter and rough weather.

Who doth ambition shun
    And loves to live i' th' sun,
Seeking the food he eats,
    And pleased with what he gets,
Come hither, come hither, come hither.
    Here shall he see no enemy
But winter and rough weather.

William Shakespeare (1564–1616), song from *As You Like It*, 1599, II.v.

Shakespeare also supplied us with a more general, and indeed definitive, celebration of England:

This royal throne of kings, this sceptered isle,
This earth of majesty, this seat of Mars,
This other Eden, demi-paradise,
This fortress built by Nature for herself
Against infection and the hand of war,
This happy breed of men, this little world,
This precious stone set in the silver sea,
Which serves it in the office of a wall,
Or as a moat defensive to a house,
Against the envy of less happier lands,
This blessèd plot, this earth, this realm, this England . . .
This land of such dear souls, this dear, dear land. . . .

William Shakespeare (1564–1616), *Richard II*, 1595, II.i.

In the Augustan Age, Dryden reconstructed the English Arcadia in more overtly Classical terms:

Fairest Isle, all Isles Excelling,
Seat of Pleasures, and of Loves;
Venus here will chuse her Dwelling,
And forsake her Cyprian Groves.

Cupid, from his Fav'rite Nation,
Care and Envy will Remove;
Jealousy that poysons Passion,
And Despair that dies for Love.

Gentle Murmurs, sweet Complaining,
Sighs that blow the Fire of Love;
Soft Repulses, kind Disdaining,
Shall be all the Pains you prove.

Ev'ry Swain shall pay his Duty,
Grateful ev'ry Nymph shall prove;
And as these Excel in Beauty,
Those shall be Renown'd for Love.

John Dryden (1631–1700), 'song of Venus', from *King Arthur*, 1691.

Pope also borrowed Classical imagery in his long topographical poem, *Windsor Forest*, which he wrote during the reign of the last Stuart monarch, Anne, and published in 1713 to celebrate the Treaty of Utrecht. The poem, which has been subjected to many political interpretations, is also an evocation of the quiet beauties of rural England, in which Nature is moderated by Order and Industry:

The groves of *Eden*, vanish'd now so long,
Live in description, and look green in song:
These, were my breast inspir'd with equal flame,
Like them in beauty, should be like in fame.
Here hills and vales, the woodland and the plain,
Here earth and water, seem to strive again;
Not *Chaos* like together crush'd and bruis'd,
But as the world, harmoniously confus'd:
Where order in variety we see,
And where, tho' all things differ, all agree.
Here waving groves a checquer'd scene display,
And part admit, and part exclude the day;
As some coy nymph her lover's warm address
Nor quite indulges, nor can quite repress.
There, interspers'd in lawns and opening glades,
Thin trees arise that shun each other's shades.
Here in full light the russet plains extend;
There wrapt in clouds the blueish hills ascend.
Ev'n the wild heath displays her purple dyes,
And 'midst the desart fruitful fields arise,
That crown'd with tufted trees and springing corn,
Like verdant isles the sable waste adorn.
Let *India* boast her plants, nor envy we
The weeping amber or the balmy tree,
While by our oaks the precious loads are born,
And realms commanded which those trees adorn.
Not proud *Olympus* yields a nobler sight,
Tho' Gods assembled grace his tow'ring height,
Than what more humble mountains offer here,
Where, in their blessings, all those Gods appear.

> See *Pan* with flocks, with fruits *Pomona* crown'd,
> Here blushing *Flora* paints th' enamel'd ground,
> Here *Ceres'* gifts in waving prospect stand,
> And nodding tempt the joyful reaper's hand;
> Rich Industry sits smiling on the plains,
> And peace and plenty tell, a *Stuart* reigns.

Alexander Pope (1688–1744), *Windsor Forest*, 1713.

Pope's view of landscape combined the aesthetic with the functional, eschewing mere decoration or escapism. He expressed his matured vision in his epistle to Richard Boyle, the 3rd Earl of Burlington, the 'presiding genius' of the Palladian movement, and the patron of the great landscape gardener William Kent:

> Another age shall see the golden ear
> Embrown the slope, and nod on the parterre,
> Deep harvests bury all his pride has plann'd,
> And laughing Ceres reassume the land.
>   Who then shall grace, or who improve the soil?
> Who plants like Bathurst, or who builds like Boyle.
> 'Tis use alone that sanctifies expense,
> And splendour borrows all her rays from sense.
>   His father's acres who enjoys in peace,
> Or makes his neighbours glad, if he increase:
> Whose cheerful tenants bless their yearly toil,
> Yet to their Lord owe more than to the soil;
> Whose ample lawns are not asham'd to feed
> The milky heifer and deserving steed;
> Whose rising forests, not for pride or show,
> But future buildings, future navies, grow:
> Let his plantations stretch from down to down,
> First shade a country, and then raise a town.

Alexander Pope (1688–1744), from 'To Lord Burlington', *Epistles to Several Persons*, 1731.

A little later in the 18th century, Joseph Warton also sang the superiorities of 'Natural' landscape over the over-formalised layouts contrived by Art. As well as useful fields of nodding corn, Warton was prepared to entertain wilder scenes, marking the beginning of a shift from a Classical towards a more Romantic sensibility:

> Ye green-rob'd *Dryads*, oft' at dusky Eve
> By wondering Shepherds seen, to Forests brown,
> To unfrequented Meads, and pathless Wilds,
> Lead me from Gardens deckt with Art's vain Pomps.
> Can gilt Alcoves, can Marble-mimic Gods,
> Parterres embroider'd, Obelisks, and Urns
> Of high Relief; can the long, spreading Lake,
> Or Vista lessening to the Sight; can *Stow*
> With all her *Attic* Fanes, such Raptures raise,

As the Thrush-haunted Copse, where lightly leaps
The fearful Fawn the rustling Leaves along,
And the brisk Squirrel sports from Bough to Bough,
While from an hollow Oak the busy Bees
Hum drowsy Lullabies? ...
Rich in her weeping Country's Spoils *Versailles*
May boast a thousand Fountains, that can cast
The tortur'd Waters to the distant Heav'ns;
Yet let me choose some Pine-topt Precipice
Abrupt and shaggy, whence a foamy Stream,
Like *Anio*, tumbling roars; or some bleak Heath,
Where straggling stand the mournful Juniper,
Or Yew-tree scath'd; while in clear Prospect round,
From the Grove's Bosom Spires emerge, and Smoak
In bluish Wreaths ascends, ripe Harvests wave,
Herds low, and Straw-rooft Cotts appear, and Streams
Beneath the Sun-beams twinkle – The shrill Lark,
That wakes the Wood-man to his early Task,
Or love-sick *Philomel*, whose luscious Lays
Sooth lone Night-wanderers, the moaning Dove
Pitied by listening Milkmaid, far excell
The deep-mouth'd Viol; the Soul-lulling Lute,
And Battle-breathing Trumpet. Artful Sounds!
That please not like the Choristers of Air,
When first they hail th'Approach of laughing *May*.

Joseph Warton (1722–1800), from *The Enthusiast: or, The Lover of Nature*, 1744.

The lure of Nature as opposed to Art was also felt by Thomas Gainsborough, the most celebrated portraitist of his time. He had to live and work in London, away from his first (and frustrated) love – landscape painting:

I'm sick of portraits, and wish very much to take my viol da gamba and walk off to some sweet village where I can paint landskips and enjoy the fag end of life in quietness and ease ... But ... we must jog on and be content with the jingling of bells, only damn it I hate a dust, the kicking up of a dust, and being confined in harness to follow the track, while others ride in the wagon, under cover, stretching their legs in the straw with ease, and gazing at green trees and blue skies without half my taste – that's damned hard.

Thomas Gainsborough (1727–88), undated letter to W. Jackson; from Ian Crofton, *A Dictionary of Art Quotations*, 1988.

By the end of the century, the full-blown Romantic Landscape had arrived. In 1798 William Wordsworth returned to Tintern on the Wye, which he had first visited in 1793:

> Five years have past; five summers, with the length
> Of five long winters! and again I hear
> These waters, rolling from their mountain-springs
> With a soft inland murmur. – Once again
> Do I behold these steep and lofty cliffs,
> That on a wild secluded scene impress
> Thoughts of more deep seclusion; and connect
> The landscape with the quiet of the sky.
> The day is come when I again repose
> Here, under this dark sycamore, and view
> These plots of cottage-ground, these orchard-tufts,
> Which at this season, with their unripe fruits,
> Are clad in one green hue, and lose themselves
> 'Mid groves and copses. Once again I see
> These hedge-rows, hardly hedge-rows, little lines
> Of sportive wood run wild: these pastoral farms,
> Green to the very door; and wreaths of smoke
> Sent up, in silence, from among the trees!
> With some uncertain notice, as might seem
> Of vagrant dwellers in the homeless woods
> Or of some hermit's cave, where by his fire
> The Hermit sits alone.

William Wordsworth (1770–1850), from 'Lines Composed a Few Miles above Tintern Abbey ... July 13th, 1798'.

Wordsworth's fellow Lakeland Poet, Samuel Taylor Coleridge, shared his friend's vision of the restorative and spiritually nurturing value of Nature:

> Dear Babe, that sleepest cradled by my side,
> Whose gentle breathings, heard in this deep calm,
> Fill up the interspersed vacancies
> And momentary pauses of the thought!
> My babe so beautiful! it thrills my heart
> With tender gladness, thus to look at thee,
> And think that thou shalt learn far other lore,
> And in far other scenes! For I was reared
> In the great city, pent 'mid cloisters dim,
> And saw nought lovely but the sky and stars.
> But thou, my babe! shalt wander like a breeze
> By lakes and sandy shores, beneath the crags
> Of ancient mountain, and beneath the clouds,
> Which image in their bulk both lakes and shores
> And mountain crags: so shalt thou see and hear

The lovely shapes and sounds intelligible
Of that eternal language, which thy God
Utters, who from eternity doth teach
Himself in all, and all things in himself
Great universal Teacher! he shall mould
Thy spirit, and by giving make it ask.

Therefore all seasons shall be sweet to thee,
Whether the summer clothe the general earth
With greenness, or the redbreast sit and sing
Betwixt the tufts of snow on the bare branch
Of mossy apple-tree, while the nigh thatch
Smokes in the sun-thaw; whether the eave-drops fall
Heard only in the trances of the blast,
Or if the secret ministry of frost
Shall hang them up in silent icicles,
Quietly shining to the quiet Moon.

Samuel Taylor Coleridge (1772–1834), from 'Frost at Midnight', 1798.

Although Coleridge 'saw nought lovely' in the city, Wordsworth's country soul could be stirred by the grandeur of the Metropolis, in the right atmospheric conditions:

Earth has not anything to show more fair:
Dull would he be of soul who could pass by
A sight so touching in its majesty:
This City now doth, like a garment, wear
The beauty of the morning; silent, bare,
Ships, towers, domes, theatres, and temples lie
Open unto the fields, and to the sky;
All bright and glittering in the smokeless air.
Never did sun more beautifully steep
In his first splendour, valley, rock, or hill;
Ne'er saw I, never felt, a calm so deep!
The river glideth at his own sweet will:
Dear God! the very houses seem asleep;
And all that mighty heart is lying still!

William Wordsworth (1770–1850), 'Lines Composed upon Westminster Bridge, September 3, 1802'.

In The Prelude, Wordsworth recalls his country boyhood among the Lakeland Fells, and gives a voice to England's wild places:

Fair seed-time had my soul, and I grew up
Fostered alike by beauty and by fear:
Much favoured in my birthplace, and no less
In that beloved Vale to which ere long
We were transplanted – there were we let loose
For sports of wider range. Ere I had told

Ten birth-days, when among the mountain-slopes
Frost, and the breath of frosty wind, had snapped
The last autumnal crocus, 'twas my joy
With store of springes o'er my shoulder hung
To range the open heights where woodcocks run
Among the smooth green turf. Through half the night,
Scudding away from snare to snare, I plied
That anxious visitation; – moon and stars
Were shining o'er my head. I was alone,
And seemed to be a trouble to the peace
That dwelt among them. Sometimes it befell
In these night wanderings, that a strong desire
O'erpowered my better reason, and the bird
Which was the captive of another's toil
Became my prey; and when the deed was done
I heard among the solitary hills
Low breathings coming after me, and sounds
Of undistinguishable motion, steps
Almost as silent as the turf they trod.

Nor less when spring had warmed the cultured Vale,
Roved we as plunderers where the mother-bird
Had in high places built her lodge; though mean
Our object and inglorious, yet the end
Was not ignoble. Oh! when I have hung
Above the raven's nest, by knots of grass
And half-inch fissures in the slippery rock
But ill sustained, and almost (so it seemed)
Suspended by the blast that blew amain,
Shouldering the naked crag, oh, at that time
While on the perilous ridge I hung alone,
With what strange utterance did the loud dry wind
Blow through my ear! the sky seemed not a sky
Of earth – and with what motion moved the clouds!

William Wordsworth (1770–1850), *The Prelude*, 1799–1805, Book I.

Painters, too, were moving away from the conventional, 'arranged' Classical landscape, and delighting in Nature's ungroomed incidentals. Here is Constable, whose pictures of particular places in Suffolk have formed what many think of as the archetypical English landscape:

The sound of water escaping from mill-dams, etc., willows, old rotten planks, slimy posts, and brickwork, I love such things. Shakespeare could make everything poetical; he tells us of poor Tom's haunts among 'sheep cotes and mills'. As long as I do paint, I shall never cease to paint such places ... Those scenes made me a painter and I am grateful.

John Constable (1776–1837), letter to the Rev. John Fisher, 1821; from Ian Crofton, *A Dictionary of Art Quotations*, 1988.

Samuel Palmer, a follower of William Blake, was a very different kind of landscape painter. His move to Shoreham in Kent in 1826 marked the beginning of an intensely visionary, almost hallucogenic, phase:

I have beheld as in the spirit, such nooks, caught such glimpses of the perfumed and enchanted twilight – of natural midsummer, as well as, at other times of day, other scenes, as passed thro' the intense purifying separating transmuting heat of the soul's infabulous alchymy, would divinely consist with the severe and stately port of the human, as with the moon thron'd among constellations, and varieties of lesser glories, the regal pomp and glistening brilliance and solemn attendance of her starry train.

Samuel Palmer (1805–81), letter to George Richmond, 1827; from Ian Crofton, *A Dictionary of Art Quotations*, 1988.

From the Romantic to the Vernacular: Thomas Hood provides a poetical inventory of a typical English village in the early 19th century:

Our village, that's to say not Miss Mitford's village, but our village of
    Bullock Smithy,
Is come into by an avenue of trees, three oak pollards, two elders, and a
    withy;
And in the middle, there's a green of about not exceeding an acre and a
    half;
It's common to all, and fed off by nineteen cows, six ponies, three
    horses, five asses, two foals, seven pigs, and a calf!
Besides a pond in the middle, as is held by a similar sort of common law
    lease,
And contains twenty ducks, six drakes, three ganders, two dead dogs,
    four drowned kittens, and twelve geese.
Of course the green's cropt very close, and does famous for bowling
    when the little village boys play at cricket;
Only some horse, or pig, or cow, or great jackass, is sure to come and
    stand right before the wicket.
There's fifty-five private houses, let alone barns and workshops, and
    pigstyes, and poultry huts, and such-like sheds;
With plenty of public-houses – two Foxes, one Green Man, three
    Bunch of Grapes, one Crown, and six King's Heads.
The Green Man is reckoned the best, as the only one that for love or
    money can raise
A postillion, a blue jacket, two deplorable lame white horses, and a
    ramshackled 'neat postchaise'.
There's one parish church for all the people, whatsoever may be their
    ranks in life or their degrees,
Except one very damp, small, dark, freezing-cold, little Methodist
    chapel of Ease;
And close by the church-yard there's a stone-mason's yard, that, when
    the time is seasonable,

Will furnish with afflictions sore and marble urns and cherubims very
low and reasonable.
There's a cage, comfortable enough; I've been in it with old Jack Jeffrey
and Tom Pike;
For the Green Man next door will send you in ale, gin, or anything else
you like.
I can't speak of the stocks, as nothing remains of them but the upright
post;
But the pound is kept in repairs for the sake of Cob's horse, as is always
there almost.
There's a smithy of course, where that queer sort of a chap in his way,
Old Joe Bradley,
Perpetually hammers and stammers, for he stutters and shoes horses
very badly.
There's a shop of all sorts, that sells everything, kept by the widow of
Mr Task;
But when you go there, it's ten to one she's out of everything you ask.
You'll know her house by the swarm of boys, like flies, about the old
sugary cask;
There's another small day-school too, kept by the respectable Mrs Gaby;
A select establishment, for six little boys and one big, and four little
girls and a baby.
There's a rectory, with pointed gables and strange odd chimneys that
never smokes,
For the rector don't live on his living like other Christian sort of folks;
There's a barber's, once a week well filled with rough black-bearded,
shock-headed churls,
And a window with two feminine men's heads, and two masculine
ladies in false curls;
There's a butcher's, and a carpenter's, and a plumber's, and a small
greengrocer's and a baker,
But he won't bake on a Sunday, and there's a sexton that's a coal-
merchant besides, and an undertaker;
And a toyshop, but not a whole one, for a village can't compare with the
London shops;
One window sells drums, dolls, kites, carts, bats, Clout's balls, and the
other sells malt and hops.
And Mrs Brown, in domestic economy not to be a bit behind her
betters,
Lets her house to a milliner, a watchmaker, a rat-catcher, a cobbler, lives
in it herself, and it's the post-office for letters.
Now I've gone through all the village – aye, from end to end, save and
except one more house,
But I haven't come to that – and I hope I never shall – and that's the
Village Poor House!

Thomas Hood (1799–1845), 'Our Village', in *Whims and Oddities*, 1826.

While Hood patiently detailed the village, John Clare – the 'peasant poet' who ended his life in a lunatic asylum – quietly evoked the countryside:

> I love to see the old heath's withered brake
> Mingle its crimpled leaves with furze and ling,
> While the old heron from the lonely lake
> Starts slow and flaps his melancholy wing,
> And oddling crow in idle motions swing
> On the half-rotten ash-tree's topmost twig,
> Beside whose trunk the gipsy makes his bed.
> Up flies the bouncing woodcock from the brig
> Where a black quagmire quakes beneath the tread;
> The fieldfares chatter in the whistling thorn
> And for the haw round fields and closen rove,
> And coy bumbarrels, twenty in a drove,
> Flit down the hedgerows in the frozen plain
> And hang on little twigs and start again.

John Clare (1793–1864), 'Emmonsail's Heath in Winter'. (A bumbarrel is a long-tailed tit.)

William Cobbett was a staunch believer in rural virtues, looking back to the Golden Age of his country childhood:

Born amongst husbandmen, bred to husbandry, delighting in its pursuits even to the minutest details, never having, in all my range of life, lost sight of the English farm-house and of those scenes in which my mind took its first spring, it is natural that I should have a strong partiality for country life, and that I should enter more in detail into the feelings of labourers in husbandry than into those of other labourers.

If the cultivators of the land be not, generally speaking, the most virtuous and most happy of mankind, there must be something at work in the community to counteract the operations of nature. This way of life gives the best security for health and strength of body. It does not teach, it necessarily produces early rising; constant forethought; constant attention; and constant care of dumb animals. The nature and qualities of all living things are known to country boys better than to philosophers. The seasons, the weather, the causes and effects of propagation, in cultivation, in tillage, are all known from habit, from incessant repetition of observation. The nature, the properties, the various uses, of different soils and woods are familiar to the mind of country boys. Riding, climbing, swimming, nothing comes amiss, and they are come, and are not sought. Rural affairs leave not a day, not an hour, unoccupied and without its cares, its promises, and its fruitions. The seasons, which wait for no man; the weather, which is no respecter of persons, and which will be what it will be, produce an habitual looking forward, and make the farmer provident, whatever might have been his natural disposition. The farmer's cares are pleasing cares. His misfortunes can seldom be more than lessons. His produce consists of things wanted by all mankind. His market-day is a ready-money one. No daybooks, bills, and ledgers haunt his mind. Envy can, in the natural state of things, find no place in his breast; for, the seasons and the weather are the same to all; and the demand for his produce has no other measure than the extent of his crops. ...

I am once more in a farm. I might have been, I am aware of it, possessed of bags of public gold or of landed domains, purchased with that gold. I trudge through the dirt, and I might have ridden in the ring at Hyde Park, with four horses to draw me along in a gilded carriage, with a coachman before me and footmen behind me. What I might have been, it is hard to say; what I have been and what I am, all the world knows; I was a plough-boy and a private soldier, and I am a Member of the House of Commons, sent thither by the free voice of a great community. ... Some generations, at least, will pass away before the name of William Cobbett will cease to be familiar in the mouths of the people of England; and, for the rest of the world, I care not a straw.

If I have one wish more ardent than all other, it is this; that I, enjoying my garden and few fields, may see England as great in the world, and her industrious, laborious, kind and virtuous people as happy as they were when I was born; and that I may at last have a few years of calm at the close of a long life of storms and of tempests.

William Cobbett (1762–1835), from the *Political Register*, June 1835.

It was once sardonically remarked (by George Sanders) that 'the most beautiful poems about England were written by poets living in Italy at the time':

> Oh, to be in England
> Now that April's there,
> And whoever wakes in England
> Sees, some morning, unaware,
> That the lowest boughs and the brushwood sheaf
> Round the elm-tree bole are in tiny leaf,
> While the chaffinch sings on the orchard bough
> In England – now!
>
> And after April, when May follows,
> And the whitethroat builds, and all the swallows!
> Hark, where my blossomed pear-tree in the hedge
> Leans to the field and scatters on the clover
> Blossoms and dewdrops – at the bent spray's edge –
> That's the wise thrush; he sings each song twice over,
> Lest you should think he never could recapture
> The first fine careless rapture!
> And though the fields look rough with hoary dew,
> All will be gay when noontide wakes anew
> The buttercups, the little children's dower
> – Far brighter than this gaudy melon-flower!

Robert Browning (1812–89), 'Home-Thoughts, from Abroad', 1845.

Some poets have been very much rooted in their own local landscapes. One such was William Barnes, the Dorset poet:

'Ithin the woodlands, flow'ry gleaded,
By the woak tree's mossy moot,
The sheenen grass-bleades, timber-sheaded,
Now do quiver under voot;
An' birds do whissle over head,
An' water's bubblen in its bed,
An' there vor me the apple tree
Do lean down low in Linden Lea.

When leaves that leately wer a-springen
Now do feade 'ithin the copse,
An' painted birds do hush their zingen
Up upon the timber's tops;
An' brown-leav'd fruit's a-turnen red,
In cloudless zunsheen, over head,
Wi' fruit vor me, the apple tree
Do lean down low in Linden Lea.

Let other vo'k meake money vaster
In the air o' dark-room'd towns,
I don't dread a peevish measter;
Though noo man do heed my frowns,
I be free to goo abrode,
Or teake agean my hwomeward road
To where, vor me, the apple tree
Do lean down low in Linden Lea.

William Barnes (1801–86), 'Linden Lea', from *Hwomely Rhymes*, 1856.

Thomas Hardy was another who wrote extensively about the landscapes of the West Country. Here is his description of Egdon Heath:

A Saturday afternoon in November was approaching the time of twilight, and the vast tract of unenclosed wild known as Egdon Heath embrowned itself moment by moment. Overhead the hollow stretch of whitish cloud shutting out the sky was as a tent which had the whole heath for its floor.

The heaven being spread with this pallid screen and the earth with the darkest vegetation, their meeting-line at the horizon was clearly marked. In such contrast the heath wore the appearance of an instalment of night which had taken up its place before its astronomical hour was come: darkness had to a great extent arrived hereon, while day stood distinct in the sky. Looking upwards, a furze-cutter would have been inclined to continue work; looking down, he would have decided to finish his faggot and go home. The distant rims of the world and of the firmament seemed to be a division in time no less than a division in matter. The face of the heath by its mere complexion added half an hour to evening; it could in like manner retard the dawn, sadden noon, anticipate the frowning of storms scarcely generated, and intensify the opacity of a moonless midnight to a cause of shaking and dread.

In fact, precisely at this transitional point of its nightly roll into darkness the great and particular glory of the Egdon waste began, and nobody could be said to understand the heath who had not been there at such a time. It could best be felt when it could not clearly be seen, its complete effect and explanation lying in this and the succeeding hours before the next dawn; then, and only then, did it tell its true tale. The spot was, indeed, a near relation of night, and when night showed itself an apparent tendency to gravitate together could be perceived in its shades and the scene. The sombre stretch of rounds and hollows seemed to rise and meet the evening gloom in pure sympathy, the heath exhaling darkness as rapidly as the heavens precipitated it. And so the obscurity in the air and the obscurity in the land closed together in a black fraternization towards which each advanced halfway.

The place became full of a watchful intentness now; for when other things sank brooding to sleep the heath appeared slowly to awake and listen. Every night its Titanic form seemed to await something; but it had waited thus, unmoved, during so many centuries, through the crises of so many things, that it could only be imagined to await one last crisis – the final overthrow.

It was a spot which returned upon the memory of those who loved it with an aspect of peculiar and kindly congruity. Smiling champaigns of flowers and fruit hardly do this, for they are permanently harmonious only with an existence of better reputation as to its issues than the present. Twilight combined with the scenery of Egdon Heath to evolve a thing majestic without severity, impressive without showiness, emphatic in its admonitions, grand in its simplicity. The qualifications which frequently invest the facade of a prison with far more dignity than is found in the facade of a palace double its size lent to this heath a sublimity in which spots renowned for beauty of the accepted kind are utterly wanting. Fair prospects wed happily with fair times; but alas, if times be not fair! Men have oftener suffered from the mockery of a place too smiling for their reason than from the oppression of surroundings over-sadly tinged. Haggard Egdon appealed to a subtler and scarcer instinct, to a more recently learnt emotion, than that which responds to the sort of beauty called charming and fair.

Thomas Hardy (1840–1928), *The Return of the Native*, 1878.

A.E. Housman is known as the poet of Shropshire – although at the time he started *A Shropshire Lad* he had not visited the county.

> Into my heart an air that kills
> From yon far country blows:
> What are those blue remembered hills,
> What spires, what farms are those?
>
> That is the land of lost content,
> I see it shining plain,
> The happy highways where I went
> And cannot come again.

A.E. Housman (1859–1936), *A Shropshire Lad*, 1896, Poem XL.

For Kipling, England meant Sussex:

> See you the ferny ride that steals
> Into the oak-woods far?
> O that was whence they hewed the keels
> That rolled to Trafalgar.
>
> And mark you where the ivy clings
> To Bayham's mouldering walls?
> O there we cast the stout railings
> That stand around St. Paul's.
>
> See you the dimpled track that runs
> All hollow through the wheat?
> O that was where they hauled the guns
> That smote King Philip's fleet.
>
> (Out of the Weald, the secret Weald,
> Men sent in ancient years,
> The horse-shoes red at Flodden Field,
> The arrows at Poitiers!)
>
> See you our little mill that clacks,
> So busy by the brook?
> She has ground her corn and paid her tax
> Ever since Domesday Book.
>
> See you our stilly woods of oak,
> And the dread ditch beside?
> O that was where the Saxons broke
> On the day that Harold died.
>
> See you the windy levels spread
> About the gates of Rye?
> O that was where the Northmen fled,
> When Alfred's ships came by.
>
> See you our pastures wide and lone,
> Where the red oxen browse?
> O there was a City thronged and known,
> Ere London boasted a house.
>
> And see you, after rain, the trace
> Of mound and ditch and wall?
> O that was a Legion's camping-place,
> When Cæsar sailed from Gaul.
>
> And see you marks that show and fade,
> Like shadows on the Downs?
> O they are the lines the Flint Men made,
> To guard their wondrous towns.

Trackway and Camp and City lost,
Salt Marsh where now is corn –
Old Wars, old Peace, old Arts that cease,
And so was England born!

She is not any common Earth,
Water or wood or air,
But Merlin's Isle of Gramarye,
Where you and I will fare!

Rudyard Kipling (1865–1936), 'Puck's Song' from *Puck of Pook's Hill*, 1906.

In *Howards End*, E.M. Forster sees England spreading out from a height in Dorset:

If one wanted to show a foreigner England, perhaps the wisest course would be to take him to the final section of the Purbeck hills, and stand him on their summit, a few miles to the east of Code. Then system after system of our island roll together under his feet. Beneath him is the valley of the Frome, and all the wild lands that come tossing down from Dorchester, black and gold, to mirror their gorse in the expanses of Poole. The valley of the Stour is beyond, unaccountable stream, dirty at Blandford, pure at Wimborne – the Stour, sliding out of fat fields, to marry the Avon beneath the tower of Christchurch. The valley of the Avon – invisible, but far to the north the trained eye may see Clearbury Ring that guards it, and the imagination may leap beyond that onto Salisbury Plain itself, and beyond the Plain to all the glorious downs of central England. Nor is suburbia absent. Bournemouth's ignoble coast cowers to the right, heralding the pine trees that mean, for all their beauty, red houses, and the Stock Exchange, and extend to the gates of London itself. So tremendous is the City's trail! But the cliffs of Freshwater it shall never touch, and the island will guard the Island's purity till the end of time. Seen from the west, the Wight is beautiful beyond all laws of beauty. It is as if a fragment of England floated forward to greet the foreigner – chalk of our chalk, turf of our turf, epitome of what will follow. And behind the fragment lies Southampton, hostess to the nations, and Portsmouth, a latent fire, and all around it, with double and treble collision of tides, swirls the sea. How many villages appear in this view. How many castles! How many churches, vanquished or triumphant! How many ships, railways and roads! What incredible variety of men working beneath that lucent sky to what final end! The reason fails, like a wave on the Swanage beach; the imagination swells, spreads and deepens, until it becomes geographic and encircles England.

E.M. Forster (1879–1970), *Howards End*, 1910.

Nearly 70 years after Browning pined 'to be in England, / Now that April's there', another poet writing from abroad chose Grantchester, in Cambridgeshire, as his little local heaven:

Here am I, sweating, sick, and hot,
And there the shadowed waters fresh
Lean up to embrace the naked flesh.
Temperamentvoll German Jews
Drink beer around; – and there the dews

Are soft beneath a morn of gold.
Here tulips bloom as they are told;
Unkempt about those hedges blows
An English unofficial rose;
And there the unregulated sun
Slopes down to rest when day is done

. . .

God! I will pack, and take a train,
And get me to England once again!
For England's the one land, I know,
Where men with Splendid Hearts may go;
And Cambridgeshire, of all England,
The shire for Men who Understand;
And of that district I prefer
The lovely hamlet Grantchester.

. . .

Ah God! to see the branches stir
Across the moon at Grantchester!
To smell the thrilling-sweet and rotten
Unforgettable, unforgotten
River-smell, and hear the breeze
Sobbing in the little trees.
Say, do the elm-clumps greatly stand
Still guardians of that holy land?
The chestnuts shade, in reverend dream,
The yet unacademic stream?
Is dawn a secret shy and cold
Anadyomene, silver-gold?
And sunset still a golden sea
From Haslingfield to Madingley?
And after, ere the night is born,
Do hares come out about the corn?
Oh, is the water sweet and cool,
Gentle and brown, above the pool?
And laughs the immortal river still
Under the mill, under the mill?
Say, is there Beauty yet to find?
And Certainty? and Quiet kind?
Deep meadows yet, for to forget
The lies, and truths, and pain? ... oh! yet
Stands the Church clock at ten to three?
And is there honey still for tea?

Rupert Brooke (1887–1915), *The Old Vicarage, Grantchester*, 1912.

From the Western Front in the First World War, England was another country, a world away:

> Yes, I remember Adlestrop –
> The name, because one afternoon
> Of heat the express-train drew up there
> Unwontedly. It was late June.
>
> The steam hissed. Someone cleared his throat.
> No one left and no one came
> On the bare platform. What I saw
> Was Adlestrop – only the name.
>
> And willows, willow-herb, and grass,
> And meadowsweet, and haycocks dry,
> No whit less still and lonely fair
> Than the high cloudlets in the sky.
>
> And for a minute a blackbird sang
> Close by, and round him, mistier,
> Farther and farther, all the birds
> Of Oxfordshire and Gloucestershire.

Edward Thomas (1878–1917), 'Adlestrop', 1917. Thomas was killed at Arras.

H.G. Wells plumped for Essex as representative of 'the real England':

Now here in Essex we're as lax as the 18th century. We hunt in any old clothes. Our soil is a rich succulent clay; it becomes semi-fluid in winter, when we go about in our waders shooting duck. ... If I wanted to play golf – which I don't, being a decent Essex man – I should have to motor 10 miles into Hertfordshire. This country is a part of the real England – England outside London and outside manufactures. It's one with Wessex and Mercia or old Yorkshire. And it's the essential England still.

H.G. Wells (1866–1946), *Mr Britling Sees It Through*, 1916.

For Siegfried Sassoon, Worcestershire was the place, and hunting the thing:

> I'd like to be the simpleton I was
> In the old days when I was whipping-in
> To a little harrier-pack in Worcestershire ...
> ...
> What a grand thing 'twould be if I could go
> Back to the kennels now and take my hounds
> For summer exercise; be riding out
> With forty couple when the quiet skies
> Are streaked with sunrise, and the silly birds
> Grown hoarse with singing; cobwebs on the furze
> Up on the hill, and all the country strange,
> With no one stirring; and the horses fresh,
> Sniffing the air I'll never breathe again.

Siegfried Sassoon (1886–1967), 'The Old Huntsman', 1917.

In 1924 Stanley Baldwin addressed the Royal Society of St George:

Now, I have very little more that I want to say to you tonight, but on an occasion like this I suppose there is no-one who does not ask himself in his heart and is a little shy of expressing it, what it is that England stands for to him, and to her. And there comes into my mind a wonder as to what England may stand for in the minds of generations to come if our country goes on during the next generation as she has done in the last two, in seeing her fields converted into towns. To me, England is the country and the country is England. And when I ask myself what I mean by England, when I think of England when I am abroad, England comes to me through my various senses – through the ear, through the eye, and through certain imperishable scents. I will tell you what they are, and there may be those among you who feel as I do.

The sounds of England, the tinkle of the hammer on the anvil in the country smithy, the corncrake on a dewy morning, the sound of the scythe against the whetstone, and the sight of a plough team coming over the brow of a hill, the sight that has been seen in England since England was a land, and may be seen in England long after the Empire has ceased to function, for centuries the one eternal sight of England. The wild anemones in the woods in April, the last load at night of hay being drawn down a lane as the twilight comes on, when you can scarcely distinguish the figures of the horses as they take it home to the farm, and above all, most subtle, most penetrating, and most moving, the smell of wood smoke coming up in an autumn evening, or the smell of the scutch fires: that wood smoke that our ancestors, tens of thousands of years ago, must have caught on the air when they were coming home with the result of the day's forage, when they were still nomads, and when they were still roaming the forests and the plains of the continent of Europe. These things strike down into the very depths of our nature, and touch chords that go back to the beginning of time and the human race, but they are chords that with every year of our life sound a deeper note in our innermost being. These are the things that make England, and I grieve for it that they are not the childish inheritance of the majority of the people today in our country. They ought to be the inheritance of every child born into this country, but nothing can be more touching than to see how the working man and woman after generations in the towns will have their tiny bit of garden if they can, will go to gardens if they can, to look at something they have never seen as children, but which their ancestors knew and loved. The love of these things is innate and inherent in our people.

Stanley Baldwin (1867–1947), Prime Minister (1923–24, 1924–29, 1935–37), 'On England and the West of England', Annual Dinner of the Royal Society of St George, 6 May 1924; collected in *On England*, 1926.

John Betjeman celebrated the role of the church spire or tower (and its lurking spiritual significance) in the English landscape, particularly in the flat lands of the east:

Greyly tremulous the thunder
Hung over the width of the wold

But here the green marsh was alight
In a huge cloud cavern of gold,
And there, on a gentle eminence,
Topping some ash trees, a tower
Silver and brown in the sunlight,
Worn by sea-wind and shower,
Lincolnshire Middle Pointed.
All around it, turning their backs,
The usual sprinkle of villas;
The usual woman in slacks,
Cigarette in her mouth,
Regretting Americans, stands
As a wireless croons in the kitchen
Manicuring her hands.
Dear old, bloody old England
Of telegraph poles and tin,
Seemingly so indifferent
And with so little soul to win.

John Betjeman (1906–84), 'A Lincolnshire Church', in *Selected Poems*, 1948.

Laurie Lee's *Cider With Rosie* is one of the best-loved celebrations of a disappearing way of life:

The last days of my childhood were also the last days of the village. I belonged to that generation which saw, by chance, the end of a thousand years' life. The change came late to our Cotswold valley, didn't really show itself till the late 1920s; I was twelve by then, but during that handful of years I witnessed the whole thing happen.

Myself, my family, my generation, were born in a world of silence; a world of hard work and necessary patience, of backs bent to the ground, hands massaging the crops, of waiting on weather and growth; of villages like ships in the empty landscapes and the long walking distances between them; of white narrow roads, rutted by hooves and cart-wheels, innocent of oil or petrol, down which people passed rarely, and almost never for pleasure, and the horse was the fastest thing moving. Man and horse were all the power we had – abetted by levers and pulleys. But the horse was king, and almost everything grew around him: fodder, smithies, stables, paddocks, distances, and the rhythm of our days. His eight miles an hour was the limit of our movements, as it had been since the days of the Romans. That eight miles an hour was life and death, the size of our world, our prison.

This was what we were born to, and all we knew at first. Then, to the scream of the horse, the change began. The brass-lamped motor-car came coughing up the road, followed by the clamorous charabanc; the solid-tyred bus climbed the dusty hills and more people came and went. Chickens and dogs were the early sacrifices, falling demented beneath the wheels. The old folk, too, had strokes and seizures, faced by speeds beyond comprehension. Then scarlet motor-bikes, the size of five-barred gates, began to appear in the village, on which our youths roared like rockets up the two-minute hills, then spent weeks making repairs and adjustments.

These appearances did not immediately alter our lives; the cars were freaks and rarely seen, the motor-bikes mostly in pieces, we used the charabancs only once a year, and our buses at first were experiments. Meanwhile Lew Ayres, wearing a bowler-hat, ran his wagonette to Stroud twice a week. The carriage held six, and the fare was twopence, but most people preferred to walk. Mr West, from Sheepscombe, ran a cart every day, and would carry your parcels for a penny. But most of us still did the journey on foot, heads down to the wet Welsh winds, ignoring the carters – whom we thought extortionate – and spending a long hard day at our shopping.

But the car-shying horses with their rolling eyes gave signs of the hysteria to come. Soon the village would break, dissolve, and scatter, become no more than a place for pensioners. It had a few years left, the last of its thousand, and they passed almost without our knowing. . . .

The death of the Squire was not the death of the church, though they drew to their end together. He died, and the Big House was sold by auction and became a Home for Invalids. The lake silted up, the swans flew away, and the great pike choked in the reeds. With the Squire's hand removed, we fell apart – though we were about to do so anyway. His servants dispersed and went into the factories. His nephew broke up the estate.

Fragmentation, free thought, and new excitements, came now to intrigue and perplex us. The first young couple to get married in a registry office were roundly denounced from the pulpit. 'They who play with fire shall be consumed by fire!' stormed the vicar. 'Ye mark my words!' Later he caught me reading *Sons and Lovers* and took it away and destroyed it. This may well have been one of his last authoritative gestures. A young apologist succeeded him soon.

Meanwhile the old people just dropped away – the white-whiskered, gaitered, booted and bonneted, ancient-tongued last of their world, who thee'd and thou'd both man and beast, called young girls 'damsels', young boys 'squires', old men 'masters', the Squire himself 'He', and who remembered the Birdlip stagecoach. Kicker Harris, the old coachman, with his top-hat and leggings, blew away like a torn-out page. Lottie Escourt, peasant shoot of a Norman lord, curled up in her relics and died. Others departed with hardly a sound. There was old Mrs Clissold, who sometimes called us for errands: 'Thee come up our court a minute, squire; I wants thee to do I a mission.' One ran to the shop to buy her a packet of bulls' eyes and was rewarded in the customary way. Bull's-eye in cheek, she'd sink back in her chair and dismiss one with a sleepy nod. 'I ain't nurn a aypence about I just now – but Mrs Crissole'll recollect 'ee ...' We wrote her off as the day's good deed, and she died still recollecting us. . . .

Time squared itself; and the village shrank, and distance crept nearer. The sun and moon, which once rose from our hill, rose from London now in the east. One's body was no longer a punching ball, to be thrown against trees and banks, but a telescoping totem crying strange demands few of which we could yet supply. In the faces of the villagers one could see one's change, and in their habits their own change also. The horses had died; few people kept pigs any more but spent their spare time buried in engines. The flutes and cornets, the gramophones with horns, the wind harps were thrown away – now wireless aerials searched the electric sky for the music of the Savoy Orpheans. Old men in the pub sang, 'As I Walked Out', then walked out and never came back.

Laurie Lee (1914–97), *Cider With Rosie*, 1959.

> Rime Intrinsica, Fontmell Magna, Sturminster Newton and
>   Melbury Bubb,
> Whist upon whist upon whist upon whist drive, in Institute,
>   Legion and Social Club.
> Horny hands that hold the aces which this morning held the
>   plough –
> While Tranter Reuben, T.S. Eliot, H.G. Wells and Edith
>   Sitwell lie in Mellstock Churchyard now.
>
> Lord's Day bells from Bingham's Melcombe, Iwerne Minster,
>   Shroton, Plush,
> Down the grass between the beeches, mellow in the evening
>   hush.
> Gloved the hands that hold the hymn-book, which this
>   morning milked the cow –
> While Tranter Reuben, Mary Borden, Brian Howard and
>   Harold Acton lie in Mellstock Churchyard now.
>
> Light's abode, celestial Salem! Lamps of evening, smelling
>   strong,
> Gleaming on the pitch-pine, waiting, almost empty evensong:
> From the aisles each window smiles on grave and grass and
>   yew-tree bough –
> While Tranter Reuben, Gordon Selfridge, Edna Best and
>   Thomas Hardy lie in Mellstock Churchyard now.

John Betjeman (1906–84), 'Dorset', from *Continual Dew*, 1937.

The Second World War concentrated many hearts and minds on the essence of England:

> There'll always be an England
> While there's a country lane,
> Wherever there's a cottage small
> Beside a field of grain.

Ross Parker (1914–74) and Hugh Charles (1907–), song, 'There'll Always Be An England', 1939.

England's might is still in her fields and villages, and though the whole weight of mechanized armies rolls over to crush them, in the end they will triumph. The best of England is a village.

C. Henry Warren, *England is a Village*, 1940.

During the war John Betjeman talked to the nation on the BBC Home Service:

Bombs and aeroplanes were falling out of the sky; guns thundered and fragments of shell whizzed about. 'I am afraid we have not everybody here,' said the head of the [Women's] Institute. 'You see, several of our members had to be up all night, but we have quite a little show all the same': and there they were, the raffia mats, the bowls of bulbs, the trailing ends of smilax writhing round mustard and pepper pots. God be praised for such dogged calm. . . .

For me, England stands for the Church of England, eccentric incumbents, oil-lit churches, Women's Institutes, modest village inns, arguments about cow-parsley on the altar, the noise of mowing machines on Saturday afternoons, local newspapers, local auctions, the poetry of Tennyson, Crabbe, Hardy and Matthew Arnold, local talent, local concerts, a visit to the cinema, branch-line trains, light railways, leaning on gates and looking across fields; for you, it may stand for some-thing else, equally eccentric to me as I may appear to you, something to do with Wolverhampton or dear old Swindon or wherever you happen to live. But just as important. But I know the England I want to come home to is not very different from that in which you want to live. If it were some efficient ant-heap which the glass and steel, flat-roof straight-road boys want to make it, then how could we love it as we do?

John Betjeman (1906–84), talk for BBC Home Service, 1943.

Perhaps there's been too much of the South in this celebration of rural England. So here, to end, is a very different, more rugged, but still essentially English landscape – that of the Yorkshire Dales, where the American writer Bill Bryson made his home:

We drove home over the tops, a winding, 6-mile drive of unutterable loveliness, up on to the Wuthering Heights-like expanses around Kirkby Fell, with bound-less views of Northern glory, and then began the descent into the serene, cupped majesty of Malhamdale, the little lost world that had been my home for seven years. Halfway down, I had my wife stop the car by a field gate. My favourite view in the world is there, and I got out to have a look. You can see almost the whole of Malhamdale; sheltered and snug beneath steep, imposing hills, with its arrow-straight drystone walls climbing up impossibly ambitious slopes, its clustered hamlets, its wonderful little two-room schoolhouse, the old church with its sycamores and tumbling tombstones, the roof of my local pub, and in the centre of it all, obscured by trees, our old stone house, which itself is far older than my native land.

It looked so peaceful and wonderful that I could almost have cried, and yet it was only a tiny part of this small, enchanted island. Suddenly, in the space of a moment, I realized what it was that I loved about Britain – which is to say, all of it. Every last bit of it, good and bad – Marmite, village fetes, country lanes, people saying 'mustn't grumble' and 'I'm terribly sorry but', people apologizing to me when I conk them with a careless elbow, milk in bottles, beans on toast, haymak-ing in June, stinging nettles, seaside piers, Ordnance Survey maps, crumpets, hot-water bottles as a necessity, drizzly Sundays – every bit of it.

What a wondrous place this was – crazy as fuck, of course, but adorable to the tiniest degree. What other country, after all, could possibly have come up with place names like Tooting Bec and Farleigh Wallop, or a game like cricket that goes on for three days and never seems to start? Who else would think it not the least odd to make their judges wear little mops on their heads, compel the Speaker of the House of Commons to sit on something called the Woolsack, or take pride in a military hero whose dying wish was to be kissed by a fellow named Hardy? ('Please, Hardy, full on the lips, with just a bit of tongue.') What other nation in the world could possibly have given us William Shakespeare, pork pies, Christopher Wren, Windsor Great Park, the Open University, *Gardeners' Question Time*, and the chocolate digestive biscuit? None, of course.

How easily we lose sight of all this. What an enigma Britain will seem to historians when they look back on the second half of the twentieth century. Here is a country that fought and won a noble war, dismantled a mighty empire in a generally benign and enlightened way, created a far-seeing welfare state – in short, did nearly everything right – and then spent the rest of the century looking on itself as a chronic failure. The fact is that this is still the best place in the world for most things – to post a letter, go for a walk, watch television, buy a book, venture out for a drink, go to a museum, use the bank, get lost, seek help, or stand on a hillside and take in a view.

All of this came to me in the space of a lingering moment. I've said it before and I'll say it again. I like it here. I like it more than I can tell you. And then I turned from the gate and got in the car and knew without doubt that I would be back.

Bill Bryson (1951–), US writer, *Notes From a Small Island*, 1995.

THE BLOODY (1): BLOODY AWFUL PLACES

A selection of informed comment and blind prejudice.

First we consider 'the great wen of all', as William Cobbett described London:

I wander thro' each charted street,
Near where the charter'd Thames does flow
And mark in every face I meet
Marks of weakness, marks of woe.

William Blake (1757–1827), 'London', 1794.

Hell is a city much like London –
A populous and a smoky city;
There are all sorts of people undone,
And there is little or no fun done;
Small justice shown, and still less pity.

Percy Bysshe Shelley (1792–1822), *Peter Bell the Third*, 1819.

London was (and is) no place to be poor:

Sur, May we beg and beseech your proteckshion and power. We are, Sur, as it may be, living in a Wilderniss, so far as the rest of London knows anything of us, or as rich and great people care about. We live in muck and filthe. We aint got no privez, no dust bins, no drains, no water splies, and no drain or suer in the whole place. The Suer Corporation, in Greek Street, Soho Square, all great, rich and powerfool men, take no notice whatsomedever of our complaints. The Stenche of a Gully-hole is disgustin. We al of us suffer, and numbers are ill, and if the Colera comes Lord help us.

Letter published in *The Times*, July 1849; quoted in Francis Wheen, *Karl Marx*, 1999.

Charles Dickens pursued a lifelong love-hate relationship with the capital – which acts as a major character in several of his novels:

LONDON. Michaelmas term lately over, and the Lord Chancellor sitting in Lincoln's Inn Hall. Implacable November weather. As much mud in the streets, as if the waters had but newly retired from the face of the earth, and it would not be wonderful to meet a Megalosaurus, forty feet long or so, waddling like an elephantine lizard up Holborn Hill. Smoke lowering down from chimney-pots, making a soft black drizzle with flakes of soot in it as big as full-grown snowflakes – gone into mourning, one might imagine, for the death of the sun. Dogs, undistinguishable in mire. Horses, scarcely better; splashed to their very blinkers. Foot passengers, jostling one another's umbrellas, in a general infection of ill temper, and losing their foot-hold at street-corners, where tens of thousands of other foot passengers have been slipping and sliding since the day broke (if this day ever broke), adding new deposits to the crust upon crust of mud, sticking at those points tenaciously to the pavement, and accumulating at compound interest.

Fog everywhere. Fog up the river, where it flows among green aits and meadows; fog down the river, where it rolls defiled among the tiers of shipping, and the waterside pollutions of a great (and dirty) city. Fog on the Essex Marshes, fog on the Kentish heights. Fog creeping into the cabooses of collier-brigs; fog lying out on the yards, and hovering in the rigging of great ships; fog drooping on the gunwales of barges and small boats. Fog in the eyes and throats of ancient Greenwich pensioners, wheezing by the firesides of their wards; fog in the stem and bowl of the afternoon pipe of the wrathful skipper, down in his close cabin; fog cruelly pinching the toes and fingers of his shivering little 'prentice boy on deck. Chance people on the bridges peeping over the parapets into a nether sky of fog, with fog all round them, as if they were up in a balloon, and hanging in the misty clouds.

Gas looming through the fog in divers places in the streets, much as the sun may, from the spongey fields, be seen to loom by husbandman and ploughboy. Most of the shops lighted two hours before their time – as the gas seems to know, for it has a haggard and unwilling look. ...

Jo lives – that is to say, Jo has not yet died – in a ruinous place, known to the likes of him by the name of Tom-all-Alone's. It is a black, dilapidated street, avoided by all decent people; where the crazy houses were seized upon, when their decay was far advanced, by some bold vagrants, who, after establishing their own possession, took to letting them out in lodgings. Now, these tumbling tenements contain, by night, a swarm of misery. As on the ruined human wretch, vermin parasites appear, so, these ruined shelters have bred a crowd of foul existence that crawls in and out of gaps in walls and boards; and coils itself to sleep, in maggot numbers, where the rain drips in; and comes and goes, fetching and carrying fever, and sowing more evil in its every footprint than Lord Coodle and Sir Thomas Doodle, and the Duke of Foodle, and all the fine gentlemen in office, down to Zoodle, shall set right in five hundred years – though born expressly to do it.

Twice, lately, there has been a crash and a cloud of dust, like the springing of a mine, in Tom-all-Alone's; and, each time, a house has fallen. These accidents have made a paragraph in the newspapers, and have filled a bed or two in the nearest hospital. The gaps remain, and there are not unpopular lodgings among the rubbish. As several more houses are nearly ready to go, the next crash in Tom-all-Alone's may be expected to be a good one.

Charles Dickens (1812–70), *Bleak House*, 1853.

A foreign visitor was not impressed:

London, black as crows and noisy as ducks, prudish with all the vices in evidence, everlastingly drunk in spite of ridiculous laws about drunkenness, immense, though it is really basically only a collection of scandal-mongering boroughs, vying with each other, ugly and dull, without any monuments except interminable docks.

Paul Verlaine (1844–96), quoted in Jonathon Green, *The Cassell Dictionary of Insulting Quotations*, 1996.

T.S. Eliot experienced London as the City of the Dead:

> Unreal City,
> Under the brown fog of a winter dawn,
> A crowd flowed over London Bridge, so many,
> I had not thought death had undone so many.
> Sighs, short and infrequent, were exhaled,
> And each man fixed his eyes before his feet.
> Flowed up the hill and down King William Street,
> To where Saint Mary Woolnoth kept the hours
> With a dead sound on the final stroke of nine.

T. S. Eliot (1888–1965), *The Waste Land*, 1922.

A London suburb which, aiming desperately at the genteel, achieves only a sordid melancholy.

W. Somerset Maugham (1874–1965), describing the London suburb of Barnes in *On a Chinese Screen*, 1922.

London! Pompous Ignorance sits enthroned there and welcomes Pretentious Mediocrity with flattery and gifts. Oh, dull and witless city! Very hell for the restless, inquiring, sensitive soul. Paradise for the snob, the parasite and the prig; the pimp, the placeman and the cheapjack.

James Bridie (1888–1951), Scottish playwright, *The Anatomist*, 1931.

What has happened to architecture since the Second World War that the only passers-by who can contemplate it without pain are those equipped with a white stick and a dog?

Bernard Levin (1928–), in *The Times*, 1983.

You have to give this much to the Luftwaffe – when it knocked down our buildings it didn't replace them with anything more offensive than rubble. We did that.

Charles, HRH the Prince of Wales, speech to the Corporation of London Planning and Communications Committee, 2 December 1987.

Off to the provinces now, starting on the south coast ...

Newhaven is spot and rash and pimple and blister; with the incessant cars like lice.

Virginia Woolf (1882–1941), diary, 1921.

Bugger Bognor.

King George V (1865–1936), attributed remark, c.1929.

This remark was prompted by the suggestion that his chosen resort be renamed 'Bognor Regis'. It still was. The phrase has also been proffered as the King's dying words, in response to the suggestion that he would soon be recuperating there.

The whole of the south coast sums up for Jeremy Taylor what amounts to 'sort of England':

I detected a strange deadness that crept like moss over certain people. It was no respecter of age and could afflict the young and the old alike. I don't know why I should have selected the south coast as the most offending region; perhaps this particular paralysis really was more prevalent there, perhaps I just encountered it there. I certainly never found it up north to the same degree.

> All along the south coast
> the sea is sort of there
> the sun is sort of shining
> through a sort of salt sea air
> there's a sort of shall we or shan't we?
> a sort of yes, or no
> a sort of rolling up of trouser legs
> and a dipping of the toe ...
>
> All along the south coast
> the day is sort of bright
> at least it's sort of brighter
> than it is at sort of night

there's a sort of should we, could we?
a sort of yes, or no
it could be sort of fun
we ought to sort of have a go...

All along the south coast
they're turning out the lights
it's sort of past eleven o'clock
and we've sort of seen the sights
there's a sort of shall we, dare we?
a sort of stroking of the thighs
a sort of gasp of sort of pleasure
and a burst of sort of sighs...

All along the south coast
the waves beat on the shore
they sound, well, sort of different
than they sort of did before
there's a sort of did we, or didn't we?
a sort of smoothing down of clothes
a sort of better take you home now
do you think it sort of shows?

All along the south coast
we sort of settle down
it's just as sort of good
as any other sort of town
only now we're sort of older
we sort of stop at home
we paint the walls and mow the lawn
and leave the world alone ...

All along the south coast
the sea is sort of there
the sun is sort of shining
through a sort of salt sea air
and all along the south coast
can still be sort of seen
a corner of sort of England
that's forever sort of green.

Jeremy Taylor (1938–), song, 'All Along the South Coast', 1971, in Ag Pleeze Deddy!, 1992.

Moving up to Surrey, the Stockbroker Belt filled H.G. Wells with fear and loathing:

Surrey is full of rich stockbrokers, company-promoters, bookies, judges, news-paper proprietors. Sort of people who fence the paths across their parks ... They do something to the old places – I don't known what they do – but instantly the countryside becomes a villadom. And little sub-estates and red-brick villas and art cottages spring up. And a kind of new, hard neatness ... Those Surrey people are not properly English at all. They are strenuous. You have to get on or get out. And they play golf in a large, expensive, thorough way because it's the thing to do.

H.G. Wells (1866–1946), *Mr Britling Sees It Through*, 1916.

Christ! I must be bored. I just thought of Catford.

Spike Milligan (1918–), quoted in Colin Jarman, *The Guinness Dictionary of More Poisonous Quotations*, 1992.

Essex, too, has its fans:

If any one were to ask me what in my opinion was the dullest and most stupid spot on the face of the Earth, I should decidedly say Chelmsford.

Charles Dickens (1812–70), letter, 1835.

... as does Berkshire:

All Berkshire women are very silly. I don't know why women in Berkshire are more silly than anywhere else.

Mr Justice Claude Duveen, Reading County Court, July 1972.

The county of Berkshire also hosts the most loathed town in England. Slough spawned a vast trading estate in the 1920s and thereafter grew and grew:

> Come, friendly bombs, and fall on Slough
> It isn't fit for humans now,
> There isn't grass to graze a cow
> Swarm over, Death!
>
> Come, bombs, and blow to smithereens
> Those air-conditioned, bright canteens,
> Tinned fruit, tinned meat, tinned milk, tinned beans
> Tinned minds, tinned breath.
>
> Mess up the mess they call a town –
> A house for ninety-seven down
> And once a week a half-a-crown
> For twenty years,
>
> And get that man with double chin
> Who'll always cheat and always win,
> Who washes his repulsive skin
> In women's tears,
>
> And smash his desk of polished oak
> And smash his hands so used to stroke
> And stop his boring dirty joke
> And make him yell.
>
> But spare the bald young clerks who add
> The profits of the stinking cad;

It's not their fault that they are mad,
They've tasted Hell.

It's not their fault they do not know
The birdsong from the radio,
It's not their fault they often go
To Maidenhead

And talk of sports and makes of cars
In various bogus Tudor bars
And daren't look up and see the stars
But belch instead.

In labour-saving homes, with care
Their wives frizz out peroxide hair
And dry it in synthetic air
And paint their nails.

Come, friendly bombs, and fall on Slough
To get it ready for the plough.
The cabbages are coming now;
The earth exhales.

John Betjeman (1906–84), 'Slough', in *Continual Dew*, 1937.

Slough has continued to get it in the neck:

The deterioration of much of England has occurred only since the cultural revolution of the 1960s. Most towns only suffered the loss of their appeal when tasteless building work and over-population became rampant. But there are some places which have always been dreadful. Slough, like Woking, is one of them.

The reason for a dedicated branch line from Slough to nearby Windsor is said to be the fact that Queen Victoria couldn't stand having to step out from her train into Slough itself to travel by road the rest of the way. I can well believe it. . . .

It's not easy to put your finger on exactly what is wrong with Slough. The name is a common Saxon word meaning 'mire'. Competing with Keats' 'And no birds sing' as the most depressing phrase in the English language is that which one hears as the train draws into the station: 'Slough, this is Slough'. . . .

Judith Hunter does quite a good job in her book *The Story of Slough*. It's a serious read, which is a shame because I thought from its title that I was going to have a laugh. I suppose I chuckled a bit when I discovered that the book, 'Town History No.7', has 11 full pages of adverts for things like 'Slough – Home of ICI Paints Division Dulux'. And 'Flexello Castors (Sales) Ltd'.

Hunter describes the difficulty historians have had mapping out an accurate description of Slough's past. One of the reasons is that there are relatively few records of the place, which I believe reflects a shortage of scribes. If that's true then it's certainly reflected in the modern Slough, where there is little call for anything in the way of a traditional library. Its local college, Thames Valley University – until recently Slough College of Higher Education – has in recent years been branded 'Britain's worst university' by the press. No small achievement.

In the 1950s, Slough's one remaining picturesque building, Hay Mill, which dated from the thirteenth century, was demolished by far-sighted town planners to make way for car parks and further trading stores.

It is not uncommon to read in the local (and national) press of savage murders committed by gangs in the town where, for instance, the victim's severed head is left by the roadside in one of the town's residential districts. A fair amount of fighting occurs in the town between different racial groups, often between black and Asian or between different Asian groups. The younger Asian generation, not just in Slough but in much of the country, is said to lack the respect and civility upheld by its elders at that age, possibly because they have undergone just that bit too much prejudice from the Anglo-Saxons. They have even developed their own variant of Estuary English. It includes the word 'innit' to replace, obviously, 'isn't it?' but also any other inverted verb formation, such as 'she's a tart, innit?'. But then you've probably seen *Goodness Gracious Me*. ...

Essentially, like so many other grim and depressing places around Britain which have less than nothing of which to be proud, Slough is sepulchral, but it is also about the only place which at least does not appear to adopt that inappropriate sense of local pride I encountered in so many other towns.

Bill Murphy, *Home Truths*, 2000.

In 2000 the local council announced plans to demolish the whole of Slough's town centre and replace it with something nicer. 'We have to admit John Betjeman had a point,' a spokesman said.

Onwards and upwards – first to the Midlands, where Birmingham has suffered its share of derision:

The longest chapter in Deuteronomy has not curses enough for an Anti-Bromingham.

John Dryden (1631–1700), 'To the Reader', 1681.

They came from Birmingham, which is not a place to promise much, you know ... One has not great hopes from Birmingham. I always say there is something direful in the sound.

Jane Austen (1775–1817), Mrs Elton in *Emma*, 1816.

It's a disgusting town with villas and slums and ready made clothes shops and Chambers of Commerce.

Evelyn Waugh (1903–66), Diary, 1925, on Birmingham.

Here's the curmudgeonly Librarian of Hull on England – and Hull in particular:

I am feeling a bit out of sympathy with England at present – God, what a hole, what witless crapulous people, delivered over gagged and bound to TV, motoring and Mackeson's stout! This is partly due to dissatisfaction with where I live – one hideous room, the sort of room you'd get at Blackpool if you tried booking now, and a kitchen the size and quality of a kitchen on an ancient, condemned one-man lugger. God knows how a single man lives unless he has about five thou. a year – even that income wouldn't help much in Hull. It's a frightful dump.

Philip Larkin (1922–85), letter to Robert Conquest, 24 July 1955.

Now it's the turn of Mancunians to be riled:

The shortest way out of Manchester is notoriously a bottle of Gordon's gin.

William Bolitho (1890–1930), 'Caliogstro and Seraphina', in *Twelve Against the Gods*, 1930.

I looked out of the train window and all I could see was rain and fog. 'I know I'm going to love Manchester,' I told Jim, 'if I can only see it.'

Mae West (1892–1980), *Goodness Had Nothing To Do With It*, 1959.

He chose to live in Manchester, a wholly incomprehensible choice for any free human being to make.

Mr Justice Melford Stevenson, quoted in the *Daily Telegraph*, 11 April 1979.

An altogether less frivolous commentator, Friedrich Engels – who for much of his life managed his family's cotton factory in Manchester – has left us an account of life in the city for the working classes in the 1840s:

Masses of refuse, offal and sickening filth lie among standing pools in all directions; the atmosphere is poisoned by the effluvia from these, and laden and darkened by the smoke of a dozen tall factory chimneys. A horde of ragged women and children swarm about here, as filthy as the swine that thrive upon the garbage heaps and in the puddles. In short, the whole rookery furnishes such a hateful and repulsive spectacle as can hardly be equalled in the worst court on the Irk. The race that lives in these ruinous cottages, behind broken windows, mended with oilskin, sprung doors, and rotten door-posts, or in dark, wet cellars, in measureless filth and stench, in this atmosphere penned in as if with a purpose, this race must really have reached the lowest stage of humanity. This is the impression and the line of thought which the exterior of this district forces upon the beholder. But what must one think when he hears that in each of these pens, containing at most two rooms, a garret and perhaps a cellar, on the average twenty human beings live? ...

On Monday, 15 January, 1844 two boys were brought before the police magistrate because, being in a starving condition, they had stolen and immediately devoured a half-cooked calf's foot from a shop. The magistrate felt called upon to investigate the case further, and received the following details from the policeman. The mother of the two boys was the widow of an ex-soldier, afterwards policeman, and had had a very hard time since the death of her husband ... When the policeman came to her, he found her with six of her children literally huddled together in a little back room, with no furniture but two old rush-bottomed chairs with the seats gone, a small table with two legs broken, a broken cup and a small dish. On the hearth was scarcely a spark of fire, and in one corner lay as many old rags as would fill a woman's apron, which served the whole family as a bed.

Friedrich Engels (1820–95), on the district of Manchester known as 'Little Ireland', in *The Condition of the Working Class in England*, 1845.

Another notable (middle-class) observer of the conditions of the working classes in the North was George Orwell. In *The Road to Wigan Pier* he describes life for many during the Great Depression:

Anyone who wants to see the effects of the housing shortage at their very worst should visit the dreadful caravan-dwellings that exist in numbers in many of the northern towns. Ever since the war, in the complete impossibility of getting houses, parts of the population have overflowed into supposedly temporary quarters in fixed caravans. Wigan, for instance, with a population of about 85,000, has round about 200 caravan-dwellings with a family in each – perhaps somewhere near 1000 people in all. How many of these caravan-colonies exist throughout the industrial areas it would be difficult to discover with any accuracy. The local authorities are reticent about them and the census report of 1931 seems to have decided to ignore them. But so far as I can discover by inquiry they are to be found in most of the larger towns in Lancashire and Yorkshire, and perhaps further north as well. The probability is that throughout the north of England there are some thousands, perhaps tens of thousands of *families* (not individuals) who have no home except a fixed caravan.

But the word 'caravan' is very misleading. It calls up a picture of a cosy gypsy-encampment (in fine weather, of course) with wood fires crackling and children picking blackberries and many-coloured washing fluttering on the lines. The caravan-colonies in Wigan and Sheffield are not like that. I had a look at several of them, I inspected those in Wigan with considerable care, and I have never seen comparable squalor except in the Far East. Indeed when I saw them I was immediately reminded of the filthy kennels in which I have seen Indian coolies living in Burma. But, as a matter of fact, nothing in the East could ever be quite as bad, for in the East you haven't our clammy, penetrating cold to contend with, and the sun is a disinfectant.

Along the banks of Wigan's miry canal are patches of waste ground on which the caravans have been dumped like rubbish shot out of a bucket. Some of them are actually gypsy caravans but very old ones and in bad repair. The majority are old single-decker buses (the rather smaller buses of ten years ago) which have been taken off their wheels and propped up with struts of wood. Some are simply wagons with semi-circular slats on top, over which canvas is stretched, so that the people inside have nothing but canvas between them and the outer air. Inside, these places are usually about five feet wide by six high (I could not stand quite upright in any of them) and anything from six to fifteen feet long. Some, I suppose, are inhabited by only one person, but I did not see any that held less than two persons, and some of them contained large families. One, for instance, measuring fourteen feet long, had seven people in it – seven people in about 450 cubic feet of space; which is to say that each person had for his entire dwelling a space a good deal smaller than one compartment of a public lavatory. The dirt and congestion of these places is such that you cannot well imagine it unless you have tested it with your own eyes and more particularly your nose. Each contains a tiny cottage kitchener and such furniture as can be crammed in – sometimes two beds, more usually one, into which the whole family have to huddle as best they can. It is almost impossible to sleep on the floor, because the damp soaks up from below.

I was shown mattresses which were still wringing wet at eleven in the morning. In winter it is so cold that the kitcheners have to be kept burning day and night, and the windows, needless to say, are never opened. Water is got from a hydrant common to the whole colony, some of the caravan-dwellers having to walk 150 or 200 yards for every bucket of water. There are no sanitary arrangements at all. Most of the people construct a little hut to serve as a lavatory on the tiny patch of ground surrounding their caravan, and once a week dig a deep hole in which to bury the refuse. All the people I saw in these places, especially the children, were unspeakably dirty, and I do not doubt that they were lousy as well. They could not possibly be otherwise. The thought that haunted me as I went from caravan to caravan was, What can happen in those cramped interiors when anybody dies? But that, of course, is the kind of question you hardly care to ask.

George Orwell (1903–50), *The Road to Wigan Pier*, 1937.

THE BLOODY (2): A PARADISE DESPOIL'D

This is the dark side of the English love of countryside: the sense of loss, of betrayal, at its degradation. The earlier extracts are from writers who knew at first hand what had been lost; the later ones express the feeling shared by the growing urban majority, that they have been 'done out of' something – that 'something' being an unconscious sense of birthright, though few would express it that way.

From the time of the first enclosures under Elizabeth I, the English have mourned the passing of something elemental to them, much as Wordsworth mourned the loss of the 'visionary gleam' of childhood. After nearly 500 years of this, one might think there was nothing left to lose, yet it is not so. Much of England, including the area I have come to know best, is not 'mere scenery'. It is not the fiefdom of hedge-destroying, environment-raping agribusiness; it is the way it is, and looks the way it does (which is much the way the visitor wants it to look) thanks to the toil of innumerable small-scale, family farmers – Cobbett would recognise them at once – who, although many of them could sell up tomorrow and put a million pounds or more in the bank, carry on for a financial reward that, in recent years (and despite all those much-derided subsidies), has not been enough to trouble the Inland Revenue, and wouldn't keep the average media pundit going much beyond a month. What has really been lost – never mind any understanding of how or why they do it – is any recognition on the part of urban England (the England of the mass media and the 'opinion-formers') that they do it at all. Cheap, high-quality food cannot be produced in a 'peasant landscape'; yet the urban English bewail their loss of 'rural heritage' while at the same time demanding the means of its destruction.

Perhaps this is, after all, merely an example of the peculiarly English desire to have one's cake and eat it.

In the 18th century, agricultural 'improvement' became all the rage among the big landowners, and the resulting increases in productivity helped to feed the growing towns and cities of the Industrial Revolution. However, 'improvement' was accompanied by large-scale enclosures of common land. Oliver Goldsmith mourned the disappearance of the English peasant farmer, and in *The Deserted Village* gives a picture of a lost way of life.

> Sweet Auburn, loveliest village of the plain,
> Where health and plenty cheared the labouring swain,
> Where smiling spring its earliest visit paid,
> And parting summer's lingering blooms delayed,
> Dear lovely bowers of innocence and ease,
> Seats of my youth, when every sport could please
>
> . . .
>
> These round thy bowers their chearful influence shed
> These were thy charms – But all these charms are fled.
>
> Sweet smiling village, loveliest of the lawn,
> Thy sports are fled, and all thy charms withdrawn;
> Amidst thy bowers the tyrant's hand is seen,
> And desolation saddens all thy green:
> One only master grasps the whole domain,
> And half a tillage stints thy smiling plain;
> No more thy glassy brook reflects the day,
> But choaked with sedges, works its weedy way.
> Along thy glades, a solitary guest,
> The hollow sounding bittern guards its nest;
> Amidst thy desert walks the lapwing flies,
> And tires their echoes with unvaried cries.
> Sunk are thy bowers in shapeless ruin all,
> And the long grass o'ertops the mouldering wall,
> And trembling, shrinking from the spoiler's hand,
> Far, far away thy children leave the land.
>
> Ill fares the land, to hastening ills a prey,
> Where wealth accumulates, and men decay;
> Princes and lords may flourish, or may fade;
> A breath can make them, as a breath has made.
> But a bold peasantry, their country's pride,
> When once destroyed, can never be supplied.
>
> A time there was, ere England's griefs began,
> When every rood of ground maintained its man;
> For him light labour spread her wholesome store,
> Just gave what life required, but gave no more.
> His best companions, innocence and health;
> And his best riches, ignorance of wealth.
>
> But times are altered; trade's unfeeling train
> Usurp the land and dispossess the swain:
> Along the lawn, where scattered hamlets rose,
> Unwieldy wealth, and cumbrous pomp repose;

And every want to oppulence allied,
And every pang that folly pays to pride.
These gentle hours that plenty bade to bloom,
Those calm desires that asked but little room,
Those healthful sports that graced the peaceful scene,
Lived in each look, and brightened all the green;
These far departing seek a kinder shore,
And rural mirth and manners are no more.

Sweet Auburn! parent of the blissful hour,
Thy glades forlorn confess the tyrant's power.
Here as I take my solitary rounds,
Amidst thy tangling walks, and ruined grounds,
And, many a year elapsed, return to view
Where once the cottage stood, the hawthorn grew,
Remembrance wakes with all her busy train,
Swells at my breast, and turns the past to pain.

Oliver Goldsmith (c.1730–74), from *The Deserted Village*, 1770.

George Crabbe wrote *The Village* as a kind of riposte to Goldsmith,
rejecting the idealisation of rural life:

Fled are those times when, in harmonious strains,
The rustic poet praised his native plains.
No shepherds now, in smooth alternate verse,
Their country's beauty or their nymphs' rehearse;
Yet still for these we frame the tender strain,
Still in our lays fond Corydons complain,
And shepherds' boys their amorous pains reveal,
The only pains, alas! they ever feel. . . .
Yes, thus the Muses sing of happy swains,
Because the Muses never knew their pains.
They boast the peasants' pipes; but peasants now
Resign their pipes and plod behind the plough;
And few, amid the rural-tribe, have time
To number syllables, and play with rhyme; . . .
I grant indeed that fields and flocks have charms
For him that grazes or for him that farms;
But, when amid such pleasing scenes I trace
The poor laborious natives of this place,
And see the mid-day sun, with fervid ray,
On their bare heads and dewy temples play;
While some, with feebler heads and fainter hearts,
Deplore their fortune, yet sustain their parts:
Then shall I dare these real ills to hide
In tinsel trappings of poetic pride?
. . .

Lo! where the heath, with withering brake grown o'er,
Lends the light turf that warms the neighbouring poor;
From thence a length of burning sand appears,
Where the thin harvest waves its wither'd ears;
Rank weeds, that every art and care defy,
Reign o'er the land, and rob the blighted rye:
There thistles stretch their prickly arms afar,
And to the ragged infant threaten war;
There poppies, nodding, mock the hope of toil;
There the blue bugloss paints the sterile soil;
Hardy and high, above the slender sheaf,
The slimy mallow waves her silky leaf;
O'er the young shoot the charlock throws a shade,
And clasping tares cling round the sickly blade;
With mingled tints the rocky coasts abound,
And a sad splendour vainly shines around.
. . .

Here joyless roam a wild amphibious race,
With sullen woe display'd in every face;
Who far from civil arts and social fly,
And scowl at strangers with suspicious eye.

George Crabbe (1754–1832), from *The Village*, 1783, Book I.

William Cobbett – who mixed radicalism with a profound conservatism – held that the adulation of the free market and the resulting drive for economic efficiency had resulted not only in an increase in rural poverty, but also in a degradation of the dignity of the common people:

In those 'dark ages' that the impudent Scotch economists talk about, we had a great many holidays. There were all the fairs of our own place, and all the fairs of the places just round about. There were several days at Christmas, at Easter, at Whitsuntide; and we had a day or two at Hollantide, as we used to call it, which came in November, I believe, and at Candlemass. Besides these, there were cricket-matches, and single-stick matches; and all these were not thought too much. I verily believe, that if I had been born in these [present] days of slavery, of rags, and of hunger, I should never have been any more known in the world, than the chap I, this very moment, see slinking by the side of a road-waggon, with scarcely a shoe on his foot, and with a smock-frock that none but actual beggars wore in the 'dark ages', when I was a boy.

I never knew a labouring man, in those 'dark ages', go out to his work in the morning without a bottle of beer and a satchel of victuals, containing cheese, if not bacon, hung upon his crook. A bottle-crook made as usual a part of the equipage of a labourer, as his smock-frock, or his hat did. Except in about five or six instances, in Essex, I have not seen a bottle-crook these twenty years.

In the 'dark ages', when I was a boy, country labourers' wives used to spin the wool, and knit the stockings and gloves that were wanted in the family. My grandmother knit stockings for me after she was blind. Farmers' wives and daughters, and servant maids, were spinning, reeling, carding, knitting, or at something or other of that sort, whenever the work of the farm-house did not demand them.

According, be it observed, that there wanted no schools, no Lancastrian or Bell work, no Tracts, no circulation of Bibles, to make the common people generally honest and obedient. I remember a little sort of fair that used to be held at a village in Surrey. I remember the white smock-frocks and red handkerchiefs, and nice clean clothes of the girls, that used to ornament that fair. By accident, I stumbled upon it in a rural ride [in 1822]. Not a tenth part of the people, and these, in general ragged and dirty, with some few girls drawn off in tawdry cottons, looking more like town prostitutes than country girls; and this was a pretty fair sample of the whole country.

The truth is, that the system which has been pursued in England from the time of the Revolution [of 1688], the system of government debt, is a system which begins by totally debasing the labouring classes, and that ends by producing its own overthrow, and, generally, that of the state along with it. It draws property into great masses; it gives to cunning the superiority over industry; it makes agriculture a subject of adventure; it puts down all small cultivators; it encloses every inch of that land which God himself seems to have intended for the poor. ...

[Look,] for a minute, to the little village of Stoke-Charity, near to Winchester, that grand scene of ancient learning, piety, and munificence. The parish formerly contained ten farms, and it contained but two [in 1824]. There used to be ten well-fed families in this parish, at any rate; and [in 1824] all were half starved except the curate and two families. The blame was not the landlord's; it was nobody's; it was due to the infernal funding and taxing system, which of necessity drove property into large masses in order to save itself; which crushed little proprietors down into labourers; and which pressed them down in that state and made them paupers, their share of food and raiment being taken away to support debt and dead-weight and army and all the rest of the enormous expenses, which were required to sustain [the] intolerable system. ...

[By the year 1830,] as the working people went on getting poorer and poorer, they became more and more immoral, in innumerable instances men committed crimes for the purpose of getting into jail; because the felons in jail were better fed and better clad than the honest working people. As the working people became poor, the laws relating to them were made more and more severe; and the Poor-Law, that famous law of Elizabeth, which was the greatest glory of England for ages, had by degrees been so much mutilated and nullified, that, at last, it was so far from being a protection for the working people, that it had, by its perversions, been made the means of reducing them to a state of wretchedness not to be described. The sole food of the greater part of them had been, for many years, bread, or potatoes, and not half enough of these. They had eaten sheep or cattle that had died from illness; children had been seen stealing food out of hog-troughs; men were found dead, [in] May [of that] year, lying under a hedge, and when opened by the surgeons nothing but sour sorrel was found in their stomachs. The spot on which these poor creatures expired was surrounded with villas of Jews, and fund-jobbers, living in luxury, and in the midst of pleasure-gardens, all the means of which living they had derived from the burdens laid on the working people.

Besides suffering from want, the working people were made to endure insults and indignities such as even Negroes were never exposed to. They were harnessed like horses or asses and made to draw carts and wagons; they were shut up in pounds made to hold stray cattle; they were made to work with bells round their necks; and they had drivers set over them, just as if they had been galley slaves; they were sold by auction for certain times, as the Negroes were sold in the West Indies; the married men were kept separated from their wives, by force, to prevent them from breeding; and, in short, no human beings were ever before treated so unjustly, with so much insolence, and with such damnable barbarity, as the working people of England had been. Such were the fruits of public debts and funds! Without them, this industrious and moral and brave nation never could have been brought into this degraded state.

William Cobbett (1763–1835), *The Autobiography of William Cobbett*, ed. William Reitzel, 1933, 1967.

For some city-dwellers, the countryside is a place of hidden sins …

By eleven o'clock the next day we were well upon our way to the old English capital. Holmes had been buried in the morning papers all the way down, but after we had passed the Hampshire border he threw them down, and began to admire the scenery. It was an ideal spring day, a light-blue sky, flecked with little fleecy white clouds drifting across from west to east. The sun was shining very brightly, and yet there was an exhilarating nip in the air, which set an edge to a man's energy. All over the countryside, away to the rolling hills around Aldershot, the little red and grey roofs of the farmsteadings peeped out from amidst the light green of the new foliage.

'Are they not fresh and beautiful?' I cried, with all the enthusiasm of a man fresh from the fogs of Baker Street.

But Holmes shook his head gravely.

'Do you know, Watson,' said he, 'that it is one of the curses of a mind with a turn like mine that I must look at everything with reference to my own special subject. You look at these scattered houses, and you are impressed by their beauty. I look at them, and the only thought which comes to me is a feeling of their isolation, and of the impunity with which crime may be committed there.'

'Good heavens!' I cried. 'Who would associate crime with these dear old home-steads?'

'They always fill me with a certain horror. It is my belief, Watson, founded upon my experience, that the lowest and vilest alleys in London do not present a more dreadful record of sin than does the smiling and beautiful countryside.'

'You horrify me!'

'But the reason is very obvious. The pressure of public opinion can do in the town what the law cannot accomplish. There is no lane so vile that the scream of a tortured child, or the thud of a drunkard's blow, does not beget sympathy and indignation among the neighbours, and then the whole machinery of justice is ever so close that a word of complaint can set it going, and there is but a step between the crime and the dock. But look at these lonely houses, each in its own fields, filled for the most part with poor ignorant folk who know little of the law. Think of the deeds of hellish cruelty, the hidden wickedness which may go on, year in, year out, in such places, and none the wiser. Had this lady who appeals to us for help gone to live in Winchester, I should never have had a fear for her. It is the five miles of country which makes the danger.'

Sir Arthur Conan Doyle (1859–1930), 'The Adventure of the Copper Beeches', from *The Adventures of Sherlock Holmes*, 1892.

For D.H. Lawrence, in melancholy mood, the end of autumn in 1915 symbolised the end of England:

When I drive across this country; with autumn falling and rustling to pieces, I am so sad, for my country, for this great wave of civilisation, 2000 years, which is now collapsing, that it is hard to live. So much beauty and pathos of old things passing away and no new things coming: this house – it is England – my God, it breaks my soul – their England, these shafted windows, the elm-trees, the blue distance – the past, the great past, crumbling down, breaking down, not under the force of the coming birds, but under the weight of many exhausted lovely yellow leaves, that drift over the lawn, and over the pond, like the soldiers, passing away, into winter and the darkness of winter – no, I can't bear it. For the winter stretches ahead, where all vision is lost and all memory dies out.

It has been 2000 years, the spring and summer of our era. What, then, will the winter be? No, I can't bear it, I can't let it go. Yet who can stop the autumn from falling to pieces, when November has come in? It is almost better to be dead, than to see this awful process finally strangling us to oblivion, like the leaves off the trees.

I want to go to America, to Florida, as soon as I can: as soon as I have enough money to cross with Frieda. My life is ended here. I must go as a seed that falls into new ground. But this, this England, these elm-trees, the grey wind with yellow leaves – it is so awful, the being gone from it altogether, one must be blind henceforth. But better leave a quick of hope in the soul, than all the beauty that fills the eyes.

It sounds very rhapsodic: it is this old house, the beautiful shafted windows, the grey gate-pillars under the elm trees: really I can't bear it: the past, the past, the falling, perishing, crumbling past, so great, so magnificent.

D.H. Lawrence (1885–1930), letter to Lady Cynthia Asquith from Garsington Manor, Oxford, 9 November 1915, from *The Letters of D.H. Lawrence*, 1932.

In *Akenfield*, Ronald Blythe's celebrated portrait of an English village, Leonard Thompson, a farm worker, recalls the years immediately after the First World War:

I want to say this simply as a fact, that village people in Suffolk in my day were worked to death. It literally happened. It is not a figure of speech. I was worked mercilessly. I am not complaining about it. It is what happened to me. ....

The slump set in during the great hot summer of 1921. I remember it well. We had no rain from March right through to October. The corn didn't grow no more than a foot high and most of it didn't even come to the ear. We harvested what we could and the last loads were leaving the field when we heard, 'the wages are coming down this week'. It was true. The farmers told the men that they would be given 42s. 6d. Then it was 38s. 6d. A fortnight later on the farm where I worked it was 'You'll have to be on short-time – the boss can only afford to give you 27s. 6d. a week'. And that is what we lived on all that bad winter.

It was the Government's fault. They ended the Corn Act less than a year after it had been made law. They said it was best if the farmers made their own bargains, which meant that they wouldn't pay the subsidies. The price of wheat was quartered in a year. Cattle were sold for next to nothing because the farmers couldn't afford to keep them. The farmers became broke and frightened, so they took it out on us men. We reminded them that we had fought in the war, and they reminded us that they had too! So it was hate all round. Then we had to close down our Union Branch because nobody could afford to pay the 4d. a week membership fee. I remember the week this happened. I drew 27s. 6d. from the farmer and after I had given my wife 24s. and paid my Union 4d. and my rent 3s. 1d., I had a penny left! So I threw it across the field. I'd worked hard, I'd been through the war and I'd married. A penny was what a child had. I wasn't having that. I would sooner have nothing.

Leonard Thompson (b.1898), in Ronald Blythe, *Akenfield*, 1969.

While Leonard Thompson experienced the agricultural depression of the 1920s at first hand and with dignity, others who bothered to look saw only a debased people, almost an alien race …

Dank thatch and slipped slates leak. Moisture runs down the inside of walls. Floors are very damp where they have always been very damp.

Two or three dumpy, blemished folk squatter on the muddy road.

At one cottage door a slattern, who was not always a slattern, takes in from the baker four ill-baked loaves that her untidy children paw.

Within another cottage door the perky, talkative credit-store man from Thurton asks the price for a skirt that poor people pay who buy on tick. In the worst cottage a labourer lies in his coffin, and his niece is wearily thankful and also a little appreciative of the drama in which death has made her a conspicuous player.

Mrs. Bloss at her back door thanking, in her kind way, the wet postman for her monthly circular of the Polynesian Mission, is just too late to hear the groans and the shrieks of a woman, wraith-like for months past, giving birth and her life to an unwanted infant in a poor cottage to which the school would be returning in two hours, but for the neighbours' mercy, six children.

The parson, cycling past to take tea with the Richardsons, has in full view the five worst cottages of the hamlet we have heard about. They are in Categories IV, V, and VI of the official transcript which gives particulars of all the cottages of the parish. . . .

Condition of Cottages	In our Hamlet	In rest of Parish
I. Up to Ministry of Health's requirements	None	None
II. Would be so with slight alterations	1	2
III. Would be so by being added to	1	2
IV. Would be so with a large outlay	2	2
V. Not worth repair	1	12
VI. Unfit for habitation	2	8
	7	26

These five cottages that the parson was passing have each two 'bedrooms', let us call them sleeping places. These sleeping places average 12 ft. long by 9 ft. wide by 7 ft. high.

If you will kindly get up from your chair and pace on the floor twelve boot-lengths by nine boot-lengths, and reach up a little on the wall beyond your height to seven feet, the facts will come home to you. The cottages are as far short of window space as they are of cubic capacity.

There slept last night in these five cottages which have two sleeping places apiece:

First Cottage: Mother, grandfather, two boys.

Second Cottage: Husband and wife, lodger, four children.

Third Cottage: Husband and wife, four girls, two boys, a baby.

Fourth Cottage: Husband and wife, a young man, two young women, two boys.

Fifth Cottage: Husband and wife, grown-up daughter, a younger girl, two young men.

In three of the cottages there is an illegitimate. In four cottages there are first-born who arrived, as so many of the firstborn in these parts do arrive, impolitely soon after the marriage of their parents.

Consider the schoolmistress's task with the physical and mental endowments, manners, sentiments, beliefs and habits of the children of these five cottages.

Consider the chances of 'social work' with their fathers and mothers.

A recent visitor to the hamlet asked if the people were interested in folk dancing. No, the people are not interested in folk dancing; and there are things most of them are more interested in than politics and the Church.

Such as, in varying degrees, what they have to eat, the weather, gossip, how to make ends meet, the growth of things, police news from the Sunday paper or local paper, old age, the day's work, sexual relations, gardens and allotments, tobacco, beer, betting. . . .

Better wages would provide the rents for better homes. But in some of these cottages, in which there are several wage-earners, there is already an income sufficient to pay the rent of a decent dwelling. There is no decent dwelling to go to, however.

And many of these people have slithered down to such a condition of fecklessness that they are incapable of putting forth the effort on their own behalf necessary to bring about the building of new cottages by the local authorities.

These people have never acted on their own behalf. They have no tradition of doing so, no memory of independence. They have not the advantage of being members of churches of 'disruptions' in which minorities have taken their stand on principles, and people have held to their views though it cost them money and homes.

Not one of these people is in a trade union. These people believe, what is true, that, sooner or later, they would 'get wrong' with Farmer Richardson and the smaller masters if they joined.

Better conditions of life are their due. Let us press forward, by every possible means, the urgent work of putting sanitary dwellings in the place of their hovels.

But to think that better housing alone will at once make very much better men and women of these afflicted people is folly. Something is lacking in them.

J.W. Robertson-Scott (1866–1962), journalist and housing adviser, from *England's Green and Pleasant Land: The Truth Attempted*, 1925.

Aesthetic and environmental changes to the countryside wrought by the modernisation of agricultural practices and creeping urbanisation have generally been of greater concern to the English middle classes than the plight of the rural poor:

The fact cannot be avoided: how much that we loved is going or gone! It is not a tremendous old age that has justified me in this exclamation. I am still merely an old young man. I have known an England in which the water mill and the windmill were regular, familiar workers; already the few of them that have not been dismantled by weather or by the improver are anxiously numbered up as antiquities which ought, if we can contrive it, to be preserved. It is a great rarity to find one that is still working – sometimes they suffer the indignity of being used as sheds for oil engines. The streams of my old home were kept clear and lively by a system of sluice-gates and tumbling-bays, when farmers flourished who understood the matter; those streams are now choked and stagnant. Ponds, that were felt to be valuable for just their beauty, are rubbish heaps; the owners have no eye for them. Rivers that poured a pure wave are defiled with the poisons that accompany our mechanical development; the radiant noonday pool in which you saw here a shoal of bluish bream, there a hundred silvery roach, and a pike or two on the warm sandy shallow beyond, is not to be seen. Paths that were as good as roads are overwhelmed with nettles and briars; or the stiles that admitted to them are uprooted, and wire fences run in their stead; although we never needed our paths so manifestly. Meadow after meadow disappears; the rabbit scarcely has time to move out before the next row of villas is affronting the retreating woods with the confectionery of the builder's yard.

Edmund Blunden (1896–1974), poet and critic, *The Face of England*, 1932.

Poets have often looked back to a lost (and usually imaginary) Arcadia. In the 1930s the poet W.H. Auden regretfully observed how the 'traditional' countryside, even then, was becoming more a leisure resource than a living, working landscape:

We would show you at first an English village: You shall choose its location
Wherever your heart directs you most longingly to look; you are loving towards it:
Whether north to Scots Gap and Bellingham where the black rams defy the pant-
    ing engine:
Or west to the Welsh Marches; to the lilting speech and the magicians' faces:
Wherever you were a child or had your first affair
There it stands amidst your darling scenery:
A parish bounded by the wreckers' cliff; or meadows where browse the Shorthorn
    and the maplike Frisian
As at Trent Junction where the Soar comes gliding; out of green Leicestershire to
    swell the ampler current.

Hiker with sunburn blisters on your office pallor,
Cross-country champion with corks in your hands,
When you have eaten your sandwich, your salt and your apple,
When you have begged your glass of milk from the ill-kept farm,
What is it you see?

I see barns falling, fences broken,
Pasture not ploughland, weeds not wheat.
The great houses remain but only half are inhabited,
Dusty the gunrooms and the stable clocks stationary.
Some have been turned into prep-schools where the diet is in the hands of an
    experienced matron,
Others into club-houses for the golf-bore and the top-hole.
Those who sang in the inns at evening have departed; they saw their hope in
    another country,
Their children have entered the service of the suburban areas; they have become typ-
    ists, mannequins and factory operatives; they desired a different rhythm of life.
But their places are taken by another population, with views about nature,
Brought in charabanc and saloon along arterial roads;
Tourists to whom the Tudor cafés
Offer Bovril and buns upon Breton ware
With leather work as a sideline: Filling stations
Supplying petrol from rustic pumps.
Those who fancy themselves as foxes or desire a special setting for spooning
Erect their villas at the right places,
Airtight, lighted, elaborately warmed;
And nervous people who will never marry
Live upon dividends in the old-world cottages
With an animal for friend or a volume of memoirs.

W.H. Auden (1907–73), from *The Dog Beneath the Skin*, 1935.

George Orwell's character George Bowling also witnessed the building-over of the country-side of his childhood with sadness – and not a little anger:

It was queer, queerer than I can tell you. Did you ever read a story of H.G. Wells's about a chap who was in two places at once – that's to say, he was really in his own home, but he had a kind of hallucination that he was at the bottom of the sea? He'd be walking round his room, but instead of the tables and chairs he'd see the wavy waterweed and the great crabs and cuttlefish reaching out to get him. Well, it was just like that. For hours on end I'd be walking through a world that wasn't there. I'd count my paces as I went down the pavement and think, 'Yes, here's where so-and-so's field begins. The hedge runs across the street and slap through that house. That petrol pump is really an elm tree. And here's the edge of the allotments. And this street (it was a dismal little row of semi-detached houses called Cumberledge Road, I remember) is the lane where we used to go with Katie Simmons, and the nut-bushes grew on both sides.' No doubt I got the distances wrong, but the general directions were right. I don't believe anyone who hadn't happened to be born here would have believed that these streets were fields as little as twenty years ago. It was as though the countryside had been buried by a kind of volcanic eruption from the outer suburbs. Nearly the whole of what used to be old Brewer's land had been swallowed up in the Council housing estate. The Mill Farm had vanished, the cow-pond where I caught my first fish had been drained and filled up and built over, so that I couldn't even say exactly where it used to stand. It was all houses, houses, little red cubes of houses all alike, with privet hedges and asphalt paths leading up to the front door. Beyond the Council Estate the town thinned out a bit, but the jerry-builders were doing their best. And there were little knots of houses dumped down here and there, wherever anybody had been able to buy a plot of land, and makeshift roads leading up to the houses, and empty lots with builders' boards, and bits of ruined fields covered with thistles and tin cans. ...

What a fool I'd been to imagine that these woods were still the same! I saw how it was. There was just the one tiny bit of copse, half a dozen acres perhaps, that hadn't been cut down, and it was pure chance that I'd walked through it on my way here. Upper Binfield, which had been merely a name in the old days, had grown into a decent-sized town. In fact it was merely an outlying chunk of Lower Binfield.

I wandered up to the edge of the pool. The kids were splashing about and making the devil of a noise. There seemed to be swarms of them. The water looked kind of dead. No fish in it now. There was a chap standing watching the kids. He was an oldish chap with a bald head and a few tufts of white hair, and pince-nez and a very sunburnt face. ...

'Upper Binfield's grown a great deal.' I said.

He twinkled at me.

'Grown! My dear sir, we never allow Upper Binfield to grow. We pride ourselves on being rather exceptional people up here, you know. Just a little colony of us all by ourselves. No interlopers – te-hee!'

'I mean compared with before the war,' I said. 'I used to live here as a boy.'

'Oh-ah. No doubt. That was before my time, of course. But the Upper Binfield

Estate is something rather special in the way of building estates, you know. Quite a little world of its own. All designed by young Edward Watkin, the architect. You've heard of him, of course. We live in the midst of Nature up here. No connexion with the town down there' – he waved a hand in the direction of Lower Binfield – 'the dark satanic mills – te-hee!'

He had a benevolent old chuckle, and a way of wrinkling his face up, like a rabbit. Immediately, as though I'd asked him, he began telling me all about the Upper Binfield Estate and young Edward Watkin, the architect, who had such a feeling for the Tudor, and was such a wonderful fellow at finding genuine Elizabethan beams in old farmhouses and buying them at ridiculous prices. And such an interesting young fellow, quite the life and soul of the nudist parties. He repeated a number of times that they were very exceptional people in Upper Binfield, quite different from Lower Binfield, they were determined to enrich the countryside instead of defiling it (I'm using his own phrase), and there weren't any public houses on the estate:

'They talk of their Garden Cities. But we call Upper Binfield the Woodland City – te-hee! Nature!' He waved a hand at what was left of the trees. 'The primeval forest brooding round us. Our young people grow up amid surroundings of natural beauty. We are nearly all of us enlightened people, of course. Would you credit that three-quarters of us up here are vegetarians? The local butchers don't like us at all – te-hee! And some quite eminent people live here. Miss Helena Thurloe, the novelist – you've heard of her, of course? And Professor Woad, the psychic research-worker. Such a poetic character! He goes wandering out into the woods and the family can't find him at mealtimes. He says he's walking among the fairies. Do you believe in fairies? I admit – te-hee! – I am just a wee bit sceptical. But his photographs are most convincing.' ...

I knew the type. Vegetarianism, simple life, poetry, nature-worship, roll in the dew before breakfast. I'd met a few of them years ago in Ealing. He began to show me round the estate. There was nothing left of the woods. It was all houses, houses – and what houses! Do you know these faked-up Tudor houses with the curly roofs and the buttresses that don't buttress anything, and the rock-gardens with concrete bird-baths and those red plaster elves you can buy at the florists? You could see in your mind's eye the awful gang of food-cranks and spook-hunters and simple-lifers with £1,000 a year that lived here. Even the pavements were crazy. ... Finally I stopped and said:

'There used to be another pool, besides the big one. It can't be far from here.'

'Another pool? Oh, surely not. I don't think there was ever another pool.'

'They may have drained it off,' I said. 'It was a pretty deep pool. It would leave a big pit behind.'

For the first time he looked a bit uneasy. He rubbed his nose.

'Oh-ah. Of course, you must understand our life up here is in some ways primitive. The simple life, you know. We prefer it so. But being so far from the town has its inconveniences, of course. Some of our sanitary arrangements are not altogether satisfactory. The dust-cart only calls once a month, I believe.'

'You mean they've turned the pool into a rubbish-dump?'

'Well, there is something in the nature of a –' he shied at the word rubbish-dump.

'We have to dispose of tins and so forth, of course. Over there, behind that clump of trees.'

We went across there. They'd left a few trees to hide it. But yes, there it was. It was my pool, all right. They'd drained the water off. It made a great round hole, like an enormous well, twenty or thirty feet deep. Already it was half full of tin cans.

I stood looking at the tin cans.

'It's a pity they drained it,' I said. 'There used to be some big fish in that pool.'

'Fish? Oh, I never heard anything about that. Of course we could hardly have a pool of water here among the houses. The mosquitoes, you know. But it was before my time.'

'I suppose these houses have been built a good long time?' I said.

'Oh – ten or fifteen years, I think.'

'I used to know this place before the war,' I said. 'It was all woods then. There weren't any houses except Binfield House. But that little bit of copse over there hasn't changed. I walked through it on my way here.'

'Ah, that! That is sacrosanct. We have decided never to build in it. It is sacred to the young people. Nature, you know.' He twinkled at me, a kind of roguish look, as if he was letting me into a little secret: 'We call it the Pixy Glen.'

The Pixy Glen. I got rid of him, went back to the car and drove down to Lower Binfield. The Pixy Glen. And they'd filled my pool up with tin cans. God rot them and bust them! Say what you like – call it silly, childish, anything – but doesn't it make you puke sometimes to see what they're doing to England, with their bird-baths and their plaster gnomes, and their pixies and tin cans, where the beechwoods used to be?

Sentimental, you say? Anti-social? Oughtn't to prefer trees to men? I say it depends what trees and what men. Not that there's anything one can do about it, except to wish them the pox in their guts.

George Orwell (1903–50), *Coming Up For Air,* 1939.

Even the land of the Hobbits was not immune to industrialisation and urban sprawl:

The travellers trotted on, and as the sun began to sink towards the White Downs far away on the western horizon they came to Bywater by its wide pool; and there they had their first really painful shock. This was Frodo and Sam's own country, and they found out now that they cared about it more than any other place in the world. Many of the houses that they had known were missing. Some seemed to have been burned down. The pleasant row of old hobbit-holes in the bank on the north side of the Pool were deserted, and their little gardens that used to run down right to the water's edge were rank with weeds. Worse, there was a whole line of the ugly new houses all along Pool Side, where the Hobbiton Road ran close to the bank. An avenue of trees had stood there. They were all gone. And looking with dismay up the road towards Bag End they saw a tall chimney of brick in the distance. It was pouring out black smoke into the evening air. ....

'It all began with Pimple, as we call him,' said Farmer Cotton; 'and it began as soon as you'd gone off, Mr. Frodo. He'd funny ideas, had Pimple. Seems he wanted to own everything himself, and then order other folk about. It soon came out that he already did own a sight more than was good for him; and he was always grabbing more, though where he got the money was a mystery: mills and malt-houses and inns, and farms, and leaf-plantations. He'd already bought Sandyman's mill before he came to Bag End, seemingly. . . .

'Take Sandyman's mill now. Pimple knocked it down almost as soon as he came to Bag End. Then he brought in a lot o' dirty-looking Men to build a bigger one and fill it full o' wheels and outlandish contraptions. Only that fool Ted was pleased by that, and he works there cleaning wheels for the Men, where his dad was the Miller and his own master. Pimple's idea was to grind more and faster, or so he said. He's got other mills like it. But you've got to have grist before you can grind; and there was no more for the new mill to do than for the old. . . . They're always a-hammering and a-letting out a smoke and a stench, and there isn't no peace even at night in Hobbiton. And they pour out filth a purpose; they've fouled all the lower Water, and it's getting down into Brandywine. If they want to make the Shire into a desert, they're going the right way about it.' . . .

It was one of the saddest hours in their lives. The great chimney rose up before them; and as they drew near the old village across the Water, through rows of new mean houses along each side of the road, they saw the new mill in all its frowning and dirty ugliness: a great brick building straddling the stream, which it fouled with a steaming and stinking outflow. All along the Bywater Road every tree had been felled.

As they crossed the bridge and looked up the Hill they gasped. . . . The Old Grange on the west side had been knocked down, and its place taken by rows of tarred sheds. All the chestnuts were gone. The banks and hedgerows were broken. Great wagons were standing in disorder in a field beaten bare of grass. Bagshot Row was a yawning sand and gravel quarry. Bag End up beyond could not be seen for a clutter of large huts. . . .

'This is worse than Mordor!' said Sam. 'Much worse in a way. It comes home to you, as they say; because it is home, and you remember it before it was all ruined.'

J.R.R. Tolkien (1892–1973), *The Lord of the Rings*, Part III, 'The Return of the King', 1955.

For John Betjeman, the urge of the town-and-country planners to rationalise was the curse and doom of the countryside:

'Yes, the Town Clerk will see you.' In I went.
He was, like all Town Clerks, from north of Trent;
A man with bye-laws busy in his head
Whose Mayor and Council followed where he led.
His most capacious brain will make us cower,
His only weakness is a lust for power –
And that is not a weakness, people think,
When unaccompanied by bribes or drink.
So let us hear this cool careerist tell
His plans to turn our country into hell.
'I cannot say how shock'd I am to see
The variations in our scenery.
Just take for instance, at a casual glance,

Our muddled coastline opposite to France:
Dickensian houses by the Channel tides
With old hipp'd roofs and weather-boarded sides.
I blush to think one corner of our isle
Lacks concrete villas in the modern style.
Straight lines of hops in pale brown earth of Kent,
Yeomen's square houses once, no doubt, content
With willow-bordered horse-pond, oast-house, shed,
Wide orchard, garden walls of browny-red –
All useless now, but what fine sites they'd be
For workers' flats and some light industry.
Those lumpy church towers, unadorned with spires,
And wavy roofs that burn like smouldering fires
In sharp spring sunlight over ashen flint
Are out of date as some old aquatint.
Then glance below the line of Sussex downs
To stucco terraces of seaside towns
Turn'd into flats and residential clubs
Above the wind-slashed Corporation shrubs.
Such Georgian relics should by now, I feel,
Be all rebuilt in glass and polished steel.
Bournemouth is looking up. I'm glad to say
That modernistic there has come to stay.
I walk the asphalt paths of Branksome Chine
In resin-scented air like strong Greek wine
And dream of cliffs of flats along those heights,
Floodlit at night with green electric lights.
But as for Dorset's flint and Purbeck stone,
Its old thatched farms in dips of down alone –
It should be merged with Hants and made to be
A self-contained and plann'd community.
Like Flint and Rutland, it is much too small
And has no reason to exist at all.

...

Hamlets which fail to pass the planners' test
Will be demolished. We'll rebuild the rest
To look like Welwyn mixed with Middle West.
All fields we'll turn to sports grounds, lit at night
From concrete standards by fluorescent light:
And over all the land, instead of trees,
Clean poles and wire will whisper in the breeze.
We'll keep one ancient village just to show
What England once was when the times were slow –
Broadway for me. But here I know I must
Ask the opinion of our National Trust.'

John Betjeman (1906–84), from 'The Town Clerk's Views', from *Selected Poems*, 1948.

In *Forty Years On,* Alan Bennett's characters ponder the new England:

HEADMASTER: In our crass-builded, glass-bloated, green-belted world Sunday is for washing the car, tinned peaches and Carnation milk.

FRANKLIN: A sergeant's world it is now, the world of the lay-by and the civic improvement scheme.

HEADMASTER: Country is park and shore is marina, spare time is leisure and more, year by year. We have become a battery people, a people of under-privileged hearts fed on pap in darkness, bred out of all taste and season to savour the shoddy splendours of the new civility. The hedges come down from the silent fields. The lease is out on the corner site. A butterfly is an event.

TEMPEST: Were we closer to the ground as children or is the grass emptier now?

MISS NISBITT: Tidy the old into the tall flats. Desolation at fourteen storeys becomes a view.

MATRON: Who now dies at home? Who sees death? We sicken and fade in a hospital ward, and dying is for doctors with a phone call to the family.

HEADMASTER: Once we had a romantic and old-fashioned conception of honour, of patriotism, chivalry and duty. But it was a duty which didn't have much to do with justice, with social justice anyway. And in default of that justice and in pursuit of it, that was how the great words came to be cancelled out. The crowd has found the door into the secret garden. Now they will tear up the flowers by the roots, strip the borders and strew them with paper and broken bottles.

LECTERN: To let. A valuable site at the cross-roads of the world. At present on offer to European clients. Outlying portions of the estate already disposed of to sitting tenants. Of some historical and period interest. Some alterations and improvements necessary.

Alan Bennett (1934–), *Forty Years On,* 1968.

Philip Larkin, in his 1972 poem 'Going, Going', is characteristically pessimistic:

I thought it would last my time –
The sense that, beyond the town,
There would always be fields and farms,
Where the village louts could climb
Such trees as were not cut down;
I knew there'd be false alarms

In the papers about old streets
And split-level shopping, but some
Have always been left so far;
And when the old part retreats
As the bleak high-risers come
We can always escape in the car.

Things are tougher than we are, just
As earth will always respond
However we mess it about;

Chuck filth in the sea, if you must:
The tides will be clean beyond.
– But what do I feel now? Doubt?

Or age, simply? The crowd
Is young in the M1 café;
Their kids are screaming for more –
More houses, more parking allowed,
More caravan sites, more pay.
On the Business Page, a score

Of spectacled grins approve
Some takeover bid that entails
Five per cent profit (and ten
Per cent more in the estuaries): move
Your works to the unspoilt dales
(Grey area grants)! And when
You try to get near the sea
In summer . . .

       It seems, just now,
To be happening so very fast;
Despite all the land left free
For the first time I feel somehow
That it isn't going to last,

That before I snuff it, the whole
Boiling will be bricked in
Except for the tourist parts –
First slum of Europe: a role
It won't be so hard to win,
With a cast of crooks and tarts.

And that will be England gone,
The shadows, the meadows, the lanes,
The guildhalls, the carved choirs.
There'll be books; it will linger on
In galleries; but all that remains
For us will be concrete and tyres.

Most things are never meant.
This won't be, most likely: but greeds
And garbage are too thick-strewn
To be swept up now, or invent
Excuses that make them all needs.
I just think it will happen, soon.

Philip Larkin (1922–85), 'Going, Going', 1972, from *High Windows*, 1974.

Auberon Waugh, like many 'countrymen', resented the intrusion of the English into their own countryside:

The roads of West Somerset are jammed as never before with caravans from Birmingham and the West Midlands. Their horrible occupants only come down here to search for a place where they can go to the lavatory free. Then they return to Birmingham, boasting in their hideous flat voices how much money they have saved.

I don't suppose many of the brutes can read, but anybody who wants a good book for the holidays is recommended to try a new publication from the Church Information Office: *The Churchyard Handbook* (CIO, £2.40).

It laments the passing of that ancient literary form, the epitaph, suggesting that many of the tombstones put up nowadays dedicated to 'Mum' or 'Dad' or 'Ginger' would be more suitable for a dog cemetery than for the resting place of Christians.

The trouble is that people can afford tombstones nowadays who have no business to be remembered at all. Few of these repulsive creatures in caravans are Christians, I imagine, but I would happily spend the rest of my days composing epitaphs for them in exchange for a suitable fee:

> He had a shit on Gwennap Head,
> It cost him nothing. Now he's dead.

> He left a turd on Porlock Hill.
> As he lies here, it lies there still.

Auberon Waugh (1939–2001), in *Private Eye*, 11 June 1976.

In *The English*, Jeremy Paxman examines the current realities and the perennial appeal of rural England:

So how did John Major's evocation of the English idyll seem to the few people who actually live in it? The Dorset town of Beaminster, whose creamy limestone houses and shops, central square and dazzling sixteen-pinnacled church tower are almost unchanged from Thomas Hardy's day (it is the 'Emminster' of his Wessex novels), was as good a place as any to find out. I was sitting on the terrace of a farmhouse high above the town, on one of those glorious late-summer days when the English countryside seems to exhale after the heat of the day and the fields and hillsides relax into their richest green. Butterflies danced around the flowers in the garden, buzzards wheeled lazily in the sky. A blue heat haze had still not quite evaporated in the valley and the tower of Beaminster church struck upwards through it, like a pencil on a sketchpad. If John Major had anywhere in mind, it surely must have been here, the quintessence of the imagined South Country.

From her terrace, Georgia Langton looks down on this glorious panorama with a cup of tea in her hand. She is a handsome, grey-haired woman of fifty-four, aware that as a relatively wealthy widow she is infinitely privileged to live in this picture of the ideal England. From the fields behind the house come the distant bleat of her sheep. On the hillside below, the beech trees rustle in the evening breeze. So what did she and her neighbours think when they heard John Major's speech? 'We all fell about with laughter. We laughed ourselves silly.' Why?

Because it's all packaging. It's all an illusion. The farmers around here can only live on subsidies. You know who's paying to keep this alive? You are, the taxpayers. And because the farmers don't need half the staff they once needed, the farmworkers have all been driven off the land. Their cottages get sold – unmodernized – for hundreds of thousands of pounds. Which means country people simply can't afford to live here any more. So new people move in. Then they start complaining about the mud on the roads, the fact that there aren't any pavements or streetlights. And soon it's all just another suburb. The whole country's just one big suburb now.

If they are honest, most country people will agree with her: where the English countryside remains, it exists only as scenery. ...

None of this is to deny the extraordinary enchantment of the English country-side. Who could resist the lure of the extraordinary names of England's villages? High Easter, New Delight, Kingston Bagpuize, Sleeping Green, Tiptoe, Nether Wallop, Nymphsfield, Christmas Common, Samlesbury Bottoms, Ryme Intrinseca, Huish Champflower, Buckland-tout-Saints, Wyre Piddle, Martin Husingtree, Norton-Juxta-Twycross and so on, a gazetteer of dreams. More, the landscape of England is the landscape of its imaginative inheritance. The Chilterns are Bunyan's Delectable Mountains, Langland's Field of Folk lies beneath the Herefordshire Beacon, Dorset belongs to Hardy, Sussex to Kipling, George Herbert claims Wiltshire as powerfully as Wordsworth the Lake District, Jane Austen Hampshire or Emily Brontë the moors of west Yorkshire.

It is the charm of small things; there is scarcely a geographical feature in the land that has any claim on world records. It is a place of tended beauties; the coun-try lane, the cottage small, the field of grain, belong to a landscape that has been shaped by generations of labour. Its appeal is charted in fields and acres. 'All is measured, mingled, varied, gliding easily one thing into another, little rivers, little plains ... little hills, little mountains ... neither prison nor palace but a decent home', as William Morris wrote, linking the landscape again to that most powerful English idea. It is still a place of short perspectives. Yet increasingly in southern England, that is all it is. Unlike France, where a peasant culture survived the twen-tieth century, in England, it died out at the time that agricultural workers were turned over to their landlords' cash crops of wheat or milk: at evening they returned not to their own smallholding but to tied cottages where the best they could hope for was the room to raise a chicken or three. The real rural life has long gone, to be replaced with suburbanism that affects farmers almost as much as it affects the commuters who live around them, for agriculture is a business, too.

Jeremy Paxman (1950–), *The English*, 1998.

Here is John Major's 'evocation of the English idyll':

Fifty years from now, Britain will still be the country of long shadows on county grounds, warm beer, invincible green suburbs, dog lovers and pools fillers and – as George Orwell said – 'old maids cycling to holy communion through the morning mist'.

John Major, Prime Minister, speech, 22 April 1993.

Orwell's list of 'characteristic fragments' was:

The clatter of clogs in the Lancashire mill towns, the to-and-fro of lorries on the Great North Road, the queues outside the Labour Exchanges, the rattle of pin-tables in the Soho pubs, the old maids biking to Holy Communion through the mists of an autumn morning ...

George Orwell (1903–50), 'England Your England', in *The Lion and the Unicorn*, 1940.

THE BLOODY (3): OTHER ENGLISH BLOODINESS

An ironic attitude towards one's country and a scepticism about one's heritage is a part of that heritage.

Alan Bennett (1934–), quoted in the *Daily Telegraph*, February 2000.

An eclectic assembly of spleen – another English speciality. Self-deprecation is inherent in every lungful of English air, and when the English really get going on themselves they put feeble foreign commentary to flight.

The great English tradition of good food and fine cooking has been celebrated by a variety of writers ...

The bread I eat in London, is a deleterious paste, mixed up with chalk, alum, and bone-ashes; insipid to the taste, and destructive to the constitution.

The milk ... should not pass unanalysed, the produce of faded cabbage-leaves and sour draff, lowered with hot water, frothed with bruised snails, carried through the streets in open pails, exposed to foul rinsings discharged from doors and windows, spittle, snot, and tobacco-quids from foot-passengers, over-flowings from mudcarts, spatterings from coach-wheels, dirt and trash chucked into it by roguish boys for the joke's sake, the spewings of infants, who have slabbered in the tin-measure, which is thrown back in that condition among the milk, for the benefit of the next customer; and finally, the vermin that drops from the rags of the nasty drab that vends this precious mixture, under the respectable denomination of milkmaid.

I shall conclude this catalogue of London dainties, with that table beer, guiltless of hops and malt, vapid and nauseous; much fitter to facilitate the operation of a vomit, than to quench thirst and promote digestion; the tallowy rancid mass called butter, manufactured with candle-grease and kitchen stuff; and their fresh eggs, imported from France and Scotland.

Tobias Smollett (1721–71), *The Expedition of Humphrey Clinker*, 1771.

Now for a chop house or coffee-room dinner! Oh, the 'orrible smell that greets you at the door! Compound of cabbage, pickled salmon, boiled beef, saw-dust, and anchovy sarce ... everything tastes flat, stale, and unprofitable.

R.S. Surtees (1805–64), *Handley Cross*, 1843.

I heard a lady who sat next to me, in a low, sweet voice, say, 'No gravy, Sir.' I had never seen her before, but I turned suddenly round and said, 'Madam, I have been looking for a person who disliked gravy all my life; let us swear eternal friendship.'

Sydney Smith (1771–1845), quoted in Lady Holland, A Memoir of Sydney Smith, 1855.

'Turbot, Sir,' said the waiter, placing before me two fishbones, two eyeballs, and a bit of black mackintosh.

Thomas Earle Welby (1881–1933), 'Birmingham or Crewe?', in The Dinner Knell, 1932.

Nearly every woman in England is competent to write an authoritative article on how not to cook cabbage.

Vyvyan Holland (1886–1967), Wine and Food, 1935.

Boiled cabbage à l'Anglaise is something compared with which steamed coarse newsprint bought from bankrupt Finnish salvage dealers and heated over smoky oil stoves is an exquisite delicacy. Boiled British cabbage is something lower than ex-Army blankets stolen by dispossessed Goanese doss-housekeepers who used them to cover down busted-down hen houses in the slum district of Karachi.

Cassandra (William Connor, 1909–67), in the Daily Mirror, 30 June 1950.

The average cooking in the average hotel for the average Englishman explains to a large extent the English bleakness and taciturnity. Nobody can beam and warble while chewing pressed beef smeared with diabolical mustard. Nobody can exult aloud while ungluing from his teeth a quivering tapioca pudding.

Karel Čapek (1890–1938), quoted in Jonathon Green, The Cassell Dictionary of Insulting Quotations, 1996.

In one such hotel ...

The beef and salad were corpse-cold and did not seem like real food at all. They tasted like water. The rolls, also, though stale, were damp. The reedy Thames water seemed to have got into everything. It was no surprise that when the wine was opened it tasted like mud. But it was alcoholic, that was the great thing.

George Orwell (1903–50), Keep the Aspidistra Flying, 1936.

The English contribution to world culture: the chip.

John Cleese (1939–) and Charles Crichton (1910–99), A Fish Called Wanda, 1988.

Catering apart, there follows a chronological miscellany of anti-Englishry, doled out impartially by non-English and English alike:

My God! This is a wonderful land and a faithless one; for she has exiled, slain, destroyed and ruined so many kings, so many rulers, so many great men, and she is always diseased and suffering from differences, quarrels and hatred between her people.

Richard II (1367–1400), attributed remark made in the Tower of London, 21 September 1399, ten days before his enforced abdication.

I think that those who accuse the English of being cruel, envious, distrustful, vindictive and libertine, are wrong. It is true, they take pleasure in seeing gladiators fight, in seeing bulls torn to pieces by dogs, seeing cocks fight, and that in the carnivals they use batons against the cocks, but it is not out of cruelty so much as coarseness.

Alain René Lesage (1668–1747), *Gil Blas*, 1715–35.

The Englishman has all the qualities of a poker except its occasional warmth.

Daniel O'Connell ('The Liberator', 1775–1847).

It is related of an Englishman that he hanged himself to avoid the daily task of dressing and undressing.

Johann Wolfgang von Goethe (1749–1832), quoted in Jonathon Green, *The Cassell Dictionary of Insulting Quotations*, 1996.

It must be acknowledged that the English are the most disagreeable of all the nations of Europe, more surly and morose, with less disposition to please, to exert themselves for the good of society, to make small sacrifices, and to put themselves out of their way.

The Rev. Sydney Smith (1771–1845), quoted in Jonathon Green, *The Cassell Dictionary of Insulting Quotations*, 1996.

Curse the blasted, jelly-boned swines, the slimy, the belly-wriggling invertebrates, the miserable sodding rotters, the flaming sods, the snivelling, dribbling, dithering, palsied, pulse-less lot that make up England today. They've got white of egg in their veins, and their spunk is that watery it's a marvel they can breed. They *can* nothing but frog-spawn – the gibberers! Why, why, why was I born an Englishman? God, how I hate them!

D.H. Lawrence (1885–1930), letter to Edward Garnett, 3 July 1912. Lawrence had just received a publisher's letter of rejection for his novel *Sons and Lovers*.

The English people on the whole are surely the nicest people in the world, and everybody makes everything so easy for everyone else, that there is almost nothing to resist at all.

D.H. Lawrence (1885–1930), 'Dull London', *Evening News*, 1928.

Your Englishman, confronted by something abnormal, will always pretend that it isn't there. If he can't pretend that, he will look through the object, or round it, or above it, or below it, or in any direction except into it. If, however, you *force* him to look into it, he will at once pretend that he sees the object not for what it is but for something that he would like it to be.

James Agate (1877–1947), *Ego 1*, entry for 14 October 1932.

In England we have come to rely upon a comfortable time-lag of a century intervening between the perception that something ought to be done and a serious attempt to do it.

H.G. Wells (1866–1946), *The Work, Wealth and Happiness of Mankind*, 1934.

The English never smash in a face. They merely refrain from asking it to dinner.

Margaret Halsey, US writer, *With Malice Toward Some*, 1938.

Curious effect, here in the sanatorium, on Easter Sunday, when the people in this (the most expensive) block of 'chalets' mostly have visitors, of hearing large numbers of upper-class English voices. I have been almost out of the sound of them for two years, hearing them at most one or two at a time, my ears growing more & more used to working-class or lower-middle-class Scottish voices. In the hospital at Hairmyres, for instance, I literally never heard a 'cultivated' accent except when I had a visitor. It is as though I were hearing these voices for the first time. And what voices! A sort of over-fedness, a fatuous self-confidence, a constant bah-bahing of laughter about nothing, above all a sort of heaviness & richness combined with a fundamental ill-will – people who, one instinctively feels, without even being able to see them, are the enemies of anything intelligent or sensitive or beautiful. No wonder everyone hates us so.

George Orwell (1903–50), entry in his manuscript notebook, 17 April 1949; from Sonia Orwell and Ian Angus, eds., *The Collected Essays, Journalism and Letters of George Orwell*, 1968.

Approved terms of abuse for East German speakers and writers when describing Britain, issued by the Communist Party of the German Democratic Republic in 1953:

Paralytic sycophants, effete betrayers of humanity, carrion-eating servile imita-tors, arch-cowards and collaborators, gang of women-murderers, degenerate rabble, parasitic traditionalists, playboy soldiers, conceited dandies.

This is a letter of hate. It is for you my countrymen, I mean those men of my country who have defiled it. The men with manic fingers leading the sightless, feeble, betrayed body of my country to its death ... damn you England.

John Osborne (1929–94), letter in *Tribune*, 18 August 1961.

Sheep with a nasty side.

Cyril Connolly (1903–74), on the English, quoted by Gavin Ewart in *Quarto*, 1980.

English Law: where there are two alternatives: one intelligent, one stupid; one attractive, one vulgar; one noble, one ape-like; one serious and sincere, one undig-nified and false; one far-sighted, one short; EVERYBODY will INVARIABLY choose the latter.

Cyril Connolly (1903–74), in D. Pryce-Jones, ed., *Journal and Memoir*, 1983.

One of the best-loved of English characters is the jobsworth ...

The British habit of being negative in response to any request to render service never ceased to amaze and infuriate me. From ... anyone, in short, who sported some sort of uniform and whose object in life was to obstruct rather than oblige, all of these people could be depended upon to declare at some stage that whatever it was you wanted of them was 'more than their job's worth'. ... I cannot resist the thought that it was the jobsworthian attitude that saved Britain in the last war. When Hitler announced his intention to invade, the English people, as one, said, 'Sorry, mate, we're closed!'

> I was just an ordinary Englishman
> till I got me uniform and hat
> and ever since that hour
> I exercise me power
> preventing you from doing this and that.
> You'll find me on the turnstiles at the Zoo
> or outside the Roxy marshalling the queue,
> and if you turn up late
> while I'm on the gate
> it's no good asking me to let you through
> 'cos I'll just say:
>
> *Jobsworth, jobsworth,*
> *it's more than my job's worth!*
> *I don't care, rain or snow,*
> *whatever you want the answer's NO!*
> *I can keep you standing*
> *for hours in the queue,*
> *and if you don't like it*
> *you know what you can do! ...*

Jeremy Taylor (1938–), song, 'Jobsworth', 1971, in *Ag Pleeze Deddy!*, 1992.

English life, while very pleasant, is rather bland. I expected kindness and gentility and I found it, but there is such a thing as too much couth.

S.J. Perelman (1904–79), quoted in the *Observer*, 24 September 1971.

England is, after all, the land where children were beaten, wives and babies bashed, football hooligans crunch, and Miss Whip and Miss Lash ply their trade as nowhere else in the Western world. Despite our belief [that] we are a 'gentle' people we have, in reality, a cruel and callous streak in our sweet natures, reinforced by a decadent puritan strain which makes some of us believe that suffering, whether useful or not, is a fit scourge to the wanton soul.

Colin MacInnes (1914–76), in *New Society*, 1976.

A soggy little island huffing and puffing to keep up with Western Europe.

John Updike (1932–), US novelist, 'London Life', 1969, in *Picked Up Pieces*, 1976.

Racial Characteristics: cold-blooded queers with nasty complexions and terrible teeth who once conquered half the world but still haven't figured out central heating. They warm their beers and chill their baths and boil all their food.

P.J. O'Rourke (1947–), 'Foreigners Around the World', in *National Lampoon*, 1976.

The English think incompetence is the same thing as sincerity.

Quentin Crisp (1908–99), quoted in the *New York Times*, 1977.

Inglan is a bitch dere's no escapin' it
Inglan is a bitch dere's no runnin' way fram it.

Linton Kwesi Johnson (1952–), 'Inglan is a Bitch', 1980.

In *A Better Class of Person*, John Osborne remembered the very English miserableness of his parents' families:

The Grove Family Rows were not masterminded but emerged from a port-wine haze of unsated disappointment. What the two families shared was the heart pumped from birth by misgiving. Not a proud misgiving of the spirit but a timid melancholy or dislike of joy, effort or courage. 'I don't suppose it'll last.' ... 'I knew it wouldn't last.' ... 'How do you know it'll work?' ... 'But aren't you worried?' ... 'Well, there's nothing we can do about it.' ... 'No use crying over it.' ... 'Can't expect too much, go too far, only get disappointed. ...'

Disappointment was oxygen to them. Their motto might have been *ante coitum triste est*. ...

For Boxing Day, Grandma Osborne had perfected a pumpkin trick which turned all the cold Christmas pudding and mince pies suddenly into funeral baked meats. She did it almost on the stroke of five and in one wand-like incantation. Lying back in the Hymnal position, she would close her eyes, smile her thin gruel of a smile and say, 'Ah, well, there's *another* Christmas over.' I dreaded the supreme satisfaction with which she laid the body of Christmas to rest. In one phrase she crushed the festive flower and the jubilant heart. On New Year's Eve she used less relish in confirming that there was little reason to feel good about the year passing and certainly less about the coming year.

Two days of bewilderment, betrayal, triumph and, above all, irredeemable and incurable disappointment ended.

John Osborne (1929–94), *A Better Class of Person*, 1981.

England has become a squalid, uncomfortable, ugly place ... an intolerant, racist, homophobic, narrow-minded, authoritarian rat-hole run by vicious suburban-minded, materialistic philistines.

Hanif Kureishi (1954–), 1988, quoted in Patrick Higgins, ed., *A Queer Reader*, 1993.

There is such relish in England for anything that doesn't succeed.

Jonathan Miller (1934–), interview in *The Sunday Times*, 4 December 1988.

Do you have any idea what it's like being English, being so correct all the time, being so stifled by this dread of doing the wrong thing? We are all terrified of embarrassment ... that's why we're so ... dead.

John Cleese (1939–), with Charles Crichton, *A Fish Called Wanda*, 1988.

To be born an Englishman – ah, what an easy conceit that builds in you, what a self-righteous nationalism, a secure xenophobia, what a pride in your ignorance. No other people speak so few languages. No other people ... have an expression that is the equivalent of 'greasy foreign muck'.

Tony Parsons (1953–), in *Arena*, 1989.

England's not a bad country. ... It's just a mean, cold, ugly, divided, tired, clapped-out, post-imperial, post-industrial slag-heap covered in polystyrene hamburger cartons.

Margaret Drabble (1939–), *A Natural Curiosity*, 1989.

England is a horrible place with horrible people, horrible food, horrible climate, horrible class system, horrible cities and horrible countryside.

Stephen Pile, in the *Sunday Times*, quoted in Colin Jarman, *The Guinness Dictionary of More Poisonous Quotations*, 1992.

Ah don't hate the English. They're just wankers. We are colonised by wankers. We can't even pick a decent, healthy culture to be colonised by. No. We're ruled by effete arseholes.

Irving Welsh (1957–), *Trainspotting*, 1993.

The English vice is not flagellation or homosexuality as some continentals suppose. It is whimsy.

A.N. Wilson (1950–), quoted in the *Observer*, 2001.

PRODUCT RECALL
BRITAIN
(No. 74732461)

The manufacturers regret that a number of serious problems have recently emerged with this product.

Millions of complaints have been received regarding the constituent parts of Britain – none of which appear to work. Furthermore, some of them are extremely dangerous and can cause serious injury.

The manufacturers regret that Britain no longer conforms to acceptable safety standards and have therefore decided to withdraw the product from the market.

Issued by UK PLC – 'Disasters R Us'

Private Eye, 22 March 2001.

If you want to get at the crux of what's wrong with *Weakest Link*, you have to look at the culture from which it sprang. ... It seems to be a game show that's predominantly about losing. ...

Now, if there's one thing that the British are better at than us Yanks, it's losing. The Brits know how to lose big. They're losing right now, in fact. In just a matter of months, the swinging England of the 90's has devolved into a dismal swamp heaped with charred cow carcasses and dysfunction. In a 'London Journal' headlined 'Soggy Pastures Where All Things Crash and Burn' that appeared in the April 7 edition of *The New York Times*, reporter Sarah Lyall listed a whole host of ills, including a tuberculosis epidemic, a problem-plagued railroad industry and, of course, hoof-and-mouth disease, before writing: 'Is anything going right in Britain these days? If so, it's hard to tell.'

But that's Britannia. As the actor Stephen Fry explained to Ms. Lyall in an e-mail: 'To be honest, I can't remember a time where one couldn't say with authority that "the wheels have come off" or "it's all gone pear-shaped." ... Perhaps we are the only people who take freude in our own schaden.'

Probably that's because deep in the damp, depressive British soul can be found great stores of resilience – what used to be called that old Dunkirk spirit – that comes to the fore in the face of abject humiliation and disaster. With their stoicism and their stiff upper lips, the British lose with such class that they look like winners. And that's one of the reasons why *Weakest Link* must appeal to their television audiences. It's a great showcase for their strength. Even the prize money over there – reportedly a paltry £20,000 – reinforces the notion of losing as winning. After running a gauntlet of needling insults, the winner of the U.K. version of *Weakest Link* barely has enough to buy a modest automobile.

One thing you can say for certain: That's not *us*.

Frank DiGiacomo, *The New York Observer*, 23 April 2001.

The Free-born English

THINK OF WHAT OUR NATION STANDS FOR,
BOOKS FROM BOOTS AND COUNTRY LANES,
FREE SPEECH, FREE PASSES, CLASS DISTINCTION,
DEMOCRACY AND PROPER DRAINS.
John Betjeman (1906–84), 'In Westminster Abbey', *Old Lights for New Chancels*, 1940.

Under an act of Elizabeth I, quoted below, it was ordained that any person exist-ing in a state of slavery should, upon reaching the shores of England – upon 'breathing English air' – immediately become freed from slavery: Britons, as the English were to become under Elizabeth's successor, never should, never could, be slaves. The hypocrisy of the fact that this did not apply to the victims of the 'Triangular Trade' – or, indeed, to slaves in British colonies – was not lost on agitators for reform. Britain abolished the slave trade in 1807, and slavery in its colonies in 1833 (some decades before the Land of the Free, rather painfully, got round to it), and after that the Royal Navy took it on itself to patrol the coasts of western and southern Africa to prevent anyone else doing it.

At home, Elizabeth's edict merely enacted a widely held truism. The assump-tion of 'liberty' as a birthright has a long pedigree in the English consciousness; and it has produced the curious paradox that, while the English have striven for centuries to secure and assert their rights and liberties, often in the face of unabashed oppression, they have all along behaved as though they had them anyway. While England might be 'Mother of the Free', those of her children who wished to assert their freedom had to leave home first to do so safely.

The following sections (which, inevitably, overlap to some extent) examine the phenomenon of 'free-born Englishness' in various contexts. The liberating prop-erty of English air blows through all of them.

'NATURAL LIBERTY, NATURAL JUSTICE'

This section takes up the theme of the Introduction above, that of 'the assumption of liberty', and goes on to look at examples of it at work in what we habitually assume to be our tradition of law. The phrase 'English common law' resonates in both our official and unofficial cultures: in the former as a body of practice established by precedent, in the latter as something 'fair' and commonsensical, and somehow pre-existent, and in both as an inviolable right (and duty) applicable to all. 'Assumption of liberty' and 'respect for law' have gone together, as if each were dependent on the other, as twin pillars of Englishness. Some writers have observed that this is essentially a fiction, albeit a necessary and wonderful one. Even the famous Clause 39 of the Magna Carta – the bit everyone thinks they know – contains a slippery little escape clause for the oppressor who chooses not to play the game of believing it: '... or by the law of the land'. Just as the Human Rights Act (surely the most thorough attempt ever made to codify the 'assumption of liberty') was passing into statute, the same 'law of the land' dismantled its central promise. Objectors (of whom there seem to have been few) were vilified (as 'forces of conservatism') for not being 'modern'; for being, indeed, enemies of the English people.

The root of English liberty is held to be the Magna Carta, the 'Great Charter' of rights and feudal obligations that the barons forced King John to sign in the 13th century. Among its provisions was that:

> No free man shall be taken or imprisoned or dispossessed, or outlawed or exiled, or in any way destroyed, nor will we go unto him, nor will we send against him except by lawful judgement of his peers or by the law of the land.

Magna Carta, 15 June 1215, Clause 39. This only applied to the 'free man', so bondsmen, serfs, villeins, etc., were excluded from its protection.

The influence of the Magna Carta can be found in the Petition of Right of 1628 and the Habeas Corpus Act of 1679, and also in the Constitution of the United States.

Some centuries later Oliver Cromwell – who had fought against another tyrannical monarch – made an eloquent plea in the cause of liberty:

> Your pretended fear lest error should come in, is like the man who would keep all wine out of the country, lest men should be drunk. It will be found an unjust and unwise jealousy to deprive a man of his natural liberty upon a supposition he may abuse it.

Oliver Cromwell (1599–1658), letter to the General Assembly of the Church of Scotland, 3 August 1650.

Once firmly in power as the Protector, however, Cromwell oversaw the imposition of a Puritan code, under which 'Merrie England' was suspended.

After the Restoration it became obligatory, whether one was Whig or Tory, to pay lip service at least to liberty. The following comes from the Tory Poet Laureate's Pindaric ode on the death of Charles II:

> Freedom, still maintain'd alive,
> Freedom which in no other Land will thrive,
> Freedom an *English* subject's sole Prerogative,
> Without whose Charms ev'n Peace would be
> But a dull, quiet Slavery.

John Dryden (1631–1700), *Threnodia Augustalis*, 1685.

However, it was the Whigs who more thoroughly wrapped themselves in the robes of liberty. Fearing James II was moving towards Catholic absolutism, they forced his abdication and brought over William of Orange as King. William and his wife Mary were obliged to agree to the 1689 Declaration of Rights, which became the Bill of Rights – formally known as An Act Declaring the Rights and Liberties of the Subject, and the basis of the country's constitutional monarchy. An extract from the Bill of Rights is given later in the chapter, under the section entitled *It's a Free Country, Isn't It?*

Immediately following this 'Glorious Revolution', the philosopher John Locke published his *Two Treatises on Government*, retrospectively justifying the Revolution by defining the state in terms of a social contract between rulers and ruled, in which the former consent to be ruled in return for the protection by the latter of their rights:

However it may be mistaken, the end of law is, not to abolish or restrain, but to preserve and enlarge freedom. ... Man being ... by nature all free, equal, and independent, no one can be put out of this estate, and subjected to the political power of another, without his own consent. ... The only way by which anyone divests himself of his natural liberty and puts on the bonds of civil society is by agreeing with other men to join and unite into a community.

John Locke (1632–1704), *Second Treatise of Civil Government*, 1690, from chapters 6 and 8.

Locke was quite clear that the most important right was the right to property:

Man ... hath by nature a power ... to preserve his property – that is, his life, liberty, and estate – against the injuries and attempts of other men. ... The great and chief end, therefore, of men's uniting into commonwealths, and putting themselves under government, is the preservation of their property.

John Locke (1632–1704), *Second Treatise of Civil Government*, 1690, from chapters 7 and 9.

The right to property was a freedom most assiduously defended during the 18th century – as long as that property was acquired by due legal process. Thus, between 1760 and 1815, some 7 million acres of common land was transferred by Acts of Enclosure into the possession of wealthy landowners, while minor thefts could be punishable by hanging. This state of affairs prompted the following anonymous verse:

> The law doth punish man or woman
> That steals the goose from off the common,

> But lets the greater felon loose
> That steals the common from the goose.

When, in 1925, the communist Harry Pollitt (later general secretary of the Communist Party of Great Britain) was imprisoned in Wandsworth for seditious libel and incitement to mutiny, a professional burglar allegedly upbraided him:

Serve you bloody well right, you've no respect for private property.

Quoted in J. Mahon, *Harry Pollitt*, 1976.

Dr Johnson, a deeply moral Tory, was sceptical whenever the banner of liberty was waved:

The notion of liberty amuses the people of England, and helps to keep off the *taedium vitae*.

Samuel Johnson (1709–84), in 1763; quoted in James Boswell, *Life of Samuel Johnson*, 1791, Vol. 1.

Johnson later attacked the hypocrisy of the American colonists, who demanded freedom and yet maintained the institution of slavery.

One of the most notable – or notorious – wavers of the flag was John Wilkes, an opportunistic politician, journalist and rake who took on the role of battling against 'tyranny'. He was a constant thorn in the side of George III and his ministers, and on several occasions, and on dubious grounds, was disbarred from his seat in Parliament (see the section below entitled *My Voice Shall Be Heard*). During the parliamentary debate on one such occasion, Pitt the Elder pronounced on the rights of every citizen to an unpartisan hearing:

The character and circumstances of Mr Wilkes have been very improperly introduced into this question, not only here, but in that court of judicature where his cause was tried, I mean the House of Commons. With one party he was a patriot of the first magnitude; with the other the vilest incendiary. For my own part I consider him merely and indifferently as an English subject, possessed of certain rights which the laws have given him, and which the laws alone can take from him. I am neither moved by his private vices nor by his public merits. In his person, though he were the worst of men, I contend for the safety and security of the best; and God forbid, my lords, that there should be a power in this country of measuring the civil rights of the subject by his moral character, or by any other rule but the fixed laws of the land.

William Pitt, Earl of Chatham (1708–78), proposing a bill for John Wilkes's reinstatement in the House of Commons, 1769. The motion was lost by 203 to 36.

The protection given to natural rights in England was widely admired at this time by Enlightenment thinkers living under the absolute monarchies of continental Europe:

The English Constitution has in fact arrived at the point of excellence, in consequence of which all men are restored to those natural rights of which in nearly all monarchies they are deprived. These rights are: Total Liberty of person and property; freedom of the press; the right of trial in all criminal cases by an inde-

pendent jury; the right of being tried only according to the strict letter of the law; and the right of each man to profess any religion he desires.

Voltaire (François-Marie Arouet, 1694–1778), *Dictionnaire philosophique*, 1764.

The radical Tom Paine blew fresh life into Locke's ideas, and spoke for the rights of the colonists during the American Revolution:

Government, even in its best state, is but a necessary evil; in its worst state, an intolerable one. Government, like dress, is the badge of lost innocence; the palaces of kings are built upon the ruins of the bowers of paradise.

Thomas Paine (1737–1809), radical political theorist, *Common Sense*, 1776.

Paine went on to defend the French Revolution:

All hereditary government is in its nature tyranny. . . . To inherit a government, is to inherit the people, as if they were flocks and herds.

Thomas Paine (1737–1809), *The Rights of Man*, 1791.

From the constitutionalism of Locke, through the radicalism of Paine, we arrive at the founding father of modern liberalism, John Stuart Mill:

If all mankind minus one were of one opinion, and only one person were of the contrary opinion, mankind would be no more justified in silencing that one person, than he, if he had the power, would be justified in silencing mankind. . . .

The liberty of the individual must be thus far limited; he must not make himself a nuisance to other people.

John Stuart Mill (1806–73), *On Liberty*, 1859.

An Englishman's heaven-born privilege of doing as he likes.

Matthew Arnold (1822–88), *Culture and Anarchy*, 1869.

In 1790 the Irish judge John Philpot Curran had warned: 'The condition upon which God hath given liberty to man is eternal vigilance.' A century and a half later, as the clouds of Fascism gathered over Europe, E.M. Forster spoke in Paris on the tradition of liberty in England, and the subtle threats to it from within:

When this committee honoured me with an invitation to speak and asked me to choose a subject, I replied that I would speak either on liberty of expression or on cultural tradition as they preferred, but that in either case I should make the same speech. Coming from an Englishman, this is not an epigram. In England, our traditions and our liberties are closely connected, and so it should be possible to treat the two at once. Freedom has been praised in my country for several hundred years. Duty and self-abnegation have been praised too, but freedom has won the larger chorus. . . .

I am actually what my age and upbringing have made me – a bourgeois who adheres to the British constitution, adheres to it rather than supports it, and the fact that this isn't dignified doesn't worry me. I do care about the past. I do care about the preservation and the extension of freedom. And I have come to this congress mainly to listen to what is being done and suffered in other lands. My own land – we're in for a bad time, too, I've no doubt about it, but the fact that our rulers have to *pretend* to like freedom is an advantage. … It is something that in England dictatorship is still supposed to be ungentlemanly, and massacres of Jews in bad form, and private armies figures of fun.

Our danger from Fascism – unless a war starts when anything may happen – is negligible. We're menaced by something much more insidious – by what I might call 'Fabio-Fascism', by the dictator-spirit working quietly away behind the façade of constitutional forms, passing a little law (like the Sedition Act) here, endorsing a departmental tyranny there, emphasizing the national need of secrecy elsewhere, and whispering and cooing the so-called 'news' every evening over the wireless, until opposition is tamed and gulled. Fabio-Fascism is what I am afraid of, for it is the traditional method by which liberty has been attacked in England. It was the method of King Charles I – a gentleman if ever there was one – the method of our enlightened authoritarian gentlemen today. This Fabio-Fascism is our old enemy, the tyrant:

He shall mark our goings, question whence we came,
Set his guards about us, as in Freedom's name.
He shall peep and mutter, and the night shall bring
Watchers 'neath our window, lest we mock the King.

'As in Freedom's name'. How well Rudyard Kipling puts it – though he will scarcely thank me for quoting him.

E.M. Forster (1879–1970), novelist and essayist, *Liberty in England*, an address delivered at the Congrès International des Ecrivains, Paris, 21 June 1935; reprinted in *Abinger Harvest*, 1936.

Another writer ever vigilant in the cause of liberty, always aware of the state's tendency to repress, was George Orwell. Here he explores the English attitude towards the law, contrasting the idea of justice with the reality:

In all societies the common people must live to some extent *against* the existing order. The genuinely popular culture of England is something that goes on beneath the surface, unofficially and more or less frowned on by the authorities. One thing one notices if one looks directly at the common people, especially in the big towns, is that they are not puritanical. They are inveterate gamblers, drink as much beer as their wages will permit, are devoted to bawdy jokes, and use probably the foulest language in the world. They have to satisfy these tastes in the face of astonishing, hypocritical laws (licensing laws, lottery acts, etc.) which are designed to interfere with everybody but in practice allow everything to happen. …

Our criminal law is as out-of-date as the muskets in the Tower. Over against the Nazi Storm Trooper you have got to set that typically English figure, the hanging judge, some gouty old bully with his mind rooted in the nineteenth century, handing out savage sentences. In England people are still hanged by the neck and flogged with the cat o' nine tails. Both of these punishments are obscene as well as cruel, but there has never been any genuinely popular outcry against them. People accept them (and Dartmoor, and Borstal) almost as they accept the weather. They are part of 'the law', which is assumed to be unalterable.

Here one comes upon an all-important English trait: the respect for constitutionalism and legality, the belief in 'the law' as something above the State and above the individual, something which is cruel and stupid, of course, but at any rate *incorruptible*.

It is not that anyone imagines the law to be just. Everyone knows that there is one law for the rich and another for the poor. But no-one accepts the implications of this, everyone takes it for granted that the law, such as it is, will be respected, and feels a sense of outrage when it is not. Remarks like 'They can't run me in; I haven't done anything wrong', or 'They can't do that; it's against the law', are part of the atmosphere of England. The professed enemies of society have this feeling as strongly as anyone else. One sees it in ... letters to the papers from eminent Marxist professors, pointing out that this or that is a 'miscarriage of British justice'. Everyone believes in his heart that the law can be, ought to be, and, on the whole, will be impartially administered. The totalitarian idea that there is no such thing as law, there is only power, has never taken root. Even the intelligentsia have only accepted it in theory... . In England such concepts as justice, liberty and objective truth are still believed in. They may be illusions, but they are very powerful illusions.

George Orwell (1903–50), *The Lion and the Unicorn*, 1941.

Sir John Mortimer QC, defender of *Lady Chatterley* and fox hunting, is a noted libertarian of a later generation. Here he speaks through his fictional mouthpiece, the barrister Horace Rumpole:

When London is but a memory and the Old Bailey has sunk back into the primeval mud, my country will still be remembered for three things: the British Breakfast, *The Oxford Book of English Verse* and the Presumption of Innocence! That presumption is the Golden Thread which runs through the whole history of the Criminal Law.

John Mortimer (1923–), *Rumpole and the Golden Thread*, 1983.

Legislation brought before Parliament in 2000 proposed the abolition of the automatic presumption of innocence in all cases and the right to a jury trial in all criminal prosecutions in England and Wales. The right to remain silent after arrest – without the fact being 'taken into consideration' by the Court – had already been taken away.

'I'LL SAY WHAT I LIKE'

The right to free speech, and in particular the right to grumble, is a universal assumption of the English, and surely their most obvious and enduring characteristic. That leaves only the question of what it is one is free to speak, and how loudly one is free to speak or publish it. ....

John Milton's *Areopagitica* – against the licensing of printing – is one of the most famous defences of free speech:

If we think to regulate printing, thereby to rectify manners, we must regulate all recreations and pastimes, all that is delightful to man. No music must be heard, no song be set or sung, but what is grave and Doric. There must be licensing dancers, that no gesture, motion, or deportment be taught our youth but what by their allowance shall be thought honest .... It will ask more than the work of twenty licensers to examine all the lutes, the violins, and the guitars in every house; they must not be suffered to prattle as they do, but must be licensed what they may say. And who shall silence all the airs and madrigals that whisper softness in chambers? The windows also, and the balconies must be thought on; there are shrewd books, with dangerous frontispieces, set to sale; who shall prohibit them, shall twenty licensers? ...

Our garments also should be referred to the licensing of some more sober workmasters to see them cut into a less wanton garb. Who shall regulate the mixed conversation of our youth, male and female together, as is the fashion of this country? Who shall still appoint what shall be discoursed, what presumed, and no further? ...

Lords and Commons of England, consider what nation it is whereof ye are, and whereof ye are the governors; a nation not slow and dull, but of a quick, ingenious and piercing spirit, acute to invent, subtle and sinewy to discourse, but beneath the reach of any point the highest that human capacity can soar to. ... Yet that which is above all this, the favour and love of heaven, we have great argument to think in a peculiar manner propitious and propending towards us. ... God is decreeing to begin some new and great period in his church, even to the reforming of Reformation itself: what does he then but reveal himself to his servants, and, as his manner is, first to his Englishmen? ...

Behold now this vast city: a city of refuge, the mansion house of liberty, encompassed and surrounded with his protection; the shop of war hath not there more anvils and hammers waking, to fashion out the plates and instruments of armed justice in defence of beleaguered truth, than there be pens and heads there, sitting by their studious lamps, musing, searching, revolving new notions and ideas wherewith to present, as with their homage and their fealty, the approaching Reformation; others as fast reading, trying all things, assenting to the force of reason and convincement. What could a man require more from a nation so pliant and so prone to seek after knowledge? What wants there to such a towardly and pregnant soil, but wise and faithful labourers, to make a knowing people, a nation of prophets, of sages, and of worthies? ...

Methinks I see in my mind a noble and puissant nation rousing herself like a strong man after sleep, and shaking her invincible locks; methinks I see her as an eagle mewing her mighty youth, and kindling her undazzled eyes at the full midday beam; purging and unscaling her long-abused sight at the fountain itself of heavenly radiance; while the whole noise of timorous and flocking birds, with those also that love the twilight, flutter about, amazed at what she means, and in their envious gabble would prognosticate a year of sects and schisms.

What should ye do then? Should ye suppress all this flowery crop of knowledge and new light sprung up and yet springing daily in this city? Should ye set an oligarchy of twenty engrossers over it, to bring a famine upon our minds again, when we shall know nothing but what is measured to us by their bushel? ...

Ye cannot make us now less capable, less knowing, less eagerly pursuing of the truth, unless ye first make yourselves, that made us so, less the lovers, less the founders of our true liberty. We can grow ignorant again, brutish, formal and slavish, as ye found us; but you then must first become that which ye cannot be, oppressive, arbitrary and tyrannous, as they were from whom ye have freed us. ... Give me the liberty to know, to utter, and to argue freely according to conscience, above all liberties.

John Milton (1609–74), Areopagitica; A Speech for the Liberty of Unlicensed Printing, to the Parliament of England, 1644. The Bill Milton opposed had been passed by Parliament the previous year.

At various points in the 18th century governments attempted to curtail freedom of expression. One such instance was the imprisonment of John Wilkes (see the previous section) for publishing 'seditious and obscene libels'. This led to violent protests:

At the sessions of the peace at Guildhall, a woman was tried for assaulting Mr Emmerton, a constable, at St Bride's parish. He had taken her into custody for bawling *Wilkes and Liberty*, when for his folly, she said, she would take the liberty to break his head, which she accordingly did. The jury found her guilty, and the court fined her one shilling.

The Gentleman's Magazine, 4 July 1768.

During the General Strike of 1926, a strike-breaking bus conductor, who had to tell his passengers to put up their umbrellas to protect themselves from flying glass, wrote to the Prime Minister, Stanley Baldwin:

... facing some of these rough mobs is not exactly a pleasant job. I find the women very bad in parts (I mean in parts of London), the language simply awful and my raincoat is well stained with spittle.

Quoted in Piers Brendon, The Dark Valley, 2000.

I have got no further than this: Every man has a right to utter what he thinks truth, and every other man has a right to knock him down for it.

Samuel Johnson (1709–84), in 1780; quoted in James Boswell's Life of Samuel Johnson, 1791, Vol. 4.

The anonymous Letters of Junius published in The Public Advertiser between 1768 and 1772 largely consisted of attacks on the government of the day. But Junius was no revolutionary, and upheld the English constitution as the guarantor of liberty:

Let me exhort and conjure you never to suffer an invasion of your political constitution, however minute the instance may appear, to pass by, without a determined, persevering resistance. ... Be assured, that the laws which protect us in our civil rights grow out of the constitution, and they must fall or flourish with it. This is not the cause of faction, or of party, or of any individual, but the common interest of every man in Britain. ...

   Let it be impressed upon your minds, let it be instilled into your children, that the liberty of the press is the *palladium* of all the civil, political, and religious rights of an Englishman: and that the right of juries to return a general verdict, in all cases whatsoever, is an essential part of our constitution, not to be controlled or limited by the judges, nor, in any shape, questioned by the legislature. The power of king, lords, and commons, is not an arbitrary power. They are the trustees, not the owners of the estate. The fee-simple is in *us*.

Dedication to *The Letters of Junius*, collected in two volumes in 1772.

The laws of seditious libel used against Wilkes continued to be invoked against publications thought threatening to the status quo. In 1793 the proprietors of the *Morning Post* appeared before Lord Kenyon, presiding over the Court of King's Bench, for publishing the minutes of a meeting of the Society for Political Information. Kenyon addressed the jury thus:

The liberty of the press has always been, and has justly been, a favourite topic with Englishmen. They have looked at it with jealousy whenever it has been invaded; and although a licenser was put over the press, and was suffered to exist for some years after the coming of William, and after the revolution, yet the reluctant spirit of English liberty called for a repeal of that law; and from that time to this it has not been shackled and limited more than it ought to be.

Gentlemen, it is placed as the sentinel to alarm us, when any attempt is made on our liberties: and we ought to be watchful, and to take care that this sentinel is not abused and converted into a traitor. It can only be protected by being kept within due limits, and by our doing those things which we ought, and watching over the liberties of the people; but the instant it degenerates into licentiousness, we ought not to suffer it to exist without punishment. ...

Reading this paper, which appears to me calculated to put the people in a state of discontent with every thing done in this country, I am bound on my oath to answer, that I think this paper was published with a wicked and malicious intent to vilify the government, and to make the people discontented with the constitution under which they live. ... That it was done with a view to vilify the constitution, and the laws, and the government of this country, and to infuse into the minds of his majesty's subjects a belief that they were oppressed: and on this ground I consider it as a gross and seditious libel.

Lord Kenyon (1732–1802), 9 December 1793; from the *Annual Register*, 1793. The jury voted for acquittal.

In 1792 Thomas Paine was indicted for an alleged seditious libel contained in Part II of *The Rights of Man*, published earlier that year. He himself had fled to France before he could be arrested, and so was tried *in absentia*. The jury was of a type called a 'special jury' – chosen by the Crown and paid two guineas each if they found for the prosecution, or one guinea each if they found for the defence. Defending Paine was Thomas Erskine:

Mr Erskine, on the Part of the Defendant.

'Gentlemen of the Jury,

'... There is an end to the freedom of England, and of that constitution we all profess to love, if every man, possessed of an opinion, may not freely write those sentiments, which he does not take up upon the spur of a particular occasion, but merely to express the sentiments of his mind. Gentlemen, the principle I mean to

THE FREE-BORN ENGLISH   99

lay down as to the liberty of the English press is this, that every man may address himself to the individuals of a whole nation, and may in that address canvass the propriety and advantage of the form of government in general, and the government in a particular country which he inhabits; that he may find fault with the constitution, that he may take it to pieces, that he may point out its errors and defects, and state what are its corruptions, and what are likely to be the consequences, and where the public, from falling into those corruptions, are long suffered to remain; and in doing all that, he is not a subject of criminal justice, unless it can be shown, that at the time he so wrote, and at the time he so published, he did it, not contemplating the happiness, but seeking the misery of the human race. . . .

'Gentlemen, I say, and I say it in the name of Thomas Paine, the Defendant, the Author of the Rights of Man, and in his words, which I shall read to you: "The end of all political associations is the preservation of the rights of man, which rights are liberty, property, and security; that the nation is the source of all sovereignty derived from it; the right of property being secured and inviolable, no one ought to be deprived of it, except in cases of evident public necessity, legally ascertained, and on condition of a previous just indemnity." Gentlemen, those are undoubtedly the rights of man. . . .

'Let me not, therefore, be suspected to be contending that it is lawful to write a book pointing out defects in the English government, and exciting individuals to destroy its sanctions and to refuse obedience. But, on the other hand, I do contend that it is lawful to address the English nation on these momentous subjects; for had it not been for this inalienable right (thanks be to God and our fathers for establishing it!), how should we have had this Constitution which we so loudly boast of? If, in the march of the human mind, no man could have gone before the establishments of the time he lived in, how could our establishment, by reiterated changes, have become what it is? If no man could have awakened the public mind to errors and abuses in our government, how could it have passed on from stage to stage, through reformation and revolution, so as to have arrived from barbarism to such a pitch of happiness and perfection that the Attorney-General considers it as profanation to touch it further or to look for any further amendment?

'Was any Englishman ever so brought as a criminal before an English court of justice? If I were to ask you, gentlemen of the jury, what is the choicest fruit that grows upon the tree of English liberty, you would answer: security under the law. If I were to ask the whole people of England the return they looked for at the hands of government, for the burdens under which they bend to support it, I should still be answered: security under the law; or, in other words, an impartial administration of justice. . . .

'France and its Constitution are the mere pretences. It is because Britons begin to recollect the inheritance of their own Constitution left them by their ancestors; it is because they are awakened to the corruptions which have fallen upon its most valuable parts, that forsooth the nation is in danger of being destroyed by a single pamphlet. . . .

'Engage the people by their affections, convince their reason – and they will be loyal from the only principle that can make loyalty sincere, vigorous or rational – a conviction that it is their truest interest, and that their government is for their good. Constraint is the natural parent of resistance, and a pregnant proof that reason is not on the side of those who use it. You must all remember Lucian's pleasant story: Jupiter and a countryman were walking together, conversing with great freedom and familiarity upon the subject of heaven and earth. The countryman listened with attention and acquiescence, while Jupiter strove only to convince him – but happening to hint a doubt, Jupiter turned hastily around and threatened him with his thunder. "Ah! ah!" says the countryman, "now, Jupiter, I know that you are wrong; you are always wrong when you appeal to thunder."

'This is the case with me – I can reason with the people of England, but I cannot fight against the thunder of authority.'

... The Attorney General rose to reply, but Mr Campbell, the foreman of the Jury, said he was instructed by his brother jurors to say that he might save himself the trouble of any observations, unless he though otherwise himself, for that they were satisfied. The Jury immediately gave their verdict *Guilty*.

Thomas Erskine (1750–1823), lawyer and MP, speech, 18 December 1792, to a special jury of the Court of King's Bench, Lord Kenyon presiding. Compiled from *The Genuine Trial of Thomas Paine* (1792) and *The Penguin Book of Historic Speeches* (1995).

The French Revolution, and the Revolutionary Wars that followed, frightened the Younger Pitt's government into increasing reaction and oppression at home. Here Charles James Fox speaks out against the Treason and Sedition Bills brought before the Commons in 1795:

Our government is valuable, because it is free. ... For my own part, I never heard of any danger arising to a free state from the freedom of the press, or freedom of speech; so far from it, I am perfectly clear that a free state cannot exist without both. The honourable and learned gentleman has said, will we not preserve the remainder by giving up this liberty? I admit that, by passing of the bill, the people will have lost a great deal. A great deal! Aye, all that is worth preserving. For you will have lost the spirit, the fire, the freedom, the boldness, the energy of the British character, and with them its best virtue. I say, it is not the written law of the constitution of England, it is not the law that is to be found in books, that has constituted the true principle of freedom in any country, at any time. No! it is the energy, the boldness of a man's mind, which prompts him to speak, not in private, but in large and popular assemblies, that constitutes, that creates, in a state, the spirit of freedom. This is the principle that gives life to liberty; without, the human character is a stranger to freedom. If you suffer the liberty of speech to be wrested from you, you will have then lost the freedom, the energy, the boldness of the British character. ... If this bill shall pass, England herself will have thrown away that ladder, by which she has risen to wealth (but that is the last consideration), to honour, to happiness, and to fame. Along with energy of thinking and liberty of speech, she will forfeit the comforts of her situation, and the dignity of her character, those blessings which they have secured to her at home, and the rank by which she has been distinguished among the nations.

Charles James Fox (1749–1806), speech against the Treason and Sedition Bills, 25 November 1795.

Freedom of speech in England is little else than the right to write or say anything which a jury of twelve shopkeepers think it expedient should be said or written.

Albert Venn Dicey (1835–1922), English jurist, *Lectures Introductory to the Study of the Law of the Constitution*, 1885.

Freedom of the press in Britain is freedom to print such of the proprietor's prejudices as the advertisers don't object to.

Hannen Swaffer (1879–1962), English journalist, in c.1928, quoted in Tom Driberg, *Swaff*, 1974.

> You cannot hope to bribe or twist,
> Thank God! the British journalist.
> But, seeing what the man will do,
> Unbribed, there's no occasion to.

Humbert Wolfe (1886–1940), 'Over the Fire', 1930.

One of the best-known locations for the exercise of free speech is Speaker's Corner in Hyde Park, to which George Orwell devoted an article in *Tribune*:

As for the meetings inside the Park, they are one of the minor wonders of the world. At different times I have listened there to Indian Nationalists, Temperance reformers, Communists, Trostkyists, the S.P.G.B. [Socialist Party of Great Britain], the Catholic Evidence Society, Freethinkers, vegetarians, Mormons, the Salvation Army, the Church Army, and a large variety of plain lunatics, all taking their turn at the rostrum in an orderly way and receiving a fairly good-humoured hearing from the crowd. Granted that Hyde Park is a special area, a sort of Alsatia where outlawed opinions are permitted to walk – still, there are very few countries in the world where you can see a similar spectacle. I have known continental Europeans, long before Hitler seized power, come away from Hyde Park astonished and even perturbed by the things they have heard Indian or Irish Nationalists saying about the British Empire.

The degree of freedom of the press existing in this country is often overrated. Technically there is great freedom, but the fact that most of the press is owned by a few people operates in much the same way as a state censorship. On the other hand, freedom of speech is real. On the platform, or in certain recognized open-air spaces like Hyde Park, you can say almost anything; and, what is perhaps more significant, no one is frightened to utter his true opinions in pubs, on the tops of buses, and so forth.

The point is that the relative freedom which we enjoy depends on public opinion. The law is no protection. Governments make laws, but whether they are carried out, and how the police behave, depends on the general temper of the country. If large numbers of people are interested in freedom of speech, there will be freedom of speech, even if the law forbids it; if public opinion is sluggish, inconvenient minorities will be persecuted, even if laws exist to protect them.

George Orwell (1903–50), 'Freedom of the Park', *Tribune*, 7 December 1945. Alsatia was an area of Whitefriars in London that had formerly had the right to grant sanctuary to fugitives.

The BBC is held to be another bastion of free speech. During the Second World War it advertised itself thus:

BRITAIN CALLS THE WORLD

Men, women, and even children, risk imprisonment and death to hear broadcasts from London. They are the inhabitants of the occupied countries of Europe. They do so because they have learned that the British broadcasts tell them the truth.

All over the world, and in many languages, you can listen to the truth from London. The British radio sticks to the facts – giving the latest, most authentic news as soon as it is known. . . .

FROM LONDON COMES

THE VOICE OF BRITAIN

. . . THE VOICE OF FREEDOM

The BBC: Second World War advertising on the dust-jackets of books, in this case the 1942 reprint of E.M. Forster's *Abinger Harvest*.

'MY VOICE SHALL BE HEARD'

It is one thing to have your say, another thing to have your voice listened to. The record of the English struggle for the effective means of bringing this about – the franchise – would itself fill an anthology. What follows is merely a flavour.

When the radical John Wilkes stood for election in Middlesex in 1768, a handbill for his campaign was entitled *A List of the Horses that are to start* . . .:

The famous horse Liberty, formerly belonging to Mr Pitt, and since sold by Lord Chatham; he was got by Magna Charta, his dam by Freedom. This horse is too well known on the turf to need much description; there has been a great deal of Jockeyship made use of to prevent his starting, as the knowing ones are too well acquainted with his mettle to wish to have him brought again on the course; however, he is now entered, and very large betts are depending; the odds on him are four to one against the field.

Accompanied by crowds shouting 'Wilkes and Liberty', Wilkes was elected on 28 March, but his election was immediately declared invalid as he had been convicted of seditious libel in the matter of *An Essay on Woman*, a privately printed pornographic poem, and Issue Number 45 of *The North Briton*, a contrarian political newspaper. A fresh election was called; Wilkes, although imprisoned, was again elected and again disbarred. This happened three times more until Wilkes, having served his sentence, took his seat. He remained an MP for the rest of his life, and became Lord Mayor of London.

As recounted above, Thomas Paine's *Rights of Man* saw him found guilty of seditious libel, and it became a criminal offence, punishable by deportation, to sell or publish the book. In the Conclusion to Part I, Paine argued that sovereignty should reside in the nation as a whole – the people – not in king or government:

When we survey the wretched condition of man, under the monarchical and hereditary systems of Government, dragged from his home by one power, or driven by another, and impoverished by taxes more than by enemies, it becomes evident that those systems are bad, and that a general revolution in the principle and construction of Governments is necessary.

What is government more than the management of the affairs of a Nation? It is not, and from its nature cannot be, the property of any particular man or family, but of the whole community, at whose expense it is supported; and though by force and contrivance it has been usurped into an inheritance, the usurpation cannot alter the right of things. Sovereignty, as a matter of right, appertains to the Nation only, and not to any individual; and a Nation has at all times an inherent indefeasible right to abolish any form of Government it finds inconvenient, and to establish such as accords with its interest, disposition and happiness. The romantic and barbarous distinction of men into Kings and subjects, though it may suit the condition of courtiers, cannot that of citizens; and is exploded by the principle upon which Governments are now founded. Every citizen is a member of the Sovereignty, and, as such, can acknowledge no personal subjection; and his obedience can be only to the laws.

When men think of what Government is, they must necessarily suppose it to possess a knowledge of all the objects and matters upon which its authority is to be exercised. In this view of Government, the republican system, as established by America and France, operates to embrace the whole of a Nation; and the knowledge necessary to the interest of all the parts, is to be found in the centre, which the parts by representation form: But the old Governments are on a construction that excludes knowledge as well as happiness; government by Monks, who knew nothing of the world beyond the walls of a Convent, is as consistent as government by Kings.

What were formerly called Revolutions, were little more than a change of persons, or an alteration of local circumstances. They rose and fell like things of course, and had nothing in their existence or their fate that could influence beyond the spot that produced them. But what we now see in the world, from the Revolutions of America and France, are a renovation of the natural order of things, a system of principles as universal as truth and the existence of man, and combining moral with political happiness and national prosperity.

'I. Men are born, and always continue, free and equal in respect of their rights. Civil distinctions, therefore, can be founded only on public utility.

'II. The end of all political associations is the preservation of the natural and imprescriptible rights of man; and these rights are liberty, property, security, and resistance of oppression.

'III. The nation is essentially the source of all sovereignty; nor can any Individual, or Any Body Of Men, be entitled to any authority which is not expressly derived from it.'

In these principles, there is nothing to throw a Nation into confusion by inflaming ambition. They are calculated to call forth wisdom and abilities, and to exercise them for the public good, and not for the emolument or aggrandisement of particular descriptions of men or families. Monarchical sovereignty, the enemy of mankind, and the source of misery, is abolished; and the sovereignty itself is restored to its natural and original place, the Nation.

Thomas Paine (1737–1809), Conclusion to Part I of *The Rights of Man*, 1791.

A target of the reformers were the rotten boroughs. These were ancient parliamentary constituencies with only a handful of voters that continued to return members to Parliament – while large new towns like Birmingham lacked any representation:

The great fount of evil is the rotten boroughs; these are the Pandora's box, from which has flowed national calamities, desolating wars, lavish expenditure and the monstrous debt and dead weight. They are the obstacle to every social melioration – civil, commercial, legal, and ecclesiastical. By means of them the nobility have been able to double their private revenues, appropriating to themselves the dignities and livings of the church; pensions and grants out of the public purse; and filling with their connexions and dependants, every lucrative office in the army, navy and public administration. ... In consequence of the boroughs, all our institutions are partial, oppressive, and aristocratic. We have an aristocratic church, an aristocratic bar, an aristocratic game-code, aristocratic taxation, aristocratic corn-laws, aristocratic laws of property; in short, the aristocratic spirit pervades every-thing – all is privilege, prescription, monopoly, association and corporation.

The Extraordinary Black Book, 1831.

The Great Reform Act of the following year abolished some rotten boroughs, gave representation to towns such as Birmingham and Manchester, and extended the franchise – a little. Although Parliament continued to be dominated by the landed classes, the principle that Parliament *could* be reformed had been established.

It was all too much for some old reactionaries:

A new democratic influence has been introduced into elections. ... To this, add the practice of requiring candidates to pledge themselves to certain measures, which is too common even among the best class of electors, and the readiness of candidates to give these pledges, and you will see reason to be astonished that we should even now exist as a nation.

The Duke of Wellington (1769–1852), letter, 6 March 1833; quoted in L.J. Jennings, ed., *The Croker Papers*, 1884.

Encouraged by the Great Reform Act, but dissatisfied by its limitations, the London Working Men's Association drew up a People's Charter in 1838. Over one million people signed the Charter, and in 1839 it was presented to Parliament, who rejected it. A similar fate befell those petitions submitted in the 1840s. The following election address contains four of the Chartists' key aims:

I solicit your support as an advocate of the following reforms:

1. UNIVERSAL SUFFRAGE, as propounded in the People's Charter, since, if Capital has a right to represent itself, Labour has the same right also, and since experience teaches that those invariably suffer who are not able to watch over their own interests.

2. VOTE BY BALLOT, as the only means of preventing undue influence and intimidation, and since it is a mode of election that has long been successfully adopted among the wealthy classes.
3. ANNUAL PARLIAMENTS, since we find that sound measures are always more readily carried at the close of a Parliament than at its commencement; and since the objection, that elections place the country in a state of excitement, is much more likely to exist after the intrigues and conflicting interests of *seven* years, than of *one*.
4. NO PROPERTY QUALIFICATION, since we do not find that a man's brains increase or decrease in proportion to his wealth; nor that amassing riches is in itself any sign of virtue, temperance, or honesty; nor that those riches guarantee the patriotism of their possessor. . . .

Ernest Jones, first election address to the electors and non-electors of Halifax, *Northern Star*, 3 July 1847.

The other two aims of the People's Charter were the establishment of equal electoral districts and payment of MPs. It should be pointed out that 'vote by ballot' meant a secret ballot, and that by 'universal suffrage' the Chartists meant universal *male* suffrage. The latter was not achieved until 1918, when some women were also given the vote. True universal suffrage did not come until 1928, when the franchise was extended to *all* women.

The introduction of the secret ballot appalled some Elder Statesmen:

I say that for men who are charged with the high and important duty of choosing the best man to represent the country in Parliament to go sneaking to the ballot-box, and, poking in a piece of paper, looking round to see that no-one could read it, is a course which is unconstitutional and unworthy of the character of straightforward and honest Englishmen.

Lord Palmerston (1784–1865), speech in Parliament opposing secret ballots, 1852.

In 1866 John Stuart Mill presented the first petition for female suffrage to Parliament. However, it took the radical action of the Suffragettes in the early years of the following century to get things really moving:

We are here to claim our rights as women, not only to be free, but to fight for freedom. It is our privilege, as well as our pride and our joy, to take some part in this militant movement, which, as we believe, means the regeneration of humanity.

Christabel Pankhurst (1880–1958), speech, 'Votes for Women', 31 March 1911.

Meanwhile, her mother was out breaking windows:

The argument of the broken window pane is the most valuable argument in modern politics.

Emmeline Pankhurst (1858–1928); quoted in George Dangerfield, *The Strange Death of Liberal England*, 1936.

'As Good As The Next Man'

England has produced reformers in plenty; some would say that few other nations ever produced so much that required to be reformed. Revolutionaries – true equalitarians – have been thin on the ground; our instinct for compromise – one that was shared by Cromwell, our most famous revolutionary – sees to that. While 'being as good as the next person' is as universal an English assumption as that of being – through class, region of birth, accent, outlook, personality – different, few have ever felt compelled to make that assumption a constitutional reality. But England has, uniquely, produced in its few true revolutionaries the phenomenon of the Anarcho-Puritan: one who, while being committed to the wholesale overturning of the existing order, chooses to justify it on the most rigorously conservative and absolutist of grounds.

Nowadays the Anarcho-Puritan is more of an endangered species than ever.

The poll tax imposed to raise money for the Hundred Years' War was the immediate provocation of the Peasants' Revolt of 1381. The peasants, who had seen their wages rise following the decimation of the labour force by the Black Death, had also long resented the Statute of Labourers of 1351, which had tried to fix wages at pre-plague levels, and prevented men from moving to work for lords who offered better money. In June 1381 the rebels were addressed by one of their leaders, the excommunicated priest John Ball, who attacked the distinction between bondsmen and free men:

When Adam delved and Eve span,
Who was then the gentleman?

From the beginning all men by nature were created alike, and our bondage or servitude came in by the unjust oppression of naughty men. For if God would have had any bondsmen from the beginning, he would have appointed who should be bond, and who free. And therefore I exhort you to consider that now the time is come, appointed to us by God, in which ye may (if ye will) cast off the yoke of bondage, and recover liberty. I counsel you therefore well to bethink yourselves, and to take good hearts unto you, that after the manner of a good husband that tilleth his ground, and riddeth out thereof such evil weeds as choke and destroy the good corn, you may destroy first the great lords of the realm, and after, the judges and lawyers, and questmongers, and all other who have undertaken to be against the commons. For so shall you procure peace and surety to yourselves in time to come; and by dispatching out of the way the great men, there shall be an equality in liberty, and no difference in degrees of nobility; but a like dignity and equal authority in all things brought in among you.

John Ball (d.1381), speech to the rebels at Blackheath, June 1381.

Ball was executed for his part in the Peasants' Revolt, which fizzled out within a month. However, no more poll taxes were levied. Also at about this time the continuing shortage of labour following the Black Death did bring about the disappearance of serfdom in England, so ending the distinction between bondsmen and free men.

It was not until the Civil Wars of three centuries later that popular revolutionary movements again came to the fore. Prominent among these were the Levellers and the Diggers. Like John Ball before him, one of the leaders of the Diggers, Gerrard Winstanley, invoked God in support of a classless society:

In the beginning of time the great creator, Reason, made the earth to be a common treasury, to preserve beasts, birds, fishes and man, the lord that was to govern this creation. ... Not one word was spoken in the beginning that one branch of mankind should rule over another. ... Selfish imaginations ... did set up one man to teach and rule over another. And thereby ... man was brought into bondage, and became a greater slave to such of his own kind than the beasts of the field were to him. And hereupon the earth ... was hedged into enclosures by the teachers and rulers, and the others were made ... slaves. And that earth that is within this creation made a common storehouse for all, is bought and sold and kept in the hands of a few, whereby the great Creator is mightily dishonoured, as if he were a respecter of persons, delighting in the comfortable livelihood of some and rejoicing in the miserable poverty and straits of others. From the beginning it was not so. ...

The power of enclosing land and owning property was brought into the creation by your ancestors by the sword; which first did murder their fellow creatures, men, and after plunder or steal away their land, and left this land successively to you, their children. And therefore, though you did not kill or thieve, yet you hold that cursed thing in your hand by the power of the sword; and so you justify the wicked deeds of your fathers, and that sin of your fathers shall be visited upon the head of you and your children to the third and fourth generation, and longer too, till your bloody and thieving power be rooted out of the land. ...

The poorest man hath as true a title and just right to the land as the richest man ... True freedom lies in the free enjoyment of the earth. ... If the common people have no more freedom in England but only to live among their elder brothers and work for them for hire, what freedom then have they in England more than we can have in Turkey or France? ...

The best laws that England hath are yokes and manacles, tying one sort of people to another. ... All laws that are not grounded upon equity and reason, not giving a universal freedom to all but respecting persons, ought to be cut off with the King's head. ...

While this kingly power reigned in one man called Charles all sorts of people complained of oppression. ... Thereupon you that were the gentry, when you were assembled in Parliament, you called upon the poor common people to come and help you. ... That top bough is lopped off the tree of tyranny, and the kingly power in that one particular is cast out. But alas, oppression is a great tree still, and keeps off the sun of freedom from the poor commons still. ...

Therefore, you Army of England's Commonwealth, look to it! The enemy could not beat you in the field, but they may be too hard for you by policy in counsel if you do not stick close to see common freedom established. For if so be that kingly authority be set up in your laws again, King Charles hath conquered you and your posterity by policy, and won the field of you, though you seemingly have cut off his head.

Gerrard Winstanley (c.1609–c.1660), one of the leaders of the Diggers and according to some sources the founder of the Quaker Movement; quoted in Christopher Hill, *The World Turned Upside Down*, 1972.

The Diggers set up a community on common land at St George's Hill, Surrey, in April 1649, and practised agrarian communism. They were constantly harassed by the locals, however, and the community broke up in 1650. The Levellers, a movement within the lower ranks of the army who agitated for a written, republican constitution, a wider franchise and the abolition of class distinctions, also disappeared after the suppression of a mutiny in 1649.

Dr Johnson celebrated the egalitarian spirit of the ordinary Englishman, while recognising that, for the 'lowest ranks' of society, liberty was severely constrained by economic circumstance:

The equality of English privileges, the impartiality of our laws, the freedom of our tenures, and the prosperity of our trade, dispose us very little to reverence of superiors. It is not to any great esteem of the officers that the English soldier is indebted for his spirit in the hour of battle, for perhaps it does not often happen that he thinks much better of his leader than of himself ... He was born without a master, and looks not on any man, however dignified by lace or titles, as deriving from nature any claims to his respect, or inheriting any qualities superior to his own. ... Liberty is, to the lowest rank of every nation, little more than the choice of working or starving.

Samuel Johnson (1709–84), 'The Bravery of the English Common Soldier' in *The British Magazine*, January 1760.

The French Revolution inspired the establishment in England of a number of working-class movements – mostly reformist, but a few revolutionary:

My friends, you are oppressed, you know it. Lord Buckingham who died the other day had thirty thousand pounds yearly for setting his arse in the House of Lords and doing nothing. Liberty calls aloud, ye who will hear her voice, may you be free and happy. He who doe not, let him starve and be DAMNED.

NB be resolute and you shall be happy. He who wishes well to the cause of Liberty let him repair to the Chapel Field at Five O'clock this afternoon, to begin a Glorious Revolution.

Broadsheet, confiscated in 1793 as a 'seditious libel'.

Despite repressive government measures against the so-called 'English Jacobins' such as Thomas Paine, and the banning of their societies, the flame of radicalism continued to burn:

Men of England, wherefore plough
For the lords who lay ye low?
Wherefore weave with toil and care
The rich robes your tyrants wear?

Wherefore feed and clothe and save,
From the cradle to the grave,
Those ungrateful drones who would
Drain your sweat – nay, drink your blood?

Wherefore, Bees of England, forge
Many a weapon, chain, and scourge,
That these stingless drones may spoil
The forced produce of your toil?

Have ye leisure, comfort, calm,
Shelter, food, love's gentle balm?
Or what is it ye buy so dear
With your pain and with your fear?

The seed ye sow another reaps;
The wealth ye find another keeps;
The robes ye weave another wears;
The arms ye forge another bears.

Sow seed, – but let no tyrant reap;
Find wealth, – let no impostor heap;
Weave robes, – let not the idle wear;
Forge arms, in your defence to bear.

Percy Bysshe Shelley (1792–1822), from *Song to the Men of England*, 1819.

Popular protests continued, often brutally dealt with by the authorities – at the Peterloo Massacre of 1819, for example, a peaceful crowd was dispersed by cavalry, leaving eleven dead. After a riot at a Durham colliery in 1831 one of the miners left a letter in the manager's house:

I was at yor hoose last neet and meyd mysel very comfortable. Ye hay nee family and yor just won man on the colliery, I see ye hey a greet lot of rooms and big cellars and plenty wine and beer in them which I got ma share on. Noo I naw some at wor colliery that has three or fower lads and lasses and they live in won room not half as gude as yor cellar. I dont pretend to naw very much but I naw there shudnt be that much difference. The only place we can gan to o the week ends is the yel hoose and heve a pint. I dinna pretend to be a profit, but I naw this, and lots of ma marrers na's te, that were not tret as we owt to be, and a great filosopher says, to get noledge is to naw yer ignerent. But weve just begun to find that oot, and ye maisters and owners may luk oot, for yor not gan to get se much o yor way, wer gan to hey some o wors now ...

Duncan Steen and Nicholas Soames, *The Essential Englishman*, 1989.

The 1830s saw the rise of the Chartists (see previous section), who pressed for parliamentary reform and universal male suffrage:

THE GOVERNMENT OF ENGLAND IS A DESPOTISM AND HER INDUSTRIOUS MILLIONS SLAVES. Her 'constitutional rights' are specious forms wanting substance; her forms of 'justice' subterfuges for legal plunder and class domination; ... her 'right of petitioning' a farce; her 'religious freedom' a cheat. ...

Shall it be said, fellow countrymen, that four millions of men, capable of bearing arms, and defending their country against every foreign assailant, allowed a few domestic oppressors to enslave and degrade them? ... We have resolved to obtain our rights, 'peaceably if we may, forcibly if we must'; but woe to those who begin the warfare with the millions, or who forcibly restrain their peaceful agitation for justice.

From the Chartist Manifesto, 1839.

In England, as Engels observed, working-class rights were advanced slowly but surely:

The English working class is moving. ... It moves, like all things in England, with a slow and measured step. ... And if the patience of the movement is not up to the impatience of some people, let them not forget that it is the working class which keeps alive the finest qualities of the English character, and that, if a step in advance is once gained in England, it is, as a rule, never lost afterwards.

Friedrich Engels (1820–95), *Socialism, Utopian and Scientific*, 1892. Engels lived for much of his life in England, where he managed his family's cotton factory in Manchester.

G.K. Chesterton opposed the 'scientific' socialism of the likes of H.G. Wells and George Bernard Shaw, favouring instead 'Distributism' – the redistribution of land. His agrarian utopianism was matched by a romantic conception of the 'people of England':

Smile at us, pay us, pass us; but do not quite forget.
For we are the people of England, that never have spoken yet.
There is many a fat farmer that drinks less cheerfully,
There is many a free French peasant who is richer and sadder than we.
There are no folk in the whole world so helpless or so wise.
There is hunger in our bellies, there is laughter in our eyes;
You laugh at us and love us, both mugs and eyes are wet:
Only you do not know us. For we have not spoken yet.
. . .
We hear men speaking for us of new laws strong and sweet,
Yet is there no man speaketh as we speak in the Street.
It may be we shall rise the last as Frenchmen rose the first,
Our wrath come after Russia's wrath and our wrath be the worst.
It may be we are meant to mark with our riot and our rest
God's scorn for all men governing. It may be beer is best.
But we are the people of England; and we have not spoken yet.
Smile at us, pay us, pass us. But do not quite forget.

G.K. Chesterton (1874–1936), from *The Secret People*, 1915.

The veteran Labour politician Tony Benn follows in the tradition of John Ball and Gerrard Winstanley, and has proved as much an irritant to his own party as to his political opponents. Whenever he meets somebody in a position of power he puts to them these questions:

What power have you got? Where did you get it from? In whose interests do you exercise it? To whom are you accountable? How do we get rid of you?

Tony Benn (1925–), lecture 'The Independent Mind', given in Nottingham, 18 June 1993.

'IT's A FREE COUNTRY, ISN'T IT?'

The assumption of personal liberty, the necessary illusion of the English, leads to the assumption that England must by definition be free. We all believe it, and we all know it isn't true. We all behave as though it must be true, but we all know that when a man protests, 'It's a free country, isn't it?' he knows, better than anyone, that it's not. It should be; so, of course, we behave as if it were. That's the free-born English for you.

The Britons themselves submit to levies, tribute and the tasks laid upon them by the government, if they are not treated oppressively. Oppression they cannot bear, being reduced far enough to give obedience, but not yet far enough to be slaves.

Tacitus (c.AD 56–after 117), *Agricola*.

William I, never loved, but respected and feared, was far from Albion. ... Whoever ruled, the mass of the populace remained English, grumbling, suspicious of authority, sceptical of 'winged words' from lords, but rebellious only if over-goaded by the rampantly unfair. They preferred the Crown to the baronage, one Devil being better than many devils. Tenacious of rights, however niggardly, they disputed boundary stones and bargained over marriages and field-strips with an unwavering obstinacy which would one day win them the right to vote, form unions, let women into Parliament, universities, the Law, the Church. ... Meanwhile, lacking an Arthur, a Hengist, an Alfred, they acquired the characteristics of the defeated: dumb insolence, irony, deviousness, understatement. Their rule for good conduct was perfectly expressed by a foreign nun, the first recognised female dramatist and wholly unknown to them, Hrotswitha of Gandersheim (c.932–1002): 'Blame not he who falls but he who fails to rise again.'

Peter Vansittart, *In Memory of England*, 1998.

'My son,' said the Norman Baron, 'I am dying, and you will be heir
To all the broad acres in England that William gave me for my share
When we conquered the Saxons at Hastings, and a nice little handful it is.
But before you go over to rule it I want you to understand this:–

'The Saxon is not like us Normans. His manners are not so polite.
But he never means anything serious till he talks about justice and right.
When he stands like an ox in the furrow with his sullen set eyes on your own,
And grumbles, "This isn't fair dealing," my son, leave the Saxon alone.

'You can horsewhip your Gascony archers, or torture your Picardy spears;
But don't try that game on the Saxon; you'll have the whole brood
    round your ears.

> From the richest old Thane in the county to the poorest chained serf
>   in the field,
> They'll be at you and on you like hornets, and, if you are wise,
>   you will yield. ...'

Rudyard Kipling (1865–1936), from *Norman and Saxon*, AD 1100, 1911.

Serfdom – where bondsmen were tied to their lord's land – had died out in England by around the end of the 14th century, and slavery was regarded as an alien institution:

One Cartwright brought a Slave from Russia, and would scourge him, for which he was questioned: and it was resolved, That England was too pure an Air for Slaves to breathe in.

'In the 11th of Elizabeth' (17 November 1568 to 16 November 1569), in John Rushworth, *Historical Collections* (1680–1722), Vol. 2.

As for slaves and bondmen we have none, naie such is the privilege of our countrie by the especiall grace of God, and bountie of our princes, that if anie come hither from other realms, so soone as they set foot on land they become so free of condition as their masters, whereby all note of servile bondage is utterlie remooved from them.

William Harrison (1534–93), *Description of England*, 1577 (second edition, 1587).

However, none of this prevented many English merchants from profiting hugely from the slave trade overseas, or English colonists using slaves on their plantations in the Americas.

Fearing that James II was moving towards the establishment of a Catholic absolutism in England, Parliament invited the Protestant William of Orange to take the throne jointly with his wife Mary, the Protestant daughter of James – on condition that they accepted the terms that were incorporated into the 1689 Bill of Rights, the foundation of constitutional monarchy in England:

The said Lords Spiritual and Temporal and Commons, pursuant to their respective letters and elections, being now assembled in a full and free representative of this nation, taking into their most serious consideration the best means for attaining the ends aforesaid, do in the first place (as their ancestors in like case have usually done) for the vindicating and asserting their ancient rights and liberties declare:

That the pretended power of suspending the laws or the execution of laws by regal authority without consent of Parliament is illegal;

That the pretended power of dispensing with laws or the execution of laws by regal authority, as it hath been assumed and exercised of late, is illegal;

That the commission for erecting the late Court of Commissioners for Ecclesiastical Causes, and all other commissions and courts of like nature, are illegal and pernicious;

That levying money for or to the use of the Crown by pretence of prerogative, without grant of Parliament, for longer time, or in other manner than the same is or shall be granted, is illegal;

That it is the right of the subjects to petition the king, and all commitments and prosecutions for such petitioning are illegal;

That the raising or keeping a standing army within the kingdom in time of peace, unless it be with consent of Parliament, is against law;

That the subjects which are Protestants may have arms for their defence suitable to their conditions and as allowed by law;

That election of members of Parliament ought to be free;

That the freedom of speech and debates or proceedings in Parliament ought not to be impeached or questioned in any court or place out of Parliament;

That excessive bail ought not to be required, nor excessive fines imposed, nor cruel and unusual punishments inflicted;

That jurors ought to be duly impanelled and returned, and jurors which pass upon men in trials for high treason ought to be freeholders;

That all grants and promises of fines and forfeitures of particular persons before conviction are illegal and void;

And that for redress of all grievances, and for the amending, strengthening and preserving of the laws, Parliaments ought to be held frequently.

An Act Declaring the Rights and Liberties of the Subject and Settling the Succession of the Crown (the 'Bill of Rights'), 1689.

After the Glorious Revolution that brought William and Mary to the throne, the playwright William Congreve celebrated English liberty:

I look upon humour to be almost of English growth; at least, it does not seem to have found such increase on any other soil. And what appears to me to be the reason of it, is the great freedom, privilege and liberty which the Common People of England enjoy. Any man that has a humour is under no restraint, or fear of giving it vent; they have a proverb among them, which, may be, will shew the bent and genius of the People, as well as a longer discourse: *He that will have a May-Pole, shall have a May-Pole.* This is a maxim with them, and their practice is agreeable to it.

William Congreve, letter to John Dennis, 1695.

Maypoles had been banned under Cromwell's Protectorate, one of many killjoy measures that had helped bring about the Restoration of 1660.

Voltaire, who spent two years in exile in England in the 1720s, was a great admirer of the English constitution:

The English are the only people upon earth who have been able to prescribe limits to the power of kings by resisting them; and who, by a series of struggles, have at last established that wise Government where the Prince is all-powerful to do good, and, at the same time, is restrained from committing evil; where the nobles are great without insolence, though there are no vassals; and where the people share in the Government without confusion.

Voltaire (François-Marie Arouet, 1694–1778), *Letters on England*, 1731.

> Slaves cannot breathe in England, if their lungs
> Receive our air, that moment they are free;
> They touch our country, and their shackles fall.
>
> William Cowper (1731–1800), *The Task*, 1785, Book 2, 'The Timepiece'.

Wordsworth, who had been in France in the early years of the French Revolution ('Bliss was it in that dawn to be alive'), later became disillusioned. During the brief Peace of Amiens of 1802 he paid a short visit to Calais to meet his former mistress and his illegitimate daughter. He wrote the following sonnet on his return:

> Here, on our native soil we breathe once more.
> The cock that crows, the smoke that curls, that sound
> Of bells, – those boys who in yon meadow-ground
> In white-sleeved shirts are playing, – and
> Of the waves breaking on the chalky shore,
> All, all are English. Oft have I looked round
> With joy in Kent's green vales; but never
> Myself so satisfied in heart before.
> Europe is yet in bonds; but let that pass,
> Thought for another moment. Thou art free,
> My country! and 'tis joy enough and pride
> For one hour's perfect bliss, to tread the grass
> Of England once again, and hear and see,
> With such a dear companion at my side.
>
> William Wordsworth (1770–1850), 'Sonnet Composed in the Valley, near Dover, on the Day of our Landing', September 1802.

In 1803, as war broke out again with Napoleon, Wordsworth wrote another sonnet to English liberty:

> It is not to be thought of that the flood
> Of British freedom, which, to the open sea
> Of the world's praise, from dark antiquity
> Hath flowed, 'with pomp of waters unwithstood,'
> Roused though it be full often to a mood
> Which spurns the check of salutary bands,
> That this most famous stream in bogs and sands
> Should perish; and to evil and to good
> Be lost forever. In our halls is hung
> Armoury of the invincible knights of old:
> We must be free or die, who speak the tongue
> That Shakespeare spake: the faith and morals hold
> Which Milton held. In everything we are sprung
> Of earth's first blood, have titles manifold.
>
> William Wordsworth (1770–1850), Sonnet, 'It is not to be thought of…', 1803.

Madame de Staël, exiled from France in 1803 following a quarrel with Napoleon, considered the role of the sea in defending English freedom:

Those who do not wish to acknowledge the influence of liberty on England's power are always repeating that the English would have been conquered by Napoleon like all the continental nations if they had not been protected by the sea … but I have no doubt that had Great Britain been lifted by Leviathan and united to the Continent of Europe although she would undoubtedly have suffered more and been more greatly impoverished, yet such is the public spirit of a free nation she would never have submitted to the foreigner's yoke.

One of the marvels of English liberty is the multitude of men who give their time to public works in every town and county and whose mind and character are formed by the occupations and duties of a citizen. … They have deposed, killed, overturned more kings, princes and governments than all Europe put together and yet they have obtained the most noble, brilliant and religious social order which exists in the old world.

Madame de Staël (1766–1817), *Considérations sur la Révolution Française*, 1813, tr. Francesca M. Wilson.

Such visions have appeared to me
        As I my ordered race have run.
Jerusalem is named Liberty
        Among the sons of Albion.

William Blake (1757–1827), *Jerusalem*, 1815, chapter 1, plate 26.

You ask me, why, tho' ill at ease,
        Within this region I subsist,
        Whose spirits falter in the mist,
And languish for the purple seas.

It is the land that freemen till,
        That sober-suited Freedom chose,
        The land, where girt with friends or foes
A man may speak the thing he will;

A land of settled government,
        A land of just and old renown,
        Where Freedom slowly broadens down
From precedent to precedent:

Where faction seldom gathers head,
        But by degrees to fullness wrought,
        The strength of some diffusive thought
Hath time and space to work and spread.

Alfred, Lord Tennyson (1809–92), 'You ask me, why…', 1842.

It would be better that England should be free than that England should be compulsorily sober.

William Connor Magee (1821–91), speech on the Intoxicating Liquor Bill, House of Lords, 2 May 1872.

Englishmen never will be slaves: they are free to do whatever the Government and public opinion allow them to do.

George Bernard Shaw (1856–1950), *Man and Superman,* 1903, Act III.

During the Second World War, George Orwell reflected on what it was about the ordinary people of England that made them so averse to Fascism:

On the day in 1936 when the Germans reoccupied the Rhineland I was in a northern mining town. I happened to go into a pub just after this piece of news, which quite obviously meant war, had come over the wireless, and I remarked to others at the bar, 'The German army has crossed the Rhine.' With a vague air of capping a quotation someone answered, 'Parley-voo'. No more response than that! Nothing will ever wake these people up, I thought. But later in the evening, at the same pub, someone sang a song which had recently come out, with the chorus:

'For you can't do that there 'ere,
No, you can't do that there 'ere;
Anywhere else you can do that there,
But you can't do that there 'ere!'

And it struck me that perhaps this was the English answer to Fascism. At any rate it is true that it has not happened here, in spite of fairly favourable circumstances. The amount of liberty, intellectual or other, that we enjoy in England ought not to be exaggerated, but the fact that it has not markedly diminished in nearly five years of desperate war is a hopeful symptom.

George Orwell (1903–50), *The English People,* written 1944, published 1947.

This is a free country. We are fighting to keep it a free country, as I understand it.

Bow Street Magistrate, 1944, dismissing the Crown's case against six Peace Pledge Union members for distributing pacifist literature; quoted in Vera Brittain, *England's Hour.*

At Runnymede, at Runnymede,
        O hear the reeds at Runnymede:–
'You mustn't sell, delay, deny,
A freeman's right to liberty.
It wakes the stubborn Englishry,
        We saw 'em roused at Runnymede!'

. . .

And still when Mob or Monarch lays
Too rude a hand on English ways,
The whisper wakes, the shudder plays,
        Across the reeds at Runnymede.

And Thames, that knows the mood of kings,
And crowds and priests and suchlike things,
Rolls deep and dreadful as he brings
   Their warning down from Runnymede!

Rudyard Kipling (1865–1936), from *The Reeds of Runnymede (Magna Charta, June 15, 1215).*

I'll tell of the Magna Charter
As were signed at the Barons' command
On Runningmead Island in t'middle oft' Thame
By King John, as were known as 'Lack Land'.
. . .
It were all right him being a tyrant
To vassals and folks of that class,
But he tried on his tricks with the Barons an' all,
And that's where he made a faux pass.
. . .
So they went to the King in a body,
And their spokesman, Fitzwalter by name,
He opened the 'ole in his 'elmet and said,
Concil-latory like, 'What's the game?'
. . .
'We'll get him a Magna Charter,'
Said Fitz when his face he had freed;
Said the Barons, 'That's right and if one's not enough,
Get a couple and happen they'll breed.'
. . .
'You'd best sign at once,' said Fitzwalter,
'If you don't, I'll tell thee for a start
The next coronation will happen quite soon,
And you won't be there to take part.'

So they spread Charter out on t' tea table,
And John signed his name like a lamb,
His writing in places was sticky and thick
Through dipping his pen in the jam.

And it's through that there Magna Charter,
As were signed by the Barons of old,
That in England to-day we can do what we like,
So long as we do what we're told.

Marriott Edgar (1880–1951), monologue written for Stanley Holloway.

A Touch of Class

THE RICH MAN IN HIS CASTLE.

THE POOR MAN AT HIS GATE,

GOD MADE THEM, HIGH OR LOWLY,

AND ORDERED THEIR ESTATE.

Cecil Francis Alexander (1818–95), hymn, 'All Things Bright and Beautiful', 1848.

There seems to be no end to the things than can (and have been) written about 'the English class system'. There is some truth in most of them, but all of them are in some degree wrong. That class is a feature solely of English society is, of course, a myth, as anyone who knows (say) France or the USA will confirm. Of the following authors, I should say that Vansittart, Barker and Critchley are most perceptive in their analyses, while Orwell, in his depiction of the sort of well-meaning person who emphasises class distinction by going around earnestly denying it, is most toe-curlingly acute. Class in England remains almost entirely a matter of others' perceptions and has very little to do with one's own self-identity, income or birth. Achieve what seems to you to be a state of perfect 'classlessness' and, likely enough, others will call you a 'natural aristocrat'; you can't win, so you may as well stop worrying about it.

It is interesting to note how much of what follows remains true today, and what has become hilariously untrue. Dialect, for example, has lost its social stigma, while Alan Ross's wonderfully ex-cathedra assertion that no 'U-speaker' could ever want to perpetrate 'non-U speech' has been swept into oblivion (at least for the time being) on a tide of Estuary English cross-cut with currents of reggae and hip-hop. Today it is doubtful if even Professor Higgins could differentiate between one aitch-dropping glottal-stopper and another. The BBC, it is reported, is getting rid of people whose voices sound too posh – which is, of course (if true), itself a form of class distinction. Perhaps the real English 'class problem' is the taking of it seriously.

'Dropping One's Aitches'

Yet it is better to drop thy friends, O my daughter, than to drop thy 'H's'.

C.S. Calverley (1831–84), British poet, 'Of Friendship', in *The Complete Works of C.S. Calverley*, 1901.

In England, more than in any other country in the world, the way one speaks has traditionally spoken volumes about one's status in society.

Dialect words – those terrible marks of the beast to the truly genteel.

Thomas Hardy (1840–1928), *The Mayor of Casterbridge*, 1886.

It is impossible for an Englishman to open his mouth without making some other Englishman hate him or despise him.

George Bernard Shaw (1856–1950), Irish-born playwright, Preface to *Pygmalion*, 1916.

After the First World War the government commissioned the poet Sir Henry Newbolt (1862–1938), author of patriotic and nautical verse such as 'Drake's Drum', to chair a committee on the teaching of English. Here is an extract from its report:

Two causes, both accidental and conventional rather than national, at present distinguish and divide one class from another in England. The first of these is a marked difference in their modes of speech. If the teaching of the language were properly and universally provided for, the difference between educated and uneducated speech, which at present causes so much prejudice and difficulty of intercourse on both sides, would gradually disappear. Good speech and great literature would not be regarded as too fine for use by the majority, nor, on the other hand, would natural gifts for self-expression be rendered ineffective by embarrassing faults of diction or composition.

Report of the Newbolt Committee, *The Teaching of English in England*, 1921. The authors of the report went on to state that 'The second cause of division amongst us is the undue narrowness of the ground on which we meet for the true purposes of social life …'

George Orwell, commissioned by the Left Book Club to write a study of poverty in England, noted the importance of geography:

In a Lancashire cotton-town you could probably go for months on end without hearing an 'educated' accent, whereas there can hardly be a town in the South of England where you could throw a brick without hitting the niece of a bishop.

George Orwell (1903–50), *The Road to Wigan Pier*, 1937, chapter 7.

The would-be hegemony of the 'educated' Southern accent was resented by some who hailed from further north. Here is the Nottinghamshire-born D.H. Lawrence on the so-called 'Oxford accent':

When you hear it languishing
and hooing and cooing and sidling through the front teeth,
the oxford voice

or worse still
the would-be oxford voice
you don't even laugh any more, you can't.

For every blooming bird is an oxford cuckoo nowadays,
you can't sit on a bus nor in the tube
but it breathes gently and languishingly in the back of your neck.

And oh, so seductively superior, so seductively
self-effacingly
deprecatingly
superior. –
We wouldn't insist on it for a moment
but we are
we are
you admit we are
superior. –

D.H. Lawrence (1885–1930), 'The Oxford Voice', in *Selected Poems*, 1950.

Vocabulary and idiom are as important as accent in establishing class distinctions. The most famous treatise on the subject of 'U and non-U' expressions is by Alan Ross:

Article (meaning 'chamber-pot') is non-U; in so far as the thing survives, U-speakers use *jerry* (a schoolboy term) or *pot*.

Bath. To TAKE *a bath* is non-U against U *to* HAVE *one's bath*.

Civil: this word is used by U-speakers to approve the behaviour of a non-U person in that the latter has appreciated the difference between U and non-U, e.g. *The guard was certainly very civil*.

Coach (meaning 'char-à-banc') is non-U, doubtless because the thing itself is. Those U-speakers who are forced, by penury, to use them call them *buses*, thereby causing great confusion (a *coach* runs into the country, a *bus* within a town).

non-U *corsets*/U *stays*.

Counterpane, bedspread, coverlet. Of these three synonyms, I think that the first is U, the second obsolete, the third non-U.

Cruet. The sentence *Pass the cruet, please* is very non-U; *cruets* are in themselves non-U. In gentlemen's houses there are, ideally, separate containers – *salt-cellars, pepper-pots (-castors, -grinders, -mills)* and *mustard-pots*, so that the corresponding U-expression will be *I wonder if you could pass the salt (pepper, mustard), please?* or the like. *Vinegar* is a fourth constituent of many cruets but many uses of vinegar (e.g. poured on fish or bacon-and-eggs) are definitely non-U. ...

Cultivated in *They're cultivated people* is non-U and so also is *cultured*. There is really no U-equivalent (some U-speakers use *civilised* in this sense). ...

Dinner. U-speakers eat lunch in the middle of the day (*luncheon* is old-fashioned U) and *dinner* in the evening; if a U-speaker feels that what he is eating is a travesty of his dinner, he may appropriately call it *supper*. Non-U-speakers (also U-children and U-dogs), on the other hand, have their *dinner* in the middle of the day. *Evening meal* is non-U. ...

non-U *mental*/U *mad*. . . .

Mention: *If you don't mind my mentioning it* is non-U.

Mirror (save in compounds such as *driving-*, *shaving-mirror*) is non-U against U *looking-glass*.

non-U *note-paper*/U *writing-paper*.

Pardon! is used by the non-U in three main ways:

(1) if the hearer does not hear the speaker properly;

(2) as an apology (e.g. on brushing by someone in a passage);

(3) after hiccupping or belching.

The normal U-correspondences are very curt, viz. (1) *What?* (2) *Sorry!* (3) [Silence], though, in the first two cases, U-parents and U-governesses are always trying to make children say something 'politer' – *What did you say?* and *I'm frightfully sorry* are certainly possible. For Case (3) there are other non-U possibilities, e.g. *Manners! Beg Pardon! Pardon me!* . . .

Pleased to meet you! This is a very frequent non-U response to the greeting *How d'you do?* U-speakers normally just repeat the greeting; to reply to the greeting (e.g. with *Quite well, thank you*) is non-U.

Posh 'smart' is essentially non-U but, recently, it has gained ground among schoolboys of all classes.

non-U *preserve*/U *jam*.

non-U *radio*/U *wireless* (but *radio* technically as in aircraft).

Rude meaning 'indecent' is non-U; there is no universal U-correspondent.

non-U *serviette*/U *table-napkin*; perhaps the best known of all the linguistic class-indicators of English. . . .

Teacher is essentially non-U, though *school-teacher* is used by the U to indicate a non-U teacher. The U equivalent is *master, mistress* with prefixed attribute (as *maths-mistress*). Non-U children often refer to their teachers without article (as, *Teacher says*. . .).

non-U *toilet-paper*/U *lavatory-paper*.

non-U *wealthy*/U *rich*.

In England today – just as much as in the England of many years ago – the question 'Can a non-U speaker become a U-speaker?'* is one noticeably of paramount importance for many Englishmen (and for some of their wives). The answer is that an adult can never attain complete success. Moreover, it must be remembered that, in these matters, U-speakers have ears to hear, so that one single pronunciation, word, or phrase will suffice to brand an apparent U-speaker as originally non-U (for U-speakers themselves never make 'mistakes'). Under these circumstances, efforts to change voice are surely better abandoned. But, in fact, they continue in full force and in all strata of society. On the whole, the effect is deleterious.

* Logically, the converse question 'Can a U-speaker become a non-U-speaker?' should also arise, but, in practice, it seems not to – even the staunchest of inverted snobs apparently draws the line here. At all events I have only come across one case of it (in Leeds).

Alan S.C. Ross (1907–80), 'U and non-U: An essay in sociological linguistics', in Nancy Mitford, ed., *Noblesse Oblige*, 1956.

CHANGING PLACES

Since every Jack became a gentleman
There's a many a gentle person made a Jack.

William Shakespeare (1564–1616), *Richard III*, I.iii.

*Various commentators have remarked on the ease – or otherwise – of abandoning one's
class for another, and on the possibility and/or desirability (or otherwise) of achieving
equality between the classes, or, indeed, of abolishing class distinctions altogether.*

Social mobility – either way – has always been a possibility in England, as Daniel Defoe noted
at the very beginning of the 18th century:

Wealth, howsoever got, in England makes
Lords of mechanics, gentlemen of rakes.
Antiquity and birth are needless here;
'Tis impudence and money makes a Peer.
Innumerable City-Knights we know,
From Bluecoat Hospitals and Bridewell flow.
Draymen and porters fill the City Chair,
And footboys magisterial purple wear.
Fate has but very small distinction set
Betwixt the counter and the coronet.
Tarpaulin Lords, pages of high renown,
Rise up by poor men's valour, not their own.
Great families of yesterday we show,
And Lords, whose parents were the Lord knows who.

Daniel Defoe (1660–1731), *The True-Born Englishman*, 1701.

Defoe did, however, acknowledge that the process might take more than one generation
to achieve:

Trade is so far here with being inconsistent with a gentleman that, in short, trade
in England makes a gentleman, and has peopled this nation with gentlemen. ...
The Tradesman's children, or at least their grandchildren, come to be as good
gentlemen, parliament men, privy councillors, judges, bishops and noblemen as
those of the highest birth and the most ancient families.

Daniel Defoe (1660–1731), *The Complete English Tradesman*, 1736.

In the 19th century Thackeray wryly observed what was involved in the upward progress
from 'trade' to 'gentleman'. In this extract from *Vanity Fair*, old Osborne, a merchant, is dining
with his officer-son, the upwardly mobile but caddish George:

'What I want to know, George,' the old gentleman said, after slowly smacking his
first bumper – 'What I want to know is, how you and – ah – that little thing
upstairs, are carrying on?'

'I think, sir, it's not hard to see,' George said, with a self-satisfied grin. 'Pretty
clear, sir. – What capital wine!'

'What d'you mean, pretty clear, sir?'

'Why, hang it, sir, don't push me too hard. I'm a modest man. I – ah – I don't set up to be a lady-killer; but I do own that she's as devilish fond of me as she can be. Anybody can see that with half an eye.'

'And you yourself?'

'Why, sir, didn't you order me to marry her, and ain't I a good boy? Haven't our Papas settled it ever so long?'

'A pretty boy, indeed. Haven't I heard of your doings, sir, with Lord Tarquin, Captain Crawley of the Guards, the Honourable Mr Deuceace, and that set. Have a care, sir, have a care.'

The old gentleman pronounced these aristocratic names with the greatest gusto. Whenever he met a great man he grovelled before him, and my-lorded him as only a free-born Briton can do. He came home and looked out his history in the Peerage: he introduced his name into his daily conversation; he bragged about his Lordship to his daughters. He fell down prostrate and basked in him as a Neapolitan beggar does in the sun. . . .

'Well, well, young men will be young men. And the comfort to me is, George, that living in the best society in England, as I hope you do; as I think you do; as my means will allow you to do – '

'Thank you, sir,' says George, making his point at once. 'One can't live with these great folks for nothing; and my purse, sir, look at it;' and he held up a little token which had been netted by Amelia, and contained the very last of Dobbin's pound notes.

'You shan't want, sir. The British merchant's son shan't want, sir. My guineas are as good as theirs, George, my boy; and I don't grudge 'em. Call on Mr Chopper as you go through the City tomorrow; he'll have something for you. I don't grudge money when I know you're in good society, because I know that good society can never go wrong. There's no pride in me. I was a humbly born man – but you have had advantages. Make a good use of 'em. Mix with the young nobility. There's many of 'em who can't spend a dollar to your guinea, my boy. And as for the pink bonnets' (here from under the heavy eyebrows there came a knowing and not very pleasing leer) – 'why, boys will be boys. Only there's one thing I order you to avoid, which, if you do not I'll cut you off with a shilling, by Jove; and that's gambling, sir.'

'Oh, of course, sir,' said George.

'But to return to the other business about Amelia: why shouldn't you marry higher than a stockbroker's daughter, George – that's what I want to know?'

'It's a family business, sir,' says George, cracking filberts. 'You and Mr Sedley made the match a hundred years ago.'

'I don't deny it; but people's positions alter, sir. I don't deny that Sedley made my fortune, or rather put me in the way of acquiring, by my own talents and genius, that proud position which, I may say, I occupy in the tallow trade and the City of London. I've shown my gratitude to Sedley; and he's tried it of late, sir, as my cheque-book can show. George! I tell you in confidence I don't like the looks of Mr Sedley's affairs. My chief clerk, Mr Chopper, does not like the looks of 'em, and he's an old file, and knows 'Change as well as any man in London.

Hulker & Bullock are looking shy at him. He's been dabbling on his own account I fear. They say the *Jeune Amélie* was his, which was taken by the Yankee privateer *Molasses*. And that's flat – unless I see Amelia's ten thousand down you don't marry her. I'll have no lame duck's daughter in my family. Pass the wine, sir – or ring for coffee.'

William Makepeace Thackeray (1811–63), *Vanity Fair* (1847–48). George duly dumps Amelia, but is later brought to a sense of shame by a fellow officer and marries her – only to be shunned by his father.

In the Gilbert and Sullivan opera *The Gondoliers*, 1889, Gilbert satirised the implications of 'levelling up' – as well, perhaps, as mocking those, such as Don Alhambra, who abhorred such egalitarian ideals:

DON ALHAMBRA:
There lived a King, as I've been told,
In the wonder-working days of old,
When hearts were twice as good as gold,
And twenty times as mellow.
Good-temper triumphed in his face,
And in his heart he found a place
For all the erring human race
And every wretched fellow.
When he had Rhenish wine to drink
It made him very sad to think
That some, at junket or at jink,
Must be content with toddy.

MARCO & GIUSEPPE:
With toddy, must be content with toddy.

DON ALHAMBRA:
He wished all men as rich as he
(And he was rich as rich could be),
So to the top of every tree
Promoted everybody.

MARCO & GIUSEPPE:
Now, that's the kind of King for me.
He wished all men as rich as he,
So to the top of every tree
Promoted everybody!

DON ALHAMBRA:
Lord Chancellors were cheap as sprats,
And Bishops in their shovel hats
Were plentiful as tabby cats –
In point of fact, too many.
Ambassadors cropped up like hay,

Prime Ministers and such as they
Grew like asparagus in May,
And Dukes were three a penny.
On every side Field-Marshals gleamed,
Small beer were Lords-Lieutenant deemed,
With Admirals the ocean teemed
All round his wide dominions.

MARCO & GIUSEPPE:
With Admirals all round his wide dominions.

DON ALHAMBRA:
And Party Leaders you might meet
In twos and threes in every street
Maintaining, with no little heat,
Their various opinions.

MARCO & GIUSEPPE:
Now that's a sight you couldn't beat –
Two Party Leaders in each street
Maintaining, with no little heat,
Their various opinions.

DON ALHAMBRA:
That King, although no one denies
His heart was of abnormal size,
Yet he'd have acted otherwise
If he had been acuter.
The end is easily foretold,
When every blessed thing you hold
Is made of silver, or of gold,
You long for simple pewter.
When you have nothing else to wear
But cloth of gold and satins rare,
For cloth of gold you cease to care –
Up goes the price of shoddy.

MARCO & GIUSEPPE:
Of shoddy, up goes the price of shoddy.

DON ALHAMBRA:
In short, whoever you may be,
To this conclusion you'll agree,
When every one is somebodee,
Then no one's anybody!

MARCO & GIUSEPPE:
Now that's as plain as plain can be,
To this conclusion we agree –

ALL:
When every one is somebodee,
Then no one's anybody!
W.S. Gilbert (1836–1911), *The Gondoliers*, 1889.

By the early 20th century the middle classes and their values seemed to dominate the country. But where one class had risen to power, another might follow … This state of affairs was noted in 1909 by C.F.G. Masterman:

England, for the nation or foreign observer, is the tone and temper which the ideals and determinations of the middle class have stamped upon the vision of an astonished Europe. It is the middle class which stands for England in most modern analyses. It is the middle class which is losing its religion; which is slowly or suddenly discovering that it no longer believes in the existence of the God of its fathers, or a life beyond the grave. It is the middle class whose inexhaustible patience fills the observer with admiration and amazement as he beholds it waiting in the fog at a London terminus for three hours beyond the advertised time, and then raising a cheer, half joyful, half ironical, when the melancholy train at last emerges from the darkness. And it is the middle class which has preserved under all its security and prosperity that elemental unrest which this same observer has identified as an inheritance from an ancestry of criminals and adventurers: which drives it out from many a quiet vicarage and rose garden into a journey far beyond the skyline, to become the 'frontiersmen of all the world'.

But below this large kingdom, which for more than half a century has stood for 'England', stretches a huge and unexplored region which seems destined in the next half-century to progress towards articulate voice, and to demand an increasing power. It is the class of which Matthew Arnold, with the agreeable insolence of his habitual attitude, declared himself to be the discoverer, and to which he gave the name of the 'Populace'. 'That vast portion of the working-class', he defined it, nearly forty years ago, 'which, raw and half-developed, has long been half hidden amid its poverty and squalor, and is now issuing from its hiding-place to assert an Englishman's heaven-born privilege of doing as he likes, and is beginning to perplex us by marching where it likes, meeting where it likes, bending what it likes, breaking what it likes.' 'To this vast residuum', he adds, 'we may with great propriety give the name of Populace.' To most observers from the classes above, this is the Deluge; and its attainment of power – if such attainment ever were realised – the coming of the twilight of the gods. They see our civilisation as a little patch of redeemed land in the wilderness; preserved as by a miracle from one decade to another. They behold the influx, as the rush of a bank-holiday crowd upon some tranquil garden: tearing up the flowers by the roots, reeling in drunken merriment on the grass plots, strewing the pleasant landscape with torn paper and broken bottles.

C.F.G. Masterman (1874–1927), *The Condition of England*, 1909.

One man who was a decided unbeliever in the importance of class was the Anglo-Irish play-wright and socialist George Bernard Shaw. In *Pygmalion* he sought to get to the heart of the matter:

HIGGINS: My manners are exactly the same as Colonel Pickering's.

LIZA: That's not true. He treats a flower girl as if she was a duchess.

HIGGINS: And I treat a duchess as if she was a flower girl. ... The great secret, Eliza, is not having bad manners or good manners, but having the same manner for all human souls: in short, behaving as if you were in Heaven, where there are no third-class carriages, and one soul is as good as another.

George Bernard Shaw (1856–1950), *Pygmalion*, 1916.

Another middle-class socialist, George Orwell, was aware of the ingrained nature of class distinctions, and thus realistic about the difficulties of getting rid of them:

In a sense it is true that almost everyone would like to see class-distinctions abolished. Obviously this perpetual uneasiness between man and man, from which we suffer in modern England, is a curse and a nuisance. Hence the temptation to believe that it can be shouted out of existence with a few scout-masterish bellows of good-will. Stop calling me 'sir', you chaps! Surely we're all men? Let's pal up and get our shoulders to the wheel and remember that we're all equal, and what the devil does it matter if I know what kind of ties to wear and you don't, and I drink my soup comparatively quietly and you drink yours with the noise of water going down a waste-pipe – and so on and so on and so on; all of it the most pernicious rubbish, but quite alluring when it is suitably expressed.

But unfortunately you get no further by merely wishing class-distinctions away. More exactly, it is necessary to wish them away, but your wish has no efficacy unless you grasp what it involves. The fact that has got to be faced is that to abolish class-distinctions means abolishing a part of yourself. Here am I, a typical member of the middle class. It is easy for me to say that I want to get rid of class-distinctions, but nearly everything I think and do is a result of class-distinctions. All my notions – notions of good and evil, of pleasant and unpleasant, of funny and serious, of ugly and beautiful – are essentially middle-class notions; my taste in books and food and clothes, my sense of honour, my table-manners, my turns of speech, my accent, even the characteristic movements of my body, are the products of a special kind of upbringing and a special niche about half-way up the social hierarchy. When I grasp this I grasp that it is no use clapping a proletarian on the back and telling him that he is as good a man as I am; if I want real contact with him, I have got to make an effort for which very likely I am unprepared. For to get outside the class-racket I have got to suppress not merely my private snob-bishness, but most of my other tastes and prejudices as well. I have got to alter myself so completely that at the end I should hardly be recognisable as the same person. What is involved is not merely the amelioration of working-class conditions, nor an avoidance of the more stupid forms of snobbery, but a complete abandonment of the upper-class and middle-class attitude to life. And whether I say Yes or No probably depends upon the extent to which I grasp what is demanded of me.

Many people, however, imagine that they can abolish class-distinctions without making any uncomfortable change in their own habits and 'ideology'. Hence the eager class-breaking activities which one can see in progress on all sides. Everywhere there are people of goodwill who quite honestly believe that they are working for the overthrow of class-distinctions. The middle-class Socialist enthuses over the proletariat and runs 'summer schools' where the proletarian and the repentant bourgeois are supposed to fall upon one another's necks and be brothers for ever; and the bourgeois visitors come away saying how wonderful and inspiring it has all been (the proletarian ones come away saying something different). And then there is the outer-suburban creeping Jesus, a hangover from the William Morris period, but still surprisingly common, who goes about saying 'Why must we level down? Why not level up?' and proposes to level the working class 'up' (up to his own standard) by means of hygiene, fruit-juice, birth-control, poetry, etc. Even the Duke of York (now King George VI) runs a yearly camp where public-school boys and boys from the slums are supposed to mix on exactly equal terms, and do mix for the time being, rather like the animals in one of those 'Happy Family' cages where a dog, a cat, two ferrets, a rabbit, and three canaries preserve an armed truce while the showman's eye is on them.

All such deliberate, conscious efforts at class-breaking are, I am convinced, a very serious mistake. Sometimes they are merely futile, but where they do show a definite result it is usually to intensify class-prejudice. This, if you come to think of it, is only what might be expected. You have forced the pace and set up an uneasy, unnatural equality between class and class; the resultant friction brings to the surface all kinds of feelings that might otherwise have remained buried, perhaps for ever. . . .

The only possible policy for the moment is to go easy and not frighten more people than can be helped. And above all, no more of those muscular-curate efforts at class-breaking. If you belong to the bourgeoisie, don't be too eager to bound forward and embrace your proletarian brothers; they may not like it, and if they show that they don't like it you will probably find that your class-prejudices are not so dead as you imagined. And if you belong to the proletariat, by birth or in the sight of God, don't sneer too automatically at the Old School Tie; it covers loyalties which can be useful to you if you know how to handle them. . . .

Perhaps this misery of class-prejudice will fade away, and we of the sinking middle class – the private schoolmaster, the half-starved free-lance journalist, the colonel's spinster daughter with £75 a year, the jobless Cambridge graduate, the ship's officer without a ship, the clerks, the civil servants, the commercial travellers, and the thrice-bankrupt drapers in the country towns – may sink without further struggles into the working class where we belong, and probably when we get there it will not be so dreadful as we feared, for, after all, we have nothing to lose but our aitches.

George Orwell (1903–50), *The Road to Wigan Pier*, 1937, chapters 12 and 13.

Mrs Thatcher, grocer's daughter and former Prime Minister, strove to persuade people that Britain is a meritocracy – a meritocracy in which one's merit is measured by one's money:

The charm of Britain has always been the ease with which one can move into the middle class.

Margaret Thatcher (1925–), quoted in *The Observer*, 'Sayings of the Week', 27 October 1974.

For others, class or classlessness is just a state of mind:

The real solvent of class distinction is a proper measure of self-esteem – a kind of unselfconsciousness. Some people are at ease with themselves, so the world is at ease with them. My parents thought this kind of ease was produced by education ... they didn't see that what disqualified them was temperament – just as, though educated up to the hilt, it disqualified me.

Alan Bennett (1934–), *Dinner at Noon*, BBC television, 1988.

'PASSING FOR WHITE'

This phrase, used ironically by Julian Critchley in the extract quoted below, suggests the difficulties experienced by those who attempt to disguise their class origins. Several of the following extracts also bear witness to the snobbish delight taken by some in exposing such 'pretenders'.

> Lord Heygate had a troubled face,
> His furniture was commonplace –
> The sort of Peer who might well pass
> For someone of the middle class.
>
> Hilaire Belloc (1870–1953), 'Lord Heygate', from *More Peers*, 1911.

Sir John Mortimer, a pupil at Harrow in the 1930s, recalls how the smallest things could give the game away:

The first boy I shared a room with was called Weaver. .... His parents, he told me, were extremely wealthy and had a large house in the New Forest. I was impressed with Weaver until I met a boy called Marsh who told me,

'Weaver's really extremely common. His parents have side-plates at dinner.'

'Side-plates?'

'Yes. Side-plates. To put your bread on. Not at luncheon. Everyone has side-plates at luncheon. At *dinner*.' He explained carefully, as though to a backward foreigner, matters which seemed to him perfectly obvious.

'But if you don't have side-plates at dinner what do you put your bread on?'

'You crumble it. On the table.' Marsh looked at me with great pity. 'Don't you know anything?'

'Not very much.'

It was clear that I didn't.

John Mortimer (1923–), *Clinging to the Wreckage*, 1982.

In 1947, in *The Character of England*, Sir Ernest Barker tried to get to the root of snobbery:

Snobbery is an appetite for false position: it is a desire to enjoy in the estimation of others a position which is not enjoyed in fact. At its best it may be, as a friendly critic has called it, 'an honest expression of social idealism': a longing to rise and to be translated, in a friendly society which is none the less a society of degrees, to a higher range and an ampler air. From that point of view we may regard it as a tension, or rather the result of a tension – a tension between the two poles of a sense of social homogeneity and a sense of the difference of social positions. But this is perhaps only a gloss; and snobbery in general, as the same friendly critic has also said, 'is really a vice: it tempts us to neglect and despise our proper virtues in aping those of other people'. Is it a modern English vice, and was it the invention, or discovery, of Thackeray; or is it an ancient English sin, as ancient as Ancient Pistol? At any rate it is there, an offence against honesty and a breach of the commandment, 'To thine own self be true'.

Sir Ernest Barker (1874–1960), *The Character of England*, 1947.

In this famous poem John Betjeman satirises the pretensions of the faux-genteel betrayed by every non-U expression, act and possession:

> Phone for the fish-knives, Norman
>   As Cook is a little unnerved;
> You kiddies have crumpled the serviettes
>   And I must have things daintily served.
>
> Are the requisites all in the toilet?
>   The frills round the cutlets can wait
> Till the girl has replenished the cruets
>   And switched on the logs in the grate.
>
> It's ever so close in the lounge, dear,
>   But the vestibule's comfy for tea
> And Howard is out riding on horseback
>   So do come and take some with me.
>
> Now here is a fork for your pastries
>   And do use the couch for your feet;
> I know what I wanted to ask you –
>   Is trifle sufficient for sweet?
>
> Milk and then just as it comes dear?
>   I'm afraid the preserve's full of stones;
> Beg pardon, I'm soiling the doileys
>   With afternoon tea-cakes and scones.

John Betjeman (1906–84), 'How to Get On in Society', from *A Few Late Chrysanthemums*, 1954.

When the romantic novelist Dame Barbara Cartland was asked in a radio interview if she thought class barriers in Britain had broken down, she replied:

Of course they have, or I wouldn't be sitting here talking to you.

Dame Barbara Cartland (1901–2000), quoted in Jilly Cooper, *Class*, 1978.

The late Conservative MP Julian Critchley revealed in his memoirs *A Bag of Boiled Sweets* the truth behind his image as a 'Tory gent':

My mother was a nurse and midwife; my father, who was thirty, a consulting neurologist at King's College Hospital, Denmark Hill and the National Hospital. ... my mother was one of six children of a Shropshire railway worker; she married the brightest young doctor on the ward. My parents lived in a rented flat in Chelsea at a time when that borough was not particularly fashionable. Today they would be classified as upwardly mobile young professionals, drawn from the thin line that divides the lower middle from the 'respectable' working class.

In later life I have been called a snob by Teresa Gorman. This could be due to a plummy voice and the portliness of late middle age; Tory MPs tend to be double-breasted. It might also be related to my invention of Essex Man ..., a character much trumpeted in the national press as representative of the 'new' working-class Conservative. It could also be due to my comment on the ideal number of buttons on an MP's cuff, the party having lost one during the thirty years I have sat in the House of Commons. This phenomenon had been pointed out to me one day at lunch by an elderly Knight of the Shire. It appears that a decent suit has four buttons on the cuff; the ready-made having three and sometimes as few as two. As I wanted to tease the more zealous Thatcherites whose role model was Norman Tebbit, I made much of the missing buttons in a newspaper article. Nicholas Soames, Churchill's grandson, was not to be outdone; he promptly instructed his tailor to make him a suit with five buttons. No doubt Alan Clark has six.

John Major's desire to achieve a classless society seems a harmless enough aspiration, although given the tendency of the English to judge people by their vowels, it is unlikely ever to come about. Class is fun, or it should be; it is also fascinating with its infinite nuances and gradations. It is every Englishman's parlour game. A snob, in the derogatory sense, is someone who takes the whole ridiculous business seriously. This, I hope, I have never done. Of my grandfathers, my paternal was a clerk in the Bristol Gas Works whose trouser pockets were especially strengthened to take the amount of copper coins he was obliged to collect going from door to door. My maternal grandfather worked as a bridge builder on the London and North Western Railway. He was killed by a rogue engine at Leominster in 1902. His moustache, according to family legend, was found a mile down the line. My father's success as a doctor catapulted him and his family into the professional middle class. In consequence, Shrewsbury, the Sorbonne and Pembroke College, Oxford, permitted me to pass for white in the Tory party. ...

I suppose my trouble was that I was, in the eyes of all right-thinking Tory MPs 'almost a gentleman'. Michael Heseltine once said to me that he passed for white (the reference was to Tavistock, the seat that he won in 1966), and we were both first-generation public school and Oxford. Michael Jopling when he was chief whip in Mrs Thatcher's government said of Michael that 'he is the kind of man who had to buy all his own furniture', a remark quoted by Alan Clark in his *Diaries*. So did I.

Julian Critchley (1930–2000), *A Bag of Boiled Sweets*, 1995.

KNOWING ONE'S PLACE

> Better a brutal starving nation
> Than men with thoughts above their station.

John Masefield (1878–1967), 'The Everlasting Mercy', 1911.

There have in the past been very many fine gradations of rank in society and, for some, the apparently minutest distinctions in occupation or parentage have meant a world of difference. Knowing exactly how you stand in relation to everybody else – above them, beneath them or on a par with them – has been of immense importance to many English men and women over the ages.

Not greatly addicted to class-hatred, the English early developed, however, a concern for degrees of status: a sixteenth century Mr Sprigg was listed as 'cloth-maker alias yeoman alias gentleman alias merchant'.

Peter Vansittart, *In Memory of England*, 1998.

A clear account of who was who in the reign of Queen Elizabeth I is given by William Harrison in his *Description of England*:

We in England divide our people commonlie into foure sorts, as gentlemen, citizens or burgesses, yeomen, and artificers, or labourers. Of gentlemen the first and cheefe (next the king) be the prince, dukes, marquesses, earls, viscounts, and barons: and these are called gentlemen of the greater sort, or (as our common usage of speech is) lords and noblemen: and next unto them be knights, esquiers, and last of all they that are simplie called gentlemen; so that in effect our gentlemen are divided into their conditions ...

Gentlemen be those whom their race and bloud, or at least their vertues, doo make noble and knowne. ... Gentlemen whose ancestors are not knowen to come in with William duke of Normandie ... do take their beginning in England, after this manner in our times. Who soever studieth the lawes of the realme, who so abideth in the universitie giving his mind to his booke, or professeth physicke and the liberall sciences, or beside his service in the roome of a captain in the warres, or good counsel given at home, whereby his commonwealth is benefited, can live without manuell labour, and thereto is able and will beare the port, charge, and countenance of a gentleman, he shall ... be called master, which is the title that men give to esquiers and gentlemen, and reputed for a gentleman ever after. ...

Citizens and burgesses have the next place to gentlemen, who be those that are free within the cities, and are of some likelie substance to beare office in the same. ...

In this place also are our merchants to be installed, as amongst the citizens (although they often change estate with gentlemen, as gentlemen doo with them, by a mutuall conversion of the one into the other) whose number is so increased in these our daies, that their onelie maintenance is the cause of the exceeding prices of forreine wares, which otherwise when everie nation was permitted to bring in hir own commodities, were farre better cheape and more plentifull to be had. ...

Yeomen are those which by our law are called *Legales homines*, free men borne English, and may depend of their owne free land in yearly revenue, to the summe of ... six pounds as monie goeth in our times. ... This sort of people have a certeine preheminence, and more estimation than labourers & the common sort of artificers, & these commonlie live wealthilie, keepe good houses, and travell to get riches. They are also for the most part farmers to gentlemen ... & with grasing, frequenting of markets, and keeping of servants (not idle servants as the gentlemen doo, but such as get both their owne and part of their masters living) do come to great welth in somuch that manie of them are able and doo buie the lands of unthriftie gentlemen, and often setting their sonnes to the schooles, to the universities, and to the Ins of the court; or otherwise leaving them sufficient lands whereupon they may live without labour, doo make them by those means to become gentlemen: these were they that in times past made all France afraid. And albeit they be not called master as gentlemen are, or sir as to knights appertaineth, but onelie John and Thomas, &c: ... . Whereto I ad ... goodmen, as goodman Smith, goodman Coot, goodman Cornell, goodman Mascall, goodman Cockswet, &c; & in matters of law these and the like are called thus, Giles Jewd yeoman, Edward Mountford yeoman, James Cocke yeoman, Herrie Butcher yeoman, &c: by which addition they are exempt from the vulgar and common sorts. ...

The fourth and last sort of people in England are daie labourers, poore husbandmen, and some retailers (which have no free land) copie holders, and all artificers, as tailers, shomakers, carpenters, brickmakers, masons, &c. As for slaves and bondmen we have none, naie such is the privilege of our countrie by the especiall grace of God, and bountie of our princes, that if anie come hither from other realms, so soone as they set foot on land they become so free of condition as their masters, whereby all note of servile bondage is utterlie remooved from them .... This fourth and last sort of people therefore have neither voice nor authoritie in the common wealth, but are to be ruled, and not to rule over: yet they are not altogither neglected, for in cities and corporat townes, for default of yeomen, they are faine to make up their inquests of such maner of people. And in villages they are commonlie made churchwardens, sidemen, aleconners, now and then constables, and manie times injoie the name of hedboroughes. Unto this sort also may our great swarmes of idle serving men be referred .... No nation cherishes such store of them as we doo here in England, in hope of which maintenance manie give themselves to idlenesse, that otherwise would be brought to labour, and live in order like subjects. Of their whoredomes I will not speake anie thing at all, more than of their swearing, yet it is found that some of them doo make the first a cheefe piller of their building, consuming not onlie the goods but also the health & welfare of manie honest gentlemen, citizens, wealthie yeomen, &c: by such unlawfull dealings.

William Harrison (1534–93), *Description of England*, 1577 (second edition, 1587).

Some classes could be luckier than others, apparently …

He bade me observe it, and I should always find, that the calamities of life were shared among the upper and lower part of mankind; but that the middle station had the fewest disasters.

Daniel Defoe (1660–1731), *Robinson Crusoe*, 1719.

Not knowing where a stranger stands in the hierarchy perhaps explains the diffidence for which the English are noted:

Unable to judge at once of the social position of those he meets, an Englishman prudently avoids all contact with them. Men are afraid lest some slight service rendered should draw them into an unsuitable acquaintance; they dread civilities, and they avoid the obtrusive gratitude of a stranger quite as much as his hatred.

Alexis de Tocqueville (1805–59), *De la Démocritie en Amérique*, 1835–40.

De Tocqueville observed a different attitude towards class in France and England:

The French want no-one to be their *superior*. The English want *inferiors*. The Frenchman constantly raises his eyes above him with anxiety. The Englishman lowers his beneath him with satisfaction. On either side it is pride, but understood in a different way.

Alexis de Tocqueville (1805–59), *Voyage en Angleterre et en Irelande de 1835*.

The fictional archetype of he who knows his place is the oleaginous Uriah Heep in Charles Dickens's *David Copperfield*:

We live in an numble abode. … I'm a very umble person. … We are so very umble. … I ate umble pie with an appetite.

Charles Dickens (1812–70), *David Copperfield*, 1850.

Not only humble but umble, which I look upon to be the comparative, or, indeed, superlative degree.

Anthony Trollope (1815–82), *Doctor Thorne*, 1858.

Nowhere are the finest of social distinctions more consciously and carefully observed than in an English village, as Mrs Gaskell acutely portrayed in *Cranford*:

Miss Betty Barker was the daughter of the old clerk at Cranford who had officiated in Mr. Jenkyns's time. She and her sister had had pretty good situations as ladies' maids, and had saved money enough to set up a milliner's shop, which had been patronised by the ladies in the neighbourhood. Lady Arley, for instance, would occasionally give Miss Barkers the pattern of an old cap of hers, which they immediately copied and circulated among the *élite* of Cranford. I say the *élite*, for Miss Barkers had caught the trick of the place, and piqued themselves upon their 'aristocratic connection'. They would not sell their caps and ribbons to any one without a pedigree. Many a farmer's wife or daughter turned away huffed from

Miss Barkers' select millinery, and went rather to the universal shop, where the profits of brown soap and moist sugar enabled the proprietor to go straight to (Paris, he said, until he found his customers too patriotic and John Bullish to wear what the Mounseers wore) London, where, as he often told his customers, Queen Adelaide had appeared, only the very week before, in a cap exactly like the one he showed them, trimmed with yellow and blue ribbons, and had been complimented by King William on the becoming nature of her head-dress.

Miss Barkers, who confined themselves to truth, and did not approve of miscellaneous customers, throve notwithstanding. They were self-denying, good people. Many a time have I seen the eldest of them (she that had been maid to Mrs. Jamieson) carrying out some delicate mess to a poor person. They only aped their betters in having 'nothing to do' with the class immediately below theirs. And when Miss Barker died, their profits and income were found to be such that Miss Betty was justified in shutting up shop and retiring from business. She also (as I think I have before said) set up her cow; a mark of respectability in Cranford almost as decided as setting up a gig is among some people. She dressed finer than any lady in Cranford; and we did not wonder at it; for it was understood that she was wearing out all the bonnets and caps and outrageous ribbons which had once formed her stock-in-trade. It was five or six years since she had given up shop, so in any other place than Cranford her dress might have been considered *passée*.

And now Miss Betty Barker had called to invite Miss Matty to tea at her house on the following Tuesday. She gave me also an impromptu invitation, as I happened to be a visitor – though I could see she had a little fear lest, since my father had gone to live in Drumble, he might have engaged in that 'horrid cotton trade,' and so dragged his family down out of 'aristocratic society'. She prefaced this invitation with so many apologies that she quite excited my curiosity. 'Her presumption' was to be excused. What had she been doing? She seemed so overpowered by it I could only think that she had been writing to Queen Adelaide to ask for a receipt for washing lace; but the act which she so characterised was only an invitation she had carried to her sister's former mistress, Mrs. Jamieson. 'Her former occupation considered, could Miss Matty excuse the liberty?' ...

'Mrs. Jamieson is coming, I think you said?' asked Miss Matty.

'Yes. Mrs. Jamieson most kindly and condescendingly said she would be happy to come. One little stipulation she made, that she should bring Carlo. I told her that if I had a weakness, it was for dogs.'

'And Miss Pole?' questioned Miss Matty, who was thinking of her pool at Preference, in which Carlo would not be available as a partner.

'I am going to ask Miss Pole. Of course, I could not think of asking her until I had asked you, madam – the rector's daughter, madam. Believe me, I do not forget the situation my father held under yours.'

'And Mrs. Forrester, of course?'

'And Mrs. Forrester. I thought, in fact, of going to her before I went to Miss Pole. Although her circumstances are changed, madam, she was born a Tyrrell, and we can never forget her alliance to the Bigges, of Biggelow Hall.'

Miss Matty cared much more for the little circumstance of her being a very good card-player.

'Mrs. Fitz-Adam – I suppose' –

'No, madam. I must draw a line somewhere. Mrs. Jamieson would not, I think, like to meet Mrs. Fitz-Adam. I have the greatest respect for Mrs. Fitz-Adam – but I cannot think her fit society for such ladies as Mrs. Jamieson and Miss Matilda Jenkyns.'

Miss Betty Barker bowed low to Miss Matty, and pursed up her mouth. She looked at me with sidelong dignity, as much as to say, although a retired milliner, she was no democrat, and understood the difference of ranks.

'May I beg you to come as near half-past six to my little dwelling, as possible, Miss Matilda? Mrs. Jamieson dines at five, but has kindly promised not to delay her visit beyond that time – half-past six.' And with a swimming curtsey Miss Betty Barker took her leave.

My prophetic soul foretold a visit that afternoon from Miss Pole, who usually came to call on Miss Matilda after any event – or indeed in sight of any event – to talk it over with her.

'Miss Betty told me it was to be a choice and select few,' said Miss Pole, as she and Miss Matty compared notes.

'Yes, so she said. Not even Mrs. Fitz-Adam.'

Now Mrs. Fitz-Adam was the widowed sister of the Cranford surgeon, whom I have named before. Their parents were respectable farmers, content with their station. The name of these good people was Hoggins. Mr. Hoggins was the Cranford doctor now; we disliked the name and considered it coarse; but, as Miss Jenkyns said, if he changed it to Piggins it would not be much better. We had hoped to discover a relationship between him and that Marchioness of Exeter whose name was Molly Hoggins; but the man, careless of his own interests, utterly ignored and denied any such relationship, although, as dear Miss Jenkyns had said, he had a sister called Mary, and the same Christian names were very apt to run in families.

Soon after Miss Mary Hoggins married Mr. Fitz-Adam, she disappeared from the neighbourhood for many years. She did not move in a sphere in Cranford society sufficiently high to make any of us care to know what Mr. Fitz-Adam was. He died and was gathered to his fathers without our ever having thought about him at all. And then Mrs. Fitz-Adam reappeared in Cranford ('as bold as a lion,' Miss Pole said), a well-to-do widow, dressed in rustling black silk, so soon after her husband's death that poor Miss Jenkyns was justified in the remark she made, that 'bombazine would have shown a deeper sense of her loss.'

I remember the convocation of ladies who assembled to decide whether or not Mrs. Fitz-Adam should be called upon by the old blue-blooded inhabitants of Cranford. She had taken a large rambling house, which had been usually considered to confer a patent of gentility upon its tenant, because, once upon a time, seventy or eighty years before, the spinster daughter of an earl had resided in it. ... Still, it was not at all a settled thing that Mrs. Fitz-Adam was to be visited, when dear Miss Jenkyns died; and, with her, something of the clear knowledge of the strict code of gentility went out too. As Miss Pole observed: 'As most of the ladies of good family in Cranford were elderly spinsters, or widows without children, if we did not relax a little, and become less exclusive, by and by we should have no society at all.'

Mrs. Forrester continued on the same side.

'She had always understood that Fitz meant something aristocratic; there was Fitz-Roy – she thought that some of the King's children had been called Fitz-Roy; and there was Fitz-Clarence, now – they were the children of dear good King William the Fourth. Fitz-Adam! – it was a pretty name, and she thought it very probably meant "Child of Adam". No one, who had not some good blood in their veins, would dare to be called Fitz; there was a deal in a name – she had had a cousin who spelt his name with two little ffs – ffoulkes – and he always looked down upon capital letters and said they belonged to lately invented families. She had been afraid he would die a bachelor, he was so very choice. When he met with a Mrs. ffarringdon, at a watering-place, he took to her immediately; and a very pretty genteel woman she was – a widow, with a very good fortune; and "my cousin," Mr. ffoulkes, married her; and it was all owing to her two little ffs.'

Mrs. Fitz-Adam did not stand a chance of meeting with a Mr. Fitz-anything in Cranford, so that could not have been her motive for settling there. Miss Matty thought it might have been the hope of being admitted into the society of the place, which would certainly be a very agreeable rise for *ci-devant* Miss Hoggins; and if this had been her hope it would be cruel to disappoint her.

So everybody called upon Mrs. Fitz-Adam – everybody but Mrs. Jamieson, who used to show how honourable she was by never seeing Mrs. Fitz-Adam when they met at the Cranford parties. There would be only eight or ten ladies in the room, and Mrs. Fitz-Adam was the largest of all, and she invariably used to stand up when Mrs. Jamieson came in, and curtsey very low to her whenever she turned in her direction – so low, in fact, that I think Mrs. Jamieson must have looked at the wall above her, for she never moved a muscle of her face, no more than if she had not seen her.

Mrs Gaskell (Elizabeth Gaskell, 1810–65), *Cranford*, 1851–53.

Even royalty has felt the need to instruct its progeny in the ways of a true gentleman. Here is Prince Albert writing to the teenage Prince of Wales, later Edward VII:

A gentleman does not indulge in careless, self-indulgent lounging ways such as lolling in armchairs or on sofas, slouching in his gait, or placing himself in unbecoming attitudes with his hands in his pockets. … He will borrow nothing from the fashions of the groom or the gamekeeper, and whilst avoiding the frivolity and foolish vanity of dandyism, will take care that his clothes are of the best quality.

Prince Albert (1819–61), letter to the Prince of Wales, 1858. Edward VII was to develop an obsession with correct attire. When a courtier appeared dressed in a loud check suit he is said to have inquired, 'Goin' rattin', 'arris?'

Writing to an Italian patriot, the philosopher and political theorist John Stuart Mill observed:

The English of all ranks and classes, are at bottom, in all their feelings, aristocrats. … The very idea of equality is strange and offensive to them. They do not dislike to have many people above them as long as they have some below them.

John Stuart Mill (1806–73), letter to Giuseppe Mazzini, quoted in Duncan Steen and Nicholas Soames, *The Essential Englishman*, 1989.

The English constitutional theorist Walter Bagehot was in no doubt as to which class had grasped hold of power:

England is the type of deferential countries, and the manner in which it is so, and has become so, is extremely curious. The middle classes – the ordinary majority of educated men – are in the present day the despotic power in England. 'Public opinion, nowadays, is the opinion of the bald-headed man at the back of the omnibus.'

Walter Bagehot (1826–77), *The English Constitution*, 1867.

In 1869 Matthew Arnold identified the beginnings of a shift in power between the classes:

Our society distributes itself into Barbarians, Philistines, and Populace; and America is just ourselves, with the Barbarians quite left out, and the Populace nearly. ... When I want to distinguish clearly the aristocratic class from the Philistines proper, or middle class, I name the former, in my own mind *The Barbarians*. ... That vast portion ... of the working-class which, raw and half-developed, has long lain half-hidden amidst its poverty and squalor, and is now issuing from its hiding-place to assert an Englishman's heaven-born privilege of doing as he likes, and is beginning to perplex us by marching where it likes, meeting where it likes, bawling what it likes, breaking what it likes – to this vast residuum we may with great propriety give the name of Populace.

Matthew Arnold (1822–88), *Culture and Anarchy*, 1869.

By the later 19th century the aristocracy's assumption that everyone else should defer to them had become something of a joke. Here are members of the House of Lords singing in chorus in Gilbert and Sullivan's *Iolanthe*:

Bow, bow, ye lower middle classes!
Bow, bow, ye tradesmen, bow, ye masses!
Blow the trumpets, bang the brasses!
Tantantara! Tzing! Boom!
We are peers of highest station,
Paragons of legislation,
Pillars of the British nation!
Tantantara! Tzing! Boom!

W.S. Gilbert (1836–1911), *Iolanthe*, 1882.

In a world of topsyturvydom Oscar Wilde was always one to point up the paradoxes:

Really, if the lower orders don't set us a good example, what on earth is the use of them?

Oscar Wilde (1854–1900), Irish-born playwright, *The Importance of Being Earnest*, 1895.

Hilaire Belloc in his poem 'The Justice of the Peace' makes it clear why the landed gentry had the upper hand:

Distinguish carefully between these two,
This thing is yours, that other thing is mine.

You have a shirt, a brimless hat, a shoe
        And half a coat. I am the Lord benign
Of fifty hundred acres of fat land
To which I have a right. You understand?

I have a right because I have, because,
        Because I have – because I have a right.
Now be quite calm and good, obey the laws,
        Remember your low station, do not fight
Against the goad, you know, it pricks
Whenever the uncleanly demos kicks.

I do not envy you your hat, your shoe,
        Why should you envy me my small estate?
It's fearfully illogical in you
        To fight with economic force and fate,
Moreover, I have got the upper hand,
And mean to keep it. Do you understand?

Hilaire Belloc (1870–1953), 'The Justice of the Peace', From *Verses and Sonnets*, 1896.

Toad, in *The Wind in the Willows*, has all the trappings and attitudes of an English country squire:

Now the gaoler had a daughter, a pleasant wench and good-hearted, who assisted her father in the duties of his post. ... They had many interesting talks together ... and the gaoler's daughter grew very sorry for Toad, and thought it a great shame that a poor little animal should be locked up in prison for what seemed to her a very trivial offence. Toad, of course, in his vanity, thought that her interest in him proceeded from a growing tenderness; and he could not help half regretting that the social gulf between them was so very wide, for she was a comely lass, and evidently admired him very much.

One morning the girl was very thoughtful, and answered at random, and did not seem to Toad to be paying proper attention to his witty sayings and sparkling comments.

'Toad,' she said presently, 'just listen, please. I have an aunt who is a washer-woman.'

'There, there,' said Toad graciously and affably, 'never mind; think no more about it. *I* have several aunts who *ought* to be washerwomen.'

Kenneth Grahame (1859–1932), *The Wind in the Willows*, 1908.

Hilaire Belloc again, this time on the social iniquity of do-it-yourself:

Lord Finchley tried to mend the Electric Light
Himself. It struck him dead: And serve him right!
It is the business of the wealthy man
To give employment to the artisan.

Hilaire Belloc (1870–1953), 'Lord Finchley', from *More Peers*, 1911.

A gentleman, after all, has responsibilities as well as rights:

We've dressed in our best and are prepared to go down like gentlemen.

Ben Guggenheim (1865–1912), having changed into evening dress to stand with his valet on the deck of the *Titanic*, 1912.

The ascendancy of the bourgeoisie could be perplexing to a 'classless' gent of the old school, such as John Buchan's fictional hero, Richard Hannay:

A man of my sort, who has travelled about the world in rough places, gets on perfectly well with the two classes, what you may call the upper and the lower. He understands them and they understand him. I was at home with herds and tramps and roadmen, and I was sufficiently at my ease with people like Sir Walter and the men I had met the night before. I can't explain why, but it is a fact. But what fellows like me don't understand is the great comfortable, satisfied middle-class world, the folk that live in villas and suburbs. He doesn't know how they look at things, he doesn't understand their conventions, and he is as shy of them as of a black mamba.

John Buchan (First Baron Tweedsmuir, 1875–1940), Scottish writer and statesman, *The Thirty-Nine Steps*, 1915.

The Victorians based their charity on a distinction between the 'deserving' and the 'undeserving' poor. Doolittle, the father of Eliza in George Bernard Shaw's *Pygmalion*, is quite clear in which category he belongs:

I ask you, what am I? I'm one of the undeserving poor: that's what I am. Think of what that means to a man. It means that he's up agen middle class morality all the time. If there's anything going, and I put in for a bit of it, it's always the same story: 'You're undeserving; so you can't have it.' But ... I don't need less than a deserving man: I need more. .... What is middle class morality? Just an excuse for never giving me anything.

George Bernard Shaw (1856–1950), Irish-born playwright, *Pygmalion*, 1916.

The young, especially, are not immune from class prejudice. Here George Orwell recalls his time at 'St Cyprian's', the preparatory school he left in 1916:

Looking back, it is astonishing how intimately, intelligently snobbish we all were, how knowledgeable about names and addresses, how swift to detect small differences in accents and manners and the cut of clothes. ... I have seen a little new boy, hardly older than eight, desperately lying his way through such a catechism:

'Have your people got a car?'
'Yes.'
'What sort of car?'
'Daimler.'
'How many horse-power?'
(Pause, and leap in the dark.) 'Fifteen.'
'What kind of lights?'
The little boy is bewildered.

'What kind of lights? Electric or acetylene?'

(A longer pause, and another leap in the dark.) 'Acetylene.'

'Coo! He says his pater's car's got acetylene lamps. They went out years ago. It must be as old as the hills.'

'Rot! He's making it up. He hasn't got a car. He's just a navvy. Your pater's a navvy.'

And so on.

George Orwell (1903–50), *Such, Such Were the Joys*, in the *Partisan Review*, September–October 1952 (written by May 1947).

Young Molesworth offered the following advice in dealing with prep-school snobbery:

CADS

Cads hav always a grandmother who is the DUCHESS of BLANK hem hem. They are inclined to cheat at conkers having baked them for 300 years in the ancestral ovens.

These conkers belong to the national trust they are so tuough and if you strike one your new conker fly into 10000000000 bits. In this case there is nothing to do about it xcept to SMILE. . . .

Back to cads. They sa wot skool are you going to. You sa well it is one of the lesser known publick skools it is called GRUNTS it is in devonshire and my pater thinks that becos it is ok for sons of retired clergymen i will be ok. to eton for you i supose? It is always eton and good luck to them they go to a good show in spite of the fog.

eton is a small paradise in the thames valley. New bugs who arive are met by the maitre d'hotel who sa Welcome sir we have to put you in suite number 2 this is only temporary sir you understand no bathroom no shower your toothpaste will be waiting for you frozen in the wash-basin.

YOU MUST HAVE PATIENCE. In 3 years you can despise EVERY-BODE the LOT. If you are lucky you can even call the matron a dame which takes a bit of doing. So wot you are still in the thames valley then you can put your shoulder againgst a wall and achive o but less than nothing.

CHEERS CHEERS WIZZ WIZZ.

Less than no marks to the dear old skool imagine me in a topper eh gosh.

As i sa i am down for GRUNTS wizz wow which is an ancient foundation and full of boys to whom masters hav said You'll never pass the CE molesworth never. But they pass into GRUNTS all right which receive them with open arms.

Cads always ask you about your pater and mater e.g.

Wot does your pater *do*, molesworth?

Not a stroke positively not a stroke (*a lite larff*)

He is in the city i suppose

Som of the time at other times he is in earls court it depends *(more larffter)*

But what is his job?

You canot get out of this one. There are a lot of jobs for which the younger gener-ation are being trained up to take the places of their fathers. There is a bird seed merchant, skoolmaster, pigeonfancier brassfounder skinner stockbroker and a lot of others in fact it is shoking how many there are. But all of them sound deadly when you sa your pater do them. Like mum you could wish sometimes that your pater was a bit more glamorous but hay ho. The only thing is to jam your monocle in your eye and sa i kno your pater is a lord pauncefoote but he could jolly well do with a new suit.

Then run like the wind. Ho jenkins sponge the mud of the county from my knees and I will stroll into deten.

Geoffrey Willans (1921–58) and Ronald Searle (1920–), *How to be Topp*, 1954.

John Betjeman also suffered from snobbery in his childhood:

> I remember the dread with which I at a quarter past four
> Let go with a bang behind me our house front door
> And, clutching a present for my dear little hostess tight,
> Sailed out for the children's party into the night
> Or rather the gathering night. . . .
> Oh who can say how subtle and safe one feels
> Shod in one's children's sandals from Daniel Neal's,
> Clad in one's party clothes made of stuff from Heal's?
> And who can still one's thrill at the candle shine
> On cakes and ices and jelly and blackcurrant wine,
> And the warm little feel of my hostess's hand in mine?
> Can I forget my delight at the conjuring show?
> And wasn't I proud that I was the last to go?
> Too overexcited and pleased with myself to know
> That the words I heard my hostess's mother employ
> To a guest departing, would ever diminish my joy,
> I WONDER WHERE JULIA FOUND THAT STRANGE,
>   RATHER COMMON LITTLE BOY?

John Betjeman (1906–84), from 'False Security', in *Poems Written after 1954*.

The feeling of affinity of the upper for the lower classes – expressed above by John Buchan's Richard Hannay – was shared, albeit satirically, by the novelist E.M. Forster:

You can remain a patriot if you will become a snob. Realise that the lower class, not the middle, is the typical Englishman, and you can love our race without difficulty. Officers, stockbrokers, politicians, grocers – they run us, but they are not England numerically, and their self-righteousness is not our national characteristic. Shuttleworth and I have decided to be snobs. We shrink, consciously, from such people, just as they shrink unconsciously from the lower class whom we love. We used to pretend we shrank from no one. But it's no good. Middle-class people smell.

E.M. Forster (1879–1970), letter to Goldsworthy Lowes Dickinson, 25 June 1917, from *Selected Letters of E.M. Forster: Volume 1: 1879–1920*.

'Sapper', the creator of Bulldog Drummond, was, along with John Buchan and Dornford Yates, one of the 'practitioners in that school of Snobbery with Violence that runs like a thread of good-class tweed through twentieth-century literature' (Alan Bennett, *Forty Years On*, 1969). The following is from one of Sapper's short stories:

Before the war Derek Vane had been what is generally described as a typical Englishman. That is to say, he regarded his own country ... whenever he thought about it ... as being the supreme country in the world. He didn't force his opinion down anyone's throat; it was simply so. If the other fellow didn't agree, the funeral was his, not Vane's. He had to the full what the uninitiated regard as conceit; on matters connected with literature, or art, or music, his knowledge was micro-scopic. Moreover, he regarded with suspicion anyone who talked intelligently on such subjects. On the other hand, he had been in the eleven at Eton, and was a scratch golfer. He had a fine seat on a horse and rode straight; he could play a passable game of polo, and was a good shot. Possessing as he did sufficient money to prevent the necessity of working, he had not taken the something he was sup-posed to be doing in the City very seriously. ... He belonged, in fact, to the Breed; the Breed that has always existed in England, and will always exist to the world's end. You may meet its members in London and Fiji; in the lands that lie beyond the mountains and at Henley; in the swamps where the stagnant vegetation rots and stinks; in the great deserts where the night air strikes cold. They are always the same, and they are branded with the stamp of the Breed. They shake your hand as a man shakes it; they meet your eye as a man meets it.

Sapper (Herman Cyril McNeile, 1888–1937), 'Mufti'.

Hilaire Belloc again, on the Rich, the Poor and the People in Between:

The Rich arrived in pairs
And also in Rolls-Royces;
They talked of their affairs
In loud and strident voices.

(The Husbands and the Wives
Of this select society
Lead independent lives
Of infinite variety.)

The Poor arrived in Fords
Whose features they resembled;
They laughed to see so many Lords
And Ladies there assembled.

The People in Between
Looked underdone and harassed
And out of place and mean,
And horribly embarrassed.

For the hoary social curse
Gets hoarier and hoarier,
And it stinks a trifle worse
Than in the days of Queen Victoria,

When they married and gave in marriage,
They danced at the County Ball,
And some of them kept a carriage,
AND THE FLOOD DESTROYED THEM ALL.

Hilaire Belloc (1870–1953), 'The Garden Party', in *Ladies and Gentlemen*, 1932.

After the First World War the effects of graduated income tax, land taxes and death duties began to hit the owners of the great country houses:

The Stately Homes of England
How beautiful they stand,
To prove the upper classes
Have still the upper hand.
Though the fact that they have to be rebuilt
And frequently mortgaged to the hilt
Is inclined to take the gilt
Off the gingerbread,
And certainly damps the fun
Of the elder son,
But still we won't be beaten,
We'll scrimp and screw and save;
The playing fields of Eton
Have made us frightf'ly brave,
And now if the Van Dykes have to go
And we've pawned the Bechstein grand,
We'll stand by the Stately Homes of England!
. . .
Reading in De Brett of us,
This fine patrician quartet of us
We can feel extremely proud.
Our ancient lineage we trace
Back to the cradle of our race,
Before those beastly Roman bowmen
Ditched our local yeomen,
Though the new Democracy
Maintains the old Aristocracy
We've not winced, nor cried alarm.
Under the bludgeonings of chance,
What will be, will be;
Our heads will still be
Bloody but quite unbowed!
. . .
Our duty to the nation,
It's only fair to state,
Lies not in procreation
But what we procreate;

And so we can cry
With grimling eye,
To married life we go:
What ho! for the Stately Homes of England.

Noël Coward (1899–1973), 'The Stately Homes of England', from *Operette*, 1938.

The Second World War was a great levelling experience – for some. The following has been attributed to one Captain Strahan, when asked for his impressions of the battle of Bastogne in 1944:

Oh my dear fellow, the noise – and the people!

The war also led to a lamentable shortage of servants:

Very stupid to kill the only servant in the house. Now we don't even know where to find the marmalade.

Line from the film *And Then There Were None* (USA, 1945), adapted from an Agatha Christie novel.

Just after the war Sir Ernest Barker, in *The Character of England*, reflected on the eternal verities of English life and values:

Perhaps enough homage has been paid to change (although even in speaking of change we have seen that the more the Englishman changes, the more he remains the same); and we may now turn back to some constants. . . .

The name of the first (one might wish that it were simpler) is *social homogeneity*. England has had little class-feeling – and that though, down to our own days, it has had, and has even cherished, a whole ladder of class-differences. The habitat has somehow produced understanding and even fusion. . . . But this tendency to social homogeneity is qualified by, or combined with, an English doctrine and practice of what may be called 'position'. England has always been full of positions, or what Shakespeare calls 'degrees' and the Catechism calls 'states of life'. She has run through the ages into a graded hierarchy, with men taking positions, and holding stations, on this rung and that of a very long ladder. But there has always been a mutual respect between different positions; and the ladder has always been a ladder of possible ascent. . . . It is in this way that English life has long been a pageant of positions – positions based on capacity – with men respecting positions because they respect capacity. There is no reason in the nature of things why this fashion of life should alter. In a new age of equality it may well become more elastic and fluid. If it does so, it will remain the same, and even more the same. A system of positions based on capacities, if it has grown under individualism, may also grow, and grow even higher, under socialism. . . .

Another constant in the English character is the figure and idea of the *gentleman*. The idea of a gentleman is not a class idea (it was ceasing to be that even in the sixteenth century): it is the idea of a type of character. It is an idea which has had its mutations. In the eighteenth century a gentleman knew his tenants, his fields, and his foxes: he helped to govern his country, and might sit in parliament at Westminster; he might even be interested in architecture and painting, and indulge himself in music. He was an amateur furnished with ability – the apotheosis of the amateur. But the essence was a code of conduct – good form: the not doing of things which are not done: reserve: a habit of understatement. The code became disengaged, and explicit, with the spread of boarding or 'public' schools during the nineteenth century. It was in many ways a curious code. It was hardly based on religion, though it might be instilled in sermons: it was a mixture of stoicism with mediæval lay chivalry, and of both with unconscious national ideals half Puritan and half secular. Yet if it contained such national ideals, it was not a national code, in the sense that it embraced the nation: it was the code of an *élite* (from whatever classes the *élite* was drawn) rather than the code of the nation at large. On the other hand ... it is impossible to think of the character of England without thinking also of the character of the gentleman. But it is also impossible to think of the character of the gentleman clearly. It has an English haze. The gentleman is shy, yet also self-confident. He is the refinement of manliness; but the manliness is sometimes more obvious than the refinement.

Sir Ernest Barker (1874–1960), *The Character of England*, 1947.

Impotence and sodomy are socially O.K. but birth control is flagrantly middle-class.

Evelyn Waugh (1903–66), 'An Open Letter', in Nancy Mitford, ed., *Noblesse Oblige*, 1956.

Bertrand Russell on the Conservative Prime Minister Sir Anthony Eden in 1955:
Not a gentleman: dresses too well.

Bertrand Russell (3rd Earl Russell, 1872–1970), quoted in Alastair Cooke, *Six Men*, 1977.

Dear Michael,
I am always hearing about the Middle Classes. What is it they really want? Can you put it down on a sheet of note paper and I will see whether we can give it to them.

Harold Macmillan (1894–1986), Conservative Prime Minister, memo to Michael Fraser, head of the Conservative Party Research Department, October 1957; quoted in the *Daily Telegraph* obituary of Lord Fraser of Kilmorack, 5 July 1996.

The one class you do *not* belong to and are not proud of at all is the lower-middle class. No one ever describes himself as belonging to the lower-middle class.

George Mikes (1912–87), Hungarian-born British author, *How to be Inimitable*, 1961.

No writer before the middle of the 19th century wrote about the working classes other than as grotesque or as pastoral decoration. Then when they were given the vote certain writers started to suck up to them.

Evelyn Waugh (1903–66), interview, *Paris Review*, 1963.

In 1963, following Harold Macmillan's resignation of the premiership, the Conservative Party chose as its leader, and as Prime Minister, the 14th Earl Home, who renounced his title to sit in the House of Commons as Sir Alec Douglas-Home:

After half a century of democratic advance, the whole process has ground to a halt with a Fourteenth Earl.

Harold Wilson (1916–95), leader of the Labour Party, 18 October 1963.

I suppose Mr Wilson, when you come to think about it, is the fourteenth Mr Wilson.

Sir Alec Douglas-Home (1903–95; formerly the 14th Earl Home), reply to the above in a television interview, 21 October 1963.

He is used to dealing with estate workers. I cannot see how anyone can say he is out of touch.

Caroline Douglas-Home (1937–), daughter of the new Prime Minister, on accusations that he was out of touch with working-class people; quoted in the *Daily Herald*, 21 October 1963.

After the death of Lord Home of the Hirsel (as Sir Alec Douglas-Home became on his retirement), the actor Alex Guinness recalled:

I met him only once, at a dinner party at which I was placed next to his wife. Conversation was a bit stiff and, in desperation, I asked her how she mostly spent her day when at home in the Border Country. 'Good heavens!' she exclaimed. 'I do what every woman in the British Isles does. I spend the morning making sandwiches and then take them down to the men in the butts.' Lord Home stretched his lips at me in a thin smile. He undoubtedly had patrician charm but he made me feel very ill-bred.

Sir Alec Guinness (1914–2000), *My Name Escapes Me*, 1996; diary entry for 12 October 1995.

Class became a prime target in the satire boom of the 1960s. The following famous sketch from the *Frost Report* featured John Cleese (6 ft 5 in), Ronnie Barker (5 ft 8½ in) and Ronnie Corbett (5 ft 1 in):

CLEESE: I look down on him (*indicating Barker*) because I am upper-class.

BARKER: I look up to him (*indicating Cleese*) because he is upper-class; but I look down on him (*indicating Corbett*) because he is lower-class. I am middle-class.

CORBETT: I know my place. I look up to them both. But I don't look up to him (*Barker*) as much as I look up to him (*Cleese*), because he has got innate breeding.

CLEESE: I have got innate breeding, but I have not got any money. So sometimes I look up (*bending knees and doing so*) to him (*Barker*).

BARKER: I still look up to him (*Cleese*) because although I have money, I am vulgar. But I am not as vulgar as him (*Corbett*), so I still look down on him.

CORBETT: I know my place. I look up to them both; but while I am poor, I am honest, industrious and trustworthy. Had I the inclination, I could look down on them. But I don't.

BARKER: We all know our place, but what do we get out of it?

CLEESE: I get a feeling of superiority over them.

BARKER: I get a feeling of inferiority from him (*Cleese*), but a feeling of superiority over him (*Corbett*).

CORBETT: I get a pain in the back of my neck.

'Class', by Marty Feldman and John Law, *The Frost Report*, BBC TV, 1967.

When interviewed in 1974 by police during their enquiry into the killing of Sandra Rivett, nanny to Lord and Lady Lucan, 'an old lady in Belgravia' remarked:

Oh dear, what a pity. Nannies are so hard to come by these days.

Reported in the *Sunday Times Magazine*, 8 June 1975.

The world is run on knowing the right people, actually. I'm sorry, but it is. Generations ago, if you were an Old Etonian, if you were a member of the aristocracy, you knew the right people. Well, it's just the same now, really. It's just a lot bigger.

Lord Charteris, Provost of Eton, interviewed in Jeremy Paxman, *Friends in High Places*, 1990.

It is extraordinary the things that can cause feelings of social inferiority. Even if the following is a spoof, it is a spoof based on some sort of perceived reality:

Q. Some years ago in White's Club I found myself standing at the urinal alongside the late Sir Iain Moncreiffe of that Ilk. Seeing me washing my hands afterwards, he admonished me with the diktat that 'no gentleman washes his hands after using a urinal'. Urinals have been a source of disquiet for me ever since. It is a question of divided loyalties. My nanny always drummed into me that I should wash my hands after going to the loo, but Sir Iain was a great hero of mine. Can you clear up this matter once and for all, Mary, and tell me what is the correct protocol?

Name and address withheld

A. Use of a full lavatory exposes the discharger of waste to a range of unsavoury surfaces, after which hand-washing is de rigueur. As far as urinals are concerned, however, Sir Iain was correct, since the only 'surface' handled by the user is his own member. Historical evidence bears out this rule of protocol. A study of architects' plans for the Palace of Westminster reveals that, while lavatories in the Lords were always equipped with washbasins, the latter were only introduced to urinals – many of which were separate – during the last war. Their introduction coincided with the relocation of the bomb-damaged Commons into the Lords, thus bringing an element of middle-class behaviour into what had been previously a purely aristocratic domain.

Mary Killen, 'Dear Mary ...', *The Spectator*, 3 March 2001.

'A People
Not Used to War'

THE DANGER OF ALL IS THAT A PEOPLE NOT USED TO WAR
BELIEVETH THAT NO ENEMY DARE VENTURE UPON THEM. . . .
WE THINK IF WE HAVE MEN AND SHIPS, OUR KINGDOM IS SAFE
AS IF MEN WERE BORN SOLDIERS. . . . WE DISBURTHEN THE PRISONS
OF THIEVES, WE ROB THE TAVERNS AND ALEHOUSES OF TOSSPOTS
AND RUFFIANS, WE SCOUR BOTH TOWNS AND COUNTRY OF ROGUES
AND VAGABONDS.
Sir Edward Cecil (d.1638), commander of the bungled Spanish expedition of 1628.

Unless we are military historians our 'national idea' of war is based almost entirely on a fading folklore of the two great conflicts of the 20th century, and these we tend to think of in 'nursery-history' terms: the First World War was a Bad Thing, a pointless slaughter caused by 'politics', and the Second World War was a Good Thing, a 'People's War' against tyranny and in heroic self-defence. When we think of the first we think of trenches and mud; when we think of the second we think of Dunkirk, the battle of Britain and the Blitz – of defeat, deliverance and desperation: of times when our backs were against the wall, which is where we most like them to be. Above all, we think of our soldiers, sailors and airmen as 'our boys' – ordinary, splendid, put-upon, decent people – just like us. We know they volunteered in their tens of thousands from 1914 until, in February 1916, a reluctant government introduced conscription; we know they were called up in 1939. They were our people; they came from us, and their survivors returned to us. From 1940 we were 'all in it together'; war came to us, on the Home Front. Seldom has any nation – particularly our own – been so engaged and united in military conflict.

But throughout most of our history our idea of the fighting man, and of his trade, has been a very different one, a legacy, perhaps, of the days of the medieval warlord-baron. Soldiers were not 'us' but The Other: a marauding underclass of mercenaries, murderers and plunderers, feared and hated; the 'rapacious and licentious soldiery' of Edmund Burke's phrase. Nobody ever thought to put up memorials to them. Their names are unrecorded, their voices unheard. Shakespeare and Kipling are among the few writers to give them a voice; William Cobbett, himself once a soldier, was almost alone in speaking out on their behalf. Pressed into service from the dregs of society, as and when required – for the concept of a 'standing army' was anathema to the English for centuries – they were used up, occasionally (and briefly) fêted, then discarded with revulsion and forgotten. Weeks after the defeat of the Armada, England's sailors, unpaid, were dying by the shipload of hunger and disease; the survivors of Trafalgar fared little better. Few of their commanders – Nelson and Marlborough are exceptions – regarded them as anything other than a necessary and repellent, scarcely human, evil. It is no coincidence that the voice of 'Sam', writing with three fingers missing of his comrades' grief at the death of their admiral, is one of the few to reach us from their ranks.

The first section of this chapter gives a flavour of England's historic awareness of the trade of war. It is followed by voices speaking of, and from, some of the conflicts that have shaped our attitudes to it. The two world wars, and their after-math, are then considered separately.

Of Tommy Atkins and Jack Tar

The ordinary soldiers and sailors of England have had a mixed press through the centuries.

They have a very high reputation in arms; and from the great fear the French entertain of them, one must believe it to be justly acquired. But I have it on the best information, that when the war is raging most furiously, they will seek for good cating, and all their other comforts, without thinking of what harm might befall them.

Andrea Trevisano (d.1534), Venetian ambassador to Henry VII, *Relation of the Island of England*, 1497; quoted in Francesca M. Wilson, *Strange Island: Britain through Foreign Eyes 1395–1940*, 1955.

Ours is composed of the scum of the earth – the mere scum of the earth.

The Duke of Wellington (1769–1852), on the British army, 1831.

Don't talk to me about naval tradition. It's nothing but rum, sodomy, and the lash.

Winston Churchill (1874–1965), quoted in Sir Peter Gretton, *Former Naval Person*, 1968.

William Cobbett (1763–1835), the great campaigning journalist, joined the army as a young man, served in Canada, and rose to the rank of regimental sergeant major. As he here recounts in his autobiography, his nose for injustice soon got him into trouble:

I like soldiers, as a class in life, better than any other description of men. Their conversation is more pleasing to me; they have generally seen more than other men; they have less of vulgar prejudice about them. Amongst soldiers, less than amongst any other description of men, have I observed the vices of lying and hypocrisy.

The object of my quitting the army, to which I was attached, was to bring certain officers to justice for having, in various ways, wronged both the public and the soldier. ... If my officers had been men of manifest superiority of mind, I should, perhaps, not have so soon conceived the project of bringing them, or some of them, at least, to shame and punishment for the divers flagrant breaches of the law, committed by them. ...

This project was conceived so early as the year 1787, when an affair happened, that first gave me a full insight into regimental justice. It was shortly this: that the Quarter-Master, who had the issuing of the men's provisions to them, kept about a fourth part to himself. This, the old sergeants told me, has been the case for many years; and they were quite astonished and terrified at the idea of my complaining of it. ...

Returning to England in 1791 Cobbett accused the officers concerned of corruption. They brought counter-charges against him, and he fled to France, then America. He returned to England again in 1800, but it was not long before another injustice got him into trouble:

In 1809, some young men at Ely, in what was called the 'local militia', had refused to march without the 'marching guinea', which the Act of Parliament awarded them. This was called Mutiny; and a body of Hanoverian horse were brought from Bury St Edmunds, to compel these young Englishmen to submit to be flogged! They were flogged, while surrounded by these Hanoverians; and the transaction was recorded in 'The Courier' ministerial paper. I, in my 'Register', expressed my indignation at this, and to express it too strongly was not in the power of man. The Attorney-General, Gibbs, was set upon me; he harassed me for nearly a year, then brought me to trial. This took place on the 15th of June, 1810, when I was found guilty of treasonous libel by a Special Jury.

Cobbett was fined £1,000 and jailed for two years.

The extracts come from William Reitzel, ed., *The Autobiography of William Cobbett*, 1967.

In his essay, 'The English at War', the historian E.L. Woodward examined the fate and status of the common soldiery:

For many years [after 1660] the fear of military despotism made parliament suspicious of proposals for establishing barracks throughout the country; soldiers were scattered in small detachments, billeted in public houses, and regarded as among the lowest of the low. Little wonder that they behaved as outcasts and sometimes even as enemies of society.

Out of this unpromising material Marlborough and Wellington won their victories.

Marlborough respected his men; Wellington also respected them, after a fashion, but thought coldly of them. They counted for very little in the public sympathy and have left practically no written records of their achievements or their sufferings. Sir John Fortesque has stated that in all the books which he read on the wars of Marlborough he found only one man under commissioned rank – a Sergeant Littler – mentioned by name. Thus the English still went away to the wars; when they were out of sight no one cared overmuch what happened to them. They had no spokesmen of their own, and civilian politicians were concerned with other matters than the fate of these men who saved the sum of things for them. At the beginning of almost every war there is the same tale of expeditions hastily sent out, badly equipped, poorly led, and often serving no wide strategic purpose.

From Ernest Barker, ed., *The Character of England*, 1947.

Come, I'll be friends with thee, Jack: thou art going to the wars; and whether I ever shall see thee again or no, there is nobody cares.

William Shakespeare (1564–1616), Doll Tearsheet to Sir John Falstaff, in *Henry IV, Part II*, 1597.

From the early 19th century the British private soldier was known as 'Tommy Atkins', from the name used in the specimen form accompanying the manual issued to all army recruits. Even at the end of the century he was still treated as the scum of the earth, as bemoaned by Kipling's 'Tommy':

> I went into a public-'ouse to get a pint o' beer,
> The publican 'e up an' sez, 'We serve no red-coats here.'
> The girls be'ind the bar they laughed an' giggled fit to die,
> I outs into the street again an' to myself sez I:
>> O it's Tommy this, an' Tommy that, an' 'Tommy, go away';
>> But it's 'Thank you, Mister Atkins,' when the band begins to play –
>> The band begins to play, my boys, the band begins to play,
>> O it's 'Thank you, Mister Atkins,' when the band begins to play.

> I went into a theatre as sober as could be,
> They gave a drunk civilian room, but 'adn't none for me;
> They sent me to the gallery or round the music-'alls,
> But when it comes to fightin', Lord! they'll shove me in the stalls!
>> For it's Tommy this, an' Tommy that, an' 'Tommy, wait outside!';
>> But it's 'special train for Atkins' when the trooper's on the tide –
>> When the trooper's on the tide, my boys, the trooper's on the tide,
>> O it's 'special train for Atkins' when the trooper's on the tide.

> Yes, makin' mock o' uniforms that guard you while you sleep
> Is cheaper than them uniforms, an' they're starvation cheap;
> An' hustlin' drunken soldiers when they're goin' large a bit
> Is five times better business than paradin' in full kit.
> . . .
>> For it's Tommy this, an' Tommy that, an' 'Chuck him out, the brute!'
>> But it's 'saviour of 'is country' when the guns begin to shoot;

> An it's Tommy this, an' Tommy that, an' anything you please;
> An' Tommy ain't a bloomin' fool – you bet that Tommy sees!

Rudyard Kipling (1865–1936), 'Tommy', 1892.

The soldier's stoicism, and his duty of obedience whatever the rights or wrongs of the conflict, is meditated upon by Shakespeare in *Henry V*. Before dawn on the day of Agincourt, the King goes unrecognised among his troops, dispensing 'a little touch of Harry in the night':

Enter three soldiers: JOHN BATES, ALEXANDER COURT and MICHAEL WILLIAMS.

COURT: Brother John Bates, is not that the morning which breaks yonder?

BATES: I think it be; but we have no great cause to desire the approach of day.

WILLIAMS: We see yonder the beginning of the day, but I think we shall never see the end of it. Who goes there?

KING HENRY: A friend. . . .

. . . By my troth, I will speak my conscience of the king: I think he would not wish himself any where but where he is.

BATES: Then I would he were here alone; so should he be sure to be ransomed, and a many poor men's lives be saved.

KING HENRY: I dare say you love him not so ill to wish him here alone, howsoever you speak this to feel other men's minds. Methinks I could not die anywhere so contented as in the king's company, his cause being just and his quarrel honourable.

WILLIAMS: That's more than we know.

BATES: Ay, or more than we should seek after; for we know enough if we know we are the king's subjects. If his cause is wrong, our obedience to the king wipes the crime of it out of us.

WILLIAMS: But if the cause be not good, the king himself hath a heavy reckoning to make; when all those legs and arms and heads, chopped off in a battle, shall join together at the latter day, and cry all, 'We died in such a place' – some swearing, some crying for a surgeon, some upon their wives left poor behind them, some upon the debts they owe, some upon their children newly left. . . . Now, if these men do not die well, it will be a black matter for the king that led them to it, whom to disobey were against all proportion of subjection. . . .

KING HENRY: I myself heard the king say he would not be ransomed.

WILLIAMS: Ay, he said so to make us fight cheerfully; but when our throats are cut he may be ransomed, and we ne'er the wiser.

KING HENRY: If I live to see it, I will never trust his word after.

WILLIAMS: You pay him then. That's a perilous shot out of an elder-gun, that a poor and private displeasure can do against a monarch. You may as well go about to turn the sun to ice with fanning in his face with a peacock's feather. You'll never trust his word after! Come, 'tis a foolish saying.

. . .

BATES: Be friends, you English fools, be friends: we have French quarrels enow, if you could tell us how to reckon.

William Shakespeare (1564–1616), *King Henry V*, 1599, IV.i.

Consider John Bates, Alexander Court, and Michael Williams on the morning of 25 October 1415. … After the battle Williams comes back, a good fighter as he was a good grouser, to discover with whom he has quarrelled. Neither Bates nor Court appears again. Who, after reading these matchless lines, has not lain awake at night wondering whether Court saw evening as well as morning on that day, and whether John Bates ever ploughed or reaped again in some field of southern England?

… John Bates, Alexander Court, and Michael Williams are known to every one who has been with an English army, whatever the time, wherever the battle. The nearest modern equivalent, the best memorial of John Bates, is the soldier standing on the plinth at Paddington railway station. This soldier is a man of the first World War. Between the wars he was almost forgotten – even in a short peace – by the English, although he was there all the time, and although he commemorated their own acts. In 1939 and for the next six years, day after day from morning until midnight and long after, hundreds upon hundreds of Englishmen like him passed in and out of Paddington Station on their way to or from the wars. As they passed, they grumbled and argued, and laughed or swore, or just 'went on'. If they noticed him at all, they thought of him as one of themselves. They did not think of him or of themselves as Milton's 'inviolable saints', accomplishing *nova gesta Dei per Anglos*, or even as deserving the special regard of bearing the burden of the English State. Yet, without John Bates, without those unwarlike soldiers and sailors and airmen, whose thoughts have been not of conquests but of their homes, English liberty would not exist.

E.L. Woodward, 'The English at War', in Ernest Barker, ed., *The Character of England*, 1947.

We aren't no thin red 'eroes, nor we aren't no blackguards too,
  But single men in barracks, most remarkable like you.
Rudyard Kipling (1865–1936), 'Tommy', 1892.

THE BLAST OF WAR

Shakespeare, not for the most part a martial tub-thumper, could turn it on when he wanted. The first passage below is less well known; the second and third are classics of blood-stirring patriotism.

A kind of conquest
Caesar made here; but not made here his brag
Of 'Came, and saw, and overcame': with shame –
The first that ever touched him – he was carried
From off our coast, twice beaten; and his shipping –
Poor ignorant baubles! – on our terrible seas,
Like egg-shells moved upon their surges, cracked
As easily 'gainst our rocks.
…
            Our countrymen
Are men more ordered than when Julius Caesar

Smiled at their lack of skill, but found their courage
Worthy his frowning at: their discipline,
Now mingled with their courages, will make known
To their approvers they are people such
That mend upon the world.

William Shakespeare (1564–1616), *Cymbeline*, 1610.

Once more unto the breach, dear friends, once more;
Or close the wall up with our English dead.
In peace there's nothing so becomes a man
As modest stillness and humility:
But when the blast of war blows in our ears,
Then imitate the action of the tiger;
Stiffen the sinews, summon up the blood.
Disguise fair nature with hard-favour'd rage;
Then lend the eyes a terrible aspect;
Let it pry through the portage of the head
Like the brass cannon . . .
                    And you, good yeomen,
Whose limbs were made in England, show us here
The mettle of your pasture; let us swear
That you are worth your breeding; which I doubt not;
For there is none of you so mean and base,
That hath not noble lustre in your eyes.
I see you stand like greyhounds in the slips,
Straining upon the start. The game's afoot:
Follow your spirit, and upon this charge
Cry 'God for Harry, England, and Saint George!'

William Shakespeare (1564–1616), *Henry V*, 1599, III.i.

If we are mark'd to die, we are enow
To do our country loss; and if to live,
The fewer men, the greater share of honour.
God will! I pray thee, wish not one man more.
. . .
Rather proclaim it, Westmoreland, through my host,
That he which hath no stomach to this fight,
Let him depart; his passport shall be made
And crowns for convoy put into his purse:
We would not die in that man's company
That fears his fellowship to die with us.
This day is call'd the feast of Crispian:
He that outlives this day, and comes safe home,
Will stand a tip-toe when this day is named,
And rouse him at the name of Crispian.
. . .

Old men forget; yet all shall be forgot,
But he'll remember with advantages
What feats he did that day.

. . .

This story shall the good man teach his son;
And Crispin Crispian shall ne'er go by,
From this day to the ending of the world,
But we in it shall be remembered;
We few, we happy few, we band of brothers;
For he today that sheds his blood with me
Shall be my brother; be he ne'er so vile,
This day shall gentle his condition:
And gentlemen in England, now a-bed
Shall think themselves accursed they were not here,
And hold their manhoods cheap whiles any speaks
That fought with us upon Saint Crispin's day.

William Shakespeare (1564–1616), *Henry V*, 1599, IV.iii.

GOD BREATHED AND THEY WERE SCATTERED

Motto on the Armada victory medal, 1588.

The defeat of the Spanish Armada in 1588 immediately became an emblem of plucky little Protestant England resisting the insolent might of the great Catholic powers of Continental Europe.

In 1587, the year before the Armada, Sir Francis Drake, regarded by some as little better than a pirate, had led 'the Enterprise of Cadiz' – a raid on the Spanish fleet in its home port:

I remember Drake, in the vaunting style of a soldier, would call the Enterprise the singeing of the King of Spain's beard.

Francis Bacon (1561–1626), *Considerations touching a War with Spain*, in the *Harleian Miscellany*, 1745.

As the Armada of King Philip II approached, the Lord High Admiral of the English fleet observed:

Their force is wonderful great and strong; and yet we pluck their feathers by little and little.

Lord Howard of Effingham (1536–1624), letter, July 1588.

It seems that insouciant calm was endemic among the English commanders. Drake is supposed to have been playing bowls on Plymouth Hoe ...

There is plenty of time to win this game, and to thrash the Spaniards too.

Sir Francis Drake (c.1540–96), attributed in the *Dictionary of National Biography*. W. Oldys, in his *Life of Raleigh*, 1736, writes: 'The tradition goes, that Drake would needs see the game up; but was soon prevail'd on to go and play the rubber with the Spaniards.'

As Effingham and Hawkins and Drake were plucking Spanish feathers in the Channel, the Queen was addressing her troops on land:

My loving people, we have been persuaded by some that are careful of our safety to take heed how we commit ourselves to armed multitudes, for fear of treachery; but I do assure you, I do not desire to live to distrust my faithful and loving people.

Let tyrants fear. I have always so behaved myself that, under God, I have placed my chiefest strength and safeguard in the loyal hearts and goodwill of my subjects, and therefore I am come amongst you, as you see, at this time, not for my recreation and disport, but being resolved in the midst and heat of the battle to live or die amongst you all, to lay down for my God and for my kingdom, and for my people, my honour and my blood, even in the dust.

I know I have the body of a weak and feeble woman, but I have the heart and stomach of a king, aye, and of a king of England too, and think it foul scorn that Parma or Spain, or any prince of Europe, should dare invade the borders of my realm; to which, rather than any dishonour shall grow by me, I myself will take up arms, I myself will be your general, judge, and rewarder of every one of your virtues.

In the meantime, my Lieutenant General shall be in my stead, than whom never a prince commanded a more noble or worthy subject, not doubting but, by your obedience to my general, by your concord in the camp and your valour in the field, we shall shortly have a famous victory over these enemies of God, of my kingdom, and of my people.

Elizabeth I (1533–1603), address to the troops at Tilbury, 9 August 1588.

The mythologising of the Armada had, by the 19th century, become quite an industry. Here is one of its most famous products:

> Drake he's in his hammock an' a thousand mile away,
>   (Capten, art tha sleepin' there below?),
> Slung atween the round shot in Nombre Dios Bay,
>   An' dreamin' arl the time o' Plymouth Hoe.
> Yarnder lumes the Island, yarnder lie the ships,
>   Wi' sailor lads a dancin' heel-an'-toe,
> An' the shore lights flashin', and the night-tide dashin'.
>   He sees it arl so plainly as he saw et long ago.
>
> Drake he was a Devon man, an' rüled the Devon seas,
>   (Capten, art tha sleepin' there below?),
> Rovin' tho' his death fell, he went wi' heart at ease,
>   An' dreamin' arl the time o' Plymouth Hoe.
> 'Take my drum to England, hang et by the shore,
>   Strike et when your powder's runnin' low;
> If the Dons sight Devon, I'll quit the port o' Heaven,
>   An' drum them up the Channel as we drummed them long ago.'
>
> Drake he's in his hammock till the great Armadas come,
>   (Capten, art tha sleepin' there below?),

Slung atween the round shot, listenin' for the drum,
    An' dreamin' arl the time o' Plymouth Hoe.
Call him on the deep sea, call him up the Sound,
    Call him when you sail to meet the foe;
Where the old trade's plyin', and the old flag flyin',
    They shall find him ware an' wakin', as they found him long ago!

Henry Newbolt (1862–1938), 'Drake's Drum', in *The Island Race*, 1897.

After his death, Drake's drum was taken to his home in Buckland Abbey, near Plymouth. The drum is said to have sounded as war broke out in 1914, again in 1918 aboard HMS *Royal Oak*, flagship of the British Grand Fleet, as the German fleet arrived to surrender, and finally during Britain's 'darkest hour', the evacuation from Dunkirk in 1940.

Old soldiers, and old admirals, like nothing better than to talk over old victories. In *No Bed For Bacon* (1941), Caryl Brahms and S.J. Simon assembled the *dramatis personae* of the Armada for a reunion:

Like a scallop of flame the Royal Barge cut through the Thames. The lutes and viols had changed their playing to a lilting dance tune. … But the flower of England was still talking about the Armada.

'The enemy had a hundred and eighty ships,' Howard was saying. 'Eight thousand seamen, nineteen hundred infantry and gentlemen volunteers, officers, priests, surgeons, and galley-slaves at least three thousand more, and all provisioned for six months.'

'A good thing,' said Sir Philip Sidney, 'that we did not know what we had to face.'

'I knew,' said Elizabeth of England.

'So did I,' said Burghley.

    ….

'We too were not without our preparations,' insisted Burghley. He rummaged in a pocket and pulled out an ancient pamphlet. 'See,' he said, 'I have it all set down.' He began to read.

'The Lords demanded five thousand men and fifteen ships: the Cittie craved two days respite for the answer, which was granted; and then entreated their Lordships, in signe of their perfect love and loyaltie to their Prince and Country, humbly to accept ten thousand menne, and thirtie ships amply furnished: and even as London, London-like, gave precendent, the whole Kingdome kept true rank and equipage,' he ended smugly.

'And in the meantime,' said Drake, 'you cut down our victuals.'

'That is as may be,' said Burghley stiffly. 'I have always maintained that sailors have too great an appetite.'

'We had our own land defences to think of,' said Leicester.

'Land!' said old man Hawkins. He turned his back on it.

    ….

It was a beautiful night. The Royal Barge had run on to a mudbank. Clearly too many admirals had spoiled the broth. Presently the tide would rise and lift the boat off, but in the meantime there was no harm in prodding a bit.

The ladies of the Court were leaning over the side watching the proceedings with interest. But the Admirals, after glaring furiously at one another, were making their way back in twos and threes to their monarch. They would wait for the tide to rise, or maybe a wind would blow up, as it always did for Drake, and in the meantime they would remember a bit more about the Armada.

But on their return they found that the landlubbers had taken charge of the conversation and Burghley was reading from his pamphlet.

'It was a pleasant sight,' he read, 'to beholde the souldiers as they marched towards Tylbury, their cheerful countenances, couragious words and gestures. ....
The Queene, upon certayne knowledge of the Spanyardes comming, forthwith settled all her forces in warlike readiness, but ordained no more camps than at Tylbury.'

'And did I not go down to Tylbury in person?' asked Elizabeth of England.

'You did, M'am,' said Sir Philip Sidney, 'and your presence and princely encouragement infused a second spirit of love, loyaltie, and resolution into every souldier in your armie, who being as it were ravished with their Souverayngnes sight, that as well as Commaunders and common souldiers quite forgate the fickleness of Fortune and the chance of Warre, and prayed heartily that the Spanyards might land quickly.'

'Indeed,' said the Master of the Revels affectionately, 'when later they heard the Spanyarde had fled the men wept. They wept,' he repeated, touched.

'I made a speech, too,' said Elizabeth of England.

. . .

The Master of the Revels waggled a finger.

'We shall miss the meaning of this high epic encounter,' he said, 'if we do not realise that both sides had the most profound conviction they were fighting the battle of the Almighty for all time.'

This was a new idea to some of the seamen. They thought it over.

'Two principles were contending for the guidance of mankind,' said Elizabeth of England. 'Freedom and authority.'

'Which side were we on?' asked Lady Meanwell, confused.

Caryl Brahms (1901–82) and S.J. Simon, *No Bed For Bacon*, 1941.

HEART OF OAK: NELSON AND TRAFALGAR

The power and glory of the Royal Navy grew and grew, and the 18th century witnessed one naval victory after another – mostly over the French, who had succeeded the Spanish and the Dutch as the overseas enemy.

Come cheer up, my lads! 'tis to glory we steer,
To add something more to this wonderful year.
To honour we call you, not press you like slaves,
For who are so free as the sons of the waves?
    Heart of oak are our ships,
    Heart of oak are our men:
    We always are ready;

> Steady, boys, steady;
> We'll fight and we'll conquer again and again.

David Garrick (1717–79), song, 'Heart of Oak', from *Harlequin's Invasion*, 1759.

The apogee of English naval glory came at Trafalgar in 1805, when England's most successful admiral died at the moment of victory, so achieving apotheosis in the eyes of his countrymen.

Many accounts survive of those who were with Nelson at the battle. The legend – already begun at the Nile and continued by a blind eye at Copenhagen – opened its final chapter with a memorable signal …

I was walking with him on the poop when he said, 'I'll now amuse the fleet with a signal', and he asked me if I did not think there was one yet wanting. I answered that I thought the whole of the Fleet seemed very clearly to understand what they were about, and to vie with each other who should first get nearest to the *Victory* or *Royal Sovereign*. These words were scarcely uttered when his last well known signal was made: 'England expects every man will do his duty'. The shout with which it was received throughout the fleet was truly sublime. 'Now,' said Lord Nelson, 'I can do no more. We must trust to the Great Disposer of all Events, and the justice of our cause. I thank God for the great opportunity of doing my duty.'

Captain Blackwood, aboard the *Victory* at the Battle of Trafalgar, 21 October, 1805; quoted in Yvonne ffrench, *News From the Past*.

The story is picked up by Second-Lieutenant Ellis of the Marines, aboard the *Ajax*:

I was desired to inform those on the main-deck of the Admiral's signal. Upon acquainting one of the quarter-masters of the order, he assembled the men with 'Avast there, lads, come and hear the Admiral's words'. When the men were mustered, I delivered with becoming dignity the sentence, rather anticipating the effect on the men to be to awe them by its grandeur. Jack, however, did not appreciate it, for there were murmurs from some, whilst others in an audible whisper, murmured, 'Do our duty! Of course we'll do our duty! I've always done mine, haven't you? Let us come alongside of 'em, and we'll soon show whether we'll do our duty.' Still the men cheered vociferously – more, I believe, from love and admiration of their Admiral and leader than from a full appreciation of this well-known signal.

Quoted in Yvonne ffrench, *News From the Past*.

Partial firing continued until 4.30, when a victory having been reported to the Right Honourable Lord Viscount Nelson, K.B., and Commander-in-Chief, he then died of his wounds.

The log of the *Victory*, 21 October 1805.

The *Redoubtable* commenced a heavy fire of musketry from the tops, which was continued for a considerable time with destructive effect to the *Victory*'s crew. … It was from this ship that Lord Nelson received his mortal wound. About fifteen minutes past one o'clock, which was in the heat of the engagement, he was walking in the middle of the quarter-deck with Captain Hardy, and in the act of turning near the hatchway, with his face towards the stern of the *Victory*, when the fatal ball was fired from the enemy's mizen top. ... The ball struck the epaulette on his left shoulder and penetrated his chest. He fell with his face on the deck. Captain Hardy, who was on his right, and had advanced some steps before his Lordship, on turning round, saw the serjeant-major of the Marines with two seamen raising him from the deck. ...

Captain Hardy expressed a hope that he was not severely wounded, to which the gallant Chief replied, 'They have done for me at last, Hardy.'

'I hope not,' said Captain Hardy.

'Yes,' replied his Lordship, 'my backbone is shot through.'

... While the men were carrying him down the ladder from the middle-deck, his Lordship observed that the tiller ropes were not yet replaced; and desired one of the midshipmen stationed there to go upon the quarter-deck and remind Captain Hardy of the circumstance, and request the new ones be immediately rove. Having delivered this order, he took his handkerchief from his pocket and covered his face with it, that he might be conveyed to the cockpit at this crisis unnoticed by the crew. ...

He evinced great solicitude for the event of the battle, and fears for the safety of his friend Captain Hardy. Doctor Scott and Mr Burke used every argument they could suggest, to relieve his anxiety. Mr Burke told him the enemy were decisively defeated, and that he hoped his Lordship would still live to be himself the bearer of the joyful tidings to his country. He replied, 'It is nonsense, Mr Burke, to suppose I can live; my sufferings are great, but they will soon be over.' ...

He then told Captain Hardy he felt that in a few minutes he should be no more, adding in a low tone, 'Don't throw me overboard, Hardy.' The Captain answered: 'Oh! no, certainly not.' 'Then,' replied his Lordship, 'you know what to do, and,' continued he, 'take care of my dear Lady Hamilton, Hardy: take care of poor Lady Hamilton. Kiss me, Hardy.' The Captain now knelt down, and kissed his cheek; when his Lordship said, 'Now I am satisfied. Thank God I have done my duty.'...

He afterwards became very low; his breathing was oppressed, and his voice faint. He said to Doctor Scott, 'Doctor, I have *not* been a *great* sinner'; and, after a short pause, 'Remember, that I leave Lady Hamilton and my daughter Horatia as a legacy to my country: and,' added he, 'never forget Horatia.' ... These words he spoke in a very rapid manner, which rendered his articulation difficult: but he every now and then with evident increase of pain, made a greater effort with his vocal powers, and pronounced distinctly these last words: 'Thank God, I have done my duty.'

Surgeon Beatty, of the *Victory*; quoted in Yvonne ffrench, *News From the Past*.

Royal Sovereign

Honoured Father,

This comes to tell you I am alive and hearty except three fingers; but that's not much, it might have been my head. I told brother Tom I should like to see a greadly battle, and I have seen one, and we have peppered the Combined rarely: and for the matter of that, they fought us pretty tightish for French and

Spanish. Three of our mess are killed, and four more of us winged. But to tell you the truth of it, when the game began, I wished myself at Warnborough with my plough again; but when they had given us one duster, and I found myself snug and tight, I set to in good earnest, and thought no more about being killed than if I were at Murrell Green Fair, and I was presently as busy and as black as a collier. How my fingers got knocked overboard I don't know, but off they are, and I never missed them till I wanted them. You see, by my writing, it was my left hand, so I can write to you, and fight for my King yet. We have taken a rare parcel of ships, but the wind is so rough we cannot bring them home, else I should roll in money, so we are busy smashing 'em, and blowing 'em up wholesale.

Our dear Admiral Nelson is killed! So we have paid pretty sharply for licking 'em. I never sat eyes on him, for which I am both sorry and glad; for, to be sure, I should like to have seen him – but then, all the men in our ship who have seen him are such soft toads, they have done nothing but blast their eyes and cry, ever since he was killed. God bless you! chaps that fought like the devil, sit down and cry like a wench. I am still in the *Royal Sovereign*, but the Admiral [Collingwood] has left her, for she is like a horse without a bridle, so he is in a frigate that he might be here and there and everywhere for he's as *cute* as a here and there one; and as bold as a lion, for all he can cry! – I saw his tears with my own eyes, when the boat hailed and said my Lord was dead. So no more at present from your dutiful son,

Sam.

Quoted in Yvonne ffrench, News From the Past.

Of course, the English have never been able to take their heroes *absolutely* seriously …

Napoleon ought never to be confused with Nelson, in spite of their hats being so alike; they can most easily be distinguished from one another by the fact that Nelson always stood with his arm *like this*, while Napoleon always stood with his arms *like that*.

Nelson was one of England's most naval officers, and despised weak commands. At one battle when he was told that his Admiral-in-Chief had ordered him to cease fire, he put the telephone under his blind arm and exclaimed in disgust: 'Kiss me, Hardy!'

By this and other intrepid manœuvres the French were utterly driven from the seas.

W.C. Sellar (1898–1951) and R.J. Yeatman (1898–1968), 1066 And All That, 1930.

At Viscount Nelson's lavish funeral,
While the mob milled and yelled about St Paul's,
A General chatted with an Admiral:
'One of your Colleagues, Sir, remarked today
That Nelson's *exit*, though to be lamented,
Falls not inopportunely, in its way.'
'He was a thorn in our flesh,' came the reply –
'The most bird-witted, unaccountable,
Odd little runt that ever I did spy. …

'He would dare lecture us Sea Lords, and then
Would treat his ratings as though men of honour
And play at leap-frog with his midshipmen!
'We tried to box him down, but up he pooped,
And when he'd banged Napoleon at the Nile
Became too much of a hero to be dropped.
'You've heard that Copenhagen "blind" eye story?
We'd tied him to Nurse Parker's apron-strings –
By G–d, he snipped them through and snatched the glory!'
'Yes,' cried the General, 'six-and-twenty sail
Captured or sunk by him off Tráfalgár –
That writes a handsome *finis* to the tale.'
'Handsome enough. The seas are England's now.
That fellow's foibles need no longer plague us.
He died most creditably, I'll allow.'
'And, Sir, the secret of his victories?'
'By his UnServicelike, familiar ways, Sir,
He made the whole Fleet love him, damn his eyes!'

Robert Graves (1895–1985), '1805', in *Selected Poems*, 1986.

WELLINGTON AND WATERLOO

Wellington's final defeat of Napoleon at Waterloo achieved a similar status in the minds of the English as Nelson's victory at Trafalgar. Wellington himself was appalled by the human cost, and later was heard to observe, on several occasions:

Next to a battle lost, the greatest misery is a battle gained.

Quoted in the *Diary of Frances, Lady Shelley, 1787–1817.*

Hard pounding this, gentlemen; let's see who will pound longest.

The Duke of Wellington at the Battle of Waterloo, 18 June 1815, reported in Sir Walter Scott, *Paul's Letters*, 1818.

The pounding was sometimes misdirected in the fog of war ... the British and the Prussians then being allies:

We suddenly became sensible of a most destructive flanking fire from a battery which had come, the Lord knows how, and established itself on a knoll somewhat higher than the ground we stood on, and only about 400 or 500 yards a little in advance of our left flank. The rapidity and precision of this fire were quite appalling. Every shot, almost, took effect, and I certainly expected we should all be annihilated. ... The whole livelong day had cost us nothing like this. Our gun-ners too – the few of them left fit for duty were so exhausted that they were unable to run the guns up after firing, consequently at every round they retreated nearer to the limbers [the detachable front parts of gun-carriages]; and as we had pointed out two left guns towards the people who were annoying us so terribly, they soon came together in a confused heap, the trails crossing each other, and the whole dangerously near the limbers and ammunition wagons, some of which were totally unhorsed, and others in sad confusion from the loss of their drivers and horses, many of them lying dead in their harness attached to their carriages. I sighed for my poor troop – it was already but a wreck. . . .

Whilst in position on the right of the second line, I had reproved some of my men for lying down when shells fell near them until they burst. Now my turn came. A shell, with a long fuse, came slop into the mud at my feet, and lay there fizzing and flaring, to my infinite discomfiture. After what I had said on the subject, I felt that I must act up to my own words, and, accordingly, there I stood, endeavouring to look quite composed until the cursed thing burst – and, strange to say, without injuring me, though so near. The effect on my men was good. We pointed our two left guns towards the people who were annoying us so terribly, but had scarcely fired many rounds at the enfilading battery when a tall man in the black Brunswick uniform came galloping up to me from the rear, exclaiming, 'Ah, mine Gott! – mine Gott! Vat is it you doose, sar? Dat is your friends de Proosiens; and you kills dem! Ah, mine Gott! – mine Gott! Vill you no stop, sare? – vill you no stop? Ah! mine Gott – mine Gott! vat for is dis? De Inglish kills dere friends de Proosiens! Vere is the Dook von Vellington?' . . . etc., etc., and so he went on raving like one demented. I observed that if these were our friends the Prussians they were treating us very uncivilly; and that it was not without sufficient provocation we had turned our guns upon them, pointing out to him at the same time the bloody proofs of my assertion. Apparently not noticing what I had said, he continued his lamentations, saying, 'Vill you stop, sare, I say?' Wherefore, thinking he might be right, to pacify him I ordered the whole to cease firing, desiring him to remark the consequences. Psieu, psieu, psieu, came our friends' shot, one after another; and our friend himself had a narrow escape from one of them. 'Now, sir,' I said, 'you will be convinced; and we will continue our firing, whilst you can ride round the way you came, and tell them they kill their friends – the English; the moment their fire ceases, so shall mine.' Still he lingered, exclaiming, 'Oh, dis is terreeble to see de Prossien and de Inglish kill von anoder!' At last darting off I saw no more of him.

General Cavalie Mercer, *Journal of the Waterloo Campaign*, 1870.

As a Field Captain of the Royal Horse Artillery at Waterloo, Mercer witnessed the terror on all sides:

A heavy column of cavalry . . . was advancing upon us at a rapid pace, so that there scarcely appeared time even to get into action, and, if caught in column, of course we were lost.

However, the order was given to deploy, and each gun as it came up immediately opened its fire; the two Infantry Squares at the same time commencing a feeble and desultory fire; for they were in such a state that I momentarily expected to see them disband.

Their ranks, loose and disjointed, presented gaps of several file in breadth, which the Officers and Sergeants were busily employed filling up by pushing and even thumping their men together; whilst these, standing like so many logs, with their arms at the recover, were apparently completely stupefied and bewildered. I should add that they were all perfect children. None of the privates, perhaps, were above eighteen years of age. In spite of our fire the column of cavalry continued advancing at a trot ... but at the very moment when we expected to be overwhelmed, those of the leading Squadron suddenly turning, and endeavouring to make way to the rear, confusion took place, and the whole broke into a disorderly crowd. The scene that ensued is scarcely to be described. Several minutes elapsed ere they succeeded in quitting the plateau, during which our fire was incessant, and the subsequent carnage frightful, for each gun (9 pounders) was loaded with a round and case shot; all of which, from the shortness of the distance, size of the object, and elevation of the ground on which they stood, *must* have taken effect.

Many, instead of seeking safety in retreat, wisely dashed through the intervals between our guns ... but the greater part, rendered desperate at finding themselves held, as it were, in front of the Battery, actually fought their way through their own ranks, and in the struggle we saw blows exchanged on all sides.

Cavalie Mercer, letter, from H.T. Silborne, *Waterloo Letters*, 1891.

Wellington's cool head was legendary. A number of versions of the following exchange have circulated:

UXBRIDGE: I have lost my leg, by God!
WELLINGTON: By God, and have you!

Quoted in Thomas Hardy, *The Dynasts*, 1904.

In the course of that morning (Monday) Wellington came over here to write his dispatch, and ... he beckoned to me out of his windows to come up to him, and having shook hands, he very gravely told me how *critical* the battle had been, and with what incredible gallantry our troops had conducted themselves. ...

On Tuesday morning, nothing would serve Barnes and Hamilton but I must ride over and see their positions, so I was mounted on your old friend the *Curate*, accompanied by Barnes's groom on a Boss Coach Horse. Two miles on this side Waterloo Wellington overtook me in his curricle with Harvey, so we went on together and he said Harvey would mount his horse at Waterloo and shew me over the field of battle, and all about it, which he did. ... Terrible as this sight was in prospect and in fact, it was most interesting, and I would not have missed it for the world. I talked with various French soldiers lying among the dead, but not dead or dying themselves. They were vary gay, and Lord Arthur got off and gave three or four of them some gin and water out of a bottle he had, and they all called him, 'Mon Général' and said he was 'bien honnête'. Harvey told me in riding home he thought the French left on the field were 15,000.

Thomas Creevey (1768–1838), *The Creevey Papers*, 1903, letter from Thomas Creevey to Charles Ord, Bruxelles, 25 June 1815.

It has been a damned serious business – Blücher and I have lost 30,000 men. It has been a damned nice thing – the nearest run thing you ever saw in your life. ... By God! I don't think it would have been done if I had not been there.

The Duke of Wellington, quoted in *The Creevey Papers*, chapter 10.

It is an honourable characteristic of the Spirit of this Age, that projects of violence and warfare are regarded among civilised states with gradually increasing aversion. The Universal Peace Society certainly does not, and probably never will, enrol the majority of statesmen among its members. But even those who look upon the Appeal of Battle as occasionally unavoidable in international controversies, concur in thinking it a deplorable necessity, only to be resorted to when all peaceful modes of arrangement have been vainly tried; and when the law of self-defence justifies a State, like an individual, in using force to protect itself from imminent and serious injury. ...

England has now been blest with thirty-seven years of peace. At no other period of her history can a similarly long cessation from a state of warfare be found. It is true that our troops have had battles to fight during this interval for the protection and extension of our Indian possessions and our colonies; but these have been with distant and unimportant enemies. The danger has never been brought near our own shores, and no matter of vital importance to our empire has ever been at stake. We have not had hostilities with either France, America, or Russia; and when not at war with any of our peers, we feel ourselves to be substantially at peace. There has, indeed, throughout this long period, been no great war, like those with which the previous history of Modern Europe abounds. There have been formidable collisions between particular states; and there have been still more formidable collisions between the armed champions of the conflicting principles of absolutism and democracy; but there has been no general war, like those of the French Revolution, like the American, or the Seven Years' War, or like the War of the Spanish Succession. It would be far too much to augur from this, that no similar wars will again convulse the world; but the value of the period of peace which Europe has gained, is incalculable; even if we look on it as only a truce, and expect again to see the nations of the earth recur to what some philosophers have termed man's natural state of warfare.

No equal number of years can be found, during which science, commerce, and civilisation have advanced so rapidly and so extensively, as has been the case since 1815. When we trace their progress, especially in this country, it is impossible not to feel that their wondrous development has been mainly due to the land having been at peace. Their good effects cannot be obliterated, even if a series of wars were to recommence. When we reflect on this, and contrast these thirty-seven years with the period that preceded them, a period of violence, of tumult, of unrestingly destructive energy, – a period throughout which the wealth of nations was scattered like sand, and the blood of nations lavished like water, – it is impossible not to look with deep interest on the final crisis of that dark and dreadful epoch; the crisis out of which our own happier cycle of years has been evolved. The great battle which ended the twenty-three years' war of the first French Revolution, and which quelled the man whose genius and ambition had so long disturbed and desolated the world, deserves to be regarded by us, not only with peculiar pride, as one of our greatest national victories, but with peculiar gratitude for the repose which it secured for us, and for the greater part of the human race.

Sir Edward Creasy (1812–78), from the Introduction and 'The Battle of Waterloo' in *Fifteen Decisive Battles*, 1851.

The Irish-born Wellington was originally Arthur Welsey, which became Wellesley in 1798, before he was ennobled as Viscount Wellington during the Peninsular War, and then became a marquess, and finally a duke. This sort of thing was guaranteed to confuse schoolchildren:

But the most important of the great men who at this time kept Britain top nation was an Irishman called John Wesley, who afterwards became the Duke of Wellington (and thus English). When he was still Wolseley, Wellington made a great name for himself at Plassaye, in India, where he

'Fought with his fiery few and one',

remarking afterwards, 'It was the bloodiest battle for numbers I ever knew.' It was, however, against Napoleon and his famous Marshals (such as Marshals Ney, Soult, Davos, Mürren, Soult, Blériot, Snelgrove, Ney, etc.) that Wellington became most memorable. Napoleon's armies always used to march on their stomachs, shouting: 'Vive l'Intérieur!' and so moved about very slowly (*ventre-à-terre*, as the French say) thus enabling Wellington to catch up and defeat them. When Napoleon made his troops march all the way to Moscow on their stomachs they got frozen to death one by one, and even Napoleon himself admitted afterwards that it was rather a Bad Thing. . . .

After losing this war Napoleon was sent away by the French, since he had not succeeded in making them top nation; but he soon escaped and returned just in time to fight on the French side at the battle of Waterloo. This utterly memorable battle was fought at the end of a dance, on the Playing Fields of Eton, and resulted in the English definitely becoming top nation. It was thus a very Good Thing. During the engagement the French came on in their usual creeping and crawling method and were defeated by Wellington's memorable order, 'Up Jenkins and Smashems.'

This time Napoleon was sent right away for ever by everybody, and stood on the deck of a ship in white breeches with his arms *like that*.

W.C. Sellar (1898–1951) and R.J. Yeatman (1898–1968), *1066 And All That*, 1930.

PAX BRITANNICA

As Sir Edward Creasy observed above, Britain's wars in the 19th century, after Waterloo, were largely colonial affairs, against 'distant and unimportant enemies'. However, as the 19th century turned into the 20th, rumours of war closer to home began to appear again.

We have got all we want in territory and our claim to be left in unmolested enjoyment of vast and splendid territories, mainly acquired by violence, largely maintained by force, often seems less reasonable to others than it does to us.

Winston Churchill (1874–1965), *A History of the English-Speaking Peoples*, 1956–58.

While the enemy remained in far-off places, he could command a certain respect, even a kind of affection. Here is Kipling on the Sudanese:

> We've fought with many men acrost the seas,
>   An' some of them was brave an' some was not;
> The Paythan an' the Zulu an' Burmese;
>   But the Fuzzy was the finest of the lot.
> We never got a ha'porth's change of 'im:
>   'E squatted in the scrub an' 'ocked our 'orses,
> 'E cut our sentries up at Sua*kim*,
>   'An 'e played the cat an' banjo with our forces.
>   So 'ere's to *you*, Fuzzy-Wuzzy, at your 'ome in the Soudan;
>   You're a poor benighted 'eathen but a first-class fightin' man;
>   We gives you your certificate, an' if you want it signed
> We'll come an' 'ave a romp with you whenever you're inclined.
>
> We took our chanst among the Khyber 'ills,
>   The Boers knocked us silly at a mile,
> The Burman give us Irriwaddy chills,
>   An' a Zulu *impi* dished us up in style:
> But all we ever got from such as they
>   Was pop to what the Fuzzy made us swaller;
> We 'eld our bloomin' own, the papers say,
>   But man for man the Fuzzy knocked us 'oller.
>   Then 'ere's to *you*, Fuzzy-Wuzzy, an' the missis an' the kid;
>   Our orders was to break you, an' of course we went an' did.
>   We sloshed you with Martinis, an' it wasn't 'ardly fair;
>   But for all the odds agin' you, Fuzzy-Wuz, you broke the square.

Rudyard Kipling (1865–1936), 'Fuzzy-Wuzzy', 1892.

Of course, the enemy didn't always play by the rules:

The Boers are not like the Sudanese, who stood up to a fair fight. They are always running away on their little ponies.

General Kitchener on the Second Boer War (1899–1902).

The Boer War, like all others, sent back its share of maimed young men. The return of one such boy to his father was witnessed by the novelist Ford Madox Ford:

I have assisted at two scenes that in my life have most profoundly impressed me with those characteristics of my countrymen. In the one case I was at a railway station awaiting the arrival of a train of troops from the front. I happened to see upon the platform an old man, a member of my club, a retired major. He, too, was awaiting the train; it was to bring back to him his son, a young man who had gone out to the war as of extraordinary promise. He had, the son, fulfilled this promise in an extraordinary degree; he was the only son, and, as it were, the sole hope for the perpetuation of an ancient family – a family of whose traditions old Major

H— was singularly aware and singularly fond. But, at the attack upon a kopje of ill-fated memory, the young man, by the explosion of some shell, had had an arm, one leg, and one side of his face completely blown away. Yet, upon that railway platform I and the old man chatted away very pleasantly. We talked of the weather, of the crops, of the lateness of the train, and kept, as it were, both our minds studiously averted from the subject that continuously was present in both our minds. And, when at last, the crippled form of the son let itself down from the train, all that happened was the odd, unembarrassing clutch of left hand to extended right – a hurried, shuffling shake, and Major H— said: 'Hullo, Bob!' his son: 'Hullo, Governor!' – And nothing more. It was a thing that must have happened, day in day out, all over these wonderful islands; but that a race should have trained itself to such a Spartan repression is none the less worthy of wonder.

Ford Madox Ford (1873–1939), *The Spirit of the People*, 1907.

Towards the end of the long European peace, some looked forward to 'a great war' as the only way out of decadence and decline:

To the man whose first thought is England, and who feels that she must sink or be saved by her gentlefolk, the contemplation of English Society is painful. I feel that a country whose upper classes live as a certain set of men and women do, can only be saved from annihilation by some such upheaval as a great war which will cost all the best families their sons, and call forth the worst animal passions and the noblest of human virtue and for a time place the very existence of the kingdom in danger.

Field Marshal Viscount Garnet Wolseley, 1913, quoted in Peter Vansittart, *In Memory of England*, 1998.

The war that did come in 1914 turned out to be a very different kind of war than the officer class were used to. Here Osbert Lancaster remembers the certainties and security of the Pax Britannica on the verge of dissolution:

Of all the extraordinary interiors of my childhood, of which the atmosphere has been rendered by subsequent events remote from all modern experience, the most difficult to convey to any reader under forty-five was Colonel Hook's study. The faded sepia ranks of brother-officers, moustachioed, whiskered, bearded, staring straight ahead from under the peaks of monstrously high topees or jaunty little pill-boxes, their gloved hands clasped on chased sword-hilts, the water-colour sketches of forgotten cantonments with long rows of bell-tents and skeletal pyramids of stacked rifles, the yellowing maps with little coloured oblongs marking the spot where the Company made their last stand and the route taken by the relieving column indicated by a straggling procession of beetle-like arrows, the knobkerries, the assegais, the Pathan knives – all spoke of a way of military life as far removed from that with which we are familiar as that of the Roman legions. For Colonel Hook belonged entirely to the world of Lady Butler and Sir Henry Newbolt, of thin red lines and broken squares, of stockades and fuzzy-wuzzies, and displayed all its very real virtues in the highest degree. Although a little bent by the years his figure, in the short-tailed old-fashioned cut-away he usually wore, remained unmistakably military; his Roman nose, thick brows and long walrus moustache combined with the high white collar to make him the very image of the fictional colonel. However, of the traditional failings of the type he was completely free, being extremely gentle in manner and the reverse of peppery so that it was quite as impossible to picture him ever losing his temper as it was to imagine that he could under any circumstances break his word.

His whole life had centred round a single-minded devotion to his regiment and he could not conceive it possible that any man could ask for a more rewarding career than the army.

Even as he had lived it Colonel Hook's life, and that of all those whiskered captains, had been, one can now see, anachronistic. It was, at this date, some fifty years since General Sherman had ravaged Georgia (the full significance of which event seems at the time to have escaped the notice of almost everyone save Napoleon III), and yet here we all were, grown-ups just as vividly as little boys, on the very eve of disaster, still envisaging war in terms of bugle-calls and charging lancers. So ridiculous does this now seem to us that we tend in retrospect to dismiss all these little colonial wars as playing at soldiers and denigrate by implication the heroism and courage of Colonel Hook and his like. What they had been spared was the realisation which only came gradually even after 1914, of the immense gravity attaching to the outcome of the fight, the large-scale anxiety transcending the personal which must lie at the back of any modern mind, however much it may be deliberately or unconsciously suppressed in action. If the relieving column did not arrive, or the ammunition run out so much the worse for the regiment; it was unthinkable, so accustomed to victory was that generation, that the ultimate outcome of the campaign would be affected. And even if by some extraordinary and terrible turn of events, or an act of betrayal on the part of Liberal politicians, the war itself should be lost, no threat to the British way of life would result; a whole battalion might be wiped out, national prestige sadly dimmed, but not a penny more would go on the income-tax, the Derby would still be run, and silk hats and frock-coats would still be worn at church parade.

Osbert Lancaster (1908–86), *All Done From Memory*, 1963; the extract refers to 1914.

'BLOOD IS DIRT': THE FIRST WORLD WAR

The First World War was joined and fought by men who sincerely professed an idealism and fervour for it that is as unimaginable to English people today as are the conditions under which it was fought. At the time of writing, the numbers of living survivors of that conflict (which ended when my own father was 12 years old, a pupil of a 'War School' near Allahabad) scarcely run into double figures. Of all those of us who observe an Act of Remembrance on the anniversary of its end – the eleventh hour of the eleventh day of the eleventh month – few have an inkling of an idea of what it is that we are remembering.

The 'Great War' has become a distant, almost mythical horror – a necessary horror, most historians would say; a horror planned by German politicians and militarists for decades beforehand. Nonetheless, it was a horror that shattered not only Europe but a settled way of life in England, where no experience so traumatising had occurred since the Civil Wars of the 17th century. It cost close on one million British and Empire lives and, for Britain, over £35 billion. Such facts and figures are easily come by: 7,500 British sailors lost off Jutland on 31 May 1916; 380,000 British dead in the Somme Offensive – 21,000 of them on the first day, 1 July 1916 – whose gains were numbered in yards rather than miles; over 300,000 British and Empire casualties at Passchendaele in 1917. But despite all that is known about this war, it has yet to be seen whole, and satisfactorily settled in all its aspects. Until it is as remote from historians as the Hundred Years' War of 1337–1453 is today, perhaps it cannot be.

One of the most resonant quotations to emerge from the war is an exchange between the German generals, Ludendorff and Hoffmann: 'The English soldiers fight like lions,' says Ludendorff; 'True,' replies Hoffman. 'But don't we know they are lions led by donkeys.' This famous exchange was cited, from an obscure and untraceable memoir, by the historian and politician Alan Clark in his history of the First World War, published in the 1960s. After the author's death, a close friend revealed that Clark had made it up.

All we have, for the time being, are the known facts – and the awe, the wonder, the puzzlement and the horror. And we have the voices of a people who are us, but who are also a world away from us.

On 3 August 1914, the eve of Britain's declaration of war against Germany, the Foreign Secretary, Sir Edward Grey, looked out of his room in the Foreign Office as the street lamps were dowsed …

The lamps are going out all over Europe. We shall not see them lit again in our life-time.

Sir Edward Grey (1862–1933), recounted in his *Twenty-five Years*, 1925.

Grey's pessimism contrasted with the innocence of most of his countrymen:

It is doubtful if the younger generation today [1940], familiarised for years through the news-reels and illustrated papers with the destructiveness of modern warfare as practised on the bodies of Jonah-countries, can realise the virgin ignorance of their counterparts in 1914–15. We were inured to colonial wars, pacifications of backward peoples, our toy soldiers had significantly bright armaments, which only differed from the more risky and expensive forms of sport in the degree of hardship involved.

Edgell Rickword (b.1898), poet and critic, *Essays and Opinions*, 1974.

To some, in anticipation, the war was going to be the most romantic of all adventures:

If I should die, think only this of me:
    That there's some corner of a foreign field
That is for ever England. There shall be
    In that rich field a richer dust concealed;
A dust whom England bore, shaped, made aware,
    Gave, once, her flowers to love, her ways to roam,

> A body of England's, breathing English air,
>   Washed by the rivers, blest by suns of home.
>
> And think, this heart, all evil shed away,
>   A pulse in the eternal mind, no less
>   Gives somewhere back the thoughts by England given;
> Her sights and sounds; dreams happy as her day;
>   And laughter, learnt of friends; and gentleness,
>   In hearts at peace, under an English heaven.

Rupert Brooke (1887–1915), 'The Soldier', 1914.

The Prime Minister, 'Old Squiffy' Asquith, addressed the Commons on 6 August 1914, characterising the war as a moral crusade:

I do not think any nation ever entered into a great conflict – and this is one of the greatest that history will ever know – with a clearer conscience or stronger conviction that it is fighting not for aggression, not for the maintenance of its own selfish ends, but in defence of principles the maintenance of which is vital to the civilisation of the world. *(Cheers.)*

H.H. Asquith (1852–1928), speech, House of Commons, 6 August 1914.

For many of the young men who rushed to the recruiting offices the motives for fighting were very different:

There came out of the unclouded blue of that summer, a challenge that was almost like a conscription of the spirit, little to do really with King and country and flag-waving and hip-hip-hurrah, a challenge to what we felt was our untested manhood. Other men who had not lived as easily as we had, had drilled and marched and borne arms – couldn't we?

J.B. Priestley (1894–1984), in *Margin Released*, 1964.

I feel … I am meant to take some active part in this war. It is to me a very fascinating thing – something, if often horrible, yet very ennobling and very beautiful, something whose elemental reality raises it above the reach of cold theorising. You will call me a militarist. You may be right.

Roland Leighton, aged 19, letter to Vera Brittain, September 1914.

Basic training in England was soon followed by embarkation. Here are two contrasting experiences of setting sail for France:

The romance of it … the mystery and uncertainty of it … the glowing enthusiasm and lofty idealism of it: of our own free will we were embarked on this glorious enterprise, ready to endure any hardship and make any sacrifice, inspired by a patriotism newly awakened by the challenge to our country's honour.

Nothing could have been more romantic than our passing out into the open sea. As I looked back on the receding coast the sun was sinking slowly behind it, forming an ever-changing colour scheme such as an artist might travel miles to feast upon. The moving boat left a visible track on the calm water, which seemed to stretch right back to the shore as though to remind us that we could never be entirely cut off from the dear land of our birth.

Good-bye, good old England, good-bye!

Private W.T. Colyer, 1st Battalion Artists Rifles, quoted in Malcolm Brown, *Tommy Goes to War*, 1978.

Whilst waiting on the quayside to embark a huge Hospital ship came in filled with wounded. From the upper deck a voice shouted, 'Are you down-hearted?' to which we replied to a man, 'No-o-o!' Back came the voice, 'Then you bloody soon will be!'

Private C.W. Mason, 10th Battalion Lincolnshire Regiment, quoted in Malcolm Brown, *Tommy Goes to War*, 1978.

Coming face to face with the enemy brought many to the realisation of the common human-ity of 'Englander' and 'Hun'. Here an ordinary soldier describes a column of German POWs:

They were not big savage hulks of men with bristling whiskers or criminal fore-heads. They were young men, bandaged and battered, a solid bunch of nerves after having I expect been through a hellish bombardment. The most savage com-ment I heard while watching the prisoners came from an infantryman. That was 'Poor buggers!' It makes one feel glad to belong to a fighting force where 'poor buggers' is said about enemy prisoners. Fancy seeing it in print in the morning newspapers: 'Our infantrymen are sorry for the enemy prisoners and wonder why he has to kill them.' Those who printed it would be on parade next day.

Gunner Hiram Sturdy, Royal Field Artillery, quoted in Malcolm Brown, *Tommy Goes to War*, 1978.

However, this kind of attitude was not officially encouraged – in fact, the very opposite was required:

The German atrocities (many of which I doubt in secret), the employment of gas in action, the violation of French women, and the 'official murder' of Nurse Cavell all help to bring out the brute-like bestiality which is so necessary for vic-tory. ... The British soldier is a kindly fellow and it is safe to say, despite the dope, seldom oversteps the mark of barbaric propriety in France, save occasionally to kill prisoners he cannot be bothered to escort back to his lines.

In order that he shall enter into the true spirit of the show, however, the fun of the fair as we may call it, it is necessary to corrode his mentality with bitter-sweet vice and keep him up to the vicious scratch on all occasions. ... It is the only way in war, and both sides follow it.

Brigadier F.P. Crozier, *A Brass Hat in No Man's Land*, 1930.

The army was determined to put every man to use, whatever his physical condition. Here an NCO recalls the methods of an MO at Divisional Base Camp in 1915:

He used to line the men up and go along the line asking each one, 'Well, and what's the matter with you my man?'

(1) 'Bad teeth, sir!'
answer 'Well, I don't want you to eat the Germans.'
(2) 'Consumption, sir!'
answer 'Go up and spit at them.'
(3) 'short-sighted, sir!'
answer 'How far can you see?'
'About 30 yards, sir.'
answer 'The trenches are only 15 yards apart at some places. Up you go and the best of luck.'
(4) 'shot in the leg, sir!'
answer 'Up you go and shoot the man who shot you.'
(5) 'Hit with shrapnel, sir!'
answer 'Up you go and get your own back.'
(6) 'Bad eyes, sir!'
answer 'Just the man we want for listening posts.'
The result of this particular doctor's methods was that one man with a varicose vein and another with his trigger finger shot off were returned to the firing line.

Lance-Sergeant Elmer Cotton, Northumberland Fusiliers, quoted in Malcolm Brown, *Tommy Goes to War*, 1978.

The official view of heroism on the Front was reflected in a plethora of stories for boys back home, in which death was heroic – and quick:

Jim had the head and shoulders of our islanders. A small, fair moustache set off a handsome face which was resolute and firm, and had none of the floppy stodginess so often found among the beer-drinking subjects of the Kaiser. ...

'Boys,' [the subaltern] shouted, and at the call the men on either side of him sat up and cheered him. 'Boys, for the sake of Old England, for the sake of the regiment, you'll hold 'em. Fire, boys!' There was a choking cough, while a shudder ran down his frame. The subaltern collapsed into Jim's kindly arms, and lay white and motionless at the bottom of the trench. He was dead; another victim of the Kaiser's murderous ambition, one more count against the German nation.

Captain F.S. Brereton (1872–1957), *With French at the Front*, 1915.

There were many such deaths; a subaltern's life expectancy on the Front was just three weeks. Siegfried Sassoon, an officer-poet who – remarkably – survived years of trench warfare, knew that many died more slowly and less willingly. This poem is 'To Any Dead Officer':

Well, how are things in Heaven? I wish you'd say,
     Because I'd like to know that you're all right.
Tell me, have you found everlasting day,
     Or been sucked in by everlasting night?
For when I shut my eyes your face shows plain;
     I hear you make some cheery old remark –
I can rebuild you in my brain,
     Though you've gone out patrolling in the dark.

You hated tours of trenches; you were proud
>Of nothing more than having good years to spend;
Longed to get home and join the careless crowd
>Of chaps who work in peace with Time for friend.
That's all washed out now. You're beyond the wire:
>No earthly chance can send you crawling back;
You've finished with machine-gun fire –
>Knocked over in a hopeless dud-attack.

Somehow I always thought you'd get done in,
>Because you were so desperate keen to live:
You were all out to try and save your skin,
>Well knowing how much the world had got to give.
You joked at shells and talked the usual 'shop',
>Stuck to your dirty job and did it fine:
With 'Jesus Christ! when will it stop?
>Three years ... It's hell unless we break their line.'

So when they told me you'd been left for dead
>I wouldn't believe them, feeling it must be true.
Next week the bloody Roll of Honour said
>'Wounded and missing' – (That's the thing to do
When lads are left in shell-holes dying slow,
>With nothing but blank sky and wounds that ache,
Moaning for water till they know
>It's night, and then it's not worth while to wake!)
...

Good-bye, old lad! Remember me to God,
>And tell Him that our Politicians swear
They won't give in till Prussian Rule's been trod
>Under the Heel of England ... Are you there? ...
Yes ... and the War won't end for at least two years;
But we've got stacks of men ... I'm blind with tears,
>Staring into the dark. Cheero!
I wish they'd killed you in a decent show.

Siegfried Sassoon (1886–1967), 'To Any Dead Officer', in *Counterattack*, 1918.

But still the lads at home were told a different story:

It is up to you boys of today to see that a similar danger never threatens your glorious Empire again. Those of you who have not yet donned khaki, see to it that when you are old enough you train yourselves to defend your homes, your mothers, your sisters, your country, all that you hold dear. ... And believe one of those whose proud privilege it has been to wear the King's uniform, that those days you will spend in khaki or blue will be among the fullest and happiest of your lives.

Escott Lynne, *In Khaki for the King*, 1915.

An England where such things were still believed was totally alien to the soldier back from the Front. In his celebrated war memoir, *Goodbye to All That*, Robert Graves, wounded at the Somme and home on leave in August 1916, remarked on this disjunction:

England looked strange to us returned soldiers. We could not understand the war-madness that ran wild everywhere, looking for a pseudo-military outlet. The civilians talked a foreign language; and it was newspaper language. I found serious conversation with my parents all but impossible. Quotations from a single typical document of this time will be enough to show what we were facing:

A MOTHER'S ANSWER TO

'A COMMON SOLDIER'

By A Little Mother

A Message to the Pacifists.   *A Message to the Bereaved.*

A Message to the Trenches.

Owing to the immense demand from home and from the trenches for this letter, which appeared in *The Morning Post*, the Editor found it necessary to place it in the hands of London publishers to be reprinted in pamphlet form, seventy-five thousand copies of which were sold in less than a week direct from the publishers.

'The Queen was deeply touched at the 'Little Mother's' beautiful letter, and Her Majesty fully realises what her words must mean to our soldiers in the trenches and in hospitals.'

To the Editor of 'The Morning Post'

Sir, – As a mother of an only child – a son who was early and eager to do his duty – may I be permitted to reply to Tommy Atkins, whose letter appeared in your issue of the 9th inst.? Perhaps he will kindly convey to his friends in the trenches, not what the Government thinks, not what the Pacifists think, but what the mothers of the British race think of our fighting men. It is a voice which demands to be heard, seeing that we play the most important part in the history of the world, for it is we who 'mother the men' who have to uphold the honour and traditions not only of our Empire but of the whole civilised world.

To the man who pathetically calls himself a 'common soldier', may I say that we women, who demand to be heard, will tolerate no such cry as 'Peace! Peace!' where there is no peace. The corn that will wave over land watered by the blood of our brave lads shall testify to the future that their blood was not spilt in vain. We need no marble monuments to remind us. We only need that force of character behind all motives to see this monstrous world tragedy brought to a victorious ending. The blood of the dead and the dying, the blood of the 'common soldier' from his 'slight wounds' will not cry to us in vain. They have all done their share, and we, as women, will do ours without murmuring and without complaint. Send the Pacifists to us and we shall very soon show them, and show the world, that in our homes at least there shall be no 'sitting at home warm and cosy in the winter, cool and "comfy" in the summer'. There is only one temperature for the women of the British race, and that is white heat. With those who disgrace their sacred trust of motherhood we have nothing in common. Our ears are not deaf to the cry that is ever ascending from the battlefield from men of flesh and blood whose indomitable courage is borne to us, so to speak, on every blast of the wind. We women pass on the human ammunition of 'only sons' to fill up the gaps, so that when the 'common soldier' looks back before going 'over the top' he may see the women of the British race at his heels, reliable, dependent, uncomplaining.

The reinforcements of women are, therefore, behind the 'common soldier'. We gentle-nurtured, timid sex did not want the war. It is no pleasure to us to have our homes made desolate and the apple of our eye taken away. We would sooner our loveable, promising, rollicking boy stayed at school. We would have much preferred to have gone on in a light-hearted way with our amusements and our hobbies. But the bugle call came, and we have hung up the tennis racquet, we've fetched our laddie from school, we've put his cap away, and we have glanced lovingly over his last report which said 'Excellent' – we've wrapped them all in a Union Jack and locked them up, to be taken out only after the war to be looked at. A 'common soldier', perhaps, did not count on the women, but they have their part to play, and we have risen to our responsibility. We are proud of our men, and they in turn have to be proud of us. If the men fail, Tommy Atkins, the women won't.

> *Tommy Atkins to the front,*
> *He has gone to bear the brunt.*
> *Shall 'stay-at-homes' do naught but snivel and but sigh?*
> *No, while your eyes are filling*
> *We are up and doing, willing*
> *To face the music with you – or to die!*

Women are created for the purpose of giving life, and men to take it. Now we are giving it in a double sense. It's not likely we are going to fail Tommy. We shall not flinch one iota, but when the war is over he must not grudge us, when we hear the bugle call of 'Lights out', a brief, very brief, space of time to withdraw into our secret chambers and share, with Rachel the Silent, the lonely anguish of a bereft heart, and to look once more on the college cap, before we emerge stronger women to carry on the glorious work our men's memories have handed down to us for now and all eternity.

Yours, etc.,
A Little Mother.

EXTRACTS AND PRESS CRITICISMS

'The widest possible circulation is of the utmost importance.' – *The Morning Post.*

'Deservedly attracting a great deal of attention, as expressing with rare eloquence and force the feelings with which the British wives and mothers have faced and are facing the supreme sacrifice.' – *The Morning Post.*

'Excites widespread interest.' – *The Gentlewoman.*

'A letter which has become celebrated.' – *The Star.*

'We would like to see it hung up in our wards.' – *Hospital Blue.*

'One of the grandest things ever written, for it combines a height of courage with a depth of tenderness which should be, and is, the stamp of all that is noblest and best in human nature.' – *A Soldier in France.*

'Florence Nightingale did great and grand things for the soldiers of her day, but no woman has done more than the 'Little Mother', whose now famous letter in *The Morning Post* has spread like wild-fire from trench to trench. I hope to God it will be handed down in history, for nothing like it has ever made such an impression on our fighting men. I defy any man to feel weak-hearted after reading it ... My God! she makes us die happy.' – *One who has Fought and Bled*.

'Worthy of far more than a passing notice; it ought to be reprinted and sent out to every man at the front. It is a masterpiece and fills one with pride, noble, level-headed, and pathetic to a degree.' – *Severely Wounded*.

'I have lost my two dear boys, but since I was shown the 'Little Mother's' beautiful letter a resignation too perfect to describe has calmed all my aching sorrow, and I would now gladly give my sons twice over.' – *A Bereaved Mother*.

'The 'Little Mother's' letter should reach every corner of the earth – a letter of the loftiest ideal, tempered with courage and the most sublime sacrifice.' – *Percival H. Monkton*.

'The exquisite letter by a 'Little Mother' is making us feel prouder every day. We women desire to fan the flame which she has so superbly kindled in our hearts.' – *A British Mother of an Only Son*.

Robert Graves (1895–1985), *Goodbye to All That*, 1929.

In such a din the voices from the Front struggled to be heard:

You love us when we're heroes, home on leave,
Or wounded in a mentionable place.
You worship decorations; you believe
That chivalry redeems the war's disgrace.
You make us shells. You listen with delight,
By tales of dirt and danger fondly thrilled.
You crown our distant ardours while we fight,
And mourn our laurelled memories when we're killed.
You can't believe that British troops 'retire'
When hell's last horror breaks them, and they run,
Trampling the terrible corpses – blind with blood.
O German mother dreaming by the fire,
While you are knitting socks to send your son
His face is trodden deeper in the mud.

Siegfried Sassoon (1886–1967), 'Glory of Women', 1917.

In September 1915 Roland Leighton, who just a year before had anticipated the war was going to be 'very ennobling and very beautiful', wrote again to Vera Brittain. He was now 20 years old:

Let him who thinks that War is a glorious thing, who loves to roll forth stirring words of exhortation, invoking Honour and Praise and Valour and Love of Country ... let him but look at a little pile of sodden grey rags that cover half a skull and a shin bone and what might have been Its ribs ... and let him realise how grand and glorious a thing it is to have distilled all Youth and Joy and Life into a foetid heap of hideous putrescence.

> Bent double, like old beggars under sacks,
> Knock-kneed, coughing like hags, we cursed through sludge,
> Till on the haunting flares we turned our backs
> And towards our distant rest began to trudge.
> Men marched asleep. Many had lost their boots
> But limped on, blood-shod. All went lame; all blind;
> Drunk with fatigue; deaf even to the hoots
> Of tired, outstripped Five-Nines that dropped behind.
>
> Gas! GAS! Quick, boys! – An ecstasy of fumbling,
> Fitting the clumsy helmets just in time;
> But someone still was yelling out and stumbling
> And flound'ring like a man in fire or lime ...
> Dim, through the misty panes and thick green light,
> As under a green sea, I saw him drowning.
>
> In all my dreams, before my helpless sight,
> He plunges at me, guttering, choking, drowning.
>
> If in some smothering dream you too could pace
> Behind the wagon that we flung him in,
> And watch the white eyes writhing in his face,
> His hanging face, like a devil's sick of sin;
> If you could hear, at every jolt, the blood
> Come gargling from the froth-corrupted lungs,
> Obscene as cancer, bitter as the cud
> Of vile, incurable sores on innocent tongues, –
> My friend, you would not tell with such high zest
> To children ardent for some desperate glory,
> The old Lie: Dulce et decorum est
> Pro patria mori.

Wilfred Owen (1893–1918), 'Dulce et Decorum Est', August 1917, *Collected Poems*, 1920.

It is considered very unlucky to be killed on a Friday.

'Soldiers' Superstitions' in *The Wipers Times* (also known as *The Somme Times* and *The BEF Times*), published by officers in the field, 1916–18. For the last issue the title was altered to *The Better Times*.

Wot a life. No rest, no beer, no nuffin. It's only us keeping so cheerful as pulls us through.

L. Ravenhill, cartoon in *Punch*, 27 September 1916.

'Good morning; good morning!' the General said
When we met him last week on our way to the line.
Now the soldiers he smiled at are most of 'em dead,
And we're cursing his staff for incompetent swine.
'He's a cheery old card,' grunted Harry to Jack
As they slogged up to Arras with rifle and pack.

But he did for them both by his plan of attack.

Siegfried Sassoon (1886–1967), 'The General', 1918.

'You! What d'you mean by this?' I rapped.
'You dare come on parade like this?'
'Please, sir, it's –' ''Old yer mouth,' the sergeant snapped.
'I takes 'is name, sir?' – 'Please, and then dismiss.'

Some days 'confined to camp' he got,
For being 'dirty on parade'.
He told me, afterwards, the damnèd spot
Was blood, his own. 'Well, blood is dirt,' I said.

'Blood's dirt,' he laughed, looking away
Far off to where his wound had bled
And almost merged forever into clay.
'The world is washing out its stains,' he said.
'It doesn't like our cheeks so red:
Young blood's its great objection.
But when we're duly white-washed, being dead,
The race will bear Field-Marshal God's inspection.'

Wilfred Owen (1893–1918), 'Inspection', in *Collected Poems*, 1920.

The most famous elegy for the war dead was actually written in 1914. 'For The Fallen' by Laurence Binyon (1869–1943) has become the memorial epitaph for the British dead of all wars, recited each year on Remembrance Day:

They shall grow not old, as we that are left grow old.
Age shall not weary them, nor the years condemn.
At the going down of the sun and in the morning
We will remember them.

Wilfred Owen's alternative elegy, 'Anthem for Doomed Youth', was written in the light of slaughter on an industrial scale:

What passing-bells for these who die as cattle?
Only the monstrous anger of the guns.
Only the stuttering rifle's rapid rattle
Can patter out their hasty orisons.
No mockeries now for them; no prayers no bells,
Nor any voice of mourning save the choirs, –

The shrill, demented choirs of wailing shells;
    And bugles calling for them from sad shires.

What candles may be held to speed them all?
    Not in the hands of boys, but in their eyes
Shall shine the holy glimmers of good-byes.
    The pallor of girls' brows shall be their pall;
Their flowers the tenderness of patient minds,
And each slow dusk a drawing-down of blinds.

Wilfred Owen (1893–1918), from *Collected Poems*, 1920.

Grey of Fallodon, who had watched the lights go out all over Europe in 1914, haunted a generation with his shade:

One afternoon I watched him as he stood
In the twilight of his wood.
Among the firs he'd planted, forty years away,
Tall, and quite still, and almost blind,
World patience in his face, stood Edward Grey;
Not listening,
For it was at the end of summer, when no birds sing:
Only the bough's faint dirge accompanied his mind
Absorbed in some Wordsworthian slow self-communing.

In lichen-coloured homespun clothes he seemed
So merged with stem and branch and twinkling leaves
That almost I expected, looking away, to find
When glancing there again, that I had daylight dreamed
His figure, as when some trick of sun and shadow deceives.

But there he was, haunting heart-known ancestral ground;
Near to all Nature; and in that nearness somehow strange;
Whose native humour, human-simple yet profound,
And strength of spirit no calamity could change.
To whom, designed for countrified contentments, came
Honours unsought and unrewarding foreign fame:
And, at the last, that darkened world wherein he moved
In memoried deprivation of life once learnt and loved.

Siegfried Sassoon (1886–1967), 'A Fallodon Memory' in *Emblems of Experience*. Sir Edward Grey, Foreign Secretary at the outbreak of war in 1914, had become Viscount Grey of Fallodon in 1916.

The descendants of that decimated generation are left to wonder, and to stare at the old photographs:

Dusty, bulging, old: they are all the same, these albums. The same faces, the same photos. Every family was touched by the war and every family has an album like this. Even as we prepare to open it, the act of looking at the album is overlaid by the emotions it will engender. We look at the pictures as if reading a poem about the experience of seeing them.

I turn the dark, heavy pages. The dust smell of old photographs.

The dead queuing up to enlist. Marching through the dark town, disappearing beyond the edge of the frame. Some turn up later, in the photos from hospital: marching away and convalescing, nothing in between. Always close to hand, the countryside seems empty in these later pictures, a register of absence. Dry stone walls and rivers. Portraits and group portraits. Officers and other ranks. The loved and the unloved, indistinguishable from each other. . . .

A nurse in round glasses and long uniform ('Myself' printed beneath in my grandmother's perfect hand). A group of men in hospital. Two with patches over their eyes, three with arms in slings. One

in his ghastly suit of grey,
Legless, sewn short at the elbow.

A stern-faced sister stands at the end of the back row, each name diligently inked beneath the picture. My mother's father is the second on the left, in the back row. Born (illegitimate) in Worthen in Shropshire, eighteen miles from Oswestry where Wilfred Owen was born. Farm labourer. Able only to read and write his name. Enlisted in 1914. Served on the Somme as a driver (of horses), where, according to family legend, he once went up to the front-line trenches in place of a friend whose courage had suddenly deserted him. Later, back in the reserve trench, he shovelled the remains of his best friend into a sandbag. (Every family has the same album, every family has a version of the same legend.) Returned to Shropshire in 1919 and resumed the life he had left.

Worked, went to war, married, worked.

He died aged ninety-one, able still only to write his name.

Everything I have said about my grandfather is true. Except he is not the man second from the left in the photograph. I do not know who that is. It makes no difference. He could be anyone's grandfather.

Like many young men, my grandfather was under age when he turned up to enlist. The recruiting sergeant told him to come back in a couple of days when he was two years older. My grandfather duly returned, added a couple of years to his age and was accepted into the army.

Similar episodes are fairly common in the repertoire of recruitment anecdotes, but I never doubted the veracity of this particular version of it, which my mother told several times over the years. It came as a surprise, then, to discover from his death certificate that my grandfather was born in November 1893 (the same year as Owen), and so was twenty when war broke out. One of the commonly circulating stories of the 1914 generation had been so thoroughly absorbed by my family that it had become part of my grandfather's biography

He is everyone's grandfather.

Geoff Dyer (1958–), *The Missing of the Somme*, 1994. The quotation is from Wilfred Owen, 'Disabled'.

'Keep Buggering On': The Second World War

So much has been written – so much is known *– about the Second World War, that it seems superfluous to write a single word more. For the purposes of this book, an anthology of voices from a shared past, all that needs to be said is that it was a time when Britain – and, it may be said without exciting undue controversy, England in particular – experienced a degree of national unity and self-realisation never attained before, perhaps never attainable again. For once, it is not bombastic hyperbole to say, 'We saved the world from terror and tyranny.' From the fall of France in June 1940 to the entry of the USA in December 1941, that is precisely what we did, against all odds and in defiance of all contemporary logical analysis. With equal reason, and as never before, we were proud of our fighting forces as we were proud of ourselves. Maybe this, our finest hour, was the hour we had been shaping ourselves for; our defining, culminating hour. We buggered on, muddled through, kept our heads down, didn't grumble ... much ... and generally got on with it. All the clichés of Englishness that ever were coined were new-minted, and true.*

We had a Good War.

[The British] are the only people who like to be told how bad things are – who like to be told the worst.

Winston Churchill (1874–1965), speech, 1921.

It's being so cheerful as keeps me going.

Joan Harben (1909–53) as 'Mona Lott', the miserable laundrywoman in *It's That Man Again* (*ITMA*), the BBC variety show that ran throughout the Second World War.

On 1 September 1939 Germany invaded Poland, which Britain had pledged to defend against Nazi aggression. In his diary, Ralph Glyn, Conservative MP for Abingdon, recorded the events that followed:

September 3. Last night in London was one of the great times in modern history. The half-hour in the Commons – 7.30 to 8 – was perhaps the most decisive half-hour that we have known.

All through the day the House had been in a schoolboyish, almost hysterical mood; they were laughing and shuffling. There was a feeling that something fishy was happening in Downing Street. The Cabinet was still sitting. Ministers were telephoning Paris – and the Germans were bombing Poland. *Why* were we not at war?

At half-past seven we met again, this time subdued and tense. Chamberlain we knew would declare war. The Ambassadors were looking down; Count Edward Raczijnsky pale and worn. Chamberlain came in looking grey – a kind of whitish-grey – and glum, dour. Captain Margesson, the Secretary to the Treasury, came behind him, purple with anxiety. Chamberlain's statement! ... In the House we thought he was only half-way through when – he sat down. There was a gasp, first of horror, then anger. His own backbenchers leant forward to cry, 'Munich, Munich!' The House seemed to rise to its feet with Mr. Arthur Greenwood, the Labour leader.

Mr. L.S. Amery [Conservative MP for Sparkbrook, Birmingham], sitting very small near Anthony Eden, jumped up to shout at Greenwood – 'speak for England.' Others took up the cry. Chamberlain white and hunched. Margesson with sweat pouring down his face, Sir John Simon, [and] the Foreign Secretary [Lord Halifax], punctiliously looking holy.

Greenwood spoke slowly and very simply. He spoke for England and what is more he saved Chamberlain by most skilfully suggesting that it was the French who were delaying. Then one or two backbenchers, Chamberlain's own supporters, got up. It was not a joint Anglo–French pledge to Poland, they said, it was a *British* pledge – why were we not fulfilling it? The House swung against Chamberlain again. Winston Churchill, I saw, was getting whiter and grimmer. He turned round to look at Eden, who nodded as if to say, 'You speak, I'll follow.' I know that Churchill was about to move a vote of censure on the Government – which would have fallen. But Chamberlain looked across at Churchill: 'I'm playing straight,' his glance seemed to say, 'there really *are* reasons for delay.' Churchill sat back, relaxed, uneasy.

Then James Maxton [Independent Labour MP for Bridgeton, Glasgow], the pacifist, rose, gaunt, a Horseman from the Apocalypse, doom written across his face: 'Don't let's talk of national honour: what do such phrases mean? The plain fact is that war means the slaughter of millions. If the Prime Minister can still maintain the peace he will have saved those lives, he mustn't be rushed.' Again the House swung and was poised. We all thought in the curious hush: What if the gaunt figure of doom were right after all? Slaughter – misery – ruin – was he right? But the alternative: Hitler trading on our fears, Germany treading on freedom, Europe under terror. The whole House was swayed in unison with the drama which itself was living.

Another backbencher spoke: 'We must keep our pledge – Hitler must be stopped.' Once again we were swinging against Chamberlain, when Margesson, damp and shapeless, rose to move the adjournment. In a kind of daze it was carried.

We broke up, some feeling sick from the reaction – two members *were* sick – all were uneasy and ashamed. I went home, lay awake all night, slept a bit towards morning, and was awakened by the air-raid warning. Had the Germans read the feelings of the country? Were they attacking first?

From my window I could look over London – it is the clearest and sunniest and freshest day we have had this year. St. Paul's dome shone blue, and to the east I could see the smoke and masts of the ships at the wharves all peaceful under a blue sky. Later – at 11.15 – I heard Chamberlain's announcement. We had gone out to meet Hitler, we were at war.

Ralph Glyn (1885–1960), diary entry for 3 September 1939.

Margery Allingham summed up the feelings of many on that day:

At eleven o'clock the next morning Mr. Chamberlain made his famous speech and, still like the family solicitor, so kindly and so very upset, told us it had come. We were at war. Still there was no band, no cheering, no noise; only this breathless feeling of relief and intolerable grief. ...

I thought: 'Well, it's come; this is the terminus. This is the explanation of the extraordinary sense of apprehension, of the unaccountable nostalgic sadness of the last few years. This is where our philosophy led. This is what was in the bag

for all of us. This is what has come of curbing our natural bossiness out of defer-
ence to the criticisms of the sophisticated cleversides of three continents. This is
what comes of putting up with wrong 'uns. This is what comes of not interfering
when you see something horrible happening, even if it isn't your business. This is
where we've been going. This was our portion after all.'

Margery Allingham (1904–68), from *The Oaken Heart*, 1941.

In that momentous month of September 1939, the Prime Minister, Neville Chamberlain,
quoted the following lines of Shakespeare:

> This England never did, nor never shall,
> Lie at the proud foot of a conqueror,
> But when it first did help to wound itself.
> Now these her princes are come home again,
> Come the three corners of the world in arms,
> And we shall shock them. Nought shall make us rue,
> If England to herself do rest but true.

William Shakespeare (1564–1616), *King John*, 1591–98.

But this war, for once, was not a war of princes ...

This is the people's war. It is our war. We are the fighters. Fight it with all that is
in us. And may God defend the right.

'Mrs Miniver' (Jan Struther) speaks to the 'Home Front' in *The Times*, from September 1939.

The following appeared in the Classified sections in that month in 1939:

CLUB with BLAST and SPLINTER-PROOF dining room – all enquiries for special
membership. Albany Club.

Burlington Magazine, 1 September.

*

CHOOSE YOUR OWN SAFETY ZONE! Full size buses to live in; existing seats
make excellent beds; electric light; £55 each, deliver anywhere.

The Sunday Times, 3 September.

*

PARENTS who wish may send girls back AT ONCE. Lindores School, Bexhill-
on-Sea.

The Daily Telegraph, 4 September.

*

ARE YOU GOING ABROAD? If so, send a postcard to publisher of *The Times*,
Printing House Square, London E. C. 4., for subscription rates.

The Times, 4 September.

*

CELLARS, spacious, dry, solid; excellent large house above. London 20 miles.

The Daily Telegraph, 6 September.

*

LIVE PEACEFULLY in Sussex free of worries. Tunbridge Wells property invisible
from the air.

Country Life, 8 September.

BREED RABBITS. Safeguard your larder. Three breeding Does produce nearly 2cwt carcases per annum. Crawley, Sussex.

Amateur Gardening, 8 September.

*

EVACUATE DOGS for holiday to neutral territory. Ten shillings a week, gun dogs £1. Donegal.

Country Life, 8 September.

*

MR. EVELYN WAUGH wishes to let Piers Court near Dursley, Glos. Furnished for duration of war. Old house recently modernised; 4 reception, 10 bed, 4 bath, etc. 4 acres or more. Low rent to civilised tenant.

The Times, 8 September.

*

VICAR of large country parish, now Head Warden ARP, would be grateful for an old car.

The *Christian Herald*, 9 September.

All quoted in Peter Haining, *The Day War Broke Out*.

Old values could be slow to change. On 30 September Sir Kingsley Wood, Minister for Air, rejected an RAF plan to attack targets in the Black Forest with the following words:

Are you aware that it is private property? Why, you will be asking me to bomb Essen next!

Most of us have stories about 'how we saw the war in', but I doubt if anyone in this country had a more bizarre experience than my friend who was at a large holiday camp. Throughout the crisis, the camp authorities refused to broadcast any news and maintained that all war-talk was 'just rumour'. It was, my friend remarked, a regime of totalitarian high spirits.

On the Friday when Poland was invaded, the two thousand-odd campers in the two great dining rooms were informed by the stentorian loud speaker that, in spite of all gossip, the camp was definitely carrying on. 'Heigh-de-he,' shouted the unseen leader. 'Heigh-de-ho,' replied the two thousand, and, clasping their hands above their heads, thundered the camp song in cheery defiance of war.

There is no doubt this censorship of politics was a great relief. News bulletins are a drug, my friend assures me, and he was better without them, although he did on occasion slip furtively out of the camp and lurk outside a private house to catch the news. But, alas! the charmed circle was broken on Friday evening.

At 4 am the holiday-makers were awakened by a reveille and my friend's last glimpse of the camp was a smartly dressed officer scanning the crowd of bathing belles and anxious mothers and remarking loudly, 'Won't be so bad when we get these dreadful people out.'

'A London Diary', *New Statesman*, 9 September 1939.

Everybody expected death to rain from the skies, but when this did not immediately happen, some began to take the air-raid exercises less seriously. One volunteer 'casualty' left the following note:

Ave bled to death and gorn ome.

The Second World War is not as renowned for its poetry as the First, but one of the most famous poems to come out of it is Henry Reed's 'Naming of Parts'. Reed was in the Army Ordnance Corps, and his poem conveys something of the tedium experienced by service-men and women when not in action. It also shows the healthily detached attitude of 'a people not used to war'.

Today we have naming of parts. Yesterday,
We had daily cleaning. And tomorrow morning
We shall have what to do after firing. But today,
Today we have naming of parts. Japonica
Glistens like coral in all of the neighbouring gardens
    And today we have naming of parts.

This is the lower sling swivel. And this
Is the upper sling swivel, whose use you will see
When you are given your slings. And this is the piling swivel,
Which in your case you have not got. The branches
Hold in the gardens their silent, eloquent gestures,
    Which in our case we have not got.

This is the safety-catch, which is always released
With an easy flick of the thumb. And please do not let me
See anyone using his finger. You can do it quite easy
If you have any strength in your thumb. The blossoms
Are fragile and motionless, never letting anyone see
    Any of them using their finger.

And this you can see is the bolt. The purpose of this
Is to open the breech, as you see. We can slide it
Rapidly backwards and forwards; we call this
Easing the spring. And rapidly backwards and forwards
The early bees are assaulting and fumbling the flowers;
    They call it easing the spring.

They call it easing the spring; it is perfectly easy
If you have any strength in your thumb; like the bolt,
And the breech, and the cocking-piece, and the point of balance,
Which in our case we have not got; and the almond-blossom
Silent in all of the gardens and the bees going backwards and forwards,
    For today we have naming of parts.

Henry Reed (1914–86), 'Naming of Parts', from *Lessons of the War*, 1946.

The 'Phoney War' did not last. On 13 May 1940, while German armies swept across the Meuse into France, Winston Churchill made his first speech as Prime Minister to the House of Commons:

I have nothing to offer but blood, toil, tears and sweat. ... You ask, What is our policy? I will say: It is to wage war, by sea, land and air, with all our might and with all the strength that God can give us: to wage war against a monstrous tyranny, never surpassed in the dark, lamentable catalogue of human crime. That is our policy. You ask, What is our aim? I can answer in one word: Victory – victory at all costs, victory in spite of all terror; victory, however long and hard the road may be; for without victory there is no survival.

One voice above all others rallied the nation on the day of the final evacuation from Dunkirk – and on many subsequent occasions:

We must be very careful not to assign to this deliverance the attributes of a victory. Wars are not won by evacuations. But there was a victory inside this deliverance, which should be noted. ...

We are told that Herr Hitler has a plan for invading the British Isles. This has often been thought of before. When Napoleon lay at Boulogne for a year with his flat-bottomed boats and his Grand Army he was told by someone: 'There are bitter weeds in England.' There are certainly a great many more of them since the British Expeditionary Force returned. ...

Even though large tracts of Europe and many old and famous States have fallen or may fall into the grip of the Gestapo and all the odious apparatus of Nazi rule, we shall not flag or fail. We shall go on to the end. We shall fight in France, we shall fight in the seas and oceans, we shall fight with growing confidence and growing strength in the air; we shall defend our Island, no matter what the cost may be. We shall fight on the beaches, we shall fight on the landing-grounds, we shall fight in the fields and in the streets, we shall fight in the hills; we shall never surrender.

Winston Churchill (1874–1965), speech, House of Commons, 4 June 1940.

On 18 June Churchill again addressed the House of Commons. The speech was subsequently broadcast:

What General Weygand called the Battle of France is over. I expect that the Battle of Britain is about to begin. Upon this battle depends the survival of Christian civilisation. Upon it depends our own British life, and the long continuity of our institutions and our Empire. The whole fury and might of the enemy must very soon be turned on us. Hitler knows that he will have to break us in this Island or else lose the war. If we can stand up to him, all Europe may be free and the life of the world may move forward into broad, sunlit uplands. But if we fail, then the whole world, including the United States, including all that we have known and cared for, will sink into the abyss of a new Dark Age, made more sinister, and perhaps more protracted, by the lights of perverted science. Let us therefore brace ourselves to our duties, and so bear ourselves that, if the British Empire and its Commonwealth last for a thousand years, men will still say: 'This was their finest hour'.

Many people in England, it seems, relished the purity and nobility of being alone and *in extremis*:

> At last the push of time has reached it; realer
> Today than for centuries England is on the map
> As a place where something happens, as a springboard or a trap.
>
> Roy Fuller (1912–91), 'August 1940', in *The Middle of a War*, 1942.

Personally I feel happier now that we have no allies to be polite to & to pamper.
George VI (1894–1952), letter to his mother, Queen Mary, 27 June 1940.

Now we know where we are! No more bloody allies!
Tug boat skipper, shouted remark to A.P. Herbert, in *Home Propaganda*, 1941. Mass Observation, (which was begun in 1937 by Tom Harrison as a survey of the habits, attitudes and experiences of ordinary British people).

People's lives took on a new significance in these circumstances, a fact that Pierre Maillaud, a Frenchman in England at the time, celebrated in his 1945 book, *The English Way*:

All nations have their peculiar weaknesses, faults, even permanent deficiencies inherent in their geography, temperament, historical heritage, as well as their periods of lowered vitality. The distinctive feature of great nations is not their ability to behave well or righteously at all times, which is impossible and, even if it were possible would probably be a sign of mere spineless mediocrity. What singles them out is their capacity to produce greatness at a vital moment and, by an act of supreme greatness, so to redeem their own failings and so to shape history as to strengthen their own fabric for a long period to come. On 19 June 1940, England redeemed all her past failings. Germany had planned to cast history 'for a thousand years' in a mould of her own. Britain broke that mould and thus set history free. On that day Winston Churchill said that, come what might, generations to be would at least proclaim: 'This was their most shining hour'. It was, and will be so recorded.

A great action consists precisely in setting oneself a task far above one's normal strength, in an act of faith transcending the normal calculation of possibilities. ... All those who were witnesses of the English people's conduct during those fateful days know it for a fact that the nation then showed a supreme sense of its own greatness and a full readiness to pay the crushing price which that greatness might exact. ... There was a sense of dramatisation – of epic stardom – in the heart of most Englishmen, as there was in the heart of the fighter pilots who fought the *Luftwaffe* above their heads, and as there always is in those whose life and death, usually humble and unnoticed, suddenly assumes a fateful meaning for a large section of mankind. ...

The twelve months or so during which Britain stood alone were not only glorious pages in her history: they will remain as an epoch of her life when her people were at their best not only in those qualities which history chooses to exalt, but in those human dispositions without which history would be little more than an absurd record of meaningless battles, pompous declarations and tiresome treaties.

For it is in those dispositions, far more than the vague and changing definitions of war or peace aims, which testify to the existence of a civilisation to fight for. That in their darkest hour this people should have remained quietly human in their daily life, that they retained their tolerance and good humour at home when they had to show Spartan defiance to a hostile world – this is the real proof that their cause was good, their defence justified, and that their championship of Europe, conscious or not, was not an empty word.

Pierre Maillaud (1909–48), *The English Way*, 1945.

Churchill himself was the first to praise the spirit of his countrymen and women:

The buoyant and imperturbable temper of Britain, which I had the honour to express, may well have turned the scale. Here was this people, who in the years before the war had gone to the extreme bounds of pacifism and improvidence, who had indulged in the sport of party politics, and who, though so weakly armed, had advanced light-heartedly into the centre of European affairs, now confronted with the reckoning alike of their virtuous impulses and neglectful arrangements. They were not even dismayed. They defied all the conquerors of Europe. They seemed willing to have their Island reduced to a shambles rather than give in. ... As the commissionaire at one of the Service clubs in London said to a rather downcast member: 'Anyhow, sir, we're in the Final, and it's to be played on the Home Ground.' ...

I have often wondered however what would have happened if two hundred thousand German storm troops had actually established themselves ashore. The massacre would have been on both sides grim and great. There would have been neither mercy nor quarter. They would have used Terror, and were prepared to go to all lengths. I intended to use the slogan 'You can always take one with you'. ... This was a time when it was equally good to live or die.

Winston Churchill (1874–1965), *Their Finest Hour*, 1949.

In the battle of Britain predicted by Churchill on 18 June, Hitler's invasion plans were thwarted by the fighter pilots of the RAF:

Never in the field of human conflict was so much owed by so many to so few.

Winston Churchill (1874–1965), speech, House of Commons, 20 August 1940.

The legend of 'the Few' was turned to cliché in a myriad stories and films of the 1940s and 1950s, thus inviting the satirical attention of a younger generation. Here are Alan Bennett, Peter Cook, Dudley Moore and Jonathan Miller in a sketch from *Beyond the Fringe*:

MOORE: Please sir, I want to join the Few.

MILLER: I'm sorry, there are far too many.

COOK: From the rugby fields into the air.

MILLER: From the squash courts into the clouds.

BENNETT: From the skiffs into the Spitfires.

MILLER: This was war.

BENNETT: I had a pretty quiet war, really. I was one of the Few. We were
    stationed down at Biggin Hill. One Sunday we got word that Jerry was coming

in – over Hastings, I think it was. We got up there as quickly as we could, and everything was very calm and peaceful. England lay like a green carpet below me, and the war seemed worlds away. I could see Tunbridge Wells, and the sun glistening on the river, and I remembered that last weekend I'd spent there with Celia that summer of '39, and her playing the piano in the cool of the evening. Suddenly, Jerry was coming at me out of a bank of cloud. I let him have it, and I think I must have got him in the wing because he spiralled past me out of control. As he did so – I will always remember this – I got a glimpse of his face, and, you know – he smiled. Funny thing, war.

(There is the sound of hearty singing. Cook enters)

COOK: Perkins! Sorry to drag you away from the fun, old boy. War's not going very well, you know.

MILLER: Oh my God!

COOK: We are two down, and the ball's in the enemy court. War is a psychological thing, Perkins, rather like a game of football. You know how in a game of football ten men often play better than eleven –?

MILLER: Yes, sir.

COOK: Perkins, we are asking you to be that one man. I want you to lay down your life, Perkins. We need a futile gesture at this stage. It will raise the whole tone of the war. Get up in a crate, Perkins, pop over to Bremen, take a shufti, don't come back. Goodbye, Perkins. God, I wish I was going too.

MILLER: Goodbye, sir – or is it – au revoir?

COOK: No, Perkins.

'Aftermyth of War', from *Beyond the Fringe*, 1961.

There were many who did not, in reality, come back. This poem is by Olivia Fitzroy, whose boyfriend, an RAF pilot, was killed near the end of the war.

'Good show!' he said, leaned back his head and laughed.
'They're wizard types!' he said, and held his beer
Steadily, looked at it and gulped it down
Out of its jam-jar, took a cigarette
And blew a neat smoke ring into the air.
'After this morning's prang I've got the twitch;
I thought I'd had it in that teased-out kite.'
His eyes were blue, and older than his face,
His single stripe had known a lonely war
But all his talk and movements showed his age.
His whole life was the air and his machine,
He had no thought but of the latest 'mod',
His jargon was of aircraft or of beer.
'And what will you do afterwards?' I said,
Then saw his puzzled face and held my breath.
There was no afterwards for him, but death.

Olivia Fitzroy (1921–69), 'Fleet Fighter'.

After the victory of 'the Few', Hitler turned to the night-time bombing of British cities – the Blitz. The English reacted with good humour, as the following pieces show.

MORE OPEN THAN USUAL
Common sign in bomb-damaged shops, from 1940.

BE GOOD – WE'RE STILL OPEN
Sign on a boarded-up window of a police station, Southampton, 1941, reported by Mass Observation.

Young woman to her boyfriend, emerging from a public surface shelter during an air raid, 1940:

I can't stop now, Tom, really. I must get down the shelter, Mum'll be worrying. But I'll see you tomorrow, same time, same sandbag.

Overheard by Barbara Nixon in *Raiders Overhead*, 1943.

One evening when I was leaving for an inspection on the East Coast, on my way to King's Cross the sirens sounded, the streets began to empty, except for long queues of very tired, pale people, waiting for the last bus that would run. An autumn mist and drizzle shrouded the scene. The air was cold and raw. Night and the enemy were approaching. I felt, with a spasm of mental pain, a deep sense of the strain and suffering that was being borne throughout the world's largest capital city. How long would it go on? ... I was coming in one night to the Annexe when there was a lot of noise and something cracked off not far away, and I saw in the obscurity seven or eight men of the Home Guard gathered about the doorway on some patrol or duty. We exchanged greetings, and a big man said from among them: 'It's a grand life, if we don't weaken.'

Winston Churchill (1874–1965), *Their Finest Hour*, 1949.

I'VE GOT A BOMB STORY TOO
Lapel badge prevalent in London, from 1940.

The East End of London took the brunt of the bombing in the Blitz, but Buckingham Palace also took a hit:

I'm glad we've been bombed. It makes me feel I can look the East End in the face.

Queen Elizabeth, wife of King George VI, reported remark to a policeman, 13 September 1940.

But the Blitz failed to break the spirit of the English:

When I warned them [the French Government] that Britain would fight on alone whatever they did, their generals told their Prime Minister and his divided Cabinet, 'In three weeks England will have her neck wrung like a chicken.' Some chicken! Some neck!

Winston Churchill (1874–1965), speech to the Canadian Parliament, 30 December 1941. The phrase had been used by the French commander in chief General Maxime Weygand on 5 June 1940.

People suffered, but mostly were not prepared to let their suffering show:

Sometimes I say if we could stand Monday, we could stand anything. But sometimes I feels I can't stand it any more. But it don't do to say so. If I says anything my girls say to me, 'Stop it, Ma! It's no good saying you can't stand it. You've got to!' My girls is ever so good.

Anonymous Portsmouth woman, in *Second Portsmouth Report*, Mass Observation.

> Still falls the Rain –
> Dark as the world of man, black as our loss –
> Blind as the nineteen hundred and forty nails
> Upon the Cross.

Edith Sitwell (1887–1964), 'Still Falls the Rain', 1942.

We must just Keep Buggering On.

Winston Churchill (1874–1965), frequent remark (abbreviated to 'KBO') from late 1940 onwards.

The following passage recalls the attitude of ordinary soldiers in the First World War – as expressed by Gunner Hiram Sturdy above – towards their captured enemy:

As I was driving home I realised that I, a civilian, had just experienced my first taste of war, and that I disliked it intensely. I was dead keen to hunt that fellow, felt the same exhilaration as I did when hounds were running, and would have shot him on the instant if need be. But, somehow, when he was caught I had no further quarrel with him.

A.G. Street, Wiltshire Home Guard, on a German airman who turned out to be 'a very ordinary, decent-looking lad', in *From Dusk to Dawn*, 1947.

Not all downed pilots were so lucky. In 1940 one man baled out of his fighter over Wapping, and landed injured in the busy street below. Because no one could understand what he said, he was taken for a German and beaten to death, in reprisal for all the raids the people there had suffered. Only later did it transpire that he was a Pole fighting with the RAF.

As the Blitz continued, demands for retaliation grew:

One day after luncheon the Chancellor of the Exchequer, Kingsley Wood, came to see me on business at No. 10, and we heard a very heavy explosion take place across the river in South London. I took him to see what had happened. The bomb had fallen in Peckham. It was a very big one – probably a land-mine. It had completely destroyed or gutted twenty or thirty small three-storey houses and cleared a considerable open space in this very poor district. Already little pathetic Union Jacks had been stuck up amid the ruins. When my car was recognised the people came running from all quarters, and a crowd of more than a thousand soon gathered. All these folk were in a high state of enthusiasm. They crowded round us, cheering and manifesting every sign of lively affection, wanting to touch and stroke my clothes. One would have thought I had brought them some fine substantial benefit which would improve their lot in life. I was completely undermined, and wept. Ismay [General Hastings Ismay, Churchill's chief of staff

1940–46], who was with me, records that he heard an old women say, 'You see, he really cares. He's crying.' They were tears not of sorrow but of wonder and admiration. … When we got back to the car a harsher mood swept over this haggard crowd. 'Give it 'em back,' they cried, and 'Let *them* have it too.' I undertook forthwith to see that their wishes were carried out; and this promise was certainly kept. The debt was repaid tenfold, twentyfold, in the frightful routine bombardment of German cities, which grew in intensity as our air-power developed, as the bombs became far heavier and the explosives more powerful. Certainly the enemy got it all back in good measure, pressed down and running over. Alas for poor humanity!

Winston Churchill (1874–1965), *Their Finest Hour*, 1949.

In his diary, George Orwell noted the brutalising effect of the war:

The Germans never admit damage to military objectives, but they acknowledge civilian casualties after our bigger raids. After the Hamburg raid of 2 nights ago they described the casualties as heavy. The papers here reproduce this with pride. Two years ago we would all have been aghast at the idea of killing civilians. I remember saying to someone during the blitz, when the RAF were hitting back as best they could, 'In a year's time you'll see headlines in the *Daily Express*: "Successful Raid on Berlin Orphanage. Babies Set on Fire".' It hasn't come to that yet, but this is the direction we are going in.

George Orwell (1903–50), diary, 28 July 1942.

In the early summer of 1941, following the German airborne attack on Crete, there were fears of a new kind of invasion:

Prime Minister to Secretary of State for War and C.I.G.S.

29 June 41

We have to contemplate the descent from the air of perhaps a quarter of a million parachutists, glider-borne or crash-landed aeroplane troops. Everyone in uniform, and anyone else who likes, must fall upon these wherever they find them and attack them with the utmost alacrity –

    'Let everyone
    Kill a Hun.'

… No building occupied by troops should be surrendered without having to be stormed. Every man should have a weapon of some kind, be it only a mace or a pike. The spirit of intense individual resistance to this new form of sporadic invasion is a fundamental necessity. I have no doubt a great deal is being done. …

I should like Sir Alan Brooke [commander in chief, Home Forces] to see this minute and enclosure, and to give me his views about it. Let me also see some patterns of maces and pikes.

Winston Churchill (1874–1965), *The Grand Alliance*, 1950, Appendix D.

For children, the war was strange, wonderful, confusing:

> My mother is ironing scraps of paper
> we've saved for the wounded soldiers.
> To patch their bullet-holes?
> To make neat chimneys
> for the smoke inside their bones
> to flow more easily away?
> To manufacture artificial limbs?
> Mr Rigby hides his limp,
> but when he leapt across the daffodils
> to catch my green balloon
> his left leg glinted in the sun.
>
> The bomb crater, up Gasworks Lane,
> is disappointing,
> cold, dry, no sign of blood,
> no face-shapes blasted in the sand.
> Too shallow, even, for the patient cow
> who died last week
> in Mr Maddock's field
> – sad, stiff-tailed,
> mourned by quiet flies.
>
> Traitorous for handling
> these shrapnel shards we swap at school,
> their colour greasy to the touch,
> we inspect our hands for warts
> or grey stigmata.
>
> Who are these enemies with silly names,
> beyond our tiptoed vision
> even from the top of Frodsham Hill,
> shapes tangled
> in the wireless hiss and crackle,
> when my father spins the yellow knob?
> 'That Mr Hitler. He's a fidget,'
> said Miss Helsby
> when the firemen pulled her out.
>
> John Latham (1937–), from *All-Clear*.

Grown-ups, too, liked to cut their 'enemies with silly names' down to size. The following wonderfully childish rhyme, sung to the tune of 'Colonel Bogey', was particularly popular with marching troops:

> Hitler
> Has only got one ball,

> Goering
> Has two, but very small;
> Himmler
> Has something sim'lar,
> But poor old Goebbels
> Has no balls
> At all.

Churchill's speeches did not appeal to all:

> You've heard of fighting on the hills and beaches
>   And down the rabbit holes with pikes and bows
>
> . . .
>
> You've heard His Nibs decanting year by year
>   The dim productions of his bulldog brain,
> While homes and factories sit still to hear
>   The same old drivel dished up once again
>
> . . .
>
> O for another vast satiric comet
>   To blast this wretched tinder, branch and root.
> The servile stuff that makes a true man vomit –
>   Suck from the works to which they cling like leeches
>   Those resurrection-puddings, Churchill's speeches.

'Obadiah Hornbooke' (Alex Comfort, 1920–2000), 'Letter to an American Visitor', *Tribune*, 4 June 1943.

To which George Orwell replied:

> I'm not a fan for 'fighting on the beaches',
> And still less for the 'breezy uplands' stuff,
> I seldom listen-in to Churchill's speeches,
> But I'd far sooner hear that kind of guff
> Than your remark, a year or so ago,
> That if the Nazis came you'd knuckle under
> And peaceably 'accept the *status quo*'.
> Maybe you would! But I've a right to wonder
> Which will sound better in the days to come,
> 'Blood, toil and sweat' or 'Kiss the Nazi's bum'.

George Orwell (1903–50), 'As One Non-Combatant to Another', *Tribune*, 18 June 1943.

The stirring oratory could be tiresome even to those to whom it was applied. Here is Richard Hillary, Battle of Britain pilot, on why he wrote his classic book *The Last Enemy* (1942). Hillary was later killed in a training accident, aged 23.

I got so sick of the sop about our 'Island Fortress' and 'The Knights of the Air' that I determined to write it anyway in the hope that the next generation might realise that, while stupid, we were not that stupid, that we could remember only too well that all this has been seen in the last war, but that in spite of that and not because of it, we still thought this one worth fighting.

The poem 'Luck', written in 1942, speaks for all servicemen and women in all wars:

> I suppose they'll say his last thoughts were of simple things,
> Of April back at home, and the late sun on his wings;
> Or that he murmured someone's name
> As earth reclaimed him sheathed in flame.
> Oh God! Let's have no more of empty words,
> Lip service ornamenting death!
> The worms don't spare the hero;
> Nor can children feed upon resounding praises of his deed.
> 'He died who loved to live,' they'll say,
> 'Unselfishly so we might have today!'
> Like hell! He fought because he had to fight;
> He died that's all. It was his unlucky night.

Wing Commander Dennis McHarrie OBE, 'Luck', 1942.

During the course of 1941, the war broadened – first with Hitler's attack on the Soviet Union:

During dinner, Mr Churchill said that a German attack on Russia was now certain, and … we should go all out to help Russia. … After dinner, when I was walking on the croquet lawn with Mr Churchill, he reverted to this theme, and I asked whether for him, the arch anti-Communist, this was [not] bowing down in the House of Rimmon. Mr Churchill replied, 'Not at all. I have only one purpose, the destruction of Hitler, and my life is much simplified thereby. If Hitler invaded Hell I would make at least a favourable reference to the Devil in the House of Commons.'

Sir John Colville, private secretary to the Prime Minister, 21 June 1941, quoted in Winston Churchill, *The Grand Alliance*, 1950.

The following day, 22 June 1941, Churchill made a speech to the nation on the German invasion of the USSR:

I have to declare the decision of His Majesty's Government – and I feel sure it is a decision in which the great Dominions will in due course concur – for we must speak out now at once, without a day's delay. I have to make the declaration, but can you doubt what our policy will be? We have but one aim and one single, irrevocable purpose. We are resolved to destroy Hitler and every vestige of the Nazi regime. From this nothing will turn us – nothing. We will never parley, we will never negotiate with Hitler or any of his gang. We shall fight him by land, we shall fight him by sea, we shall fight him in the air, until, with God's help, we have rid the earth of his shadow and liberated its peoples from his yoke. Any man or state who fights on against Nazidom will have our aid. Any man or state who marches with Hitler is our foe. … That is our policy and that is our declaration. … This is no class war, but a war in which the whole British Empire and Commonwealth of Nations is engaged, without distinction of race, creed, or party.

In December Japan entered the war against the Allies with its attacks on Pearl Harbor and on British possessions in east Asia:

The War Cabinet authorised the immediate declaration of war upon Japan, for which all the formal arrangements had been made. As Eden had already started on his journey to Moscow and I was in charge of the Foreign Office I sent the following letter to the Japanese Ambassador:

> *Foreign Office, December 8th 1941*
>
> *Sir,*
>
> *On the evening of December 7th His Majesty's Government in the United Kingdom learned that Japanese forces without previous warning either in the form of a declaration of war or an ultimatum with a conditional declaration of war had attempted a landing on the coast of Malaya and bombed Singapore and Hong Kong.*
>
> *In view of these wanton acts of unprovoked aggression committed in flagrant violation of International Law and particularly of Article I of the Third Hague Convention relative to the opening of hostilities, to which both Japan and the United Kingdom are parties, His Majesty's Ambassador at Tokyo has been instructed to inform the Imperial Japanese Government in the name of His Majesty's Government in the United Kingdom that a state of war exists between our two countries.*
>
> *I have the honour to be, with high consideration,*
>
>   *Sir,*
>
>   *Your obedient servant,*
>
>   WINSTON S. CHURCHILL

Some people did not like this ceremonial style. But after all when you have to kill a man it costs nothing to be polite.

Winston Churchill (1874–1965), *The Grand Alliance*, 1950.

Meanwhile, back on the Home Front, everybody was doing their bit. For example, there was the salvage drive for iron, as recorded in one provincial newspaper:

'SMACK IN THE EYE FOR HITLER'
Burnham-on-Sea Railings for Scrap

'I can see Mr Hitler getting a nasty smack in the eye before long,' remarked Mr W. H. Hatcher at a special meeting of Burnham-on-Sea Urban Council when proposals of the Ministry of Works for appropriation of iron railings and gates were discussed.

Mr W. E. Pring inquired the position of gates of historic value or erected as memorials, and the surveyor replied that it had been arranged for the memorial gates at the seaward end of St Andrew's churchyard to remain.

Mr Cox said they should protest against taking the church gates, and also those at the entrances to the Manor Gardens, because of the possibility of cattle straying, but Mr Pring declared, 'People would rather see them take these gates than go in the cemetery robbing graves.'

The Chairman: 'We must not look at it like that. Someone else would rob them if we didn't.'

The clerk reported that it was intended to take cemetery railings and also chains and railings round graves. Altogether eighteen graves would be affected.

He also stated that people who wished to appeal could obtain the necessary forms at his office.

The *Western Daily Press*, 22 February 1943.

But things could still be serious on the Home Front – especially with the advent of Hitler's secret weapon, the V-1 flying bomb or 'doodlebug', which terrorised southern England from the middle of 1944:

Life in the civilised world.
(The family are at tea.)
Zoom–zoom–zoom!
'Is there an alert on?'
'No, it's all clear.'
'I thought there was an alert on.'
Zoom–zoom–zoom!
'There's another of those things coming!'
'It's all right, it's miles away.'
Zoom–zoom–ZOOM!
'Look out, here it comes! Under the table, quick!'
Zoom–zoom–zoom!
'It's all right, it's getting fainter.'
Zoom–zoom–ZOOM!
'It's coming back!'
'They seem to kind of circle round and come back again.
    They've got something on their tails that makes them do it.
    Like a torpedo.'
ZOOM–ZOOM–ZOOM!
'Christ! It's bang overhead!'
Dead silence.
'Now get *right* underneath. Keep your head well down.
    What a mercy baby isn't here!'
'Look at the cat! He's frightened too.'
'Of course animals *know*. They can feel the vibrations.'
BOOM!
'It's all right, I told you it was miles away.'
(Tea continues.)

George Orwell (1903–50), 'As I Please', *Tribune*, 7 July 1944.

This is my doodle-bug face. Do you like it?
It's supposed to look dreadfully brave.
Not jolly of course – that would hardly be tactful,
But ... well, sort of loving and grave.

You are meant to believe that I simply don't care
And am filled with a knowledge supernal,

Oh, well ... about spiritual things, don't you know,
Such as man being frightfully eternal.

This is my doodle-bug voice. Can you hear it?
It's thrillingly vibrant, yet calm.
If it weren't in the office, which *isn't* the place,
I'd read you a suitable psalm.

This is my doodle-bug place. Can you see me?
It's really amazingly snug.
Lying under my desk with my doodle-bug face
And my doodle-bug voice in the rug.

Virginia Graham (1912–98), 'Losing Face', in *Consider the Years*.

In May 1945 victory came at last – in Europe at least:

God bless you all. This is your victory! This is not a victory of any party or of any class. It is the victory of the cause of freedom in every land. In all our long history we have never seen a greater day than this. Everyone, man or woman, has done their best. Everyone has tried. Neither the long years, not the dangers, nor the fierce attacks of the enemy, have in any way weakened the independent resolve of the British nation. God bless you all.

Winston Churchill (1874–1965), speech, VE Day, 8 May 1945.

Well, it certainly is a great day; a great historic day. It is hard to realise now, but we shall know better later on. I feel rather like a patient coming round after a severe but successful operation. Deep down there is a feeling that all is well, and that a great oppression has been lifted, but other feelings are not so pleasant, and the nurse who pats one on the arm and shouts that all is over is excessively exasperating.

Sir Henry Tizard (1885–1959), diary entry for VE Day, 8 May 1945.

The nation had the lion's heart. I had the luck to give the roar.

Winston Churchill (1874–1965), speech on his 80th birthday, 1954.

At the time of the Dunkirk evacuation ... when Churchill made his often-quoted fighting speech, it was rumoured that what he actually said, when recording the speech for broadcasting, was: 'We will fight on the beaches, we will fight on the streets ... We'll throw bottles at the b—s, it's about all we've got left' – but, of course, the BBC's switch-censor pressed his thumb on the key at the right moment. One may assume that this story is untrue, but at the time it was felt that it ought to be true. It was a fitting tribute from ordinary people to the tough and humorous old man whom they would not accept as a peace-time leader but whom in the moment of disaster they felt to be representative of themselves.

George Orwell (1903–50), review of W.S. Churchill, *Their Finest Hour*, 1949, in the *New Leader* (New York), 14 May 1949.

Despite the final victory, there were those who felt something had been lost. Here is one anonymous woman's reaction to the nuclear bombing of Japan:

I was happier when I lay listening to bombs and daring myself to tremble; when I got romantic letters from abroad; when I cried over Dunkirk; when people showed their best sides and we still believed we were fighting to gain something.

From *Peace and the Public*, Mass Observation.

DE-MOBBED

What is left, after supreme effort, but exhaustion and ennui? Some see our post-war military role as playing our part in a global settlement in which we undertake a defining and continuing part; others, that we are flogging the dead and decomposing horse that we once rode so assuredly. Today, we tend to think of our armed forces as a cross between armed policemen and aid workers with added (but strictly limited) firepower. Some see the Falklands War as a necessary and splendid affirmation of our refusal, at no matter what cost, to allow our own people to fall under tyranny; others as the last fatuous twitching of a colonial corpse. Those who subscribe to the view that our military commanders have always fought every new war as if it were a continuation of the last one point to the Falklands campaign as evidence, and despair. Others point to it with pride as a piece of unfinished business from 1939–45. Either way, twenty years on, we could not do the same again; we don't have the ships. Opinion on our actions, as a small part of a US-led, and -dominated, force in Kosovo and Iraq, divides between seeing us as playing our part on a global stage, and playing our bit-part as a global stooge.

In under a hundred years we seem to have become, once again, a people unused to war. Perhaps the attitudes we had in the first half of the 20th century were an aberration; perhaps the only argument we now have is over whether our soldiery are a necessary evil, or one we would be better off without. It is a classically English dilemma.

In 1955, Geoffrey Gorer meditated on the martial nature or otherwise of the English nation:

I would make the assumption that fundamentally English character has changed very little in the last 150 years, and possibly longer; that the Roaring Boys and the Boys' Brigade, the ardent bull-baiters and the ardent anti-vivisectionists, the romantically criminal mobs and the prosaically law-abiding queues are made up of people of the same basic type of character. Underlying the enormous superficial changes, I believe there is a basic historical continuity.

The superficial changes are enormous, of that there is no doubt. One of the most lawless populations in the world has turned into one of the most law-abiding; a society which uninhibitedly enjoyed public floggings and public executions, dog-fights and animal baiting has turned into an excessively humanitarian, even squeamish society. ...

The reversals can, I think, all be accounted for on one principle. Up till a century ago the English were openly aggressive (John Bull, in fact) and took pleasure and pride in their truculence, their readiness to fight and to endure, and, by a simple process of partial identification, in 'game' animals which would fight, in 'game' criminals who finished a slashing career fittingly on the public gallows, and in the comical spectacles afforded by the physical mishaps and pains of others. There was little or no guilt about the expression of aggression in the appropriate situations; and there was no doubt, except in odd and rather comical cases, that every English man and woman had sufficient aggression for every possible event; there was always more potential strength than could be used, unless one had 'one's back to the wall'.

Today, unless 'one's back is to the wall', almost any overt expression of aggression is fused with guilt. ... But I do not think the aggression has disappeared, nor even much diminished in potentiality. ... If nearly all the 'human' strength is involved in keeping the forces of aggression under control, there is relatively little energy left for other pursuits. ...

The simile ... of the man keeping the door shut against the emotional force implied that this was an invariable state of affairs, that the conscience always disapproved of the release of aggression. But this is an oversimplified picture; there are occasions or situations when the conscience gives its approval to the release of aggression and then the enormous potential strength of righteous anger, of righteous indignation is released. A war in a good cause is the most obvious example: courage, daring, and the most lethal ingenuity suddenly manifest themselves in practically the whole of a most civilian population. John Citizen is transformed into John Bull with a completeness which regularly confounds our enemies and surprises our friends; instead of the strong conscience keeping the strong aggression in check, the two, in the literal as well as the metaphorical sense of the word, join forces and shape the world.

Geoffrey Gorer (1905–85), *Exploring English Character*, 1955.

During the era of National Service, the British refusal to take things military terribly seriously continued:

Last week I went into hospital with the reappearance of a minor infection from some bullet wounds received in Cyprus many years ago. A sympathetic editor to whom I reported this circumstance said he remembered the incident well, when I was machinegunned from behind by my own men.

I am not sure whether it makes one more or less ridiculous to be machinegunned from behind by one's own men or to be machinegunned from in front by oneself, which is my memory of the incident. An even more persistent piece of gossip – always emanating from someone known to the speaker who was in Cyprus at the time – is that I shot my testicles off.

Here, then, is my version of the events which led to my retirement from the Cyprus problem: The date was 9 June 1958. I was a slim, suntanned 18-year-old national service officer in a famous cavalry regiment. The morning of 9 June 1958 found me posted on the Kyrenia-Nicosia road between a Greek village called Autokoi (or something like that) and a Turkish village called Guinyeli (or something like that) with three or four armoured cars, hoping to discourage the villagers from massacring each other, if I had read my map correctly and was in the right place.

I had noticed an impediment in the elevation of the Browning machinegun in the turret of my particular armoured car and, having nothing else to do, resolved to investigate it. Seizing hold of the end with quiet efficiency, I was wiggling it up and down when I noticed it had started firing. Six bullets later I was alarmed to observe that it was firing through my chest, and got out of the way pretty sharpish. It may encourage those who have a fear of being shot to learn that it is almost completely painless, at any rate from close range with high-velocity bullets. You feel a slight tapping and burning sensation and (if shot through the chest) a little winded, but practically no pain for about three quarters of an hour afterwards when, with luck, someone will have arrived with morphine, if you are still alive. My first reaction to shooting myself in this way was not one of sorrow or despair so much as mild exhilaration. I lay down behind the armoured car and explained what had happened in words of few syllables, to incredulous murmurs of 'coo' and 'cor', while an enterprising corporal climbed into the turret and tried to stop the machinegun. That, then is my memory of the incident, although there is no particular reason why people should prefer it to other versions. The incident deprived me of a lung, a spleen, several ribs and a finger *but nothing else* (my italics).

Finally, I have a vivid memory of how I disgusted and shocked my corporal of horse (platoon sergeant) by playing a silly joke on him. He was a tough parachutist from Bristol called Chudleigh. As I lay on the ground waiting for an ambulance, I facetiously said: 'Kiss me, Chudleigh.' Plainly he did not spot the reference, and treated me with an unaccustomed reserve from that moment, even when he came to bid me goodbye on my return to England. But in the past few years I have grown to mistrust my memory. Too many people have disbelieved the story, and it is just the sort of thing one would invent whether it was true or not. Or perhaps I heard it from a friend and, ever credulous, believed it implicitly.

Auberon Waugh (1939–2001), *New Statesman,* 27 September 1974.

However, to their cost, foreigners sometimes misjudged just how martial the English could be:

The English public will not fight for the Malvinas. The English will never again go to war for a colony. ... The English will not go to war again except to defend England directly.

Report from Argentina's London Embassy to the Argentinian Foreign Ministry concerning the proposed annexation of the Falkland Islands, February 1982; quoted in John Laffin, *Fight for the Falklands,* 1982.

But some who served and died in the Falklands were disgusted at what they were being asked to do by the politicians. The following is from a letter written by Lieutenant David Tinker, RN, written on board HMS *Glamorgan* in the Falklands. He was killed in action two weeks later.

I cannot think of a single war in Britain's history which has been so pointless. ... This one is to recapture a place which we were going to leave undefended from April, and to deprive its residents of British citizenship in October. And to recapture it, having built up *their* forces with the most modern Western arms. ... Let us just hope it ends quickly. ...

The sad thing about all this, of course, is that the professional forces of both sides (not the conscripts) do what they are told. So if two megalomaniac idiots tell them to beat each other's brains out, they do; and there is no stopping them. ... I am sure the troops of both sides are a peace-loving lot (although I do wonder about the Paras and the Marines) and the news that we listen for is that of peace moves, not damage inflicted on the enemy. That, we regard as unfortunately necessary because it is the only way to end this business, which our political masters have sent us into with such glee.

Lieutenant David Tinker, RN (1957–82), letter, 28 May 1982.

The outstanding and – by contemporary standards – highly original quality of the English is their habit of not killing one another. ... It is – and this was true long before the rise of Fascism – the only country where armed men do not prowl the streets and no one is frightened of the secret police. And the whole British Empire, with all its crying abuses, its stagnation in one place and exploitation in another, at least has the merit of being internally peaceful. It has always been able to get along with a very small number of armed men, although it contains a quarter of the population of the earth. Between the wars its total armed forces amounted to about 600,000 men, of whom a third were Indians. At the outbreak of war the entire Empire was able to mobilize about a million trained men. Almost as many could have been mobilized by, say, Rumania.

George Orwell (1903–50), 'The English People', written in 1944, published in *Britain in Pictures*, 1947.

Religio Anglicorum

AND DID THOSE FEET, IN ANCIENT TIME,

WALK UPON ENGLAND'S MOUNTAINS GREEN?

AND WAS THE HOLY LAMB OF GOD

ON ENGLAND'S PLEASANT PASTURES SEEN?

AND DID THE COUNTENANCE DIVINE

SHINE FORTH UPON THOSE CLOUDED HILLS,

AND WAS JERUSALEM BUILDED HERE,

AMONG THOSE DARK SATANIC MILLS?

William Blake (1757–1827), preface to *Milton* (1802–10). Blake's verse – which has become the anthem of the Women's Institute and was the 'official' song of England football supporters in the 2000 European Championships – refers to what may be called the creation-myth of the English: that Christ voyaged to England as a boy and later stayed at Glastonbury, which became an outpost of God's kingdom on earth, and where Joseph of Aramathea brought the cup in which the crucified Christ's blood was caught: the Holy Grail. 'Jerusalem', however, refers to Blake's personal creation myth, in which Liberty (Jerusalem) is brought to the English by 'the giant Albion'. Like the Glastonbury myth, it is entirely fabulous.

England, at the start of the 21st century, has officially attained the status of almost the least religious country in the world, second only to Holland: 40% of us either don't believe in the existence of a Deity, or actively disbelieve it. Most of the rest of us have a vague sort of half-belief in the possibility of a Something, but have no inclination to investigate It, far less to exert ourselves to obey whatever It might want us to do on Its behalf. While attendance at 'fringe' churches – charismatic, evangelical, rapturous and variously fundamentalist – has increased a little, from a very small base, attendance at the 'traditional' churches – Anglican, Roman Catholic and Nonconformist – steeply and consistently declines. A small but well-publicised minority claims to adhere to a mish-mash of misunderstood and made-up bits of 'ancient religion' spiced up with stones, crystals, smelly oils and whatnot, but the sacred shrine of this quasi-religion is located in Hollywood rather than Cricklewood. Some of us are practising and religiously conscientious Muslims, Hindus or Sikhs, while Judaism in England would appear to be in much the same state as Christianity, consisting of the 'liberal', the orthodox and (easily in the majority) the indifferent.

In no other respect is England more different from America, where lack of

Christian belief is regarded by the vast majority as weird and dangerous. American politicians are required to proclaim and practise their religion loudly and frequently; if ours did that, most of us would smell a rat. Even in Scotland – where there has never been a law against Sunday trading, because until quite recently there was no need for one – attendance at the National Church has fallen by 20% in a decade. It is the English disease, perhaps; one that, in England, seems to have entered a terminal phase. For the story of the decline of Christianity in England, of religious belief itself, is like the story of its foundation and establishment, its triumphs and controversies, a peculiarly English one.

FIRST LIGHT

No one knows the extent of our powers better than He who gave us those powers. ... And He who is righteous has not will to command anything impossible; neither would He who is holy condemn a man for what he cannot help.

Pelagius (c.360–c.431), British (possibly Welsh) monk, *Epistle to Demetriades, Patrologia Latina.*

Pelagius was not English, but a Briton who may have hailed from what was later called Wales; nonetheless his voice, among the earliest Christian voices heard in these isles, has an authentic ring of Englishness in its refutation of the extreme, the unreasonable and the uncomfortable. Rejecting the doctrine of predestination and original sin, he taught that we may achieve salvation by our own conscientious efforts, and that God, a reasonable Deity, does not expect us to achieve what, by creating us, He has made unachievable. For this he was excommunicated by Pope Innocent I in 417 and subsequently persecuted, and his Celtic Church was suppressed. But his message was not lost, and his remains an authentic voice of English religious moderation. His basic tenets persisted among his own people, and were appealed to during the English Reformation; later, Charles II was, at least in part, a Pelagian.

In the words of the English King Ethelbert, and of the unknown adviser to his son-in-law Edgar, we can hear a very English sort of easy-going tolerance – and bet-hedging caution. Theirs, like Samuel Johnson's and Clement Attlee's, is a God of amelioration, of charitable judgement, of sensible morality; a God of Mitigating Circumstances; one of us.

To go back to the beginning ... Frank Morley came up with an intriguing theory about how Christianity might have taken hold in England:

In Britain, Mithra was worshipped in Roman London, and along the main Roman roads. Why was it that this religion failed, as also the Latin language failed, to get off the roads? It is possible, and without irreverence, to consider some of the adventitious aids which may have helped Christianity in the contest with Mithraism. Mithraism was a soldiers' religion; it was identified with the legionaries; it was identified with the roads. That brings me to a small and trivial thought, which I present as being no better than it is. We had a glimpse of a Roman Centurion in charge of a working-party slicing one of the Roman roads across Britain, compelling British slaves to make a scar across the native wildness. I reflect a moment on the engineering. I have made no special study of Vitruvius, but I would wager that in his time a customary method of Roman road-engineers for sighting ahead and obtaining the levels of the road to be built, was the use of what have subsequently in our language been called boning-rods. Boning-rods are commonly used in the construction of new roads today; it would require a lot of contradiction to persuade me they were not used in the time of Vitruvius. A boning-rod is a vertical upright with a horizontal cross-piece – a miniature Christian Cross. My thought is that in a mere engineering way the Roman roads in Britain were preceded by the planting ahead of the miniature crosses: that what the remorseless effort of the Roman road-builders was effecting, was the posting of a symbol before it was a symbol. I am sure the boning-rods which preceded the roads would have been signals for resentment and hostility such as a modern landholder may now feel when served with notice that pylons are about to be marched across his property by authority which he is powerless to resist. According to my speculation, the signal of the cross may have been made familiar and hateful to the Britons by the very same Roman soldiery who were advancing their own civilization and their own religion of supremacy. Looking at the cross as a British slave might see it, as symbol only at first of the contemptuous humiliation of a powerless people – so soon as it was put about that it was on the cross that Christ had been crucified, it would help to make Him one of us.

Frank Morley, *The Great North Road*, 1961.

When the Romans left in the early 5th century and the Angles and Saxons poured in to become the English, Christianity largely died out in England. The wave of missionaries that later arrived from Ireland, Scotland and Rome were given a reasonable hearing:

I see you believe what you say, or you would not have come all this way to say it. But you must not expect me to renounce immediately the customs which I and the English have followed from one generation to another. So, go on talking; no-one will interfere with you: and, if you convince us, well, of course, it follows that we will accept your message.

Ethelbert (c.552–616), Saxon King of Kent, greets Pope Gregory I's emissary Augustine at Thanet in 596. Augustine (d. 604) became the first Archbishop of Canterbury.

King Edwin of Northumbria, who was married to Ethelbert's daughter, called a council to discuss the merits of Christianity. According to Bede, he was advised as follows by a Saxon nobleman:

'Such,' he said, 'O King, seems to me the present life of men on earth, in comparison with that time which to us is uncertain, as if when on a winter's night you sit feasting with your ealdormen and thegns, a single sparrow should fly swiftly into the hall, and coming in at one door, instantly fly out through another. In that time in which it is indoors it is indeed not touched by the fury of the winter, but yet, this smallest space of calmness being passed almost in a flash, from winter going into winter again, it is lost to your eyes. Somewhat like this appears the life of man; but of what follows or what went before, we are utterly ignorant. Wherefore if this new learning has brought us any better surety, it may be worthy to be followed.'

Bede (673–735), *Ecclesiastical History of England*, Book 2, chapter 13.

Who liveth alone longeth for mercy,
Maker's mercy. Though he must traverse
tracts of sea, sick at heart,
– trouble with oars, ice-cold waters,
the ways of exile, – Wyrd is set fast.

The Wanderer, copied c.975 and contained in the 'Exeter Book', presented by Bishop Leofric (d.1072) to Exeter Cathedral. *Wyrd* means 'Fate'.

Whoever he may be that is willing to suffer for his faith, whether he be little lad or grown man, Jew or Gentile, Christian or Infidel, man or woman, it matters not at all; whoever dies for justice dies a martyr, a defender of Christ's cause.

John of Salisbury (c.1115–80), Bishop of Chartres. Quoted in Peter Vansittart, *In Memory of England*, 1998.

TURBULENCE, SCHISM AND SETTLEMENT

Protestantism, rising in Europe in revulsion at the excesses and corruptions of Rome and finding its religious expression in a desire to commune directly with God, had spread to England by the reign of Henry VIII. But the King himself was no Protestant; the title 'Defender of the Faith' was bestowed on him by Pope Leo X in recognition of his zeal against the Protestants. It was the Church in England, not a 'Church of England' that he desired to lead. The same power struggle that had arisen between Henry II and Thomas à Becket – simply, the question of whether King or Pope were to exercise supreme authority in the realm – was carried on in Henry's reign, and it was brought to a head by the King's desire to divorce Catherine of Aragon and marry Anne Boleyn. A book by William Tyndale, quoted below, brought matters to a head: Henry declared himself to be, in effect, his own Pope, divorced his wife, set about plundering the religious houses to restore his depleted Treasury, commissioned an official translation of the Bible, and declared England an Empire. Anne was crowned Queen by a new Archbishop of Canterbury, Thomas Cranmer, and the English Catholic Church, with Henry as its Supreme Head – its doctrines unchanged but its Pope reduced to the title of 'Bishop of Rome' – became a practical and increasingly efficient expression of a new, xenophobic nationalism under a 'Vicar General', Thomas Cromwell. Henry's former Chancellor, Thomas More, a burner of heretics and books (including many of Tyndale's) refused to swear the new Oath of Supremacy and was executed in 1535; 400 years later Pope Leo XIII canonised him, and in 2000 Pope John Paul II made him the patron saint of politicians.

Reformation was political under Henry, and became nationalistic; under his successor, the zealously Protestant boy-king Edward VI, it finally became religious. Now the customs and doctrines of Catholicism were extirpated and the Church stripped – quite literally – to its bare essentials. The Faith of which Henry had begun as the Defender and ended as the Supreme Head, was outlawed, though nobody was burned for it. No sooner had the new Protestant Church of England – with its Book of Common Prayer and over 60 translations of the Bible – been established than it was itself outlawed; Edward VI died and was succeeded by his fanatically Catholic elder sister, Mary I, daughter of Catherine of Aragon and wife of Philip of Spain. Not only were its bishops and ministers, including Cranmer, its scholars and leading adherents tortured and burned; so were ordinary people, in their hundreds. Mary, a popular and sympathetic queen at her accession, died largely unmourned.

Elizabeth, Mary's younger sister, was crowned Queen and instructed the priests in the royal chapel to extinguish the candles, 'for we see very clearly'. Elizabeth I styled herself Supreme Governor, rather than Supreme Head, of the Church of England, and set about uniting her country under a more benign, but always watchful, Protestantism. In 1570 the Pope promised a martyr's throne in heaven to anyone who would assassinate her. In 1588 a Holy Armada sailed from Spain to attempt conquest. Church – the Reformed, Established, Protestant Church of England – and State were now inextricably inter-linked: 'God breathed', announced the medals coined to celebrate the Armada's defeat, 'and they were scattered'. The religion of the English was a matter not only of devotion and salvation but also of national security, civic order and public peace; any threat to it, either from Rome or from Puritans at home, must be squeezed out. Elizabeth chose as her successor the Protestant King James VI of Scotland; as James I of England he published an Authorised edition of the Bible in 1611, as much to consolidate as to enlighten.

Under James's despotic successor Charles I, the opposition came not from Rome but from the anti-establishment party, the Puritans, and their 'chief of men', the army general Oliver Cromwell. Under his Commonwealth, England was a republican fundamentalist theocracy; after it, fundamentalism and fanaticism were banished to the fringes of English religious life. The Puritans, once feared, could now be satirised. But a new constitution prevailed, in fact if not in word, under the restored King Charles II – and his successor, the Roman Catholic James II, was found to be in breach of it. A Declaration of Indulgence, promising liberty of conscience for all denominations, might be one thing if proclaimed by a Protestant prince with a proper sense of his place in the State; coming from a potential absolutist, suspected of wishing to open the gate to England's enemies, it was not acceptable – especially after a Protestant rebellion, led by Charles II's bastard son James, Duke of Monmouth, was put down with bloody severity, as if the nightmare days of 'Bloody Mary' had returned. James was driven out in 1688, and the Dutch prince, William of Orange – married to James's Protestant daughter Mary – was invited to succeed him. The high summer of Anglicanism had begun.

Henry VIII dissolved the monasteries and left them to fall into ruin. Centuries later they were to provide Gothic novelists with haunted settings and Romantic poets with objects of melancholy contemplation:

> Threats come which no submissions may assuage;
> No sacrifice avert, no power dispute;
> The tapers shall be quenched, the belfries mute.
> And, 'mid their choirs unroofed by selfish rage,

The warbling wren shall find a leafy cage;
The gadding bramble hang her purple fruit;
And the green lizard and the gilded newt
Lead unmolested lives, and die of age.
The owl of evening and the woodland fox
For their abodes the shrines of Waltham choose:
Proud Glastonbury can no more refuse
To stoop her head before these desperate shocks –
She whose high pomp displaced, as story tells,
Arimathean Joseph's wattled cells.

William Wordsworth (1770–1850), 'Dissolution of the Monasteries' in *Ecclesiastical Sonnets*,
1822. The Glastonbury Thorn, supposedly sprung from the staff of Joseph of Arimathea
(who was believed to be buried there), was chopped down by a zealous Puritan.

In the 14th century the reformer John Wyclif (c.1330–84) commissioned the first translation
of the Bible into English – a move decried by the Church authorities, as it would allow the
common people to make their own interpretations of the Gospels:

This Master John Wyclif translated from Latin into English – the Angle not the
angel speech – and so the pearl of the Gospel is scattered abroad and trodden
underfoot by swine.

Anonymous contemporary of Wyclif; quoted in McCrum, Cran and McNeil, *The Story of English*,
1986. In 1379 Wyclif was sentenced to death for rejecting the doctrine of transubstantiation, but
was saved by a riot.

Reformers continued to translate the Bible into the common tongue. Here are the opening
verses of the Gospel of St John as translated by William Tyndale in the early 16th century:

In the beginning was that word, and that word was with god: and god was that
word. All things were made by it, and without it was made nothing that made was.
In it was life; And life was the light of men; and the light shineth in darkness; and
darkness comprehended it not.

William Tyndale (c.1494–1536), translation of the New Testament from the Greek, printed in
Worms, Germany, 1526.

One king, one law, is God's ordinance in every realm.

William Tyndale (c.1494–1536), *On the Obedience of a Christian Man and how Christian Rulers
Ought to Govern*, 1528.

The English Bible was published, according to Archbishop Cranmer, for 'all manner of persons of
whatever estate or condition'. However, in 1546 Henry VIII forbade women and the lower
orders from reading it. Around this time, a shepherd inscribed the following in a religious tract:

I bought this book when the testament was abrogated that shepherds might not
read it. I pray God amend that blindness. Writ by Robert Williams, keeping sheep
upon Saintbury Hill.

Quoted in Simon Schama, *A History of Britain*, 2000.

Henry VIII conducted the English version of Mao Zedong's Cultural Revolution. In 1536 he kicked off with an attack on the smaller religious houses:

Forasmuch as manifest sin, vicious, carnal and abominable living is daily used and committed amongst the little and small abbeys, priories, and other religious houses of monks, canons, and nuns, where the congregation of religious persons is under the number of twelve persons, whereby the governors of such religious houses and their convents, spoil, destroy, consume, and utterly waste as well their churches, monasteries, priories, principal houses, farms, granges, lands, tenements, and hereditatements, as the ornaments of their churches and their goods and chattels to the high displeasure of Almighty God, slander of good religion, and to the greater infamy of the King's Highness and realm, if redress should not be had thereof, and albeit that many continual visitations hath been heretofore had by the space of 200 years and more, for an honest and charitable reformation of such unthrifty, carnal, and abominable living, yet nevertheless little or none amendment, and by cursed custom so rooted, and infested, that a great number of the religious persons in such small houses do choose to rove abroad in apostasy than to conform to the observation of good religion, so that without such small houses be utterly suppressed and the religious persons therein committed to great and honorable monasteries of religion in this realm, where they may be compelled to live religiously for reformation of their lives ... there can else be no reformation in this behalf.

An Act for the Dissolution of the Monasteries, 1536.

Later, the 'great and honorable monasteries' were themselves suppressed and plundered.

Some scholars bemoaned the loss of the monasteries' libraries:

To destroye all without consyderacyon, is and wyll be unto England for ever, a most horrible infamy among the grave senyours of other nacyons. A great nombre of them which purchased those superstycyouse mansions [the monasteries], reserved of those lybrarye bokes, some to serve theyr iakes [to use as lavatory paper], some to scoure theyr candelstyckes, & some they sent over see to the boke-bynders, not in small nombre, but at tymes whole shyppes full, to the wonderynge of the foren nacyons.

John Bale (1495–1563), bibliophile, prelate and author, Preface to John Leland (c.1506–52), *The Laboryouse Journey and Serche for Englandes Antiquitees*, 1549.

Leland, on commission from Henry VIII to seek and catalogue the libraries of the monasteries, was one of the last people to visit Glastonbury before its destruction. Leland's request to Thomas Cromwell, that his commission be extended to allow him to rescue the libraries' contents, to give 'profit to students and great succour to this realm', was refused; of the many thousand books in Glastonbury's library, forty are known to survive.

Daniel Defoe, writing at the end of the following century, was as cynical about Henry VIII's motives as he was censorious of the goings-on in the dissolved monasteries:

When I review the past times, and look back upon the various scenes, which they present us as to ecclesiastical transactions within this kingdom, there seems nothing more strange than the turns we have had from Popish to regal supremacy, from the Romish religion to reformed, from reformed back again to Romish, and then to reformed again, and so on through several degrees of reformation, and back again from those degrees to the first steps of reformation, and then forward again.

King Henry the 8th, a prince of a haughty spirit, disdaining the insolence with which his predecessors were treated by the Popes, gave the first shock to the Roman power in these kingdoms. I won't say he acted from any principles of conscience, whatever his ambition and interest led him to pretend; but that, as it is in most cases of public revolutions, was the gloss; however it was, having satisfied his pride by subduing the supremacy of the Pope, and establishing his own; his interest next guided him to the suppression of abbeys and monasteries; the horrible vices which were protected, as well as practised in those nests of superstition, giving his pretence of piety the larger scope; and I'll for once be so free with the character of that prince, as to suppose what to me seems plain, that neither this religion, or that, were of much moment in his thoughts, but his interest, as the sequel made plain, by the seizure he made of the revenues of the Church. And yet the justice of Providence seemed very conspicuous in that point, that those houses who under the specious pretences of religion and extraordinary devotion, had amassed to themselves vast revenues to the impoverishing many families, and in the meantime practised secretly most unheard-of wickedness, should under the same pretence of zeal and piety be suppressed and impoverished by a person, who merely to serve his own glory, triumphed over them, pretending, Jehu-like, *to shew his zeal for the Lord.*

Some do assure us, that the eyes of this prince were really opened as to the point of religion; and that had he lived longer, he would most effectually have established the Reformation in his time; but God, who gave him that light, *if he had it,* however he might accept his intention, as he did that of David's building his house, yet he reserved the glory of the performance to his son.

King Edward the 6th, of whom wondrous things are spoken in all our English writers, and more than we need suppose should be literally true; yet was, without doubt, a prince of the strictest piety, not only that ever reigned, but that ever lived, perhaps, since the days of Josiah, whose parallel our writers say he was.

The Reformation began in his hand; not but that the Protestant religion had been received in England many years before, by the preaching of John Wickliff, William Tindall, and others, and had many professors, and those such, who gallantly offered their lives in defence of the truth.

But it got but little ground; for religion has but few votaries, while all its professors must also be confessors, and while exile or martyrdom is all the present prospect of advantage to be got by it.

None will dare to be Dissenters in times of danger, but such whose consciences are so awakened that they dare not be otherwise.

But in the hands of this young prince, the great work was begun, and in a shorter time than could be imagined, was finished and established; the Romanists fled or conformed; for we find but very few had any inclination to martyrdom if it had been put upon them.

Daniel Defoe (c.1660–1731), *An Enquiry into the Occasional Conformity of Dissenters*, 1697.

It was under Henry VIII's son, Edward VI, that the real *theological* Reformation got under way. One of the main points at issue is here laid out by Archbishop Thomas Cranmer – and it was for these words that he was later to be burnt at the stake (see below):

The roots of the weeds, is the popish doctrine of transubstantiation, of the real presence of Christ's flesh and blood in the sacrament of the altar (as they call it), and of sacrifice and oblation of Christ by the priest, for the salvation of the quick and dead.

Thomas Cranmer (1489–1556), Archbishop of Canterbury; quoted in E.P. Echlin, *The Story of Anglican Ministry*, 1974.

It was Cranmer who introduced The Book of Common Prayer. The extract that follows is taken from his Preface:

It hath been the wisdom of the Church of England, ever since the compiling of her first public Liturgy, to keep the mean between the two extremes, of too much stiffness in refusing, and of too much easiness in admitting any variation from it. For, as on the one side common experience sheweth, that where a change hath been made of things advisedly established (no evident necessity so requiring) sundry inconveniences have thereupon ensued; and those many times more and greater than the evils that were intended to be remedied by such change; So on the other side, the particular Forms of Divine worship, and the Rites and Ceremonies appointed to be used therein, being things in their own nature indifferent, and alterable, and so acknowledged; it is but reasonable, that upon such weighty and important considerations, according to the various exigency of times and occasions, such changes and alterations should be made therein, as to those that are in Authority should from time to time seem either necessary or expedient. ...

Though it be appointed, that all things shall be read or sung in the Church in the English Tongue, to the end that the congregation may be thereby edified; yet it is not meant, but that when men say Morning and Evening prayer privately, they may say the same in any language that they themselves do understand.

Thomas Cranmer (1489–1556), Archbishop of Canterbury, Preface to The Book of Common Prayer, 1548, revised 1552.

While Henry VIII had destroyed the monasteries, the Protestant reformers set about the churches: the vast majority of wall paintings were whitewashed or plastered over, while statues, carvings and stained glass windows were smashed. However, as this 'post-Reformation decorators' bill' from Telscombe, Sussex, shows, some churches managed to keep their decorations:

To renovating heaven and adjusting the stars, washing servant of the High Priest and putting carmine on his cheeks, and brightening up the flames of hell, putting a new tail on the Devil, and doing odd jobs for the damned, and correcting the Ten Commandments.

Quoted in Peter Vansittart, *In Memory of England*, 1998.

O my Lord God, deliver this realm from papistry.

The supposed last words of Edward VI (1537–53).

It was not to be. After Edward's death an attempt to place the Protestant Lady Jane Grey on the throne was foiled, and she was beheaded as the Catholic Mary took the crown and set about reversing the Protestant Reformation:

There were burnt 5 bishops, 21 divines, 8 gentlemen, 84 artificers, 100 husband-men, servants and labourers, 26 wives, 9 virgins, 2 boys, and 2 infants. 64 more were persecuted for their religion, whereof 7 were whipped, 16 perished in prison and 12 were buried in dunghills.

John Foxe (1516–87), *Acts and Monuments*, 1563, better known as 'Foxe's Book of Martyrs', detailing the depredations of Queen Mary from 1555 to 1558. The last five victims, three men and two women, were burned at Canterbury a week before Mary's death.

Among the victims were Nicholas Ridley, formerly Bishop of London, and the popular preacher Hugh Latimer. Both refused to accept papal authority and doctrine, and were burnt together at the stake:

Be of good comfort, Master Ridley, and play the man. We shall this day light such a candle by God's grace in England, as (I trust) shall never be put out.

Hugh Latimer (c.1485–1555), 16 October 1555.

The following year it was the turn of Cranmer, who was forced to recant his Protestant beliefs under torture. However, at the service before his execution in Oxford he renounced all that he had signed under duress:

I renounce and refuse as things written with my hand contrary to the truth which I thought in my heart, and written in fear of death and to save my life if it might be; and that is, all such bills which I have written or signed with mine own hand since my degradation: wherein I have written many things untrue. And forasmuch as my hand offended in writing contrary to my heart, therefore my hand shall be first punished; for if I may come to the fire, it shall be first burned. And as for the Pope, I refuse him as Christ's enemy and anti-Christ, with all false doctrine. And as for the Sacrament –

Cranmer was dragged away before he could finish but, at the stake, he stretched out his hand into the fire and cried:

This hand hath offended.

Thomas Cranmer (1489–1556), Archbishop of Canterbury, 21 March 1556.

Mary was succeeded by her half-sister, the Protestant Elizabeth, who took a very English, no-nonsense approach to theological matters:

There is only one Jesus Christ. The rest is a dispute over trifles.

Elizabeth I (1533–1603) to the French Ambassador, André Hurault.

Indeed, Elizabeth is said to have described theology as:

Ropes of sand or sea-slime leading to the moon.

She summarised her approach to the vexed question of transubstantiation thus:

> Christ was the Word that spake it,
> He took the bread and brake it,
> And what his words did make it,
> That I believe and take it.

Elizabeth I (1533–1603), attributed verses in Richard Baker's *Chronicle*, 1645.

The Authorised Version of the Bible, published in 1611, was produced by a committee chaired by John Bois (1560–1643) and employed a vocabulary of just 8,000 words (Shakespeare used over 30,000). Apart from its religious importance, the Authorised, or King James, Version, along with Shakespeare and The Book of Common Prayer, has had an immense influence on the English language and its literature down the ages. One could quote endless magnificent passages, but one alone will have to serve here:

> For I am persuaded, that neither death, nor life, nor angels, nor principalities, nor powers, nor things present, nor things to come,
> Nor height, nor depth, nor any other creature, shall be able to separate us from the love of God, which is in Christ Jesus our Lord.

Authorised Version of the Bible, 1611, Romans, 8:38.

The translators, in their preface, outlined their purpose – to steer a middle course between Romishly enforced ignorance and Nonconforming waywardness:

> So that if, on the one side, we shall be traduced by Popish persons at home or abroad, who therefore will malign us, because we are poor instruments to make God's holy truth to be yet more and more known unto the people, whom they desire to keep in ignorance and darkness; or if, on the other side, we shall be maligned by self-conceited brethren, who shall run their own ways, and give liking unto nothing but what is framed by themselves, and hammered on their anvil, we may rest secure . . . .

'To the Most High and Mighty Prince James, by the Grace of God, King of Great Britain, France, and Ireland, Defender of the Faith, Etc …': from the translators' preface to the Authorised Bible, 1611.

Here is Wordsworth on the Authorised Version:

> But to outweigh all harm, the sacred Book,
> In dusty sequestration wrapt too long,
> Assumes the accents of our native tongue;
> And he who guides the plough, or wields the crook,
> With understanding spirit now may look
> Upon her records, listen to her song,
> And sift her laws – much wondering that the wrong,
> Which faith has suffered, Heaven could calmly brook.
> Transcendent boon! noblest that earthly king
> Ever bestowed to equalise and bless
> Under the weight of moral wretchedness!

But passions spread like plagues, and thousands wild
With bigotry shall tread the offering
Beneath their feet – detested and defiled.

William Wordsworth (1770–1850), 'Translation of the Bible' in *Ecclesiastical Sonnets*, 1822.

I die a Christian, according to the profession of the Church of England, as I found it left me by my father.

Charles I (1600–49), speech on the scaffold, 30 January 1649.

I desire from my heart, I have prayed for it, I have waited for the day to see union and right understanding between godly people, Scots, English, Jews, Gentiles, Presbyterians, Independents, Anabaptists, and all.

Oliver Cromwell (1599–1658), Lord Protector of the Commonwealth (1653–58), letter to the French minister Cardinal Mazarin.

With the Restoration, Puritanism once more received a bad press:

Not a religion for gentlemen.

Charles II (1630–85), on Presbyterianism.

Indeed, Charles II restored a kind of Pelagianism:

He said once to myself, he was no atheist, but he could not think God would make a man miserable only for taking a little pleasure out of the way.

Bishop Gilbert Burnet, *History of My Own Time*, 1724.

Samuel Butler satirised the Puritans in his mock romance *Hudibras*:

For his religion, it was fit
To match his learning and his wit;
'Twas Presbyterian true blue;
For he was of that stubborn crew
Of errant saints, which all men grant
To be the true Church Militant;
Such as do build their faith upon
The holy text of pike and gun;
Decide all controversies by
Infallible artillery;
And prove their doctrine orthodox
With apostolic blows and knocks;
Call fire, and sword, and desolation
A godly, thorough Reformation,
Which always must be carried on,
And still be doing, never done;
As if religion were intended
For nothing else but to be mended;

A sect whose chief devotion lies
In odd perverse antipathies;
In falling out with that and this,
And finding somewhat still amiss;
More peevish, cross, and splenetic,
Than dog distract or monkey sick;
That with more care keep holiday
The wrong, than others the right way;
Compound for sins they are inclin'd to,
By damning those they have no mind to:
Still so perverse and opposite,
As if they worshipp'd God for spite.

Samuel Butler (1612–80), *Hudibras*, 1663.

Rhymes such as the following were revived with glee:

To Banbury came I, O profane one!
Where I saw a Puritane one
Hanging of his cat on Monday
For killing of a mouse on Sunday.

Richard Brathwaite (c.1588–1673), *Barnabee's Journal*, 1638.

The Puritans' constant poring over the Scriptures, with its multiplicity of possible interpretations, exasperated many:

Scrutamini scripturas [Let us look at the Scriptures]. These two words have undone the world.

John Selden (1584–1654), 'Bible Scripture' in *Table Talk*, 1689.

The puritan hated bear-baiting, not because it gave pain to the bear, but because it gave pleasure to the spectators.

Thomas Babington, 1st Lord Macaulay (1800–59), *History of England*, 1849.

In his long poem of 1682, *Religio Laici* ('The Layman's Faith'), the Tory Poet Laureate John Dryden defended clarity, practicality, custom, individuality, community, restraint, common sense and the Anglican Church against obscurity, theoreticism, novelty, authority, faction, fanaticism, 'enthusiasm' and dissension:

The Book thus put in every vulgar hand,
Which each presum'd he best cou'd understand,
The *Common rule* was made the *common Prey*;
And at the mercy of the *Rabble* lay.
The tender Page with horny Fists was gaul'd;
And he was gifted most that loudest baul'd;
The *Spirit* gave the *Doctoral Degree*,
And every member of a *Company*
Was of *his* Trade and of the *Bible free*.

Plain *Truths* enough for needfull *use* they found;
But men wou'd still be itching to *expound*;
Each was ambitious of th'obscurest place,
No measure ta'n fro *Knowledge*, all from GRACE.
Study and *Pains* were now no more their *Care*;
Texts were explain'd by *Fasting* and by *Prayer*:
This was the Fruit the *private Spirit* brought;
Occasion'd by *great Zeal* and *little Thought*.
While crouds unlearn'd, with rude Devotion warm,
About the Sacred Viands buz and swarm,
The *Fly-blown Text* creates a *crawling brood*;
And turns to *Maggots* what was meant for *Food*.
A Thousand daily Sects rise up, and dye;
A Thousand more the perish'd Race supply:
So all we make of Heaven's discover'd Will
Is, not to have it, or to use it ill.
The Danger's much the same; on several Shelves
If *others* wreck us or *we* wreck our *selves*.

What then remains, but, waving each Extreme,
The Tides of Ignorance, and Pride to stem?
Neither so rich a Treasure to forgo;
Nor proudly seek beyond our pow'r to know:
Faith is not built on disquisitions vain;
The things we *must* believe, are *few* and *plain*;
But since men *will* believe more than they *need*;
And every man will make *himself* a Creed,
In doubtfull questions 'tis the safest way
To learn what unsuspected Ancients say:
For 'tis not likely *we* should higher Soar
In search of Heav'n than *all the Church before*:
Nor can we be deceiv'd, unless we see
The *Scripture* and the *Fathers disagree*.
If after all, they stand suspected still,
(For no man's Faith depends upon his Will;)
'Tis some Relief, that points not clearly known,
Without much hazard may be let alone:
And after hearing what our Church can say,
If still our Reason runs another way,
That private Reason 'tis more just to curb,
Than by Disputes the publick Peace disturb.
For points obscure are of small use to learn:
But *Common quiet* is *Mankind's concern*.

John Dryden (1631–1700), *Religio Laici* ('The Layman's Faith'), 1682.

Dryden steers a middle way towards the Church of England because it accommodates individual freedom within a traditional body. ... In a tone of weary yet satisfied finality the concluding passage points decisively away from appearance to the self-evidently real, regarded equally as a matter of truth and consensus. English empiricism has few better monuments.

Antony Easthope, *Englishness and National Culture*, 1999.

However, in 1685, the year that the Catholic James II mounted the throne, Dryden converted to Catholicism. In another long poem, *The Hind and the Panther* (1687), he not only attacked the Puritans but also the Church of England itself.

Among the Puritans, the best-known voice is that of John Bunyan, the son of a tinker who served with the Parliamentary Army during the Civil Wars. He went on to experience a spiritual crisis, and joined a Baptist sect in Bedford. At the Restoration he was charged with holding a Nonconformist service, and imprisoned for twelve years. During this time he began his allegorical account of a spiritual journey, *Pilgrim's Progress*, which conveys the Puritan emphasis on the importance of the individual conscience. The work, though largely in prose, contains the following verses, which have become one of the best loved of English hymns:

> Who would true valour see
> Let him come hither;
> One here will constant be,
> Come wind, come weather;
> There's no discouragement
> Shall make him once relent
> His first avow'd intent
> To be a pilgrim.
>
> Whoso beset him round
> With dismal stories,
> Do but themselves confound;
> His strength the more is.
> No lion shall him fright;
> He'll with a giant fight,
> But he will have the right
> To be a pilgrim.
>
> No goblin nor foul fiend
> Can daunt his spirit;
> He knows he at the end
> Shall life inherit.
> Then, fancies, fly away;
> He'll not fear what men say;
> He'll labour night and day
> To be a pilgrim.

John Bunyan (1628–88), from *The Pilgrim's Progress*, 1678.

Even in the religion-riven 17th century, there were voices of reason and toleration:

One religion is as true as another.

Robert Burton (1577–1640), scholar and clergyman, *The Anatomy of Melancholy*, 1621–51.

The Earl of Shaftesbury was a minister under both Cromwell and Charles II, but fled to Holland after opposing James II. He is best remembered as one of the first Deists, whose belief in God was based on reason, and largely restricted to acknowledging an initial Creator as a necessary First Cause. Of course, it did not do to publish such near-atheistical views abroad, as can be seen from this exchange:

'People differ in their discourse and profession about these matters, but men of sense are really but of one religion.' ... 'Pray, my lord, what religion is that which men of sense agree in?' 'Madam,' says the earl immediately, 'men of sense never tell it.'

Anthony Ashley Cooper, 1st Earl of Shaftesbury (1621–83), quoted in Bishop Gilbert Burnet, *History of My Own Time*, 1724.

But such voices were rare. Just as the Puritans were despised, so were the Catholics hated. During the 'Popish Terror' of 1681, Nell Gwyn, mistress of Charles II, was mistaken for the King's Catholic mistress by a hostile crowd in Oxford. With magnificent aplomb she shouted:

Pray, good people, let me pass. I am the Protestant whore.

Quoted in B. Bevan, *Nell Gwyn*, 1969.

Dean Swift, as usual, got to the quick of the matter:

We have just enough religion to make us hate, but not enough to make us love one another.

Jonathan Swift (1667–1745), Anglo-Irish poet, satirist and Dean of St Patrick's Cathedral, Dublin, *Thoughts on Various Subjects*, 1711.

Also sick of religious dispute, another embittered satirist advised:

Know then thyself, presume not God to scan;
The proper study of mankind is man.

Alexander Pope (1688–1744), *An Essay on Man*, Epistle 2, 1733.

HIGH SUMMER

The Vicar of Bray is the embodiment of the sort of Anglican clergyman who had emerged in the decades following the Restoration: a broad-bottomed self-preservationist. Under the Test Acts of William III and the Occasional Conformity Acts of Anne – measures designed to prevent religious dissenters holding office – he took on a Tory, High Church hue; under the Georges, and the threat of Jacobite Catholicism, he inclined to Whiggishness. As the 18th century gave way to the 19th, the establishment of the Church of England found room for almost the whole range of theological interior décor, from high Baroque to stripped pine. Like George Crabbe's vicar in The Village, *it sought to embrace everyone without bothering itself overmuch about theology. It became 'the one Church for the whole people of England, in its religious aspect' – assuming, that is, the whole people of England to be Protestant and Episcopalian. Towards the end of the 18th century it stood, together with the whole apparatus of the State, against the atheism and anarchy of the French Revolution, and its suspected imitators at home. Thoroughly well established and broader bottomed than ever, its opposition came not from Rome but from those who felt themselves excluded from the political and social establishment: Methodists, fighting for souls rather than preferment; Deists seeking an unsuperstitious explanation for the workings of heaven and earth alike; and 'enthusiasts' and troublemakers generally. These lessons the Church of England had learned in its three centuries of existence: that enthusiasm always causes trouble, and that those who rock the boat risk being thrown out of it. The Church absorbed what it could, bore satire with a patient smile, and shrugged off the rest.*

John Arbuthnot, the creator of John Bull, personified the Established Church thus:

The Character of John Bull's *Mother* (The C—h of E—d).

John had a Mother, whom he lov'd and honour'd extreamly, a discreet, grave, sober, good-condition'd, cleanly old Gentlewoman as ever liv'd; she was none of your cross-grain'd, termagent, scolding Jades, that one had as good be hang'd as live in the house with, such as are always censuring the conduct, and telling scandalous stories of their Neighbours, extolling their own good Qualities, and undervaluing those of others. On the contrary, she was of a meek Spirit, and as she was strictly virtuous herself, so she always put the best conjectures upon the Words and Actions of her Neighbours, except when they were irreconcileable to the Rules of Honesty and Decency. She was neither one of your precise *Prudes*, nor one of your fantastical old *Belles*, that dress themselves like Girls of Fifteen; as she neither wore a Ruff, Forehead-cloth, nor High-crown'd Hat, so she cast aside Feathers, Flowers, and crimpt Ribbons in her Head-dress, Furbelo-Scarfs, and Hoop'd Petticoats. She scorn'd to patch and paint, yet she lov'd to keep her hands and her face clean. ... She was not like some Ladies, hung about with Toys and Trinkets, Tweezer-cases, Pocket-glasses and Essence-bottles; she used only a Gold Watch and an Almanack, to mark the Hours and the Holy-days.

John Arbuthnot (1667–1735), *The History of John Bull,* 1712.

Voltaire, though generally an admirer of English tolerance, could not resist a little irony when describing its limits:

England is properly the country of sectarists. *Multae sunt mansiones in domo patris mei* (in my Father's house are many mansions). An Englishman, as one to whom liberty is natural, may go to heaven his own way. Nevertheless, though every one is permitted to serve God in whatever mode or fashion he thinks proper, yet their true religion, that in which a man makes his fortune, is the sect of Episcopalians or Churchmen, called the Church of England, or simply the Church, by way of eminence. No person can possess an employment either in England or Ireland unless he be ranked among the faithful, that is, professes himself a member of the

Church of England. This reason (which carries mathematical evidence with it) has converted such numbers of Dissenters of all persuasions, that not a twentieth part of the nation is out of the pale of the Established Church. The English clergy have retained a great number of the Romish ceremonies, and especially that of receiving, with a most scrupulous attention, their tithes. They also have the pious ambition to aim at superiority. Moreover, they inspire very religiously their flock with a holy zeal against Dissenters of all denominations.

Voltaire (François-Marie Arouet, 1694–1778), *Letters on England*, 1731.

The Vicar of Bray, eponymous 'hero' of the famous song of unknown authorship, may have been based on one Symon Symonds, vicar of Bray in Berkshire during the reigns of Henry VIII, Edward VI, Mary I and Elizabeth I, who was 'twice a Papist and twice a Protestant'. Symonds apparently stated 'If I changed my religion, I am sure I kept true to my principle, which is to live and die the vicar of Bray.'

In good King Charles's golden days
When loyalty no harm meant,
A furious High-Church man I was,
And so I gain'd preferment.
Unto my flock I daily preach'd,
Kings are by God appointed,
And damn'd are those who dare resist,
Or touch the Lord's anointed.

And this is Law I will maintain
Unto my dying day, Sir:
That whatsoever king may reign,
I will be the Vicar of Bray, Sir!

When Royal James possest the Crown
And Popery grew in fashion,
The Penal Law I hooted down
And read the Declaration;
The Church of Rome I found would fit
Full well my Constitution,
And I had been a Jesuit
But for the Revolution.

And this is Law, etc.

When William our Deliv'rer came
To heal the Nation's grievance,
I turn'd the cat in pan again,
And swore to him allegiance;
Old principles I did revoke,
Set conscience at a distance,
Passive obedience is a joke,
A jest is non-resistance.

And this is Law, etc.

When Royal Ann became our Queen
Then Church of England's glory,
Another face of things was seen,
And I became a Tory;
Occasional Conformists base
I damn'd, and Moderation,
And thought the Church in danger was
From such prevarication.

And this is Law, etc.

When George in pudding-time came o'er
And Moderate men looked big, Sir,
My principles I chang'd once more
And so became a Whig, Sir.
And thus preferment I procur'd
From our Faith's great Defender,
And almost ev'ry day abjur'd
The Pope, and the Pretender.

And this is Law, etc.

Th' illustrious House of Hanover
And Protestant succession:
To these I lustily will swear
Whilst they can keep possession;
For in my Faith, and loyalty,
I never once will falter,
But George my lawful King shall be
Except the times should alter.

And this is Law I will maintain
Until my dying day, Sir:
That whatseoever King may reign,
I will be the Vicar of Bray, Sir!

Anon., 'The Vicar of Bray', in *The British Musical Miscellany*, 1734.

When I mention religion, I mean the Christian religion; and not only the Christian religion but the Protestant religion; and not only the Protestant religion but the Church of England.

Henry Fielding (1707–54), *Tom Jones*, 1749.

They seem to know no medium between a mitre and a crown of martyrdom. If the clergy are not called to the latter, they never deviate from the pursuit of the former. One would think their motto was, *Canterbury or Smithfield*.

Horace Walpole, 4th Earl of Oxford (1717–97), *Memoirs of the Reign of King George II*, 1757.
Smithfield in London was the scene of several executions during the Reformation period.

I am afraid he has not been in the inside of a church for many years; but he never passes a church without pulling off his hat. That shows that he has good principles.

Samuel Johnson, in James Boswells, *Life of Samuel Johnson*, 1791, 1 July 1763.

I never saw, heard, nor read, that the clergy were beloved in any nation where Christianity was the religion of the country. Nothing can render them popular, but some degree of persecution.

Jonathan Swift (1667–1745), poet, satirist and Dean of St Patrick's Cathedral, Dublin, *Thoughts on Religion*, published 1765.

There were some clergymen who were 'beloved', however. One such is the vicar in Oliver Goldsmith's idealised village:

> A man he was to all the country dear,
> And passing rich on forty pounds a year;
> Remote from towns he ran his godly race,
> Nor e'er had changed, or wished to change, his place;
> Unpractised he to fawn, or seek for power,
> By doctrines fashioned to the varying hour;
> Far other aims his heart had learned to prize,
> More skilled to raise the wretched than to rise.
> His house was known to all the vagrant train,
> He chid their wanderings, but relieved their pain. ...
>   At church, with meek and unaffected grace,
> His looks adorned the venerable place;
> Truth from his lips prevailed with double sway,
> And fools, who came to scoff, remained to pray.
> The service past, around the pious man,
> With steady zeal, each honest rustic ran; ...
> To them his heart, his love, his griefs were given,
> But all his serious thoughts had rest in Heaven.

Oliver Goldsmith (1730–74), *The Deserted Village*, 1770.

George Crabbe's *The Village* is a riposte to Goldsmith's rose-tinted view of rural life. Crabbe's vicar is altogether less creditable:

> And doth not he, the pious man, appear,
> He, 'passing rich on forty pounds a year'?
> Ah! no; a shepherd of a different stock,
> And far unlike him, feeds this little flock:
> A jovial youth, who thinks his Sunday's task
> As much as God or man can fairly ask;
> The rest he gives to loves and labours light,
> To fields the morning, and to feasts the night;
> None better skill'd the noisy pack to guide,
> To urge their chase, to cheer them or to chide;

A sportsman keen, he shoots through half the day,
And, skill'd at whist, devotes the night to play.
Then, while such honours bloom around his head,
Shall he sit sadly by the sick man's bed,
To raise the hope he feels not, or with zeal
To combat fears that e'en the pious feel? ...
      Now once again the gloomy scene explore,
Less gloomy now; the bitter hour is o'er.
The man of many sorrows sighs no more. ...
Him now they follow to his grave, and stand
Silent and sad, and gazing, hand in hand;
While bending low, their eager eyes explore
The mingled relics of the parish poor. ...
The busy priest, detain'd by weightier care,
Defers his duty till the day of prayer;
And, waiting long, the crowd retire distress'd,
To think a poor man's bones should lie unbless'd.

George Crabbe (1754–1832), from *The Village*, 1783, Book I .

The later 18th century saw the Church of England – and sometimes religion more generally – attacked by Radicals and Romantics alike.

Prisons are built with stones of Law, brothels with bricks of Religion.

William Blake (1757–1827), *The Marriage of Heaven and Hell*, 1790–93, 'Proverbs of Hell'. The Church of England, in its capacity as landowner, derived a substantial income from the ground-rents of 'immoral earnings' establishments.

As to religion, I hold it to be the indispensable duty of government to protect all conscientious professors thereof, and I know of no other business which government hath to do therewith.

Thomas Paine (1737–1809), radical political theorist, and a Deist in religion, *Common Sense*, 1776.

Persecution is not an original feature of *any* religion; but it is always the strongly marked feature of all law-religions, or religions established by law. ... I do not believe that any two men, on what are called doctrinal points, think alike who think at all. It is only those who have not thought that appear to agree.

Thomas Paine (1737–1809), *The Rights of Man*, Part 2, 1792.

Paine set out his Deist principles in *The Age of Reason*:

I believe in one God, and no more; and I hope for happiness beyond this life.

    I believe the equality of man, and I believe that religious duties consist in doing justice, loving mercy, and endeavouring to make our fellow-creatures happy. ...

    I do not believe in the creed professed by the Jewish church, by the Roman church, by the Greek church, by the Turkish church, by the Protestant church, nor by any church that I know of. My own mind is my own church.

All national institutions of churches, whether Jewish, Christian, or Turkish, appear to me no other than human inventions set up to terrify and enslave mankind, and monopolize power and profit.

I do not mean by this declaration to condemn those who believe otherwise. They have the same right to their beliefs as I have to mine. But it is necessary to the happiness of man, that he be mentally faithful to himself. Infidelity does not consist in believing, or in disbelieving; it consists in professing to believe what he does not believe.

Thomas Paine (1737–1809), *The Age of Reason*, 1794, Part I.

For Blake, the Church was a polluter of innocence:

I went to the garden of love,
And saw what I never had seen:
A chapel was built in the midst,
Where I used to play on the green.

And the gates of this chapel were shut,
And *Thou shalt not* writ over the door;
So I turned to the garden of love,
That so many sweet flowers bore,

And I saw it was filled with graves,
And tomb-stones where flowers should be –
And priests in black gowns were walking their rounds,
And binding with briars my joys and desires.

William Blake (1757–1827), 'The Garden of Love', in *Songs of Experience*, 1794.

The 18th century also witnessed a great religious revival, in the form of Methodism, in which the Wesley brothers played an important role. Initially it was a Low Church movement within the Church of England, before setting up its own organisation in the 1790s. In most doctrinal matters Methodists were close to Anglicans – but not in all …

Men may call me a knave or a fool, a rascal, a scoundrel, and I am content; but they shall never by my consent call me a Bishop!

John Wesley (1703–91), a founder of Methodism; in Betty M. Jarboe, *Wesley Quotations*, 1990.

John's brother Charles is best known as a writer of hymns, of which the following is a typically muscular example:

Soldiers of Christ, arise,
    And put your armour on;
Strong in the strength which God supplies
    Through His Eternal Son;

Strong in the Lord of Hosts,
    And in His mighty power;
Who in the strength of Jesus trusts
    Is more than conqueror.

Stand then in His great might,
    With all His strength endued;
And take, to arm you for the fight,
    The panoply of God.

From strength to strength go on,
    Wrestle, and fight, and pray;
Tread all the powers of darkness down,
    And win the well-fought day.

Charles Wesley (1707–88), Methodist preacher and hymn-writer, 'The Whole Armour of God' in *Hymns and Sacred Poems*, 1749.

Not everybody regarded the Methodists and other Dissenters as models of piety and virtue. Here is a broadside from William Cobbett:

Now, as to the moral benefit arising from the teaching of Dissenting Ministers, it is sometimes very great, and I believe it is sometimes very small indeed, and, in many cases, I believe, their teaching tends to immorality and to misery.

Amongst the Ministers of some of the sects there are many truly learned and most excellent men; and even amongst the sects called Methodists there have been, and doubtless are, many men of the same description. But, on the other hand, it must be allowed that there are many of the Methodist Preachers who are fit for anything rather than *teaching* the people *morality*. I am willing to give most of them full credit for sincerity of motive, but to believe that the Creator of the Universe can be gratified with the ranting and raving and howling that are heard in some of the Meeting-Houses, is really as preposterous as any part of the Mahommedan Creed; and if possible it is still more absurd to suppose that such incoherent sounds should have a tendency to mend the *morals* of the people, to make them more honest, industrious, and public-spirited, for this last is a sort of morality by no means to be left out of the account. . . .

I must say that when I hear the Dissenters complaining of persecution, I cannot help reflecting on the behaviour of some of them towards the *Catholics*, with respect to whom common decency ought to teach them better behaviour. But, whether I hear in a Churchman or a Dissenter abuse of the Catholics, I am equally indignant; when I hear men, no two of whom can agree in any one point of religion, and who are continually dooming each other to perdition; when I hear them join in endeavouring to shut the Catholic out from political liberty on account of his religious tenets*, which they call idolatrous and damnable, I really cannot feel any compassion for either of them, let what will befall them. There is, too, something so impudent; such cool impudence in their affected contempt of the understanding of the Catholics, that one cannot endure it with any degree of patience. You hear them all boasting of their *ancestors*; you hear them talking of the English Constitution as the pride of the world; you hear them bragging of the deeds of the Edwards and the Henrys; and of their wise and virtuous and brave forefathers;

---

* Until the 1829 Emancipation Act, Roman Catholics were barred from public office.

and, in the next breath, perhaps, you will hear them speak of the Catholics as the vilest and most stupid of creatures, and as wretches doomed to perdition; when they ought to reflect that all these wise and virtuous and brave forefathers of theirs were *Catholics*; that they lived and died in the Catholic faith; and that notwithstanding their Catholic faith they did not neglect whatever was necessary to the freedom and greatness of England. ... There is something so unnatural, so monstrous, in a line of conduct in which we say *that our forefathers are all in Hell*, that no one but a brutish bigot can hear of it with patience. ...

But *my* great dislike to them is grounded on their politics, which are the very worst in the country; and though I am aware that there must be many very honourable exceptions amongst them I must speak of them as *a body*; and as a body I know of none so decidedly hostile to public liberty. This is an age of *cant*. The country has been ruined by cant; and they have been the principal instruments in the work, and have had their full share of the profit.

William Cobbett (1762–1835), *The Dissenters*, May 1811.

Cobbett saw in the religious revivalists a political conspiracy against radical action:
One of the Tracts put forth by canting hypocrites who pretended to exclusive grace, was entitled 'The Life of Peter Kennedy, who lived on, and saved money out of eighteen pence a week'. And this to his praise, mind! I never considered empty bellies and ragged backs as marks of the grace of God. [Never] did we, until these days, hear of millions of 'Tracts, Moral and Religious' for the purpose of keeping the poor from cutting the throats of the rich. The parson's sermon, once a week or a fortnight, used to be quite sufficient for the religion and morals of a village. Now we had a busy creature or two in every village, dancing about with 'Tracts' for the benefit of the souls of the labourers and their families. The gist of the whole of the 'Tracts' was to inculcate content in a state of misery! To teach people to starve without making a noise! What did all this show? Why, a consciousness on the part of the rich, that the poor had not fair play; and that the former wished to obtain security against the latter by coaxing.
     ... The fact is, I am no Doctor of Divinity, and like a religion, any religion, that tends to make men innocent and benevolent and happy, by taking the best possible means of furnishing them with plenty to eat and drink and wear.
     Once, coming through the village of Benenden, I heard a man talking very loudly about houses! houses! houses! It was a Methodist parson, in a house, close by the roadside. I pulled up, and stood still, in the middle of the road, but looking up, in silent soberness, into the window (which was open) of the room in which the preacher was at work. I believe my stopping rather disconcerted him; for he got into a shocking repetition. 'Do you KNOW', said he, laying great stress on the word KNOW, 'that you have ready for you houses, houses I say; I say do you KNOW; do you KNOW that you have houses in the heavens not made with hands?' And, on he went to say, that, if Jesus had told them so, they would be saved, and that if he had not, and did not, they would be damned. Some girls whom I saw in the room, plump and rosy as could be, did not seem at all daunted by these menaces; and indeed, they appeared to me to be thinking much more about getting

houses in this world first: houses with pig-styes and little snug gardens attached to them, together with all other domestic and conjugal circumstances. The truth is, these fellows had no power over the minds of any but the miserable.

William Cobbett (1762–1835), from William Reitzel, ed., *The Autobiography of William Cobbett*, 1933; the above selection is from *Rural Rides* and *The Political Register*.

I dearly loved to go to the church, it was so solemn. I never knew rightly that I had much sin till I went there. When I found out that I was a great sinner, I was very sorely grieved, and very much frightened.

Mary Prince (c.1788–c.1833), Bermudan slave and writer.

Others were against Dissenters for the sake of the status quo:

I'm against you, by God! I am for the Established Church, damme! Not that I have any more regard for the Established Church than for any other Church, but because it *is* established. And if you can get your own damned church established, I'll be for that too!

Edward, Baron Thurlow (1731–1806), Lord Chancellor and patron of Samuel Johnson and George Crabbe, addressing a Nonconformist from the Bench; quoted in Peter Vansittart, *In Memory of England*, 1998.

Prosperity to the Establishment and confusion to all Enthusiasts.

An Anglican toast of the early 19th century, quoted in Lord Radcliffe, *Not in Feather Beds*, 1968.

A typical Anglican vicar – untroubled by controversy or, indeed, thought – is portrayed by George Crabbe in *The Borough*. Although still critical, this portrait of a country clergyman is more mellow than that painted in Crabbe's earlier poem *The Village* (see above):

> To what famed college we our Vicar owe,
> To what fair county, let historians show.
> Few now remember when the mild young man,
> Ruddy and fair, his Sunday-task began;
> Few live to speak of that soft soothing look
> He cast around, as he prepared his book;
> It was a kind of supplicating smile,
> But nothing hopeless of applause, the while;
> And when he finish'd, his corrected pride
> Felt the desert, and yet the praise denied.
> Thus he his race began, and to the end
> His constant care was, no man to offend;
> No haughty virtues stirr'd his peaceful mind,
> Nor urged the priest to leave his flock behind;
> He was his Master's soldier, but not one
> To lead an army of his martyrs on ...
> Mild were his doctrines, and not one discourse
> But gain'd in softness what it lost in force:
> Kind his opinions; he would not receive

An ill report, nor evil act believe;
'If true, 'twas wrong; but blemish great or small
'Have all mankind; yea, sinners are we all'.
    If ever fretful thought disturb'd his breast,
If aught of gloom that cheerful mind oppress'd,
It sprang from innovation; it was then
He spake of mischief made by restless men,
Not by new doctrines: never in his life
Would he attend to controversial strife;
For sects he cared not; 'They are not of us,
'Nor need we, brethren, their concerns discuss;
'But 'tis the change, the schism at home I feel;
'Ills few perceive, and none have skill to heal: ...
'Churches are now of holy song bereft;
'And half our ancient customs changed or left;
'Few sprigs of ivy are at Christmas seen,
'Nor crimson berry tips the holly's green;
'Mistaken choirs refuse the solemn strain
'Of ancient Sternhold, which from ours amain
'Comes flying forth, from aile to aile about,
'Sweet links of harmony and long drawn out.'
    These were to him essentials; all things new
He deem'd superfluous, useless, or untrue;
To all beside indifferent, easy, cold,
Here the fire kindled, and the woe was told.
    Habit with him was all the test of truth,
'It must be right: I've done it from my youth'.
Questions he answer'd in as brief a way,
'It must be wrong – it was of yesterday'.
    Though mild benevolence our priest posses'd,
'Twas but by wishes or by words express'd:
Circles in water, as they wider flow,
The less conspicuous in their progress grow;
And when at last they touch upon the shore,
Distinction ceases, and they're viewed no more.
His love, like that last circle, all embraced,
But with effect that never could be traced.
    Now rests our Vicar. They who knew him best
Proclaim his life t'have been entirely rest –
Free from all evils which disturb his mind
Whom studies vex and controversies blind.

George Crabbe (1754–1832), *The Borough*, 1810, 'Letter III, The Vicar'.

Becoming more conservative as he grew older, the poet Coleridge valued the Church as an instrument of benevolence:

This unobtrusive, continuous agency of a Protestant Church Establishment, this it is, which the patriot and the philanthropist, who would fain unite the love of peace with the faith in the progressive amelioration of mankind, cannot estimate at too high a price.

Samuel Taylor Coleridge (1772–1834), *On the Constitution of Church and State*, 1830.

MERE SENTIMENT

The Church of England in the first quarter of the 19th century stood at the peak of its power, influence and wealth, yet its story thereafter is one of slow dissolution. As the century progressed it seemed to sicken from within as its very foundations were undermined. Complacency and sheer size, with its attendant mediocrity, were to blame for some of it, as well as competition from other, more vigorous churches; but England's changing social and economic life, and the rise of science and education, accounted for most of it. The Established Church started to become, in the word that was to haunt it to the end of the following century, irrelevant.

Nonconformist faiths found increasing favour among the working classes of the newly industrialised towns and cities, while intellectual and middle-class Anglicans were attracted by the 'Oxford Movement' of Pusey, Keble, Newman and Manning, Oxford scholars and clerics who sought to bring the Church closer to its pre-Reformation Catholic roots in liturgy, theology and outward show. The intellectual vigour they brought to their 'Tractarian' campaign proved refreshing for a while, but in the end intolerable to the Anglican mainstream; Newman and Manning became Roman Catholics, the latter becoming the first cardinal to be enthroned in England since Henry VIII broke with Rome. Many clergymen and congregations went with them; those who remained were bitter. An orgy of church-building (and ill-conceived restoration) followed, but the popular mood was turning away from unquestioning obedience.

Charles Darwin, who held off publishing On the Origin of Species *for fear of the opprobrium it would attract, lived to see agnosticism become respectable, and was buried with full honours in Westminster Abbey. His work asked the Church the question: If some of Holy Scripture is to be regarded as untrustworthy, or at best metaphorical, how is one to rely on the rest of it, save as an ideal guide to good behaviour? And what is the point, then, in worshipping a moral guidebook? While other Churches dealt with the question by denying its validity (as is still the case in much of the USA), Anglicanism sought to embrace it, suggesting that since science and religion ought to be reconciled, then somehow they would be; but still it could not answer the question. What remained was a habit of observance, and 'mere sentiment'; even belief in personal immortality, hitherto as 'sure and certain' as the burial service itself, became wistful, or was quietly discarded. As Rupert Brooke sent 'Heaven' to the printers, the First World War was about to deliver the last fatal blow.*

Somehow, people were just not taking the Church seriously …

Many of our clergy suppose that if there was no Church of England, cucumbers and celery would not grow; that mustard and cress could not be raised. If

Establishments are connected so much with the great laws of nature, this makes all the difference.

Anonymous commentator on the conservative Anglican view, c.1837, quoted in Adrian Desmond and James Moore, *Darwin*, 1991.

Merit, indeed! … We are come to a pretty pass if they talk of *merit* for a bishopric.

John Fane (1759–1841), 10th Earl of Westmorland, quoted in the diary of Lady Salisbury, 9 December 1835.

Damn it! Another Bishop dead! I believe they die to vex me.

William Lamb, 2nd Lord Melbourne (1779–1848), Prime Minister 1834, 1835–41; quoted in Lord David Cecil, *Lord M*, 1954. As Prime Minister, it was Melbourne's job to appoint Church of England bishops.

What bishops like best in their clergy is a certain dropping-down-deadness of manner.

The Rev. Sydney Smith (1771–1845), 'First Letter to Archdeacon Singleton, 1837' in *Works*, vol. 2, 1859.

Giving sermons seems not to have been an English forte. In fact the activity appears to have been as much a penance for those sermonising as for those sermoned at. As Byron dolefully wrote in *Don Juan*:

Let us have wine and women, mirth and laughter,
Sermons and soda water the day after.

Lord Byron (1788–1824), *Don Juan*, Canto 2, Stanza 178, 1819–24.

The English, generally remarkable for doing very good things in a very bad manner, seem to have reserved the maturity and plenitude of their awkwardness for the pulpit.

The Rev. Sydney Smith (1771–1845), quoted in Lady Holland, *Memoir of Sydney Smith*, 1855.

Jane Carlyle, wife of Thomas Carlyle, the essayist and historian, recounts her experience of a typical English sermon:

The service went off quite respectably; it is wonderful how little faculty is needed for saying prayers *perfectly well*! But when we came to the sermon! – greater nonsense I have often enough listened to – for, in fact, the sermon (Mrs Buller with her usual sincerity informed me before I went) 'was none of *his*; he had scraped together as many written by other people as would serve him for years – *which was much better for the congregation*', but he delivered it exactly as daft Mr Hamilton used to read the newspaper – with a noble disdain of everything in the nature of a *stop* – pausing just when he needed breath at the end of a sentence, or in the middle of a word, as it happened! In the midst of this extraordinary exhortation an infant screamed out, 'Away, mammy! Let's away!' and another bigger child went off in whooping cough! For my part, I was all the while in a state between laughing and crying – nay, doing both alternately. … And this was the Gospel of

Christ I was hearing – made into something worse than the cawing of rooks. I was glad to get out, for my thoughts rose into my throat at last, as if they would choke me; and I privately vowed never to go there, when worship was going on again!

Jane Carlyle (1801–66), letter to her husband, 15 August 1842.

Anthony Trollope suffered similarly:

There is, perhaps, no greater hardship at present inflicted on mankind in civilized and free countries, than the necessity of listening to sermons. No one but a preaching clergyman has, in these realms, the power of compelling an audience to sit silent, and be tormented. No one but a preaching clergyman can revel in platitudes, truisms, and untruisms, and yet receive, as his undisputed privilege, the same respectful demeanour as though words of impassioned eloquence, or persuasive logic, fell from his lips. ... He is the bore of the age, the old man whom we Sinbads cannot shake off, the nightmare that disturbs our Sunday's rest, the incubus that overloads our religion and makes God's service distasteful. We are not forced into Church! No: but we desire more than that. We desire not to be forced to stay away. We desire, nay, we are resolute, to enjoy the comfort of public worship; but we desire also that we may do so without an amount of tedium which ordinary human nature cannot endure with patience; that we may be able to leave the house of God, without that anxious longing to escape, which is the common consequence of common sermons.

With what complacency will a young parson deduce false conclusions from misunderstood texts, and then threaten us with all the penalties of Hades if we neglect to comply with the injunctions he has given us! Yes, my all too self-confident juvenile friend, I do believe in those mysteries which are so common in your mouth; I do believe in the unadulterated word which you hold there in your hand; but you must pardon me if, in some things, I doubt your interpretation. The Bible is good, the Prayer-book is good, nay, you yourself would be acceptable, if you would read to me some portion of those time-honoured discourses which our great divines have elaborated in the full maturity of their powers. But you must excuse me, my insufficient young lecturer, if I yawn over your imperfect sentences, your repeated sentences, your repeated phrases, your false pathos, your drawlings and denouncings, your humming and hawing, your ohing and ahing, your black gloves and your white handkerchief. To me, it all means nothing; and hours are too precious to be so wasted – if one could only avoid it.

Anthony Trollope (1815–82), *Barchester Towers*, 1857.

In reaction to the vague amateurishness of the average English clergyman there arose, in the 1830s, a fierce new spiritual force in the form of the Anglo-Catholic Oxford Movement. One of the leading lights of this movement, John Henry Newman, later summarised the rigorous basis of his faith:

From the age of fifteen, dogma has been the fundamental principle of my religion; I cannot enter into the idea of any other sort of religion; religion, as a mere sentiment, is to me a dream and a mockery.

John Henry Newman (1801–90), cardinal and leader of the Oxford Movement, *Apologia pro Vita Sua*, 'History of my Religious Opinions from 1833 to 1839', 1864.

Newman loathed the wishy-washiness of English religion:

I will not shrink from uttering my firm conviction that it would be a gain to this country, were it more bigoted, more gloomy, more fierce in its religion than at present it shows itself to be. Not, of course, that I think the tempers of mind herein implied desirable, which would be an evident absurdity; but I think them infinitely more desirable and more promising than a heathen obduracy, and a cold, self-sufficient, self-wise tranquillity.

John Henry Newman (1801–90), cardinal and leader of the Oxford Movement, *Parochial and Plain Sermons*, 1834–42.

His brother, meanwhile, moved from Christian belief to scientific theism:

I felt no convulsion of mind, no emptiness of soul, no inward practical change.

Francis William Newman (1805–97), scholar and rationalist, *Phases of Faith*, 1850.

While John Henry Newman converted to Catholicism in 1845, his colleagues Keble and Pusey remained in the Established Church. Under their influence more ritual and ceremony was introduced, which was not to the taste of Low Church members:

Yesterday the parish church of St George's-in-the-East was reopened for Divine service, after the mediation of the Bishop of London in reference to the ecclesiastical disputes which have for some time past agitated the parish. Unhappily the mediation has ended in nothing, except, indeed, in inducing a fiercer and more outrageous display of passion on the part of the parishioners then has hitherto been experienced. ...

It was understood throughout the parish that the Rev. Bryan King, M.A., the rector, would take the morning service. He did so, and the congregation was a very large one. ... It will be remembered that the Bishop of London, on his mediation, decided that the coloured stoles should not be used, and Mr King got over his dislike to this part of the mediation in a very ingenious manner. Yesterday being within the octave of All Saints, the stole, according to the model hitherto observed, would have been green, but Mr King wore none of any kind, being habited simply in his surplice with his hood representing his degree of Master of Arts in the University of Oxford. As soon as he commenced the service there was a hiss, but this soon subsided, and there was no further interruption until the reverend gentleman commenced his sermon. Preparatory to this Mr King turned his back to the congregation, and, bowing to the altar, said, 'In the name of the Father, the Son, and the Holy Ghost,' instead of the ordinary prayers. This was followed by hisses, stamping of feet, and the slamming of pew doors. ...

When the reverend gentleman appeared with his choristers in the church, a loud determined shout of disapproval burst forth. Unmoved, however, by this violent demonstration, the rev. gentleman knelt before the altar and went through the Litany service. He was hissed, hooted, and yelled at during the whole of the service, and at its close made his way with difficulty to the vestry.

'Anti-Puseyite Riots', *The Observer*, 7 November 1859.

The Roman Catholic hierarchy had been restored in England in 1850. Henry Edward Manning, like Newman, began as a reactionary Anglo-Catholic but in 1851 'went over to Rome', along with many other clergy, over the Privy Council's interference (as they saw it) in matters of doctrine. In 1865 he became Archbishop of Westminster:

Dr Manning is the first Roman catholic archbishop who has ever been consecrated in England since the Reformation, for the late Cardinal Wiseman had that dignity conferred upon him at Rome. It is singular enough that the first archbishop who is thus consecrated should be an Oxford man, and not the less curious that of the many priests who stood round the high altar of St Mary's, Moorfields, yesterday, there were not less than a hundred who had either been in orders of the church of England, or who had been fellows of English colleges in their day.

The *Daily News*, 9 June 1865.

A much more fundamental challenge to the Church came on 1 July 1858, when a joint paper by Alfred Russel Wallace and Charles Darwin was read to the Linnaean Society in London. This outlined the theory of evolution by natural selection that both men had independently arrived at. The following year Darwin published On the Origin of Species, *which, with its alternative – and, to most scientists, irrefutable – account of the development of life on earth, challenged the story of creation given in Genesis. It rocked the faith of millions.*

In some cases, this shower of scientific rationalism fell on fertile ground. Tennyson had already written in 1850:

There lives more faith in honest doubt,
Believe me, than in half the creeds.

Alfred, Lord Tennyson (1809–92), *In Memoriam A.H.H.*, Canto 96, 1850.

At a meeting of the British Association for the Advancement of Science in Oxford on 30 June 1860 the evolution issue was debated by 'Soapy Sam' Wilberforce, the Bishop of Oxford, and 'Darwin's Bulldog', the eminent biologist T.H. Huxley. During the course of the debate Wilberforce addressed the following question to Huxley:

Was it through his grandfather or his grandmother that he claimed his descent from a monkey?

Samuel Wilberforce (1805–73).

Huxley's famous riposte was crushing:

I asserted – and I repeat – that a man has no reason to be ashamed of having an ape for his grandfather. If there were an ancestor whom I should feel shame in recalling it would rather be a *man* – a man of restless and versatile intellect – who, not content with an equivocal success in his own sphere of activity, plunges into scientific questions with which he has no real acquaintance, only to obscure them by an aimless rhetoric, and distract the attention of his hearers from the real point at issue by eloquent digressions and skilled appeals to religious prejudice.

T.H. Huxley (1825–95).

Darwin's theory prompted the greatest intellectual upheaval since Copernicus – and also many individual crises of faith. For not only did natural selection deny Genesis, it left us in a crueller, more indifferent universe, where any ultimate purpose for human existence was denied. The shock of this chilling new dispensation is movingly evoked in Matthew Arnold's 'Dover Beach', one of the finest poems from the Victorian era:

> The sea is calm to-night.
> The tide is full, the moon lies fair
> Upon the Straits; – on the French coast, the light
> Gleams, and is gone; the cliffs of England stand,
> Glimmering and vast, out in the tranquil bay.
> Come to the window, sweet is the night air!
> Only, from the long line of spray
> Where the ebb meets the moon-blanch'd sand,
> Listen! you hear the grating roar
> Of pebbles which the waves suck back, and fling,
> At their return, up the high strand,
> Begin, and cease, and then again begin,
> With tremulous cadence slow, and bring
> The eternal note of sadness in.
>
> Sophocles long ago
> Heard it on the Ægean, and it brought
> Into his mind the turbid ebb and flow
> Of human misery; we
> Find also in the sound a thought,
> Hearing it by this distant northern sea.
>
> The sea of faith
> Was once, too, at the full, and round earth's shore
> Lay like the folds of a bright girdle furl'd;
> But now I only hear
> Its melancholy, long, withdrawing roar,
> Retreating to the breath
> Of the night-wind down the vast edges drear
> And naked shingles of the world.
>
> Ah, love, let us be true
> To one another! for the world, which seems
> To lie before us like a land of dreams,
> So various, so beautiful, so new,
> Hath really neither joy, nor love, nor light,
> Nor certitude, nor peace, nor help for pain;
> And we are here as on a darkling plain
> Swept with confused alarms of struggle and flight,
> Where ignorant armies clash by night.

Matthew Arnold (1822–88), 'Dover Beach', in *New Poems*, 1867.

Darwin himself was something of an agnostic Agnostic:

I think that generally (and more and more as I grow older), but not always, that an Agnostic would be a more correct description of my state of mind.

Charles Darwin (1809–82), letter, 1879. The word 'agnostic' had been coined in 1869 by T.H. Huxley.

While all these great ructions were occurring, some clung to a simpler and more complete faith:

On Tuesday night an adjourned inquiry was held at the Sir Robert Peel Tavern, Plumstead, before Mr C J Carttar, coroner for West Kent, relative to the death of George Walker, a labourer, aged 48, who expired on Saturday, the 25th ult. The deceased belonged to a sect called 'The Peculiar People', who held the doctrine that faith in God alone will heal the sick. ... On the Friday night before his death a prayer meeting, attended by the elders, was held at the house where the deceased lodged, at 141, Sandy-hill-road. One of the sisters asked the deceased if he would have a doctor, and he replied, 'No,' he had every faith in the Lord. The oil used was olive oil. ... Mr J B Riley, a surgeon, who made the *post mortem* examination, proved that death had resulted from a long-standing disease of the lungs. Medical aid at an earlier period would have been of service.

The Times, 7 July 1870.

That such sects as the Peculiar People might thrive among the poor was perhaps not surprising in the light of the following observations:

Anglican ministers and bishops are proud and rich, live in wealthy parishes and dioceses and wax fat with an entirely untroubled conscience. ... It is a religion of the rich, and undisguised at that. ... They travel all over the earth, penetrate into darkest Africa to convert one savage, and forget the million savages in London because they have nothing to pay them with.

Fyodor Dostoevsky (1821–81), *Summer Impressions*, tr. Philippe Julian, 1955.

A survey on Sunday 30 March 1851 showed that two-thirds of the population of London did not go to church; east and south London had the lowest rate of church attendance in the country.

For some, the Stoicism of the ancient Romans replaced orthodox Christian faith:

Out of the night that covers me,
Black as the pit from pole to pole,
I thank whatever gods may be
For my unconquerable soul.

In the fell clutch of circumstance
I have not winced nor cried aloud.
Under the bludgeonings of chance
My head is bloody, but unbowed.

Beyond this place of wrath and tears
Looms but the horror of the shade,
And yet the menace of the years
Finds, and shall find, me unafraid.

It matters not how strait the gate,
How charged with punishments the scroll,
I am the master of my fate:
I am the captain of my soul.

W.E. Henley (1849–1903), 'Invictus, In Memoriam R.T.H.B.', 1888.

Meanwhile, the Church of England bumbled along amiably, trying to be all things to all men:

I am a loyal Anglican,
    A Rural Dean and Rector;
I keep a wife and pony-trap,
    I wear a chest-protector.
I should not like my name to be
    Connected with a party:
But still my type of service is
    Extremely bright and hearty.

Of course, one has to keep abreast
    Of changing times and manners;
A Harvest Festival we keep,
    With special Psalms and banners;
A Flower-Service in July,
    A Toy-Fund Intercession.
And, when the hens lay well, we hope
    To start an Egg-Procession.

My wife and I composed a form
    For dedicating hassocks,
Which (slightly changed) we also use
    For surplices and cassocks;
Our Bishop, when we sent it for
    His Lordship's approbation,
Remarked: 'A very primitive
    And pleasing compilation.'

To pick the best from every school
    The object of my art is,
And steer a middle course between
    The two contending parties.
My own opinions would no doubt
    Be labelled 'High' by many;
But all know well I would not wish
    To give offence to any.

One ought, I'm certain, to produce
    By gradual education
A tone of deeper Churchmanship
    Throughout the population.
There are, I doubt not, even here

Things to be done in plenty;
But still – you know the ancient saw –
'Festina lentè – *lentè*.'

I humbly feel that my success,
        My power of attraction,
Is mainly due to following
        This golden rule of action:
'See us from all men's point of view,
        Use all men's eyes to see with,
And never preach what anyone
        Could ever disagree with.'

G.W.E. Russell (1853–1919), *Lines from a Parish Magazine.*

As long as the rich man was in his castle, the poor man at his gate – and God stayed in His heaven – all would be well with the world …

Mr. Ellison in the pulpit was the Mr. Ellison of the Scripture lessons, plus a white surplice. To him, his congregation were but children of a larger growth, and he preached as he taught. A favourite theme was the duty of regular churchgoing. He would hammer away at that for forty-five minutes, never seeming to realize that he was preaching to the absent, that all those present were regular attendants, and that the stray sheep of his flock were snoring upon their beds a mile and a half away.

Another favourite subject was the supreme rightness of the social order as it then existed. God, in His infinite wisdom, had appointed a place for every man, woman, and child on this earth and it was their bounden duty to remain contentedly in their niches. A gentleman might seem to some of his listeners to have a pleasant, easy life, compared to theirs at field labour; but he had his duties and responsibilities, which would be far beyond their capabilities. He had to pay taxes, sit on the Bench of Magistrates, oversee his estate, and keep up his position by entertaining. Could they do these things? No. Of course they could not; and he did not suppose that a gentleman could cut as straight a furrow or mow or thatch a rick as expertly as they could. So let them be thankful and rejoice in their physical strength and the bounty of the farmer, who found them work on his land and paid them wages with his money.

Less frequently, he would preach eternal punishment for sin, and touch, more lightly, upon the bliss reserved for those who worked hard, were contented with their lot and showed proper respect to their superiors. The Holy Name was seldom mentioned, nor were human grief or joys, or the kindly human feelings which bind man to man. It was not religion he preached, but a narrow code of ethics, imposed from above upon the lower orders, which, even in those days, was out of date.

Once and once only did inspiration move him. It was the Sunday after the polling for the General Election of 1886, and he had begun preaching one of his usual sermons on the duty to social superiors, when suddenly something, perhaps the memory of the events of the past week, seemed to boil up within him. Flushed with anger – 'righteous anger', he would have called it – and his frosty blue eyes flashing like swords, he cast himself forward across the ledge of his pulpit and roared: 'There are some among you who have lately forgotten that duty, and we know the cause, the *bloody* cause!'

Laura shivered. Bad language in church! and from the Rector! But, later in life, she liked to think that she had lived early enough to have heard a mild and orthodox Liberalism denounced from the pulpit as 'a bloody cause'. It lent her the dignity of an historic survival.

The sermon over, the people sprang to their feet like Jacks-in-a-box. With what gusto they sang the evening hymn, and how their lungs expanded and their tongues wagged as they poured out of the churchyard! Not that they resented anything that was said in the Rector's sermons. They did not listen to them. After the Bloody Cause sermon Laura tried to find out how her elders had reacted to it; but all she could learn was: 'I seems to have lost the thread just then', or, more frankly, 'I must've been nodding'; the most she could get was one woman's, 'My! didn't th' old parson get worked up to-day!'

Flora Thompson (1876–1947), *Lark Rise to Candleford*, 1945.

Peter Vansittart, in his *In Memory of England* (1998), provides a splendid survey of the English parson through the ages:

A feature of the village – and the town, for that matter – was the Parson, often what Wodehouse terms a stately procession of one, supposedly above Class or Party. Absence of 'enthusiasm', spiritual intensity, after the Restoration could benefit local goodwill, appealing, if not to the soul, at least to the charitable conscience, suggesting that good living need not be godly living, that aimlessness was un-Christian. The Parson, as against pastor, minister, elder, was an English compromise between mysticism, austerity intolerant or intolerable, and jovial or reclusive bone-laziness.

Literary men, scholars, indigent younger sons, unfulfilled geniuses, could be slid into livings by private patrons. Tennyson's father was forced into holy orders to save the family estates from his incompetence. The parson's social standing could be ambiguous, often midway between the gentleman and the upstart farmer or lawyer, his own personality the final determinant of how often he was invited to dine at the Big House or town mansion. Within village life, Thomas Hinde adjudicates,

> Taken as a whole, country parsons suggest some sociological experiment: give a reasonably-educated middle-class Englishman a modest income, a house in the country and job security for life, and see what he will do. He does remarkable things; he invents a theory of history which makes the Druids a tribe of Phoenicean pre-Christian Christians; he plants 5,000 roses in his garden and the surrounding countryside, runs his own foxhound pack, makes his rectory into a monastery; collects folk-songs, breeds winning race-horses or green mice, rides from Land's End to John o'Groats.

Much can be added for a catalogue of ordained worthies. John Skelton, Henry VIII's Laureate, venomously satirical against Wolsey, was poignant and tender in religious verse, and grandly exhibited his bastard baby from the pulpit. William Lee devised a mechanical stocking-frame, though dying in want in 1610. Dr

Dodd, Royal Chaplain, linguist, compiler of Thoughts in Prison and The Beauties of Shakespeare, whose translations introduced the latter to a number of undiscerning Germans, was hanged for forgery in 1777, despite a growling plea from Johnson. Among parsons were Sydney Smith, George Herbert, Robert Herrick, Laurence Sterne, George Crabbe, Charles Kingsley, Andrew Young, R.S. Thomas. There were Marxists, like Conrad Noel who flaunted the Red Flag above Thaxted Church, and Hewlett Johnson who advertised Stalin's Russia as 'that new and richer freedom that all the world's great minds looked for and prayed for'. Francis Kilvert's famous diary logs a frog-woman; Sabine Baring-Gould of Lew Trenchard was essayist, novelist, mythologist, folk-lorist, anthropologist, historian, travel-writer and authority on Devonshire churches: he wrote 'Onward, Christian Soldiers', and investigated 3,600 saints, many imaginary. Hugh Eyton-Jones preached at Cowes in 1972 on 'British Sea-Power Decisive in Recent Wars'.

Physical prowess was not neglected. J.H. Parsons, E.T. Killick, D.S. Shepherd were notable cricketers; K.R.G. Hunt played in the 1908 Cup Final. James Adams won the VC in Afghanistan; J. Bradford roamed the countryside seeking someone to wrestle with. William Wilkes of Shirley spent a decade perfecting the Shirley Poppy. Elisha Fawcett, dying in the Admiralty Islands, had his wooden leg buried with him; it took root, and gave abundant material for cricket bats. Harold Davidson, of Stiffkey, was known as the Prostitutes' Padre; ejected from his parish he was prosecuted for obstructing the highway, financed his costs by exhibiting himself at fairs in a barrel, then in a glass-topped coffin. Defrocked, assaulted, he made public fasts, was unsuccessfully charged with attempting suicide, addressed crowds from the lions' cage in a circus before fatally allowing a lion the last word.

Theological niceties could be inexact. A Victorian cleric jibbed at embarking on HMS *Infernal* but accepted HMS *Destruction*. Nevertheless, the saintly are recorded amid the humdrum or bizarre. John Stevens Henslow of Hitcham championed many popular rights. Once Cambridge Professor of Botany, admired by Darwin, in 1837 he found Hitcham in Suffolk famous for violence, arson, harassment of rectors, sheep-stealing. He cured this by fostering local pride, founding a school, clubs, allotments, against landowners' opposition, and transforming village shows into great social occasions. What Britain absorbed from pre-1914 pulpits and ceremonies is hard to fathom. Many parsons must have respected Christ's ethic but, in the age of Darwin, Huxley, Spencer, German Higher Thought, Comte ..., dispensed with supernatural dogma.

Peter Vansittart, In Memory of England, 1998. The Thomas Hinde quotation is taken from *The Field Guide to the English Country Parson*, 1983.

Interior design and general church make-over was another popular pastime among parsons:

> The Church's Restoration
>> In eighteen eighty-three
> Has left for contemplation
>> Not what there used to be.

How well the ancient woodwork
 Looks round the Rect'ry hall,
Memorial of the good work
 Of him who plann'd it all.

He who took down the pew-ends
 And sold them anywhere
But kindly spared a few ends
 Work'd up into a chair.
O worthy persecution
 Of dust! O hue divine!
O cheerful substitution
 Thou varnishéd pitch-pine!

Church furnishing! Church furnishing!
 Sing art and crafty praise!
He gave the brass for burnishing,
 He gave the thick red baize,
He gave the new addition,
 Pull'd down the dull old aisle,
– To pave the sweet transition
 He gave th'encaustic tile.

Of marble brown and veinéd
 He did the pulpit make;
He ordered windows stainéd
 Light red and crimson lake.
Sing on, with hymns uproarious,
 Ye humble and aloof,
Look up! and oh how glorious
 He has restored the roof!

John Betjeman (1906–84), 'Hymn', in *Mount Zion*, 1932.

If for some church furnishing provided an image of heaven, others might hold a loftier conception …

My idea of heaven is, eating *paté de fois gras* **to the sound of trumpets.**

The Rev. Sydney Smith (1771–1845), quoted in Hesketh Pearson, *The Smith of Smiths*, 1934.

On the eve of the First World War, it was safe for an established poet to question – indeed, to satirise – the very idea of heaven:

Fish (fly-replete, in depth of June,
Dawdling away their wat'ry noon)
Ponder deep wisdom, dark or clear,
Each secret fishy hope or fear.
Fish say, they have their Stream and Pond;
But is there anything Beyond?
This life cannot be All, they swear,

For how unpleasant, if it were!
One may not doubt that, somehow, Good
Shall come of Water and of Mud;
And, sure, the reverent eye must see
A Purpose in Liquidity.
We darkly know, by Faith we cry,
The future is not Wholly Dry.
Mud unto mud! – Death eddies near –
Not here the appointed End, not here!
But somewhere, beyond Space and Time,
Is wetter water, slimier slime!
And there (they trust) there swimmeth One
Who swam ere rivers were begun,
Immense, of fishy form and mind,
Squamous, omnipotent, and kind;
And under what Almighty Fin,
The littlest of fish may enter in.
Oh! never fly conceals a hook,
Fish say, in the Eternal Brook,
But more than mundane weeds are there,
And mud, celestially fair;
Fat caterpillars drift around,
And Paradisal grubs are found;
Unfading moths, immortal flies,
And the worm that never dies.
And in that Heaven of all their wish,
There shall be no more land, say fish.

Rupert Brooke (1887–1915), 'Heaven', 1913.

A MELANCHOLY, LONG, WITHDRAWING WHIMPER

'What does the Church of England stand for?' asks a parish priest towards the end of this section. 'A vague theism and an intermittent belief in life after death,' in George Orwell's words of forty years earlier, would seem to be the answer – and perhaps even that is putting it a little strongly. The terminal decline of England's Church can be measured from Cosmo Lang's 'witness to some ultimate sanction' in 1913, to the Bishop of Liverpool, writing in the Daily *Telegraph of 5 December 2000: 'Religion is in the soul of Britain. Church attendance figures are only one of the indicators of how religious a society is. Titles of contemporary novels and lyrics of modern songs show that there is a residual spirituality within the population.' It is hardly an inspiring mission statement for a national religion: 'The one Church for the whole people of England, in its residual spiritual aspect'.*

Traditional Nonconformism has fared little better, while the Roman Catholic Church – despite, as in the days of Manning and Newman, a boost from a few prominent creative intellectuals, and Anglicans defecting from the prospect of female clergy – has declined in proportion to the inability of its leadership to understand, among other things, the basic facts of human sexuality, as most human beings practise them.

If the Archbishop of Canterbury himself likens the Church to a dotty old woman gibbering to herself in a chimney corner, who are we to disagree? Would we take it more seriously if he came out fighting, as his predecessor did during the Abdication crisis of 1936? Assuredly not – no more now than we did then. The plain fact would seem to be this: that the Church of England exercised a religious influence over us only in the days when we were already inclined to be religious, and that its role in our national life waned from the moment religion and national identity began to part company. With successive revisions of Bible and Prayer Book, recasting both in 'contemporary' language that was out of date the moment it left the press, it has lost most of its power to inspire or awe. Its public discourse now is largely limited to its own internal affairs; as the old millennium has given way to the new, the Church has hotly debated the issue of homosexual priests, but very few people, apart from the Anglican clergy and certain homosexual activists, care one way or the other what the outcome might be. Here and there it is one of many organisations doing various Good Works. That is all.

And we, the English? We are every bit as lonely as the Anglo-Saxon Wanderer, but without hope of Maker's mercy. Our lives flit from nothingness to nothingness, winter going into winter again, but we do not look for better surety from the clergy. Still, we let them go on talking, and do not interfere with them.

In 1913 Archbishop Cosmo Lang pondered on the role of the Church in national life. The question was, according to Lang ...

... whether just there, in that inward region of the national life, where anything that can be called its unity and character can be expressed, there is or is not to be this witness to some ultimate sanction to which the nation looks, some ultimate ideal which it professes. It is in our judgement a very serious thing for a state to take out of that corporate heart of its life any acknowledgement at all of its concern with religion.

Cosmo Gordon Lang (1864–1945), Scottish-born Archbishop of York (1908) and Canterbury (1928), on the establishment of the Church of England; quoted in Jeremy Paxman, *Friends in High Places*, 1990.

But by this time not many were listening ...

Religion beats me. I'm amazed at folk
Drinking the gospels in and never scratching
Their heads for questions. When I was a lad
I learned a bit from mother, and never thought
To educate myself for prayers and psalms.

But now I'm old and bald and serious-minded,
With days to sit and ponder. I'd no chance
When young and gay to get the hang of all

> This Hell and Heaven: and when the clergy hoick
> And holloa from their pulpits, I'm asleep,
> However hard I listen; and when they pray
> It seems we're all like children sucking sweets
> In school, and wondering whether master sees.

Siegfried Sassoon (1886–1967), 'The Old Huntsman', 1917.

D.H. Lawrence looked back to a time of greater religious vigour, before the era of 'ghastly sentimentalism':

I liked our chapel, which was tall and full of light, and yet still; and colour-washed pale green and blue, with a bit of lotus pattern. And over the organ-loft, 'O worship the Lord in the beauty of holiness,' in big letters.

That was a favourite hymn too:

> O worship the Lord, in the beauty of holiness,
>   Bow down before Him, His glory proclaim;
> With gold of obedience and incense of lowliness
>   Kneel and adore Him, the Lord is His name.

I don't know what the 'beauty of holiness' is, exactly. It easily becomes cant, or nonsense, but if you don't think about it – and why should you? – it has a magic. The same with the whole verse. It is rather bad, really, 'gold of obedience' and 'incense of lowliness'. But in me, to the music, it still produces a sense of splendour. . . .

In Sunday School I am eternally grateful to old Mr Remington, with his round white beard and his ferocity. He made us sing! And he loved the martial hymns:

> Sound the battle-cry,
> See the foe is nigh.
> Raise the standard high
> For the Lord.

The ghastly sentimentalism that came like a leprosy over religion had not yet got hold of our colliery village. I remember when I was in Class II in the Sunday School, when I was about seven, a woman teacher trying to harrow us about the Crucifixion. And she kept saying: 'And aren't you sorry for Jesus? Aren't you sorry?' And most of the children wept. I believe I shed a crocodile tear or two, but very vivid is my memory of saying to myself: 'I don't really care a bit.' And I could never go back on it. I never cared about the Crucifixion, one way or another. Yet the wonder of it penetrated very deep in me.

Thirty-six years ago men, even Sunday School teachers, still believed in the fight for life and the fun of it. 'Hold the fort, for I am coming.' It was far, far from any militarism or gun-fighting. But it was a battle-cry of a stout soul, and a fine thing, too.

> Stand up, stand up for Jesus,
>   Ye soldiers of the Lord.

Here is the clue to the ordinary Englishman – in the Nonconformist hymns.

D.H. Lawrence (1885–1930), 'Hymns in a Man's Life' in *Selected Essays*. ('Stand up, stand up for Jesus' was written in 1858 by the American Presbyterian George Duffield.)

There is a hilarious parody of Nonconformist hellfire preaching in Stella Gibbons's *Cold Comfort Farm*, when urbanite Flora Poste attends the Church of the Quivering Brethren:

Flora found a hymn-book being pressed into her hand by a female on her left.

'It's number two hundred, "Whatever shall we Do, O Lord?"' said the female, in a loud conversational voice. ...

The hymn went like this:

Whatever shall we do, O Lord,
When Gabriel blows o'er sea and river,
Fen and desert, mount and ford?
The earth may burn, but we will quiver.

Flora approved of this hymn, because its words indicated a firmness of purpose, a clear plan in the face of a disagreeable possibility, which struck an answering note in her own character. She sang industriously in her pleasing soprano. The singing was conducted by a surely excessively dirty old man with long, grey hair who stood on the platform and waved what Flora, after the first incredulous shock, decided was a kitchen poker.

'Who is that?' she asked her friend.

''Tes Brother Ambleforth. He leads the quiverin' when we begins to quiver.'

'And why does he conduct the music with a poker?'

'To put us in mind o' hell fire,' was the simple answer. ...

After the hymn, which was sung sitting down, everybody crossed their legs and arranged themselves more comfortably, while Amos rose from his seat with terrifying deliberation, mounted the little platform, and sat down.

For some three minutes he slowly surveyed the Brethren, his face wearing an expression of the most profound loathing and contempt, mingled with a divine sorrow and pity. He did it quite well. Flora had never seen anything to touch it except the face of Sir Henry Wood when pausing to contemplate some latecomers into the stalls at the Queen's Hall just as his baton was raised to conduct the first bar of the *Eroica*. Her heart warmed to Amos. The man was an artist.

At last he spoke. His voice jarred the silence like a broken bell.

'Miserable, crawling worms, are ye here again, then? Have ye come like Nimshi son of Rehoboam, secretly out of yer doomed houses to hear what's comin' to ye? Have ye come, old and young, sick and well, matrons and virgins (if there is any virgins among ye, which is not likely, the world bein' in the wicked state it is), old men and young lads, to hear me tellin' o' the great crimson lickin' flames o' hell fire?'

A long and effective pause, and a further imitation of Sir Henry. The only sound (and it, with the accompanying smell, was quite enough) was the whickering hissing of the gas flares which lit the hall....

Amos went on:

'Ay, ye've come.' He laughed shortly and contemptuously. 'Dozens of ye. Hundreds of ye. Like rats to a granary. Like field-mice when there's harvest home. And what good will it do ye?'

Second pause, and more Sir Henry stuff.

'Nowt. Not the flicker of a whisper of a bit o' good.'

He paused and drew a long breath, then suddenly he leaped from his seat and thundered at the top of his voice:

'Ye're all damned!'

An expression of lively interest and satisfaction passed over the faces of the Brethren, and there was a general rearranging of arms and legs as though they wanted to sit as comfortably as possible while listening to the bad news.

'Damned,' he repeated, his voice sinking to a thrilling and effective whisper. 'Oh, do ye ever stop to think what that word *means* when ye use it every day, so lightly, o' yer wicked lives? No. Ye doan't. Ye never stop to think what anything means, do ye? Well I'll tell ye. It means endless horrifyin' torment, with yer poor sinful bodies stretched out on hot grid-irons in the nethermost pit of hell, and demons mockin' ye while they waves cooling jellies in front of ye, and binds ye down tighter on yer dreadful bed. Ay, an' the air'll be full of the stench of burnt flesh and the screams of your nearest and dearest . . . .'

He took a gulp of water, which Flora thought he more than deserved. She was beginning to feel that she could do with a glass of water herself.

Amos's voice now took on a deceptively mild and conversational note. His protruding eyes ranged slowly over his audience.

'Ye know, doan't ye, what it feels like when ye burn yer hand in takin' a cake out of the oven or wi' a match when ye're lightin' one of they godless cigarettes? Ay. It stings wi' a fearful pain, doesn't it? And ye run away to clap a bit o' butter on it to take the pain away. Ah, but' (an impressive pause) *'there'll be no butter in hell!'* Yer whoal body will be burnin' and stingin' wi' that unbearable pain, and yer blackened tongues will be stickin' out of yer mouth, and yer cracked lips will try to scream out for a drop of water, but no sound woan't come because yer throat is drier nor the sandy desert and yer eyes will be beatin' like great red hot balls against yer shrivelled eyelids . . . .'

It was at this point that Flora quietly rose. . . .

Stella Gibbons (1902–89), *Cold Comfort Farm*, 1932.

The true nature of puritanism became a subject of debate in relation to D.H. Lawrence's novel, *Lady Chatterley's Lover*, whose publishers, Penguin Books, were charged with obscenity when they issued it in 1960:

[Mr Hutchinson, for the Defence, asked]: 'The book has been described as little more than vicious indulgence in sex and sensuality. In your view is that a valid description of this novel?' – 'I think it is invalid on all three counts. It is not in any sense vicious; it is highly virtuous and, if anything, puritanical.'

'Did you say 'virtuous and puritanical'?' interrupted Mr Justice Byrne. And Mr Hoggart . . . said he did. . . .

[Mr Griffith-Jones, Prosecuting]: 'You described this book as highly virtuous, if not puritanical. Please do not think that I am suggesting it with any bad faith against you. This is your genuine and considered view, is it?' – 'Yes.'

'I thought I had lived my life under a misapprehension as to the meaning of the word "puritanical". Will you help me?' Mr Hoggart took this as a genuine cry for help. 'Yes,' he said, 'many people do live their lives under a misapprehension of the meaning of the word "puritanical". This is the way in which language decays. In England today and for a long time the word "puritanical" has been extended to mean somebody who is against anything which is pleasurable, particularly sex.

The proper meaning of it, to a literary man or to a linguist, is somebody who belongs to the tradition of British puritanism generally, and the distinguishing feature of that is an intense sense of responsibility for one's conscience. In this sense this book is puritanical.'

'I am obliged for that lecture upon it.'

C.H. Rolph, ed., *The Trial of Lady Chatterley: Regina* v *Penguin Books Limited*, 1961. Richard Hoggart, author of *The Uses of Literacy* and at that time Senior Lecturer in English at Leicester University, was giving evidence for the Defence. Lawrence's novel *Lady Chatterley's Lover* was first published privately in 1928.

There is a species of person called a 'Modern Clergyman' who draws the full salary of a beneficed clergyman and need not commit himself to any religious belief.

Evelyn Waugh (1903–66), *Decline and Fall*, 1928.

One of the greatest tests of the relation of Church and State came with the Abdication Crisis of 1936 when Edward VIII renounced the throne, and with it the Supreme Governorship of the Church of England, in order to marry the divorcée Wallis Simpson. Cosmo Lang (1864–1945), the Archbishop of Canterbury ('Cantuar' in his Latin designation), who had conducted a bitter campaign against the partial liberalisation of England's divorce laws the previous year, refused to countenance the husband of a divorced woman as King, and continued to censure him after his departure from Britain in the belief that such a 'moral' campaign would revive church-going. It didn't. It did, however, inspire the following anonymous ditty:

> My Lord Archbishop, what a scold you are,
> And when a man is down, how bold you are,
> Of Christian charity how scant you are,
> You auld Lang Swine, how full of cant you are!

The Second World War also proved testing at times:

BBC Board. We discuss whether the clergy should use the microphone to preach forgiveness of our enemies. I say I prefer that to the clergy who seek to pretend that the bombing of Cologne was a Christian act. I wish the clergy would keep their mouths shut about the war. It is none of their business.

Harold Nicolson (1886–1968), *Diaries and Letters*, 11 June 1942.

By this time ethics was about all that was left of Christianity for many people:

For perhaps a hundred and fifty years organised religion, or conscious religious belief of any kind, have had very little hold on the mass of English people. Only about ten per cent of them ever go near a place of worship except to be married and buried. A vague theism and an intermittent belief in life after death are probably fairly widespread, but the main Christian doctrines have been largely forgotten. Asked what he meant by 'Christianity', the average man would define it wholly in ethical terms ('unselfishness', or 'loving your neighbour', would be the kind of definition he would give). This was probably much the same in the early days of the Industrial Revolution, when the old village life had been suddenly broken up and the Established Church had lost touch with its followers. But in recent times the Nonconformist sects have also lost much of their vigour, and within the last generation the Bible reading which used to be traditional in England has lapsed. It is quite common to meet with young people who do not know the Bible stories even as *stories*.

George Orwell (1903–50), *The English People*, written 1944, published 1947.

I do not mind a conscience, but I do object to an organised conscience.

Arthur Henderson (1863–1935), Labour MP and minister, quoted in Peter Vansittart, *In Memory of England*, 1998.

Accept the Christian ethic. Can't stand the mumbo-jumbo!

Clement Attlee (1883–1967), Labour Prime Minister, quoted in Peter Vansittart, *In Memory of England*, 1998.

What then is the purpose of the Church of England?

The Church of England exists for the sake of those outside it.

Dr William Temple (1881–1944), Archbishop of Canterbury, attributed remark, 1944.

The following passage suggests some other answers:

[Mr. Chorlton] paused at the lych-gate to light his pipe, and looked back at the airy spire of our lovely church, and said:

'You know, John, it is a very curious thing. I am an agnostic, and I find in all religions, including the Christian one, a perpetual affront to my reason; and yet I find too, deep in my heart, a real and growing affection for this Church of England. Why?'

He paused and puffed hard to get his pipe going.

'Now why?' he went on. 'Historically it is absurd, being the bastard child of a king's folly and a pope's obstinacy; born of accident and compromise, with a breath of puritanical brimstone at its christening which doesn't seem to have done it any harm. Its dogma is so confused that even its Bishops have difficulty in defining it, and end up by allowing their flock to believe anything, everything or nothing so long as they refrain from causing a scandal. The structure of its doctrine is as much a mixture of different styles and periods as the physical structure of our church, which is a blend of early Norman, late Norman, fourteenth century and Perp., with a three-decker pulpit and an octagonal font in which old Mountjoy, rest his soul, used to keep his little fishes. And a lot of perfectly odious late-Victorian windows presented by Lord Orris' father. But the building is homogeneous, isn't it – almost as much part of the landscape as the hedges and the trees? Now look at its doctrine; take a slice of the Reformation, spice it with English puritanism and butter it with English tolerance, add a pinch of popery, boil it in English Conservatism, and garnish it with all the extraordinary odds and ends such as Establishment and Tithe, Queen Anne's Bounty and the Parson's Glebe and the Ecclesiastical Commissioners. What a recipe! And then bear in mind the fact that a country living may be in the gift of a layman who doesn't believe in Christianity at all or a squire whose only anxiety is to appoint a clergy-man who hunts and plays a good game of bridge! And yet,' repeated Mr. Chorlton, leaning on the wall beside the wicket-gate, 'I love it. Agnostic though I am, I want to be buried in this churchyard when I die, and I should be very con-tent for some absurd old clergyman such as Mountjoy to say over me those splen-did words in the Burial Service: dust to dust and ashes to ashes.

'The funny thing is that thousands of people who don't believe in it have the same feeling. I suppose in Greece and Rome, when the old Gods fell out of favour and people ceased to believe in their thunderbolts and their power, the crumbling ivy-grown altars were still regarded with a sort of half-amused, half-apologetic affection, and people made an occasional shame-faced sacrifice at them for old time's sake. That is how I feel about the C. of E. and I still wonder why!'

John Moore (1907–67), *Brensham Village*, 1946.

Philip Larkin's poem 'Church Going' is marked by an awkward ambivalence many of us share:

Once I am sure there's nothing going on
I step inside, letting the door thud shut.
Another church: matting, seats, and stone,
And little books; sprawlings of flowers, cut
For Sunday, brownish now; some brass and stuff
Up at the holy end; the small neat organ;
And a tense, musty, unignorable silence,
Brewed God knows how long. Hatless, I take off
My cycle-clips in awkward reverence,

Move forward, run my hand around the font.
From where I stand, the roof looks almost new –
Cleaned, or restored? Someone would know: I don't.
Mounting the lectern, I peruse a few
Hectoring large-scale verses, and pronounce
'Here endeth' much more loudly than I'd meant.
The echoes snigger briefly. Back at the door
I sign the book, donate an Irish sixpence,
Reflect the place was not worth stopping for.

Yet stop I did: in fact I often do,
And always end much at a loss like this,
Wondering what to look for; wondering, too,
When churches fall completely out of use
What we shall turn them into, if we shall keep
A few cathedrals chronically on show,
Their parchment, plate and pyx in locked cases,
And let the rest rent-free to rain and sheep.
Shall we avoid them as unlucky places?

Or, after dark, will dubious women come
To make their children touch a particular stone;
Pick simples for a cancer; or on some
Advised night see walking a dead one?
Power of some sort or other will go on
In games, in riddles, seemingly at random;
But superstition, like belief, must die,
And what remains when disbelief has gone?
Grass, weedy pavement, brambles, buttress, sky.

A shape less recognizable each week,
A purpose more obscure. I wonder who
Will be the last, the very last, to seek
This place for what it was; one of the crew
That tap and jot and know what rood-lofts were?
Some ruin-bibber, randy for antique,
Or Christmas-addict, counting on a whiff
Of gown-and-bands and organ-pipes and myrrh?
Or will he be my representative,

Bored, uninformed, knowing the ghostly silt
Dispersed, yet tending to this cross of ground
Through suburb scrub because it's held unspilt
So long and equably what since is found
Only in separation – marriage, and birth,
And death, and thoughts of these – for which was built
This special shell? For, though I've no idea
What this accoutred frowsty barn is worth,
It pleases me to stand in silence here;

A serious house on serious earth it is,
In whose blent air all our compulsions meet,
Are recognized, and robed as destinies.
And that much never can be obsolete,
Since someone will forever be surprising
A hunger in himself to be more serious,
And gravitating with it to this ground,
Which, he once heard, was proper to grow wise in,
If only that so many dead lie round.

Philip Larkin (1922–85), 'Church Going', 1954.

Early post-war England still had room for 'characters' whose mere presence could evangelise:

Canon Edwyn Young [1913–87], who has died aged 74, was one of the Church of England's most colourful priests and claimed to be the first-ever chaplain to a strip-tease club, officiating at the Raymond Revue Bar in Soho. ...

In 1953 the Bishop of London persuaded him to leave Islington in order to become rector of Stepney, a parish of some 32,000 people and containing five pre-war parishes. Here he built up a staff of six curates, three women church workers, two club leaders and a secretary, and through a combination of hard work and audacity the Church infiltrated virtually every aspect of Stepney's community life. At one time Young was a member of 44 committees.

The parish newspaper, reflecting the life of the whole community and … sold in public houses, was called *Stepahoy*; on one occasion, a member of the staff suggested that from time to time it might have a religious supplement. In fact, it contained many pictures of the rector in the company of actors and actresses, for he was also chaplain of the London Palladium and often invited 'stars' to church services and parish events. Every summer he moved down to Kent for three weeks to minister to East Enders working in the hop fields.

Hugh Massingberd, ed., *The Daily Telegraph Book of Obituaries: Eccentric Lives*, 1995.

I am not a pillar of the church but a buttress. I support it from the outside.

Winston Churchill (1874–1965), quoted by Montague Brown in a speech to the International Churchill Society, 25 September 1985.

As to the British churchman, he goes to church as he goes to the bathroom, with the minimum of fuss and no explanation if he can help it.

Ronald Blythe (1922–), *The Age of Illusion*, 1963.

My view of God is a simple one, namely that if He exists at all He must be an outstandingly disagreeable old gentleman.

Arthur Marshall (1910–89), writer, quoted in Hugh Massingberd, ed., *The Daily Telegraph Book of Obituaries: Eccentric Lives*, 1995.

I am not sure of anything nowadays. I am lost. I am adrift. Everywhere one looks, decadence. I saw a bishop with a moustache the other day.

Alan Bennett (1934–), *Forty Years On*, 1969.

In *Akenfield*, Ronald Blythe's portrait of an English village, he quotes the views of various members of the community on religion and the Church. First, the village doctor:

I've thought of following Christ – many, many times. But it would have to be the real thing – not this business going on in the church. St Paul altered it, spoilt it all at the very start, didn't he? Yes, I'd certainly have a go at the original idea if I had the nerve, but I wouldn't waste my time on the rest of it.

Then the retired Brigadier:

The church is going to pot because of all these young inexperienced parsons. Servicemen make the best parsons. They are men of the world who are used to handling people. You take these chaps getting ordained in their twenties – what do they know about life? What you need is the padre type, somebody who will have a drink with you in the bar and who has the right to say to you, 'Now look here, old boy. You've been grizzling away about your Ethel and her shortcomings, but do you ever think about how she feels being left alone all the evening while you are lining them up here? I mean, fair's fair …' A man shouldn't be a parson until he's in his forties; he can't know about life till then. The best advice I ever had was given me by a padre, you know. Changed my life, you know. 'Think of the other fellow,' he said – something like that. Made me a different person, you know.

Ronald Blythe (1922–), *Akenfield,* 1969.

Whither the Church of England? This question, which had been asked now and again ever since the Church's establishment, repeated itself with ever-growing frequency as the second millennium of Christ's dispensation drew to its close. And the questioners asked not only 'Whither?', but also 'What for?' and 'Why?' and 'Who cares anyway?' …

'There is a large part of the community quite indifferent to religion,' said the Archbishop of Canterbury in 1969, in an understatement of sublime dimensions. … Everywhere men longed for a scientific form of myth, a non-compulsory set of commandments, an undivine God. Such demands were not new; they had been made afresh in every age, and always been sternly refused. The refusals had, in the past, been met in a variety of ways: some of those refused had run mad, or heretical, or launched Reformations, or communed secretly with the Devil, or accepted the refusal as best they might. Now, however, and indeed for a long time, men had met refusal with indifference, so that instead of running their heads against the stone front of the Church they had turned away and found better things to do.

Bernard Levin (1928–), *The Pendulum Years,* 1970.

There was a stir, now largely forgotten, when Bishop Robinson of Woolwich published *Honest to God* in 1963; a fuss as forgotten as that stirred up when Bishop Jenkins of Durham denied the literal truth of the Resurrection (and much else) a decade or two later …

'It is not every day,' said the *Church Times* in an editorial, 'that a bishop goes on public record as apparently denying almost every Christian doctrine of the Church in which he holds office.' Nowadays, of course, it is, or at least it seems as though it is, but when John Robinson, then Bishop of Woolwich, published *Honest to God* in 1963, it was more of a novelty.

Bernard Levin (1928–), *The Pendulum Years,* 1970.

GOD IS NOT A DADDY IN THE SKY

Banner headline, *Daily Herald,* after the publication of *Honest to God* in 1963.

Bishop Robinson himself observed:

What is dissolving is the *casing* of the Church, and … this process could be one of release and liberation. … The pains of disintegration are salutary. … The next five years, I suspect, will tell which way the Church will die.

John Robinson (1919–83), Bishop of Woolwich (1959–69), author of *Honest to God,* 1963; from articles in the *Sunday Pictorial* quoted in Bernard Levin, *The Pendulum Years,* 1970.

There were some in the Church who were prepared to kick back. One such was the Anglo-Catholic Canon Gareth Bennett, who, in the unsigned Preface to the 1987 edition of *Crockford's Clerical Directory*, launched a powerful attack on Robert Runcie, then Archbishop of Canterbury. When Bennett's identity was subsequently revealed, he committed suicide. Here is some of what he wrote:

He has the disadvantage of the intelligent pragmatist: the desire to put off all questions until someone else makes a decision. One recalls a lapidary phrase of Mr Frank Field that the archbishop is usually to be found nailing his colours to the fence.

(Frank Field, a Labour MP, is a member of the Church of England Synod.)

But Canon Bennett was fighting a losing battle …

It's just called 'The Bible' now. We dropped the word 'Holy' to give it a more mass-market appeal.

An editor at Hodder & Stoughton, quoted in the *Daily Telegraph*, 30 December 1989.

Between 1914 and 1987 the number of Anglican clergymen fell from 22,000 to 10,500; between 1969 and 1989 1,215 churches were deconsecrated or pulled down …

The Church is spending money on bureaucrats. I met a former pupil of mine recently. Impressive young man. He'd become a Clerk in Holy Orders. I asked him what he was doing. He told me he was diocesan education officer, whatever that is. He'd no parish, you see. That's what the Church is spending money on, and that's why – all these canons and others with no proper job – they haven't got any parish priests. … This family has been in love with the Church. But it's at an end. What does the Church of England stand for any longer?

The Rev. Henry Thorold, squire and parson of Marston, Lincolnshire, quoted in Jeremy Paxman, *Friends in High Places*, 1990.

In 1990 the playwright Alan Bennett addressed the Prayer Book Society, which campaigns to preserve the original language of the Book of Common Prayer against the depredations of modernisers:

I begin with a poem by Stevie Smith. … It's called 'Why are the Clergy … ?'

    Why are the clergy of the Church of England
    Always changing the words of the prayers in the Prayer Book?
    Cranmer's touch was surer than theirs, do they not respect him?
    For instance last night in church I heard
    (I italicize the interpolation)
    'The Lord bless you and keep you *and all who are dear unto you*'
    As the blessing is a congregational blessing and meant to be
    This is questionable on theological grounds
    But is it not offensive to the ear and also ludicrous?
    That 'unto' is a particularly ripe piece of idiocy
    Oh how offensive it is. I suppose we shall have next
    'Lighten our darkness we beseech thee O Lord
      and also the darkness of all those who are dear unto us'

    It seems a pity. Does Charity object to the objection?
    Then I cry, and not for the first time to that smooth face
    Charity, have pity.

The poem is pretty self-explanatory apart from the last two lines ... I think what Stevie Smith means is that living in fellowship with other believers might seem to require her to be silent. Don't rock the boat, in other words. Whereas she begs to be allowed, as you in this Society beg to be allowed, to differ.

    Stevie Smith brings me to the first of my difficulties: God, put bluntly. Stevie Smith regarded God much as she regarded producers with whom she worked at the BBC: He had to be kept in His place, not allowed to go too far, and on occasion needed to be taken down a peg or two. But, though she and God didn't always get on, she undoubtedly believed in Him and so was entitled to weigh in with her opinions and objections, including her opinions about the Prayer Book. I'm not sure that I do believe in God. If I don't, it could reasonably be objected that I shouldn't be talking about the Prayer Book at all. Those who rewrote the Prayer Book complained very much at the time – and understandably – that many of the protests came from those, such as myself, whose connection with the Church was tenuous, the argument implicit in this being that the clergy know what is best for their congregations. That is the same argument that is advanced by farmers in answer to protests about the grubbing-up of hedges and the destruction of field patterns. The land is the farmer's bread and butter, the argument goes, and so he must therefore have its welfare more at heart than the occasional visitor. So in their own field the liturgical reformers grub up the awkward thickets of language that make the harvest of souls more difficult, plough in the sixteenth-century hedges that are hard to penetrate but for that reason shelter all manner of rare creatures: poetry, mystery, transcendence. All must be flat, dull, accessible and rational. Fields and worship.

    The folly in this reform of institutions is to fix on an essential or a primary function. The land is there to produce food. The Prayer Book is there to net souls. Once one function has been given priority, all other considerations go by the board. But there is an ecology of belief as well as of nature. Poetry, mystery, the beauty of language – these may be incidental to the primary purpose of the Church, which is to bring people to God, but one doesn't have to be Archbishop Laud to see that these incidental virtues of the Prayer Book are not irrelevant or dispensable. If they were, architecture would be irrelevant too; the logical end of rewriting the Prayer Book being that serious-minded congregations would worship in Nissen huts. And a small voice says, 'Well, perhaps that is what they do.'

    Of course in the Anglican Church whether or not one believes in God tends to be sidestepped. It's not quite in good taste. Someone said that the Church of England is so constituted that its members can really believe anything, but of course almost none of them do.

    One of the aims of the liturgical reformers was to make God more accessible; but that didn't mean that they weren't also a bit embarrassed by Him, and I think it's this embarrassment that has got into their language. God is like an aged father taken in by his well-intentioned children. They want to keep him presentable and a useful member of society, so they scrap his old three-piece suit, in which he looked a little old-fashioned (though rather distinguished), and kit him out instead in pastel-coloured leisurewear in which he looks like everybody else. The trouble is, though, they can't change the habits of a lifetime. It's not so much that he spits in the fire or takes his teeth out at the table but that, given the chance, he is so forthright. He's always laying down the law and seems to think nobody else exists, and his family might be servants the way he treats them. It's a bit embarrassing – particularly when those warm, friendly people from the religion next door come round. Still, it's only a matter of time. Father's old. He may die soon.

Alan Bennett (1934–   ), from 'Comfortable Words', an address to the Prayer Book Society, Blackburn Cathedral, 12 May 1990, in *Writing Home*, 1994.

An insider proffered the following view of the Church of England:

I see it as an elderly lady, who mutters away to herself in a corner, ignored most of the time.

Dr George Carey (1935–   ), interviewed in *Reader's Digest* following his appointment as Archbishop of Canterbury, March 1991.

Meanwhile, the future Supreme Governor of the Church was waxing multicultural:

I personally would much rather see my title as Defender of Faith, not the Faith, because it means just one interpretation of the faith, which I think is sometimes something that causes a great deal of a problem.

H.R.H. The Prince of Wales, in the ITV programme *Charles: The Private Man, The Public Role*, 29 June 1994.

In the same year, a Sussex rector who had declared his non-belief in God was deprived of his living by his bishop, despite protests from parishioners and other clergy. *Private Eye*, which had run a series of parodies of the revised Prayer Book ever since its introduction in the late 1970s, offered a fitting service for such an eventuality …

THE ALTERNATIVE ROCKY HORROR SERVICE BOOK
No. 94: SERVICE OF CARING AND SHARING FOR AN INCUMBENT DEPRIVED OF HIS LIVING BY A REACTIONARY BISHOP ON THE GROUNDS OF HIS SINCERELY HELD NON-BELIEF IN THE DEITY.

PRESIDENT: We are gathered here in the presence of No One At All, remembering that when two or three are gathered together nothing much happens.

ALL: That's the way we see it.

PRESIDENT: We would like to give thanks to ourselves at this time for the work of thy servant N or M (as it may be, Kevin or Tracey). He or she has faithfully served this community, forming pastoral relationships on a one-to-one basis at all levels.

ALL: The Karaoke Evening/pub quiz/Summer Fayre was a great success.

PRESIDENT: We shall now join together in the words of the Non-Credo.

ALL: We do not believe in God in the sense of a sort-of Father Christmas figure sitting on a cloud, but more of a sort of Life Force thingie, like the

Buddhists. Did you see that programme on the Paranormal, makes you think, doesn't it? Amen.

HYMN (No. 94) 'God moves in a mysterious way. In fact He doesn't move at all.'
The President shall then ask the congregation to join with him in a General Commination of the Bishop.

PRESIDENT: Our Father who isn't in heaven, but if you were we feel sure you would send this bigoted Bishop to Hell, which doesn't exist, obviously, but if it did, then this would be the place where this bastard should go for sacking Kevin (or he may say Mariella) when his only crime was to be honest enough to say what most of us vicars think, i.e. that there is nothing out there.

ALL: For God's sake, this is the twentieth century.

PRESIDENT: *(addressing the ex-incumbent)*
Did you get many letters of support?

KEITH: Yea, even an hundredfold.

PRESIDENT: Have you been on the media?

KEITH: Indeed I hath. *South Today* and *Good Morning Chichester.*

ALL: And there was a letter in the *Independent.*
The choir shall then sing an Anthem: 'I know my Redeemer doesn't liveth'.

THE DISMISSAL

PRESIDENT: The Lord isn't with you.

ALL: And He isn't with you either.

PRESIDENT: Go in peace.

ALL: And get another job.

KEITH: Yea, I have already been offered a part in the Government's Multi-Faith Education Programme.

ALL: Great. Thank God for that.

Private Eye, 12 August 1994.

In his book, *The English,* Jeremy Paxman took a cool look at the Church of England:

I once asked the Bishop of Oxford what you needed to believe to be a member of his Church. A look of slight bafflement crossed his face. 'An intriguing question,' he answered, as though it had not occurred to him before. ... 'It depends on which church you go to. An evangelical church will say you need to be sincerely converted. A traditional Anglo-Catholic church will teach you a Christian ortho-doxy virtually indistinguishable from Roman Catholic teaching. ... The Church of England doesn't believe in laying down rules. ... It prefers to give people space and freedom. It's enough to make the effort to attend and take communion. That shows you believe.' ...

What kind of an organization is it that makes itself as available as a local post office and requires virtually nothing of its adherents? The most characteristic English statement about belief is 'Well, I'm not particularly religious,' faintly embarrassed by the suggestion that there might be somthing more to life. It sometimes seems the Church of England thinks God is just the ultimate 'good chap'. ...

When I asked the Very Reverend David Edwards, the author of over thirty books on modern Christianity, for his assessment of the state of spirituality in England, he just told me bleakly that 'The English have lost any sense of what religion is.'

Jeremy Paxman (1950–), *The English*, 1998.

A tacit atheism prevails. Death is assumed to be the end of life, bleak though that thought is. If we need hope to clutch to our breast at all it will be in such greatly scaled down forms, such as our longings for family happiness, the next holiday, or personal fulfilment.

Dr George Carey (1935–), Archbishop of Canterbury, sermon, 27 October 2000.

Where Dr Carey is wrong is in his claim that 'a tacit atheism prevails'. A nation of real atheists would be much easier for Dr Carey to take on. ... The worst of all worlds is the one Dr Carey is presented with. It is a world in which most people believe in a ruling spirit of some sort, but not necessarily one rooted in religion and requiring thought. 'When men stop believing in God, they don't believe in nothing; they believe in anything,' Chesterton is supposed to have said. 'Anything' means horoscopes, ouija boards and alternative medicine. And those who believe in these things are unaffected by whatever Dr Carey says: indifference is more frustrating than agreement.

Daily Telegraph, editorial, 28 October 2000.

I have, alas, only one illusion left, and that is the Archbishop of Canterbury.

The Rev. Sydney Smith (1771–1845), quoted in Lady Holland, *Memoirs*, 1855.

An English Education

I CAN'T DO WITH ANY MORE EDUCATION.
I WAS FULL UP YEARS AGO.
P. G. Wodehouse (1881–1975), *The Code of the Woosters*, 1938.

Intellect has never been highly valued in England; nor, in its purest or philosophical sense, has education ever featured prominently in national debates. Schools, on the other hand – and, more recently, universities – have exercised us mightily. Who they are for, what they are for, how they are to achieve it, what to do about them when they don't, and how to do it: these are subjects on which the English become warm and voluble. No other nation has had so many Great Debates on education; no other nation has succeeded quite so often in coming to no definite conclusion. No other developed nation produces, in each generation, so many functionally illiterate and innumerate school leavers. Each new attempt to raise educational standards appears, in the popular psyche, to lower them still further. They are like Louis MacNeice's barometer in Bagpipe Music: *'The glass is falling hour by hour, the glass will fall forever, / But if you break the bloody glass you won't hold up the weather.'*

We begin with a brisk trot through the history of schooling, then do some hard pounding through the many aspects of the English School. Finally comes an agreeable ramble round the mellow stone, red brick, white tile, and leprous grey cement of the English University.

SCHOOLING: A BRIEF SORRY HISTORY

Lord God, howe many good and clene wittes of children, be nowe a days peris-shed by ignorant schole maisters.

Sir Thomas Elyot (c.1490–1546), *The Boke Named the Governour.*

It is pitie, that commonlie more care is had, yea and that emonges verie wise men, to finde out rather a cunnynge man for their horse than a cunnynge man for their children. They say nay in worde, but they do so in deede. For, to the one they will glad-lie give a stipend of 200 Crounes by year, and loth to offer to the other 200 shillings.

Roger Ascham (1515–68), *The Scholemaster.*

The following extract from an Elizabethan statute explains how the now misleadingly named 'Public' Schools ended up being, in fact, private institutions for the well-off:

They were created by their founders at the first, onelie for pore men's sons, whose parents were not able to bring them up unto learning: but now they have the least benefit of them, by reason the rich do so incroach upon them. In some grammar schooles likewise, which send scholers to these universities, it is lamentable to see what briberie is used; for yet the scholer can be preferred, such briberye is made that pore men's children are commonly shut out, and the richer sort received.

Statute 31 Elizabeth, cap. 6, 1589.

By the end of the 17th century, John Aubrey noted some progress in the spread of education:

Before printing, Old-Wives Tales were ingeniose, and since printing came into fashion, till a little before the Civill-warres, the ordinary sort of People were not taught to reade. Now-a-dayes Bookes are common, and most of the poor people understand letters; and the many good Bookes, and variety of Turnes of Affaires, have putte the old Fables out of doors: and the divine art of Printing and Gunpowder have frighted away Robin-good-fellow and the Fayries.

John Aubrey (1626–97), *Miscellanies,* 1696.

However, in contrast to Scotland, where the parishes provided more or less universal ele-mentary education, schooling in England up to the Education Act of 1870 could be a very hit-or-miss affair. There were parish schools and charity schools – and, for a few, the endowed grammar schools – but most children probably had little or no formal schooling. Various com-mentators thought that this was for the best …

It is manifest that in a free nation where slaves are not allowed, the surest wealth consists in a multitude of laborious poor. … To make society happy and people easy under the meanest circumstances, it is requisite that great numbers of them should be ignorant as well as poor. … A man who has had some education, may follow husbandry by choice … but he won't make a good hireling and serve as a farmer for a pitiful reward, at least he is not so fit for it as a day labourer that has always been employed about the plough and dung-cart, and remembers not that ever he has lived otherwise.

Bernard Mandeville (c.1670–1733), *Essay on Charity and Charity Schools.*

The charity school is another universal nursery of idleness: nor is it easy to conceive or invent anything more destructive to the interests and very foundation principles of a nation than the giving of an education to the children of the lowest class of her people that will make them contemn those drudgeries for which they were born.

Anon., 1763: *Consideration of the Fatal Effects to a Trading Nation of the Excess of Public Charity.*

In addition to the parish schools and charity schools, many individuals made a living as unregulated instructors:

It is not at all uncommon to see on doors in one continued succession, 'children educated here'; 'shoes mended here'; 'foreign and spirituous liquors sold here'; and 'funerals furnished here'.

Karl Philipp Moritz (1757–93), *Travels of a German in England.*

In his preface to *Nicholas Nickleby,* Dickens railed against the lack of regulation and standards in England's schools:

Of the monstrous neglect of education in England, and the disregard of it by the State as a means of forming good or bad citizens, and miserable or happy men, [private] schools long afforded a notable example. Although any man who had proved his unfitness for any other occupation in life, was free, without examination or qualification, to open a school anywhere; although preparation for the functions he undertook, was required in the surgeon who assisted to bring a boy into the world, or might one day assist, perhaps, to send him out of it; in the chemist, the attorney, the butcher, the baker, the candlestick maker; the whole round of crafts and trades, the schoolmaster excepted; and although schoolmasters, as a race, were the blockheads and impostors that might naturally be expected to spring from such a state of things, and to flourish in it; these Yorkshire schoolmasters [such as Squeers] were the lowest and most rotten round in the whole ladder. Traders in the avarice, indifference, or imbecility of parents, and the helplessness of children; ignorant, sordid, brutal men, to whom few considerate persons would have entrusted the board and lodging of a horse and dog; they formed the worthy cornerstone of a structure, which, for absurdity and a magnificent high-minded laissez-aller neglect, has rarely been exceeded in the world.

We hear sometimes of an action for damages against the unqualified medical practitioner, who has deformed a broken limb in pretending to heal it. But, what of the hundreds and thousands of minds that have been deformed for ever by the incapable pettifoggers who have pretended to form them!

Charles Dickens (1812–70), preface to *Nicholas Nickleby,* 1839.

In England, at any rate, education produces no effect whatsoever. If it did, it would prove a serious danger to the upper classes, and would probably lead to acts of violence in Grosvenor Square.

Oscar Wilde (1854–1900), *The Importance of Being Earnest,* 1895.

We don't need no education,
We don't need no thought control,
No dark sarcasm in the classroom,
Teachers leave them kids alone.
Hey! Teachers! Leave them kids alone!
All in all it's just another brick in the wall.
All in all you're just another brick in the wall.

Pink Floyd, *The Wall*, 1979 (Roger Waters).

As the 20th century drew to a close, the state sector was plagued by inadequate funding and low morale:

There's a fish tank
In our class
With no fish in it;
A guinea-pig cage
With no guinea-pig in it;
A formicarium
With no ants in it;
And according to Miss Hodge
Some of our heads
Are empty too.

There's a stock-cupboard
With no stock,
Flowerpots without flowers,
Plimsolls without owners,
And me without a friend
For a week
While he goes on holiday.

There's a girl
With no front teeth,
And a boy with hardly any hair
Having had it cut.
There are sums without answers,
Paintings unfinished,
And projects with no hope
Of ever coming to an end.
According to Miss Hodge
The only thing that's brim-full
In our class
Is the waste-paper basket.

Allan Ahlberg (1938–), 'There's a Fish Tank', from *Please Mrs Butler*, 1983.

Privation and Cruelty

There is a long English tradition of making schooldays the unhappiest of one's life. The many opportunities to curb, correct and coerce the Youth of England, by various virtuously sadistic means, often prove too tempting to resist . . .

At Jane Eyre's school, Lowood Institution, the fee per girl is 'fifteen pounds a year'. Jane asks why they are called 'charity-children' if they pay such fees. It is explained that this is insufficient for board and teaching, so 'the deficiency is supplied by subscription' – and by cutting costs wherever possible, notably on the catering front:

Ravenous, and now very faint, I devoured a spoonful or two of my portion without thinking of its taste; but the first edge of hunger blunted, I perceived I had got in hand a nauseous mess: burnt porridge is almost as bad as rotten potatoes; famine itself soon sickens over it. . . .

 . . . the summons sounded for dinner: all re-entered the house. The odour which now filled the refectory was scarcely more appetising than that which had regaled our nostrils at breakfast: the dinner was served in two huge tin-plated vessels, whence rose a strong steam redolent of rancid fat. I found the mess to consist of indifferent potatoes and strange shreds of rusty meat . . .

Charlotte Brontë (1816–55), *Jane Eyre*, 1847, chapter 5.

Extreme meanness on the food front – and in other areas – was still going on seventy years later, as Stephen Spender discovered:

When I was nine, I was sent to a preparatory school. This was during the [First World] War. At the end of the hall of this school there was a platform and under that platform there was a hole, where, for some reason, the remnants of the day's food were always put, so that it was called the 'Bloater Hole'. For four terms, I was unceasingly shoved down the 'Bloater Hole' by other boys. One day, I and a few other boys, being hungry during the 'break', ate four quarters of a slice of bread, instead of only a quarter, as we were allowed to. This was discovered. The housemaster assembled all the boys, and standing on the platform (above the 'Bloater Hole'), said words to this effect: 'These boys are worse than Huns, they're FOOD HOGS. I'm not going to try to discover the culprits. I leave it to the remainder of you to do what you like with them. I outlaw them.' We were soon discovered. Some boys tied pieces of rope round my arms and legs and pulled in different directions.

It so happened that immediately afterward the incident I was to have a music lesson. The music master was called Greatorex, a man whom all the boys loved. I could not play the piano, and I burst into tears. He asked me very gently what was the matter. I told him, and he said, 'You may go on being unhappy until you are twenty or so, and a year comes when you are free and only waiting to go up to the University. You will probably travel abroad and then that will perhaps be the happiest time of your life.' In the completest sense, I understood what he meant. I think that I shall be grateful to him all my life for having told me that one got happy when one was older. Everyone else used to say, 'How I wish I was young. How happy one is when one is a boy.'

My father, realising that all was not well with me, took me away from this school, just as I was getting used to it, and sent me to another that was far worse. ... This school was run in the most dishonest way. For example, one summer term the amazed but sceptical boys returned from their homes to discover that it was quite transformed. The head master's drawing room had been turned into a boys' study. There was a tennis court. The boys had gardens. I, as the son of a literary man, was appointed school librarian. The next term, as suddenly, all these benefits had evaporated, and we lived in the old way, cooped up in a minute changing room and made to play in a back yard of asphalt. But a lovely photogravure school prospectus had been published with captions such as 'Boys playing tennis', 'What book, please?', 'The boys' study', 'Gardening', etc., under the photographs.

Stephen Spender, 'Day Boy', in Graham Greene, ed., *The Old School*, 1934.

As a boy, George Orwell also suffered in a less-than-lavish prep school:

Part of the trouble was that in winter, after about the age of ten, I was seldom in good health, at any rate during term-time. I had defective bronchial tubes and a lesion in one lung which was not discovered till many years later. Hence I not only had a chronic cough, but running was a torment to me. In those days however, 'wheeziness', or 'chestiness', as it was called, was either diagnosed as imagination or was looked on as essentially a moral disorder, caused by overeating. Sambo [the Headmaster] would say disapprovingly as he stood behind my chair, 'You're perpetually stuffing yourself with food, that's why.' My cough was referred to as a 'stomach cough', which made it sound both disgusting and reprehensible. The cure for it was hard running, which, if you kept it up long enough, ultimately 'cleared your chest'. ...

As usual, I did not see the sound commercial reason for this underfeeding. On the whole I accepted Sambo's view that a boy's appetite is a sort of morbid growth which should be kept in check as much as possible. A maxim often repeated to us at St Cyprian's was that it is healthy to get up from a meal feeling as hungry as when you sat down. ... At some schools, [a boy] would literally not have had enough to eat unless he had bought in regular supplies of eggs, sausages, sardines, etc.; and his parents had to allow him money for this purpose. At Eton, for instance, at any rate in College, a boy was given no solid meal after midday dinner. ... Sambo went down to see his eldest son at Eton and came back in snobbish ecstasies over the luxury in which the boys lived. 'They give them fried fish for supper!' he exclaimed, beaming all over his chubby face. 'There's no school like it in the world!' Fried fish! The habitual supper of the poorest of the working class! At very cheap boarding schools it was no doubt worse. A very early memory of mine is of seeing the boarders at a grammar school – the sons, probably, of farmers and shopkeepers – being fed on boiled lights. ...

I do not think I exaggerate the squalor of school life, when I remember how health and cleanliness were neglected, in spite of the hoo-ha about fresh air and cold water and keeping in hard training. ... A little boy of eight or nine will not necessarily keep himself clean unless there is someone to see that he does it.

There was a new boy named Hazel, a pretty, mother's darling of a boy, who came a little while before I left. The first thing I noticed about him was the beautiful pearly whiteness of his teeth. By the end of that term his teeth were an extraordinary shade of green. During all that time, apparently, no one had taken sufficient interest in him to see that he brushed them.

George Orwell (1903–50), 'Such, Such Were the Joys', in the *Partisan Review*, September–October 1952 (written by May 1947).

Orwell left 'St Cyprian's' (which Cyril Connolly, in *The Enemies of Promise*, dubbed 'St Wulfric's') in 1916. The conditions he described were not untypical, and, like those in the slums, were perfect breeding grounds for the tubercle bacillus. Orwell himself died of pulmonary tuberculosis at the age of 46.

A shy, sensitive boy, he was much bullied at Brockhurst preparatory school, where he developed a lifelong phobia of water as a result of being constantly ducked on the end of a rope by a master who believed it was the way to teach timid pupils how to swim.

Daily Telegraph, obituary of Sir Julian Critchley (1930–2000), 11 September 2000.

Show me the man who has enjoyed his schooldays and I will show you a bully and a bore.

Robert Morley (1908–92), *Robert Morley: Responsible Gentleman*, 1966.

Any one who has been sent to an English public school will always feel comparatively at home in prison. It is the people brought up in the gay intimacy of the slums, Paul learned, who find prison so soul-destroying.

Evelyn Waugh (1903–66), *Decline and Fall*, 1928.

There is nothing on earth intended for innocent people so horrible as a school. It is in some respects more cruel than a prison. In a prison, for instance, you are not forced to read books written by the warders and the governor.

George Bernard Shaw (1856–1950), *Parents and Children*, 1914.

It's rightly said that the great advantage of an English public school education is that no subsequent form of captivity can hold any particular terror for you. A friend who was put to work on the Burma railway once told me that he was greeted, on arrival, by a fellow prisoner-of-war who said, 'Cheer up. It's not half as bad as Marlborough.'

John Mortimer (1923–), *Clinging to the Wreckage*, 1982.

As far as the physical miseries go, I am sure I will cope. I lived at Eton in the 1950s and I know all about life in uncomfortable quarters.

Jonathan Aitken (1942–), former Conservative MP and cabinet minister, on the prospect of going to prison, 19 January 1999.

Headmasters all work v. hard. (See plan below)

TIMTABLE OF DAY

0700.	Jump out of bed singing cheerfull songs chase the matron round the dorms pull sheets off masters beds rout out all boys to wash basins freeze freeze.
0710.	Chase out all boys who hav climbed back into bed.
0730.	Drive boys matron and masters into brekfast. eat wot the good lord hav provided as if truly thankful.
0736.	Greet wife with luving kiss.
0736.00001.	Stop greeting wife wipe moustache and eat more hadock.
0900.	Drive boys and masters into class. Lock them in. Take latin class qui quae quod stoke boiler peel potatoes more latin quibus quibus quibus rush out to garden to pick sprouts mend punkture and answer leters.
1000.	Break. Milk buns boys for the kane.
1015.	Drive in boys and masters agane lay table clean silver feed hens teach 3A more latin. Romans v benevenuti. Treble chance pool forum packed.
1300.	lunch stew and prunes. eat with relish.
1330.	eat secret lunch smoked salmon duck green peas strubres and cream.
1430.	Flay boys and masters from changing room to foopball field, coach boys remove corpses blow up foopball mend net. Demonstrate how to head ball. Fall stunned. Wake up in time to beat boys and masters back to change.
1600.	More latin. Benevenuti playing at home sla romans with spears and arows from ditches and ramparts. Wizz! About time romans got some new players put Caesar on the transfer list Aurelius inside-right and Remus into gole.
1800.	Tea bred and scrape.
1830.	Eat second tea meringues eclairs honey and sossages. Flog boys to bed. Chase matron round dorm. Lock masters in cells.
1930.	*BEER!*
2000.	Frugal super haunch of venison or rosted ox folowed by soup partridge wine jely and trifle. Push stale bred into masters cells. Prowl round dorm and kane raggers. Confiskate dormy feast and eat same.
2100.	Latin corections with left hand xxxxxxxxxxxxx do pools with the other xx oooxxxxxx.
2200.	Snore.

Geoffrey Willans (1921–58) and Ronald Searle (1920–), *Down With Skool!*, 1953.

Now outlawed by the European Court of Human Rights, corporal punishment was for centuries taken to be an integral part of the educational method – although an occasional dissenting voice was to be heard:

Beating is the worst, and therefore, the last means to be used in the correction of children. ... Children learn to dance and fence without whipping; nay, arithmetic, drawing, etc., they apply themselves well enough to without beating: which would make one suspect that there is something strange, unnatural and disagreeable to that age, in the things required in grammar schools or in the methods used there, that children cannot be brought to, without the severity of the lash, and hardly with that too.

John Locke (1632–1704), *Some Thoughts Concerning Education*, 1693.

Dr Johnson regretted this backsliding tendency:

There is now less flogging in our great schools than formerly, but then less is learned there; so that what the boys get at one end they may lose at the other.

Samuel Johnson (1709–84), in James Boswell, *Life of Samuel Johnson*, 1791.

He was sent, as usual, to a public school, where a little learning was carefully beaten into him, and from thence to the university, where it was carefully taken out of him.

Thomas Love Peacock (1785–1866), *Nightmare Abbey*, 1818.

Charles Lamb offered this portrait of a typical whacker – one John Boyer, or Bowyer, classics master at Christ's Hospital:

J.B. had a heavy hand. I have known him double his knotty fist at a poor trembling child (the maternal milk hardly dry upon his lips) with a 'sirrah, do you presume to set your wits at me?' – Nothing was more common than to see him make a headlong entry into the schoolroom from his inner recess, or library, and, with a turbulent eye, singling out a lad, roar out, 'Od's my life, Sirrah' (his favourite adjuration), 'I have a great mind to whip you,' – then, with as sudden a retractive impulse, fling back into his lair – and, after a cooling lapse of some minutes (during which all but the culprit had totally forgotten the context) drive headlong out again, piecing out his imperfect sense, as if it had been some Devil's Litany, with the expletory yell – '*and I WILL too.*' ....

Perhaps we cannot dismiss him better than with the pious ejaculation of C. [Samuel Taylor Coleridge, former pupil at Christ's Hospital] – when he heard that his old master was on his death-bed – 'Poor J.B.! – may all his faults be forgiven; and may he be wafted to bliss by little cherub boys, all head and wings, with no *bottoms* to reproach his sublunary infirmities.'

Charles Lamb (1775–1834), 'Christ's Hospital Five and Thirty Years Ago'.

Beating was not just a prerogative of boys' public schools – it was as widely used in other schools, and against both sexes. The first passage below is from *Jane Eyre*; as a girl, Jane is sent to Lowood Institution, where Miss Scatcherd picks on Helen Burns:

'You dirty, disagreeable girl! you have never cleaned your nails this morning!'

Burns made no answer: I wondered at her silence.

'Why,' thought I, 'does she not explain that she could neither clean her nails nor wash her face, as the water was frozen?'

My attention was now called off by Miss Smith ... till she dismissed me, I could not pursue my observations on Miss Scatcherd's movements. When I returned to my seat, that lady was just delivering an order, of which I did not catch the import; but Burns immediately left the class, and, going into the small inner room where the books were kept, returned in half a minute, carrying in her hand a bundle of twigs tied together at one end. This ominous tool she presented to Miss Scatcherd with a respectful courtesy; then she quietly, and without being told, unloosed her pinafore, and the teacher instantly and sharply inflicted on her neck a dozen strokes with the bunch of twigs. Not a tear rose to Burns' eye; and, while I paused from my sewing, because my fingers quivered at this spectacle with a sentiment of unavailing and impotent anger, not a feature of her pensive face altered its ordinary expression.

'Hardened girl!' exclaimed Miss Scatcherd; 'nothing can correct you of your slatternly habits: carry the rod away.'

Burns obeyed; I looked at her narrowly as she emerged from the book-closet; she was just putting back her handkerchief into her pocket, and the trace of a tear glistened on her thin cheek.

Charlotte Brontë (1816–55), *Jane Eyre*, 1847, chapter 6.

Corporal punishment was also a feature of the English village school:

In the bottom drawer of my desk are three massive books, with leather covers and mottled edges. Embossed on their fronts are the words 'Log Book' and they cover, between them, the history of this school. ...

Our first entry at Fairacre School is at the latter end of 1880 when the first headmistress set down the details of her appointment and that of her sister as 'An assistant in the Babies' Class'. It has thus been a two-teacher school since its inception.

These two ladies would appear to have been kindly, conscientious, and religious. Their discipline seems to have been maintained with some difficulty, and the rule, laid down by the local authority and still in force, that canings must be entered in the log book, leads to several poignant entries. The ink has faded to fawn in this first battered book, but there, in rather agitated handwriting, we can read:

February 2nd, 1881. Had occasion to cane John Pratt (3) for Disobedience.

And a little later on:

April 4th, 1881. After repeated warnings, which have in nowise been heeded, had occasion to punish Tom East (2), William Carter (2), and John Pratt (3) the Ringleader, for Insolence and Damage to School Property.

The figures in brackets refer to the number of strokes of the cane, usually (2) or (3) seemed to be the rule, but gentle Miss Richards was evidently driven to distraction by John Pratt, for before long we read, in a badly shaken hand:

July, 1882. Found John Pratt standing on a Stool, putting on the Hands of the Clock with the greatest Audacity, he imagining himself unobserved. For this Impudence received six (6).

During the following two years there are several entries about the sisters' ill-health and in 1885 a widow and daughter took over the school. Their first entry reads:

April, 1885. Found conditions here in sore confusion. Children very backward and lacking, in some cases, the first Rudiments of Knowledge. Behaviour, too, much to be deplored.

This is interesting because it is echoed, at every change of head, throughout the seventy-odd years of Fairacre School's history. The new head confesses himself appalled and shocked at his predecessor's slackness, sets down his intention of improving standards of work and conduct, runs his allotted time and goes, only to be replaced by just such another head, and just such another entry in the log book.

'Miss Read' (Dora Saint, b.1913), *Village School*, 1955.

When D.H. Lawrence wrote *The Rainbow*, corporal punishment was considered the first line of defence against 'the unteachable'; when the author of the present volume started teaching, six decades later, one of the first pieces of 'professional advice' he was given was: 'Don't hit 'em after three o'clock, then the marks won't show when they get home.' The boy in this extract goes home covered in marks, and it turns out he has a heart condition …

The afternoon came again. Williams was there, glancing at her, and her heart beat thick, for she knew it was a fight between them. She watched him.

During the geography lesson, as she was pointing to the map with her cane, the boy continually ducked his whitish head under the desk, and attracted the attention of other boys.

'Williams,' she said, gathering her courage, for it was critical now to speak to him, 'what are you doing?'

He lifted his face, the sore-rimmed eyes half smiling. There was something intrinsically indecent about him. Ursula shrank away.

'Nothing,' he replied, feeling a triumph.

'What are you doing?' she repeated, her heart-beat suffocating her.

'Nothing,' replied the boy, insolently, aggrieved, comic.

'If I speak to you again, you must go down to Mr Harby,' she said.

But this boy was a match even for Mr Harby. He was so persistent, so cringing, and flexible, he howled so when he was hurt, that the master hated more the teacher who sent him than he hated the boy himself. For of the boy he was sick of the sight. Which Williams knew. He grinned visibly.

Ursula turned to the map again, to go on with the geography lesson. But there was a little ferment in the class. Williams' spirit infected them all. She heard a scuffle, and then she trembled inwardly. If they all turned on her this time, she was beaten.

'Please Miss –' called a voice in distress.

She turned round. One of the boys she liked was ruefully holding out a torn celluloid collar. She heard the complaint, feeling futile.

'Go in front, Wright,' she said.

She was trembling in every fibre. A big, sullen boy, not bad but very difficult, slouched out to the front. She went on with the lesson, aware that Williams was making faces at Wright, and that Wright was grinning behind her. She was afraid. She turned to the map again. And she was afraid.

'Please Miss, Williams –' came a sharp cry, and a boy on the back row was standing up, with drawn, pained brows, half a mocking grin on his face, half real resentment against Williams – 'Please Miss, he's nipped me,' – and he rubbed his leg ruefully.

'Come in front, Williams,' she said.

The rat-like boy sat with his pale smile and did not move.

'Come in front,' she repeated, definite now.

'I shan't,' he cried, snarling, rat-like, grinning. Something went click in Ursula's soul. Her face and eyes set, she went through the class straight. The boy cowered before her glowering, fixed eyes. But she advanced on him, seized him by the arm, and dragged him from his seat. He clung to the form. It was a battle between him and her. Her instinct had suddenly become calm and quick. She jerked him from his grip, and dragged him, struggling and kicking, to the front. He kicked her several times, and clung to the forms as he passed, but she went on. The class was on its feet in excitement. She saw it, but made no move.

She knew if she let go the boy he would dash to the door. Already he had run home once out of her class. So she snatched her cane from the desk, and brought it down on him. He was writhing and kicking. She saw his face beneath her, white, with eyes like the eyes of a fish, stony, yet full of hate and horrible fear. And she loathed him, the hideous writhing thing that was nearly too much for her. In horror lest he should overcome her, and yet at the heart quite calm, she brought down the cane again and again, whilst he struggled making inarticulate noises, and lunging vicious kicks at her. With one hand she managed to hold him, and now and then the cane came down on him. He writhed, like a mad thing. But the pain of the strokes cut through his writhing, vicious, coward's courage, bit deeper, till at last, with a long whimper that became a yell, he went limp. She let him go, and he rushed at her, his teeth and eyes glinting. There was a second of agonized terror in her heart: he was a beast thing. Then she caught him, and the cane came down on him. A few times, madly, in a frenzy, he lunged and writhed, to kick her. But again the cane broke him, he sank with a howling yell on the floor, and like a beaten beast lay there yelling.

Mr Harby had rushed up towards the end of this performance.

'What's the matter?' he roared.

Ursula felt as if something were going to break in her.

'I've thrashed him,' she said, her breast heaving, forcing out the words on the last breath. The headmaster stood choked with rage, helpless. She looked at the writhing, howling figure on the floor.

'Get up,' she said. The thing writhed away from her. She took a step forward.

She had realized the presence of the headmaster for one second, and then she was oblivious of it again.

'Get up,' she said. And with a little dart the boy was on his feet. His yelling dropped to a mad blubber. He had been in a frenzy.

'Go and stand by the radiator,' she said.

As if mechanically, blubbering, he went.

The headmaster stood robbed of movement and speech. His face was yellow, his hands twitched convulsively. But Ursula stood stiff not far from him. Nothing could touch her now: she was beyond Mr Harby. She was as if violated to death.

The headmaster muttered something, turned, and went down the room, whence, from the far end, he was heard roaring in a mad rage at his own class.

The boy blubbered wildly by the radiator. Ursula looked at the class. There were fifty pale, still faces watching her, a hundred round eyes fixed on her in an attentive, expressionless stare.

'Give out the history readers,' she said to the monitors.

There was dead silence. As she stood there, she could hear again the ticking of the clock, and the chock of piles of books taken out of the low cupboard. Then came the faint flap of books on the desks. The children passed in silence, their hands working in unison. They were no longer a pack, but each one separated into a silent, closed thing.

'Take page 125 and read that chapter,' said Ursula.

There was a click of many books opened. The children found the page, and bent their heads obediently to read. And they read, mechanically.

Ursula, who was trembling violently, went and sat in her high chair. The blubbering of the boy continued. The strident voice of Mr Brunt, the roar of Mr Harby, came muffled through the glass partition. And now and then a pair of eyes rose from the reading-book, rested on her a moment, watchful, as if calculating impersonally, then sank again.

She sat still without moving, her eyes watching the class, unseeing. She was quite still, and weak. She felt that she could not raise her hand from the desk. If she sat there for ever, she felt she could not move again, nor utter a command. It was a quarter past four. She almost dreaded the closing of the school, when she would be alone.

The class began to recover its ease, the tension relaxed. Williams was still crying. Mr Brunt was giving orders for the closing of the lesson. Ursula got down.

'Take your place, Williams,' she said.

He dragged his feet across the room, wiping his face on his sleeve. As he sat down, he glanced at her furtively, his eyes still redder. Now he looked like some beaten rat.

At last the children were gone. Mr Harby trod by heavily, without looking her way, or speaking. Mr Brunt hesitated as she was locking her cupboard.

'If you settle Clarke and Letts in the same way, Miss Brangwen, you'll be all right,' he said, his blue eyes glancing down in a strange fellowship, his long nose pointing at her.

'Shall I?' she laughed nervously. She did not want anybody to talk to her.

D.H. Lawrence (1885–1930), *The Rainbow*, 1915.

In his autobiographical *Summoned by Bells,* John Betjeman recalled his boyhood suffering at Marlborough:

> Upper School captains had the power to beat:
> Maximum six strokes, usually three.
> My frequent crime was far too many books,
> So that my desk lid would not shut at all:
> 'Come to Big Fire then, Betjeman, after prep.'
> I tried to concentrate on delicate points –
> *Ut,* whether final or consecutive?
> (Oh happy private-school days when I knew!) –
> While all the time I thought of pain to come.
> Swift after prep all raced towards 'Big Fire',
> Giving the captain space to swing his cane:
> '*One,*' they would shout and downward came the blow;
> '*Two*' (rather louder); then, exultant, '*Three!*'
> And some in ecstasy would bellow '*Four.*'
> These casual beatings brought us no disgrace,
> Rather a kind of glory. In the dorm,
> Comparing bruises, other boys could show
> Far worse ones that the beaks and prefects made.
>   No, Upper School's most terrible disgrace
> Involved a very different sort of pain.
> Our discontents and enmities arose
> Somewhere about the seventh week of term:
> The holidays too far off to count the days
> Till our release, the weeks behind, a blank.
> 'Haven't you heard?' said D.C. Wilkinson.
> 'Angus is to be basketed tonight.'
> Why Angus ... ? Never mind. The victim's found.
> Perhaps he sported coloured socks too soon,
> Perhaps he smarmed his hair with scented oil,
> Perhaps he was 'immoral' or a thief.
> We did not mind the cause: for Angus now
> The game was up. His friends deserted him,
> And after his disgrace they'd stay away
> For fear of being basketed themselves.
> '*By* the boys, *for* the boys. The boys know best.
> Leave it to them to pick the rotters out
> With that rough justice decent schoolboys know.'
> And at the end of term the victim left –
> Never to wear an old Marlburian tie.
>   In quieter tones we asked in Hall that night
> Neighbours to pass the marge; the piles of bread
> Lay in uneaten slices with the jam.
> Too thrilled to eat we raced across the court

Under the frosty stars to Upper School.
Elaborately easy at his desk
Sat Angus, glancing through *The Autocar*.
Fellows walked past him trying to make it look
As if they didn't know his coming fate,
Though the boy's body called 'Unclean! Unclean!'
And all of us felt goody-goody-good,
Nice wholesome boys who never sinned at all.
At ten to seven 'Big Fire' came marching in
Unsmiling, while the captains stayed outside
(For this was 'unofficial'). Twelve to one:
What chance had Angus? They surrounded him,
Pulled off his coat and trousers, socks and shoes
And, wretched in his shirt, they hoisted him
Into the huge waste-paper basket; then
Poured ink and treacle on his head. With ropes
They strung the basket up among the beams,
And as he soared I only saw his eyes
Look through the slats at us who watched below.
Seven. 'It's prep'. They let the basket down
And Angus struggled out. 'Left! Right! Left! Right!'
We stamped and called as, stained and pale, he strode
Down the long alley-way between the desks,
Holding his trousers, coat and pointed shoes.
'You're for it next,' said H.J. Anderson.
'I'm not.' 'You are. I've heard.' So all that term
And three terms afterwards I crept about,
Avoiding public gaze. I kept my books
Down in the basement where the boot-hole was
And by its fishtail gas-jet nursed my fear.

John Betjeman (1906–84), *Summoned by Bells*, 1960.

George Orwell remembered beating as being completely routine:

On some days nothing seemed to go right, and then it would be: 'All right, then, I know what you want. You've been asking for it the whole morning. Come along, you useless little slacker. Come into the study.' And then whack, whack, whack, and back one would come, red-wealed and smarting. ... I do remember, more than once, being led out of the room in the middle of a Latin sentence, receiving a beating and then going straight ahead with the same sentence, just like that. ... There was a boy named Beacham, with no brains to speak of .... He went up for a scholarship at Uppingham, came back with a consciousness of having done badly, and a day or two later received a severe beating for idleness. 'I wish I'd had that caning before I went up for the exam,' he said sadly – a remark which I felt to be contemptible, but which I perfectly well understood.

George Orwell (1903–50), 'Such, Such Were the Joys', 1947, in *Partisan Review*,
September–October 1952.

By the end of the 20th century, beating had become a historical curiosity:

The teacher
had some thin springy sticks
for making kites.

Reminds me
of the old days, he said;
and swished one.

The children
near his desk laughed nervously,
and pushed closer.

A cheeky girl
held out her hand.
Go on, Sir!

said her friends.
Give her the stick, she's always
playing up!

The teacher
paused, then did as he was told.
Just a tap.

Oh, Sir!
We're going to tell on you,
The children said.

Other children
left their seats and crowded round
the teacher's desk.

Other hands
went out. Making kites was soon
forgotten.

My turn next!
He's had one go already!
That's not fair!

Soon the teacher,
to save himself from the crush,
called a halt.

(It was
either that or use the cane
for real.)

> Reluctantly,
> the children did as they were told
> and sat down.
>
> If you behave
> yourselves, the teacher said,
> I'll cane you later.

Allan Ahlberg (1938–), 'The Cane', from *Please Mrs Butler*, 1983.

EARLY DAYS . . . AND BEYOND

From downy-cheeked and/or sweetly simpering Mixed Infant to spotty and/or nubile adolescent (at whatever age Parliament may have fixed for this transition), the English Pupil is supposed to proceed along a smooth, expertly crafted educational continuum, emerging as a fully formed, fully educated proto-adult. That's the idea, anyway . . .

When he was eight, John Aubrey attended the 'Latin schoole' at the church of Yatton Keynel, Wiltshire. The Curate taught the older boys – and they taught some lessons of their own ...

I was 8 yeares old before I knew what theft was, *scilicet*, I had a fine Box top which was stolen from me. . . .

In the next yeare ... I was entered in ... Latin Grammar by Mr R Latimer, Rector of Leigh de-la-mere, who had an easie way of teaching: and every time we askt leave to goe forth, we had a Latin word from him which at our return we were to tell him again – which in a good while amounted to a good number of Wordes. 'Twas my unhappiness in half a yeare to lose this good Enformer by his death ... [after which] I was under severall ignorant rest-in-house teachers.

John Aubrey (1626–97), letter to Anthony Wood, in Oliver Lawson Dick, ed., *Aubrey's Brief Lives*, 1949.

Nursery, for many in the 20th century, was a first introduction to school:

Children – we're going to do our nice 'Moving to Music' this morning, so let's make a lovely fairy ring, shall we? And then we'll all be flowers growing in the grass.

Let's make a big circle – spread out – wider – wider – just finger-tips touching – that's it.

Sue, let go of Neville – Because flowers don't hold hands, they just touch finger-tips.

SUE. Let go of Neville.

And Sue, we don't want GRUMBLERS in our fairy ring, do we? We only want *smilers*.

Yes David, you're a smiler – so is Lavinia – and Peggy and Geoffrey. Yes, you're *all* smilers.

QUIET, PLEASE.

Don't get so excited.

And Sue is going to be a smiler too, aren't you Sue? That's better.

George – don't do that ...

Now then, let's all put on our Thinking Caps, shall we, and think what flower we are going to choose to be.

Lavinia? – What flower are you?

A bluebell. Good.

Peggy?

A red rose. That's nice.

Neville?

A *wild* rose. Well done, Neville!

Sidney? – Sidney, pay attention, dear, and don't pummel Rosemary – what flower are you going to choose to be?

A *horse* isn't a flower, Sidney.

No children, it isn't funny, it's very silly. If Sidney can't think of a better flower than that we'll have to go on to someone else until he can.

Now then Sue, what are you?

Another rose! Oh I *have* got a lovely bunch of roses, haven't I? Peggy is a *red* one and Neville is a *wild* one, so I expect you are a beautiful *white* one, aren't you?

Oh, you're another red one! I see ... Now then Sidney?

A carrot *isn't a flower*, Sidney. *Think* dear, and don't blow like that. How about a tulip?

A holly-leaf isn't a flower, Sidney. All right, you'd better be a holly-leaf.

Now, children, listen very carefully. Elvis, stop bouncing, please.

No, bouncing isn't dancing, Elvis. Don't argue, dear – just stop bouncing. You watch the others – you'll see.

When Miss Boulting plays her music I want you all to get up on to your tip-most toes, light as feathers, and dance away all over the room where-ever the music takes you. And remember: you are all lovely flowers in the grass.

Everybody ready?

Just a minute, Miss Boulting.

Sidney – come here, please.

What have you got in your mouth?

I can't hear a word you're saying, Sidney, so go out of the room and spit it out, whatever it is, and then come back and tell me what it was. And Sidney. Both feet. Don't hop.

Now then, children, we're not going to wait for a boy who puts things in his mouth like a baby – we're going to be lovely flowers growing in the grass, and the sun is shining down on us to make us grow tall and beautiful and – Geoffrey, stand up – flowers don't look backwards through their legs, do they?

What flower are you?

A fat daisy! Good.

Hazel, what do we do with our heads?

We hold them up.

I should think so.

Come in, Sidney!

COME IN. There's no need to knock the door down, is there?

Now what did you have in your mouth?

It can't have been nothing, Sidney, because I distinctly saw something.

Yes, I know it's nothing *now* but what was it *then?*

A big button! Well, I'm very glad you spat it out, aren't you?

You didn't? Do you feel all right, Sidney? Sure?

Well, get back into your place, then. Incidentally, where did you get the button? Off Rosemary's pink frock. I'm ashamed of you, Sidney, a big boy of four to go around eating buttons off little girls' frocks. What flower are you going to be? I've forgotten. You'd better be a hollyhock.

No, you can't be a *super-jet,* and if you are going to be a crosspatch you'd better go and sit down over there till you are a nice boy again. You can be thinking what flower you are going to be. Go along ...

George – what did I say before? Well, don't ... Come along, children. Listen carefully to the music and then dance like a flower to it.

We're ready at last, Miss Boulting. I'm so sorry.

One – two – Off we go.

Dance, Neville, don't just stand there. Dance.

Head up, Hazel, and use your arms.

Peggy, dear – don't forget to breathe.

Rhythm, George. And cheer up – you're a *happy* flower, George.

Yes, you are.

Because I say so.

Oh good, Sidney, I knew you'd think of something.

All right, you shall be a cauliflower – only be it *gently.*

Joyce Grenfell (1910–79), 'George – Don't Do That ...', 1977.

In *Cider with Rosie*, Laurie Lee recalled his experiences in Slad Village School, from Mixed Infants to Upper Juniors:

The village school at that time provided all the instruction we were likely to ask for. It was a small stone barn divided by a wooden partition into two rooms – The Infants and The Big Ones. There was one dame teacher, and perhaps a young girl assistant. Every child in the valley came crowding there, remained till he was fourteen years old, then was presented to the working field or factory with nothing in his head more burdensome than a few mnemonics, a jumbled list of wars, and a dreamy image of the world's geography. It seemed enough to get by with, in any case; and was one up on our poor old grandparents.

This school, when I came to it, was at its peak. Universal education and unusual fertility had packed it to the walls with pupils. Wild boys and girls from miles around – from the outlying farms and half-hidden hovels way up at the ends of the valley – swept down each day to add to our numbers, bringing with them strange oaths and odours, quaint garments and curious pies. They were my first amazed vision of any world outside the womanly warmth of my family; I didn't expect to survive it for long, and I was confronted with it at the age of four.

The morning came, without any warning, when my sisters surrounded me, wrapped me in scarves, tied up my boot-laces, thrust a cap on my head, and stuffed a baked potato in my pocket.

'What's this?' I said.

'You're starting school today.'

'I ain't. I'm stopping 'ome.'

'Now, come on, Loll. You're a big boy now.'

'I ain't.'

'You are.'

'Boo-hoo.'

They picked me up bodily, kicking and bawling, and carried me up to the road.

'Boys who don't go to school get put into boxes, and turn into rabbits, and get chopped up Sundays.'

I felt this was overdoing it rather, but I said no more after that. I arrived at the school just three feet tall and fatly wrapped in my scarves. The playground roared like a rodeo, and the potato burned through my thigh. Old boots, ragged stockings, torn trousers and skirts, went skating and skidding around me. The rabble closed in; I was encircled; grit flew in my face like shrapnel. Tall girls with frizzled hair, and huge boys with sharp elbows, began to prod me with hideous interest. They plucked at my scarves, spun me round like a top, screwed my nose, and stole my potato.

I was rescued at last by a gracious lady – the sixteen-year-old junior-teacher – who boxed a few ears and dried my face and led me off to The Infants. I spent that first day picking holes in paper, then went home in a smouldering temper.

'What's the matter, Loll? Didn't he like it at school, then?'

'They never gave me the present!'

'Present? What present?'

'They said they'd give me a present.'

'Well, now, I'm sure they didn't.'

'They did! They said: "You're Laurie Lee, ain't you? Well, just you sit there for the present." I sat there all day but I never got it. I ain't going back there again!'

But after a week I felt like a veteran and grew as ruthless as anyone else. Somebody had stolen my baked potato, so I swiped somebody else's apple. The Infant Room was packed with toys such as I'd never seen before – coloured shapes and rolls of clay, stuffed birds and men to paint. Also a frame of counting beads which our young teacher played like a harp, leaning her bosom against our faces and guiding our wandering fingers. . . .

. . . My brother Jack, who was with me in the Infants, was too clever to stay there long. Indeed, he was so bright he made us uncomfortable, and we were all of us glad to get rid of him. Sitting pale in his pinafore, gravely studying, commanding the teacher to bring him fresh books, or to sharpen his pencils, or to make less noise, he was an Infant freak from the start. So he was promoted to the Big Room with unprecedented promptness, given a desk and a dozen atlases to sit on, from which he continued to bully the teachers in that cold clear voice of his.

But I, myself, was a natural Infant, content to serve out my time, to slop around and whine and idle; and no one suggested I shouldn't. So I remained long after bright Jack had moved on, the fat lord of my nursery life, skilled at cutting out men from paper, chalking suns on the walls, making snakes from clay, idling voluptuously through the milky days with a new young teacher to feed on. But my time was slowly running out; my Big Room bumps were growing. Suddenly, almost to my dismay, I found that I could count up to a hundred, could write my name in both large and small letters, and subtract certain numbers from each other. ... Infant no longer, I was being moved up – the Big Room was ready for me.

I found there a world both adult and tough, with long desks and inkwells, strange maps on the walls, huge boys, heavy boots, scratching pens, groans of labour, and sharp and sudden persecutions. Gone for ever were the infant excuses, the sanctuary of lisping charms. Now I was alone and unprotected, faced by a struggle which required new techniques, where one made pacts and split them, made friends and betrayed them, and fought for one's place near the stove.

The stove was a symbol of caste among us, the tub of warmth to which we cleaved during the long seven months of winter. It was made of cast-iron and had a noisy mouth which rattled coke and breathed out fumes. It was decorated by a tortoise labelled 'Slow But Sure', and in winter it turned red hot. If you pressed a pencil against it, the wood burst into flames; and if you spat on the top, the spit hopped and gambolled like tiny ping-pong balls.

My first days in the Big Room were spent in regret for the young teacher I'd left in the Infants, for her braided breasts and unbuttoning hands and her voice of sleepy love. Quite clearly the Big Room boasted no such comforts; Miss B, the Head Teacher, to whom I was now delivered, being about as physically soothing as a rake.

She was a bunched and punitive little body and the school had christened her Crabby; she had a sour yellow look, lank hair coiled in earphones, and the skin and voice of a turkey. We were all afraid of the gobbling Miss B; she spied, she pried, she crouched, she crept, she pounced – she was a terror.

Each morning was war without declaration; no one knew who would catch it next. We stood to attention, half-crippled in our desks, till Miss B walked in, whacked the walls with a ruler, and fixed us with her squinting eye. 'Good a-morning, children!' 'Good morning, Teacher!' The greeting was like a rattling of swords. Then she would scowl at the floor and begin to growl 'Ar Farther ...'; at which we said the Lord's Prayer, praised all good things, and thanked God for the health of our King. But scarcely had we bellowed the last Amen than Crabby coiled, uncoiled, and sprang, and knocked some poor boy sideways.

One seldom knew why; one was always off guard, for the punishment preceded the charge. The charge, however, followed hard upon it, to a light shower of angry spitting.

'Shuffling your feet! Playing with the desk! A-smirking at that miserable Betty! I will not have it. I'll not, I say. I repeat – I will not have it!'

Many a punch-drunk boy in a playground battle, outnumbered and beaten to his knees, would be heard to cry:

'I will not have it! I'll not, I say! I repeats I will not have it!' It was an appeal to the code of our common suffering, and called for immediate mercy.

So we did not much approve of Crabby – though she was responsible for our excellent reflexes. Apart from this, her teaching was not memorable. She appears in my recollection as merely a militant figure, a hunched-up little creature all spring-coils and slaps – not a monster by any means, but a natural manifestation of what we expected of school.

For school in my day, that day, Crabby's day, seemed to be designed simply to keep us out of the air and from following the normal pursuits of the fields. Crabby's science of dates and sums and writing seemed a typical invention of her own, a sour form of fiddling or prison-labour like picking oakum or sewing sacks.

So while the bright times passed, we sat locked in our stocks, our bent backs turned on the valley. The June air infected us with primitive hungers, grass-seed and thistledown idled through the windows, we smelt the fields and were tormented by cuckoos, while every out-of-door sound that came drifting in was a sharp nudge in the solar plexus. The creaking of wagons going past the school, harness-jingle, and the cries of the carters, the calling of cows from the 17-Acre, Fletcher's chattering mower, gunshots from the warrens – all tugged and pulled at our active wishes till we could have done Miss B a murder.

And indeed there came the inevitable day when rebellion raised its standard, when the tension was broken and a hero emerged whom we would willingly have named streets after. At least, from that day his name was honoured, though we gave him little support at the time . . . .

Spadge Hopkins it was, and I must say we were surprised. He was one of those heavy, full-grown boys, thick-legged, red-fisted, bursting with flesh, designed for the great outdoors. He was nearly fourteen by then, and physically out of scale – at least so far as our school was concerned. The sight of him squeezed into his tiny desk was worse than a bullock in ballet-shoes. He wasn't much of a scholar; he groaned as he worked, or hacked at his desk with a jack-knife. Miss B took her pleasure in goading him, in forcing him to read out loud; or asking him sudden unintelligible questions which made him flush and stumble.

The great day came; a day of shimmering summer, with the valley outside in a state of leafy levitation. Crabby B was at her sourest, and Spadge Hopkins had had enough. He began to writhe in his desk, and roll his eyes, and kick with his boots, and mutter; 'She'd better look out. 'Er, – Crabby B. She'd better, that's all. I can tell you …'

We didn't quite know what the matter was, in spite of his meaning looks. Then he threw down his pen, said; 'Sod it all,' got up, and walked to the door.

'And where are you going, young man, may I ask?' said Crabby with her awful leer.

Spadge paused and looked her straight in the eye.

'If it's any business of yourn.'

We shivered with pleasure at this defiance, Spadge leisurely made for the door.

'Sit down this instant!' Crabby suddenly screamed. 'I won't have it!'

'Ta-ta,' said Spadge.

Then Crabby sprang like a yellow cat, spitting and clawing with rage. She caught Spadge in the doorway and fell upon him. There was a shameful moment of heavy breathing and scuffling, while the teacher tore at his clothes. Spadge caught her hands in his great red fists and held her at arm's length, struggling.

'Come and help me, someone!' wailed Crabby, demented. But nobody moved; we just watched. We saw Spadge lift her up and place her on the top of the cupboard, then walk out of the door and away. There was a moment of silence, then we all laid down our pens and began to stamp on the floor in unison. Crabby stayed where she was, on top of the cupboard, drumming her heels and weeping.

Laurie Lee (1914–97), *Cider with Rosie*, 1959.

The experiences of new boys at St Custards (the immortal Molesworth's prep school) were perhaps not entirely different ... perhaps rather worse:

New bugs are wets and weeds their mummies blub when they kiss them goodby while seniors such as me hem-hem stand grimly by licking their slobering chops. No more dolies or William the bear to cuddle and hug, no more fairy stories at nanny's knee it is all aboard the fairy bus for the dungeons. You hav to hav a bit of patience but once the trane moves out the little victims are YOURS. You put them in the lugage rack with molesworth 2.

Paters at the moment are patting the blubing maters.

'It is all right old gurl,' they sa. 'Skools are not wot they were in my day. Boys are no longer cruel to each other and the masters are frends.'

'But my Eustace hav been taken away. He is only a baby.'

(You are dead right he is. Fancy sending him to skool with a name like Eustace. They deserve it all.)

Pater stare at his glass of gin reflectively. It will be peaceful at home now. He can relax at the weekends and if it is a good skool Eustace will soon be strong and brany enuff to bring in the coal. He sa:

'Now in my day it was diferent. When i first went to Grunts they tosted me on a slo fire. Then i ran the gauntlet being flicked with wet towels. Then they stood me aganst the mantelpeace as i am standing now –'

BANG! CRASH!

Mater gives him sharp uper cut folowed by right cross then zoom up to bed leaving pater wondering why women are so unprediktable. Glumly he pours himself another gin.

MEANWHILE AT ST CUSTARDS
Eustace hav been trussed to a chair and a pair of socks are stuffed in his mouth to stifle his desperate cries. 'Now,' sa molesworth the Pukon 'we will submit you to three trillion volts of the nuclear torture.' . . .

DOWN BELOW IN THE STUDY
Tinkle, tinkle.

Is that the telephone, my dere?

Nothing else go tinkle, tinkle, swetehart, unless it be the photograph of that repulsive old custardian in its brite silver frame. Shall I answer?

Pray do.

Tinkle, tink – It is mrs togglington to enquire after Eustace. Oh yes he hav setled down very well. He was as quiet and as good as a lamb.

(Thinks: Which one was he?)

Yes, there is no need to wory. He hav no spots his head do not ache his knok knees hav given him no trouble. He is as far as we kno unlikely to develop a disease tonite. He hav changed his socks and cleaned his fangs. I have put him in the charge of a v. reliable boy e.g. dere little nigel molesworth.

Eustace mater ring off very relieved cheers cheers and telephone all the other lades about it. Headmaster and wife continue to make wool rug. Masters shiver in their cells. An owl hoot and Eustace is insensible. St custard's hav begun another term.

Geoffrey Willans (1921–58) and Ronald Searle (1920–), *How to be Topp*, 1954.

Jennings is another famously subversive schoolboy. Here his class give the teacher a hard time:

Mr Wilkins was on duty in Form 3 classroom that evening. After patrolling the room for five minutes to make sure that all the boys were working properly, he retired to the master's desk and settled down to mark a pile of geography notebooks. Presently he became conscious of a hand upraised in query which was flapping at him from a desk in the back row. ...

There was no response from the master's desk. The voice went on: 'Sir ... Mr Wilkins, sir ...' increasing in volume until it became impossible to ignore it any longer.

The duty master looked up from his books. 'If you are addressing me, Jennings,' he said with dignity, 'you should know that I don't reply to ill-mannered little boys who shout at masters as though they were calling the cattle home across the sands of Dee.'

'I'm sorry, sir. I *did* put my hand up first, only you wouldn't look,' the boy explained. 'My arm was almost dropping off at the roots, I'd been holding it up so long.'

The arm-aching ordeal evoked no sympathy from Mr Wilkins. 'What is your question, anyway?'

'Well, sir, it's about this prep that Mr Carter set us,' Jennings went on. 'He said we'd got to write *Macbeth*, sir.'

'Did he, indeed! I was under the impression that Shakespeare had already done so.'

'In our own words, I mean, sir. Mr Carter said we were to write out the story ...'

The explanation was cut short by Temple who had not been listening attentively when the work had been set. 'No he didn't, sir!' he called out loudly. 'He said we were to *read* it, not *write* it.'

'He never did! You've got it all wrong, Darbishire chimed in. 'He said we'd got to read it first and then write it out afterwards.'

'You don't know what you're talking about,' Temple persisted. 'I can distinctly remember thinking to myself that ...'

A babble of voices broke out on all sides of the room as different boys proffered their version of what Mr Carter had said.

'It's a *written* prep. I jotted it down on my blotch, so that proves it,' announced Bromwich I, raising his voice above the tumult.

'He didn't say writing it out was compulsory!' argued Atkinson, who was hoping to avoid the effort of putting pen to paper. 'He said we could write it out if we wanted to.'

'Silence! Be quiet, all of you!' Mr Wilkins thundered. 'This is a preparation class, not a free-for-all shouting match.'

When the noise had abated, the master turned once more to the earnest questioner. 'Now, then, Jennings, what's the trouble?'

'It's this scene about Lady Macbeth, sir. It doesn't make sense.'

'Surely you mean that *you* can't make sense of it,' Mr Wilkins reproved. 'Or do you imply that the fault is Shakespeare's?'

'I suppose it *must* be, sir,' Jennings decided. 'Perhaps he didn't read it through carefully after he'd written it, sir. Mr Carter's always telling us to do that, and I expect Shakespeare was in a hurry or something, and didn't bother.'

Mr Wilkins tut-tutted like thimbles on a washing-board. 'Don't talk such ridiculous nonsense. Bring the book up here and let me have a look at it.'

The boy made his way up to the front of the room and laid the book on the master's desk. 'There, sir. Top of the page.'

'Ah, yes, this is a very famous scene,' Mr Wilkins observed as he scanned the page proffered for his inspection. 'This is the passage where Lady Macbeth walks in her sleep.'

Jennings looked puzzled. 'It doesn't *say* she walks in the passage, sir,' he objected. 'Mr Carter said she comes down the stairs.'

'Not that sort of passage, you silly little boy,' Mr Wilkins replied impatiently. 'I'm talking about a scene – an excerpt.'

'Oh, I see, sir.' Jennings formed a picture of the scene in his mind's eye. Then he said: 'Still, I suppose there *could* be a passage at the top of the stairs, couldn't there, sir? Or at any rate a landing or something, so that she could get back to her bedroom afterwards, don't you think, sir?'

'That's neither here nor there,' Mr Wilkins retorted. 'Now come along, boy, what is it you don't understand?'

A sticky forefinger traced a path down the page until it came to the line in question. 'Look, sir. It says here: "Enter Lady Macbeth with a *tapper*," sir, but it doesn't say what she taps with it.'

'Eh! Let me see.' Mr Wilkins followed the direction of the sticky forefinger and then clicked his tongue in mild despair. 'What it says is: "Enter Lady Macbeth with a *taper*," you silly little boy. Taper, not tapper. She's carrying a lighted candle, don't you see? It's the middle of the night.'

There was a pause while this information sank in. Then Jennings said: 'And is she *really* asleep, sir?'

'Yes, of course.'

'Well, in that case, sir, what does she want a candle for?'

A wave of speculation rippled round the desks as Jennings propounded this fascinating query. And before Mr Wilkins had time to think out the answer, the question was being hotly debated on all sides.

'She couldn't possibly need a taper if she was asleep because her eyes would be shut,' Martin-Jones decided.

'Perhaps she wasn't really asleep. Perhaps she was just pretending,' suggested Rumbelow.

'She was asleep, right enough,' Venables decided. 'With her eyes open, of course. Otherwise she couldn't have seen where she was going, not even with a taper.'

'How could they be open? You're bound to close your eyes when you're asleep,' Atkinson pointed out.

'Ah yes, for *going* to sleep, but not for *walking* in it. After all, you can walk with your eyes shut when you're awake, so surely you can walk with them open when you're asleep. Besides, how could she have found the taper if she couldn't see what she was doing?'

'She had to grope around for it in the dark. I bet you a million pounds they were shut. I bet you Shakespeare meant them to be.'

The uproar rose to a crescendo. Seldom in the history of dramatic criticism had scholars argued so forcibly about what Shakespeare really meant.

Anthony Buckeridge (1912–), *The Trouble With Jennings*, 1960.

Allan Ahlberg's Mrs Butler is perhaps rather more effective in dealing with children who are troublesome …

Please Mrs Butler
This boy Derek Drew
Keeps copying my work, Miss.
What shall I do?

Go and sit in the hall, dear.
Go and sit in the sink.
Take your books on the roof, my lamb.
Do whatever you think.

Please Mrs Butler
This boy Derek Drew
Keeps taking my rubber, Miss.
What shall I do?

Keep it in your hand, dear.
Hide it up your vest.
Swallow it if you like, my love.
Do what you think best.

Please Mrs Butler
This boy Derek Drew
Keeps calling me rude names, Miss.
What shall I do?

Lock yourself in the cupboard, dear.
Run away to sea.
Do whatever you can, my flower.
But *don't ask me!*

Allan Ahlberg (1938–), 'Please Mrs Butler', from *Please Mrs Butler*, 1983.

The 1944 Education Act established the Eleven-Plus exam, by which state pupils were herded either into Grammar Schools or the local Secondary Modern. The Public Schools were unaffected, and the tripartite structure of English education nicely reflected the class structure of English society:

> Crocodile from Grey Towers, Ancient Seat of Learning,
> Trailing down the avenue, pair by snooty pair,
> With a cargo of snobbery,
> Hauteur, prejudice,
> Exaggerated accents and upper-class stare.
>
> Arnold-haunted small fry from the local Grammar,
> Standing in a huddle, waiting for the bus,
> With cargo of sniggers,
> Spectacles, horseplay,
> Brashness and Angst stemming from Eleven-plus.
>
> Hordes of little bastards from the Secondary Modern,
> Gadarening home to the Children's Hour and News,
> With a cargo of comics,
> Candy floss, ice cream,
> Hollywood values and low I.Q.s.

Stanley J. Sharples, parody of Masefield's 'Cargoes', entered for a *New Statesman* competition, 1956.

The school portrayed in Barry Hines's novel, *A Kestrel for a Knave* (filmed by Ken Loach as *Kes*), is of a sort now abolished: the Secondary Modern. These schools catered for 'less academic' pupils who had failed the Eleven-Plus examination in their last year at junior school; the pass-rate was dictated by the number of places available at the local Grammar School. Some of the teachers who worked in these schools were superb; most were not. However, Hines's Games Master, Mr Sugden, is of a type known to everyone who ever was a boy shivering in the mud of any school playing field, anywhere in England …

'Right! We'll play down hill!'

The team broke for their appropriate halves, and while they were arguing their claims for positions, Mr Sugden jogged to the sideline, dropped the ball, and took off his tracksuit. Underneath he was wearing a crisp red football shirt with white cuffs and a white band round the neck. A big white 9 filled most of the back, whiter than his white nylon shorts, which showed a slight fleshy tint through the material. He pulled his socks up, straightened the ribs, then took a fresh roll of half inch bandage from his tracksuit and ripped off two lengths. The torn bandage packet, the cup of its structure still intact, blew away over the turf like the damaged shell of a dark blue egg. Mr Sugden used the lengths of bandage to secure his stockings just below the knees, then he folded his tracksuit neatly on the ground, looked down at himself, and walked on to the pitch carrying the ball like a plum pudding on the tray of his hand. Tibbut, standing on the centre circle, with his hands down his shorts, winked at his Left Winger and waited for Mr Sugden to approach.

'Who are you today, Sir, Liverpool?'

'Rubbish, lad! Don't you know your club colours yet?'

'Liverpool are red, aren't they, Sir?'

'Yes, but they're all red, shirts, shorts and stockings. These are Manchester United's colours.'

'Course they are, Sir. I forgot. What position are you playing?'

Mr Sugden turned his back on him to show him the number 9.

'Bobby Charlton. I thought you were usually Denis Law when you were Manchester United.'

'It's too cold to play as a striker today. I'm scheming this morning, all over the field like Charlton.'

'Law plays all over, Sir. He's not only a striker.'

'He doesn't link like Charlton.'

'Better player though, Sir.'

Sugden shook his head. 'No, he's been badly off form recently.'

'Makes no odds, he's still a better player. He can settle a game in two minutes.'

'Are you trying to tell *me* about football, Tibbut?'

'No, Sir.'

'Well shut up then. Anyway Law's in the wash this week.' He placed the ball on the centre spot and looked round at his team. There was only Billy out of position. He was standing between the full backs, the three of them forming a domino pattern with the half backs. The goal was empty. Mr Sugden pointed at it.

'There's no one in goal!'

His team looked round to confirm this observation, but Tibbut's team had beaten them to it by just looking straight ahead.

'Casper! What position are you supposed to be playing?' Billy looked to the Right Back, the Left Back, the Right Back again. Neither of them supplied the answer, so he answered the question himself.

'I don't know, Sir. Inside Right?'

This answer made 1: Mr Sugden angry. 2: the boys laugh. 'Don't talk ridiculous, lad! How can you be playing Inside Right back there?'

He looked up at the sky.

'God help us; fifteen years old and still doesn't know the positions of a football team!'

He levelled one arm at Billy.

'Get in goal lad!'

'O, Sir! I can't goal. I'm no good.'

'Now's your chance to learn then, isn't it?'

'I'm fed up o' goin' in goal. I go in every week.'

Billy turned round and looked at the goal as though it was the portal leading into the gladiatorial arena.

'Don't stand looking lad. Get in there!'

'Well don't blame me then, when I let 'em all through.'

'Of course I'll blame you, lad! Who do you expect me to blame?'

Billy cursed him quietly all the way back to the nets. Sugden (commentator): 'And both teams are lined up for the kick off in this vital fifth-round cup-tie,

Manchester United versus …?' Sugden (teacher): 'Who are we playing, Tibbut?'

'Er … we'll be Liverpool, Sir.'

'You can't be Liverpool.'

'Why not, Sir?'

'I've told you once, they're too close to Manchester United's colours aren't they?'

Tibbut massaged his brow with his fingertips, and under this guise of thinking, glanced round at his team: Goalkeeper, green polo. Right Back, blue and white stripes. Left Back, green and white quarters. Right Half, white cricket Centre Hall, all blue. Left Half, all yellow. Right Wing, orange and green rugby. Inside Right, black T. Centre Forward, blue denim tab collar. Tibbut, red body white sleeves. Left Wing, all blue.

'We'll be Spurs then, Sir. They'll be no clash of colours then.'

'… And it's Manchester United v. Spurs in this vital fifth-round cup-tie.'

Mr Sugden (referee) sucked his whistle and stared at his watch, waiting for the second finger to twitch back up to twelve. 5 4 3 2. He dropped his wrist and blew. Anderson received the ball from him, sidestepped a tackle from Tibbut then cut it diagonally between two opponents into a space to his left. Sugden (player) running into this space, raised his left foot to trap it, but the ball rolled under his studs. He veered left, caught it, and started to cudgel it upfield in a travesty of a dribble, sending it too far ahead each time he touched it, so that by the time he had progressed twenty yards, he had crash-tackled it back from three Spurs defenders. His left winger, unmarked and lonely out on the touchline, called for the ball, Sugden heard him, looked at him, then kicked the ball hard along the ground towards him. But even though the wingman started to spring as soon as he read its line, it still shot out of play a good ten yards in front of him. He slithered to a stop and whipped round.

'Heyup, Sir! What do you think I am?'

'You should have been moving, lad. You'd have caught it then.'

'What do you think I wa' doin', standing still?'

'It was a perfectly good ball!'

'Ar, for a whippet perhaps!'

'Don't argue with me, lad! And get that bell fetched!'

The ball had rolled and stopped on the roped-off cricket square. The left winger left the pitch and walked towards it He scissor-jumped the rope, picked the ball up off the lush lawn, then volleyed it straight back on to the pitch without bouncing it once on the intervening stretch of field.

Back in the goal, Billy was giant-striding along the goal line, counting the number of strides from post to post: five and a bit. He turned, propelled himself off the post and jump-strode across to the other side: five. After three more attempts he reduced this record to four and a half, then he returned along the line, heel-toe, heel-toeing it: thirty pump lengths.

After fourteen minutes' play he touched the ball for the first time. Tibbut, dribbling in fast, pushed the ball between Mr Sugden's legs, ran round him and delivered the ball out to his right winger, who took it in his stride, beat his Full Back and centred for Tibbut, who had continued his run, to outjump Mr Sugden and head the ball firmly into the top right-hand corner of the goal. Billy watched it fly in, way up on his left, then he turned round and picked it up from under the netting.

'Come on Casper! Make an effort, lad!'

'I couldn't save that, Sir.'

'You could have tried.'

'What for, Sir, when I knew I couldn't save it?'

'We're playing this game to win you know, lad.'

'I know, Sir.'

'Well, try then!'

He held his hands out to receive the ball. Billy obliged, but as it left his hand the wet leather skidded off his skin and it dropped short in the mud, between them. He ran out to retrieve it, but Sugden had already started towards it, and when Billy saw the stare of his eyes and the set of his jaw as he ran at the ball, he stopped and dropped down, and the ball missed him and went over him, back into the net. He knelt up, his left arm, left side and left leg striped with mud.

'What wa' that for, Sir?'

'Slack work, lad. Slack work.'

He retrieved the ball himself, and carried it quickly back to the centre for the restart. Billy stood up, a mud pack stuck to each knee. He pulled his shirt sleeve round and started to furrow the mud with his finger nails.

'Look at this lot. I've to keep this shirt on an' all after.' The Right Back was drawn by this lament, but was immediately distracted by a chorus of warning shouts, and when he turned round he saw the ball running loose in his direction. He ran at it head down, and toed it far up field, showing no interest in its flight or destination, but turning to commiserate with Billy almost as soon as it had left his boot. It soared over the halfway line, and Sugden started to chase. It bounced, once, twice, then rolled out towards the touchline. He must catch it, and the rest of his forward line moved up in anticipation of the centre. But the ball, decelerating rapidly as though it wanted to be caught, still crossed the line before he could reach it. His disappointed Forwards muttered amongst themselves as they trooped back out of the penalty area.

'He should have caught that, easy.'

'He's like a chuffing carthorse.'

'Look at him, he's knackered.'

'Hopeless tha means.'

Tibbut picked the ball up for the throw in.

'Hard luck, Sir.'

Sugden, bands on hips, chest heaving, had his Right Back in focus a good thirty seconds before he had sufficient control over his respiration to remonstrate with him.

'Come on, lad! Find a man with this ball! Don't just kick it anywhere!'

The Right Back, his back turned, continued his conversation with Billy.

'SPARROW!'

'What, Sir?'

'I'm talking to you, lad!'

'Yes, Sir.'

'Well pay attention then and get a grip of your game. We're losing, lad.'

Manchester United equalised soon after when the referee awarded them a penalty. Sugden scored.

Barry Hines (1939–), *A Kestrel for a Knave*, 1968.

In the late 1960s all Secondary Moderns, and most Grammar Schools, were abolished and subsumed into one-size-fits-all schools called Comprehensives. Scotland had been getting on very nicely with this system for over a hundred years, but in England the transition was rather more traumatic. As with all schools, some Comprehensives (whether 'bog-standard' or not) are excellent, many competent, and some appalling. This one would seem to fall somewhere between the latter categories:

'You're the new boy, aren't you?' said someone beside him. 'I'm Miss Beale, who are you?'

'I'm Mitchell,' said Andrew. 'Andrew Mitchell, Miss.' It sounded like a silly sort of tongue twister.

'How do you like it here?' said Miss Beale. Andrew didn't intend to be side-tracked.

'What are we supposed to be doing?' he asked.

'That rather depends on you,' said Miss Beale. 'In General Studies you can choose your own subject and follow it through. You'll be rather behind the others but you can start on a project now and work on it through the holidays. That's what most of the others will do, if they haven't finished by next week.'

Andrew found this hard to believe.

'What are you interested in?' asked Miss Beale.

'Motor racing, guinea-pigs,' said Andrew.

'Well, either of those would do for a start,' said Miss Beale. 'Perhaps Victor would show you round so that you can see how the others set about it.' ...

'Miss Beale said you would show me round, to look at the projects,' said Andrew.

'Why, do you want to copy one?' asked Victor, lifting a strand of hair and exposing one eye. 'You could copy mine, only someone might recognize it. I've done that three times already.'

'Whatever for?' said Andrew. 'Don't you get tired of it?'

Victor shook his head and his hair.

'That's only once a year. I did that two times at the junior school and now I'm doing that again,' he said. 'I do fish, every time. Fish are easy. They're all the same shape.'

'No, they're not,' said Andrew.

'They are when I do them,' said Victor. He spun his book round, with one finger, to show Andrew the drawings. His fish were not only all the same shape, they were all the same shape as slugs. Underneath each drawing was a printed heading: BRAEM; TENSH; CARP; STIKLBAK; SHARK. It was the only way of telling them apart. The shark and the bream were identical, except that the shark had a row of teeth like tank traps.

'Isn't there a 'c' in stickleback?' said Andrew. Victor looked at his work.

'You're right.' He crossed out both 'k's, substituted 'c's and pushed the book away, the better to study it. 'I got that wrong last year.'

Andrew flipped over a few pages. There were more slugs: PLACE; COD; SAW-FISH; and a stringy thing with a frill round its neck: EEL.

'Don't you have to write anything?' asked Andrew.

'Yes, look. I wrote a bit back here. About every four pages will do,' said Victor. 'Miss Beale, she keep saying I ought to write more but she's glad when I don't. She's got to read it. Nobody can read my writing.'

Andrew was not surprised. Victor's writing was a sort of code to deceive the enemy, with punctuation marks in unlikely places to confuse anyone who came too close to cracking the code. He watched Andrew counting the full stops in one sentence and said, 'I put those in while I think about the next word. I like doing question marks better.' He pointed out two or three specimens, independent question marks, without questions. They looked like curled feathers out of a pillow. One had a face.

'Do you put a question mark in every sentence?' said Andrew.

'Oh, yes. I know you don't actually need them,' said Victor, 'but they're nice to do.'

Andrew turned to the last page of the book. There was a drawing of a whale.

'Whales aren't fish,' said Andrew.

'Aren't they?' said Victor. He wrote 'This.is.not.a.fish?' under his whale and closed the book. 'Come and see the others.' ...

Andrew thought that he had seen most of Tim's project before. It featured a man in a tree, knotty with muscles and wearing a leopard skin.

'Tarzan,' said Tim.

'Why do a project about Tarzan?' said Andrew.

'Tarzan's easy,' said Tim. 'You just cut him out and stick him in.'

'Fish are easier,' said Victor.

'Why not do worms then?' said Andrew. 'Nothing could be easier than worms. Wiggle-wiggle-wiggle: all over in a second. Page one: worms are long and thin. Page two, worms are round.'

Victor began to grin but Tim sat down to give the idea serious consideration.

Victor's grin became wider, revealing teeth like Stonehenge.

'I reckon you're catching on,' he said. 'Why don't you do worms?'

'I want to do something interesting,' said Andrew.

'Ho,' said Victor. 'You'll come to a bad end, you will.'

Jan Mark (1943–), *Thunder and Lightnings*, 1973.

A LIBERAL EDUCATION

'But we don't want to teach 'em,' replied the Badger. 'We want to learn 'em ...'
Kenneth Grahame (1859–1932), *The Wind in the Willows*, 1908, chapter 11.

An English education is supposed to implant into the mind of growing youth a mysterious thing called Character, which then becomes Well-Rounded. In order to do this, it must be a Liberal Education: the sort of education much valued in the wake of Dickens's merciless portrayal of its opposite, Mere Instruction ...

In *Nicholas Nickleby*, Mr Wackford Squeers' Academy, Dotheboys Hall, advertises its curriculum grandly. Boys will be:

... instructed in all languages living and dead, mathematics, orthography, geometry, astronomy, trigonometry, the use of the globes, algebra, single stick (if required), writing, arithmetic, fortification, and every other branch of classical literature. Terms, twenty guineas per annum. No extras, no vacations, and diet unparalleled.

Charles Dickens (1812–70), *Nicholas Nickleby*, 1839, chapter 3.

The reality at Dotheboys Hall is somewhat different. Physical privation dominates, and intellectual instruction turns out to be combined with what might politely be termed vocational training:

C-l-e-a-n, clean, verb active, to make bright, to scour. W-i-n, win, d-e-r, der, winder, a casement. When the boy knows this out of the book, he goes and does it.

Charles Dickens (1812–70), *Nicholas Nickleby*, 1839, chapter 8.

The school run by Thomas Gradgrind, the 'eminently practical man' in Dickens's *Hard Times*, is run on principles of strict utility, as befits the requirements of the new industrial era. Gradgrind explains it thus to the new teacher, Mr M'Choakumchild:

'Now, what I want is, Facts. Teach these boys and girls nothing but Facts. Facts alone are wanted in life. Plant nothing else, and root out everything else. You can only form the minds of reasoning animals upon Facts: nothing else will ever be of any service to them. This is the principle on which I bring up my own children, and this is the principle on which I bring up these children. Stick to Facts, sir!'

Charles Dickens (1812–70), *Hard Times*, 1854, book 1, chapter 1.

A little later Gradgrind asks Bitzer, a well-drilled boy, to define a horse:

'Quadruped. Graminivorous. Forty teeth, namely twenty-four grinders, four eye-teeth, and twelve incisive. Sheds coat in the spring; in marshy countries, sheds hoofs too. Hoofs hard, but requiring to be shod with iron. Age known by marks in mouth.' Thus (and much more) Bitzer.

Charles Dickens (1812–70), *Hard Times*, 1854, book 1, chapter 2.

At the turn of the twentieth century it was the boast of the British Empire that only the very best were sent out to work in it; the highest fliers in the Civil Service examinations were posted to India. The following extract suggests that the flame of the English Liberal Education burned most brightly not in Amersham or Ampleforth, but in Allahabad:

While dealing with the subject of fees, I fancy many parents ask themselves 'What is the use of the education you are giving to my sons?' And too often what he means is distinctly 'What return shall I get for the fees? What sort of an income are you training him to earn?'

We endeavour to provide a 'liberal' education which has no end beyond itself, except the enjoyment and natural pleasure which necessarily attend it. The educated man is not imprisoned within himself. He is at home everywhere and at all times. This expansion of personality is the real test of liberal education. A boy whose mind has been really awakened by his boyhood education will be able to turn to and fit himself for a particular walk in life after leaving school. His intelligence will be a sharpened instrument with which he can do mental tasks quickly and well. We do not educate to secure a mechanical competence acquired by getting early into the destined rut, but we aspire to awaken the intellect, inculcate the habit of employing the mind, of rejoicing in the exercise of it, and to awaken a wider curiosity in life and ideas. A school which chills the exploratory eagerness of youth is not quite playing up to the requirements of 'liberal education'. . . .

The School is a moral gymnasium, an arena for contest, a republic community in which personal rights have to be maintained for one's self and respected in others, a training ground for the business and struggle of life and for the duties of a world in which men have to contend with men. . . . In the boarding house you will find the words:–

'God gives every bird its food, but he does not throw it into the nest.'

This I think expresses the intention we have here of making boys fend for themselves; the cry for 'Bearer! Bearer!' is little heard in the land, and most have learned that as school boys they ARE the School and that the School is not an Institution provided for them to patronise by coming here.

W.P.S. Milsted, Head Master of The Boys' High School, Allahabad, Report for the Year 1913.

In his reply to Milsted's address, the Lieutenant-Governor, Lord Meston, showed that not all late 20th-century political slogans are new-minted. He is reported as saying: 'The idea that the Anglo-Indian community to which they all belonged in this country could live on prestige alone was nearly finished and it was only by grit and ability, by showing themselves as good as others and a little better, that they could hope to hold their own and do the work and achieve the success of their forefathers in India. This could only be done by education, education, education.'

Back in England, the limited ambitions of the public-school curriculum were recalled by Evelyn Waugh:

To sum up my schooling:

My knowledge of English literature derived chiefly from my home. Most of my hours in the form room for ten years had been spent on Latin and Greek, History and Mathematics. Today I remember no Greek. I have never read Latin for pleasure and should now be hard put to it to compose a single epitaph. But I do not regret my superficial classical studies. I believe that the conventional defence of them is valid; that only by them can a boy fully understand that a sentence is a logical construction and that words have basic inalienable meanings, departure from which is either conscious metaphor or inexcusable vulgarity. Those who have not been so taught – most Americans and most women – unless they are guided by some rare genius, betray their deprivation. . . .

Those who passed through the Sixth at Lancing might spell atrociously, for our written work was seldom read and then only to criticise style or meaning; spelling was regarded as too elementary for attention. Those of us who 'specialised' in History had a vague conspectus of the succession of events in the Mediterranean from the time of Pericles, a rather more detailed knowledge of English History from the time of Henry VII, and of European History from the War of the Austrian Succession to the battle of Sedan. We could translate literary French unseen, but spoke it with outrageous accents and without knowledge of idiom. ... We were completely ignorant of Geography and all the natural sciences. In Mathematics we had advanced scarcely at all since we left our preparatory schools. Our general information was of the kind that makes *The Times* crossword-puzzle soluble.

My education, it seems to me, was the preparation for one trade only; that of an English prose writer. It is a matter of surprise that so few of us availed ourselves of it.

Evelyn Waugh (1903–66), *A Little Learning*, 1964.

Even Oxford University had fairly un-academic ambitions for its undergraduates. There was something more important to learn ...

Gentlemen, you are now about to embark upon a course of studies which will occupy you for two years. Together, they form a noble adventure. But I would like to remind you of an important point. Some of you, when you go down from the University, will go into the Church, or to the Bar, or to the House of Commons, or to the Home Civil Service, or the Indian or Colonial Services, or into various professions. Some may go into the Army, some into industry and commerce; some may become country gentlemen. A few – I hope a very few – will become teachers or dons. Let me make this clear to you. Except for those in the last category, nothing that you will learn in the course of your studies will be of the slightest possible use to you in after life – save only this – that if you work hard and intelligently you should be able *to detect when a man is talking rot*, and that, in my view, is the main, if not the sole, purpose of education.

J.A. Smith, professor of moral philosophy, opening a lecture course in 1914; quoted by Harold Macmillan in *The Times*, 1965.

In *Let Dons Delight*, a work featuring conversations in a senior common room at fifty-year intervals, Ronald Knox pondered the varying qualities of undergraduates and the importance or otherwise of their education:

MORDAUNT: That blasted gramophone again! I wish somebody would tell me what you ought to do with a man like Carruthers .... He's quite charming, adequately athletic, and has none of the squalid vices. But I'm supposed to teach him, you see; and he's got the sort of mind you just can't establish any contact with. ... Ought we to take on those people at all, when they're just nature's thirds?

BEITH: That's the examination system; thank God, my men are all doing research. In my department, the whole thing works itself out quite simply; if a man's a dud, you spot it in less than a term, and you just tell him to go and read something else. ... Education's nonsense, I've always said, unless there's some kind of bond between tutor and pupil.

MASSINGHAM: I haven't any bond at all with my pupils. If they seem hopeless, I'm very, very rude to them, and tell them they will plough. Which makes them so angry that they quite often pass, simply to spite me. I think kindness is wasted on the young. ... No, but seriously, Beith, if Carrutherses are prepared to pay for the privilege of being uneducated here, why shouldn't we let them? All these ornamental young men form a kind of puddle, in which you and your friends can make a culture of pure students. They don't do much harm, and when they've finished playing here they can go out like good little boys and govern the Empire.

Ronald Knox (1888–1957), *Let Dons Delight*, 1939.

PUBLIC SCHOOLS – THE GOOD, THE BAD AND THE UGLY

We class schools, you see, into four grades: Leading School, First-Rate School, Good School, and School.

Evelyn Waugh (1903–66), *Decline and Fall*, 1928.

After the closure of the monasteries, which had provided education in England for centuries, public schools were, as we have seen, established to provide education for the children of the poor. They didn't stay that way for long. The English Public School soon reinvented itself as the Nursery of the Establishment, the place where its seedlings were pricked out, thinned, hardened off and forced on, prior to being bedded out in their allotted niches in Parliament, business, the Law, banking, the armed forces, the City, the media, the arts, the Church – and, of course, in order to perpetuate the process, the public schools themselves. The British Empire was ruled (though certainly not made) by the Public School Ethos, as devised in the middle years of the 19th century by Dr Arnold. The best and the worst of the public school is, or was, widely perceived as the best and the worst of Englishness itself.

These days, Englishness (particularly in other countries) is defined in other ways, some better than the best, some worse than the worst of the old ethos. But public schools flourish into the third millennium. They (and their cousins in the 'independent sector') offer, for some parents, an alternative to the corrosive hopelessness of what the State, where they live, has to offer; for others they remain what they have always been – bastions of privilege and the Establishment.

In the words of an acquaintance, pondering his sons' schooling, 'It's not that they'll necessarily get a better education there; it's just that they'll meet the sort of people who'll be useful to them later on.' Applaud it or deplore it: in England, it continues to be true.

Standards in the public schools had badly declined by the early 19th century, and the quality of the education – intellectual, spiritual and moral – left a lot to be desired:

I should like to know ... how much ruin has been caused by that accursed system which is called in England 'the education of a gentleman'. Go, my son, for ten years to a public school, that 'world in miniature'; learn 'to fight for yourself' against the time that your real struggles shall begin. Begin to be selfish at ten years of age; study for another ten years; get a competent knowledge of boxing, swimming, rowing, and cricket, with a pretty knack of Latin hexameters and a decent smattering of Greek plays – do this and a fond father shall bless you – bless the two thousand pounds which he has spent in acquiring all these benefits for you. And, besides, what else have you learned? You have been many hundreds of times to chapel, and have learned to consider the religious service performed there as the vainest parade in the world. If your father is a grocer, you have been beaten for his sake, and have learned to be ashamed of him. You have learned to forget (as how should you remember, being separated from them for three-fourths of the time?) ties and natural affections of home. You have learned, if you have a kindly heart and an open hand, to compete with associates much more wealthy than yourself; and to consider money as not much, but honour – the honour of dining and consorting with your betters – as a great deal. All this does the public-school and college boy learn; and woe to his knowledge! Alas! what natural tenderness and kindly clinging filial affection is he taught to trample on and despise!

William Makepeace Thackeray (1811–1863), 'A Shabby Genteel Story'.

All this began to change (at least in intention) when Thomas Arnold became headmaster of Rugby in 1828, instituting widespread reforms. In *Tom Brown's School-Days*, Thomas Hughes recounted, in fictional guise, how pre-Arnoldian beastliness came to be replaced by a new ethos, that of 'muscular Christianity'. The aims of the new public-school ethos were neither primarily spiritual nor intellectual …

To condense the Squire's meditation, it was somewhat as follows: 'I won't tell him to read his Bible and serve God; if he don't do that for his mother's sake and teaching, he won't for mine. Shall I go into the sort of temotations he'll meet with? No, I can't do that. Never do for an old fellow to go into such things with a boy. He won't understand me. Do him more harm than good, ten to one. Shall I tell him to mind his work, and say he's sent to school to make himself a scholar? Well, but he isn't sent to school for that – at any rate, not for that mainly. I don't care a straw for Greek particles, or the digamma; no more does his mother. What is he sent to school for? Well, partly because he wanted so to go. If he'll only turn out a brave, helpful, truth-telling Englishman, and a gentleman, and a Christian, that's all I want.'

Thomas Hughes (1822–96), *Tom Brown's School-Days*, 1857.

Here Hughes elaborates on the character-building purpose of the good school:

In no place in the world has individual character more weight than at a public school. Remember this, I beseech you, all you boys who are getting into the upper forms. Now is the time in all your lives, probably, when you may have more influence for good or evil on the society you live in than you ever can have again. Quit yourselves like men, then; speak up, and strike out if necessary, for whatsoever is true, and manly, and lovely, and of good report; never try to be popular, but only to do your duty and help others to do theirs, and you may leave the tone of feeling in the school higher than you found it, and so be doing good which no living soul can measure to generations of your countrymen yet unborn. ... It is the leading boys for the time being who give the tone to all the rest, and make the School either a noble institution for the training of Christian Englishmen, or a place where a young boy will get more evil than he would if he were turned out to make his way in London streets. ...

The evil that men, and boys too, do, lives after them; Flashman was gone, but our boys, as hinted above, still felt the effects of his hate. ... So it is, and must be always, my dear boys. If the angel Gabriel were to come down from heaven, and head a successful rise against the most abominable and unrighteous vested interest which this poor world groans under, he would most certainly lose his character for many years, probably for centuries, not only with the upholders of said vested interest, but with the respectable mass of the people whom he had delivered. They wouldn't ask him to dinner, or let their names appear with his in the papers; they would be very careful how they spoke of him in the Palaver, or at their clubs. What can we expect, then, when we have only poor gallant blundering men like Kossuth [Lajos Kossuth (1802–94), Hungarian nationalist leader], Garibaldi, Mazzini [Guiseppe Garibaldi (1807–82) and Guiseppe Mazzini (1805–72), Italian nationalists], and righteous causes which do not triumph in their hands; men who have holes enough in their armour, God knows, easy to be hit by respectabilities sitting in their lounging chairs, and having large balances at their bankers? But you are brave gallant boys, who hate easy-chairs, and have no balances or bankers. You only want to have your heads set straight to take the right side; so bear in mind that majorities, especially respectable ones, are nine times out of ten in the wrong; and that if you see a man or boy striving earnestly on the weak side, however wrong-headed or blundering he may be, you are not to go and join the cry against him. If you can't join him and help him, and make him wiser, at any rate remember that he has found something in the world which he will fight and suffer for, which is just what you have got to do for yourselves; and so think and speak of him tenderly. ...

After all, what would life be without fighting, I should like to know? From the cradle to the grave, fighting, rightly understood, is the business, the real, highest, honestest business of every son of man. Every one who is worth his salt has his enemies, who must be beaten, be they evil thoughts or habits in himself, or spiritual wickedness in high places, or Russians, or Border-ruffians, or Bill, Tom, or Harry, who will not let him live his life in quiet till he has thrashed them.

It is no good for Quakers, or any other body of men, to uplift their voices against fighting. Human nature is too strong for them, and they don't follow their own precepts. Every soul of them is doing his own piece of fighting, somehow and somewhere. The world might be a better world without fighting, for anything I know, but it wouldn't be our world; and therefore I am dead against crying peace when there is no peace, and isn't meant to be. I am as sorry as any man to see folk fighting for the wrong people, and the wrong things, but I'd a deal sooner see them doing that, than that they should have no fight in them. ...

'And then the Captain of the Eleven!' said the master, 'what a post that is in our

School-world! almost as hard as the Doctor's [Dr Thomas Arnold]; requiring skill and gentleness and firmness and I know not what other rare qualities.'

'Which don't he may wish he may get!' said Tom, laughing; 'at any rate he hasn't got them yet, or he wouldn't have been such a flat tonight as to let Jack Ruggles go in out of his turn.'

'Ah, the Doctor never would have done that,' said Arthur, demurely. 'Tom, you've got a great deal to learn in the art of ruling.'

'Well, I wish you'd tell the Doctor so then, and get him to let me stop till I'm twenty. I don't want to leave, I'm sure.'

'What a sight it is,' broke in the master, 'Doctor as a ruler! Perhaps ours is the only little corner of the British Empire which is so thoroughly, wisely, and strongly ruled just now. I'm more and more thankful every day of my life that I came here to be under him.'

'So am I, I'm sure,' said Tom; 'and more and more sorry that I've got to leave.'

Thomas Hughes (1822–96), *Tom Brown's School-Days*, 1857.

One disadvantage of the Arnold approach was that it could result in a sterile conformism:

It makes me very sad sometimes to see these well-groomed, well-mannered, rational, manly boys all taking the same view of things, all doing the same things, smiling politely at the eccentricity of anyone who finds matter for serious interest in books, in art or music.

A.C. Benson, house master at Eton (quoted in 1904); from *The World of the Public Schools*, 1979.

From George Orwell's own report, the prep school he attended was little more than a crammer, a business that acquired richer and richer clients by achieving the right results:

St Cyprian's was an expensive and snobbish school which was in process of becoming more snobbish and, I imagine, more expensive. The public school with which it had special connexions was Harrow, but during my time an increasing proportion of the boys went to Eton. Most of them were the children of rich parents, but on the whole they were the un-aristocratic rich, the sort of people who live in huge shrubberied houses in Bournemouth or Richmond, and who have cars and butlers but not country estates. ... Sambo [the Headmaster] had two great ambitions. One was to attract titled boys to the school, and the other was to train up pupils to win scholarships at public schools, above all at Eton. ...

All the very rich boys were more or less undisguisedly favoured. ... The rich boys had milk and biscuits in the middle of the morning, they were given riding lessons once or twice a week. Flip [the Headmaster's wife] mothered them and called them by their Christian names, and above all they were never caned. Apart from the South Americans, whose parents were safely distant, I doubt whether Sambo ever caned any boy whose father's income was much above £2,000 a year. ...

Over a period of two or three years the scholarship boys were crammed with learning as cynically as a goose is crammed for Christmas. And with what learning! This business of making a gifted boy's career depend on a competitive examination, taken when he is only twelve or thirteen, is an evil thing at best, but there do appear to be preparatory schools which send scholars to Eton, Winchester, etc.

without teaching them to see everything in terms of marks. At St Cyprian's the whole thing was frankly a preparation for a sort of confidence trick. Your job was to learn exactly those things that would give an examiner the impression that you knew more than you did know, and as far as possible to avoid burdening your brain with anything else. ... Latin and Greek, the main scholarship subjects, were what counted, but even these were taught in a deliberately flashy, unsound way. We never, for example, read right through even a single book of a Greek or Latin author: we merely read short passages which were picked out because they were the kind of thing likely to be set as an 'unseen translation'. During the last year or so before we went up for our scholarships, most of our time was spent in simply working our way through the scholarship papers of previous years. ... But the greatest outrage of all was the teaching of History.

There was in those days a piece of nonsense called the Harrow History Prize, an annual competition for which many preparatory schools were entered. It was a tradition for St Cyprian's to win it every year, as well we might, for we had mugged up every paper that had been set since the competition started, and the supply of possible questions was not inexhaustible. ... Who plundered the Begams? Who was beheaded in an open boat? Who caught the Whigs bathing and ran away with their clothes? Almost all our historical teaching was on this level. History was a series of unrelated, unintelligible but – in some mysterious way that was never explained to us – important facts with resounding phrases attached to them. Disraeli brought peace with honour. Clive was astonished at his moderation. Pitt called in the New World to redress the balance of the Old. And the dates, and the mnemonic devices! (Did you know, for example, that the initial letters of 'A black Negress was my aunt: that's her house behind the barn' are also the initial letters of the battles of the Wars of the Roses?) Flip, who 'took' the higher forms in history, revelled in this kind of thing. I recall positive orgies of dates ...
'1587?'
'Massacre of St Bartholomew!'
'1707?'
'Death of Aurangzeeb!'
'1713?'
'Treaty of Utrecht!'
'1773?'
'Boston Tea Party!'
'1520?'
'Oo, Mum, please, Mum – '
'Please, Mum, please, Mum! Let me tell him, Mum!'
'Well! 1520?'
'Field of the Cloth of Gold!'
And so on. ...
Very early it was impressed upon me that I had no chance of a decent future unless I won a scholarship at a public school. Either I won my scholarship, or I must leave school at fourteen and become, in Sambo's favourite phrase, 'a little office boy at forty pounds a year'. In my circumstances it was natural that I should

believe this. Indeed, it was universally taken for granted at St Cyprian's that unless you went to a 'good' public school (and only about fifteen schools came under this heading) you were ruined for life. It is not easy to convey to a grown-up person the sense of strain, of nerving oneself for some terrible, all-deciding combat, as the date of the examination crept nearer – eleven years old, twelve years old, then thirteen, the fatal year itself! ... And yet curiously enough I was also tormented by an almost irresistible impulse *not* to work. ... Then Sambo or Flip would send for me, and this time it would not even be a caning.

Flip would search me with her baleful eyes. ... She would start off in her peculiar, wheedling, bullying style, which never failed to get right through one's guard and score a hit on one's better nature.

'I don't think it's awfully decent of you to behave like this, is it? Do you think it's quite playing the game by your mother and father to go on idling your time away, week after week, month after month? Do you *want* to throw all your chances away? You know your people aren't rich, don't you? You know they can't afford the same things as other boys' parents. How are they going to send you to a public school if you don't win a scholarship? I know how proud your mother is of you. Do you *want* to let her down?'

'I don't think he wants to go to a public school any longer,' Sambo would say, addressing himself to Flip with a pretence that I was not there. 'I think he's given up on that idea. He wants to be a little office boy at forty pounds a year.' ...

Flip would bring out her ace of trumps.

'And do you think it's quite fair to *us*, the way you're behaving? After all we've done for you? You *do* know what we've done for you, don't you? ... We don't *want* to have to send you away, you know, but we can't keep a boy here just to eat up our food, term after term. *I* don't think it's very straight, the way you're behaving. Do you?' ...

By the social standards that prevailed about me, I was no good, and could not be any good. But all the different kinds of virtue seemed to be mysteriously interconnected and to belong to much the same people. It was not only money that mattered: there were also strength, beauty, charm, athleticism and something called 'guts' or 'character', which in reality meant the power to impose your will on others. I did not possess any of these qualities. ...

I did not question the prevailing standards, because so far as I could see there were no others. How could the rich, the strong, the elegant, the fashionable, the powerful, be in the wrong? It was their world, and the rules they made for it must be the right ones. ...

There was a line of verse that I came across not actually while I was at St Cyprian's, but a year or two later, and which seemed to strike a sort of leaden echo in my heart. It was: 'The armies of unalterable law'. I understood to perfection what it meant to be Lucifer, defeated and justly defeated, with no possibility of revenge. The schoolmasters with their canes, the millionaires with their Scottish castles, the athletes with their curly hair – these were the armies of unalterable law. It was not easy, at that date, to realise that in fact it *was* alterable. And according to that law I was damned. I had no money, I was weak, I was ugly, I was unpopular, I had a chronic cough, I was cowardly, I smelt. ... The conviction that it was *not possible* for me to be a success went deep enough to influence my actions till far into adult life. Until I was about thirty I always planned my life on the assumption not only that any major undertaking was bound to fail, but that I could only expect to live a few years longer. . . . I could not invert the existing scale of values, or turn myself into a success, but I could accept my failure and make the best of it. I could resign myself to being what I was, and then endeavour to survive on those terms. . . .

My situation was that of countless other boys, and if potentially I was more of a rebel than most, it was only because, by boyish standards, I was a poorer speci-men. But I never did rebel intellectually, only emotionally. I had nothing to help me except my dumb selfishness, my inability – not, indeed, to despise myself, but to *dislike* myself – my instinct to survive.

George Orwell (1903–50), 'Such, Such Were the Joys', in the *Partisan Review*, September–October 1952 (written by May 1947).

Public schools for girls were at this time really no more than public schools for boys – only in drag:

'Run about, girls, *like* boys, and then you won't think *of* them.' That was Sherborne. Not that anything of the kind could ever be said openly, of course, because this would be to admit not only the existence of boys – horrid – but also that unless kept on the hop nice-minded English girls in their teens occasionally speculated about them. Horrid with three stars, in the unwritten Baedeker of the Nasty which ruled our young lives. Almost every human activity seemed to be in it, except cricket. Cricket was compulsory at Sherborne. . . .

I know I am being unjust to the school because I was unhappy there; presum-ably there must have been something good about it, for everyone was not as unhappy as I was. Indeed, lots of the girls ran about even more than they were required to do by a curriculum that made little allowance for time spent in getting from one place to another. (Hockey in the winter, also compulsory: run, girls, run!)

Perhaps the teaching was good. Certainly I can still remember, as one of the few relics of my education, that

Common are to either sex
Artifex and opifex,

and something effective must have been done to impress this on my memory because I have no idea now what either of them means, and I doubt that I ever knew, not having an enquiring mind in this direction. . . .

It is very difficult to convey the atmosphere of an English public school for girls to anyone who has the good fortune not to have been sent to one. They are – or at least this one was in my time – run on a male system imperfectly adapted to female needs. We were terribly, terribly keen on games. A carefully fostered and almost totally spurious interest in house matches was our main subject of conver-sation. . . . Trying to remember now the inter-girl talks that took place when authority was not in hearing, I remember snatches of discussion, in which we vied with one another in the single-minded animation expected of us, as to whether

Wingfield's second eleven was likely to do better than last year against Aldhelmsted Juniors, these being two of the houses. Now I do not believe that sporting conjecture of this kind comes natural to one girl in twenty; but this was the tradition of the place (officially described as The High Moral Tone of the School) and so this was how we talked, even when alone. . . .

Hardy as well as sporting, that was the Sherborne Type, of which we heard a great deal. I was frequently asked whether I did not want to be it – a rhetorical question which I never had the moral courage to answer truthfully. . . . The one thing about which the school and I saw eye to eye was that I was not the best raw material for the Sherborne Type. The headmistress once told me in an expansive moment that she had prayed about me more than about any other girl then under her care. The failure of these intercessions to 'take' on me satisfactorily was one of the first things to shake my belief in the efficacy of prayer. . . .

It was supposed to break one's School Honour to disregard a rule. Everything affected one's 'honour', the hardest worked word in our narrow world. And if one broke a rule one was expected to confess it to a prefect and have a nice spiritual wallow together. This system produced the most thoroughgoing prigs imaginable. At my first, smaller, healthy minded school we all smuggled in sweets whenever we could: at Sherborne when I managed to bring some back one term everyone refused them smugly because they were against the rules, and I was forced by public opinion to give them up to authority. . . .

I was an extremely ordinary child in every way; or every way but one. Indeed, if there could have been competitions in ordinariness, I should have come out high, being more ordinary than most, only much less suggestible: this was the snag. The slightly hysterical atmosphere of 'Oh-goody-goody-we-ought-to-do-well-in-lacrosse-this-term. Hurrah-for-the-House-and-I'm-so-glad-I'm-not-pretty' fostered no seeds of enthusiasm in my mind. And without that enthusiasm, vague but ready for anything that could reflect credit on the House, life at Sherborne was either one long pretence or one long nag. The School Type, which was our pattern, was the epitome of the team spirit. . . . I still feel that I was instinctively sound in regarding the House as a collection of thirty affectedly boyish little girls and nothing more. At intervals I said so, which was not so sound. . . .

After I left it took me two or three years to get over my schooldays in health. . . . And it took me much longer than that to get over the horrible feeling with which we were subtly inoculated about sex – that it was something so beastly lying in wait for us that we were not to think about it (run, girls, run). On the other hand it was made very difficult to forget because of the frequent references to purity. I remember the headmistress . . . telling us in an emotional address that she trusted us alone in the bathrooms. What she trusted us about I had at the time no idea. . . . The remark 'I'm glad I'm not pretty', quoted before and made by a member of my house who certainly had much to be thankful for, reflects equally well the general level of our intelligence and the feeling about sex in the school. . . .

I was handicapped by having a cousin who was the perfect example of the Type into which we were all supposed to be compressed. Bright and enthusiastic about almost everything by nature, she revelled in Stiff-Upper-Lippery, sending back glowing reports of jolly Sixth Form doings, while I, a squidgy part of Upper

Fourth (b), wrote home monotonous and incoherent complaints, trying vainly to convey, with the vocabulary of fifteen or sixteen years old, that it was not any specific thing I hated but all that the school stood for. ... If only I had had the sense to stick to describing the food, meal by meal, I might have got away earlier. ...

Release came eventually through my happy decision not to be confirmed when the time came. My reason for this was no more profound than that of the unwisely handled mule when it refuses to budge in any direction: 'they' wanted it, so there must be a catch somewhere. My loss of faith would not have been sufficient reason for letting myself be nagged at by the unfortunate prefects, who were set to walking round the grounds with me after lunch on Sunday to try to persuade me. ... I could find no reason for my continued refusal. They, poor conscientious girls, could find very few reasons to advance in favour of confirmation, except that the preparation classes were 'simply topping'; but then so, I had been given to understand, was cricket, and I knew all about that. They were agonising walks.

Eventually, in desperation, one of the prefects asked me whether I did not think religion 'so sensible', and suddenly this crystallised Sherborne for me. A place where a collection of incredible legends – among them, in the New Testament, the most moving and lovely human story I had heard – could be described as 'so sensible'. ...

I sat up, hunched on the corner of my bed, all my last night at Sherborne, unwilling to waste in sleep a moment of gloating over the fact that my public school life was over: how exquisitely delightful it would be to be an adult! And it is: the state of not being a child has surpassed even my expectations of joy. The simple pleasure that I take in this is the best thing my education gave me; apart, of course, from the cultural value of knowing the hermaphroditic qualities of artifex and opifex, whatever they are.

E. Arnot Robertson, 'Potting Shed of the English Rose', in Graham Greene, ed., *The Old School*, 1934.

E.M. Forster saw the public schools as manufacturers of a powerfully monolithic but blinkered outlook:

Just as the heart of England is the middle classes, so the heart of the middle classes is the public-school system. This extraordinary institution is local. It does not even exist all over the British Isles ... [and] remains unique, because it was created by the Anglo-Saxon middle classes, and can flourish only where they flourish. How perfectly it expresses their character – far better, for instance, than does the university, into which social and spiritual complexities have already entered. With its boarding-houses, its compulsory games, its system of prefects and fagging, its insistence on good form and on *esprit de corps*, it produces a type whose weight is out of all proportion to its numbers.

... Many men look back on their school days as the happiest of their lives. They remember with regret that golden time when life, though hard, was not yet complex; when they all worked together and played together and thought together, so far as they thought at all; when they were taught that school is the world in miniature, and believed that no-one can love his country who does not love his school. And they prolong that time as best they can by joining their Old Boys' society; indeed, some of them remain Old Boys and nothing else for the rest of their lives. They attribute all good to the school. They worship it. They quote the remark that 'the battle of Waterloo was won on the playing fields of Eton'. It is nothing to them that the remark is inapplicable historically and was never made by the Duke of Wellington, and that the Duke of Wellington was an Irishman. They go on quoting it because it expresses their sentiments; they feel that if the Duke of Wellington didn't make it he ought to have, and that if he wasn't an Englishman he ought to have been. And they go forth into a world that is not entirely composed of public-school men or even of Anglo-Saxons, but of men who are as various as the sands of the sea; into a world of whose richness and subtlety they have no conception. They go forth into it with well-developed bodies, fairly developed minds, and undeveloped hearts.

E.M. Forster (1879–1970), 'Notes on the English Character', in *Abinger Harvest*, 1936.

> Here you see the four of us,
> And there are so many more of us,
> Eldest sons who must succeed:
> We know how Cæsar conquered Gaul
> And how to whack a cricket ball –
> Apart from this our education
> Lacks co-ordination.
>
> Noël Coward (1899–1973), song, 'The Stately Homes of England', from *Operette*, 1938.

The 'school story' was an immensely popular genre of children's literature in the first half of the 20th century. Such stories featured in a number of boys' weeklies, including the *Gem* and *Magnet*, both of which remained popular until the late 1950s:

The mental world of the *Gem* and *Magnet* ... is something like this:

The year is 1910 – or 1940, but it is all the same. You are at Greyfriars, a rosy-cheeked boy of fourteen in posh, tailor-made clothes, sitting down to tea in your study on the Remove passage after an exciting game of football which was won by an odd goal in the last half-minute. There is a cosy fire in the study, and outside the wind is whistling. The ivy clusters thickly round the old grey stones. The King is on his throne and the pound is worth a pound. Over in Europe the comic foreigners are jabbering and gesticulating, but the grim grey battleships of the British Fleet are steaming up the Channel and at the outposts of Empire the monocled Englishmen are holding the niggers at bay. Lord Mauleverer has just got another fiver and we are all settling down to a tremendous tea of sausages, sardines, crumpets, potted meat, jam and doughnuts. After tea we shall sit round the study fire having a good laugh at Billy Bunter and discussing the team for next week's match against Rookwood. Everything is safe, solid and unquestionable. Everything will be the same for ever and ever.

George Orwell (1903–50), 'Boys' Weeklies', in *Horizon*, March 1940.

Private Eye sent up, in its own inimitably impish fashion, the ritual-ridden ethos and arcane language of the English public school:

ST CAKE'S SCHOOL

Boot term begins today. There are 2.5 million boys in the School, and 3 girls in Uppers. J.P.R. Raj-Quartet (Ballard's) is Custodian of the Grove. L.L.L. Crocodile-Dundee (Odeon's) is Lictor of Lower Mattress. Mr P.J. Rentboy is on an exchange with the Centre of Human Interface Studies, New Proctor, Cal. His place is taken by Mr Conrad Q. Roughtrade, who will be in charge of Lower Trunks. Elders Day is on 17 June. The Van der Post Sermon will be given by the Rev N'Tiny M'Rowland, O. C., Dean of North Rumbabwe. Ruddocks will be run over Waldegrave's Piece. There will be a performance of *The Resistable Rise of Gryff Rhys Jones* by Berthold Brecht in the new Sainsbury Arts Complex (formerly the Armoury). Old Cake's Dinner will be held in the Ernest Saunders Suite of the Al-Fayed Holiday Inn, Rumpole-on-Stour on 23 August. Tickets from the Bursar, Maj. N.F. Hamilton-Howarth. Ejaculations will be on 26 July.

Private Eye, I May 1987.

In the Thatcher era, some public-school heads found themselves at odds with the new spirit abroad in the land:

Whatever their private misgivings, the schools endorse the priorities of the age: every man for himself in the competition for good 'A' levels, a good university, a well-paid job and red Porsche to roar up the school drive, scattering your former teachers like nature's rejects in the race of life.

Dr John Rae, headmaster of Westminster School, 'Tom Brown's Porsche Days', *The Times,* 31 July 1987.

When I observe the shallow materialism of some of the homes from which our boys come, and the glib expectation that a school such as mine will provide the culture, sensitivity and spirituality that are so flagrantly inconspicuous in the domestic *mise-en-scène*, I feel a twinge of despair.

David Newsome, headmaster of Wellington School, unpublished address to the 27 Club, May 1987; in *Friends in High Places* by Jeremy Paxman, 1990.

A critique of the whole system came in 2000 from a surprising source:

The Michaelmas Term begins, the football season gets under way, there is a nip in the evening air and the heart sinks as one reads those announcements posted by the fee-paying schools .... Yes, the dreaded Y K Swotski is Head Boy, the Fourth of November will be held on Nov 6, together with a performance of *If* in College Chapel. J S B Outstanding-Greaser is Keeper of the Mixed Grill. What memories seem to rise within me as I look on those cryptic blocks of text.

Think of the smell of carbolic; the awful afflatus of the organ on that first Sunday evening, as hundreds of pupils, their mothers' Mitsouko still on their cheeks, whimper their way through *Abide With Me*. Think of that little British microcosm, with nothing ahead but violent games and teasing and the howling of the school dog, and no girls save the Chaplain's daughter. Think of the privations, think of the cabbage, think of what it felt like to have your head kicked in as you lay face down in the mud at four o'clock as darkness fell and the sleet intensified.

And what did it feel like, my friends? It felt absolutely marvellous, of course. Totally top-hole. It made me what I am. It was a first-rate preparation for life; and the only reason my heart sinks is that ... if you want a boarding school private education for your nippers, these days you won't get much change from £15,000 a year, while the average London day school now demands £7,000 a year. Multiply that by four, and you understand the whole crippling insanity of the British educational apartheid. ...

Boris Johnson, editor of the *Spectator*, in the *Daily Telegraph*, 17 September 2000.

Buggery

Public schools are the nurseries of all vice and immorality.

Henry Fielding (1707–54), *Joseph Andrews*, 1742.

One further aspect of English public-school life deserves a little outing ...

You can't expect a boy to be depraved until he has been to a good school.

Saki (H.H. Munro, 1870–1916), 'The Baker's Dozen', 1910.

I expect you'll be becoming a schoolmaster, sir. That's what most of the gentle-men does, sir, that gets sent down for indecent behaviour.

Evelyn Waugh (1903–66), *Decline and Fall*, 1928.

Assistant masters came and went. ... Some liked little boys too little and some too much.

Evelyn Waugh (1903–66), *A Little Learning*, 1964.

At Harrow you could have any boy for a box of Cadbury's milk chocolate. But I didn't want boys.

John Mortimer (1923–), quoted in the *Daily Telegraph*, 24 September 1998.

In the 1930s Derek Verschoyle examined the confused attitude towards homosexuality in the public schools:

The objection to homosexuality is fundamentally not a question of ethics but a question of orthodoxy, except in so far as orthodoxy is considered as identical with morality. The Public Schools confess (and some of them confess it with pride) that they do not cater for 'abnormal' boys. When they speak of 'character' (which they do, in the context of 'development', with monotonous frequency) they mean, not a well-developed personal identity in which the idiosyncrasies of the individual have been fused with a sense of obligation to the community, but a composite of certain standardised qualities, more frequently invoked than analysed, in whose perpetration the system has a vested interest. The boy who exhibits noticeable affection for another boy offends by his unorthodoxy more than by his specific conduct, in that he demonstrates that he has not been moulded into the standard condition of insensient asexuality at which the system aims. The system is thus threatened with a failure to standardise . . . . What is least to the credit of the Public Schools is that it is generally attachments that have grown on a valuable and fertilising basis of common interests and temperamental compatibility that are noticed and penalised, while the grosser examples of physical lust, being of their essence fugitive and secret, pass undetected. . . .

Meanwhile we still have the Public School Boy, the product of the present system . . . at his best a practical man, a little limited in his views but tolerant towards those of different opinion, well mannered and polite, neat in his appearance and punctual in his ways, a shade superficial perhaps but perfectly adapted to climb gradually to the top of any of the professions for which he has been produced, a smoothly turning cog in the machine; at his worst a complacent philistine, unable to think for himself and leaning on a code for moral conviction, lacking in imagination and in vision, eager for popularity, emotionally dwarfed and blandly adolescent in sexual matters, insensitive to beauty and confused towards truth, a creature lost to progress in his obsequiousness towards convention, his inability for innovation, his class-consciousness and smug confidence in his own superiority, his faith in his own powers in a crisis ('It was the Public Schools which pulled the country through the General Strike'), his narrowness and prejudice, above all his absurd Loyalty: 'I have to thank the Old School for making me what I am.'

Derek Verschoyle, 'Indian Innocence, Ltd.', in Graham Greene, ed., *The Old School*, 1934.

Decades later, Stephen Fry found a similar double-standard at work in attitudes towards what Verschoyle called 'attachments' on the one hand, and what he termed 'the grosser examples of physical lust' on the other:

At my last year at prep school, it had become very much the thing amongst a handful of us in our senior dormitory to do a fair amount of fooling around when the others were asleep. A couple of the boys were equipped with a set of fully operational testicles and bushy pubic undergrowth, others like me were not. I greatly enjoyed creeping over to another boy's bed and having a good old rummage about. I never quite knew what it was that I enjoyed, and certainly the first time I saw semen erupt from a penis it gave me the fright of my life. I have to confess I found it frankly rather disgusting and wondered at nature's eccentricity: like Noel Coward's Alice I felt that things could have been organised better. One of the boys in that dorm, we'll call him Halford, like me not fully ripened but of a sportive disposition, took the same pleasure that I did in wandering around the school naked. Together we would, with roaring stiffies, or what passed for roaring stiffies in our cases, creep around the bathrooms simply glorying in the fact of our nakedness. We might point and prod and giggle and fondle each other a little, and experiment with that curious squashing of dicks in closing doors and desk-lids that seems to please the young, but it was the nakedness and the secrecy that provided all the excitement we needed.

One afternoon, this same Halford was climbing out of the swimming pool when he suddenly got the most terrible cramp in one leg. He yowled with pain, flopped forward on to the grass and started to thrash his legs up and down in agony. I was standing close by so I went and helped him up and then walked him around the pool until the cramp had gone. Fully recovered, he streaked away to change and I thought no more about it.

As the afternoon wore on it became apparent to me that I seemed suddenly to have become extremely unpopular. One is highly sensitive to these things at twelve, I was at least. Highly. My popularity rating was something I was more aware of than the most sophisticated political spin-doctor. But I simply couldn't understand it. It must have been one of those rare afternoons when I knew I had done absolutely nothing wrong. It was bewildering, but inescapable: boys were cutting me dead, sneering openly at me, sending me to Coventry and falling sullenly silent when I entered rooms.

At last I ran into someone who could explain. I found myself approaching a fat boy called McCallum in the corridor and he whispered something as I passed.

'What did you say?' I asked, stopping and spinning round.

'Nothing,' he said and tried to move on. McCallum was someone of little account and I knew that I could master him.

'You muttered something just now,' I said grasping him by both shoulders, 'you will tell me what it was or I will kill you. It is that simple. I will end your life by setting fire to you in bed while you are asleep.'

McCallum was the sort of gullible panicky fool who took that kind of threat very seriously indeed.

'You wouldn't dare!' he said, proving my point.

'I most certainly would,' I replied. 'Now. Tell me what it was that you said just now.

'I just said ... I said ...' he spluttered to a halt and coloured up.

'Yes?' I said. 'I'm waiting. You just said ...?'

'I just said "Queer".'

'Queer?'

'Yes.'

'You said "Queer', did you? And why was that?'

'Everyone knows. Let me go.'

'Everyone knows,' I said, strengthening my grip on his shoulders, 'but me. What is it that everyone knows?'

'This afternoon ... ow! You're hurting me!'

'Of course I'm bloody hurting you! Do you think I would be exerting this much pressure for any other reason? Go on. "This afternoon ..." you said.'

'When Halford got out of the pool ...'

'Yes, what about it?'

'You, you put your arm round him like a queer. Halford is hopping mad. He wants to beat you up.'

In my shock, outrage, horror and indignation I let go of McCallum completely and he took his opportunity, scuttling away like a fat beetle, shouting 'Queer!' as he rounded the corner out of sight.

I didn't even remember putting my arm round Halford's shoulder. I suppose I must have done as I had walked him round the pool.

All the blood drained from my face and I came close to one of those early adolescent fainting fits which sometimes stay with you till late in life, a physical sensation that can overwhelm you if you stand up very suddenly – a feeling that you
are close to blacking out and falling down.

Halford thought I was queer because I had put my arm round him. Put my arm
round him to support him! The very same Halford who was wandering naked
with me around the bathroom not two nights previously. The Halford who taught
me how to shut my cock in a door. The Halford who did a backward somersault
naked on the floor at me and pushed his finger up his arse, giggling. He thought
I was queer? Queer for putting an arm round him when he had cramp? Jesus.

I stumbled to a back stairway to try and find a private place to go and weep. I had
got no further than the first landing when I walked straight into the hairy tweed
jacket of Mr Bruce, history master and quondam internee of the Japanese Army.

'Hello, hello, hello! What's up here?'

The tears were streaming down my face and it was no good pretending it was
hayfever. Racked with sobs, I explained about Halford's cramp and the disgust
I had apparently caused him when just trying to be helpful. I did not, of course,
mention our night-time prowls in the nude, the sheer *hypocrisy* of Halford's reaction, the unfairness and injustice and cruelty of which was what had really knocked
me for six. Mr Bruce nodded gravely, gave me a handkerchief and disappeared.

I crawled my way on up to a bed and lay there weeping until tea, when I decided
that I might as well get used to my unpopularity and face the howling mob in the
senior refectory.

As I tried to wedge myself into my place on the bench, an artificially huge gap
appeared as the boys either side made a huge show of distancing themselves from the
disgusting homo who was polluting their table. Pale but resolute I started to eat my tea.

Halfway through the meal a gong sounded. Everybody looked up in surprise.

Mr Bruce was standing at the end of the room, an arm upraised for silence.

'Boys,' he said. 'I have a special announcement to make. I have just heard of a
heroic act of kindness that took place by the swimming-pool this afternoon.
It seems that Halford got into difficulties with cramp and that Fry helped him to
his feet and did exactly the right thing. He walked him about, supporting him
carefully all the way. I am awarding Fry five merits for this sensible, cool action.'

I stared down at my plate, unable to move a single muscle.

'Oh, by the way,' continued Bruce, as if the thought had just struck him. 'It has
also come to my ears that some of the younger, sillier boys, who are ignorant about
such things, think that someone putting their arm around a friend in distress is a
sign of some sort of perversion. I look to you senior boys, who have a rather more
sophisticated understanding of sexual matters, to quash this sort of puerile nonsense. I hope, incidentally, that Halford has thanked Fry properly for his promptness and consideration. I should think a hearty handshake and good manly
bear-hug would be appropriate. That's all.'

A squeak of brogues on floorboards and he was gone. After one and a half seconds of unbearable silence, palms began to rain down congratulatory thumps
upon my back, Halford rose sheepishly from his bench to thank me and I was in
favour once more.

Ant Cromie writes me that Jim Bruce died a couple of years ago, God rest, nourish and soothe his immortal soul. He walks now with Montrose, William Wallace and Bonnie Prince Charlie himself. He saved my last term at Stouts Hill and I will honour his memory for ever.

But does that, or does that not tell you something of the psychological minefield one trod through in those days, when it came to questions of sexual nature, of *sexuality*, as we would say now? The difference between sexual play and *queering*; the blind terror that physical affection inspired, but the easy acceptance of erotic games.

At Uppingham, much the same views obtained. Those whose morning prongers one brushed as Morning Fag did not think of themselves or of me as queer in any way at all. I am not sure anyone really knew what queer really, *really* meant. The very idea of it made everyone so afraid that each created their own meaning, according to their own dread of their own impulses.

You could openly admire a pretty boy, and all the middle and senior boys did. It was a sign of manliness indeed to do so.

'Just ten minutes alone, me and that arse ...' a sixth former might say as a cute junior walked past. 'That's all I ask,' he would add looking skywards in prayer.

'Oh no!' One senior would clutch another as they caught sight of a comely new boy, 'I'm in love. Save me from myself.'

I *think* that the logic of it was that new boys, pretty boys, were the closest approximation Uppingham offered to *girls*. They were hairless in the right places and sweet and cute and comely like girls, they had fluffy hair and kissable lips like girls, they had cute little bottoms like ... well, they had cute little bottoms like *boys*, but hell, any port in a storm, and there's no storm like pubescence and no port like a pretty boy's bum. All that public swooning however, was no more than macho posture. It proved their heterosexuality.

Stephen Fry (1957–), *Moab is my Washpot*, 1997.

Educated: in the holidays from Eton.

Sir Osbert Sitwell (1892–1969), entry in *Who's Who*, 1929.

CAMFORD, OXBRIDGE, AND OTHER SEATS OF LEARNING

'Oxford-and-Cambridge'; pressed to define that concept, the majority come up with something that is recognisably Oxford.
This section takes account of that perception, but not slavishly.

Undergraduate Life

Oxford in the 18th century was at a low ebb of intellectual vigour. Although it was the place to go, higher education was the last thing on anyone's mind ...

... if I am to make any acquaintance that may be usefull to me in future life, which is the only reason I am sent to this colledge....

Richard Congreve, letter from Oxford to his mother, 13 April 1733.

To the University of Oxford I acknowledge no obligation; and she will as cheerfully renounce me for a son. I spent fourteen months at Magdalen College: they proved the fourteen months the most idle and unprofitable of my whole life.

Edward Gibbon (1737–94), *Memoirs of My Life*, 1796.

Cambridge was no better:

Surely it was of this place, now Cambridge but formerly known by the name of Babylon, that the prophet spoke when he said: 'the wild beasts of the desert shall dwell there, and their houses shall be full of doleful creatures, and owls shall build there, and satyrs shall dance there'.

Thomas Gray (1716–71), letter to Richard West, December 1736.

West, who was at Oxford, replied, 'Oxford, I can assure you, has owls that match yours.'

Hail, horrors, hail! ye ever gloomy bowers,
Ye gothic fanes, and antiquated towers
Where rushy Camus' slowly winding flood
Perpetual draws his humid train of mud.

Thomas Gray (1716–71), 'Hymn to Ignorance'.

In the 19th century, the colleges began to take their responsibilities a little more seriously:

Anyone who tries to get hold of young men of rank or wealth must expect to be accused of snobbishness, but one must remember how important it is to influence towards good those who are going to have an influence over hundreds of thousands of other lives.

Benjamin Jowett (1817–93), Master of Balliol College, Oxford, quoted in Jan Morris, ed., *The Oxford Book of Oxford*.

Oxford indeed began to produce men well equipped to hold sway over others:

One can tell an Oxford man ... almost at a glance. He is full of opinions and of the ability to defend them. He sets his mind at yours with a conscious briskness which seems to foreknow victory. He uses his culture like a weapon always drawn – with a flourish wonderfully easy and graceful. ... His trim dress and carefully poised voice, his brisk movements and the precise elaboration of his speech, all seem deliberately and yet easily accomplished, all part of his armoury, weapons fit for his confident attack upon the universe. Not even the world-old traditions, the crumbling towers and quiet quadrangles of his own city, have succeeded in luring him into the past. Not even the study of Literae Humaniores has seduced him into abstraction; not even the rich seclusion of the Thames Valley has availed to enervate him: he has pressed all into the service of his own ambitions.

Charles Tennyson, *Cambridge from Within*, 1913.

An observation of Cambridge from this period:

Trinity is like a dead body in a high state of putrefaction. The only interest of it is in the worms that come out of it.

Lytton Strachey (1880–1932), letter, 1903.

For some, sport or other diversions were more important than study:

Lionel Hedges had come up from Tonbridge [to Trinity College, Oxford] with a tremendous reputation as a schoolboy cricketer, having already played for Kent. A seedy looking middle-aged gentleman called on him one morning of a match. Imagining him to be a reporter, Lionel said to him brusquely, 'I have nothing to say to you.' The man tried to expostulate but Lionel repeated, 'I have nothing to say to you.' It only afterwards transpired that the seedy man was not a reporter but his tutor, with whom he was not otherwise acquainted.

Christopher Hollis (1902–1977), *Oxford in the Twenties*, 1976.

In *Autumn Journal*, Louis MacNeice pondered the advantages of an Oxford education:

... certainly it was fun while it lasted
And I got my honours degree
And was stamped as a person of intelligence and culture
For ever wherever two or three
Persons of intelligence and culture
Are gathered together in talk
Writing definitions on invisible blackboards
In non-existent chalk.
But such sacramental occasions
Are nowadays comparatively rare;
There is always a wife or a boss or a dun or a client
Disturbing the air.
Barbarians always, life in the particular always,
Dozens of men in the street,
And the perennial if unimportant problem
Of getting enough to eat.

But in case you should think my education was wasted
I hasten to explain
That having once been to the University of Oxford
You can never really again
Believe anything that anyone says and that of course is an asset
In a world like ours;
Why bother to water a garden
That is planted with paper flowers?

Louis MacNeice (1907–63), *Autumn Journal*, 1939.

Oxford has supplied a high proportion of prime ministers and top civil servants. Maurice Bowra, Warden of Wadham College, recalled the early promise of the man who was to be Harold Macmillan's Cabinet Secretary:

Very quick, Brook. Learned the tricks, learned the tricks. Came up with a front pocket stuffed full of pens. Soon disappeared inside. Learned the tricks.

Maurice Bowra, in conversation with Harold Macmillan about Norman Brook (afterwards Lord Normanbrook); quoted in Jeremy Paxman, *Friends in High Places*, 1990.

The essential training ground for the political Establishment was the Oxford Union, where undergraduates cut their debating teeth. In the early 1920s Evelyn Waugh reported on the goings-on at the Union for the student newspaper. On this occasion no future prime ministers were speaking …

Mr. M.A. Thomson (Exeter) was almost wholly fatuous and successful.

Mr. J.L. Parker (New College) was much in favour of blood, iron, Bismarck, France and all those sorts of thing.

Mr. H. Lloyd-Jones (Jesus) gave the impression of having been suddenly stirred from a deep slumber by the previous speaker's mention of Wales.

Mr. R.H. Bernays (Worcester) was, as always, vehement, long-winded, biblical, homely, and not ineffective. He quoted French with an accent for which he thought he need not apologize.

Mr. Alfonso de Zulueta (New College) told an enchanting story about a school where the matron was wanton.

Mr. S.F. Villiers-Smith (New College) made the sort of speech which one associates with aged colonels.

Mr. Nobbs (Wadham) actually used the expression 'made the Empire what it is'.

Mr. H.J.V. Wedderburn (Balliol) addressed some of Shakespeare's more unrestrained love poems to the President in a most shameless manner.

Mr. D.J. Dawson (Christ Church) was brief almost to the point of insignificance.

Mr. I.B. Lloyd (of Exeter) said something in a foreign tongue of which I happened to know the meaning, but could not see the interest.

I detest all that Mr. A. Gordon Bagnall (St. John's) says always.

Evelyn Waugh (1903–66), reporting an Oxford Union debate for *Isis*, c.1923.

Jan Morris, of a later generation of Oxford graduates, gives a more measured assessment of the Oxford Union:

You cannot actually learn kingship at Oxford, except by the study of your predecessors, but there is probably nowhere on earth where so many men have learnt how to be politicians. The most famous of political nurseries is the Oxford Union, the debating society of the University, which is a House of Commons in epitome – often as pompous as Westminster, sometimes as boorish, and frequently just as far-sighted. The Union Society is a club, physically the most depressing I know, with a gloomy bar and a restaurant like an indigent church vestry. The core of it, though, is the debating hall, a humped red-brick structure at the bottom of the garden. Here each Thursday evening the members, reinforced by a few eminent guests, meet in debate to all the protocol of Parliament – interruptions on points of order, references to the Honourable Gentlemen on the other side of the House, invitations to the Honourable the ex-Treasurer to take the chair, Tellers for the Ayes and Noes, hoity-toity references to the rules and angry interventions by young men with beards who want to know why the President had the heartless effrontery to say good morning to the South African Ambassador during his recent offensive visit to the city.

Around them there meditate, long hardened to it all, busts of distinguished predecessors – Gladstone, Asquith, Curzon, F.E. Smith, Macmillan. They represent a predominantly patrician past, but today the elected officers of the Union more faithfully represent the social spectrum. The President may be a Socialist from a Bradford secondary school, the secretary the son of a Scottish duke, the treasurer a Bengali in white trousers, the librarian the jolly decent son of a former colonial Civil Servant. They debate most of the obvious political issues of the day, helped along by visiting Ministers of the Crown, Opposition leaders, journalists and miscellaneous experts, except in the farewell debate of the term, when the motion is usually funny – 'That this Union be Consummated', for instance – and the guests are likely to be erudite comedians.

Visiting foreigners often like to attend a Union debate, to see how decadent the young English are these days, and often the affairs of this society get into the newspapers. When the famous 'King and Country' motion was carried in 1933 – 'That this House will on no account fight for its King and Country' – it was interpreted as proof that England had gone soft at last (though it was really a reflection of the confused idealism, part pacifist, part Communist, then aflame in the English universities). Public opinion was severely shocked by it, and though *The Times* tried to shrug it off with an editorial headed 'Children's Hour', Winston Churchill called it disquieting, disgusting, squalid, shameless and abject, all in one speech – 'one can almost feel', said he, 'the curl of contempt upon the lips of the manhood of Germany, Italy and France'. The curl faded in time, and for once *The Times* was probably wiser than Winston, but in the days when the privileged classes ruled England, and Oxford educated the privileged classes, the Union could usefully be watched as a political weather-gauge, to show how things were likely to go when the young gentlemen graduated from St. Michael's Street, and took the train to Parliament Square.

It is not so seminal now, because English politicians are drawn from a much wider background, and 25 new universities have been founded in the past half-century. Nowadays an evening at the Union is only a convincing, and sometimes alarming, demonstration of the fragile artificiality of the English democracy – quivering always on the edge of anarchy, and apparently at the mercy of strong characters. Sometimes you feel, when the president seems to be losing control, that the whole evening is going to break up in abuse and violence. Sometimes you can see how a swift and graceful stroke of repartee can dissolve an ugly situation in a trice, and instantly restore the discipline of the debate. Sometimes, when the tough in the hairy jacket persists in his interruptions, ignoring the instructions of the chair and loudly supported by cronies at his side – sometimes you may imagine how easily a forceful demagogue may break down the whole structure of democracy. Sometimes a supercilious lisp from the other side of the house, languidly suggesting that if the *spluttering* is to continue, the house might perhaps be provided with what one must assume the Honourable Gentleman opposite would call *serviettes*, reminds us how recently the caste system controlled this country, and how long it takes an English prejudice to die.

Like the city itself, the Union is always poised in a tricky balance – ready, you would think, to be pushed into chaos by a shove from any ill-wisher. It has been debating now, however, for more than a century, and visiting Cassandras are repeatedly surprised to find that when all the shouting is over, the obstreperous revolutionary has sat down at last, the insufferable true-blue has been hissed into silence, and the impossible pedant has been briskly squashed – 'You are out of order yourself, you silly little man' – when the time for a division comes, the house carries the motion with orderly restraint, and does not even trip each other up, as it files out through the glazed doors into the Oxford night.

Jan Morris (1926–), *Oxford*, 1965/1978.

If you go to Oxford or Cambridge, you're given a different class of map of the world. It has a different projection. Instead of looking up at the institutions of power, you look down upon them, and you can see the way into them, the links between them.

Robert McCrum, interviewed in Jeremy Paxman, *Friends in High Places*, 1990.

Meanwhile, at a lesser provincial university:

Term had just begun. Professor Treece, head of the department of English, sat at his desk, his back to the window, with the cold, clear October light shining icily over his shoulders on to the turbulent heaps of papers upon his desk, on to the pale young faces of his three new students. As the rain rattled against the panes behind him, and the students stared speculatively out at the last leaves falling damply from the trees, Professor Treece spoke sonorously. His comments were academic and solid. . . .

This tutorial, the first of the new academic year, had already assumed a character-istic tone of embarrassment and uncertainty. Learning lay heavily in the air like pipe-smoke. Treece leapt up jerkily from time to time to pull books suddenly from off their shelves, and it was like throwing stones into a pool; the students jumped visibly in their seats, as if they expected to be attacked. The cold light shone on the pupils of their eyes. Students (it was at Oxford and Cambridge that one called them undergraduates) were not at all cast in the heroic mould when it came to the study of literature; they plodded along the towpath like barge horses. And, for the teacher, the desire to mould the great spirit, along with the search to lead one's own life on the heroic level, was soon defeated by the pressures of a heavy routine. Thus these three sat before him, the usual unpromising examination material which three years of tuition and, more importantly, self discipline, concentration, good influences, would bring to degree level – gauche youths, shuffling their feet, opening and shut-ting their new briefcases, noting down with ostentation the not-always-valuable points, turning red when spoken to, propounding the too-glib possibility ('Wouldn't you say that was because of the influence of Marlowe?'), furtively inspecting their new watches to see how much longer this was going to continue. . . .

They were youths straight from some grammar school sixth-form, rejects of Oxford, Cambridge and the better provincial universities, whose course could be charted easily enough; one could name almost the haphazard collection of books that they would read, one could sketch out beforehand the essays they would write, indicate simply their primary values. They appeared each year, to eat for three more years in the university refectory, to join sports clubs and attend the students' union dances held each Saturday night, sliding gracelessly through weekly waltzes and tangos, drinking down beer at the impromptu bar, tempting girls out into the grounds in order to kiss them on damp benches; to throw tomatoes at policemen on three successive rag days, to go out in three years with perhaps as many girl friends, and finally to leave with a lower second or third class degree, passing on into teaching or business seemingly untouched by what, Treece thought, the university stood for – whatever that was. Each year he wondered, is it worth it? Each year he planned to send out into the world, at last, a little group of discontented men who would share his own disgusts, his own firm assurance in the necessity for good taste, honest feeling, integrity of motive; and each year the proposition came to seem odious as he foresaw the profound weariness and depression of spirit that would overcome such people when, with too few vacancies in the faculties of universities, they would find themselves teaching in grammar schools in Liverpool or working in the advertising department of soap factories in Newcastle.

Malcolm Bradbury (1932–2001), *Eating People is Wrong*, 1959.

David Lodge, another 'campus novelist', here examines the oddities of the whole business:

In America, it is not too difficult to obtain a bachelor's degree. The student is left very much to his own devices, he accumulates the necessary credits at his leisure, cheating is easy, and there is not much suspense or anxiety about the eventual outcome. He (or she) is therefore free to give full attention to the normal interests of late adolescence – sport, alcohol, entertainment and the opposite sex. It is at the postgraduate level that the pressure really begins, when the student is burnished and tempered in a series of gruelling courses and rigorous assessments until he is deemed worthy to receive the accolade of the PhD. By now he has invested so much time and money in the process that any career other than an academic one has become unthinkable, and anything less than success in it unbearable. He is well primed, in short, to enter a profession as steeped in the spirit of free enterprise as Wall Street, in which each scholar-teacher makes an individual contract with his employer, and is free to sell his services to the highest bidder.

Under the British system, competition begins and ends much earlier. Four times, under our educational rules, the human pack is shuffled and cut – at eleven-plus, sixteen-plus, eighteen-plus and twenty-plus – and happy is he who comes top of the deck on each occasion, but especially the last. This is called Finals, the very name of which implies that nothing of importance can happen after it. The British postgraduate student is a lonely, forlorn soul, uncertain of what he is doing or whom he is trying to please – you may recognize him in the tea-shops around the Bodleian and the British Museum by the glazed look in his eyes, the vacant stare of the shell-shocked veteran for whom nothing has been real since the Big Push. As long as he manages to land his first job, this is no great handicap in the short run, since tenure is virtually automatic in British universities, and everyone is paid on the same scale. But at a certain age, the age at which promotions and Chairs begin to occupy a man's thoughts, he may look back with wistful nostalgia to the days when his wits ran fresh and clear, directed to a single, positive goal.

Philip Swallow had been made and unmade by the system in precisely this way. He liked examinations, always did well in them. Finals had been, in many ways, the supreme moment of his life. He frequently dreamed that he was taking the examinations again, and these were happy dreams. Awake, he could without difficulty remember the questions he had elected to answer on every paper that hot, distant June. In the preceding months he had prepared himself with meticulous care, filling his mind with distilled knowledge, drop by drop, until, on the eve of the first paper (Old English Set Texts) it was almost brimming over. Each morning for the next ten days he bore this precious vessel to the examination halls and poured a measured quantity of the contents on to pages of ruled quarto. Day by day the level fell, until on the tenth day the vessel was empty, the cup was drained, the cupboard was bare. In the years that followed he set about replenishing his mind, but it was never quite the same. The sense of purpose was lacking – there was no great Reckoning against which he could hoard his knowledge, so that it tended to leak away as fast as he acquired it. . . .

There was one respect alone in which Philip was recognized as a man of distinction, though only within the confines of his own Department. He was a superlative examiner of undergraduates: scrupulous, painstaking, stern yet just. No one could award a delicate mark like B+/B+?+ with such confident aim, or justify it with such cogency and conviction.

David Lodge (1935–2001), *Changing Places*, 1975.

Very much at the other end of the academic spectrum are the students at local colleges, such as that at Slough:

The local college itself is a national disgrace, with about the country's lowest academic standards and passes for anyone who bothers to enrol. I shouldn't complain. I went there for two years, spent most of the time in the bar and left with a merit-graded HND. I topped up my grant by copying on my Amstrad computer any work I had bothered to do, altering the layout and putting at the top the name of whoever was paying me a fiver to do so. A fellow student who never even bothered to return for her final year rang me soon after I'd completed my course to say she had received a certificate from the college which gave her a pass.

Bill Murphy, *Home Truths*, 2000.

I don't think one 'comes down' from Jimmy's university. According to him, it's not even red brick, but white tile.

John Osborne (1929–94), *Look Back in Anger*, 1956.

Another initially angry young man famously remarked of the expansion of higher education:

More will mean worse.

Kingsley Amis (1922–95), in *Encounter*, July 1960.

Alan Bennett was a Cambridge graduate:

My degree was a kind of inoculation. I got just enough education to make me immune from it for the rest of my life.

Alan Bennett (1934–), *Getting On*, 1972.

Dons

Men unscoured, grotesque
In character, tricked out like aged trees.

William Wordsworth (1770–1850) on Cambridge dons, in *The Prelude*. Wordsworth was at St John's College.

Oxford has specialised in eccentric dons, such as the wonderful William Buckland:

Most of the professors in science were impresarios for their subjects. They did not do experimental work; their task, they believed, was to tell their audience what had already been discovered. They supplemented the theology of the Church of England by providing new proofs of God's design – not as meticulous as those of Newton but still evidence that 'in all His works most wonderful, Most sure in all His ways', as Newman's hymn asserted. Nevertheless, there was one professor who lived in an apartment in Christ Church – which is at once a college and a cathedral – set aside for the canons, a clergyman unlike the orthodox run of canons. Christ Church was the citadel of the High and Dry party within the Church of England and this canon was a liberal latitudinarian. What was more he was a geologist. He had made his name with his research into the rocks of south-west England and his patron was no less than the Prince Regent himself, who created a special professorship for him in 1819. He was the first president of the newly formed British Association, which had been formed to publicise advances in science. This was William Buckland. . . .

Buckland became a legend not so much for his scientific studies as for his remorseless application of the scientific practice of experiment and observation in his private life. He used to say that he had eaten his way through the whole animal creation and that the worst thing was a mole – 'perfectly horrible' – though afterwards he told Lady Lyndhurst that there was one thing worse than a mole and that was a blue-bottle fly. Mice in batter and bison steaks were served at his table in London. A guest wrote in his diary: 'Dined at the Deanery. Tripe for dinner last night, don't like crocodile for breakfast.' He had a Protestant's scepticism of Catholic miracles. Pausing before a dark stain on the flagstones of an Italian cathedral where the martyr's blood miraculously renewed itself, he dropped to his knees and licked it. 'I can tell you what it is: it is bat's urine.'

Like many scientists his mind subconsciously continued to work on the problems preoccupying him. 'My dear,' he said to his wife, starting up from sleep at two o'clock in the morning, 'I believe that *Cheirotherium*'s footsteps are undoubtedly testudinal.' They hurried downstairs and while he fetched the pet tortoise from the garden, his wife mixed paste on the kitchen table. To their delight they saw that the impression left by the tortoise's feet in the paste were almost identical with those of the fossil.

Their apartments in the quad were at once a natural history museum and a menagerie. They and their children lived surrounded on all sides by specimens, dead and alive, that Buckland had collected. When you entered the hall you might as easily mount a stuffed hippopotamus as the children's rocking horse. Monsters of different eras glared down on you from the walls. The sideboard in the dining room groaned under the weight of fossils and was protected from the children by a notice: PAWS OFF. The very candlesticks were carved out of the bones of Saurians. Toads were immured in pots to see how long they could survive without food. There were cages full of snakes, and a pony with three children up would career round the dining-room table and out into the quad. Guinea pigs, owls, jackdaws and smaller fry had the run of the house. The children imbibed science with their mother's milk. One day a clergyman excitedly brought Buckland some fossils for identification. 'What are these, Frankie?' said the professor to his four-year-old son. 'They are the vertebuae of an ichthyosauwus,' lisped the child. The parson retired crestfallen to his parish.

Noel Annan (1917–2000), *The Dons*, 1999.

Hilaire Belloc was an admirer of dons generally, with the exception of one who had written a critical review of his friend G.K. Chesterton:

> Remote and ineffectual Don
> That dared attack my Chesterton,
> With that poor weapon, half-impelled,
> Unlearnt, unsteady, hardly held,
> Unworthy for a tilt with men –
> Your quavering and corroded pen;
> Don poor at Bed and worse at Table,
> Don pinched, Don starved, Don miserable;
> Don stuttering, Don with roving eyes,
> Don nervous, Don of crudities;
> Don clerical, Don ordinary,
> Don self-absorbed and solitary;
> Don here-and-there, Don epileptic;
> Don puffed and empty, Don dyspeptic;
> Don middle-class, Don sycophantic,
> Don dull, Don brutish, Don pedantic;
> Don hypocritical, Don bad,
> Don furtive, Don three-quarters mad;
> Don (since a man must make an end),
> Don that shall never be my friend.
>
> Don different from those regal Dons!
> With hearts of gold and lungs of bronze,
> Who shout and bang and roar and bawl
> The Absolute across the hall,
> Or sail in amply billowing gown
> Enormous through the Sacred Town,
> Bearing from College to their homes
> Deep cargoes of gigantic tomes;
> Dons admirable! Dons of Might!
> Uprising on my inward sight
> Compact of ancient tales, and port
> And sleep – and learning of a sort.

Dons English, worthy of the land;
Dons rooted; Dons that understand.
Good Dons perpetual that remain
A landmark, walling in the plain –
The horizon of my memories –
Like large and comfortable trees.

Hilaire Belloc (1870–1953), *Lines to a Don*, 1910.

Maurice Bowra, a witty and hospitable Fellow, then Warden, of Wadham College, Oxford, is
here fondly remembered by John Betjeman:

Dinner with Maurice Bowra sharp at eight –
High up in Wadham's hospitable quad:
The Gilbert Spencers and the Campbell Gray
Bright in the inner room; the brown and green
Of rows and rows of Greek and Latin texts;
The learning lightly worn; the grand contempt
For pedants, traitors and pretentiousness.
A dozen oysters and a dryish hock;
Claret and *tournedos*; a *bombe surprise*.
The fusillade of phrases ('I'm a man
More dined against than dining') rattled out
In that incisive voice and chucked away
To be re-used in envious common-rooms
By imitation Maurices. I learned,
If learn I could, how not to be a bore,
And merciless was his remark that touched
The tender spot if one were showing off.
Within those rooms I met my friends for life.
True values there were handed on a plate
As easily as sprouts and aubergines:
'A very able man.' 'But what's he like?'
'I've told you. He's a very able man.'
Administrators, professorial chairs
In subjects such as Civics, and the cad
Out for himself, pretending to be kind –
He summed them up in scathing epigram,
Occasionally shouting out the truth
In forceful nineteen-fourteen army slang;
And as the evening mellowed into port,
He read us poems. There I learned to love
That lord of landscape, Alfred Tennyson;
There first heard Thomas Hardy's poetry,
Master of metre, local as his lanes,
The one expressive village fatalist.
Yeats he would chant in deep sonórous voice;
Bring Rudyard Kipling – then so out-of-date –

> To his full stature; show that wisdom was
> Not memory-tests (as I had long supposed),
> Not 'first-class brains' and swotting for exams,
> But humble love for what we sought and knew.
> King of a kingdom underneath the stars,
> I wandered back to Magdalen, certain then,
> As now, that Maurice Bowra's company
> Taught me far more than all my tutors did. ...
>
> John Betjeman (1906–84), *Summoned by Bells*, 1960.

A much less rosy picture of English academia outside Oxbridge is given in Kingsley Amis's *Lucky Jim*. Two interdependent imperatives assail the junior member of an English university faculty: the need to achieve tenure, and the need to publish. In Amis's novel, Dixon — a mediocre member of a mediocre faculty at a mediocre university, and accountable to the mediocre Professor Welch — is acutely pressed by both, as in these two extracts:

'I was wondering about that article of yours.'

'Oh yes. I don't ...'

'Have you heard from Partington yet?'

'Well yes, actually I sent it to him first of all, if you remember, and he said the pressure of other stuff was ...'

'What?'

Dixon had lowered his voice below the medium shout required by the noise of the car, in an attempt to half-conceal from Welch Welch's own lapse of memory, and so protect himself. Now he had to bawl out: 'I told you he said he couldn't find room for it.'

'Oh, couldn't he? Couldn't he? Well, of course they do get a lot of the most ... a most terrific volume of stuff sent to them, you know. Still, I suppose if anything really took their eye, then they ... they ... Have you sent it off to anyone else?'

'Yes, that Caton chap who advertised in the *T.L.S.* a couple of months ago. Starting up a new historical review with an international bias, or something. I thought I'd get in straight away. After all, a new journal can't very well be bunged up as far ahead as all the ones I've ...'

'Ah yes, a new journal might be worth trying. There was one advertised in the *Times Literary Supplement* a little while ago. Paton or some such name the editor fellow was called. You might have a go at him, now that it doesn't seem as if any of the more established reviews have got room for your ... effort. Let's see now; what's the exact title you've given it?'

Dixon looked out of the window at the fields wheeling past, bright green after a wet April. It wasn't the double-exposure effect of the last half-minute's talk that had dumbfounded him, for such incidents formed the staple material of Welch colloquies; it was the prospect of reciting the title of the article he'd written. It was a perfect title, in that it crystallized the article's niggling mindlessness, its funereal parade of yawn-enforcing facts, the pseudo-light it threw upon non-problems. Dixon had read, or begun to read, dozens like it, but his own seemed worse than most in its air of being convinced of its own usefulness and significance. 'In considering this strangely neglected topic,' it began. This what neglected topic? This strangely what topic? This strangely neglected what? His thinking all this without having defiled and set fire to the typescript only made him appear to himself as more of a hypocrite and fool. 'Let's see,' he echoed Welch in a pretended effort of memory: 'oh yes; *The Economic Influence of the Developments in Shipbuilding Techniques, 1450 to 1485.* After all, that's what it's ...'

Unable to finish his sentence, he looked to his left again to find a man's face staring into his own from about nine inches away. The face, which filled with alarm as he gazed, belonged to the driver of a van which Welch had elected to pass on a sharp bend between two stone walls. A huge bus now swung into view from further round the bend. Welch slowed slightly, thus ensuring that they would still be next to the van when the bus reached them, and said with decision: 'Well, that ought to do it nicely, I should say.'

Before Dixon could roll himself into a ball or even take off his glasses, the van had braked and disappeared, the bus-driver, his mouth opening and shutting vigorously, had somehow squirmed his vehicle against the far wall, and, with an echoing rattle, the car darted forward on to the straight. Dixon, though on the whole glad at this escape, felt at the same time that the conversation would have been appropriately rounded off by Welch's death. He felt this more keenly when Welch went on: 'If I were you, Dixon, I should take all the steps I possibly could to get this article accepted in the next month or so. I mean, I haven't the specialized knowledge to judge ...' His voice quickened: 'I can't tell, can I? what it's worth. It's no use anybody coming to me and asking "What's young Dixon's stuff like?" unless I can give them an expert opinion of what it's worth, is it now? But an acceptance by a learned journal would ... would ... You, well you don't know what it's worth yourself, how can you?'

Dixon felt that, on the contrary, he had a good idea of what his article was worth from several points of view. From one of these, the thing's worth could be expressed in one short hyphenated indecency; from another, it was worth the amount of frenzied fact-grubbing and fanatical boredom that had gone into it; from yet another, it was worthy of its aim, the removal of the 'bad impression' he'd so far made in the College and in his Department. But he said: 'No, of course not, Professor.'...

'After all, it's important to you, isn't it?'

This was the cue he'd been hoping for. 'Yes, sir. Actually I've been meaning to ask you about that.'

Welch's shaggy eyebrows descended a little. 'About what?'

'Well, I'm sure you appreciate, Professor, that I've been worrying rather about my position here, in the last few months.'

'Oh yes?' Welch said cheerfully, his eyebrows restored.

'I've been wondering just how I stand, you know.'

'How you stand?'

'Yes, I ... I mean, I'm afraid I got off on the wrong foot here rather, when I first came. I did some rather silly things. Well, now that my first year's nearly over, naturally I can't help feeling a bit anxious.'

'Yes, I know a lot of young chaps find some difficulty in settling down to their first job. It's only to be expected, after a war, after all. I don't know if you've ever met young Faulkner, at Nottingham he is now; he got a job here in nineteen hundred', here he paused, 'and forty-five. Well, he'd had rather a rough time in the war, what with one thing and another; he'd been out East for a time, you know, in the Fleet Air Arm he was, and then they switched him back to the Mediterranean. I remember him telling me how difficult he found it to adapt his way of thinking, when he bad to settle down here and ...'

Stop himself from dashing his fist into your face, Dixon thought. He waited for a time, then, when Welch produced another of his pauses, said: 'Yes, and of course it's doubly difficult when one doesn't feel very, secure in one's – I'd work much better, I know, if I could feel settled about ...'

'Well, insecurity is the great enemy of concentration, I know. And, of course, one does tend to lose the habit of concentration as one grows older. It's amazing how distractions one wouldn't have noticed in one's early days become absolutely shattering when one ... grows older. I remember when they were putting up the new chemistry labs here, well, I say new, you could hardly call them new now, I suppose. At the time I'm speaking of, some years before the war, they were laying the foundations about Easter time it must have been, and the concrete-mixer or whatever it was ...'

Dixon wondered if Welch could hear him grinding his teeth. If he did, he gave no sign of it. Like a boxer still incredibly on his feet after ten rounds of punishment, Dixon got in with: 'I could feel quite happy about everything, if only my big worry were out of the way.'

Welch's head lifted slowly, like the muzzle of some obsolete howitzer. The wondering frown quickly began to form. 'I don't quite see ...'

'My probation,' Dixon said loudly.

The frown cleared. 'Oh. That. You're on two years' probation here, Dixon, not one year. It's all there in your contract, you know. Two years.'

'Yes, I know, but that just means that I can't be taken on to the permanent staff until two years are up. It doesn't mean that I can't be ... asked to leave at the end of the first year.'

'Oh no,' Welch said warmly; 'no.' He left it open whether he was reinforcing Dixon's negative or dissenting from it.

'I can be asked to leave at the end of the first year, can't I, Professor?' Dixon said quickly, pressing himself against the back of his chair.

'Yes, I suppose so,' Welch said, coldly this time, as if he were being asked to make some concession which, though theoretically due, no decent man would claim.

'Well I'm just wondering what's happening about it, that's all.'

'Yes, I've no doubt you are,' Welch said in the same tone. Dixon waited, planning faces. He looked round the small, cosy room with its fitted carpet, its rows of superseded books, its filing cabinets full of antique examination papers and of dossiers relating to past generations of students, its view from closed windows on to the sunlit wall of the Physics Laboratory. Behind Welch's head hung the departmental timetable, drawn up by Welch himself in five different-coloured inks corresponding to the five teaching members of the Department. The sight of this seemed to undam Dixon's mind; for the first time since arriving at the College he thought he felt real, over-mastering, orgiastic boredom, and its companion, real hatred. If Welch didn't speak in the next five seconds, he'd do something which would get himself flung out without possible question – not the things he'd often dreamed of when sitting next door pretending to work. He no longer wanted, for example, to inscribe on the departmental timetable a short account, well tricked-out with obscenities, of his views on the Professor of History, the Department of History, medieval history, history, and Margaret and hang it out of the window for the information of passing students and lecturers, nor did he, on the whole, now intend to tie Welch up in his chair and beat him about the head and shoulders with a bottle until he disclosed why, without being French himself, he'd given his sons French names, nor ... No, he'd just say, quite quietly and very slowly and distinctly, to give Welch a good chance of catching his general drift: Look here, you old cockchafer, what makes you think you can run a history department, even at a place like this, eh, you old cockchafer? I know what you'd be good at, you old cockchafer ...

'Well, these things aren't as easy as you might imagine, you know,' Welch said suddenly. 'This is a very difficult matter, Dixon, you see. There's a great deal, a lot of things you've got to keep in mind.'

'I see that, of course, Professor. I just wanted to ask when the decision will be taken, that's all. If I'm to go, it's only fair I should be told soon.' He felt his head trembling slightly with rage as he said this.

Welch's glance, which had flicked two or three times at Dixon's face, now dropped to a half-curled-up letter on the desk. He muttered: 'Yes ... well ... I ...'

Dixon said in a still louder voice: 'Because I shall have to start looking for another job, you see. And most of the schools will have made their appointments for September before they break up in July. So I shall want to know in good time.'

An expression of unhappiness was beginning to settle on Welch's small-eyed face. Dixon was at first pleased to see this evidence that Welch's mind could still be reached from the outside; next he felt a momentary compunction at the spectacle of one man disliking to reveal something that would cause pain to another; finally panic engulfed him. What was Welch's reluctance concealing? He, Dixon, was done for. If so, he would at any rate be able to deliver the cockchafer speech, though he wished his audience were larger.

'Let you know as soon as anything's decided,' Welch said with incredible speed. 'Nothing is yet.'

Kingsley Amis (1922–95), *Lucky Jim*, 1954.

In an age when academics are increasingly called on to diversify their activities to justify their existences, some mourn the passing of the 'remote and ineffectual Don':

Don in Office, Don in power,
Don talking on Woman's Hour,
Don knocking up a constitution,

Don with ideas on prostitution ...
Don brassy, Don belligerent,
Don tipping off for ten percent,
Don christian-naming with the stars,
Don talking aloud in public bars
Remote and ineffectual Don
Where have you gone, where have you gone?

A.N.L. Munby, 'Thoughts on rereading Belloc's famous lines on Dons'; quoted in Jeremy Paxman, *Friends in High Places*, 1990.

Despite these changes, dons like to preserve their curious little traditions ...

As the citizens of Oxford readied themselves for bed last night, some of the city's most learned Fellows were eating and drinking to excess in preparation to march around their college behind a wooden duck held aloft on a pole.

The bizarre ritual of 'hunting the mallard' occurs once every 100 years at All Souls in commemoration of the chase after a huge wild duck which flew from a drain during 15th-century building work.

Archbishop Henry Chichele, who established All Souls in 1438, is said to have had a premonition of the duck in a dream.

This rowdy torchlit event is, however, no undergraduate prank. All Souls has no undergraduates and its Fellows are considered to be among the finest minds in the world.

Leading the midnight procession, carried high on a sedan chair, was Dr Martin West, a classics don and current holder of the office of Lord Mallard.

The last Lord Mallard to lead a 'hunt' was Cosmo Gordon Lang, who held the unofficial title in 1901 and later became Archbishop of Canterbury. ...

Lang remembered: 'I was carried in a chair by four stalwart Fellows – Wilbrahim [First Church Estates Commissioner], Gwyer [later Chief Justice of India], Steel-Maitland [later Minister of Labour] and Fossie Cunliffe – for nearly two hours after midnight round the quadrangles and roofs of the college, with a dead mallard borne in front on a long pole (which I still possess) singing the Mallard Song all the time, preceded by the seniors and followed by the juniors, all of them carrying staves and torches, a scene unimaginable in any place in the world except Oxford, or there in any society except All Souls.

'The whole strange ceremony had been kept secret; only late workers in the night can have heard the unusual sound, though it is said that Provost McGrath of Queen's muttered in his sleep, "I must send the Torpid down for this noise."' ...

J G Lockhart, Lang's biographer, said, 'Such elaborate junketing may sound a little odd to anyone unconnected with All Souls, but presumably, if Homer may be excused an occasional nod, a Fellow of All Souls may be allowed, once in a hundred years, to play the fool.'

Linus Gregordiadis and Sean O'Neill, *Daily Telegraph*, 15 January 2001.

The English Way
of Sex, and So On

THE ENGLISH TAKE THEIR PLEASURES SADLY
AFTER THE FASHION OF THEIR COUNTRY.
Attributed to Maximillien de Béthune, Duc de Sully (1559–1641).

This anthology, as a whole, variously confirms and explodes one and a half millennia of prejudice and stereotyping. In this chapter the confirmations are more resounding and the explosions more deafening.

Matters of the heart – not to mention the loins – are, of course, universal. But cultural and religious traditions set their own parameters, within which national characteristics may be discovered and national stereotypes promulgated. The stereotypical English person is (as the whole world knows) diffident in love, cold in marriage, and bad at sex. We even believe it ourselves, sometimes.

As one might expect, the extent to which our characteristics and stereotypes are confirmed in this chapter is matched only by the extent to which they are confounded. For every Lady Hillingdon there is a Wife of Bath; for every Thomas Carew there is a Philip Larkin. They are all quite typically English. In spite of everything, the English still manage, somehow, to love, breed, fornicate and marry. Some of us, indeed, are moderately accomplished, and get quite a kick out of it.

A Bit of the Other

It has to be admitted that we English have sex on the brain, which is a very unsatisfactory place to have it.

Malcolm Muggeridge (1903–90), 'Ideas and Men', in *The New York Times*, 11 October 1964.

Much has been said and written about the English Way of Sex. In various ages we have been renowned for concupiscence, lust, incontinence, bawdy, prurience, skill, tenderness, brutishness, chastity, faithfulness, indifference, prudishness, clumsiness, frigidity, ignorance .... Some of it is true, some false; most of it is both.

One of our first and greatest bawdy poets was Geoffrey Chaucer. Here is an extract from 'The Miller's Tale', in Nevill Coghill's translation. Young Alison, wife of an aged carpenter, is in bed with the lodger, Nicholas, when Absalon, Nicholas's rival, comes a-calling …

> The first cock crew at last, and thereupon
> Up rose this jolly lover Absalon
> In gayest clothes, garnished with that and this;
> But first he chewed a grain of liquorice
> To charm his breath before he combed his hair.
> Under his tongue, the comfit nestling there
> Would make him gracious. He began to roam
> To where old John and Alison kept home
> And by the casement window took his stand.
> Breast-high it stood, no higher than his hand.
> He gave a cough, no more than half a sound:
> 'Alison, honey-comb, are you around?
> Sweet cinnamon, my little honey-bird,
> Sweetheart, wake up and say a little word!
> You seldom think of me in all my woe,
> I sweat for love of you wherever I go!
> No wonder if I do, I pine and bleat
> As any lambkin hungering for the teat,
> Believe me, darling, I'm so deep in love
> I croon with longing like a turtle-dove,
> I eat as little as a girl at school.'
> 'You go away,' she answered, 'you Tom-fool!
> There's no come-up-and-kiss-me here for you.
> I love another and why shouldn't I too?
> Better then you, by Jesu, Absalon!
> Take yourself off or I shall throw a stone.
> I want to get some sleep. You go to Hell!'
> 'Alas!' said Absalon. 'I knew it well;
> True love is always mocked and girded at;
> So kiss me, if you can't do more than that,
> For Jesu's love and for the love of me!'
> 'And if I do, will you be off?' said she.

'Promise you, darling,' answered Absalon.
'Get ready then; wait, I'll put something on,'
She said and then she added under breath
To Nicholas, 'Hush … we shall laugh to death!'
　　　This Absalon went down upon his knees;
'I am a lord!' he thought, 'And by degrees
There may be more to come; the plot may thicken.'
'Mercy, my love!' he said, 'Your mouth, my chicken!'
　　　She flung the window open then in haste
And said, 'Have done, come on, no time to waste,
The neighbours here are always on the spy.'
　　　Absalon started wiping his mouth dry.
Dark was the night as pitch, as black as coal,
And at the window out she put her hole,
And Absalon, so fortune framed the farce,
Put up his mouth and kissed her naked arse
Most savorously before he knew of this.
　　　And back he started. Something was amiss;
He knew quite well a woman has no beard,
Yet something rough and hairy had appeared.
'What have I done?' he said. 'Can that be you?'
'Teehee!' she cried and clapped the window to.

Geoffrey Chaucer (c.1340–1400), 'The Miller's Tale' from *The Canterbury Tales*, tr. Nevill Coghill, 1951.

In 'The Merchant's Tale', old Januarie's young wife May also seeks satisfaction with a young buck, this time by name of Damyan. At the climax of the story, Damyan helps May up into a tree … and thereafter the original Middle English of the Merchant's narrative is not hard to follow …

Ladyes, I pray yow that ye be nat wrooth;
I kan nat glose, I am a rude man –
And sodeynly anon this Damyan
Gan pullen up the smok, and in he throng.

Geoffrey Chaucer (c.1340–1400), 'The Merchant's Tale' from *The Canterbury Tales*.

During the English Renaissance, some poets put a courtly and melancholy spin on the subject:

They flee from me, that sometime did me seek,
With naked foot stalking within my chamber:
Once have I seen them gentle, tame, and meek,
That now are wild, and do not once remember,
That sometime they have put themselves in danger
To take bread at my hand; and now they range
Busily seeking with a continual change.

Thanked be Fortune, it hath been otherwise
Twenty times better; but once in special,
In thin array, after a pleasant guise,
When her loose gown did from her shoulders fall,
And she me caught in her arms long and small,
And therewithal so sweetly did me kiss,
And softly said, 'Dear heart, how like you this?'

It was no dream; for I lay broad awaking:
But all is turned now through my gentleness
Into a bitter fashion of forsaking,
And I have leave to go of her goodness,
And she also to use new-fangledness.
But since that I unkindly so am served,
'How like you this?' – What hath she now deserved?

Sir Thomas Wyatt (c.1503–42), 'The Forsaken Lover'.

Other poets were more cheerfully earthy:

It fell on a summer's day,
While sweet Bessy sleeping lay
In her bower on her bed,
Light with curtains shadowed,
Jamie came; she him spies,
Opening half her heavy eyes.

Jamie stole in through the door,
She lay slumbering as before,
Softly to her he drew near;
She heard him, but would not hear.
Bessy vowed not to speak;
He resolved that dump to break.

First a soft kiss he did take;
She lay still and would not wake.
Then his hands learned to woo;
She dreamt not what he would do,
But still slept, while he smiled
To see love by sleep beguiled.

Jamie then began to play;
Bessy as one buried lay,
Gladly still through this sleight
Deceivèd in her own deceit.
And since this trance begun,
She sleeps every afternoon.

Thomas Campion (1567–1620), 'It Fell on a Summer's Day'.

The Reverend Dr John Donne tended more to the erotic than the bawdy:

Come, Madam, come all rest my powers defie,
Until I labour, I in labour lie.
The foe oft-times having the foe in sight,
Is tir'd with standing though they never fight.
Off with that girdle, like heavens Zone glistering,
But a far fairer world incompassing.
Unpin that spangled breastplate which you wear
That th'eyes of busie fooles may be stopt there.
Unlace your self, for that harmonious chyme,
Tells me from you, that now 'tis your bed time.
Off with that happy busk, whom I envie,
That still can be, and still can stand so nigh.
Your gowne's going off, such beautious state reveals,
As when from flowry meads th'hills shadow steales.
Off with your wyerie Coronet and shew
The haiery Diademe which on you doth grow:
Off with those shooes, and then safely tread
In this loves hallow'd temple, this soft bed.
In such white robes, heaven's Angels us'd to be
Receav'd by men; Thou Angel bringst with thee
A heaven like Mahomets Paradise; and though
Ill spirits walk in white, we easily know,
By this these Angels from an evil sprite,
They set our hairs, but these the flesh upright.
        Licence my roaving hands, and let them go,
Behind, before, above, between, below.
O my America! my new-found-land,
My kingdome, safeliest when with one man man'd,
My Myne of precious stones, My Emperie,
How blest am I in this discovering thee!
To enter into these bonds, is to be free;
Then where my hand is set, my seal shall be.
        Full nakedness! All joyes are due to thee,
As souls unbodied, bodies uncloth'd must be,
To taste whole joyes. Gems which you women use
Are as Atlanta's balls, cast in mens views,
That when a fools eye lighteth on a Gem,
His earthly soul may covet theirs, not them.
Like pictures, or like books gay coverings made
For lay-men, are all women thus array'd;
Themselves are mystick books, which onely wee
(Whom their imputed grace will dignifie)
Must see reveal'd. Then since I may know;

As liberally, as to a Midwife, shew
Thy self: cast all, yea, this white lynnen hence,
Here is no pennance, much lesse innocence.
        To teach thee, I am naked first: why then
What needst thou have more covering than a man.

John Donne (1572–1631), 'Elegie; Going to Bed', c.1595, published posthumously in *Poems*,
1669.

After the death of Andrew Marvell, Member of Parliament for Hull, his housekeeper Mary
Palmer – who also claimed to be his widow – found a manuscript volume containing his poems,
which were published posthumously in 1681. The volume included 'To His Coy Mistress':

Had we but World enough, and Time,
This coyness Lady were no crime.
We would sit down, and think which way
To walk, and pass our long Loves Day.
Thou by the *Indian Ganges* side
Should'st Rubies find: I by the Tide
Of *Humber* would complain. I would
Love you ten years before the Flood:
And you should if you please refuse
Till the Conversion of the Jews.
My vegetable Love should grow
Vaster than Empires, and more slow.
An hundred years should go to praise
Thine Eyes, and on thy Forehead Gaze;
Two hundred to adore each Breast:
But thirty thousand to the rest.
An Age at least to every part,
And the last Age should show your Heart.
For Lady you deserve this State;
Nor would I love at lower rate.

But at my back I alwaies hear
Times winged Charriot hurrying near:
And yonder all before us lye
Deserts of vast Eternity.
Thy Beauty shall no more be found;
Nor, in thy marble Vault, shall sound
My ecchoing Song: then Worms shall try
That long preserv'd Virginity:
And your quaint Honour turn to dust;
And into ashes all my Lust.
The Grave's a fine and private place,
But none I think do there embrace.

Now therefore, while the youthful hew
Sits on thy skin like morning dew,

And while thy willing Soul transpires
At every pore with instant Fires,
Now let us sport us while we may;
And now, like am'rous birds of prey,
Rather at once our Time devour,
Than languish in his slow-chapt pow'r.
Let us roll all our Strength, and all
Our sweetness, up into one Ball:
And tear our Pleasures with rough strife,
Thorough the Iron gates of Life.
Thus, though we cannot make our Sun
Stand still, yet we will make him run.

Andrew Marvell (1621–78), 'To His Coy Mistress', published 1681.

The 17th century marked perhaps the high point of guilt-free sexual frankness and glorying eroticism:

Come, then, and mounted on the wings of Love
We'll cut the flitting air and soar above
The monster's head, and in the noblest seats
Of those blest shades quench and renew our heats.
There shall the queens of love and innocence,
Beauty and Nature, banish all offence
From our close ivy-twines; there I'll behold
Thy bared snow and thy unbraided gold;
There my enfranchised hand on every side
Shall o'er thy naked polish'd ivory slide. ...
    Now in more subtle wreaths I will entwine
My sinewy thighs, my legs and arms with thine;
Thou like a sea of milk shalt lie display'd
Whilst I the smooth calm ocean invade
With such a tempest, as when Jove of old
Fell down on Danaë in a storm of gold;
Yet my tall pine shall in the Cyprian strait
Ride safe at anchor and unlade her freight:
My rudder with thy bold hand, like a tried
And skilful pilot, thou shalt steer, and guide
My bark into love's channel, where it shall
Dance, as the bounding waves do rise or fall.
Then shall thy circling arms embrace and clip
My willing body, and thy balmy lip
Bathe me in juice of kisses, whose perfume
Like a religious incense shall consume,
And send up holy vapours to those powers
That bless our loves and crown our sportful hours,
That with such halcyon calmness fix our souls
In steadfast peace, as no affright controls.

There no rude sounds shake us with sudden starts;
No jealous ears, when we unrip our hearts,
Such our discourse in; no observing spies
This blush, that glance traduce; no envious eyes
Watch our close meetings; nor are we betray'd
To rivals by the bribèd chambermaid.
No wedlock bonds unwreathe our twisted loves,
We seek no midnight arbour, no dark groves
To hide our kisses: there, the hated name
Of husband, wife, lust, modest, chaste, or shame,
Are vain and empty words, whose very sound
Was never heard in the Elysian ground.
All things are lawful there, that may delight
Nature or unrestrainèd appetite.
Like and enjoy, to will and act is one:
We only sin when Love's rites are not done.

Thomas Carew (1595–1639), from *A Rapture*.

Have ye beheld (with much delight)
A red rose peeping through a white?
Or else a cherry (double graced)
Within a lily's centre placed?
Or ever marked the pretty beam,
A strawberry shows half drowned in cream?
Or seen rich rubies blushing through
A pure smooth pearl, and orient too?
So like to this, nay all the rest,
Is each neat niplet of her breast.

Robert Herrick (1591–1674), 'Upon the Nipples of Julia's Breast'.

The English female orgasm was not, as some have suggested, discovered in the late 1960s …

Whilst Alexis lay prest
In her arms he loved best,
With his hands round her neck,
And his head on her breast,
He found the fierce pleasure too hasty to stay,
And his soul in the tempest just flying away.

When Celia saw this,
With a sigh and a kiss,
She cried, 'Oh, my dear, I am robbed of my bliss!
'Tis unkind to your love, and unfaithfully done,
To leave me behind you, and die all alone.'

The youth, though in haste,
And breathing his last,

In pity died slowly, while she died more fast
Till at length she cried, 'Now, my dear, now let us go:
Now die, my Alexis, and I will die too!'

Thus entranced they did lie,
Till Alexis did try
To recover new breath, that again he might die:
Then often they died; but the more they did so,
The nymph died more quick, and the shepherd more slow.

John Dryden (1631–1700), 'While Alexis Lay Prest', from *Marriage à la Mode*, 1672.

Dr John Overall was Deane of St Paule's, London. . . . I know not what he wrote or whether he was any more than a common-prayer Doctor: but most remarque-able by his Wife, who was the greatest Beautie of her time in England. That she was so, I have it attested from the famous Limmer Mr. Hoskins, and other old Painters, besides old Courtiers. She was not more beautifull than she was oblige-ing and kind, and was so tender-hearted that (truly) she could scarce denie any one. She had (they told me) the loveliest Eies that were ever seen, but wondrous wanton. When she came to Court, or to the Play-house, the Gallants would so flock about her. Richard the Earle of Dorset, and his brother Edward, since Earle, both did mightily adore her. And by their report he must have had a hard heart that did not admire her. Bishop Hall sayeth in his Meditations that there is none so old, that a beautifull person loves not; nor so young, whom a lovely feature moves not.

The good old Deane, notwithstanding he knew well enough that he was horned, loved her infinitely: in so much that he was willing she should enjoy what she had a mind to.

Among others who were charmed by her was Sir John Selby, of Yorkshire. Old Mrs. Tyndale (who knew her) remembres a song made of her and Sir John, part whereof was this, viz:–

The Deane of Paule's did search for his wife, and where d'ee thinke he found her?
Even upon Sir John Selbye's bed, as flatte as any Flounder.

Of these two Lovers was made this following copie of Pastorall verses: . . .

Sweet she was, as kind a Love
    As ever fetter'd Swayne;
Never such a daynty one
    Shall man enjoy again.
Sett a thousand on a rowe
    I forbid that any showe
Ever the like of her
    Hye nonny nonny noe. . . .

With her Mantle tuck't up high
    She foddered her flock
So bucksome and alluringly

> Her knee upheld her smock
> So nimbly did she use to goe
> So smooth she danc't upon tip-toe,
> That all the men were fond of her
> *Hye nonny nonny noe. . . .*
>
> But gonne she is the prettiest Lasse
> That ever trod on plaine.
> What ever hath betide of her
> Blame not the Shepherd Swayne
> For why? she was her owne Foe,
> And gave herselfe the overthrowe
> By being so franke of her
> *Hye nonny nonny noe.*

John Aubrey (1626–97), *Brief Lives*.

Samuel Pepys, renowned for his diary, is also remembered as something of a philanderer. On one occasion he offered advancement to the husband of a woman in return for her favours; she happily complied. Below he relates his sexual adventures with the 'mighty pretty' Deborah Willett:

27 September 1667   Up and to the office, where very busy all the morning. While I was busy at the office, my wife sends for me to come to home, and what was it but to see the pretty girl [Deborah Willett] which she is taking to wait upon her; and though she seems not altogether so great a beauty as she had before told me, yet endeed she is mighty pretty; and so pretty, that I find I shall be too much pleased with it, and therefore could be contented as to my judgment, though not to my passion, that she might not come, lest I may be found too much minding her, to the discontent of my wife. She is to come next week. She seems by her discourse to be grave beyond her bigness and age, and exceeding well-bred as to her deportment, having been a scholar in a school at Bow these seven or eight year. To the office again, my thoughts running on this pretty girl. . . .

11 January 1668   With my wife for half an hour walking by moonlight and, it being cold frosty weather, walking in the garden; and then home to supper, and so by the fireside to have my head combed, as I do now often do, by Deb, whom I love should be fiddling about me; and so to bed.

31 March 1668   I called Deb to take pen, ink, and paper and write down what things came into my head for my wife to do, in order to her going into the country; and the girl writing not so well as she would do, cried, and her mistress construed it to be sullenness and so was angry, and I seemed angry with her too; but going to bed, she undressed me, and there I did give her good advice and beso la, ella weeping still; and yo did take her, the first time in my life, sobra mi genu and did poner mi mano sub her jupes and toca su thigh, which did hazer me great pleasure; and so did no more, but besando-la went to my bed.

26–27 October 1668 Lords day. Up, and discoursing with my wife about our house and many new things we are doing of; and so to church I, and there find Jack Fen come, and his wife, a pretty black woman; I never saw her before, nor took notice of her now. So home and to dinner; and after dinner, all the afternoon got my wife and boy to read to me. And at night W. Batelier comes and sups with us; and after supper, to have my head combed by Deb, which occasioned the greatest sorrow to me that ever I knew in this world; for my wife, coming up suddenly, did find me imbracing the girl con my hand sub su coats; and endeed, I was with my main in her cunny. I was at a wonderful loss upon it, and the girl also; and I endeavoured to put it off, but my wife was struck mute and grew angry, and as her voice came to her, grew quite out of order; and I do say little, but to bed; and my wife said little also, but could not sleep all night; but about 2 in the morning waked me and cried, and fell to tell me as a great secret that she was a Roman Catholique and had received the Holy Sacrament; which troubled me but I took no notice of it, but she went on from one thing to another, till at last it appeared plainly her trouble was at what she saw; but yet I did not know how much she saw and therefore said nothing to her. But after her much crying and reproaching me with inconstancy and preferring a sorry girl before her, I did give her no provocations but did promise all fair usage to her, and love, and foreswore any hurt that I did with her – till at last she seemed to be at ease again; and so toward morning, a little sleep; and so I, with some little repose and rest, rose, and up and by water to Whitehall, but with my mind mightily troubled for the poor girl, whom I fear I have undone by this, my [wife] telling me that she would turn her out of door. ...

7 December 1668   This afternoon, passing through Queen's street, I saw pass by our coach on foot, Deb; which God forgive me, did put me into some new thoughts of her and for her, but durst not show them; and I think my wife did not see her, but I did get my thoughts free of her as soon as I could.

Samuel Pepys (1633–1703), *Diary* (ed. Robert Latham).

There are few women's voices on the subject surviving from this period, a notable exception being that of Aphra Behn, the first Englishwoman to have a career as a professional writer. This is her 'Willing Mistriss':

Amyntas led me to a Grove,
    Where all the Trees did shade us;
The Sun it self; though it had Strove,
    It could not have betray'd us:

The place secur'd from humane Eyes,
    No other fear allows,
    But when the Winds that gently rise,
Doe Kiss the yielding Boughs.

Down there we satt upon the Moss,
    And did begin to play
A Thousand Amorous Tricks, to pass

> The heat of all the day.
> A many Kisses he did give:
>   And I return'd the same
> Which made me willing to receive
>   That which I dare not name.
>
> His Charming Eyes no Aid requir'd
>   To tell their softning Tale;
> On her that was already fir'd,
>   'Twas Easy to prevaile.
> He did but Kiss and Clasp me round,
>   Whilst those his thoughts Exprest:
> And lay'd me gently on the Ground;
>   Ah who can guess the rest?

Aphra Behn (1640–89), 'Song: The Willing Mistriss', in *Poems upon Several Occasions*, 1684.

Here are the male fantasies of *Fanny Hill*, that lushly elegant perennial of English pornography:

After breakfast, Charles (the dear familiar name I must take the liberty hencefor-ward to distinguish my Adonis by), with a smile full of meaning, took me gently by the hand, and said: 'Come, my dear, I will show you a room that commands a fine prospect over some gardens'; and without waiting for an answer, in which he relieved me extremely, he led me up into a chamber, airy and lightsome, where all seeing of prospects was out of the question, except that of a bed, which had all the air of having recommended the room to him.

Charles had just slipp'd the bolt of the door, and running, caught me in his arms, and lifting me from the ground, with his lips glew'd to mine, bore me, trembling, panting, dying, with soft fears and tender wishes, to the bed; where his impatience would not suffer him to undress me, more than just unpinning my handkerchief and gown, and unlacing my stays.

My bosom was now bare, and, rising in the warmest throbs, presented to his sight and feeling the firm hard swell of a pair of young breasts, such as may be imagin'd of a girl not sixteen, fresh out of the country, and never before handled; but even their pride, whiteness, fashion, pleasing resistance to the touch, could not bribe his restless hands from roving; but; giving them the loose, my petticoats and shift were soon taken up, and their stronger centre of attraction laid open to their tender invasion.

I lay fairly exposed to the examination of his eyes and hands, quiet and unresist-ing; which confirm'd him the opinion he proceeded so cavalierly upon, that I was no novice in these matters, since he had taken me out of a common bawdy-house, nor had I said one thing to prepossess him of my virginity; and if I had, he would sooner have believ'd that I took him for a cully that would swallow such an improb-ability, than that I was still mistress of that darling treasure, that hidden mine, so eagerly sought after by the men, and which they never dig for, but to destroy.

I complain'd, but tenderly complain'd that I could not bear it ... indeed he hurt me!. ... Still he thought no more, that possibly I had not been enjoy'd by any so advantageously made in that part as himself: for still, that my virgin flower was yet uncrop'd, never enter'd into his head, and he would have thought it idling with time and words to have question'd me upon it.

He tries again, still no admittances, still no penetration; but he had hurt me yet more, whilst my extreme love made me bear extreme pain, almost without a groan. At length, after repeated fruitless trials, he lay down panting by me, kiss'd my falling tears, and ask'd me tenderly what was the meaning of so much complaining? and if I had not borne it better from others than I did from him? I answered, with a simplicity fram'd to persuade, that he was the first man that ever serv'd me so. Truth is powerful, and it is not always that we do not believe what we eagerly wish.

Charles, already dispos'd by the evidence of his senses to think my pretences to virginity not entirely apocryphal, smothers me with kisses, begs me, in the name of love, to have a little patience, and that he will be as tender of hurting me as he would be of himself.

Alas! it was enough I knew his pleasure to submit joyfully to him, whatever pain I foresaw it would cost me.

He now resumes his attempts once more: now, outrageous and no longer his own master, but borne headlong away by the fury and over-mettle of that member, now exerting itself with a kind of native rage, he breaks in, carries all before him, and one violent merciless lunge sent it, imbrew'd, and reeking with virgin blood, up to the very hilt in me ... Then! then all my resolution deserted me.

When I recover'd my senses, I found myself undress'd and a-bed, in the arms of the sweet relenting murderer of my virginity, who hung mourning tenderly over me, and holding in his hand a cordial, which, coming from the still dear author of so much pain, I could not refuse; my eyes, however, moisten'd with tears and languishingly turn'd upon him, seemed to reproach him with his cruelty, and ask him if such were the rewards of love. But Charles, to whom I was now infinitely endear'd by this complete triumph over a maidenhead, where he so little expected to find one, in tenderness to that pain which he had put me to, in procuring himself the height of pleasure, smother'd his exultation, and employ'd himself with so much sweetness, so much warmth, to soothe, to caress, and comfort me in my soft complainings, which breath'd, indeed, more love than resentment, that I presently drown'd all sense of pain in the pleasure of seeing him, of thinking that I belong'd to him: he who was now the absolute disposer of my happiness, and, in one word, my fate.

The sore was, however, too tender, the wound too bleeding fresh, for Charles' good nature to put my patience presently to another trial; but as I could not stir, or walk across the room, he order'd the dinner to be brought to the bed-side, where it could not be otherwise than my getting down the wing of a fowl, and two or three glasses of wine, since it was my ador'd youth who both serv'd, and urged them on me, with that sweet irresistible authority with which love had invested him over me.

After dinner, and as everything but the wine was taken away, Charles very impudently asks leave, he might read the grant if in my eyes, to come to bed with me, and accordingly falls to undressing; which I could not see the progress of without strange emotions of fear and pleasure.

I felt no more the smart of my wounds below; but, curling round him like the tendril of a vine, as if I fear'd any part of him should be untouch'd or unpress'd by me, I return'd his strenuous embraces and kisses with a fervour and gusto only known to true love, and which mere lust could never rise to.

How often, when the rage and tumult of my senses had subsided after the melting flow, have I, in a tender meditation ask'd myself coolly the question, if it was in nature for any of its creatures to be so happy as I was? Or, what were all fears of the consequence, put in the scale of one night's enjoyment of anything so transcendently the taste of my eyes and heart, as that delicious, fond, matchless youth?

Thus we spent the whole afternoon till supper time, in a continued circle of love delights, kissing, turtle-billing, toying, and all the rest of the feast.

John Cleland (1710–89), *Memoirs of a Woman of Pleasure*, better known as *Fanny Hill*, 1748–49.

Cleland, an impecunious former British consul in Smyrna, was paid 20 guineas for the book, which was immediately suppressed. Called before the Privy Council, Cleland pleaded poverty as an extenuating circumstance. Rather than receiving punishment, Cleland was awarded a pension, in the hope that his talent might be diverted along more acceptable lines. His most famous work, however, continued to be printed and banned – it was last seized by the police in 1963.

A rather pathetic real-life English love affair of the 1820s was reported to Prince Metternich by Princess Lieven, the London society hostess (and probable mistress of Lord Palmerston):

Society is all affairs of gallantry – there is a positive epidemic of them – and yesterday a clandestine marriage took place under the most extraordinary auspices. What strange beings these Englishwomen are! Think of it, a little miss running away at nine in the morning from her parents' home, arriving at the church door, seizing two passers-by in the street and forcing them to be witnesses of the ceremony! The young man for his part had hired a parson and caught a passer-by too. They were married and left at once, meaning to cross to France. When they got to Rochester, they realised that they had not a halfpenny; and there they are stuck, living presumably on love, for they have nothing else. The girl is own niece to the Duke of Wellington, and the young man is the Marquis of Worcester, future Duke of Beaufort. He lost his wife a year ago; it is his wife's sister he has just married. The canons of the Church do not allow this, so that his present wife must be regarded from now on as his mistress. The whole town is talking about the incident. The young woman's beauty consists in large black eyebrows and a great deal of hair on her face and arms – Englishmen cannot resist hairy arms. Isn't that an odd taste?

Princess Lieven, *Private Letters of Princess Lieven to Prince Metternich, 1820–1826*; quoted in Francesca M. Wilson, *Strange Island*, 1955.

We tend to think of the Victorians as being squeamish and/or perverse about sex – one thinks of Ruskin failing to consummate his marriage owing to the shock of seeing his wife's pubic hair – but it seems that privately many led happy and fulfilling sex lives. The Reverend Charles Kingsley, author of *The Water Babies*, looked forward to even better sex in heaven:

A more perfect delight when we be naked in each other's arms clasped together toying with each other's bodies, struggling, panting, dying for a moment. Shall we not feel then, even then, that there is more in store for us, that those thrilling writhings are but dim shadows of a union which shall be perfect?

The Reverend Charles Kingsley (1819–75), letter to his wife of 1845, quoted in Susan Chitty, *The Beast and the Monk*, 1974.

In *My Secret Life*, 'Walter' – who, according to recent research, was probably a seedy London pornographic bookseller – kicks against the pricks of conventional, 'respectable' morality in a fiercely moral defence of sex that in some ways echoes the Rev. Kingsley and anticipates D.H. Lawrence:

Yet this divine function, this coupling of the man and woman in the supremest ecstasy of mind and body. This sexual conjunction, this fucking, which is the foundation and stay of love between the sexes. This act which may form and give life to a sentient being, to a being with a soul, to one partaking of the ethereal life – of the Divine essence. This act which by the law of nature may create in God's own image a being with a soul to be hereafter called by him either blessed or damned in all eternity. This act of mighty power and eternal endowments is called foul, bestial, abominable! It may not be mentioned or talked about. – Yea, even when the law has sanctioned it, and the Priest has blest it, it may not be even hinted at in public! Nor may the sexual organs, those blessed implements of coition with which pleasure is got, and the act is done, be named or alluded to. – Age after age has wasted its thoughts in inventing words to refer to the act and its organs which shall puzzle and perplex as to their meaning, but which are called for the time decent, under the false notion that the penis and pudenda are indecent, filthy things. Yet thoughts about these organs or the sensations they afford are ever present to the sexes, and a delight to both sexes in health. The hopes of earthly happiness are mainly derived from them, and without their function life is worthless. – Yet this grave inevitable necessity of life is thought obscene!

Man and woman are joint participants in the sexual pleasure, and in the voluptuous thoughts which are the cause and consequence. Such minutes are paradise in life, are heaven before life has left us.

'Walter', *My Secret Life*, privately printed in Brussels, 1888–92.

It doesn't matter what you do in the bedroom so long as you don't do it in the street and frighten the horses.

Mrs Patrick Campbell (Beatrice Stella Tanner, 1865–1940); quoted in Daphne Fielding, *The Duchess of Jermyn Street*, 1964.

'Lightsome', 'frivolous' and 'satirical' are not words that readily spring to mind when one thinks of Thomas Hardy writing on the subject of sex. But then, on the other hand, there is this:

> 'O Melia, my dear, this does everything crown!
> Who could have supposed I should meet you in town?
> And whence such fair garments, such prosperi-ty?'
> 'O didn't you know I'd been ruined?' said she.

– 'You left us in tatters, without shoes or socks,
Tired of digging potatoes, and spudding up docks;
And now you've gay bracelets and bright feathers three!' –
'Yes: that's how we dress when we're ruined,' said she.

– 'At home in the barton you said "thee" and "thou,"
And "thik oon," and "theas oon!" and "t'other"; but now
Your talking quite fits 'ee for high compa-ny!' –
'Some polish is gained with one's ruin,' said she.

– 'Your hands were like paws then, your face blue and bleak,
But now I'm bewitched by your delicate cheek,
And your little gloves fit as on any la-dy!'–
'We never do work when we're ruined,' said she.

– 'You used to call home life a hag-ridden dream,
And you'd sigh, and you'd sock; but at present you seem
To know not of megrims or melanchol-ly!'
'True. There's an advantage in ruin,' said she.

– 'I wish I had feathers, a fine sweeping gown,
And a delicate face, and could strut about town!' –
'My dear – a raw country girl, such as you be,
Isn't equal to that. You ain't ruined!' said she.

Thomas Hardy (1840–1928), 'The Ruined Maid'.

D.H. Lawrence's *Lady Chatterley's Lover* brought a new frankness to the literary treatment of sex. Here Lady Chatterley's gamekeeper lover, Mellors, decries 'cold-hearted fucking':

The mass of women are like this: most of them want a man, but don't want the sex, but they put up with it, as part of the bargain. The more old-fashioned sort just lie there like nothing and let you go ahead. They don't mind afterwards: then they like you. But the actual thing itself is nothing to them, a bit distasteful. And most men like it that way. I hate it. But the sly sort of women who are like that pretend they're not. They pretend they're passionate and have thrills. But it's all cockaloopy. They make it up. – Then there's the ones that love everything, every kind of feeling and cuddling and going off, every kind except the natural one. They always make you go off when you're *not* in the only place where you should be, when you go off. – Then there's the hard sort, that are the devil to bring off at all, and bring themselves off, like my wife. They want to be the active party. – Then there's the sort that's just dead inside: but dead: and they know it. Then there's the sort that puts you out before you really 'come', and go on writhing their loins till they bring themselves off against your thighs. But they're mostly the Lesbian sort. It's astonishing how Lesbian women are, consciously or unconsciously. Seems to me they're nearly all Lesbian. ...

I wanted to have my pleasure and satisfaction of a woman, and I never got it: because I could never get my pleasure and satisfaction of *her* unless she got hers of me at the same time. And it never happened. It takes two. ...

I believe in being warm-hearted. I believe especially in being warm-hearted in love, in fucking with a warm heart. I believe if men could fuck with warm hearts, and the women take it warm-heartedly, everything would come all right. It's all this cold-hearted fucking that is death and idiocy.

D.H. Lawrence (1885–1930), *Lady Chatterley's Lover*, 1928.

Although privately published in 1928, *Lady Chatterley's Lover* remained unavailable to a wider public in its unexpurgated version until Penguin Books brought out an edition in 1960 – and was promptly charged with obscenity. An extract from the trial proceedings appears later in this section.

English prudery is well illustrated in the following exchange:

OFFICIAL: Excuse me, that little lad must have a top to 'is bathing dress.

MR. F: Why? What for?

OFFICIAL: Corporation's rules.

MRS. F: Lot of nonsense – the child's under age.

OFFICIAL: Can't 'elp that, madam.

ALICE: 'E 'asn't got a top.

OFFICIAL: The Corporation's very strict about indecent exposure.

MR. F: Well, it's coming to something if a child of ten can't enjoy a state of nature without giving a lot of old ladies ideas.

OFFICIAL: England don't 'old with states of nature.

Noël Coward (1899–1973), *The English Lido*, 1928.

The gap between the (male) ideal of how sex and/or love might be and the reality is exasperatedly explored in the following poem by D.H. Lawrence:

I wish I knew a woman
who was like a red fire on the hearth
glowing after the day's restless draughts.

So that one could draw near her
in the red stillness of the dusk
and really take delight in her
without having to make the polite effort of loving her
or the mental effort of making her acquaintance.
Without having to take a chill, talking to her.

D.H. Lawrence (1885–1930), 'I Wish I Knew A Woman', *Selected Poems*, 1950.

Complaints have also been voiced from the woman's point of view:

English lovemaking is not an amusement but a function. ... My real objection to the English male is that he will not give enough time, trouble or attention to the sexual act, and thereby makes it as flat, stale and deadly as a slab of one his cold suet puddings.

Odette Keun (1888–1978), *I Discover the English*, 1934.

In 1938 a Frenchman observed:

Victorian prudery is dying out. Freud and his disciples have at last allowed Anglo-Saxons to express their passions behind a scientific mask. In London theatres you will see plays far riskier than you would have dared to put on the boards in Paris. You will read English and American novels which will seem to you incredibly cynical. All the same, take care. Even in the very violence of this cynicism there is still quite a large element of Puritanism. That makes for an inimitable explosive mixture, which a foreigner should treat with caution. Besides, the great mass of the British people have not been touched by the 'new morals.' Julian Huxley tells a typical story. At the London Zoo a lady went up to the Keeper of the hippopotami. 'Tell me,' she said, 'is that hippopotamus a male or a female?' The Keeper looked at her in a shocked manner: 'That, ma'am,' he replied, 'is a question which should only interest another hippopotamus.' The Keeper of the hippopotami was also the Keeper of Victorian prudery.

André Maurois (1885–1967), *Three Letters on the English*, 1938.

> This Englishwoman is so refined
> She has no bosom and no behind.

Stevie Smith (1902–71), 'This Englishwoman', 1937.

Not all Englishwomen have been so inhibited. For many, the Second World War was a liberating experience, of a sort – or so many men appear to have encouraged many women to believe. Here the artist (and sometime artist's model) Joan Wyndham cautiously finds out for herself:

1 March 1940   What happened after that was so quick and unexpected that I had no time to protest. My neck and shoulders were bare, and Jo was covering them with kisses. I could feel the unshaven bristles rasping against my skin. To my amazement, I felt a great shiver of pure delight run through me, rather like the way I felt in church when I was thinking about Gerhardt.

Well, I thought, I'm not going to be so stupid the second time round, so this time when I saw Jo's face looming over me, blue stubbly chin and rather thick sensuous lips pouting for a kiss, I decided to shut my eyes and bear it. Actually it wasn't as bad as I had expected. In fact I even found myself responding a little, kissing him back. A pity he smelt of garlic.

Just as things were beginning to get hectic the doorbell rang furiously. It was the dustman. Jo said, 'This pisshole is just one damn thing after another,' and went to the back door. By the time he had disposed of the dustman the atmosphere of passion had somewhat evaporated and so we resumed the sitting.

26 March 1940   Had to leave at six to go to Sadler's Wells with Rowena. During the interval we had cocoa and Welsh rarebit at the Angel Café, while Rowena told me about her 'uncle', and how nice sex is. She says it's the best indoor recreation she has yet discovered, particularly in the afternoon which is the only time he can get away from his wife. She says it's like an old French song that just goes on and on, and I really ought to try it. . . .

I told her all about Gerhardt and Jo, and she said it sounded very boring and rather decadent. Of course I'm not decadent at all really, I only wish I was.

13 May 1940   Return of Jo from Cornwall. . . .

We had a wonderful morning, all young and excited again like it was at the beginning, kissing and fighting and hurling insults, laughing till we had to stuff our fingers in our mouths. Jo bit me till my neck was marked, and said, 'Oh, how good and soft you are to feel! How do I feel? Do you like it?' But I wouldn't let him undo my blouse.

'Christ, this is bad for me,' Jo said. 'I really shouldn't do it, it gets me all worked up and nowhere to go, because if there's one thing I don't do it's sleep with virgins.'

'Too much trouble, I suppose.'

'My God, yes, and no fun for the virgin either. I'll give you one word of advice – when it does happen go all out and give it everything you've got, don't hold back or have any inhibitions, because if you do it's the one thing that can turn a young girl into a lesbian. Didn't your mother ever talk about these things?'

'No, she never told me much – I don't think she knew much herself, in spite of being married. Oh, she sort of told me how it's done, driving around Hyde Park in her little Austin 7, with the engine revving up very loud to hide her embarrassment – actually, her own mother didn't tell her very much either, just to use lots of scent and not let her husband see her cleaning her teeth.'

20 May 1940   [Leonard] started teaching me words like bugger, fuck, cunt, cock etc., which he thinks should not be thought of as vulgar but should become part of the English language.

After he had gone on about this for quite a long time with the air of an Oxford don, he moved his chair nearer to me and said, 'I'm being terribly curious, and I suppose your friends would think me either silly or a cad to speak to a young girl like this, but have you ever thought you would like to indulge in certain practices other than mere face-to-face copulation?'

I told him that quite honestly I didn't know there were any, which is probably why I'd never thought about it. Leonard looked rather taken aback, but went on to describe, with scholarly enthusiasm, how a woman could lie on top of a man or sit astride him, or how she could kneel upright with a man coming in from behind, or how they could do it standing up, or the woman could lean back over a table.

'But of course,' he went on, 'it's more difficult for a woman to come in those attitudes than when you're face to face – do you follow? I'll demonstrate if you like.'

'Oh no – thank you very much, I'd really rather you didn't – what does come mean?'

Leonard stared at me in amazement. 'An orgasm, of course. My goodness, I keep forgetting how young you are.'

'So what else can a woman do?' I went on, beginning to get interested.

'Well, she can hold a man's penis in her mouth – the only objection to that is that it's rather difficult to know what to do with the semen when it comes. I know some women like swallowing it – it acts like a tonic and makes them feel marvellous.'

I said I couldn't see myself enjoying that very much, so he steered the conversation back to masturbation, which we had just been starting on the day Holland and Belgium were invaded. When I said I had never done it, he seemed very startled and said, 'Good heavens, not even at your convent? I thought all convent girls did it? Well you really ought to, you've missed a lot! Goodness,' he went on, looking for some more cake, 'I'm being extraordinarily perverse this afternoon.'

Leonard believes that any normally attractive man can get any woman in the end if he is patient and soft with her. I looked at Leonard's skinny legs and decided it wasn't true.

24 July 1940   'By the way,' asked Rupert, as we sat in the cafeteria and ate a Lyon's fresh cream sandwich for tea, 'why are you a virgin?'

'I don't really know,' I said. 'It's never occurred to me to be anything else.'

He picked up my hand and studied my palm. 'I think it's because you sit in an ivory tower, like me. ... You're like me, you look as if you're always expecting something to happen, but it doesn't unless you make it. I'm the same, I bore myself to tears, but I'm far too lazy to try to make contact with life.'

When I got up to go home at six he said, 'How would you like it if I robbed you of your virginity?'

I thought for a minute.

'I don't *think* I should mind very much, but then I hardly know you well enough to say.'

16 September 1940   This morning Sid and I nearly got bombed in the bus on our way to the first-aid post. ... Then Prudey and I went off to try and salvage some more of her stuff....

When we got there it looked very dangerous, and Prudey said, 'Don't go in, you can't die a virgin!'

'But I'm *not* a virgin,' I announced proudly. Prudey did a double take.

'Oh really? Well that's fine, I expect you feel much better for it, don't you?'

'Well, yes, I suppose I do.'

'I'm so pleased – did you use Volpar Gels?'

'No, but I'm going to.'

'You were lucky to have Rupert, of course. He's very sweet, isn't he? It's terribly important to be poked by someone nice the first time. Most girls get awful men, and it puts them off poking for good.'

25 September 1940   By this morning I had worked myself up into such a state of passion over the absent Rupert – I hadn't seen him for a week – that I didn't know what to do with myself. All morning at the post I was thinking about him and wondering how much longer I could bear life without him.

On the way home I saw seventeen German planes in arrow formation cutting through the blue sky, with hundreds of shells bursting around them. The guns were so loud I took shelter in the door of the Servite church. As I was cowering there I heard a yell – 'Woo hoo! Joanie!' – and there was old R. lurching down the street with a cheery smile on his face, completely ignoring the guns.

'Lunch?' he said happily, pushing me ahead of him just as though nothing was happening. He was all brown and glowing, his thin cheeks flushed like pomegranates, talking about *Heloïse and Abelard*, which he had been reading at his ma's – that is, he read all the sexy bits and skipped the rest. ...

I explained that what with the bombs and working at the first-aid post I really didn't have time for art any more.

'All the more time for looking after Rooples,' he chortled with satisfaction. I choked down my happiness and got lunch ready. Rupert had bought minute steak – it took the whole of his meat ration. I hadn't had any for weeks. He set about frying the onions and I sat watching him, marvelling more and more at his extraordinary physical charm. Why the handsomest man in Chelsea and Fulham should want to sit around my dump frying onions is more than I can fathom. . . .

After we had eaten he wanted to lie down with me but I resisted, and we crashed down together on the sofa, most undignified.

'Now this here Heloïse,' Rupert said reprovingly, sitting on my stomach, 'she used to *glide* down to Abelard's couch, clad only in a loose-bodied gown and carrying a lamp. Now let's see *you* glide down to me, Joanie, ten stone or no ten stone.' Looking v. intense, I glided. 'You know, I think I almost missed you,' R. said.

After that we quit being funny and made love very seriously, and I was filled with peace and delight. You can't write about sensuality mingled with tenderness and pity, it just becomes maudlin or goes bad on you in some way – so call it love and leave it at that, one of the few transcendent and satisfying things left in this bloody awful life.

Joan Wyndham (1922–), *Diary*.

The poet and university librarian Philip Larkin (1922–85) typified a particular sort of Englishman of a particular time: sexual, frustrated, fearful, distrustful, doubting that what he saw as 'face-value' could be true all the way through (or else fearing that it would be), equally fearful of rebuff and acceptance, seeking solace in just-less-than-satisfyingly-explicit porn. Suspecting throughout his life that *he was missing out on something everyone else took for granted*, he lived his life in such a way as to ensure he always would. The type is not extinct, though it has become a smaller and sadder minority. Here is a selection of his letters on the subject:

To Kingsley Amis, 9 August 1945.
I really do not think it likely I shall ever get into the same bed as anyone again because it is so much trouble, almost as much trouble as standing for Parliament. I have formed a very low opinion of women and the idea of having one perpetually following me abait [sic] is wearisome. And indeed the only advance I ever made to a woman was productive of such scorching embarrassment that the wound is still rawly open. (In response to your unspoken question, it wasn't anyone you knew.) That was over two years ago and if I forget it in ten I shall be agreeably surprised.

To Kingsley Amis, 17 July 1946.
Miss Isobel has come for a bit. I don't care much about that, as it means I have to PAY for TWO women at the PUB and the FLICKS instead of ONE and I DON'T get my COCK into EITHER of them, EVER.

To Kingsley Amis, 26 February 1947.
I have experienced rather a 'change of heart' about misruth [sic] lately. She was seriously considering going off with the young homo recently & this led me to

think that after all we got on much better than I should ever get on with Miss G.C. Evans, or Miss Jane Exall, or anybody else, because we are really quite alike, and that a pock is a pock, and that pocking Miss Jane Exall wouldn't be nearly so nice in reality as it is in my imagination WHEN I'M TOSSING MYSELF, and that it would be all right if I even intended doing anything about Miss G.C. Evans, but I don't, and therefore is it not better to take what is to hand & be thankful, particularly when what is to hand is comparatively so amusing and sympathetic? It seems to me that while pocking Miss Jane Exall is infinitely desirable, preparing Miss Jane Exall to be pocked and dealing with Miss Jane Exall after pocking is not at all desirable – and that pocks do not exist in the void. All this is very elementary, but it seems to me I am wasting a lot of energy doing s.f.a. at present & that it wd be a good thing to resign myself to misruth (perhaps not to the extent of wedding bells o'boy) and to start thinking about something else.

To J.B. Sutton, 26 January 1950.
My relations with women are governed by a shrinking sensitivity, a morbid sense of sin, a furtive lechery & a deplorable flirtatiousness – all of which are menaced by the clear knowledge that I should find marriage a trial. 'One hates the person one lives with.' So much for me. ... I resist the current, even if it means staying in the same spot all one's life. 'Never accept what you don't want. Keep refusing, & in time you may get what you do want. On the other hand you may end up with *FUCK ALL.*'

To Robert Conquest, 4 July 1959.
Yes, I got the pictures – whacko. I admired the painstaking realism of it – I mean, the teacher did really look like a teacher, & I greatly appreciated the school-like electric bell on the wall. The action & standard of definition left something to be desired – I'll leave you to guess what.

To Robert Conquest, 15 September 1959.
Send me some spanking & bondage, cleverly got up to look like the Kenyon Review, for the English mags are 'way down. Am off to London this weekend but may not reach Gerrard St.

To Robert Conquest, 5 March 1966.
Yes, life is pretty grey up in Hull. Maeve wants to marry me, Monica wants to chuck me, I feel I want to be something other than a man – a rosebush, or some ivy, or something. Something noncontroversial. Feel it would be a good time to have a year in the USA. Life's colourful pageant seems to be passing me by. How is it with you? You never said where the chief porno shop had gone. I've rather gone off the mags; I sent a 6 month sub to *Paris Hollywood*, but after sending one issue they've gone dead – next sign will be the heavy tread of the British law enforcement officer, come along o me, my bucko, we know your sort. Librarian charged.

Anthony Thwaite, ed., *Selected Letters of Philip Larkin 1940–1985*, 1992.

Continental people have a sex life; the English have hot-water bottles.

George Mikes (1912–87), *How To Be An Alien*, 1946.

Hooray, hooray,
The first of May,
Outdoor sex
Begins today.

'Traditional' Oxford University rhyme.

On the whole, however, the English have preferred rather different outdoor pursuits, such as gardening ... Here Sir John Mortimer recalls his father's views:

Sex, like love, my father thought, had been greatly overestimated by the poets. He would often pause at tea-time, his biscuit half-way to his mouth, to announce, 'I have never had many mistresses with thighs like white marble.' ... Like most children I found my father's sex life a subject on which it was best to avoid speculation. ...

'Love affairs aren't much of a subject for drama really,' he told me at an early age. 'Consider this story of a lover, a husband, and an unfaithful wife. The wife confesses all to her husband. He sends for her lover. They are closeted in the living-room together. The wife stands outside the door, trembling with fear. She strains her ears to discover what's going on in the room. Some terrible quarrel? A duel or fight to the death perhaps? At last she can stand the suspense no longer. She flings open the door and what does she see? Blood? Broken furniture? One of them stretched out on the carpet? Not at all. The two men are sitting by the fire drinking bottled ale and discussing the best method of pruning apple trees. Naturally the woman's furious. She packs and leaves for her mother's.' ...

It follows from all this that my father's advice on the subject of sex was not of much practical value.

John Mortimer (1923–), *Clinging to the Wreckage*, 1982.

A change came with the 'Swinging Sixties', heralded by the *Lady Chatterley* trial of 1960, in which the prosecuting counsel, Mr Griffith-Jones, despite his protestations, betrayed himself as a relic from an earlier time:

Let me emphasise it on behalf of the Prosecution: do not approach this matter in any priggish, high-minded, super-correct, mid-Victorian manner. ... Members of the Jury, when you have seen this book, making all such allowances in favour of it as you can, the Prosecution will invite you to say that it does tend, certainly that it may tend, to induce lustful thoughts in the minds of those who read it. It goes further, you may think. It sets upon a pedestal promiscuous and adulterous intercourse. It commends, and indeed it sets out to commend, sensuality almost as a virtue. It encourages, and indeed even advocates, coarseness and vulgarity of thought and of language. You may think that it must tend to deprave the minds certainly of some and you may think many of the persons who are likely to buy it at the price of 3s 6d and read it, with 200,000 copies already printed and ready for release.

You may think that one of the ways in which you can test this book, and test it from the most liberal outlook, is to ask yourselves the question, when you have read it through, would you approve of your young sons, young daughters – because girls can read as well as boys – reading this book. Is it a book that you would even wish your wife or your servants to read?

Mr Griffith-Jones, senior Treasury Counsel, opening address for the Prosecution in *Regina v. Penguin Books Ltd.*, 20 October 1960.

Philip Larkin famously noted the impact of the trial:

> Sexual intercourse began
> In nineteen sixty-three
> (Which was rather late for me) –
> Between the end of the *Chatterley* ban
> And the Beatles' first LP.
>
> Up till then there'd only been
> A sort of bargaining,
> A wrangle for a ring,
> A shame that started at sixteen
> And spread to everything.
>
> Then all at once the quarrel sank:
> Everyone felt the same,
> And every life became
> A brilliant breaking of the bank,
> A quite unlosable game.
>
> So life was never better than
> In nineteen sixty-three
> (Though just too late for me) –
> Between the end of the *Chatterley* ban
> And the Beatles' first LP.

Philip Larkin (1922–85), 'Annus Mirabilis', 16 June 1967; from *High Windows*, 1974.

Suddenly sex was everywhere, leading to a variety of reactions, mostly dismissive …

This sort of thing may be tolerated by the French – but we are British, thank God.

Viscount Montgomery of Alamein (1887–1976), speech on the Homosexual Law Reform Bill, House of Lords, 1965.

No more about sex, it's too boring.

Lawrence Durrell (1912–90), *Tunc*, 1968.

Sex is the last refuge of the miserable.

Quentin Crisp (1908–2000), *The Naked Civil Servant*, 1968.

I tend to believe that cricket is the greatest thing that God ever created on earth … certainly greater than sex, although sex isn't too bad either.

Harold Pinter (1930–), interviewed in the *Observer*, 5 October 1980.

Cricket-playing nations are capable of only limited amounts of sexual activity.

Letter published in the *Bangkok Post*, 1991.

Sex has never been an obsession with me. It's just like eating a bag of crisps. Quite nice, but nothing marvellous.

Boy George, quoted in the *Sun*, 21 October 1982.

Yes. I haven't had enough sex.

John Betjeman (1906–84), Poet Laureate, when asked if he had any regrets: *Time With Betjeman*, BBC TV, February 1983.

I know it does make people happy but to me it is just like having a cup of tea.

Cynthia Payne, London woman, on her acquittal on a charge of controlling prostitutes, 8 November 1987.

As time went by, women – no doubt fed up with being treated by men as a bag of crisps or a cricket substitute – increasingly voiced their dissatisfaction:

STEPHANIE: Have you ever had the feeling that they don't know where it is?
RHODA: Oh God, yes.
DENISE: Oh, yeah.
STEPHANIE: Now, sometimes I show them. I say, 'This is where you put your cock in and where the babies come out. And *this* is the clitoris, up *here*.' Otherwise they fiddle away down there for ages, and you have to keep saying, 'Up a bit.' '*Oh*,' they say, '*up?*' And you say, 'Ye-es.' And they're clearly thinking, 'Very strange, all this "up a bit". It's like *The Golden Shot.*'
JULIA: At least at the end of that you got a toaster.

'What Women Want in Bed', *GQ* magazine, 1989.

English culture is basically homosexual in the sense that the men only really care about other men.

Germaine Greer (1939–), in the *Daily Mail*, 18 April 1988.

In Anglo-Saxon countries men prefer the company of other men. … In England 25% of men are homosexual.

Edith Cresson (1934–), Prime Minister of France, 1991.

You see, I like men. I like warm, sexy men who like me. Men who like to make love to me. I like it when men make love to me and as I'm not one to stint myself on life's pleasures when they come man-sized, men make love to me quite often. Great. I love it. Only, after a man has given me a good time, made me melt with pleasure, filled me with his more interesting bits and then done very interesting (and sometimes peculiar) things with those interesting bits, for a short space of time I adore him so much I'll do anything he asks.
Anything.

Nadia Adamant (Jan Holt, 1949–93), *Fondle All Over*, 1993.

Love in a Mild, Damp Climate

I've fallen in love. I'm an ordinary woman. I didn't think such violent things could happen to ordinary people.

Noël Coward (1899–1973), film script, *Brief Encounter*, 1945.

Everybody knows the stereotype: the English are cold, passionless, awkward, clumsy, unfeeling in love; yet somehow they have contrived to produce some of the world's greatest love poetry. It's a puzzle ...

There follows a selection of some of the best of it, touching on love's many-splendoured aspects: love adoring, love undemanding, love lustful, love companionate, love hopeless and unrequited, love unbidden and unwanted, love equal and love tyrannical, love coquettish, love cruel, love kindly, love unfaithful, love despairing, love desperate, love timid, love exultant, love platonic, love ironic, love turned to contempt, love trusting, love suspecting, love betrayed and love betraying ...

The selection, which spans 600 years, is not categorised. The Englishness of it all lies in its sensibility, not its subject.

>   Merry Margaret,
>   As midsummer flower,
>   Gentle as falcon
>   Or hawk of the tower:
>   With solace and gladness,
>   Much mirth and no madness,
>   All good and no badness;
>   So joyously,
>   So maidenly,
>   So womanly
>   Her demeaning
>   In every thing,
>   Far, far passing
>   That I can indite,
>   Or suffice to write
>   Of Merry Margaret
>   As midsummer flower,
>   Gentle as falcon
>   Or hawk of the tower
>   And patient and still
>   And as full of good will
>   As fair Isaphill,
>   Coliander
>   Sweet pomander,
>   Good Cassander,
>   Steadfast of thought,
>   Well made, well wrought,
>   Far may be sought

Ere that he can find
So courteous, so kind
As Merry Margaret,
This midsummer flower
Gentle as falcon
Or hawk of the tower.

John Skelton (c.1460–1529), 'To Mistress Margaret Hussey'.

Let me not to the marriage of true minds
Admit impediments, love is not love
Which alters when it alteration finds,
Or bends with the remover to remove.
O no, it is an ever fixèd mark
That looks on tempests and is never shaken;
It is the star to every wandering bark,
Whose worth's unknown, although his height be taken.
Love's not Time's fool, though rosy lips and cheeks
Within his bending sickle's compass come,
Love alters not with his brief hours and weeks,
But bears it out even to the edge of doom:
If this be error and upon me proved,
I never writ, nor no man ever loved.

William Shakespeare (1564–1616), Sonnet 116, 1609.

Shall I compare thee to a Summer's day?
Thou art more lovely and more temperate:
Rough winds do shake the darling buds of May,
And Summer's lease hath all too short a date:
Sometimes too hot the eye of heaven shines,
And often is his gold complexion dimm'd,
And every fair from fair some-time declines,
By chance, or nature's changing course untrimm'd:
But thy eternal Summer shall not fade,
Nor lose possession of that fair thou ow'st,
Nor shall death brag thou wandr'st in his shade,
When in eternal lines to time thou grow'st,
So long as men can breathe or eyes can see,
So long lives this, and this gives life to thee.

William Shakespeare (1564–1616), Sonnet 18, 1609.

Take, oh take those lips away,
That so sweetly were forsworn,
And those eyes, the break of day,
Lights that do mislead the morn.
But my kisses bring again,
Seals of love, but sealed in vain.

Hide, oh hide those hills of snow,
    Which thy frozen bosom bears,
On whose tops the pinks that grow
    Are yet of those that April wears.
But first set my poor heart free,
Bound in those icy chains by thee.

John Fletcher (1579–1625), 'Take, oh take …'; the first stanza appears in Shakespeare's *Measure for Measure*.

I wonder by my troth, what thou, and I
Did, till we lov'd? were we not wean'd till then?
But suck'd on countrey pleasures, childishly?
Or snorted we in the seaven sleepers den?
T'was so; But this, all pleasures fancies bee.
If ever any beauty I did see,
Which I desir'd, and got, t'was but a dreame of thee.

And now good morrow to our waking soules,
Which watch not one another out of feare;
For love, all love of other sights controules,
And makes one little roome, an every where.
Let sea-discoverers to new worlds have gone,
Let Maps to other, worlds on worlds have showne,
Let us possesse one world, each hath one, and is one.

My face in thine eye, thine in mine appeares,
And true plaine hearts doe in the faces rest,
Where can we finde two better hemispheares
Without sharpe North, without declining West?
What ever dyes, was not mixt equally;
If our two loves be one, or, thou and I
Love so alike, that none doe slacken, none can die.

John Donne (1572–1631), 'The Good-morrow'.

Tell me not (Sweet) I am unkinde,
    That from the Nunnerie
Of thy chaste breast, and quiet minde,
    To Warre and Armes I flie.

True; a new Mistresse now I chase,
    The first Foe in the field;
And with a stronger Faith imbrace
    A Sword, a Horse, a Shield.

Yet this inconstancy is such,
    As you too shall adore;

I could not love thee (Deare) so much,
    Lov'd I not Honour more.

Richard Lovelace (1618–58), 'To Lucasta, Going to the Wars'.

Stella this day is thirty-four,
(We shan't dispute a year or more:)
However, Stella, be not troubled,
Although thy size and years are doubled
Since first I saw thee at sixteen,
The brightest virgin on the green;
So little is thy form declined;
Made up so largely in thy mind.
    O, would it please the gods to split
Thy beauty, size, and years, and wit!
No age could furnish out a pair
Of nymphs so graceful, wise, and fair;
With half the lustre of your eyes,
With half your wit, your years, and size.
And then, before it grew too late,
How should I beg of gentle fate,
(That either nymph might have her swain,)
To split my worship too in twain.

Jonathan Swift (1667–1745), 'Stella's Birth-Day'.

St. Patrick's Dean, your country's pride,
My early and my only guide,
You taught how I might youth prolong,
By knowing what was right and wrong;
How from my heart to bring supplies
Of lustre to my fading eyes;
How soon a beauteous mind repairs
The loss of changed or failing hairs;
How wit and virtue from within
Send out a smoothness o'er the skin:
Your lectures could my fancy fix,
And I can please at thirty-six.
The sight of Chloe at fifteen,
Coquetting, gives me not the spleen;
The idol now of every fool
Till time shall make their passions cool;
Then tumbling down Time's steepy hill,
While Stella holds her station still.

Esther Johnson (1681–1728), 'To Dr Swift on his Birthday, 30th November 1721'.

When I loved you, I can't but allow
    I had many an exquisite minute;
But the scorn that I feel for you now
    Hath even more luxury in it!

Thus, whether we're on or we're off,
    Some witchery seems to await you;
To love you is pleasant enough,
    But oh! 'tis delicious to hate you!

Thomas Moore (1779–1852), 'To …'.

Last night, ah, yesternight, betwixt her lips and mine
There fell thy shadow, Cynara! thy breath was shed
Upon my soul between the kisses and the wine;
And I was desolate and sick of an old passion,
    Yea, I was desolate and bow'd my head:
I have been faithful to thee, Cynara! in my fashion.

All night upon mine heart I felt her warm heart beat,
Night-long within mine arms in love and sleep she lay;
Surely the kisses of her bought red mouth were sweet;
But I was desolate and sick of an old passion,
    When I awoke and found the dawn was gray:
I have been faithful to thee, Cynara! in my fashion.

I have forgot much, Cynara! gone with the wind,
Flung roses, roses, riotously with the throng,
Dancing, to put thy pale lost lilies out of mind;
But I was desolate and sick of an old passion,
    Yea, all the time, because the dance was long:
I have been faithful to thee, Cynara! in my fashion.

I cried for madder music and for stronger wine,
But when the feast is finish'd and the lamps expire,
Then falls thy shadow, Cynara! the night is thine;
And I am desolate and sick of an old passion,
    Yea, hungry for the lips of my desire:
I have been faithful to thee, Cynara! in my fashion.

Ernest Dowson (1867–1900), 'Non sum qualis eram bonae sub regno Cynarae'.

At nine in the morning there passed a church,
At ten there passed me by the sea,
At twelve a town of smoke and smirch,
At two a forest of oak and birch,
    And then, on a platform, she:

A radiant stranger, who saw not me.
I said, 'Get out to her do I dare?'

But I kept my seat in my search for a plea,
And the wheels moved on. O could it but be
      That I had alighted there!

Thomas Hardy (1840–1928), 'Faintheart in a Railway Train'.

When I had met my love the twentieth time,
      She put me to confession day and night:
Did I like woman far above all things,
      Or did the songs I make give more delight?

'Listen, you sweeter flower than ever smiled
      In April's sunny face,' I said at last –
'The voices and the legs of birds and women
      Have always pleased my ears and eyes the most.'

And saying this, I watched my love with care,
      Not knowing would my words offend or please:
But laughing gaily, her delighted breasts
      Sent ripples down her body to her knees.

W.H. Davies (1871–1940), 'Her Merriment'.

Evening falls on the smoky walls,
      And the railings drip with rain,
And I will cross the old river
      To see my girl again.

The great and solemn-gliding tram,
      Love's still-mysterious car,
Has many a light of gold and white,
      And a single dark red star.

I know a garden in a street
      Which no one ever knew;
I know a rose beyond the Thames,
      Where flowers are pale and few.

J.E. Flecker (1884–1915), 'Ballad of the Londoner'.

I am worn out
with the effort of trying to love people
and not succeeding.

Now I've made up my mind
I love nobody, I'm going to love nobody,
I'm not going to tell any lies about it
and it's final.

If there's a man here and there, or a woman
whom I can really like,
that's quite enough for me.

And if by a miracle a woman happened to come along
who warmed the cockles of my heart
I'd rejoice over the woman and the warmed cockles of my heart
so long as it didn't all fizzle out in talk.

D.H. Lawrence (1885–1930), 'The Effort of Love', *Selected Poems*, 1950.

I am a lamp, a lamp that is out;
      I am a shallow stream;
In it are neither pearls or trout,
      Nor one of the things that you dream.

Why do you smile and deny, my lover?
      I will not be denied.
I am a book, a book with a cover,
      And nothing at all inside.

Here is the truth, and you must grapple,
      Grapple with what I have said.
I am a dumpling without any apple,
      I am a star that is dead.

Frances Cornford (1886–1960), 'She Warns Him'.

'Let us not speak, for the love we bear one another –
      Let us hold hands and look.'
She, such a very ordinary little woman;
      He, such a thumping crook:
But both, for the moment, little lower than the angels
      In the teashop inglenook.

John Betjeman (1906–84), 'In a Bath Teashop', from *New Bats for Old Belfries*, 1945.

Miss J. Hunter Dunn, Miss J. Hunter Dunn,
Furnish'd and burnish'd by Aldershot sun,
What strenuous singles we played after tea,
We in the tournament – you against me!

Love thirty, love forty, oh! weakness of joy,
The speed of a swallow, the grace of a boy,
With carefullest carelessness, gaily you won,
I am weak from your loveliness, Joan Hunter Dunn.

Miss Joan Hunter Dunn, Miss Joan Hunter Dunn,
How mad I am, sad I am, glad that you won.
The warm-handled racket is back in its press,
But my shock-headed victor, she loves me no less.
. . .
Miss Joan Hunter Dunn, Miss Joan Hunter Dunn,
I can hear from the car-park the dance has begun.

Oh! full Surrey twilight! importunate band!
Oh! strongly adorable tennis-girl's hand!

Around us are Rovers and Austins afar,
Above us, the intimate roof of the car,
And here on my right is the girl of my choice,
With the tilt of her nose and the chime of her voice,

And the scent of her wrap, and the words never said,
And the ominous, ominous dancing ahead.
We sat in the car park till twenty to one
And now I'm engaged to Miss Joan Hunter Dunn.

John Betjeman (1906–84), 'A Subaltern's Love-song', in *New Bats in Old Belfries*, 1945.

On Waterloo Bridge, where we said our goodbyes,
The weather conditions bring tears to my eyes.
I wipe them away with a black woolly glove
And try not to notice I've fallen in love.

On Waterloo Bridge I am trying to think:
This is nothing. You're high on the charm and the drink.
But the juke-box inside me is playing a song
That says something different. And when was it wrong?

On Waterloo Bridge with the wind in my hair
I am tempted to skip. *You're a fool.* I don't care.
The head does its best but the heart is the boss –
I admit it before I am halfway across.

Wendy Cope (1945–), 'After the Lunch' in *Serious Concerns*, 1992.

To Have and To Hold

Matrimony was ordained ... for the procreation of children ... for a remedy
against sin, and to avoid fornication ... for the mutual society, help, and comfort,
that the one ought to have of the other, both in prosperity and adversity.

The Book of Common Prayer, 1662.

*The English, it might be said, woo in poetry and marry in prose: a justifiable epigram,
though not entirely true.*

The most seriously serially married person in English literature must be Chaucer's Wife of Bath:

Blessed be God that I have wedded five!
Welcome the sixth, whenever he appears.
I can't keep continent for years and years.
No sooner than one husband's dead and gone

Some other Christian man shall take me on,
For then, so says the Apsotle, I am free
To wed, o'God's name, where it pleases me.
Wedding's no sin, so far as I can learn.
Better it is to marry than to burn.

. . .

    Had God commanded maidenhood to all
Marriage would be condemned beyond recall,
And certainly if seed were never sown,
How ever could virginity be grown?

. . .

    The Apostle was a virgin, well I know;
Nevertheless, though all his writings show
He wished that everyone were such as he,
It's all mere counsel to virginity.
And as for being married, he lets me do it
Out of indulgence, so there's nothing to it
In marrying me, suppose my husband's dead;
There's nothing bigamous in such a bed.

. . .

    Virginity is indeed a great perfection,
And married continence, for God's delection,
But Christ, who of perfection is the well,
Bade not that everyone should go and sell
All that he had and give it to the poor
To follow in His footsteps, that is sure.
He spoke to those who would live perfectly,
And by your leave, my lords, that's not for me.
I will bestow the flower of life, the honey,
Upon the acts and fruit of matrimony.
    Tell me to what conclusion or in aid
Of what were generative organs made?
And for what profit were those creatures wrought?
Trust me, they cannot have been made for naught.
Gloze as you will and plead the explanation
That they were only made for the purgation
Of urine, little things of no avail
Except to know a female from a male,
And nothing else. Did somebody say no?
Experience knows well it isn't so.
The learned may rebuke me, or be loath
To think it so, but they were made for both,
That is to say both use and pleasure in
Engendering, except in use of sin.
Why else the proverb written down and set
In books: 'A man must yield the wife her debt'?

What means of paying her can he invent
Unless he use his silly instrument?
. . .

   Now of my fifth, last husband let me tell.
God never let his soul be sent to Hell!
And yet he was my worst, and many a blow
He struck me still can ache along my row
Of ribs, and will until my dying day.
   But in our bed he was so fresh and gay,
So coaxing, so persuasive . . . Heaven knows
Whenever he wanted it – my *belle chose* –
Though he had beaten me in every bone
He still could wheedle me to love, I own.
I think I loved him best, I'll tell no lie,
He was disdainful in his love, that's why.
. . .

   Now let me tell you all that came to pass.
We sauntered in the meadow through the grass
Toying and dallying to such extent,
Johnny and I, that I grew provident
And I suggested, were I ever free
And made a widow, he should marry me.
And certainly – I do not mean to boast –
I ever was more provident than most
In marriage matters and in other such.
I never think a mouse is up to much
That only has one hole in all the house;
If that should fail, well, it's good-bye the mouse.
. . .

   To church they bore my husband on the morrow
With all the neighbours round him venting sorrow,
And one of them of course was handsome Johnny.
So help me God, I thought he looked so bonny
Behind the coffin! Heavens, what a pair
Of legs he had! Such feet, so clean and fair!
I gave my whole heart up, for him to hold.
He was, I think, some twenty summers old,
And I was forty then, to tell the truth.
But still, I always had a coltish tooth . . .
. . .

And was unable to deny, in truth,
My chamber of Venus to a likely youth.
The mark of Mars is still upon my face
And also in another privy place.
For as I may be saved by God above,
I never used discretion when in love

But ever followed on my appetite,
Whether the lad was short, long, black or white.
Little I cared, if he was fond of me,
How poor he was, or what his rank might be.

Geoffrey Chaucer (c.1340–1400), 'The Wife of Bath's Prologue' from *The Canterbury Tales*, tr. Nevill Coghill, 1951.

Two centuries later, Thomas More's Utopians went about selecting a mate in a frank and straightforward fashion:

Furthermore, in choosing wives and husbands, they observe earnestly and straightly a custom which seemed to us very fond and foolish. For a grave and honest matron showeth the woman, be she maid or widow, naked to her wooer: and likewise a sage and discreet man exhibiteth the wooer naked to the woman. At this custom we laughed, and disallowed it as foolish. But they, on the other part, do greatly wonder at the folly of other nations, which in *buying a colt* (whereas a little money is in hazard) be so chary and circumspect, that though he be almost all bare, yet will not buy him, unless the saddle and all the harness be taken off – least under those coverings may be hid some gall or sore. And yet in *choosing a wife*, which shall be a pleasure or displeasure to them all their life after, they be so reckless, that all the residue of the woman's body being covered by clothes, they esteem her scarcely by one hand breadth (for they can see no more but her face).

Sir Thomas More (1478–1535), *Utopia*, 1516.

More himself employed a similar approach:

Sir William Roper, of Eltham in Kent, came one morning, pretty early, to my lord, with a proposal to marry one of his daughters. My lord's daughters were then both together abed in a truckle-bed in their father's chamber asleep. He carries Sir William into the chamber and takes the sheet by the corner and suddenly whips it off. They lay on their backs, and their smocks up as high as their armpits. This awakened them, and immediately they turned on their bellies. Quoth Roper, 'I have seen both sides,' and so gave a pat on her buttock he made choice of, saying, 'Thou art mine.' Here was all the trouble of the wooing.

John Aubrey (1626–97), *Brief Lives*, 'Sir Thomas More'. Aubrey explains how this story came to him 'from my honoured friend, old Mistress Tyndale, whose grandfather, Sir William Stafford, was an intimate acquaintance of this Sir W. Roper, who told him the story'.

The framers of the following statute shared More's concern for honest dealing in the matrimonial trade:

Any woman who shall impose upon, seduce, and betray into matrimony any of His Majesty's subjects by virtue of her scents, paints, cosmetic washes, artificial teeth, false hair, iron stays, hoops, high-heeled shoes, or bolstered hips, shall incur the penalty against witchcraft, and the marriage ... shall be null and void.

Act of Parliament, 17th century.

A moving tribute to a 17th-century marriage survives in the form of Lady Catherine Dyer's epitaph for her husband:

My dearest dust, could not thy hasty day
Afford thy drowszy patience leave to stay
One hower longer: so that we might either
Sate up, or gone to bedd together?
But since thy finisht labor hath possest
Thy weary limbs with early rest,
Enjoy it sweetly: and thy widdowe bride
Shall soone repose her by thy slumbring side.
Whose business, now, is only to prepare
My nightly dress, and call to prayre:
Mine eyes wax heavy and ye day growes cold.
Draw, draw ye closed curtaynes: and make room:
My deare, my dearest dust; I come, I come.

Lady Catherine Dyer (fl.1630), Epitaph on the Monument of Sir William Dyer at Colmworth, 1641.

The Earl of Rochester, Restoration rake and wit, is well known as the author of exuberantly racy poems. However, the reality of his own marriage to the heiress Elizabeth Malet was somewhat different:

My most neglected Wife, till you are a much respected Widow, I find you will scarce be a contented woman, and to say no more than the plain truth, I do endeavour so fairly to do you that last good service, that none but the most impatient would refuse to rest satisfy'd; what evil Angel Enemy to my repose does inspire my Lady Warr to visit you once a year & leave you bewitch'd for elev'n months after? Doe but propose to me any reasonable thing upon Earth I can do to set you at quiet, but it is like a mad woman to lie roaring out of pain and never confess in what part it is.

John Wilmot, Earl of Rochester (1647–80), letter to his wife, 20 November 1677.

In the early 18th century a Swiss commentator, B.L. de Muralt, observed the English way of love and marriage. According to de Muralt, the English are said to be …

… capable of great determination in favour of a lover; gentle, artless and without finesse, unaffected in conversation and little spoilt by the attentions of men who give but a small part of their time to them. Indeed most men prefer wine and gaming to women, in this they are the more to blame as women are much better than the wine in England. It is true that Englishmen when they fall in love do it with violence; love with them is not a weakness of which they are ashamed, it is a serious and important matter in which often enough it is a question either of succeeding or of losing reason or life. But usually when they look for pretty women they do not want to owe the favours they have from them to delicate attentions; lazy even in love they ask only for easy pleasure. … The truth is that London is the city of the world where lazy debauchees can most easily get satisfaction. But apart from that Englishmen seem little made for gallantry, they know no mean between complete familiarity and respectful silence. ... I have seen amongst the quality pipes and tobacco handed out at the end of a meal, the women retiring and the men calmly watching them leave, as they fill their pipes.

Something still more disagreeable for English women, at least for London women, is that most husbands have mistresses. Sometimes they bring them into their homes and to meals with their wives, without anything unpleasant happening. I think if the whim took them they would bring them to lie in the same bed. ... What I find rather extraordinary and not a small proof of the extraordinary kindness of English women is that these mistresses do not appear to be particularly discredited in society; you see them sometimes received by married women, indistinguishable from them except that they are prettier, better dressed and more at their ease. ... I believe that most women suffer these mistresses out of pure kindness but it is not impossible that some have another motive, are afraid that if they disdain them they may set up some bad habit (in their husbands) from which later on they themselves may suffer.

B.L. de Muralt (1665–1749), *Lettres sur les Anglais,* Zürich, 1725.

That Englishmen are 'little made for gallantry' is illustrated by Tristram Shandy's father, who insists on a domestic routine, even in matters conjugal:

I wish either my father or my mother, or indeed both of them, as they were in duty both equally bound to it, had minded what they were about when they begot me; ...

Pray, my dear, quoth my mother, *have you not forgot to wind up the clock?*——*Good G–!* cried my father, making an exclamation, but taking care to moderate his voice at the same time,–*Did ever woman, since the creation of the world, interrupt a man with such a silly question?* Pray, what was your father saying?–Nothing. ...

My father, you must know, who was originally a Turkey merchant, but had left off business for some years, in order to retire to, and die upon, his paternal estate in the county of ——, was, I believe, one of the most regular men in everything he did, whether 'twas matter of business, or matter of amusement, that ever lived. As a small specimen of this extreme exactness of his, to which he was in truth a slave,–he had made it a rule for many years of his life,–on the first Sunday night of every month throughout the whole year,–as certain as ever the Sunday night came,–to wind up a large house-clock, which we had standing upon the backstairs head, with his own hands:–And being somewhere between fifty and sixty years of age, at the time I have been speaking of,–he had likewise gradually brought some other little family concernments to the same period, in order, as he would often say to my uncle Toby, to get them all out of the way at one time, and be no more plagued and pestered with them the rest of the month.

Laurence Sterne (1713–68), *Tristram Shandy,* 1759, Book I.

Marriage in the Shandean world involves more duties than pleasures:

Whilst a man is free,–cried the corporal, giving a flourish with his stick thus–

A thousand of my father's most subtle syllogisms could not have said more for celibacy.

Laurence Sterne (1713–68), *Tristram Shandy*, 1759, Book IX.

A contrary opinion comes from the distaff side:

It is a truth universally acknowledged, that a single man in possession of a good fortune, must be in want of a wife.

Jane Austen (1775–1817), *Pride and Prejudice*, opening words, 1813.

Obtaining the right partner for the right reasons is one of the key objectives in Austen's world:

Without thinking highly either of men or matrimony, marriage had always been her object; it was the only honourable provision for well-educated young women of small fortune, and however uncertain of giving happiness, must be their pleasantest preservative from want.

Jane Austen (1775–1817), *Pride and Prejudice*, chapter 22.

'Pray, my dear aunt, what is the difference in matrimonial affairs, between the mercenary and the prudent motive? Where does discretion end, and avarice begin? Last Christmas you were afraid of his marrying me, because it would be imprudent; and now, because he is trying to get a girl with only ten thousand pounds, you want to find out that he is mercenary.'

'If you will only tell me what sort of girl Miss King is, I shall know what to think.'

'She is a very good kind of girl, I believe. I know no harm of her.'

'But he paid her not the smallest attention till her grandfather's death made her mistress of his fortune.'

'No – why should he? If it were not allowable for him to gain *my* affections because I had no money, what occasion could there be for making love to a girl whom he did not care about, and who was equally poor?'

'But there seems indelicacy in directing his attention towards her so soon after this event.'

'A man in distressed circumstances has not time for all those elegant decorums which other people may observe. If *she* does not object to it, why should *we?*'

'*Her* not objecting does not justify *him*. It only shows her being deficient in something herself – sense or feeling.'

'Well,' cried Elizabeth, 'have it as you choose. *He* shall be mercenary, and *she* shall be foolish.'

'No, Lizzy, that is what I do *not* choose. I should be sorry, you know, to think ill of a young man who has lived so long in Derbyshire.'

'Oh! if that is all, I have a very poor opinion of young men who live in Derbyshire; and their intimate friends who live in Hertfordshire are not much better. I am sick of them all. Thank Heaven! I am going tomorrow where I shall find a man who has not one agreeable quality, who has neither manner nor sense to recommend him. Stupid men are the only ones worth knowing, after all.'

'Take care, Lizzy; that speech savours strongly of disappointment.'

Jane Austen (1775–1817), *Pride and Prejudice*, chapter 27.

In an earlier work, not published in her lifetime, Austen wrote:

To be so bent on marriage, to pursue a man merely for the sake of situation, is a sort of thing that shocks me; I cannot understand it. Poverty is a great evil; but to a woman of education and feeling it ought not, it cannot be the greatest.

Jane Austen (1775–1817), *The Watsons*, written c.1804.

Austen became increasingly sceptical about the whole marriage business (she herself remained unmarried):

'An engaged woman is always more agreeable than a disengaged. She is satisfied with herself. Her cares are over, and she feels that she may exert all her powers of pleasing without suspicion. All is safe with a lady engaged; no harm can be done.'

'Why, as to that, Mr. Rushworth is a very good sort of young man, and it is a great match for her.'

'But Miss Bertram does not care three straws for him; *that* is your opinion of your intimate friend. *I* do not subscribe to it. I am sure Miss Bertram is very much attached to Mr. Rushworth. I could see it in her eyes, when he was mentioned. I think too well of Miss Bertram to suppose she would ever give her hand without her heart.'

'Mary, how shall we manage him?'

'We must leave him to himself, I believe. Talking does no good. He will be taken in at last.'

'But I would not have him *taken in;* I would not have him duped; I would have it all fair and honourable.'

'Oh dear! let him stand his chance and be taken in. It will do just as well. Everybody is taken in at some period or other.'

'Not always in marriage, dear Mary.'

'In marriage especially. With all due respect to such of the present company as chance to be married, my dear Mrs. Grant, there is not one in a hundred of either sex who is not taken in when they marry. Look where I will, I see that it *is* so; and

I feel that it *must* be so, when I consider that it is, of all transactions, the one in which people expect most from others, and are least honest themselves'

'Ah! You have been in a bad school for matrimony, in Hill Street.'

'My poor aunt had certainly little cause to love the state; but, however, speaking from my own observation, it is a manœuvring business. I know so many who have married in the full expectation and confidence of some one particular advantage in the connection, or accomplishment, or good quality in the person, who have found themselves entirely deceived, and been obliged to put up with exactly the reverse. What is this but a take in?'

Jane Austen (1775–1817), *Mansfield Park*, 1814, chapter 5.

Austen herself was all too aware of the consequences of remaining unmarried:

Single women have a dreadful propensity for being poor – which is one very strong argument in favour of matrimony.

Jane Austen (1775–1817), letter to Fanny Knight, 13 March 1817.

With his usual directness of style and bluntness of manner, William Cobbett published in 1829 a series of 'letters' entitled *Advice to Young Men*. He met his own wife when she was 13 and he was nearly 21; he decided she was the one for him and, four years later, they were married. His was an extremely happy marriage, and he desired – nay, insisted – that others should follow this example. Here is a selection from this early version of 'The Rules':

The things which you ought to desire in a wife are, 1. Chastity; 2. Sobriety; 3. Industry; 4. Frugality; 5. Cleanliness; 6. Knowledge of domestic affairs; 7. Good temper; 8. Beauty.

Chastity, perfect modesty, in word, deed, and even thought, is so essential, that, without it, no female is fit to be a wife. It is not enough that a young woman abstain from everything approaching towards indecorum in her behaviour towards men; it is, with me, not enough that she cast down her eyes, or turn aside her head with a smile, when she hears an indelicate allusion: she ought to appear not to understand it, and to receive from it no more impression than if she were a post. A loose woman is a disagreeable acquaintance: what must she be then, as a wife? Love is so blind, and vanity is so busy in persuading us that our own qualities will be sufficient to ensure fidelity, that we are very apt to think nothing, or, at any rate, very little of trifling symptoms of levity; but if such symptoms show themselves now, we may be well assured that we shall never possess the power of effecting a cure. If prudery mean false modesty, it is to be despised; but if it mean modesty pushed to the utmost extent, I confess that I like it. Your 'free and hearty' girls I have liked very well to talk and laugh with; but never, for one moment, did it enter into my mind that I could have endured a 'free and hearty' girl for a wife. The thing is, I repeat, to last for life; it is to be a counterbalance for troubles and misfortunes; and it must, therefore, be perfect, or it had better not be at all. To say that one despises jealousy is foolish: it is a thing to be lamented; but the very elements of it ought to be avoided. Gross indeed is the beast, for he is unworthy the name of man; nasty indeed is the wretch, who can even entertain a thought of putting himself between a pair of sheets with a wife of whose infidelity he possesses the proof; but, in such cases, a man ought to be very slow to believe appearances: and he ought not to decide against his wife but upon the clearest proof. The last, and, indeed, the only effectual safeguard, is to begin well; to make a good choice; to let the beginning be such as to render infidelity and jealousy next to impossible. If you begin in grossness; if you couple yourself on to one with whom you have taken liberties, infidelity is the natural and just consequence. ...

Beauty. Though I have reserved this to the last of the things to be desired in a wife, I by no means think it the last in point of importance. The less favoured part of the sex say, that 'beauty is but skin deep'; and this is very true; but it is very agreeable, though, for all that. Pictures are only paint-deep, or pencil-deep; but we admire them, nevertheless. 'Handsome is that handsome does,' used to say to me an old man, who had marked me out for his not over-handsome daughter. 'Please your eye and plague your heart,' is an adage that want of beauty invented, I dare say, more than a thousand years ago. These adages would say, if they had but the courage, that beauty is inconsistent with chastity, with sobriety of conduct, and with all the female virtues. The argument is, that beauty exposes the possessor to greater temptation than women not beautiful are exposed to; and that, therefore, their fall is more probable. Let us see a little how this matter stands.

It is certainly true that pretty girls will have more, and more ardent, admirers than ugly ones; but as to the temptation when in their unmarried state, there are few so very ugly as to be exposed to no temptation at all; and which is the most likely to resist; she who has a choice of lovers, or she who, if she let the occasion slip, may never have it again? Which of the two is most likely to set a high value upon her reputation; she whom all beholders admire, or she who is admired, at best, by mere chance? And as to women in the married state, this argument assumes, that when they fall, it is from their own vicious disposition; when the fact is, that, if you search the annals of conjugal infidelity, you will find that, nine cases out of ten, the fault is in the husband. It is his neglect, his flagrant disregard, his frosty indifference, his foul example; it is to these that, nine times out of ten, he owes the infidelity of his wife; and if I were to say ninety-nine times out of a hundred, the facts, if verified, would, I am certain, bear me out. And whence this neglect, this disregard, this frosty indifference; whence this foul example? Because it is easy, in so many cases, to find some woman more beautiful than the wife. This is no justification for the husband to plead; for he has, with his eyes open, made a solemn contract: if she have not beauty enough to please him, he should have sought it in some other woman: if, as is frequently the case, he have preferred rank or money to beauty, he is an unprincipled man, if he do anything to make her unhappy who has brought him the rank or the money. At any rate, as conjugal infidelity is ... generally caused by the want of affection and due attention in the husband, it follows, of course, that it must more frequently happen in the case of ugly than in that of handsome women. ...

When promises have been made to a young woman; when they have been relied on for any considerable time; when it is manifest that her peace and happiness, and perhaps her life, depend upon their fulfilment; when things have been carried to this length, the change in the lover ought to be announced in the manner most likely to make the disappointment as supportable as the case will admit of; for though it is better to break the promise than to marry one while you like another better; though it is better for both parties, you have no right to break the heart of her who has, and that, too, with your own accordance, and, indeed, at your instigation, or at least by your encouragement, confided it to your fidelity. You cannot help your change of affections; but you can help making the transfer in such a way as to cause the destruction, or even probable destruction, nay, if it were but the deep misery, of her, to gain whose heart you had pledged your own. You ought to proceed by slow degrees; you ought to call time to your aid in executing the painful task; you ought scrupulously to avoid everything calculated to aggravate the sufferings of the disconsolate party.

Nor has a man any right to sport with the affections of a young woman, though he stop short of positive promises. Vanity is generally the tempter in this case; a desire to be regarded as being admired by the women: a very despicable species of vanity, but frequently greatly mischievous, notwithstanding. You do not, indeed, actually, in so many words, promise to marry; but the general tenor of your language and deportment has that meaning; you know that your meaning is so understood; and if you have not such meaning; if you be fixed by some previous engagement with, or greater liking for, another; if you know you are here sowing the seeds of disappointment; and if you, keeping your previous engagement, or greater liking, a secret, persevere, in spite of the admonitions of conscience, you are guilty of deliberate deception, injustice, and cruelty: you make to God an ungrateful return for those endowments which have enabled you to achieve this inglorious and unmanly triumph; and if, as is frequently the case, you glory in such triumph, you may have person, riches, talents to excite envy; but every just and humane man will abhor your heart.

William Cobbett (1762–1835), *Advice to Young Men*, 1829.

Charlotte Brontë gives a powerful voice to those who fear that marriage – or, at least, the wrong marriage – will crush their individuality. Here Jane Eyre describes her feelings about the Reverend St John Rivers:

As his curate, his comrade, all would be right ... There would be recesses in my mind which would be only mine, to which he never came; and sentiments growing there, fresh and sheltered, which his austerity could never blight, nor his measured warrior-march trample down. But as his wife ... forced to keep the fire of my nature continually low, to compel it to burn inwardly and never utter a cry ... *this* would be unendurable.

Charlotte Brontë (1816–55), *Jane Eyre*, 1847, chapter 34.

Charlotte's sister Emily challenged the very institution of marriage – and personal identity itself – in *Wuthering Heights*. Cathy, who is to marry Edgar Linton, cannot escape her passionate destiny:

My love for Linton is like the foliage in the woods; time will change it, I'm well aware, as winter changes the trees – My love for Heathcliff resembles the eternal rocks beneath:– a source of little visible delight, but necessary. Nelly, I *am* Heathcliff! He's always, always in my mind: not as a pleasure, any more than I am always a pleasure to myself, but as my own being. So don't talk of our separation again …

Emily Brontë (1818–48), *Wuthering Heights*, chapter 9, 1847.

The goings-on in *Wuthering Heights* – well …

How different, how very different from the home life of our own dear Queen.

Anonymous woman watching Sarah Bernhardt play Cleopatra on the London stage.

Queen Victoria was indeed one of the most happily married of monarchs, as can be seen from her letters to her Uncle Leopold, King of the Belgians:

15 July 1839
MY DEAR UNCLE, – I have no letter from you, but hope to get one soon. ….

I shall send this letter by a courier, as I am anxious to put several questions to you, and to mention some feelings of mine upon the subject of my cousins' visit, which I am desirous should not transpire. First of all, I wish to know if Albert is aware of the wish of his *Father* and *you* relative to *me*? Secondly, if he knows that there is *no engagement* between us? I am anxious that you should acquaint Uncle Ernest, that if I should like Albert, that I can make *no final promise this year*, for, at the very earliest, any such event could not take place till *two or three years hence*. For, independent of my youth, and my *great* repugnance to change my present position, there is *no anxiety* evinced in *this country* for such an event, and it would be more prudent, in my opinion, to wait till some such demonstration is shown, – else if it were hurried it might produce discontent.

Though all the reports of Albert are most favourable, and though I have little doubt I shall like him, still one can never answer beforehand for *feelings*, and I may not have the *feeling* for him which is requisite to ensure happiness. I *may* like him as a friend, and as a *cousin*, and as a *brother*, but not *more*; and should this be the case (which is not likely), I am *very* anxious that it should be understood that I am *not* guilty of any breach of promise, for *I never gave any*. I am sure you will understand my anxiety, for I should otherwise, were this not completely understood, be in a very painful position. As it is, I am rather nervous about the visit, for the subject I allude to is not an agreeable one to me. …

15 October 1839
MY DEAREST UNCLE, – This letter will, I am sure, give you pleasure, for you have always shown and taken so warm an interest in all that concerns me. My mind is quite made up – and I told Albert this morning of it; the warm affection he showed me on learning this gave me *great* pleasure. He seems *perfection*, and I think that I have the prospect of very great happiness before me. I *love* him *more* than I can say, and I shall do everything in my power to render the sacrifice he has made (for a *sacrifice* in my opinion it is) as small as I can. He seems to have a very great tact – a very necessary thing in his position. These last few days have passed like a dream to me, and I am so much bewildered by it all that I know hardly how to write; but I *do* feel *very, very* happy. ….

We also think it better, and Albert quite approves of it, that we should be married very soon after Parliament meets, about the beginning of February; and indeed, loving Albert as I do, I cannot wish it should be delayed. My feelings are a *little* changed, I must say, since last Spring, when I said I couldn't *think* of marrying for *three or four years*; but seeing Albert has changed all this.

11 February 1840
MY DEAREST UNCLE, – I write to you from here, the happiest, happiest Being that ever existed. Really, I do not think it *possible* for any one in the world to be *happier*, or AS happy as I am. He is an Angel, and his kindness and affection for me is really touching. To look in those dear eyes, and that dear sunny face, is enough to make me adore him. What I can do to make him happy will be my greatest delight. Independent of my great personal happiness, the reception we both met with yesterday was the most gratifying and enthusiastic I ever experienced; there was no end of the crowds in London, and all along the road. I was a good deal tired last night, but am quite well again to-day, and happy.

Victoria was shattered by Albert's sudden early death:

20 December 1861
MY OWN DEAREST, KINDEST *FATHER*, – For as such have I *ever* loved you! The poor fatherless baby of eight months is now the utterly broken-hearted and crushed widow of forty-two! My *life* as a *happy* one is *ended!* the world is gone for *me!* If I *must live* on (and I will do nothing to make me worse than I am), it is henceforth for our poor fatherless children – for my unhappy country, which has lost *all* in losing him – and in *only* doing what I know and *feel* he would wish, for he *is* near me – his spirit will guide and inspire me! But oh! to be cut off in the prime of life – to see our pure, happy, quiet, domestic life, which *alone* enabled me to bear my *much* disliked position, CUT OFF at forty-two – when I *had* hoped with such instinctive certainty that God never *would* part us, and would let us grow old together (though *he* always talked of the shortness of life) – is too *awful*, too cruel! And yet it *must* be for *his* good, his happiness! His purity was too great, his aspiration *too high* for this poor, *miserable* world! His great soul is *now only* enjoying *that* for which it *was* worthy! And I will *not* envy him – only pray that mine may be perfected by it and fit to be with him eternally, for which blessed moment I earnestly long. . . .

Ever your devoted, wretched Child,
VICTORIA R.

Queen Victoria (1819–1901), letters to her Uncle Leopold, King of the Belgians, from *The Letters of Queen Victoria 1837–1861*, 1908.

Charles Dickens, whose own married life was some way short of idyllic, gives a happy picture of a good marriage in his depiction of Mr and Mrs Bagnet in *Bleak House*. In this extract, Trooper George — an old friend and comrade-in-arms of Matthew Bagnet — has a certain proposition to put to him. Mr Bagnet will, of course, make the decision, when his mind is made up to it; but only Mrs Bagnet can be relied on to know what is in his mind …

By the cloisterly Temple, and by Whitefriars (there, not without a glance at Hanging-Sword Alley, which would seem to be something in his way), and by Blackfriars Bridge, and Blackfriars Road, Mr George sedately marches to a street of little shops lying somewhere in the ganglion of roads from Kent and Surrey .... To one of the little shops in this street, which is a musician's shop, having a few fiddles in the window, and some Pan's pipes and a tambourine, and a triangle, and certain elongated scraps of music, Mr George directs his massive tread. And halting at a few paces from it, as he sees a soldierly-looking woman, with her outer skirts tucked up, come forth with a small wooden tub, and in that tub commence a whisking and a splashing on the margin of the pavement, Mr George says to himself, 'She's as usual, washing greens. I never saw her, except upon a baggage-waggon, when she wasn't washing greens!'

The subject of this reflection is at all events so occupied in washing greens at present, that she remains unsuspicious of Mr George's approach; until, lifting up herself and her tub together, when she has poured the water off into the gutter, she finds him standing near her. ...

Mrs Bagnet is not at all an ill-looking woman. Rather large-boned, a little coarse in the grain, and freckled by the sun and wind which have tanned her hair upon the forehead; but healthy, wholesome, and bright-eyed. A strong, busy, active, honest-faced woman of from forty-five to fifty. Clean, hardy, and so economically dressed (though substantially), that the only article of ornament of which she stands possessed appears to be her wedding-ring; around which her finger has grown to be so large since it was put on, that it will never come off again until it shall mingle with Mrs Bagnet's dust. ...

... Mr Bagnet is an ex-artilleryman, tall and upright, with shaggy eyebrows, and whiskers like the fibres of a cocoa-nut, not a hair upon his head, and a torrid complexion. His voice, short, deep, and resonant, is not at all unlike the tones of the instrument to which he is devoted. Indeed there may be generally observed in him an unbending, unyielding, brass-bound air, as if he were himself the bassoon of the human orchestra. Young Woolwich is the type and model of a young drummer.

Both father and son salute the trooper heartily. He saying, in due season, that he has come to advise with Mr Bagnet, Mr Bagnet hospitably declares that he will hear of no business until after dinner; and that his friend shall not partake of his counsel, without first partaking of boiled pork and greens. The trooper yielding to this invitation, he and Mr Bagnet, not to embarrass the domestic preparations, go forth to take a turn up and down the little street, which they promenade with measured tread and folded arms, as if it were a rampart.

'George,' says Mr Bagnet. 'You know me. It's my old girl that advises. She has the head. But I never own to it before her. Discipline must be maintained. Wait till the greens is off her mind. Then, we'll consult. Whatever the old girl says, do – do it!'

'I intend to, Mat,' replies the other. 'I would sooner take her opinion than that of a college.'

'College,' returns Mr Bagnet, in short sentences, bassoon-like. 'What college could you leave – in another quarter of the world – with nothing but a grey cloak and an umbrella – to make its way home to Europe? The old girl would do it tomorrow. Did it once!'

'You are right,' says Mr George.

'What college,' pursues Bagnet, 'could you set up in life – with two penn'orth of white lime – a penn'orth of fuller's earth – a ha'porth of sand – and the rest of the change out of sixpence, in money? That's what the old girl started on. In the present business.'

'I am rejoiced to hear it's thriving, Mat.'

'The old girl,' says Mr Bagnet, acquiescing, 'saves. Has a stocking somewhere. With money in it. I never saw it. But I know she's got it. Wait till the greens is off her mind. Then she'll set you up.'

'She is a treasure!' exclaims Mr George.

'She's more. But I never own to it before her. Discipline must be maintained. It was the old girl that brought out my musical abilities. I should have been in the artillery now, but for the old girl. Six years I hammered at the fiddle. Ten at the flute. The old girl said it wouldn't do; intention good, but want of flexibility; try the bassoon. The old girl borrowed a bassoon from the bandmaster of the Rifle Regiment. I practised in the trenches. Got on, got another, get a living by it!'

George remarks that she looks as fresh as a rose, and as sound as an apple.

'The old girl,' says Mr Bagnet in reply, 'is a thoroughly fine woman. Consequently, she is like a thoroughly fine day. Gets finer as she gets on. I never saw the old girl's equal. But I never own to it before her. Discipline must be maintained!' . . .

The dinner done, Mrs Bagnet, assisted by the younger branches (who polish their own cups and platters, knives and forks), makes all the dinner garniture shine as brightly as before, and puts it all away; first sweeping the hearth, to the end that Mr Bagnet and the visitor may not be retarded in the smoking of their pipes. These household cares involve much pattening and counter-pattening in the backyard, and considerable use of a pail, which is finally so happy as to assist in the ablutions of Mrs Bagnet herself. That old girl reappearing by-and-by, quite fresh, and sitting down to her needlework, then and only then – the greens being only then to be considered as entirely off her mind – Mr Bagnet requests the trooper to state his case.

This, Mr George does with great discretion; appearing to address himself to Mr Bagnet, but having an eye solely on the old girl all the time, as Bagnet has himself. She, equally discreet, busies herself with her needlework. The case fully stated, Mr Bagnet resorts to his standard artifice for the maintenance of discipline.

'That's the whole of it, is it, George?' says he.

'That's the whole of it.'

'You act according to my opinion?'

'I shall be guided,' replies George, 'entirely by it.'

'Old girl,' says Mr Bagnet, 'give him my opinion. You know it. Tell him what it is.'

Charles Dickens (1812–70), *Bleak House*, 1853.

Free-thinking George Eliot (Mary Ann Evans) – who co-habited for years with George Lewes without marrying him – examined the limited opportunities open to women in several of her novels. In *The Mill on the Floss*, for example, when Lucy Deane is obliged to help in the preparations for the local bazaar, Stephen Guest exclaims:

'Here is another of the moral results of this idiotic bazaar,' Stephen burst forth, as soon as Miss Torry had left the room, 'taking young ladies from the duties of the domestic hearth into scenes of dissipation among urn-rugs and embroidered reticules! I should like to know what is the proper function of women, if it is not to make reasons for husbands to stay at home, and still stronger reasons for bachelors to go out. If this goes on much longer, the bonds of society will be dissolved.'

George Eliot (1819–80), *The Mill on the Floss*, 1860, book 6, chapter 6.

Eliot knew that for many married women, 'domestic bliss' was an illusion. In reality they were more likely to be doomed to frustration, ennui and uselessness:

A little daily embroidery had been a constant element in Mrs Transome's life; that soothing occupation of taking stitches to produce what neither she nor any one else wanted, was then the resource of many a well-born and unhappy woman.

George Eliot (1819–80), *Felix Holt*, 1866, chapter 7.

In *Middlemarch* the passionate, fiercely intelligent Dorothea Brooke, a 'St Theresa' figure, marries Mr Casaubon, an elderly scholar, out of reverence for his work, only to find out too late that he is not only a dry pedant, but also a mean-spirited fool. In the Prelude to the novel Eliot writes:

Many Theresas have been born who found for themselves no epic life wherein there was a constant unfolding of far-resonant action; perhaps only a life of mistakes, the offspring of a certain spiritual grandeur ill-matched with the meanness of opportunity; perhaps a tragic failure which found no sacred poet and sank unwept into oblivion.

George Eliot (1819–80), *Middlemarch*, 1871–72, Prelude.

Elsewhere in the novel Eliot dryly remarks:

A woman dictates before marriage in order that she may have an appetite for submission afterwards.

George Eliot (1819–80), *Middlemarch*, 1871–72, book 1, chapter 9.

'I'm afraid Fred is not to be trusted, Mary,' said the father, with hesitating tenderness. 'He means better than he acts, perhaps. But I should think it a pity for anybody's happiness to be wrapped up in him, and so would your mother.'

'And so should I, father,' said Mary, not looking up, but putting the back of her father's hand against her cheek.

'I don't want to pry, my dear. But I was afraid there might be something between you and Fred, and I wanted to caution you. You see, Mary' – here Caleb's voice became more tender; he had been pushing his hat about on the table and looking at it, but finally he turned his eyes on his daughter – 'a woman, let her be as good as she may, has got to put up with the life her husband makes for her. Your mother has had to put up with a good deal because of me.'

George Eliot (1819–80), *Middlemarch*, 1871–72, book 3, chapter 25.

The Dorset dialect poet William Barnes wrote some of his finest lyrics after the death of his wife:

> Since I noo mwore do zee your feäce,
>   Up steärs or down below,
> I'll zit me in the lwonesome pleäce,
>   Where flat-bough'd beech do grow:
> Below the beeches' bough, my love,
>   Where you did never come,
> An' I don't look to meet ye now,
>   As I do look at hwome.
>
> Since you noo mwore be at my zide,
>   In walks in zummer het,
> I'll goo alwone where mist do ride,
>   Through trees a-drippen wet:
> Below the rain-wet bough, my love,
>   Where you did never come,
> An' I don't grieve to miss ye now,
>   As I do grieve at hwome.
>
> Since now bezide my dinner-bwoard
>   Your vaice do never sound,
> I'll eat the bit I can avword,
>   A-yield upon the ground;
> Below the darksome bough, my love,
>   Where you did never dine,
> An' I don't grieve to miss ye now,
>   As I at hwome do pine.
>
> Since I do miss your vaice an' feäce
>   In prayer at eventide,
> I'll pray wi oone sad vaice vor greäce
>   To goo where you do bide;
> Above the tree an' bough, my love,
>   Where you be gone avore,
> An' be a-waiten vor me now,
>   To come vor evermwore.

William Barnes (1800–86), 'The Wife A-Lost'.

Sexuality was one thing the Victorian Englishwoman was supposed not to possess, according to the best medical opinion:

She assured me that she felt no sexual passions whatever. Her passion for her husband was of a platonic kind, and far from wishing to stimulate his frigid feelings, she doubted whether it would be right or not. She loved him as he was, and would not desire him to be otherwise except for the hope of having a family. I believe this lady is the perfect ideal of an English wife and mother. . . .

The majority of women (happily for them) are not very much troubled with sexual feelings of any kind. . . . As a general rule, a modest woman seldom desires any sexual gratification for herself. She submits to her husband's embraces, but principally to gratify him; and, were it not for the desire of maternity, would far rather be relieved from his attentions.

Dr William Acton (1878–1939), *The Functions and Disorders of the Reproductive Organs in Youth, in Adult Age and in Advanced Life*, 1857.

Some Englishwomen have been exasperated by this asexual image:

Contrary to popular belief, English women do not wear tweed nightgowns.

Hermione Gingold, in *Saturday Review*, 1955.

. . . although one suspects that Lady Hillingdon might have favoured such a garment . . .

I am happy now that Charles calls on my bedchamber less frequently than of old. As it is, I now endure but two calls a week and when I hear his steps outside my door I lie down on my bed, close my eyes, open my legs, and think of England.

Lady Hillingdon (1857–1940), *Journal*, 1912.

Such trials and tribulations were not restricted to the upper classes. In 1914 an older married woman remarked to a young wife whose husband had just joined up:

You don't know what you're up agen yet. But you wait till you've been to bed over three thousand nights with the same man, like me, and had to put up with everything, then you'll be bloomin' glad the old Kaiser went potty.

Quoted in Paul Ferris, *Sex and the British*, 1993.

Sex – and its consequences – before marriage was common in mid-Victorian England; a century later, many married English people recommended it. In his survey of the English Character Geoffrey Gorer explored attitudes to pre-marital sex, and found that while the majority of us were against it (especially for women – although women themselves were more disapproving), a significant minority bitterly regretted the fact that they, or their spouses, had been so inexperienced and ignorant. Here is a short selection of such responses:

A 41-year-old married woman of the middle class from north London:

My personal experience with a virgin husband was most distressing.

A 26-year-old divorced woman from northwest London:

My marriage was recked [*sic*] mainly through a lack of sexual knowledge. My husband had never had an affair before marriage. [for young women?] Yes, because one can be disillusioned or shocked by sex – and to be afraid can have a bad sycological [*sic*] effect if one does not know what to expect.

A 24-year-old married woman from West Bromwich:

A man should have had some experience because a woman expects a man to be able to love make. I was bitterly disappointed when I married. I had to teach him. Sexual experience teaches you things about each other you can't possibly know otherwise.

A 41-year-old married woman from Walsall:

The cause for much unhappiness for myself was because my husband had no sexual experience before marriage.

A 49-year-old re-married man from Willesden:

Lack of sexual experience was the cause of my first marriage breakdown.

A 40-year-old separated man from Yateley (Hants.):

Because I got married myself without any sexual experience whatsoever, to my sorrow. [for young women?] To help young men as unfortunate as myself as I have written about.

A divorced man, middle class, from Leigh-on-Sea, 45-year-old:

I didn't and my marriage went on the rocks from the beginning through shyness and ignorance of women.

A 30-year-old divorced working class man from Coventry:

My own failure in marriage was due to a lack of sexual experience.

Geoffrey Gorer (1905–85), *Exploring English Character*, 1955.

Quotations with the same underlying theme could be continued over several pages; they strongly suggest that ignorance, particularly on the part of the men, is a major hazard in English marriages. A 36-year-old married worker from Nottingham says 'I met men in the forces who were Married and were dead ignorant about sexual Matters'. A great deal of my evidence bears out his observation.

In a sex manual of 1939, author Anthony Havil examines the relationship between marriage and prostitution:

Those girls who are prostitutes because that is the only way in which they can find enough to eat ... have brought their sex instinct to the aid of their self-preservation instinct. In doing so, they often so abuse the sex instinct as to let it be entirely dominated by the self-preservation instinct. Sex means nothing to them but a way of earning money. Disgustingly enough, many 'respectably married' wives are like that. The husband provides the home, and in return – 'Well, if the brute wants to possess my body, I suppose it is his right.' Even in the case of prostitutes and the woman who has married as a kind of life insurance, something may remain of the strong sex feeling. Some circumstance may suddenly awaken a real sexual desire and a mind in which the sex element has seemed to play a small part, although the body was occupied with sexual matters, reawakens to a knowledge of the presence of real sex instincts. ...

There are thousands of prostitutes in England, and there will be till strong measures are taken. Their evil effects are very real. Physically, they are responsible for the spread of a large proportion of the venereal disease treated in clinics and hospitals. Mentally, without dispute they are a strong influence in the degeneration of the morals and thoughts of thousands of men. Of the inmates of one of our biggest prisons, nearly all the men, when at liberty, frequented prostitutes. Prostitutes are a strong temptation to married men who are temporarily away from home, and they have been the cause of disease and rupture in countless families that would otherwise have been happy.

In spite of all that, the author dares to say they are a necessity to many men. Many prostitutes, with all the troubles they have had to suffer, have good hearts for other people and are sympathetic listeners. They have saved many a man from suicide by being the only person to whom he dare unfold his troubles, and from craziness, by being an outlet for his over-repressed sexual feelings. That they are a necessity is a sad reflection on the sexual upbringing and arrangements of modern society.

Anthony Havil, *The Technique of Sex*, 1939.

In the recumbent effigies on a medieval tomb at Arundel, Philip Larkin found an enduring emblem of conjugal tenderness:

> Side by side, their faces blurred,
> The earl and countess lie in stone,
> Their proper habits vaguely shown
> As jointed armour, stiffened pleat,
> And that faint hint of the absurd –
> The little dogs under their feet.
>
> Such plainness of the pre-baroque
> Hardly involves the eye, until
> It meets his left-hand gauntlet, still
> Clasped empty in the other; and
> One sees, with a sharp tender shock,
> His hand withdrawn, holding her hand.
>
> They would not think to lie so long.
> Such faithfulness in effigy
> Was just a detail friends would see:
> A sculptor's sweet commissioned grace
> Thrown off in helping to prolong
> The Latin names around the base.
>
> They would not guess how early in
> Their supine stationary voyage
> The air would change to soundless damage,
> Turn the old tenantry away;
> How soon succeeding eyes begin
> To look, not read. Rigidly they
>
> Persisted, linked, through lengths and breadths
> Of time. Snow fell, undated. Light

Each summer thronged the glass. A bright
Litter of birdcalls strewed the same
Bone-riddled ground. And up the paths
The endless altered people came,

Washing at their identity.
Now, helpless in the hollow of
An unarmorial age, a trough
Of smoke in slow suspended skeins
Above their scrap of history,
Only an attitude remains:

Time has transfigured them into
Untruth. The stone fidelity
They hardly meant has come to be
Their final blazon, and to prove
Our almost-instinct almost true:
What will survive of us is love.

Philip Larkin (1922–85), 'An Arundel Tomb', from *The Whitsun Weddings*, 1964.

Marriage, well. I think of it as a marvellous thing for other people, like going to
the stake.

Philip Larkin (1922–85), letter to Pamela Kitson, 12 March 1965, in Anthony Thwaite, *Selected Letters of Philip Larkin 1940–85*, 1992.

As Larkin noted elsewhere, 'Sexual intercourse began / In nineteen sixty-three'. In *How Far Can You Go?* David Lodge explored the 'liberated' sexual and marital mores of that and the following decade – mores that could bring their own anxieties:

Ruth glanced at the page folded back for her perusal. It was an agony column of a
familiar type, entitled, *Ask Ann Field*. '*Dear Ann Field*,' the first letter began, '*I am
seventeen and have been going out with a boy who I love very much for about six
months ...*' And underneath, in bold type, was Ann Field's answer:

*Many people today believe that if the couple concerned have a loving and stable
relationship, sex before marriage is not necessarily wrong and may be a way of putting
a future marriage on a firm foundation. Only you and your boyfriend can decide
whether this, for you, would be an expression of genuine love or merely selfish exploitation. But if you do decide to commit yourself to such a relationship, for heaven's sake get
advice about contraception first. There is, incidentally, no reason why you should not
have a white wedding when the time comes.*

'If that isn't encouraging young people to jump into bed with each other, what
is?' said the teacher. 'How are a couple of teenagers supposed to know the difference between selfish pleasure and true love, I'd like to know?'

Ruth sighed again. 'It must be a great responsibility to receive such letters,' she
said. 'I suppose this, whatshername, Ann Field, I suppose she tries to help according to her lights.'

The teacher looked surprised at this mild response, and reclaimed the magazine with a slightly aggrieved air, as though confiscating it for a second time. 'Well, ten years ago, even five, you'd never have found a magazine like this approving sex before marriage,' she said. 'I don't know what things are coming to.'

Polly would have been gratified by Ruth's remark, had she overheard it, for as it happened she was Ann Field at this particular time. She was also married, to a successful television producer, to whom she had borne, precisely two years apart, a handsome son and pretty daughter; and she lived in a converted oast-house near Canterbury, with an *au pair* to help with the children and a milk-white Mini of her own to run about in. She led a busy, enjoyable life, only slightly marred by occasional twinges of anxiety about Jeremy's fidelity and perpetual worry about putting on weight, the two being connected. ...

Polly believed fervently in every woman's right to frequent orgasms, and tried out conscientiously most of the things she read about in the sex manuals and magazines that Jeremy brought back with him from his travels. Jeremy, who had been rather repressed in youth, was making up for lost time. The rediscovery of sex, he was fond of saying, was what the sixties were all about. Every now and then, they sent the children out with the *au pair*, drew the curtains, and chased each other naked around the house, having it off in various unorthodox places, on the stairs, or under the dining-room table, even in the kitchen, where Polly would spread jam or chocolate syrup on her nipples and Jeremy would lick them clean. Their private code-word for sex was 'research'. ...

Edward and Tessa experimented with positions not so much for the sake of erotic variety as to ease the strain on Edward's back. They found that the most satisfactory arrangement was for Edward to lie supine and for Tessa to squat on top of him, jigging up and down until she brought them both to climax. At first Edward found this very exciting, but the passivity of his own role in the proceedings worried him, and he frightened himself sometimes with the thought that one day he might be incapable of even this style of copulation.

Tessa herself was in a constant fever of vague sexual longing to which she dared not give definition. Her body sent messages which her mind refused to accept. Her body said: you are bored with this clumsy form of intercourse, you want to lie back and close your eyes and be possessed by a strong male force for a change, your body is a garden of unawakened pleasures and time is running out. Her mind said: nonsense, you are a happily married woman with four fine, healthy children and a good, kind, faithful husband. Count your blessings and find something to occupy yourself now that the children are growing up. So Tessa joined keep-fit classes and a tennis club. But the physical wellbeing that accrued only fuelled the fires of her libido. She exulted in the power and grace of her movements across the court or in the gym. In the changing-rooms afterwards she followed the example of the younger women who walked unconcernedly naked from their lockers to the communal shower heads, while the older and less shapely ones waited timidly for the curtained cubicles to become free. The full-length mirrors on the walls reassured her that her body could stand such exposure. From this exercise she returned home, glowing euphorically, to a jaded and weary spouse. Her body said: it would be nice to fuck. Her mind, deaf to the indelicacy, said: he's tired, he was called out last night, his back is paining him.

Tessa, in short, was classically ripe for having an affair, and in another milieu, or novel, might well have had one. Instead, she bought lots of clothes and changed more times a day than was strictly necessary, collected cookbooks and experimented with complicated recipes, read novels from the library about mature, sensitive women having affairs, and enrolled in the Open University. ...

Polly wasn't Ann Field any more. Now she wrote a weekly column under her own name on the women's page of a quality newspaper, a column in which radical and progressive ideas were put forward in a subtly ironic style that undermined them even as it expressed them, an effect which perfectly suited the paper's readership, mostly middle-class professionals and their wives, with leftish views and bad consciences about their affluent life-styles.

Polly herself, who had been an early apostle of the sexual revolution, was beginning to wonder whether things hadn't gone too far. She had of course been happily doing n things with Jeremy for years, but when he showed signs of wanting to do them with n partners, she jibbed.

They received an invitation to a swinging party at a country house owned by a film producer Jeremy knew; he pressed her to go, and sulked when she refused. Anxiously she strove to show more gusto in their lovemaking, proposing games and variations that she knew he liked, though she herself found them a little tedious, bondage and dressing up in kinky clothes and acting out little scenarios – The Massage Parlour, The Call Girl, and Blue Lagoon. These efforts diverted Jeremy for a while, but eventually he began pressing her again about going to swinging parties.

'Why do you want to go?' she said.

'I'm just curious.'

'You want to have another woman.'

He shrugged. 'All right, perhaps I do. But I don't want to do it behind your back.'

'Why do you want to? Don't we have fun in bed?'

'Of course we do, darling. But let's face it, we've been right through the book together, there's nothing new we can do, just the two of us. It's time to introduce another element. You know, sometimes when we're fucking, my mind wanders completely off the subject, I find myself thinking about shooting schedules or audience ratings. That worries me. And you needn't look at me like that. It's nothing personal. It's the nature of the beast.'

'Beast is the word.' Polly felt a cold dread at her heart. Was it possible that the flame of sex could be kept burning only by the breaking of more taboos? After group sex and orgies, what then? Rubber fetishism? Fladge? Child porn? Snuff movies? 'Where does it end?' she said. ...

David Lodge (1935–), *How Far Can You Go?*, 1980.

In any permissive age, there will always be counter-blasts:

Every man has been brought up with the idea that decent women don't always pop in and out of bed; he has always been told by his mother that 'nice girls don't'. He finds, of course, when he gets older that this may be untrue – but only in certain sections of society. ...

A man will teach his wife what is needed to arouse his desires. And there is no reason for a woman to know any more than what her husband is prepared to teach her. If she gets married knowing far too much about what she wants and doesn't want then she will be ready to find fault with her husband.

Barbara Cartland (1901–2000), romantic novelist, quoted in Wendy Leigh, *Speaking Frankly*, 1978.

As the millennium drew to a close, monogamy (with or without benefit of clergy or registrar) was still being held up as the respectable norm in English society – to the secret dissatisfaction of many:

They travelled north as far as Milan and picked up the Orient Express. They went through Switzerland and into France. He was charming, amusing, simply beautiful in bed and quite distant. In Paris they had to change from the Gare de Lyons to the Gare du Nord. He went with her until they were about to board the train to Calais. 'I'll just get a paper,' he said and he disappeared.

When the train pulled out Kate didn't worry. She was almost relieved. He would have been an embarrassment back home in her tidy life. He wasn't a Home Counties man. If he had moved in with her she would have found him hard to dis- lodge. He was a rogue, a delicious naughty enterprise. England would have dimin- ished him, made him vulgar and weak. He would have become petty and small. It was better that it was all over. Now she could enjoy the wickedness of the memory, especially the sex, uncluttered by the guilt of his presence. It was okay to break the rules on holiday. It was not okay back home in stuffy England. ... It was romantic to be dumped in Paris rather than, say, Wantage, but it didn't change your life. ...

She was bored with the received wisdom on the subject. None of it seemed to fit with her own feelings and she had, unthinkingly, accepted that she was wrong and what the world said was right. The truth was she wanted to make a carnal exploration and couldn't see why it should cause feelings of guilt. Food and sex were the two great sensual pleasures of life. No one attacked the gourmet as cor- rupt. Television was dedicated to cookery, endless cookery, and when it wasn't going on about cooking, it was advertising food. Constantly. Yet sex was undoubt- edly the superior pleasure and it was subverted, cloaked, presented slantwise as romance. Any serious exploration of the subject became risible just because the seriousness was so inappropriate. Sex was joyful. Sex was fun. Morality crowded and twisted and perverted honest enjoyment of a harmless human activity till people became guilt-ridden, repressed, furtive or alienated.

Paul had offered her love and given her bad sex. Maybe it was time she forgot about love and tenderness and equality, and went straight for what her body craved. She was a passionate woman. She lusted for men. She got hot between her thighs. It had never exactly made her ashamed, but in some mysterious way she had felt odd and at fault.

Sex should be dangerous. It was a dark fire. It should be an adventure. Society trained its members for the dullness and routine of monogamy, that most unnat- ural state. Kate had only escaped it herself through a chance set of circumstances. She had been engaged when she was twenty-one, deeply in love so she had thought, and on the brink of marriage. Colin had died in a road accident, and within three months she was in bed with another man, enjoying it.

She learned her lesson and learned it well. Had she and Colin married, she would have desired other men. Not immediately, perhaps, and no doubt she would have concealed her emotions from herself for as long as was possible. But she would have tired of him. Her feelings were not as all-important and profound as she had believed them to be. They were temporary and exciting and shallow.

Marriage was convenient socially and economically and fiscally. It was very useful if you wanted to raise a family and if the State wanted to tax you. For all other purposes and notable among them was sex, it was useless. Indeed, it was counterproductive.

They were conned. All of them, men and women. They were set an ideal, that of monogamous sex, and told it was decent, it was good, it was worth aspiring to. Most of them fell by the wayside, of course, and felt guilty according to their natures. But it was no ideal; it was emotionally degrading to aspire to sex with only one person. Through being corralled and straitjacketed, a huge human happiness was systematically destroyed.

Saskia Hope (Jan Holt, 1949–93), *No Lady*, 1993.

Playing the Game

FOR WHEN THE ONE GREAT SCORER COMES
  TO MARK AGAINST YOUR NAME,
HE WRITES – NOT THAT YOU WON OR LOST –
  BUT HOW YOU PLAYED THE GAME.

These lines, irresistibly redolent of England's one true game, were in fact written by the US sportswriter Grantland Rice (1880–1954) and their subject is American football. But never mind; Rice might just as well have been English, and writing about cricket. Few other quotations so encapsulate the game as it ought to be (and sometimes is).

Cricket – not football, variations of which have been traced in many other cultures – is the English Game, and has been for a very long time. Joseph of Exeter, writing about 1190, noted that youths played at 'cricks ... throughout the merry day' – and the fact that it took them all day to finish almost certainly means that cricket was being played. Cricket crops up in the wardrobe accounts of Edward I in 1300, and in an Italian-English dictionary of 1598. Sir Thomas Urquhart, translating the French of Rabelais into equally robust English in 1653, has Gargantua playing cricket, and in 1676 one Henry Teonge was fortunate to witness a game played by English sailors and residents in the port of Aleppo. Dr Johnson, apparently unsure whether it was played with bats or sticks, put it in his dictionary. The London Club published the first Laws of the game in 1744; Thomas Lord opened his first ground in 1787, and the MCC was formed to play on it. The game was exported to France in 1789 (but rioting at the Bastille stopped play in the inaugural match); in 1829 a player at Dieppe, having completed his innings, was asked by a French spectator when the game was going to start – the first recorded instance of a joke used many times since by the wilfully uninitiated. By the time John Nyren published The Young Cricketer's Tutor *in 1833 (dedicating it to William Wordsworth), cricket had established itself firmly in the national psyche. Bliss was it in that dawn to be alive, but to time the perfect leg glance was very heaven.*

The English Game

Considering the Englishness of cricket in all its aspects: heroic, stoic, moral, obsessional; pompous, even, and often impenetrable to the outsider.

Where the English language is unspoken there can be no real cricket.

Neville Cardus (1889–1975), cricket writer, quoted in *A Century of Great Cricket Quotes*, 1998.

I'll be at your Board, when at leisure from cricket.

John Montagu, 4th Earl of Sandwich (1718–92), on being appointed a Lord Commissioner of the Admiralty, 11 June 1745

I do love cricket – it's so very English.

Sarah Bernhardt (1844–1923), French actress, watching a game of football in Manchester.

There is a widely held and quite erroneously held belief that cricket is just another game.

H.R.H. Prince Philip, Duke of Edinburgh, Greek-born consort of Queen Elizabeth II, 'The Pleasures of Cricket', *Wisden*, 1975.

Cricket can represent many different things to many different people. For E.M. Forster, in a novel not published until after his death, it provided the field on which 'the love that dare not speak its name' – or any other persecuted minority, perhaps – could find a voice:

When he went out to bat, it was a new over, so that Alec received first ball. His style changed. Abandoning caution, he swiped the ball into the fern. Lifting his eyes, he met Maurice's and smiled. Lost ball. Next time he hit a boundary. He was untrained, but had the cricketing build, and the game took on some semblance of reality. Maurice played up too. His mind had cleared, and he felt that they were against the whole world, that not only Mr Borenius and the field but the audience in the shed and all England were closing around the wickets. They played for the sake of each other and of their fragile relationship – if one fell the other would follow. They intended no harm to the world, but so long as it attacked they must punish, they must stand wary, then hit with full strength, they must show that when two are gathered together majorities shall not triumph.

E.M. Forster (1879–1970), *Maurice*, written in 1914, published 1971.

The meanings of cricket are largely moral:

With a thorough knowledge of the Bible, Shakespeare and *Wisden* you cannot go far wrong.

Arthur Waugh, quoted in his son Evelyn's autobiography *A Little Learning*, 1964. *Wisden*, or *Wisden's Cricketers' Almanac*, first published in 1864, is the 'bible' of cricket.

The very word 'cricket' has become a synonym for all that is true and honest. To say 'that is not cricket' implies something underhand, something not in keeping with the best ideals.

Sir Pelham Warner (1873–1963), Trinidad-born English cricketer, quoted in *A Century of Great Cricket Quotations*, 1998: the one thing everybody knows about cricket, and Englishness.

You will do well to love it, for it is more free from anything sordid, anything dishonourable, than any game in the world. To play it keenly, honourably, self-sacrificingly is a moral lesson in itself, and the class-room is full of God's own air and children. Foster it, my brothers, so that it may attract all who can find the time to play it; protect it from anything that would sully it, so that it may grow in favour with all men.

Lord Harris, speech to half-holiday cricketers, quoted in a letter to *The Times* on his 80th birthday, 1930.

If Stalin had learned to play cricket, the world might now be a better place.

Richard Downey (1881–1953), English bishop, 1948; quoted in *Cassell's Sports Quotations*, 2000.

Beyond morals, cricket can also stand in for spirituality:

Cricket – a game which the English, not being a spiritual people, have invented in order to give themselves some conception of eternity.

Lord Mancroft (1914–), 'Scorecard', *Sports Illustrated*, 11 November 1963.

My wife had an uncle who could never walk down the nave of an abbey without wondering whether it would take spin.

Sir Alec Douglas-Home (1903–95), Prime Minister 1963–64, in *The Twentieth Century Revisited*, 1982.

Watching cricket may be a form of meditation – and even offer, if one surrenders oneself to the spirit of it, a glimpse of paradise:

> Watching cricket is habit-forming, it can become habitual.
> It's a kind of long-lasting white-robed ritual;
> and (until recently) it's been a male prerogative,
> played by big hairy bowlers and blacksmiths who were slogative.
> And in village cricket, which was where it all began,
> it was a straightforward matter (as in Milton) between God and Man –
> in spite of the bumpy pitch and the blinding light
> the idea was that, if you tried hard, the Deity would see you right.
> The ladies just watched – in crinolines that were both broad and high,
> which would have made the l.b.w. law hard to apply.
> Notice, by the way, that cricket doesn't have Rules, like any ordinary game;
> it has LAWS
> and many a staunch cricketer is ready to die for the Cause.
> In low-grade cricket they sometimes get hit on the head
> and left on the field (as at Eton and Waterloo) for dead.

Personally I think you don't have to be much of a detective
to work out that all those devices categorised as protective,
gloves, pads, boxes, helmets, are a good thing. Though the fans,
          stiff-upper-lipping and bobbysoxing,
consider it should be A Man's Game and lethal – like boxing.

You can imagine cricket going on eternally in Heaven.
Perhaps the Devil would be allowed up to bowl, with the Seven
Deadly Sins all clustered round the bat, fielding.
They once had Demon Bowlers and 'fast' meant yielding
(in the case of young ladies) to sexual attraction;
but I think the Devil would bowl leg-breaks with an off-break action,
the classical googly, as invented by Bosie.
Such games, going on for ever, could get quite cosy.

Or perhaps the angels would be fielding, in their white flannels,
and it would be compulsory viewing on all heavenly channels.
Certainly many Englishmen are so enamoured of cricket
that in Paradise, rather than a pretty girl, they'd like to see a wicket.

Gavin Ewart (1916–95), 'Not Quite Cricket?', in *Summer Days: Writers on Cricket*, 1983.

There are even those, such as the Arch Druid of Wiltshire, who would claim an overarching mystical significance for the game:

The three stumps are the triplefold muse or three fates – which must be held in balance. The two bails, as a man and a woman, are balanced on their fates to make up the fivefold wicket which must be defended against the fiery red sun.

Tim Sebastian, Arch Druid of Wiltshire and village cricketer, in 1995.

This observation was made as the Arch Druid presented a petition calling for Stonehenge Cricket Club to be given its ground back in order to play 'the sacred national game on the sacred site'. Cricket was last played at Stonehenge in 1860.

Cricket may itself be the highest good:

I tend to believe that cricket is the greatest thing that God ever created on Earth ... certainly greater than sex although sex isn't too bad either. But everyone knows which comes first when it's a question of cricket or sex.

Harold Pinter (1930–), playwright, quoted in the *Observer*, 5 October 1980.

It is certainly worth suffering minor inconveniences for cricket's sake. One spectator at Lord's in 1938 was unluckily struck by a Bill Edrich hook shot off the bowling of Harold Larwood while reading his newspaper. He promptly wrote to *The Times*:

Dear Mr Edrich, I would like you to know that, if I did want to have all my teeth extracted in one go, that is the way I wanted it done. Well played, sir.

Foreigners have found themselves utterly perplexed by the game:

I feel greatly hampered by my ignorance of cricket because I am aware that it is a metaphor everywhere in English life. I know I'm missing something. I don't know what it is.

Paul Theroux (1941–), US writer, quoted in *Summer Days: Writers on Cricket*, 1983.

Another American travel writer also found himself puzzled. In *Notes from a Small Island*, Bill Bryson begins his study of the English in a mental institution:

When I returned to the ward, I discovered that several of the patients had returned in my absence. Most of them were slumped in chairs in the day-room, sleeping off the exertions of a morning spent leaning on a rake or counting Rawlplugs into boxes, except for one dapper and well-spoken fellow in tweeds who was watching a test match on the television. He invited me to join him and, upon discovering that I was an American, enthusiastically explained to me this most bewildering of sports. I took him to be a member of staff, ... possibly a visiting psychiatrist, until he turned to me, in the midst of a detailed explanation of the intricacies of spin bowling, and said suddenly and conversationally: 'I have atomic balls, you know.'

'Excuse me?' I replied, my mind still on the other type of balls.

'Porton Down. 1947. Government experiments. All very hush-hush. You mustn't tell a soul.'

'Ah ... no, of course.'

'I'm wanted by the Russians.'

'Oh ... ah?'

'That's why I'm here. Incognito.' He tapped his nose significantly and cast an appraising glance at the dozing figures around us. 'Not a bad place really. Full of madmen, of course. Positively teeming with lunatics, poor souls. But they do a lovely roly-poly on Wednesdays. Now this is Geoff Boycott coming up. Lovely touch. He'll have no trouble with Benson's delivery, just you see.' ...

It is an interesting experience to become acquainted with a country through the eyes of the insane, and, if I may say so, a particularly useful grounding for life in Britain.

Bill Bryson (1956–), *Notes from a Small Island*, 1995.

Sir – When cricket fans discuss why the game has never caught on in America, the usual explanation is that people there just cannot understand a contest that goes on for several days without necessarily producing a clear result. This may not be such a problem now.

Tim de Lisle, editor of *Wisden Online*, letter to the *Daily Telegraph*, 16 November 2000, on the phenomenon of the US presidential election turning into a 'timeless Test match' in Florida.

THE REAL THING

Celebrating Village Cricket, whether played in villages or not.

Who would think that a little bit of leather, and two pieces of wood, had such a delightful and delighting power?

Mary Russell Mitford (1787–1855), novelist and playwright, *Our Village*, 1824–32.

Cricket has appealed to all sorts and conditions of men, from officers and gentlemen to blacksmiths, carters – and visionary poets. Here's William Blake out on the green:

> Oh, I say, you Joe,
> Throw us the ball.
> I've a good mind to go
> And leave you all.
> I never saw such a bowler –
> To bowl the ball in a tansy
> And to clean it with my handkercher
> Without saying a word!
>
> That Bill's a foolish fellow,
> He has given me a black eye;
> He does not know how to handle a bat
> Any more than a dog or cat.
> He has knocked down the wicket
> And broke the stumps,
> And runs without shoes to save his pumps.

William Blake (1757–1827), *Songs from an Island in the Moon*, V, Chapter II, ll. 50–64, c.1784.

It is surely the loveliest scene in England and the most disarming sound. From the ranks of the unseen dead for ever passing along country lanes, the Englishman falls out for a moment to look over the gate of the cricket field and smile.

J.M. Barrie (1860–1937), Scots playwright, quoted in *Cassell's Sports Quotations*, 2000.

Few things are more deeply rooted in the collective imagination of the English than the village cricket match. It stirs a romantic illusion about the rustic way of life, it suggests a tranquil and unchanging order in an age of bewildering flux.

Geoffrey Moorhouse (1931–), *The Best Loved Game*, 1979.

> Where else, you ask, can England's game be seen
> Rooted so deep as on the village green?
> Here, in the slum, where doubtful sunlight falls
> To gild three stumps chalked on decaying walls.

G. Rostrevor Hamilton, quoted in Godfrey Smith, 'Cricket in Poetry', *Summer Days: Writers on Cricket*, 1983.

They watched the landscape, sitting side by side
– An Odeon went past, a cooling tower,
And someone running up to bowl

Philip Larkin (1922–85), 'The Whitsun Weddings', 1964.

The charm of village cricket often lies in the vagaries and idiosyncrasies of the pitch:

One of the most unbalanced, yet beautiful, of cricket fields in my local district is the one that stands high on its hill above the village of Sheepscombe. Its gentle contour is that of a pony's back, with head held erect – the pavilion built somewhere between the ears, then the pitch itself starting halfway down the neck, levelling off for a bit along the saddle then plunging down the hind-quarters and away to the boundary. A straight drive from one end runs slap into the hill, and after trickling for a few yards, stops dead; while from the other end it soars out and disappears over the brow of the hill, and then the players get lost for a while, or sit around in the grass, till the ball is returned by some passing cowman.

Laurie Lee (1914–97), 'Hill Cricket', in *Summer Days: Writers on Cricket*, 1983.

Among many magical accounts of village matches is this, from John Moore's *Brensham Village*:

The match was against a team called Woody Bourton and it was a match we particularly wanted to win; for the plain reason that we detested Woody Bourton, whose captain was a dull humourless stone-waller, whose one-eyed umpire had never been known to give an l.b.w. against his own side, and whose wicket-keeper appealed almost ceaselessly in a cracked voice like that of a raven prophesying doom. Do not let yourself be misled by romantic writers into the belief that village cricket is played in a cheerful, 'sporting' spirit of 'Never mind who wins'. I have said that when we took to the field we were Brensham going to war. Therefore we minded very much who won. And especially we should mind if we were defeated by Woody Bourton, who were known to us as Bloody Bourton. They had beaten us (or, as some said, their umpire had beaten us) the previous year; and we thirsted for revenge.

But from the first ball, which took Mr Chorlton's off stump out of the ground, things went ill with us. Sir Gerald Hope-Kingley, who was next in, ran out Mr Mountjoy and shortly afterwards ran out himself. ('Like two old hens scampering up and down the wicket they are,' commented Dai.) Sammy Hunt batted for a while with the heroic determination of one who maintains a crumbling citadel against an innumerable enemy; then the wicket-keeper appealed for a catch and up went the loathéd umpire's cigarette-stained finger. Sammy walked slowly back, his bald head bright scarlet, which meant, we rightly guessed, that he was furious about the verdict. . . .

So far we had lost six wickets for thirty runs, most of which were byes off the fast bowler. Then there was a brief gallant stand by Briggs and Billy Butcher. Briggs for once in a way forgot his ambition to chop every ball County-fashion between the slips; he threw caution to the winds, took hold of his bat by the top of the handle as one would hold a sledge-hammer – and used it as a sledge-hammer. He had a private reason for disliking the Bloody Bourton captain: the man was Conservative agent for the constituency. So when Briggs smote the ball, he felt that he was smiting the Tories. Thus inspired he walloped it three times to the boundary and once over the willow-trees: three fours and a six, eighteen runs for Brensham, four hearty blows struck for the proletariat. . . .

Billy would have been a very fine batsman indeed if he could only have achieved the necessary co-ordination between hand and eye; the whisky got in the way of that. Today, however, he suddenly pulled himself together and made three successive strokes in which the timing was quite perfect. They were sublime: they were a poet's strokes. The first was a drive through the covers which flowed like a slow river with lovely, lazy grace. The next was a cheeky glance to leg carried out as casually as if it had been an impertinent aside during a serious conversation. The third was a glorious pull off his middle stump made with a sort of despairing gaiety, a laughing challenge to the gods, a wild unorthodox defiant shot which you realised, if you knew him well, was Billy cocking a snook at the world. The ball went sailing over the brook and into the buttercups beyond. 'Oh, lovely, lovely, lovely!' cried Lord Orris, clapping his thin pale hands. The Colonel, wiping the mouth of his flask, muttered: 'By God, I'll have a drink on that one,' and did so. A full half-minute later Goaty Pegleg, travelling slowly in the Fourth Dimension, declared loudly: 'He's hit a six.' ...

Brensham was all out for seventy-six and the teams came in to tea. ...

Now Bloody Bourton had an hour and a half in which to score eighty runs. They could have done it easily; but being Bloody Bourton they scratched and scraped and niggled and fiddled about, as Dai put it, so that by half-past five – we drew stumps at six, which was opening-time – they had only scored forty for the loss of three wickets. The game looked like ending in a dreary draw; but Bloody Bourton, realising too late that they would have to score much faster in order to have a chance of winning, suddenly began to hit; and hitting was not in their nature. After Mr Mountjoy had missed an easy catch, because he was listening to the curlews and the drumming snipe in the meadows beyond Cuckoo Pen, Alfie Perks took two wickets in the same over. A curious sort of desperation had overtaken them; for they delighted as a rule to make little pernickety shots along the ground, to score in singles, and to keep their opponents running about in the hot sun for two or three hours while they enjoyed themselves in their prim puritanical cautious way. But now they waved their bats wildly at every ball and called each other frantically for short runs. I heard Mr Chorlton say to Mr Mountjoy between overs: *Quem Deus vult perdere, prius dementat*; and sure enough next ball he was able to stump a batsman who had run half-way down the pitch to one of Alfie's leg-breaks and missed it altogether. ...

The last man walked out to the wicket as slowly as he dared and as eagerly as if he went blindfold towards the scaffold, snicked a two and a four off Sammy, and got a present of another four from one of Sir Gerald's overthrows. The score was seventy-two when Alfie bowled a long hop to the Bloody Bourton captain, who astonished even himself by hitting it for six.

This was the last over, and Bloody Bourton wanted two runs to win. Even the Colonel sat up tensely and put his flask away in his pocket. Everybody was on his toes with the solitary exception of Briggs, who was standing deep at long-on where for a long time he had nothing to do. I noticed a faint blue haze hanging about him in the still evening air; I looked again, and perceived that Briggs was lighting his pipe.

Alfie came up to the wicket with his familiar hop, skip and jump, tousled fair hair falling into his eyes. The Bloody Bourton captain, whose success in hitting a six had gone to his head, ran down the pitch and hit the ball a full toss. He caught it awkwardly high up on the blade of the bat but it was a hefty clout all the same, and the ball flew high towards long-on. Everybody looked at Briggs; but Briggs, with his big hands cupping a match, was still puffing away at his pipe. The whole team yelled at him. Sammy shouted terrible sea-oaths at the top of his voice. I shouted, the Colonel shouted, even Lord Orris shouted in his small piping voice. Only Goaty Pegleg, who had not yet tumbled to what was happening, remained silent. At last Briggs looked up, and saw the ball falling towards him. He did not move. Without hurry he put the box of matches into his left pocket and the pipe into his right pocket. Then, as one who receives manna from heaven he extended his enormous hands in front of him. The ball fell into them, the strong fingers closed as if they would squeeze it out of shape. Finally, still without hurry, he removed his pipe from his pocket lest it burn his trousers.

When the cheering was over there was a little silence while Joe Trentfield pulled up the stumps and the team came back towards the pavilion. The Goaty Pegleg announced in a loud voice *urbi et orbi*: 'He's caught it! We've won!' as if he were an astronomer who watches the stars through a telescope and sees, a hundred light-years after the event, the flaming destruction of a far-distant sun which, at the moment of earth-time when he witnesses it, has long been black and dead.

So off go Bloody Bourton with perfunctory handshakes and insincere smiles and with black hatred in their hearts. 'It was a good game,' we say, rubbing it in. 'Just the right sort of finish,' they agree without enthusiasm. Mr Mountjoy hurries off to his Evening Service – he's two minutes late already. The Colonel mounts his motor-bike and chugs off towards the Swan. Lord Orris untethers from the gate Tom Pearce's grey mare and rides slowly back towards his ruined mansion. Goaty Pegleg stumps away, the girls wash up the tea things, Mrs Hartley puts back her ham in its muslin bag. The persistent cuckoo, whose voice is breaking already, calls his last throaty cuck-cuck-cuck-oo from the top of the willow-tree.

'And now,' says Sammy Hunt, wiping the sweat-beads off his bald head, 'now for a pint at the Adam and Eve, and a game of darts!'

John Moore (1907–67), 'The Cricket Team', in *Brensham Village*, 1946.

If the French noblesse had been capable of playing cricket with their peasants, their châteaux would never have been burnt.

G.M. Trevelyan (1876–1962), *English Social History*, 1944.

Lord Frederick had royal blood in'en, so 'twere said,
For his grammer were Nelly Gwyn, King Charles's fancy,
But when Billy and him walked out to the pitch, side by side,
You couldn't tell which were the farmer and which the gentleman,
The pair on 'em looked that majestic, and when they got set
You'ld a'thought they was brothers born, the way they gloried
In blasting the bowling between 'em.

Francis Brett Young, quoted in Godfrey Smith, 'Cricket in Poetry', *Summer Days: Writers on Cricket*, 1983.

The social hierarchy could occasionally have an adverse effect on 'playing the game':

When I read of the goings-on in the House of Commons the week before last, I could not help being reminded of a little incident that I witnessed twenty years ago and more.

It was at a village cricket match. The captain of one side was the local squire, who, besides being exceedingly rich, was a vain, childish man to whom the winning of the match seemed extremely important. Those playing on his side were all or nearly all his own tenants.

The squire's side were batting, and he himself was out and was sitting in the pavilion. One of the batsmen accidentally hit his own wicket at about the same moment as the ball entered the wicketkeeper's hands. 'That's not out,' said the squire promptly, and went on talking to the person beside him. The umpire, however, gave a verdict of 'out', and the batsman was half-way back to the pavilion before the squire realized what was happening. Suddenly he caught sight of the returning batsman, and his face turned several shades redder.

'What!' he cried, 'he's given him out? Nonsense! Of course he's not out!' And then, standing up, he cupped his hands and shouted to the umpire: 'Hi, what did you give that man out for? He wasn't out at all!'

The batsman had halted. The umpire hesitated, then recalled the batsman to the wicket and the game went on.

I was only a boy at the time, and this incident seemed to me about the most shocking thing I had ever seen. Now, so much do we coarsen with the passage of time, my reaction would merely be to inquire whether the umpire was the squire's tenant as well.

George Orwell (1903–50), 'As I Please', *Tribune*, 14 April 1944.

SOME FLANNELLED ENGLISHMEN

Gentlemen and Players of the National Game.

Cricket, of course, was an obvious topic for an English Epic. In 1744 James Love supplied *Cricket: An Heroic Poem*; the following extract involves Kent vs. All England:

Now *Kent* prepares her better Skill to shew;
Loud rings the Ground, at each tremendous Blow.
With nervous Arm, performing God-like Deeds,
Another, and another Chief succeeds:
'Till, tired with Fame, the conq'ring Host give Way;
And lead by *thirteen* Strokes, the toilsome Fray.
Fresh rous'd to Arms, each Labour-loving Swain
Swells with new Strength, and dares the Field again.
Again to *Heav'n* aspires the cheerful Sound;
The *Strokes* re-echo o'er the spacious Ground.
The *Champion* strikes. When, scarce arriving fair,
The glancing Ball mounts upward in the Air!
The *Batsman* sees it; and with mournful Eyes,

Fix'd on th'ascending *Pellet* as it flies,
Thus suppliant claims the Favour of the Skies.
O mighty *Jove*! and all ye Pow'rs above!
Let my regarded Pray'r your Pity move!
Grant me but this. Whatever Youth shall dare
Snatch at the Prize, descending thro' the Air;
Lay him extended on the Grassy Plain,
And make his bold, ambitous Effort vain.

He said. The Powers, attending his Request
Granted one Part, to Winds consign'd the rest.

And now illustrious *S*[ackvill]*e*, where he stood,
Th'approaching Ball with cautious Pleasure view'd;
At once he sees the Chief's impending Doom,
And pants for mighty Honours yet to come:
Swift as the *Falcon*, darting on its Prey,
He springs elastic o'er the verdant Way;
Sure of Success, flies upward with a Bound,
Derides the slow Approach, and spurns the Ground.
Prone slips the Youth; yet glorious in his Fall,
With Arm extended shows the captive Ball.
Loud Acclamations ev'ry Mouth employ,
And Eccho rings the undulating Joy.

James Love (1722–74), actor and writer, *Cricket: An Heroic Poem*, Book III, 1744. Sackville was Lord John Sackville, son of the Duke of Dorset.

The great W.G. Grace (1848–1915), the Gloucestershire and England batsman, owed some of his success to blatant one-upmanship:

Playing for Essex against Gloucestershire, in two successive and snorting deliveries, the distinctly nippy fast bowler [Charles Kortright] had W G Grace transparently lbw, then palpably caught at the wicket. Both times the timorous umpire, under the batsman's famously beady stare, gave our bearded wonder the benefit of the doubt. Third ball, Kortright's vindictive yorker savagely spreadeagled both the Doc's middle and off stumps, and as the great batsman unbelievingly surveyed the wreckage of his castle, Korty, following through down the pitch, was unable to resist the immortal:

Surely you're not going, Doctor? – Why, there's one stump still standing!

Frank Keating, Foreword to *A Century of Great Cricket Quotations*, 1998.

Grace had been known to replace the bails after being clean bowled.

Barlow and Hornby were Lancashire's opening batsmen during the youth of the poet Francis Thompson, and inspired one of the best-loved of cricketing elegies:

It is little I repair to the matches of the Southron folk,
    Though my own red roses there may blow;
It is little I repair to the matches of the Southron folk,
    Though the red roses crest the caps, I know.

For the field is full of shades as I near the shadowy coast,
And a ghostly batsman plays to the bowling of a ghost,
And I look through my tears on a soundless-clapping host
As the run-stealers flicker to and fro,
To and fro: –
O my Hornby and my Barlow long ago!

Francis Thompson (1859–1907), 'At Lord's', 1913.

Bury me 22 yards away from Arthur, so I can send him down a ball now and again.

Alfred Shaw, Nottinghamshire bowler, 1907, last request; quoted in *A Century of Great Cricket Quotations*, 1998.

In the event, Shaw was buried 27 yards from his old team-mate, Arthur Shrewsbury; the extra 5 yards were to allow for his run-up.

Wisden has a way with its obituaries. Here is the first of several quoted in this chapter:

HEMINGWAY, GEORGE EDWARD, a brother of Messrs. W.M'G. and R.E. Hemingway, died at Rangoon on March 11, 1907. He was born in Macclesfield in 1872, was in the Uppingham XI in 1888, and in 1898 appeared for Gloucestershire against Yorkshire, at Sheffield. He was a free batsman and in the field generally stood mid-off or cover-point, but business and weak sight handicapped his game considerably. On one occasion, when playing a single-wicket match against his two brothers, he hit the ball into a bed of nettles; the fieldsmen quarrelled as to who should recover it, and during the argument the batsman ran about 250.

Wisden, 1908.

OATES, CAPT. LAWRENCE EDWARD GRACE, who died on March 17, 1912, his thirty-second birthday, whilst returning from the South Pole with Capt. Scott's ill-fated party, played cricket for his House as a lower boy at Eton.

Wisden, 1914.

Conventional wisdom has it that Scott's detestation of Amundsen was the direct result of the Norwegian's cheating and entering into a race for the South Pole. Absolute balderdash.

The whole can of worms was created by one event and one event alone – a cricket match played at Cape Evans in Antarctica on 18 September 1911, between elevens representing the respective polar expeditions of Captain Scott and Roald Amundsen. ...

As I sit in my study now with the lapwings wheeling and diving above the water meadows, the fat black rooks purring in the vicarage elms and the milkman's horse ambling heavily down the honeysuckled lane for all the world like Tom Goddard plodding back to his mark at Cheltenham, my mind wanders back in time, soaring weightlessly over storm-thrashed oceans, gliding gracefully over gnashing floes of ice and silent wastes of dazzling snow.

And like a great brooding skua it skims down tumbling mountain ramparts, cascading ice falls and lumbering glaciers and alights on a broken-backed wooden crate, and its glinting steely eyes survey the scene.

A hut.

Scott's hut at Cape Evans.

Scott's specially constructed hut with its score-box, its balconies for home side and visitor's side, its separate entrances for gentlemen and players and the broad sweep of its long room windows.

And outside on the snow a hive of activity.

Two ponies pulling a heavy roller.

The unmistakable figure of Petty Officer Evans erecting a sight-screen.

Captain Oates in the nets bowling his distinctive leg breaks and googlies to Lieutenant Bowers. ...

Chief Stoker Lashly digging a popping crease and Cecil Meares feeding the remnants of a matting wicket to his beloved huskies.

All is ready for the historic match. ...

Unfortunately, the score-book is no longer extant.

By an extreme and profoundly irritating stroke of fate it was in the hip pocket of Captain Oates when he set off on his final and heroic last journey into the polar night and eternal oblivion.

Peter Tinniswood, 'Polar Games', *Tales From a Long Room*, 1981.

RAE, EDWARD, who introduced the game into Russian Lapland, died at Birkenhead on June 26, 1923, aged 76.

Wisden, 1924.

Did I ever tell you the story about Harry Smith of Leicester? Arthur went on. He had a stutter. One day they went out in the field against Notts. Harry likes the look of the wicket, he thinks it'll suit him. I'll tell you what, S-s-skip, he says to his skipper, I think I'll b-b-bounce one or two. Wait a minute, says the skip, you know who they've got on the other side? They've got Larwood and Voce. I'll just b-b-bounce one or two, says Harry. So he bounces one or two and Notts don't like it much. Anyway, Leicestershire go in before the end of the day and Larwood and Voce knock them over like tin soldiers and suddenly old Harry finds he's at the wicket. Larwood and Voce go for him, Harry's never seen so many balls around his ears. He thinks they're going to kill him. Suddenly he gets a touch and Sam Staples dives at first slip and it looks as though he's caught it. Harry takes off his gloves and walks. Wait a minute, Harry, says Sam, it was a bump ball, I didn't catch it. Yes, you f-f-f-fucking-well did, says Harry, and he's back in the pavilion before you can say Jack Robinson.

Harold Pinter, 'Arthur Wellard', in *Summer Days: Writers on Cricket*, 1983.

During an Oxford University vs. Yorkshire match at The Parks, a nervous undergraduate batsman was at the wicket. Yorkshire wicketkeeper Don Brennan remarked to left-arm spinner Johnny Wardle:

Don't get him out just yet, Johnny, he smells so bloody lovely.

Quoted in David Hopps, *A Century of Great Cricket Quotes*, 2000.

Sir Jack Hobbs (1882–1963), 'The Master', Surrey and England, scored 5,410 runs in Test cricket and a record 197 centuries, and 61,237 runs in first-class cricket; he was the first English cricketer to be knighted. He attracted this 70th-birthday tribute from John Arlott:

> There falls across this one December day
> The light, remembered from those suns of June,
> That you reflected, in the summer play
> Of perfect strokes across the afternoon.
>
> No yeoman ever walked his household land
> More sure of step or more secure of lease
> Than you, accustomed and unhurried, trod
> Your small, yet mighty, manor of the crease.
>
> The game the Wealden rustics handed down
> Through growing skill became, in you, a part
> Of sense, and ripened to a style that showed
> Their country sport matured to balanced art.
>
> There was a wisdom so informed your bat
> To understanding of the bowler's trade
> That each resource of strength or skill he used
> Seemed but the context of the stroke you played.
>
> The Master: records prove the title good:
> Yet figures fail you, for they cannot say
> How many men whose names you never knew
> Are proud to tell their sons they saw you play.
>
> They share the sunlight of your summer day
> Of thirty years; and they, with you, recall
> How, through those well-wrought centuries, your hand
> Reshaped the history of bat and ball.

John Arlott (1914–91), broadcaster and writer, 'To John Berry Hobbs on his Seventieth Birthday, 16 December 1952'.

H.M. KING GEORGE VI, died at Sandringham on February 6, 1952. He was Patron of the Marylebone, Surrey and Lancashire clubs. When Prince Albert he performed the hat-trick on the private ground on the slopes below Windsor Castle, where the sons and grandsons of Edward VII used to play regularly. A left-handed batsman and bowler, the King bowled King Edward VII, King George V and the present Duke of Windsor in three consecutive balls, thus proving himself the best Royal cricketer since Frederick, Prince of Wales, in 1751, took a keen interest in the game. The ball is now mounted in the mess-room of the Royal Naval College, Dartmouth.

Wisden, 1953.

STICKY WICKETS

Cricket as a metaphor for the English way of war … or vice-versa.

There's a breathless hush in the Close tonight –
     Ten to make and the match to win –
A bumping pitch and a blinding light,
     An hour to play and the last man in.
And it's not for the sake of a ribboned coat,
     Or the selfish hope of a season's fame,
But his Captain's hand on his shoulder smote –
     'Play up! Play up! and play the game!'

The sand of the desert is sodden red, –
     Red with the wreck of the square that broke; –
The Gatling's jammed and the Colonel dead,
     And the regiment blind with dust and smoke.
The river of death has brimmed his banks,
     And England's far, and Honour's a name,
The voice of the schoolboy rallies the ranks:
     'Play up! Play up! and play the game!'

This is the word that year by year,
     While in her place the School is set,
Every one of her sons must hear,
     And none that hears it dare forget.
This they all with a joyful mind
     Bear through life like a torch in flame,
And falling fling to the host behind –
     'Play up! Play up! and play the game!'

Sir Henry Newbolt (1862–1938), 'Vitaï Lampada', 1897.

No Lord's this year: no silken lawn on which
A dignified and dainty throng meanders.
The schools take guard upon a fiercer pitch
Somewhere in Flanders.

Bigger the cricket here: yet some who tried
In vain to earn a colour while at Eton
Have found a place upon an England side
Which can't be beaten.

E.W. Hornung (1866–1921), 'Lord's Leave: 1915'. Hornung was the creator of Raffles, the 'amateur cracksman' – and first-class cricketer.

A visit to Lord's on a dark December day was a sobering experience; there were sandbags everywhere, and the Long Room was stripped and bare, with its treasures safely stored beneath ground, but the turf was a wondrous green, old Time on the Grand Stand was gazing serenely at the nearest balloon, and one felt that somehow it would take more than totalitarian war to put an end to cricket.

Major H.S. Altham, *Wisden*, 1940.

BIGGEST RAID EVER – SCORE 78 TO 26 – ENGLAND STILL BATTING
Newspaper placard, London, August 1940, during the battle of Britain.

It is not easy to write notes on our First-Class cricket season of 1940, because no competitive First-Class cricket was played. Nearly all the County players were occupied in some form of National Service. The war was critical. Our ally France fell; and the British forces were evacuated from Dunkirk. There are those who still think that the MCC might have done more....

R.C. Robertson-Glasgow, 'Notes on the 1940 Season', *Wisden*, 1941.

It was a bit close the other night. Several high explosives nearby, a few incendiaries on the ground and an oil bomb at deepish mid-on, if you were bowling from the Nursery end. After a little clearing up we shall be all right to start again soon.

Sir Pelham Warner, in *Lord's*, on Lord's cricket ground: letter to W.J. Edrich.

At times it seemed like a strange dream. ... Both cricket teams played well, and it was a hard and exciting game. Every now and then would come the old, accustomed cry – 'OWZATT?' – and then one's mind would flicker off to the briefing, and to joking with a pal whose broken body was now washing in the long, cold tides, and one saw again his machine cartwheeling down flaming from nose to tail and in the distance the village clock would strike and the mellow echoes would ring through the lazy air of that perfect summer afternoon.

Squadron Leader W.J. Edrich, former England Test cricketer, in *Round the Wicket*, 1959.

Edrich was recalling a match between his men and the local village team. It was interrupted by an order to scramble for a bombing raid off the Dutch coast, in which two planes were shot down. The umpires permitted the match to be concluded using substitutes on the RAF team.

There should have been a last line of defence during the war. It would have been made up entirely of the more officious breed of cricket stewards. If Hitler had tried to invade these shores he would have been met by a short, stout man in a white coat who would have said: 'I don't care who you are, you're not coming in here unless you're a member.'

Ray East, Essex spin bowler, *A Funny Turn*, 1983.

No captain worth his salt would now issue orders as daft and imprecise. 'Drop your bat on everything and leave it all to Blenkinsop' would be a sight more sensible; or even 'For heaven's sake don't get run out or you're for the high jump, mate.' But: 'Play up and play the game' – what sort of a captain would say that? ... This is intolerable. Newbolt never saw a shot fired in anger or he would never have perpetrated such patent balderdash.

Godfrey Smith on 'Vitaï Lampada', 'Cricket in Poetry', in *Summer Days: Writers on Cricket*, 1983.

THE NURSERY END

Cricket as experienced by the young – and those employed to coach them.

Cricket has provided the subject matter for countless inspiring stories for boys. This anonymous example dates from 1918:

Cyril Finch had withdrawn a little way from the mass of the spectators, and was sitting by himself under the shade of a tall hedge. He had taken his full share of the enemy's wickets, and was not paying much more than a drowsy sort of attention to the rest of the game. He knew that his name was down last but one on the batting list; no one ever expected him to make a score; his share in the contest was practically over. In an absent-minded way he watched Archer go to the wicket, and heard a lot of shouting whenever the latter made a good hit, but he did not join in the applause.

'Cad!' he muttered. 'I wish I was bowling; I'd put him in a few hot 'uns!'

The time slipped by; three more players performed the journey between the pitch and the pavilion without achieving much distinction by their performances, and Cyril began to buckle the straps of his own pads. He was thus engaged when a boy named Kenny came trotting over the grass.

'Hullo, Finch! I've been looking for you,' began the newcomer breathlessly. 'I say, you're in next; and, look here, for goodness' sake keep your end up, and don't slog. If Archer can make fifty he'll win the average; he's got twenty-six, and he's playing a ripping good game. It'll be a beastly shame if he doesn't get a chance of finishing his innings. I say, "Squib",' concluded the speaker with great earnestness, 'you will try and keep your end up, won't you, old chap?' ...

Cyril made no reply ... He didn't care tuppence how long his own innings lasted, and very much less whether Archer won the bat. There was that other little account to be balanced; the thing would be to give the fellow a glance and a nod, and then purposely miss the first straight ball. The 'Squib' could not help chuckling at the thought of how neatly Fate had delivered his enemy into his hands.

He reached the pitch, and there was a momentary delay while the bowler repaired a shoe-lace. Archer stood leaning on his bat, his face flushed and anxious; he evidently knew exactly how matters stood with regard to his chances of the average, and he greeted his new partner with a look which plainly repeated the words spoken by Kenny: 'Keep your end up, old chap!'

The smooth green turf, the shining, brass-topped stumps, the white creases, the ruts worn by the bowlers' feet: what curious influence could they all have upon a boy's mind; and why should they cause him suddenly to remember two pictures, one of a rather stout, clean-shaven gentleman, wearing a preposterous top hat, and balancing a ball on the tips of his fingers, as if he were about to perform a conjuring-trick; the other a dim and spotted photograph of a younger man, leaning on a bat, with one leg crossed accurately over the other, wearing a flannel cap and highly ornamented shirt, and with side whiskers adorning his face?

Father and grandfather – they had neither of them lived to witness the performance of the present bearer of their name; the cricket which they played and delighted in would now be voted out of date, and even absurd; but, oh! that the true spirit and chivalry of the game they handed on might ever remain the same!

Perhaps some such thought flashed through the batsman's mind as he grasped his weapon and watched the bowler's arm. It was a most tempting ball, just the sort to invite a mighty swipe, but Cyril merely returned it carefully.

'I say,' exclaimed Kenny, ten minutes later, 'it's a jolly sporting game the "Squib's" playing! He's only made two himself, and I haven't seen him slog once. He's doing all he knows to keep his end up for Archer. Give him a cheer, you fellows!' ...

'It was jolly sporting of you, "Squib",' said Archer. 'If you hadn't given me the chance, I should never have made 'em.'

'I'd a jolly good mind to get out first ball,' answered the other curtly. 'I quite intended to – only – only I didn't.'

'What ever for?'

'Why, because you spoiled my board with your beastly darts.'

'Look here,' cried Archer, laughing. 'I meant to have told you this morning, but you wouldn't listen when I called you to come back. I sold my air pistol to Peters, and it must have been his doing. He went home yesterday, but you wait till next term, and I'll make him pay for the damage, or punch the beggar's head.'

'Then it wasn't your doing, after all?' muttered Cyril, looking rather astonished.

'No,' answered the other laughing. 'I'm jolly glad you didn't slog. What made you change your mind?'

'Oh, I don't know,' answered the 'Squib', flushing, and possibly wondering in some distant manner what answer the stout old gentleman in the top hat, and the original of the spotted photograph, would have returned to such a question. 'I don't know; it wouldn't have been sporting; and of course – well, only cads play mean tricks at cricket.'

Anon., 'Playing The Game', in *Young England, an Annual for Boys,* 1918.

Molesworth, of course, has sound advice on 'criket', as on all other matters pertaining to Skool:

There is only one thing in criket and that is the STRATE BAT. Keep yore bat strate boy and all will be all right in life as in criket. So headmasters sa, but when my bat is strate I still get bowled is that an omen chiz. Aktually i usually prefer to hav a slosh: I get bowled just the same but it is more satisfactory.

For the reason that it is extremely dificult to hit the ball with a STRATE BAT or not criket matches are a bit of a strane. When you are a new bug or a junior in the 3rd game it is all right becos then you can sit around the boundary and keep the score in a notebook. When you get tired with that which is about 3 minits you can begin to tuough up your frendes and neighbours who look so sweet and angelic in their clean white criket shirts hem-hem. This is super. You look up long enuff to sa Good shot, grabber or Couldn't hit a squashed tomato and then back to the fray.

But it is a funy thing when you grow biger you always get into a criket team you cannot avoid it chiz. Tremble tremble you arive and see the pitch which is 2388 miles approx from the pavilion. Captain win toss and choose to bat chiz chiz chiz chiz. Moan drone tremble tremble you sit with white face and with everybode's knees knoking together it sound like a cocnut shy. Wot is the pleasure of it eh I would like to kno. Give me a thumbscrew or slo fire every time.

When your turn come the folowing things can hapen

    (A) You lose bat.
    (B) You fante dead away.
    (C) Your trousis fall down.
    (D) You trip over your shoe laces.

Captain then come up to you and sa BLOCK EVERYTHING molesworth and do not slosh we need 6 to win.

When he sa this all the things above hapen all at once. They revive you with a buket of water and drive you out to the wicket. This is not as you guessed 2398 miles away it is 6000 now and they hav men with gats covering all the exits so you canot run away.

AT THE WICKET
Of course it is the fast bowler you hav to face he is wating there at the other end of the pitch looking very ferce. Umpire is v. kind he can aford to be he hav not go to bat. He sa

We are very pleased to see you do make yourself at home. Of course you would like guard what guard would you like us to give you?

Squeak.

Come agane?

Squeak squeak.

I will give you centre hold your bat up strate to you a trifle now away agane. That is centre. Your position is 120 miles NNE of beachy head you may come in and land. There are 5 balls to come. At the 5th pip it will be 4.2 precisely. Able Baker Out.

PLAY!
Fast bowler retreat with the ball mutering and cursing. He stamp on the grass with his grate hary feet he beat his chest and give grate cry. Then with a trumpet of rage he charge towards you. Quake quake ground tremble birdseed fly in all directions if only you can run away but it is not done. Grit teeth close eyes. Ball hit your pads and everyone go mad.

OWSATSIR OW WASIT EHOUT!
Umpire look for a long time he is bent double at last he lift one finger.

He is a difrent man now from the kindly old gentleman who made you feel at home. His voise is harsh.

Out. No arguments. Get cracking. Take that xpresion off your face. On course at 20000 feet return to base. Out.

Distance back to pavilion is now 120000 miles and all the juniors sa yar boo sucks couldn't hit a squashed tomato. It is no use saing you were not out by a mile

team give you the treatment behind the pav just the same. There is only one consolation you can give it up when you grow up. Then you rustle the paper and sa
Wot a shocking show by m.c.c. most deplorable a lot of rabits ect. ect. Well, you
kno how they go on. Enuff.

Geoffrey Willans and Ronald Searle, *How to be Topp*, 1954.

After Oxford, John Betjeman had a brief career as a schoolmaster. Lack of cricketing prowess
proved something of an impediment:

'The sort of man we want must be prepared
To take our first eleven. Many boys
From last year's team are with us. You will find
Their bowling's pretty good and they are keen.'
'And so am I, Sir, very keen indeed.'
Oh where's mid-on? And what is silly point?
Do six balls make an over? Help me, God!
'Of course you'll get some first-class cricket too;
The MCC send down an A team here.'
My bluff had worked. I sought the common-room,
Of last term's pipe-smoke faintly redolent.
It waited empty with its worn arm-chairs
For senior bums to mine, when in there came
A fierce old eagle in whose piercing eye
I saw that instant-registered dislike
Of all unhealthy aesthetes such as me.
'I'm Winters – you're our other new recruit
And here's another new man – Barnstaple.'
He introduced a thick Devonian.
'Let's go and have some practice in the nets.
You'd better go in first.' With but one pad,
No gloves, and knees that knocked in utter fright,
Vainly I tried to fend the hail of balls
Hurled at my head by brutal Barnstaple
And at my shins by Winter. Nasty quiet
Followed my poor performance. When the sun
Had sunk behind the fringe of Hadley Wood
And Barnstaple and I were left alone
Among the ash-trays of the common-room,
He murmured in his soft West-country tones:
'D'you know what Winters told me, Betjeman?
He didn't think you'd ever held a bat.'
      The trusting boys returned. 'We're jolly glad
You're on our side, Sir, in the trial match.'
'But I'm no good at all.' 'Oh yes, you are.'
When I was out first ball, they said 'Bad luck!
You hadn't got your eye in.' Still I see

Barnstaple's smile of undisguised contempt,
Still feel the sting of Winters' silent sneer.
Disgraced, demoted to the seventh game,
Even the boys had lost their faith in me.
God guards his aesthetes. If by chance these lines
Are read by one who in some common-room
Has had his bluff called, let him now take heart:
In every school there is a sacred place
More holy than the chapel. Ours was yours:
I mean, of course, the first-eleven pitch. . . .
The prize day neared. . . .
Barnstaple drove his round-nosed Morris out
And he and I and Vera Spencer-Clarke,
Our strong gymnasium mistress, squashed ourselves
Into the front and rattled to The Cock. . . .
   Prize-day nerves? Or too much bitter beer?
What had that evening done to Barnstaple?
I only know that singing we returned;
The more we sang, the faster Barnstaple
Drove his old Morris, swerving down the drive
And in and out the rhododendron clumps,
Over the very playing-field itself,
And then – oh horror! – right across the pitch
Not once, but twice or thrice. The mark of tyres
Next day was noticed at the Parents' Match.
That settled Barnstaple and he was sacked,
While I survived him, lasting three more terms.

John Betjeman (1906–84), 'Cricket Master', from *High and Low*, 1966.

THE ESSENCE OF CRICKET:
AGONY, ECSTASY, AND POINTS IN BETWEEN

Expanding on some themes touched on in the first section and ending, appropriately enough, on a note of restrained but unqualified rapture.

Some games just never seem to take off:
As they stood a-blocking, a-blocking, a-blocking,
Wearily I yawned while I sat and watched the play:
  The bowling was all right,
  But they did not try to smite,
  Though many balls they might
   Have put away:
As they stood a-blocking, I sat yawning at the play.
. . .
As I sat a-yawning, a-yawning, a-yawning,

> The pack'd spectators were all yawning far and nigh;
>> They yawned the innings through,
>> It was more than they could do
>> To prevent it; nor could you
>>> If you try
> Keep from yawning if you fix on me your eye.

Douglas Moffat, *County Cricket*, 1897.

If county cricket can at times be boring, village cricket has filled some spectators with despair:

Having, the other day, once again spent an afternoon watching a village cricket match, I am again perplexed by the passion for the game which is displayed by those who cannot shine at it. They cannot bat, they cannot bowl, they leave their place in the field, they miss catches, they fumble returns; and yet, every Saturday, there they are, often in perfect flannels, ready to fail once more. What is this lure, this attraction, that cricket exercises, and why is it that so few village elevens can ever muster more than two or three players who know anything? No wonder it is so hard for first-class teams to be brought together. As, the other day, I saw this lack of any kind of skilled resistance to the bowler, I meditated afresh on the difficulties of those observant pilgrims from green to green whose duty it is to build up the country's nursery; and as one defeated batsman after another, with a nought to his name and no sense of humiliation, sank into his deck-chair, I deplored anew the absence of national pride. Why on earth, I wondered, don't they watch better men and learn something? Why do they think they can hit before they have tried to defend? Why do they want to make four off the first ball? But so it is, and so it will be until September, when football again comes in, and if they make mistakes they will hear about it.

E.V. Lucas (1868–1938), essayist and biographer, *Only the Other Day*, 1936.

Of course it's frightfully dull! That's the whole point! Any game can be exciting – football, dirt track racing, roulette . . . . To go to cricket to be thrilled is as stupid as to go to a Chekov play in search of melodrama.

Terence Rattigan (1911–77), playwright, filmscript for the character of Alexander Whitehead (Robert Morley) in *The Final Test*, 1953.

Some leading commentators agree that cricket's yawn-inducing quality is, indeed, a virtue:

In his autobiography, *Tiger by the Tail*, Lord MacLaurin, the chairman of the ECB, has the following passage: 'It is no longer possible to capture the somnolence of John Arlott's poem "Cricket at Worcester, 1938", when "Drowsing in deck-chair's gentle curve, through half-closed eyes, I watched the cricket." Those times are long gone.'

I am not entirely sure what Lord MacLaurin is on about. He is right in the sense that there are no deck-chairs at Worcester these days, rather those plastic tip-up thingies, which are less conducive to drowsing. I still don't find it impossible. I half-dozed very happily on a sunny September afternoon last year; there was even someone called Hutton batting. Does he think county cricket isn't somnolent any more? Has he *been* to Worcester lately?

Heaven knows, I am not against reforming cricket where it is desirable and essential. ... But he really ought to leave us snoozers alone. They have done away with the deck-chairs. There are those whose future plans for cricket would include doing away with Worcester. Do away with somnolence, and you will do away with cricket once and for all. And England with it, probably.

Matthew Engel, editor, *Wisden*, 2000.

Those in an English crowd who remain awake display their own virtues:

A fine day at the Oval makes us all akin, and a pleasant sight it is to see the vast assembly, every man with his eyes riveted on the wicket, every man able to appreciate the most delicate strokes in the game, and anxious to applaud friend or adversary. An English cricketing crowd is as fair and as generous as any assembly of mortals may be. When the Australians defeat us, though we do not like it, we applaud them until these bronzed Colonists almost blush. It is not so in all countries, nor in all countries is there the ready acceptance of the umpire's verdict, without which cricket degenerates into a wrangle.

Andrew Lang, Introduction to Richard Daft, *Kings of Cricket*, 1893.

Cricket ... gives expression to a well-marked trait in the English character, the tendency to value 'form' or 'style' more highly than success. In the eyes of any true cricket-lover it is possible for an innings of ten runs to be 'better' (i.e. more elegant) than an innings of a hundred runs: cricket is also one of the very few games in which the amateur can excel the professional. It is a game full of forlorn hopes and sudden dramatic changes of fortune, and its rules are so ill-defined that their interpretation is partly an ethical business. ... For the whole nation it is bound up with such concepts as 'good form', 'playing the game', etc., and it has declined in popularity just as the tradition of 'don't hit a man when he's down' has declined. It is not a twentieth-century game, and nearly all modern-minded people dislike it. The Nazis, for instance, were at pains to discourage cricket, which had gained a certain footing in Germany before and after the last war.

George Orwell (1903–50), 'Raffles and Miss Blandish', *Horizon*, October 1944.

If you are Pakistani or Indian you might just as well commit suicide when the team is humiliated; if you're West Indian, you might feel the world has fallen apart when things go wrong at the Oval. But these are countries where cricket is one of the leading suppliers of national pride. In England, you don't support cricket teams, you follow them. It's the game you support, not the team.

Robert Winder (1959–), *Hell for Leather*, 1996.

Teaching foreigners how to play the game is surely every Englishman's duty:

I taught my kidnappers cricket. They lent me a machete and I took great pains to carve a bat – a really heavy, Gooch-type bat. The first ball took ages to carve but I had to make a whole batch because every time a boundary was hit into the jungle it was as good as lost.

Phillip Halden, British businessman kidnapped by Colombian guerrillas, on passing the time during his eight-month captivity, 1996.

A tour of England by the Homies and Popz, a team of street kids from the tough Compton area of Los Angeles, was launched at Lord's. Many of the players, mostly Hispanic teenagers, were involved in gangs before they discovered cricket. 'It's more exciting than baseball,' said bowler Steve Aranda, 'more of a man's game.' 'Cricket teaches you life,' said coach Ted Hayes. 'You play hard but you obey the rules.' They later presented the Sinn Fein leader, Gerry Adams, with a bat.

Wisden, 2000; drawn from *The Times*, 18 September 1999, and the *Daily Mail*, 28 September 1999.

The English can be rightly proud of the fact that most of the games now played around the world were conceived in these isles, but it is in developing cricket that the English sporting genius reached its peak. Cricket still enshrines the three great English attributes: a love of irony, a general desire to avoid hype, which can almost make an art form of understatement, and above all a deep distaste for anything that smacks of too much effort and detailed premeditation.

Mihir Bose, 'Village Cricket', in *British Greats*, 2000.

There is nothing quite so poignant as the close of play...
There is always a sense of sadness about the drawing of the stumps. Standing alone upon the Heath, filled an hour ago with a crowd of excited people, now deserted by all but the workmen taking down the tent, hearing the voices of the players departing in twos and threes dying away in the lanes as the stars come out, you feel the very air breathe a chastened melancholy. But at the end of the season it is doubly sad. To know that the last ball is bowled, the last run made – 'tears inhibit my tongue' as I think of it. Before next season a hundred changes may have happened. The goodly fellowship of our eleven may never meet again unbroken; the calls of business – or that louder call – will have taken some, at least, away. And one change is already determined on, to me as serious almost as any could be. We have played over last match on the Heath. We finished the season gloriously just now, beating the Shalford men after a close match by three wickets; and when old Martin, our umpire, drew the stumps and walked gravely to the tent, the last game upon the old Heath was ended; the scene of a thousand pleasant contests will see us no more.

I protest I feel a choky sensation as I write it, but it is true. The turf, they said, is bad; the furze grows too near; they urged a hundred trifles such as these in favour of the change. The real reason, I believe, is that the mile walk from the village across the Park deters some spectators, and even some lazy players, from coming up. And they are going instead to the new Playing Fields close to the village. The turf there may be as good, the outfielding a little better, but to me the change is bitterness and vexation of spirit. To break the old associations; to get no more fours up to the Park palings, no more late cuts up to the window where my cousin Frank sits watching us from his invalid chair; to turn no more to look at the clouds rising over the firwoods, or to note between the overs the Peaslake mill standing clear against the August sky – this to me will be like losing an arm.

E.B.V. Christian, *At the Sign of the Wicket*, 1894.

The summer of 2000 epitomised for some the highest virtues of English cricket – itself a microcosm of the best of England:

There is bigotry in England. There is also prejudice based on race and class, just as there is everywhere. Yet, compared with any other country in Europe, this is a remarkably tolerant land and that tolerance found expression at the final Test which, I venture to suggest, was the most pleasing sporting event that has taken place anywhere in the kingdom this year.

It wasn't just that England won, and thereby took a series against the West Indies for the first time in three decades, though that was worth cheering. What made it a magnificent event was the stupendous last day . . . .

Apart from one daft afternoon when half of Manchester, it seemed, disrobed, the crowds have behaved with impeccable sportsmanship all summer, and the series reached its climax at the Oval, off as well as on the field. The ovations given spontaneously to Courtney Walsh and Curtly Ambrose [the two West Indian fast bowlers who had announced their retirement from international cricket] as they left the field on Sunday and again when they came out to bat the following day, confirmed the essential generosity of the English cricket lover.

The Oval crowd showed that, most of the time, most of the people on this crowded island get on pretty well, to the consternation of 'race advisers' who like to sniff conflict where none exists.

Walsh, who has always come across as a gracious man, and Ambrose, who has not, were clearly moved by the response of the crowd and of the players, who formed a guard of honour to welcome them to the crease. Relations between the teams have been good, as they usually are with the West Indies, many of whose players opt to live here when their careers end.

The current England team reflects pretty much the society the players have grown up in, for better or worse. It is led by a man who was born in Madras but who moved to East London in boyhood, and nobody has questioned Nasser Hussain's commitment, nor his right to lead the team out. Far from it. . . .

For three centuries English cricket has yoked together the squire and the tenant, and it still does. The only recognisable difference this summer is that Duncan Fletcher, the winning coach, is a transplanted Zimbabwean.

Last Monday was a truly happy day. There was no triumphalism, no immodesty, no drum-banging, no crowing. There was only great joy at a feat accomplished by an honest group of cricketers, a joy shared by performers and watchers and by the public beyond the Oval.

Victory doesn't make us better, any more than defeat would have made us worse. But it makes people a bit happier, and nobody need apologise for that.

Michael Henderson, in the *Daily Telegraph*, 11 September 2000.

Essentially English: An A to Z

A

THE AMATEUR

It is beginning to be hinted at that we are a nation of amateurs.

Lord Rosebery (1847–1929), Prime Minister 1894–95, Rectorial Address, University of Glasgow, 16 November 1900.

And all the world over, each nation's the same:
They've simply no notion of Playing the Game.
They argue with umpires, they cheer when they've won,
And they practise beforehand, which ruins the fun.

Michael Flanders (1922–75), 'A Song of Patriotic Prejudice', from *At the Drop of Another Hat*, performed with Donald Swann, 1964.

That stuff about gentlemanly amateurishness I found rather attractive. I liked the way in which brash, aggressive American types like myself were told to tone down and slow down. I took to that and I liked understatement. Some of those clichés are true: I like the wonderfully subtle strategies of English misdirection. I really enjoy it. I can't do them myself but they're fun.

Michael Ignatieff (1947–), quoted in Jonathon Green, *Them: Voices from the Immigrant Community in Contemporary Britain*, 1990.

B

BEER

Sot comme un Anglois. [Drunk as an Englishman.]

François Rabelais (c.1494–c.1553), *Gargantua*, 1534.

Back and side go bare, go bare,
Both foot and hand go cold:
But belly God send thee good ale enough,
Whether it be new or old.

Anon., *Gammer Gurton's Needle*, 1575.

In Shakespeare's *Henry VI, Part II*, a couple of the characters get beered up and dream:

CADE: There shall be in England seven halfpenny loaves sold for a penny; the three-hooped pot shall have ten hoops; and I will make it a felony to drink small beer. All the realm shall be in common, and in Cheapside shall my palfrey go to grass. And when I am king, – as king I will be, – ... there shall be no money; all shall eat and drink on my score; and I will apparel them all in one livery, that they may agree like brothers, and worship me their lord.
DICK: The first thing we do, let's kill all the lawyers.

William Shakespeare (1564–1616), *Henry VI, Part II*, 1592.

Would I were in an alehouse in London! I would give all my fame for a pot of ale, and safety.

William Shakespeare (1564–1616), *Henry V*, 1599.

Dost thou think, because thou art virtuous, there shall be no more cakes and ale?

William Shakespeare (1564–1616), *Twelfth Night*, 1601.

England, where, indeed, they are most potent in potting: your Dane, your German, and your swag-bellied Hollander, are nothing to your English.

William Shakespeare (1564–1616), *Othello*, 1602–4.

Flow, Welsted, flow! like thine inspirer, Beer,
Tho' stale, not ripe; tho' thin, yet never clear;
So sweetly mawkish, and so smoothly dull;
Heady, not strong; o'erflowing tho' not full.

Alexander Pope (1688–1744), *The Dunciad*, 1742.

What two ideas are more inseparable than Beer and Britannia?

The Rev. Sydney Smith (1771–1845), in Hesketh Pearson, *The Smith of Smiths*, 1934.

O Beer! O Hodgson, Guinness, Allsopp, Bass!
Names that should be on every infant's tongue!

C.S. Calverley (1831–84), 'Beer', 1861.

Say, for what were hop-yards meant,
Or why was Burton built on Trent?
Oh many a peer of England brews
Livelier liquor than the Muse,
And malt does more than Milton can

To justify God's ways to man.
Ale, man, ale's the stuff to drink
For fellows whom it hurts to think.

A.E. Housman (1859–1936), *A Shropshire Lad*, 1896, No. 62.

St George he was for England,
And before he killed the dragon
He drank a pint of English ale
Out of an English flagon.
For though he fast right readily
In hair-shirt or in mail,
It isn't safe to give him cakes
Unless you give him ale.

G.K. Chesterton (1874–1936), 'The Englishman', in *The Flying Inn*, 1914.

Before the Roman came to Rye or out to Severn strode,
The rolling English drunkard made the rolling English road.
A reeling road, a rolling road, that rambles round the shire,
And after him the parson ran, the sexton and the squire;
A merry road, a mazy road, and such as we did tread
The night we went to Birmingham by way of Beachy Head.

I knew no harm of Bonaparte and plenty of the Squire,
And for to fight the Frenchman I did not much desire;
But I did bash their baggonets because they came arrayed
To straighten out the crooked road an English drunkard made,
Where you and I went down the lane with ale-mugs in our hands,
The night we went to Glastonbury by way of Goodwin Sands.

His sins they were forgiven him; or why do flowers run
Behind him; and the hedges all strengthening in the sun?
The wild thing went from left to right and knew not which was which,
But the wild rose was above him when they found him in the ditch.
God pardon us, nor harden us; we did not see so clear
The night we went to Bannockburn by way of Brighton Pier.

My friends, we will not go again or ape an ancient rage,
Or stretch the folly of our youth to be the shame of age,
But walk with clearer eyes and ears this path that wandereth,
And see undrugged in evening light the decent inn of death;
For there is good news yet to hear and fine things to be seen,
Before we go to Paradise by way of Kensal Green.

G.K. Chesterton (1874–1936), 'The Rolling English Road', in *The Flying Inn*, 1914.

My love affair with beer began in Fleet Street during the early 1930s. We didn't know about pot in those days, and took our relaxation in half-pints, usually of mild and bitter, in one of the numerous pubs that beckoned journalists in that region of London. In the pub I liked most, called 'Aunties', which was just off Tudor Street, half a pint cost threepence halfpenny, which was more than it sounds but less than we pay now.

I spent much of my time in that pub for what I persuaded myself were sound business reasons. In my earliest days with the *Morning Post*, I worked 'on space', which meant I was paid for what I got into the newspaper. It paid to stick around, particularly in the early night hours when unexpected things happen in the capital and late interviews were sometimes called for. The *Morning Post*'s reporters' room was small and comfortless. The newsroom knew in which pub to find me, if required. Life was more easygoing than it is today.

There were big brewing combines in those days, but there were also many more small, independent brewers. Socially, brewers ranked pretty high, some of them not far behind the county families. Their daughters went to Ascot, fox-hunted and usually married well. The number of illustrious brewing names on the Conservative benches of the House of Commons was considered a matter for reproach by members of the Labour party.

So beer went with high life. In the now defunct Junior Carlton Club to which I belonged in those days, and at my golf club, I drank the beer out of tankards; in pubs out of half-pint glasses. I cannot remember when in the more affluent post-war years we took to pints. In the 1930s, when times were hard and we had three million unemployed, it was almost invariably half-pints. We had a way of dealing with publicans who made small profits out of froth. 'S'cuse me, miss, could you slip a small gin into this?' one would ask beguilingly. 'Yes, certainly.' Kindly smile – no point in upsetting her. 'Then, d'you mind filling it up with beer?' No hard feelings, simply a matter of business.

Now and again, when the weather was cold, we would break training and go a bust on black velvet, or 'blackers', which Evelyn Waugh and his characters drank copiously. But I always had an inner feeling that both the champagne and the stout lost something in the deal. Anyway, you can't go on drinking the stuff. The consequences are more abrupt than with a simple pint of bitter.

There is tremendous satisfaction in knowing where the best beer is to be found. My drinking companions and I came to know pubs out of London where the beer was special. We were keen on the Benskin's country of East Anglia. There was an inn at Winchelsea near Rye, I remember, with the fastest shove-ha'penny board I ever played on. The local man who always took our money was called Chummy Barden. He had inherited an ancient post which required him to go down to the beach first thing every morning with a telescope and report whether or not Napoleon was coming over.

The stipend for this duty, though inconsiderable by today's standards, together with his winnings on the shove-ha'penny board, kept him in beer. 'Us don't allow tight 'uns,' he would say when your halfpenny stopped on the brink of the line. There were worse ways of spending a summer evening than in the company of such a man.

Two men enjoying a pint of beer together do not have to be of the same intellectual weight. Beer wipes out such superficial distinctions. It affords the clever man a matchless opportunity to learn from a less clever man something he would never otherwise have found out. Beer is the most companionable of all drinks. Furthermore, there is nothing like a pint of beer in a pub for resolving small differences. In the days when I held tenuous responsibility for a newspaper, I found that most misunderstandings between rational individuals could be sorted out over a second pint. If there were more pubs in the world, there would be fewer wars. But you need to be under the roof of a landlord who knows how to keep beer well, without too much gas. I am allergic to gassy beers. And having to send back a cloudy pint interrupts the flow of intercourse. Keeping good beer calls for experience and taking pains.

The war years were hard for beer-drinkers. When war ended in my corner of Germany, we extravagantly sent three-ton lorries to France for champagne, because we'd won and, bottles being chronically short, you could exchange a couple of empties for a full bottle. I drank the stuff in our mess because there was nothing else; but I would have exchanged a bottle of Krug for a pint of bitter. Later, I came to know and respect German lager. China, incidentally, has imported a German brewery and knows how to make the stuff impressively well.

When things settled down after the war, I took to keeping a small barrel of beer in my cellar at home. If you kept it at the right temperature and made sure that the bung was always replaced tightly, there was little wastage. Then our local brewery, Shepherd Neame of Faversham, came up with bitter in a polypin, which held about four and a half gallons, and was simpler than a barrel.

Ideally, I enjoy bitter best out of a tankard, particularly if it's pewter. But it is never worth making a song and dance about it. A pint of beer drunk solo or in company tastes best when you feel on good terms with yourself. It is not quite as good if you have just had an altercation with someone behind the bar who insists that all the tankards hanging up are privately owned by the pub's regular customers.

Now and again, breweries celebrate Christmas or some anniversary of their own by producing a special ale. It will almost certainly be a point or two up on the average strength of bitter and I am wary of it outside the home. Our head – and bladder – for beer varies according to age. After you qualify for a bus-pass, stay with beer of the same strength.

Early in my days as a parliamentary candidate, a member of an otherwise rather stuffy local committee in a small town offered to take me on a pub-crawl. He ran a garage, and was the token artisan who in those days Tories thought it right to bring into the fold. There were, I remember, 12 pubs and in each of them we drank half a pint of beer. Well short of William Hague's score, but enough. Three hours later, we met the local committee for a final chaser and to report progress. Slightly pissed, I slapped the chairman on the back and gave the woman vice-chairman, who was quite good-looking, a rapturous kiss. They were very much taken aback. Silly old so-and-sos, I thought, and felt contemptuous of their sobriety. If you are going to behave badly, beer's the right stuff to do it on. Oh, the joy of that encounter! It's with me still.

W.F. Deedes (1912–), journalist and former MP, 'Memories of a beer hunter', in the *Spectator*, 11 November 2000.

C

'CHARACTER'

One quotation says it all ...

There are people who are neither very clever, nor very industrious, nor very strong, and who would probably be nowhere in an examination, and who yet exert a great influence in virtue of what is called 'force of character'. They may not know much, but they take care that what they do know they know well. They may not be very quick, but the knowledge they acquire sticks. They may not even be particularly industrious or enduring, but they are strong of will and firm of purpose, undaunted by fear of responsibility, single-minded, and trustworthy. In practical life a man of this sort is worth any number of merely learned and clever people.

T.H. Huxley (1825–95), speech, 1880.

D

DICKENS

George Orwell was one of many admirers:

I have been discussing Dickens simply in terms of his 'message', and almost ignoring his literary qualities. But every writer, especially every novelist, *has* a 'message', whether he admits it or not, and the minutest details of his work are influenced by it. All art is propaganda. Neither Dickens himself nor the majority of Victorian novelists would have thought of denying this. On the other hand, not all propaganda is art. As I said earlier, Dickens is one of those writers who are felt to be worth stealing. He has been stolen by Marxists, by Catholics and, above all, by Conservatives. The question is, What is there to steal? Why does anyone care about Dickens? Why do *I* care about Dickens?

That kind of question is never easy to answer. As a rule, an aesthetic preference is either something inexplicable or it is so corrupted by non-aesthetic motives as to make one wonder whether the whole of literary criticism is not a huge network of humbug. In Dickens's case the complicating factor is his familiarity. He happens to be one of those 'great authors' who are ladled down everyone's throat in childhood. At the time this causes rebellion and vomiting, but it may have different after-effects in later life. For instance, nearly everyone feels a sneaking affection for the patriotic poems that he learned by heart as a child, 'Ye Mariners of England', 'The Charge of the Light Brigade' and so forth. What one enjoys is not so much the poems themselves as the memories they call up. And with Dickens the same forces of association are at work. Probably there are copies of one or two of his books lying about in an actual majority of English homes. Many children begin to know his characters by sight before they can even read, for on the whole Dickens was lucky in his illustrators. A thing that is absorbed as early as that does not come up against any critical judgement. And when one thinks of this, one thinks of all that is bad and silly in Dickens – the cast-iron 'plots', the characters who don't come off, the *longueurs*, the paragraphs in blank verse, the awful pages of 'pathos'. And then the thought arises, when I say I like Dickens, do I simply mean that I like thinking about my childhood? Is Dickens merely an institution?

If so, he is an institution that there is no getting away from. How often one really thinks about any writer, even a writer one cares for, is a difficult thing to decide; but I should doubt whether anyone who has actually read Dickens can go a week without remembering him in one context or another. Whether you approve of him or not, he is there, like the Nelson Column. At any moment some scene or character, which may come from some book you cannot even remember the name of, is liable to drop into your mind. Micawber's letters! Winkle in the witness box! Mrs Gamp! Mrs Wititterly and Sir Tumley Snuffim! Todgers's! (George Gissing said that when he passed the Monument it was never of the Fire of London that he thought, always of Todgers's.) Mrs Leo Hunter! Squeers! Silas Wegg and the Decline and Fall-off of the Russian Empire! Miss Mills and the Desert of Sahara! Wopsle acting Hamlet! Mrs Jellyby! Mantalini! Jerry Cruncher! Barkis! Pumblechook! Tracy Tupman! Skimpole! Joe Gargery! Pecksniff! – and so it goes on and on. It is not so much a series of books, it is more like a world. And not a purely comic world either, for part of what one remembers in Dickens is his Victorian morbidness and necrophilia and the blood-and-thunder scenes – the death of Sikes, Krook's spontaneous combustion, Fagin in the condemned cell, the women knitting round the guillotine. To a surprising extent all this has entered even into the minds of people who do not care about it. A music-hall comedian can (or at any rate could quite recently) go on the stage and impersonate Micawber or Mrs Gamp with a fair certainty of being understood, although not one in twenty of the audience had ever read a book of Dickens's right through. Even people who affect to despise him quote him unconsciously.

Dickens is a writer who can be imitated, up to a certain point. In genuinely popular literature – for instance, the Elephant and Castle version of *Sweeney Todd* – he has been plagiarized quite shamelessly. What has been imitated, however, is simply a tradition that Dickens himself took from earlier novelists and developed, the cult of 'character', i.e. eccentricity. The thing that cannot be imitated is his fertility of invention, which is invention not so much of characters, still less of 'situations', as of turns of phrase and concrete details. The outstanding, unmistakable mark of Dickens's writing is the *unnecessary detail*. ... An interesting example, too long to quote, is Sam Weller's story of the obstinate patient in Chapter XLIV of *The Pickwick Papers*. As it happens, we have a standard of comparison here, because Dickens is plagiarizing, consciously or unconsciously. The story is also told by some ancient Greek writer. I cannot now find the passage, but I read it years ago as a boy at school, and it runs more or less like this:

> A certain Thracian, renowned for his obstinacy, was warned by his physician
> that if he drank a flagon of wine it would kill him. The Thracian thereupon
> drank the flagon of wine and immediately jumped off the house-top and
> perished. 'For,' said he, 'in this way I shall prove that the wine did not kill me.'

As the Greek tells it, that is the whole story – about six lines. As Sam Weller tells it, it takes round about a thousand words. Long before getting to the point we have been told all about the patient's clothes, his meals, his manners, even the newspapers he reads, and about the peculiar construction of the doctor's carriage, which conceals the fact that the coachman's trousers do not match his coat. Then there is the dialogue between the doctor and the patient. '"Crumpets is wholesome, sir," said the patient. "Crumpets is not wholesome, sir," says the doctor, wery fierce,' etc. etc. In the end the original story has been buried under the details. And in all of Dickens's most characteristic passages it is the same. His imagination overwhelms everything, like a kind of weed. Squeers stands up to address his boys, and immediately we are hearing about Bolder's father who was two pounds ten short, and Mobbs's stepmother who took to her bed on hearing that Mobbs wouldn't eat fat and hoped Mr Squeers would flog him into a happier state of mind. Mrs Leo Hunter writes a poem, 'Expiring Frog'; two full stanzas are given. Boffin takes a fancy to pose as a miser, and instantly we are down among the squalid biographies of eighteenth-century misers, with names like Vulture Hopkins and the Rev. Blewberry Jones, and chapter headings like 'The Story of the Mutton Pies' and 'The Treasures of a Dunghill'. Mrs Harris, who does not even exist, has more detail piled on to her than any three characters in an ordinary novel. Merely in the middle of a sentence we learn, for instance, that her infant nephew has been seen in a bottle at Greenwich Fair, along with the pink-eyed lady, the Prussian dwarf and the living skeleton. Joe Gargery describes how the robbers broke into the house of Pumblechook, the corn and seed merchant – 'and they took his till, and they took his cashbox, and they drinked his wine, and they partook of his wittles, and they slapped his face, and they pulled his nose, and they tied him up to his bedpust, and they give him a dozen, and they stuffed his mouth full of flowering annuals to perwent his crying out'. Once again the unmistakable Dickens touch, the flowering annuals; but any other novelist would only have mentioned about half of these outrages. Everything is piled up and up, detail on detail, embroidery on embroidery. It is futile to object that this kind of thing is rococo – one might as well make the same objection to a wedding-cake. Either you like it or you do not like it. . . .

If Dickens had been *merely* a comic writer, the chances are that no one would now remember his name. Or at best a few of his books would survive in rather the same way as books like *Frank Fairleigh*, *Mr Verdant Green* and *Mrs Caudle's Curtain Lectures*, as a sort of hangover of the Victorian atmosphere, a pleasant little whiff of oysters and brown stout. Who has not felt sometimes that it was 'a pity' that Dickens ever deserted the vein of *Pickwick* for things like *Little Dorrit* and *Hard Times*? What people always demand of a popular novelist is that he shall write the same book over and over again, forgetting that a man who would write the same book twice could not even write it once. . . . The thing that drove Dickens forward into a form of art for which he was not really suited, and at the same time caused us to remember him, was simply the fact that he was a moralist, the consciousness of 'having something to say'. He is always preaching a sermon, and that is the final secret of his inventiveness. For you can only create if you can care. Types like Squeers and Micawber could not have been produced by a hack writer looking for something to be funny about. A joke worth laughing at always has an idea behind it, and usually a subversive idea. Dickens is able to go on being funny because he is in revolt against authority, and authority is always there to be laughed at. There is always room for one more custard pie.

His radicalism is of the vaguest kind, and yet one always knows that it is there. . . .

As a matter of course he is on the side of the underdog, always and everywhere. To carry this to its logical conclusion one has got to change sides when the underdog becomes an upperdog, and in fact Dickens does tend to do so. He loathes the Catholic Church, for instance, but as soon as the Catholics are persecuted (*Barnaby Rudge*) he is on their side. He loathes the aristocratic class even more, but as soon as they are really overthrown (the revolutionary chapters in *A Tale of Two Cities*) his sympathies swing round. Whenever he departs from this emotional attitude he goes astray. A well-known example is at the ending of *David Copperfield*, in which everyone who reads it feels that something has gone wrong. What is wrong is that the closing chapters are pervaded, faintly but noticeably, by the cult of success. It is the gospel according to Smiles, instead of the gospel according to Dickens. The attractive, out-at-elbow characters are got rid of, Micawber makes a fortune, Heep gets into prison – both of these events are flagrantly impossible – and even Dora is killed off to make way for Agnes. If you like, you can read Dora as Dickens's wife and Agnes as his sister-in-law, but the essential point is that Dickens has 'turned respectable' and done violence to his own nature. Perhaps that is why Agnes is the most disagreeable of his heroines, the real legless angel of Victorian romance, almost as bad as Thackeray's Laura.

No grown-up person can read Dickens without feeling his limitations, and yet there does remain his native generosity of mind, which acts as a kind of anchor and nearly always keeps him where he belongs. It is probably the central secret of his popularity. A good-tempered antinomianism rather of Dickens's type is one of the marks of western popular culture. One sees it in folk-stories and comic songs, in dream-figures like Mickey Mouse and Popeye the Sailor (both of them variants of Jack the Giant-Killer), in the history of working-class Socialism, in the popular protests (always ineffective but not always a sham) against imperialism, in the impulse that makes a jury award excessive damages when a rich man's car runs over a poor man; it is the feeling that one is always on the side of the underdog, on the side of the weak against the strong. In one sense it is a feeling that is fifty years out of date. The common man is still living in the mental world of Dickens, but nearly every modern intellectual has gone over to some or other form of totalitarianism. From the Marxist or Fascist point of view, nearly all that Dickens stands for can be written off as 'bourgeois morality'. But in moral outlook no one could be more 'bourgeois' than the English working classes. The ordinary people in the western countries have never entered, mentally, into the world of 'realism' and power politics. They may do so before long, in which case Dickens will be as out of date as the cab-horse. But in his own age and ours he has been popular chiefly because he was able to express in a comic, simplified and therefore memorable form the native decency of the common man. And it is important that from this point of view people of very different types can be described as 'common'. In a country like England, in spite of its class-structure, there does exist a certain cultural unity. All through the Christian ages, and especially since the French

Revolution, the western world has been haunted by the idea of freedom and equality; it is only an idea, but it has penetrated to all ranks of society. The most atrocious injustices, cruelties, lies, snobberies exist everywhere, but there are not many people who can regard these things with the same indifference as, say, a Roman slave-owner. Even the millionaire suffers from a vague sense of guilt, like a dog eating a stolen leg of mutton. Nearly everyone, whatever his actual conduct may be, responds emotionally to the idea of human brotherhood. Dickens voiced a code which was and on the whole still is believed in, even by people who violate it. It is difficult otherwise to explain why he could be both read by working people (a thing that has happened to no other novelist of his stature) and buried in Westminster Abbey.

When one reads any strongly individual piece of writing, one has the impression of seeing a face somewhere behind the page. It is not necessarily the actual face of the writer. I feel this very strongly with Swift, with Defoe, with Fielding, Stendhal, Thackeray, Flaubert, though in several cases I do not know what these people looked like and do not want to know. What one sees is the face that the writer ought to have. Well, in the case of Dickens I see a face that is not quite the face of Dickens's photographs, though it resembles it. It is the face of a man of about forty, with a small beard and a high colour. He is laughing, with a touch of anger in his laughter, but no triumph, no malignity. It is the face of a man, who is always fighting against something, but who fights in the open and is not frightened, the face of a man who is generously angry – in other words, of a nineteenth-century liberal, a free intelligence, a type hated with equal hatred by all the smelly little orthodoxies which are now contending for our souls.

George Orwell (1903–50), 'Charles Dickens', 1939.

He had a large loving mind, and the strongest sympathy with the poorest classes. He felt sure a better feeling, and much greater union of the classes, would take place in time. And I pray earnestly it may.

Queen Victoria (1819–1901), on the death of Charles Dickens, 1870.

E

ECCENTRICS

Other nations have people who are barking mad. England has eccentrics.

Among the great gallery of characters in John Aubrey's *Brief Lives* is William Butler (1535–1618):

Will Butler, physitian; he was of Clare-hall in Cambridge, never tooke the Degree of Doctor, though he was the greatest Physitian of his time.

The occasion of his first being taken notice of was thus: About the comeing in of King James, there was a Minister a few miles from Cambridge, that was to preach before his Majestie at Newmarket. The parson heard that the King was a great Scholar, and studyed so excessively that he could not sleepe, so somebody gave him some opium, which had made him sleep his last, had not Doctor Butler used this following remedy. He was sent for by the Parson's wife. When he came and sawe the Parson, and asked what they had donne, he told her that she was in danger to be hanged for killing her husband, and so in great choler left her. It was at that time when the Cowes came into the Backside to be milkt. He turnes back and asked whose Cowes those were. She sayd, her husband's. Sayd he, Will you give one of those Cowes to fetch your husband to life again? That she would, with all her heart. He then causes one presently to be killed and opened, and the parson to be taken out of his Bed and putt into the Cowes warme belly, which after some time brought him to life, or els he had infallibly dyed.

He was a man of great Moodes, a humorist. One time King James sent for him to Newmarket, and when he was gonne halfe-way left the Messenger and turned back; so then the messenger made him ride before him.

I think he was never maried. He lived in an Apothecary-shop in Cambridge, Crane's, to whom he left his estate, and he in gratitude erected the Monument for him at his own chardge, in the fashion he used. He was not greedy of money, except choice Pieces of Golde, or Rarities.

Once, on the rode from Cambridge to London, he took a fancy to a chamber-layne or tapster in his Inne, and took him with him and made him his favourite, by whom only accession was to be had to him, and thus enriched him.

He would many times (I have heard say) sitt among the Boyes at St. Maries' Church in Cambridge (and just so would the famous attorney general Noy in Lincoln's Inne, who had many such froliques and humours).

He kept an old mayd whose name was Nell. Dr. Butler would many times go to the Taverne, but drinke by himself. About 9 or so at night old Nell comes for him with a candle and lanthorne, and sayes, Come you home, you drunken Beast. By and by Nell would stumble; then her Master calls *her* drunken beast; and so they did drunken beast one another all the way till they came home.

A Serving man brought his Master's water to Doctor Butler, being then in his Studie (with turn'd Barres) but would not bee spoken with. After much fruitlesse importunity the man tolde the doctor he was resolved he should see his Master's water; he would not be turned away, threw it on the Dr.'s head. This humour pleased the Dr., and he went to the Gent. and cured him.

A gent. lying a-dyeing, sent his Servant with a horse for the doctor. The horse, being exceeding dry, ducks downe his head strongly into the water, and plucks downe the Dr. over his head, who was plunged in the water over head and ears. The Dr. was madded, and would return home. The man swore he should not; drewe his sword, and gave him ever and anon (when he would returne) a little prick, and so drove him before him.

The Dr. lyeing at the Savoy in London next the water side, where there was a Balcony look't into the Thames, a Patient came to him that was grievously tormented with an Ague. The Dr. orders a boate to be in readinesse under his windowe, and discoursed with the patient (a Gent.) in the Balcony, when, on a signall given, two or three lusty Fellowes came behind the Gentleman and threwe him a matter of 20 feete into the Thames. This surprize absolutely cured him.

A Gent. with a red ugly, pumpled face came to him for a cure. Said the Dr., I must hang you. So presently he had a device made ready to hang him from a Beame in the roome, and when he was e'en almost dead, he cutt the veines that fed these pumples and lett out the black ugley Bloud, and cured him.

That he was chymical I know by this token, that his mayd came running in to him one time like a slutt and a Furie; with her haire about her eares, and cries, Butler! come and looke to your Devilles your selfe, and you will; the stills are all blowne up! She tended them, and it seems gave them too greate a heate. Old Dr. Ridgely knew him, and I thinke was at that time with him.

He was much addicted to his humours, and would suffer persons of quality to wayte sometimes some hours at his dore, with Coaches, before he would receive them. Dr. Gale, of Paule's School, assures me that a French man came one time from London to Cambridge, purposely to see him, whom he made staye two howres for him in his Gallery and then he came out to him in an old blew gowne. The French gentleman makes him 2 or 3 very lowe Bowes to the ground. Dr. Butler whippes his Legge over his head, and away goes into his chamber, and did not speake with him.

John Aubrey (1626–97), *Brief Lives*, ed. Oliver Lawson Dick, 1949.

William Spooner (1844–1930) was for 21 years the Warden of New College, Oxford. A kindly eccentric, known affectionately as 'The Spoo', he suffered from a speech impediment which, as 'a Spoonerism', entered the Oxford English Dictionary during his lifetime.

One by one we were taken up to him for a little conversation. When my turn came he put to me a few conventional questions – what School was I reading? Had I pleasant rooms? What was the general nature of my interests? – and when these were duly answered he went on to say: 'I hope you will have a happy time at Oxford. I am sure you will. But, if you will take the advice of an old man' – I am a little doubtful about that introductory sentence, not at all about the words that followed – '*beware of the lure of men and women*'. This surprising injunction, quickly and quietly uttered, impressed itself indelibly upon my mind, and though I have never been sure what exactly was the warning it was intended to convey, I have always done my best to follow the general line it seemed to indicate.

John Sparrow, quoted in William Hayter, *Spooner*, 1977.

His oddities were numerous. I was to dine with him alone one night, and arriving rather early, was asked to go straight to his bedroom and talk to him while he finished dressing. I found him struggling with his tie. We chatted a little. The door to an adjoining room was slightly ajar, and I heard a low drone coming from it. Presently the tie was satisfactorily adjusted, and we were just about to leave when 'Wait a minute,' he said, 'I'd forgotten.' He went to the door I have spoken of, opened it wider, put his head in, and said, almost peevishly, 'Very bad, very bad indeed. Write for next week on the Epistle of St. Paul to the Ephesians.' Then we went down and dined.

Victor Gollancz (1893–1967), *My Dear Timothy*, 1952.

There are, of course, many surviving Spoonerisms, not all of which involve the classic transposition of consonants:

In the sermon I have just preached, whenever I said Aristotle, I meant St. Paul.

'Mr. Coupland, you read the lesson very badly.'
'But, Sir, I didn't read the lesson.'
'Ah, I thought you didn't.'

'Do come to dinner tonight to meet our new Fellow, Casson.'
'But Warden, I *am* Casson.'
'Never mind, come all the same.'

SPOONER: Ah, let me see, what is your initial?
UNDERGRADUATE: V.
SPOONER: And V. stands for what?
UNDERGRADUATE: Victor.
SPOONER *(after a short pause)*: Victor what?

Kinquering Kongs their Tikles Tate.

You have tasted a whole worm. You have hissed my mystery lectures. You will leave by the town drain.

Which of us has not felt in his heart a half-warmed fish?

Undergraduates recur.

All quoted in Jan Morris (1926–), *The Oxford Book of Oxford*, 1978.

The Church of England has always had its fair share of eccentrics:

At St. John's sermons were taken seriously and the congregation included many cognoscenti of fine preaching. The Vicar in my earliest childhood was a certain Canon, of whom only a vision of an angry red face remains to me as the children's service was invariably left to the Curate. Originally a fine preacher he had come of recent years increasingly to deviate from the path of strict orthodoxy, which had caused considerable dissension among his flock, so that his departure, which took place in circumstances sufficiently remarkable, was neither wholly unforeseen nor altogether regretted. In the course of one of his most rousing sermons, fortunately at Evensong, he announced that it had recently been revealed to him in a dream that there were no women in Heaven, the female part of mankind having finally been judged incapable of salvation. While those of his hearers who were acquainted with the Canon's wife could quite appreciate the obvious satisfaction with which the Vicar promulgated this new dogma, few among a congregation that was largely female could be expected to share it, and complaints to the Bishop led to the Canon's sudden retirement for a long rest in the country from which, in fact, he never returned.

Osbert Lancaster (1908–86), *All Done From Memory*, 1963.

And then there are the Forces … Claud Cockburn remembers his Uncle Philip:

His imagination was powerful and made holes in the walls of reality. He used to shout up at the nursery for someone to come and hold his walking-stick upright at a certain point on the lawn while he paced off some distances. These were the measurements of the gunroom of the shooting lodge he was going to build on the estate he was going to buy in Argyllshire when he had won £20,000 in the Calcutta Sweep. Sometimes he would come to the conclusion that he had made this gunroom too small – barely room to swing a cat. Angrily he would start pacing again, and often find that this time the place was too large. 'I don't want a thing the size of a barn, do I?' he would shout.

Once, some years earlier, his imagination functioned so powerfully that it pushed half the British Fleet about. That was at Queen Victoria's Diamond Jubilee in 1897, when the Fleet was drawn up for review at Spithead in the greatest assembly of naval power anyone had ever seen. Uncle Philip and my father were invited by the Admiral commanding one of the squadrons to lunch with him on his flagship. An attaché of the Admiral Commanding-in-Chief was also among those present.

Half-way through lunch Uncle Philip began to develop an idea. Here, he said, was the whole British Fleet gathered at Spithead, without steam up, immobile. Across there, was Cherbourg. (At that time, the war, when it came, was going to be against the French.) Well, suppose one night – tonight, for instance – some passionately Anglophobe commander of a French torpedo-boat were to get the notion of dashing across the Channel in the dark and tearing between the lines of the great ships, loosing off torpedoes. The ships helpless, without steam up. In twenty minutes, half of them sinking. In an hour, Britain's power reduced to the level of Portugal's. By dawn, the Solent strewn with the wreckage of an Empire. Before noon, mobs crazed with triumph and wine sweeping along the Paris boulevards, yelling for the *coup de grâce*.

He spoke of this, my uncle said, not as an idle speculation, but because he happened to have recalled, on his way to this lunch, that in point of fact a French officer, just mad enough to carry out such a project, was at this moment in command of a torpedo-boat at Cherbourg. (His voice, as he said this, compelled a closer attention by the Admiral and the attaché of the Commander-in-Chief.)

Certainly, he said, he had met the man himself, a Captain Moret, a Gascon. Hot-blooded, hating the English for all the ordinary French reasons, and for another reason, too: his only sister – a young and beautiful girl, Uncle Philip believed – had been seduced and brutally abandoned by an English Lieutenant, name of Hoadley, or Hoathly, at Toulon. A fanatic, this Moret. Had a trick of gesturing with his cigar – like this (Uncle Philip sketched the gesture) – as he, Moret, expatiated on his favourite theory, the theory of the underrated powers of the torpedo-boat as the guerrilla of the sea.

'And there,' said Uncle Philip, in a slightly eerie silence, 'he is.' He nodded ominously in the direction of Cherbourg.

On the way back to Cowes in the Admiral's launch, my father upbraided Uncle Philip. A nice exhibition he had made of himself – a mere Major of Hussars, lecturing a lot of Admirals and Captains on how to run their business. Also they had undoubtedly seen through this yarn, realized that this Moret was a figment of Uncle Philip's imagination, invented half-way through the fish course. Then, and during the remainder of the afternoon and early evening, Uncle Philip was abashed, contrite. After dinner that evening they walked by the sea, taking a final look at the Fleet in the summer dusk. Silently my uncle pointed at the far-flung line. Every second ship in the line was getting up steam.

Claud Cockburn (1904–81), *I, Claud …*, 1956.

'Take my camel, dear,' said my Aunt Dot, as she climbed down from this animal on her return from High Mass.

Rose Macaulay (1881–1958), opening sentence of *The Towers of Trebizond*, 1956.

The English aristocracy has specialised in breeding oddballs:

The fifth Duke of Portland, one W.J.C. Scott-Bentinck (1800–1879), has long been something of a hero of mine. Old W.J.C., as I like to think of him, was one of history's great recluses and went to the most extraordinary lengths to avoid all forms of human contact. He lived in just one small corner of his stately home and communicated with his servants through notes passed to him through a special message box cut into the door to his rooms. Food was conveyed to him in the dining room by means of a miniature railway running from the kitchen. In the event of chance encounters, he would stand stock still and servants were instructed to pass him as they would a piece of furniture. Those who transgressed this instruction were compelled to skate on the duke's private skating-rink until exhausted. Sightseers were allowed to tour the house and grounds – 'so long,' as the duke put it, 'as you would be good enough not to see me.'

For reasons that can only be guessed at, the duke used his considerable inheritance to build a second mansion underground. At its peak, he had 15,000 men employed on its construction, and when completed it included, among much else, a library nearly 250 feet long and the largest ballroom in England, with space for up to 2,000 guests – rather an odd thing to build if you never have guests. A network of tunnels and secret passageways connected the various rooms and ran for considerable distances out into the surrounding countryside. It was as if, in the words of one historian, 'he anticipated nuclear warfare'. When it was necessary for the duke to travel to London, he would have himself sealed in his horse-drawn carriage, which would be driven through a mile-and-a-half-long tunnel to a place near Worksop Station and loaded onto a special flatcar for the trip to the capital. There, still sealed, it would be driven to his London residence, Harcourt House.

When the duke died, his heirs found all of the above-ground rooms devoid of furnishings except for one chamber in the middle of which sat the duke's commode. The main hall was mysteriously floorless. Most of the rooms were painted pink. The one upstairs room in which the duke resided was packed to the ceiling with hundreds of green boxes, each of which contained a single dark brown wig. This was, in short, a man worth getting to know.

Bill Bryson (1951–), *Notes From a Small Island*, 1995.

Political parties were once not as cautious in selecting their candidates as they tend to be today:

David James, who retired from Parliament as Member for Dorset North in 1979, was dotty. His reputation for eccentricity dated from 1964 when as Tory MP for Brighton, Kemptown, he lost his seat to Labour by seven votes. When, a few days after Alec Douglas-Home's defeat (and my own at Rochester), I went to Conservative Central Office to interview the then chairman of the party, John Hare, I murmured some words of sympathy. ... 'It's all that silly bugger David James's fault,' cried Hare. 'The fool spent most of the three-week election campaign in Scotland looking for the Loch Ness Monster.' Indeed, he had, and the tabloid press had been full of it. The papers claimed that every so often a cable would arrive from some godforsaken Scottish village addressed to the Kemptown Tory agent: 'Have almost found the Monster. Hope all goes well with the campaign.' I reminded the chairman of these communications. Hare became very animated, that is for a Conservative. 'Seven fuckin' votes, a marginal seat lost,' he shouted, 'and we're lumbered with Harold Wilson.'

James, or Guthrie-James as he later became, managed for some inexplicable reason to get himself adopted for Dorset North, returning to the House in 1970. I expressed some surprise at this one evening to Sir Harwood Harrison ... 'Quite mad,' he said, 'but he had a good war.' It appears that he had tried twice to escape from a German prisoner-of-war camp: on the first occasion he adopted the identity of a Bulgarian naval officer, Lieutenant Buggeroff. This improbable disguise served him well for a time, but he was eventually picked up by the Gestapo. ... Had he succeeded in finding Nessie he would undoubtedly have been returned for Brighton and the course of history would have been very different.

Julian Critchley (1930–2000), Conservative MP, *A Bag of Boiled Sweets*, 1995.

Labour won the 1964 general election with a majority of four seats, soon reduced to two; a James victory in Brighton would thus have produced a 'hung' Parliament.

The 4th Earl Russell, who has died aged 66, was the eccentric elder son of the philosopher Bertrand Russell and caused the occasional sensation in the House of Lords with his outrageous speeches.

In 1978, during a debate on aid for victims of crime, Lord Russell had to be called to order after a singularly rambling and incoherent discourse. As he was advocating total abolition of law and order, and saying that the police should be prevented from raping youngsters in cells, he was interrupted by Lord Wells-Pestell, from the Labour Government's Front Bench, and reminded of the length of time he had been speaking. Without any further comment the Earl left the Chamber.

In his speech from the cross-benches Russell referred to modern society and the effects of automation in factories. Then he said: 'There should be universal leisure for all, and a standing wage sufficient to provide life without working ought to be supplied ... so that everybody becomes a leisured aristocrat – aristocrats are Marxists ... Police ought to be totally prevented from ever molesting young people at all, from ever putting them into jails and raping them and putting them into brothels or sending them out to serve other people sexually against their wills.'

Peers seemed startled as he continued: 'In a completely reorganised modern society, women's lib would be realised by girls being given a house of their own by the age of 12 and three-quarters of the wealth of the State being given to the girls so that marriage would be abolished and the girl could have as many husbands as she liked ...' Finally Russell told the House of Lords: 'Mr Brezhnev and Mr Carter are really the same person ...'

The full text of this extraordinary outburst was published subsequently by Lord Russell's mother, Dora, and the old Etonian anarchist and playwright Heathcote Williams, who described Russell as 'the first man since Guy Fawkes to enter the House of Parliament with an honest intention'. The pamphlet, illustrated by Ralph Steadman, quickly became a collectors' item and essential reading for the 'psychedelic Left'.

In 1985 Russell received a less courteous hearing from Their Lordships when he read out a carefully prepared question on the leadership of the IRA and suggested that the organisation might have a legitimate role in resolving Ireland's problems.

John Conrad Russell was born in 1921 and received his early education at his parents' experimental co-education school in Hampshire where there were no compulsory lessons and the children were permitted to call their teachers rude names. At the age of 13 he proceeded to the progressive Dartington Hall in Devon and after his parents' divorce he joined his mother in America, attending the University of California at Los Angeles, and Harvard.

From 1943 to 1946 he served with the RNVR and subsequently worked briefly for the Food and Agriculture Organisation of the United Nations in Washington and as an administrative assistant with the Treasury.

Following the dissolution of his own marriage to Susan Lindsay (daughter of the American poet Nicholas Vachel Lindsay) in the mid 1950s, Russell – or Viscount Amberley as he was styled by courtesy – became something of a recluse, spending his time writing and crocheting. His published works included a slim volume entitled *Abandon Spa, Hot Springs.*

To one visitor in the early 1960s he said: 'I like to sit and think and write my thoughts. The few people who have seen my work find it too deep for them.' He then pointed proudly to a pair of trousers hanging on the wall by a nail, 'I crocheted these out of string,' he said. 'It took me a long while because I didn't have a pattern. I had to keep trying them on.'

From Hugh Massingberd, ed., *The Daily Telegraph Book of Obituaries: Eccentric Lives,* 1995.

Stanley Green, who has died aged 78, paraded Oxford Street for 25 years with a placard warning against the dangers of protein, and sold thousands of hand-printed leaflets (at 12p each) explaining why lustful feelings were induced by 'fish, bird, meat, cheese, egg, peas, beans, nuts and sitting'.

'Protein makes passion,' he said. 'If we eat less of it, the world will be a happier place.'

Stanley Owen Green was born on Feb 22 1915 and worked in the Civil Service before launching his campaign against lust in 1968. He had learnt from experience, he said, that 'passion can be a great torment'.

He produced his leaflets on a press in his small council flat at Northolt, west London: the tenants below often complained about the relentless thumping on printing days.

Until he qualified for a free travel pass, Green would bicycle to Oxford Street each day in his raincoat, cap and wire-rimmed spectacles. He recalled with pleasure that motorists reading the board on the back of his bicycle would toot their horns and wave. 'I've known coaches pass,' he said, 'and everyone has stood up and cheered at me.'

His own diet comprised porridge, fruit, steamed vegetables, lentils, home-baked bread and barley-water mixed with milk powder. He took his lunch in 'a warm and secret place' near Oxford Street – 'I think it is justified,' he said, 'because I am doing a public service and I need to be warm.'

The campaign was not without its hazards. Green was twice arrested for causing an obstruction, and wore green overalls as protection against spit. But he held no grudges, explaining that people attacked him only because they mistook him for a religious man.

He liked nothing better than to distribute leaflets in Leicester Square on a Saturday night. He would home in on cinema queues, using such opening gambits as 'You cannot deceive your groom that you are a virgin on your wedding night,' and often sold 50 leaflets in an evening.

As well as inveighing against 'love play', Green told passers-by that to prevent drug-taking, promiscuity and vandalism they should spend more time talking to their children.

The Museum of London plans to exhibit Green's placard and a selection of his leaflets.

From Hugh Massingberd, ed., *The Daily Telegraph Book of Obituaries: Eccentric Lives*, 1995.

Essex

Essex. Essex girl. A type of unintelligent and materialistic young woman who emerged in the late 1980s as the female equivalent of ESSEX MAN and who became the butt of a variety of politically incorrect jokes.

Essex man. A type of socially ungraced Conservative voter, typically a self-made businessman, who lives in Essex or London and southeast England and who in the late 1980s worshipped the consumer-oriented gospel of Thatcherism.

Brewer's Dictionary of Phrase and Fable, 1999.

One such politically incorrect joke will suffice to give a flavour:

Q: Does an Essex girl make love with the light on?
A: Only if she keeps the car door open.

An early incarnation of Essex man was Billericay Dickie:

> Good evening! I'm from Essex, in case you couldn't tell,
> My given name is Dickie, I come from Billericay,
> And I'm doin' very well.

'ad a love affair with Nina
In the back of my Cortina,
A seasoned-up hyena
Could not've been more obscener.
She took me to the cleaner's
And uvver misdemeanours,
But I got right up between 'er
Rum and 'er Ribena. . . .

I'm not a blinkin' thickie –
I'm Billericay Dickie,
And I'm doin' very well.

I bought a lot of brandy
When I was courtin' Sandy,
It took eight to make 'er randy
And all I 'ad was shandy. . . .
I'd rendezvous wiv Janet
Quite near the Isle of Thanet –
She looked more like a gannet,
She wasn't 'alf a prannit –
Her muvver tried to ban it,
Her farver 'elped me plan it,
And when I captured Janet
She bruised 'er pomegranate.

Oh you ask Joyce and Vicky
If I ever shaped up tricky –
I'm not a bloomin' thicky –
I'm Billericay Dickie,
And I'm doin' very well.

Ian Dury (1942–2000), 'Billericay Dickie', in *New Boots and Panties*, 1977.

F

FOOTBALL

There are early references to the English game that isn't Cricket: Chaucer mentions it, for example. But it was not until the nineteenth century that it began to be organised into anything like the game it has become: Association Football, or Soccer. Before then it had no rules to speak of, and no limit to the number of players on each side, or the number of balls – or even, for that matter, sides. It was played in the streets, with scant regard for silky skills:

Up and by coach to Sr Ph. Warwickes, the street being full of footballs, it being a great frost.

Samuel Pepys (1633–1703), Diary, 2 January 1665.

Me thinks I am stopt by one of your heroic games, call'd football, which I conceive not very conveniently civil in the streets, especially in such irregular and narrow roads as Crooked Lane.

Sir William Davenant (1606–68), poet and playwright, quoted in David Pickering, *Cassell's Sports Quotations*, 2000.

Even in this century, those forced to play it have found it little evolved from Davenant's day. George Orwell, who endured it as a prep school boy, reported:

I loathed the game, and since I could see no pleasure or usefulness in it, it was very difficult for me to show courage at it. Football, it seemed to me, is not really played for the pleasure of kicking a ball about, but is a species of fighting.

George Orwell (1903–50), *Such, Such Were the Joys*, 1947.

Among the earliest practitioners of Association Football – the codified sport – was John Goodall. He wrote:

The one passion in my life has been football – the most exhilarating game I know, and the strongest protest against selfishness, without sermonizing, that was ever put before a thoughtful people.

John Goodall (1863–1942), quoted in Andrew Ward and Anton Rippon, *The Derby County Story*, 1983.

Others, with something of an axe to grind, took up Goodall's theme:

Football, in itself, is a grand game for developing a lad physically and also morally, for he learns to play the game with good temper and unselfishness, to play in his place and 'play the game', and these are the best training for any game of life. But it is a vicious game when it draws crowds of lads away from playing the game themselves to be merely onlookers at a few paid performers.

Lord Baden-Powell (1857–1941), founder of the Boy Scout Movement, *Scouting for Boys*, 1908.

Not everyone agreed with Baden-Powell when it came to spectating, however:

A man who had missed the last home match of 't' United' had to enter social life on tiptoe in Bruddersford. ... To say that these men paid their shillings to watch twenty-two hirelings kick a ball is merely to say that a violin is wood and catgut, that *Hamlet* is so much paper and ink. For a shilling Bruddersford United AFC offered you Conflict and Art.

J.B. Priestley (1894–1984), *The Good Companions*, 1928.

The point about football in Britain is that it's not just a sport people take to, like cricket or tennis or running long distances. It is inherent in the people. It is built into the urban psyche, as much a common experience to our children as are uncles and schools. It is not a phenomenon; it is an everyday matter. There is more eccentricity in deliberately disregarding it than in devoting a life to it. It has more significance in the national character than theatre has.

Arthur Hopcraft (1932–), Introduction, *The Football Man*, 1968.

Football is the opera of the people.

Stafford Higginbottom (1934–95), Chairman of Bradford City, 1985.

Football, like opera, has villains as well as heroes:

I never comment on referees and I'm not going to break the habit of a lifetime for that prat.

Ron Atkinson (1939–), football manager, after a game in 1979, quoted in David Pickering, *Cassell's Sports Quotations*, 2000.

Ron Atkinson again, on a linesman …

I know where he should have put his flag up, and he'd have got plenty of help.

… and again:

If that was a penalty, I'll plait sawdust.

Sometimes it is all too much for the referee:

I was sorely provoked.

Melvin Sylvester (1956–), referee, after sending himself off for punching a player, quoted in the *Guardian*, 'Quotes of the Year', 24 December 1998.

But the Man in Black is not the only baddie on the pitch:

Nobby Stiles a dirty player? No, he's never hurt anyone. Mind you, he's frightened a few.

Sir Matt Busby (1909–94) on the player known to England's World Cup opponents in 1966 as 'El Bandito', quoted in David Pickering, *Cassell's Sports Quotations*, 2000.

I have a little black book with two players in it, and if I get a chance to do them I will. I will make them suffer before I pack this game in. If I can kick them four yards over the touch-line, I will.

Jack Charlton (1935–), Leeds United and England defender, speaking to journalists in 1970. He subsequently became manager of the Republic of Ireland team.

Norman Hunter doesn't tackle opponents so much as break them down for scrap.

Julie Welch (1948–), journalist, referring to Norman 'Bite Yer Legs' Hunter of Leeds United, quoted in David Pickering, *Cassell's Sports Quotations*, 2000.

I love tackling, love it. It's better than sex. I love hearing the noise of a crunching tackle, the 'arrgh!' from the other player.

Paul Ince (1967–), Liverpool and England player, quoted in the *Daily Telegraph*, 20 June 1998.

But these hard men are heirs to a great English tradition of The Beautiful Game:

There was plenty of fellers who would kick your bollocks off. The difference was that at the end they'd shake your hand and help you look for them.

Nat Lofthouse (1925–), footballer, recalling the 1950s, quoted in David Pickering, *Cassell's Sports Quotations*, 2000.

As in the youth of J.B. Priestley, it has been the English Football Fan who has made the game what it is:

Most people are in a factory from nine till five. Their job may be to turn out 263 little circles. At the end of the week they're three short and somebody has a go at them. On Saturday afternoons they deserve something to go and shout about.

Rodney Marsh (1944–), footballer, quoted in David Pickering, *Cassell's Sports Quotations*, 2000.

The natural state of the football fan is bitter disappointment, no matter what the score. ... Be tolerant of those who describe a sporting moment as their best ever. We do not lack imagination, nor have we had sad and barren lives; it is just that real life is paler, duller, and contains less potential for unexpected delirium.

Nick Hornby (1957–), *Fever Pitch*, 1992.

... Some fans, of course, have more experience of unexpected delirium than others.

It says on my birth certificate that I was born in the borough of West Bromwich, in the district of West Bromwich. I said all right, all right, I'll support the bloody Albion – there's no need to twist my arm.

Frank Skinner (1957–), comedian and West Bromwich Albion supporter, 1995, quoted in David Pickering, *Cassell's Sports Quotations*, 2000.

The fans' attentions are not, of course, always welcome:

The fans who give me stick are the sort of people who still point at aeroplanes.

Ian Wright (1963–), Arsenal and England player, 1997, quoted in David Pickering, *Cassell's Sports Quotations*, 2000.

English people go to matches as a form of psychoanalysis – they turn up, have a good shout and then go home. That goes for everybody, bankers in their Rolls-Royces and ordinary working people too. You'll see them all letting rip with a mouthful.

Emmanuel Petit (1970–), French footballer then with Arsenal, 1999, quoted in David Pickering, *Cassell's Sports Quotations*, 2000.

Sometimes they let rip with more than a mouthful; the Fan Abroad can be a very bad advertisement for England ...

If we were doing this in the Falklands they would love it. It's part of our heritage. The British have always been fighting wars.

Anonymous English hooligan, answering charges of violence, criminal damage and riot, quoted in the *Independent*, 23 December 1988.

Now that we don't have a war, what's wrong with a good punch-up? We are a nation of yobs. Without that characteristic, how did we colonise the world? I don't agree with broken glass and knives. But what an English guy does is fight with his fists; a good clean fight. With so many milksops, left-wing liberals and wetties around, I just rejoice that there are people who keep up our historic spirit.

The Dowager Marchioness of Reading (1919–), on English fans who rioted during the 1998 World Cup Finals in France, quoted in David Pickering, *Cassell's Sports Quotations*, 2000.

Is this what Baden-Powell meant by the viciousness of being 'merely onlookers', or would he have approved?

As we embark on the third millennium even the fan may be obsolescent, along with the game as we know it:

Do you remember when it cost seven shillings and sixpence on the terraces at Higbbury to keep Ian Ure in shorts? Happy days. ... You could watch Brady, Stapleton and O'Leary in the reserves for sixpence. It probably bought them no more than a bottle of pop. Now footballers marry into pop and that is what the Premiership has gone. Pop, bust, bubble exploded. ... The blatant black-and-white – and red – bottom line of a £34.5 million pre-tax loss last season is a stark reminder that football is a poorly run, short-term, wham-bam enterprise that its players and their exploitive agents mistake for a bottomless pit. ...

And it's all fine. Fine while the broadcasting rights run to such multiple digits that the *average* Premiership player is on £400,000 a year. But heaven help the sport if the media whim switches to golf or a greater emphasis on European football, leaving the bulk of the domestic product to perish.

And fans, thank you for being television extras, but your money is in the chicken-feed category compared to the television deals. Expect more noon kick-offs, Sunday games and the summary edicts of Sky. You are now, officially, peripheral. ...

What happened to the era when Birmingham City bought Trevor Francis from his mum for the price of a new washing machine? Domestic football, the beautiful game, is on a collision course with an ugly ending if it is not very, very careful.

Sue Mott, in the *Daily Telegraph*, 12 April 2001.

Whither English football? Some are philosophical ...

Football's football; if it weren't the case it wouldn't be the game it was.

Garth Crooks (1958–), Tottemham Hotspur footballer, quoted in David Pickering, *Cassell's Sports Quotations*, 2000.

Football today would certainly not be the same if it had not existed.

Elton Welsby, ITV sports commentator, quoted in David Pickering, *Cassell's Sports Quotations*, 2000.

I don't know. Football? Bloody hell!

Sir Alex Ferguson, manager of Manchester United, on their last-minute-of-injury-time victory (after being 1–0 down at 89 minutes) against Bayern Munich in the 1999 European Cup Final; quoted in the *Independent*, 31 December 1999.

Others are content to be merely quotable:

They think it's all over – it is now!

Kenneth Wolstenholme, BBC TV commentator, as fans ran on to the Wembley pitch moments before England's fourth goal in the 4–2 win over West Germany in the last seconds of Extra Time in the 1966 World Cup Final.

FOREIGNERS

They do not believe that there are any other people than themselves, or any other world than England: and whenever they see some handsome foreigner, they say 'He looks like an Englishman' and 'What a pity he is not English'.

Andrea Trevisano (d.1534), Venetian Ambassador in London, *Relation of the Island of England*, 1497.

A Frenchman must always be talking, whether he knows anything of the matter or not; an Englishman is content to say nothing, when he has nothing to say.

Samuel Johnson (1709–84), in James Boswell's *Life of Samuel Johnson,* 1791, Vol. IV.

In 1748 Hogarth took a short holiday in France. By all accounts, he was a complete pain in the neck, carping non-stop about the foul food, the pathetic natives and the buildings, which he saw fit to describe as 'all gilt and beshit'. In Calais, on his way home, he paused to sketch the ancient gateway which had been built by the English. As he drew, an official hand descended and he was marched off to the Governor's residence, where he was accused of being an English spy. After exchanges that verged on the farcical he was packed off back to England.

Oh, the indignity of it! Determined on revenge, he settled down and painted a strapping great picture – quickly turned into a print – that not only memorialized his version of the affair but became an enduring icon of English patriotic xenophobia. For better or for worse, he provided the English with art that pandered to their steadfast distaste for 'foreign-neers' and to their conviction that they were the elect, or something like it. As a founding member of the Sublime Society of Beefsteaks, he had no trouble coming up with a logo for these sentiments. Roast Beef, it was obvious, was the food of real men, large men, prosperous men, free men, men who spoke their minds – in short, Protestant Englishmen. By way of obvious contrast, the French in his picture were effeminate, impoverished, servile, affected – in short, credulous Papists condemned to eat frogs and other abominations. Hogarth never stopped protesting that his comic pictures were not caricatures, but it did him no good; the rich stew of gastronomic chauvinism cooked up in *The Calais Gate* was to become a staple of the caricature tradition for the next hundred years.

The inclusion of a smirking self-portrait was important; it was Hogarth's way of proclaiming that he was an 'English' artist whose work embodied and articulated 'English' values.

Haley & Steele (Boston, USA), online gallery page at www.haleysteele.com, on *The Calais Gate, or O The Roast Beef of Old England,* 1748, by William Hogarth (1697–1764).

I do not dislike the French from the vulgar antipathy between neighbouring nations, but for their insolent and unfounded airs of superiority.

Horace Walpole (1717–97), Letter to Hannah More, 14 October 1787.

You must consider every man your enemy who speaks ill of your king: and ... you must hate the Frenchman as you hate the devil.

Horatio, Lord Nelson (1758–1805), in Robert Southey, *Life of Nelson*, 1813.

We cannot bring ourselves to believe it possible that a foreigner should in any respect be wiser than ourselves. If any such point out to us our follies, we at once claim those follies as the special evidences of our wisdom.

Anthony Trollope (1815–82), *Orley Farm*, 1862.

Stereotyping can extend into name-calling, which in turn leads to further stereotyping as George Orwell observes:

All peoples who have reached the point of becoming nations tend to despise for-eigners, but there is not much doubt that the English-speaking races are the worst offenders. One can see this from the fact that as soon as they become fully aware of any foreign race, they invent an insulting nickname for it. Wop, Dago, Froggy, Squarehead, Kike, Sheeny, Nigger, Wog, Chink, Greaser, Yellowbelly – these are merely a selection. Any time before 1870 the list would have been shorter because the map of the world was different from what it is now, and there were only three or four foreign races that had fully entered into the English consciousness. But towards these, and especially towards France, the nearest and best-hated nation, the English attitude of patronage was so intolerable that English 'arrogance' and 'xenophobia' are still a legend. And of course they are not a completely untrue legend even now. Till very recently nearly all English children were brought up to despise the southern European races, and history as taught in schools was mainly a list of battles won by England. But one has got to read, say, the *Quarterly Review* of the thirties to know what boasting really is. Those were the days when the English built up their legend of themselves as 'sturdy islanders' and 'stubborn hearts of oak' and when it was accepted as a kind of scientific fact that one Englishman was the equal of three foreigners. All through nineteenth-century novels and comic papers there runs the traditional figure of the 'Froggy' – a small ridiculous man with a tiny beard and a pointed top-hat, always jabbering and ges-ticulating, vain, frivolous and fond of boasting of his martial exploits, but gener-ally taking to flight when real danger appears. Over against him was John Bull, the 'sturdy English yeoman', or (a more public-school version) the 'strong, silent Englishman' of Charles Kingsley, Tom Hughes and others.

Thackeray, for instance, has this outlook very strongly, though there are moments when he sees through it and laughs at it. The one historical fact that is firmly fixed in his mind is that the English won the battle of Waterloo. One never reads far in his books without coming upon some reference to it. The English, as he sees it, are invincible because of their tremendous physical strength, due mainly to living on beef. Like most Englishmen of his time, he has the curious illusion that the English are larger than other people (Thackeray, as it happened, *was* larger than most people), and therefore he is capable of writing passages like this:

> I say to you that you are better than a Frenchman. I would lay even money that you who are reading this are more than five feet seven in height, and weigh eleven stone; while a Frenchman is five feet four and does not weigh nine. The Frenchman has after his soup a dish of vegetables, where you have one of meat. You are a different and superior animal – a French-beating animal (the history of hundreds of years has shown you to be so), etc. etc.

George Orwell (1903–50), 'Charles Dickens', 1939.

Abroad is bloody.

George VI (1895–1952), in W.H. Auden, *A Certain World*, 1970.

Don't let's be beastly to the Germans,
When our Victory is ultimately won.

Noël Coward (1899–1973), 'Don't Let's be Beastly to the Germans', 1943.

There's something Vichy about the French.

Ivor Novello (1893–1951), in Edward Marsh, *Ambrosia and Small Beer*, 1964.

How appallingly thorough these Germans always managed to be, how emphatic! In sex no less than war – in scholarship, in science. Diving deeper than anyone else and coming up muddier.

Aldous Huxley (1894–1964), *Time Must Have a Stop*, 1944.

Frogs ... are slightly better than Huns or Wops, but abroad is unutterably bloody and foreigners are fiends.

Nancy Mitford (1904–73), *The Pursuit of Love*, 1945.

The arrival of millions of GIs during the Second World War prompted this piece of advice to their English hosts:

In fairness to our guests, we should remember these few but fundamental facts:

1. That they are foreigners. Only a small percentage have any British forbears.
2. That the similarity between our languages is misleading. Try out the word 'homely' on an American, and you will see what I mean.
3. That they are all young in spirit as well as in body, and that the mistakes that they make are likely to spring from too quick enthusiasm and too little background.
4. That though we may be spiritually far more civilized, materially they have the advantage. They know the value of comfort, we don't.
5. That they are no more superior to us than we are to them. ...
6. That like all children they are very sensitive. They mistake our British reticence and reserve for the cold shoulder and positive dislike. They come from a land

where everybody knows everybody, and everybody entertains everybody at sight. The contrast makes us seem unfriendly.

S.P.B. Mais, *Bristol Evening Post*, 29 February 1944.

The points i wish to make about the world are contained in the molesworth newsletter.
(a) the russians are roters.
(b) americans are swankpots.
(c) the french are slack.
(d) the germans are unspeakable.
(e) the rest are as bad if not worse than the above.
(f) the british are brave super and noble cheers cheers cheers.

Geoffrey Willans (1921–58) and Ronald Searle (1920–), *Down With Skool!*, 1953.

The meal was of course filthy. It began with glazed seafood and continued with ridiculously tough veal or something, the whole washed down with vile wine. Spanish food and drink were never up to much in my experience, but you used to be able to depend on simplicities like tomatoes, onions, olives, oranges and the local red. Not now. The bread has gone too. The only things that are always all right are potatoes, tinned fruit, ice cream and sherry. And Coca Cola, I dare say.

Pondering on this, I thought for a moment I had discovered a straightforward inverse correlation between nations and their food-and-drink. Spanish, like English, nice people, nasty food; French, nasty people, nice food. Oh yes, and Greeks, nice people, terrifying food. But then, Italians, nice people, nice food. Danes too. Surely there must be … Got it: Germans, nasty people, nasty food (drink better, but beer overrated, wine no good with food, schnappses often delicious but not enough on their own). Also Belgians – Walloons anyway. So no little article there.

Kingsley Amis (1922–95), 'Amis Abroad', in *The Spectator*, 23 November 1963.

And crossing the Channel, one cannot say much
For the French or the Spanish, the Danish or Dutch –
The Germans are German, the Russians are Red,
And the Greeks and Italians eat garlic in bed.

Michael Flanders (1922–1975), 'A Song of Patriotic Prejudice',
from *At the Drop of Another Hat*, performed with Donald Swann, 1964.

G

GARDENING

God Almighty first planted a garden. And indeed it is the purest of human pleasures. It is the greatest refreshment to the spirits of man; without which buildings and palaces are but gross handyworks: and a man shall ever see that when ages grow to civility and elegancy, men come to build stately sooner than to garden finely; as if gardening were the greater perfection.

Francis Bacon (1561–1626), *Essays*, 'Of Gardens'.

When England was at war with the Dutch, their national flower came in for some odium:

There is lately a *Flower* (shal I call it so? in courtesie I will tearme it so, though it deserve not the appellation) a *Toolip*, which hath engrafted the love and affection of most people unto it; and what is this *Toolip*? a well-complexion'd stink, an ill favour wrapt up in pleasant colours.

Thomas Fuller (1606–61), *Antheologia, or The Speech of Flowers: Partly Moral, Partly Misticall*, 1660.

> What wond'rous Life in this I lead!
> Ripe Apples drop about my head;
> The Luscious Clusters of the Vine
> Upon my Mouth do crush their Wine;
> The Nectaren, and curious Peach,
> Into my hands themselves do reach;
> Stumbling on melons, as I pass,
> Insnar'd with Flow'rs, I fall on Grass.
>
> Mean while the Mind, from pleasure less,
> Withdraws into its happiness:
> The Mind, that Ocean where each kind
> Does straight its own resemblance find;
> Yet it creates, transcending these,
> Far other Worlds, and other Seas;
> Annihilating all that's made
> To a green Thought in a green Shade.

Andrew Marvell (1621–78), from *The Garden*, 1681.

The taste of the English in the cultivation of land, and in what is called landscape-gardening, is unrivalled. They have studied nature intently, and discover an exquisite sense of her beautiful forms and harmonising combinations.

Those charms, which in other countries she lavishes in wild solitudes, are here assembled rounds the haunts of domestic life. They seem to have caught her coy and furtive graces, and spread them, like witchery, about their rural abodes ... all these are managed with a delicate tact, a pervading yet quiet assiduity, like the magic touchings with which a painter finishes up a favourite picture.

Washington Irving (1753–1859), *The Sketch Book*, 'Rural Life in England', 1820.

EAR-WIG. – This is a most pernicious insect, which feeds on flowers and on fruit, and which, if it congregated like the ant, would actually destroy every thing of this sort. Its favourite flowers are those of the carnation kind. To protect very curious plants against them, the florists put their stages on legs, and surround each leg with a circle of water contained in a dish which is so constructed as to admit the leg through the middle of it, seeing that the ear-wig is no swimmer.

Others make little things of paper like extinguishers, and put them on the tops of the sticks to which the carnation-stalks are tied. The ear-wigs commit their depredations in the night, and they find these extinguishers most delightful retreats from the angry eye of man and from the burning rays of the sun. Take off the extinguishers, however, in the morning, give them a rap over a basin of water, and the enjoyments of the ear-wigs are put an end to at once. They are very nasty things in fruit of the stone kind, and particularly the apricot. They make a way in the foot-stalk of the fruit, get to the stone and live there day and night: so that, when you open a fine apricot, you frequently find its fine juice half-poisoned by three or four of these nasty insects. As soon, therefore, as the wall-fruit begins to change its colour, the tree should be well furnished with extinguishers made of cartridge-paper, and able to resist a shower. By great attention in this way you destroy them all before the fruit be ripe enough for them to enter. But one great protection against all these creeping things is to stir the ground very frequently along the foot of the wall. That is their great place of resort; and frequent stirring and making the ground very fine, disturbs the peace of their numerous families, gives them trouble, makes them uneasy, and finally harasses them to death.

William Cobbett (1762–1835), *The English Gardener*, 1829.

Charles Dickens gives an early description of the popularity of gardens in what were then the outer London suburbs:

If the regular City man, who leaves Lloyd's at five O'Clock, and drives home to Hackney, Clapton, Stamford Hill, or elsewhere, can be said to have any daily recreation beyond his dinner, it is his garden. He never does anything to it with his own hands, but he takes great pride in it, notwithstanding; and if you are desirous of paying your addresses to the youngest daughter, be sure to be in raptures with every flower and shrub that it contains. ... He always takes a walk round it before he starts for town in the morning, and is particularly anxious that the fish-pond should be kept specially neat. If you call on him on Sunday in summer time, about an hour before dinner, you will find him sitting in an armchair on the lawn behind the house, with a straw hat on, reading a Sunday paper. ... Beyond these occasions, his delight in his garden appears to arise more from the consciousness of possession than actual enjoyment of it. ... [He] descants at considerable length upon its beauty, and the cost of maintaining it. This is to impress you – who are a young friend of the family – with a due sense of the excellence of the garden and the wealth of its owner; and when he has exhausted the subject, he goes to sleep.

There is another and a very different class of men whose recreation is their garden. An individual of this class resides some short distance from town – say in the Hampstead Road, or the Kilburn Road, or any other road where the houses are small and neat, and have little slips of back-garden. ...

In fine weather the old gentleman is almost constantly in the garden; and, when it is too wet to go into it, he will look out of the window at it by the hour together. He has always something to do there, and you will see him digging, and sweeping, and cutting, and planting, with manifest delight. In spring time there is no end to the sowing of seeds, and sticking little bits of wood over them, with labels, which look like epitaphs to their memory; and in the evening, when the sun has gone down, the perseverance with which he lugs a great watering-pot about is perfectly astonishing. ... The old lady is very fond of flowers, as the hyacinth-glasses in the parlour window, and geranium-pots in the little front court, testify. She takes great pride in the garden too; and when one of the four fruit-trees produces a rather larger gooseberry than usual, it is carefully preserved under a wine-glass on the sideboard, for the edification of visitors, who are duly informed that Mr So-and-so planted the tree which produced it with his own hands. On a summer's evening, when the large watering-pot has been filled and emptied some fourteen times, and the old couple have quite exhausted themselves by trotting about, you will see them sitting happily together in the little summer-house, enjoying the calm and peace of the twilight, and watching the shadows as they fall upon the garden, and, gradually growing thicker and more sombre, obscure the tints of their gayest flowers – no bad emblem of the years that have silently rolled over their heads, deadening in their course the brightest hues of early hopes and feelings which have long since faded away. These are their only recreations, and they require no more. They have within themselves the materials of comfort and content; and the only anxiety of each is to die before the other.

Charles Dickens (1812–70), 'London Recreations' in *Sketches by Boz*, 1839.

And now to sum up as to a garden. Large or small, it should look both lively and rich. It should be well fenced from the outside world. It should by no means imitate either the wilfulness or the wildness of Nature, but should look like a thing never to be seen except near a house. It should, in fact, look like a part of the house.

William Morris (1834–96), *Hopes and Fears for Art*, 1882.

A garden is a lovesome thing, God wot!
   Rose plot,
   Fringed pool,
Fern'd grot –
   The veriest school
   Of peace; and yet the fool
Contends that God is not –
Not God! in gardens! when the eve is cool?
   Nay, but I have a sign;
   'Tis very sure God walks in mine.

Thomas Edward Brown (1830–97), 'My Garden', 1893.

Gertrude Jekyll was the pioneer of the informal, natural look that has made the English garden the envy of the world:

I hold that the best purpose of a garden is to give delight and to give refreshment of mind, to soothe, to refine, and to lift-up the heart in a spirit of praise and thankfulness. It is certain that those who practise gardening in the best ways find it to be so. ...

And a garden is a grand teacher. It teaches patience and careful watchfulness; it teaches industry and thrift; above all, it teaches entire trust. 'Paul planteth and

Apollos watereth, but God giveth the increase.' The good gardener knows with absolute certainty that if he does his part, if he gives the labour, the love, and every aid that his knowledge of his craft, experience of the conditions of his place, and exercise of his personal wit can work together to suggest, that so surely as he does this diligently and faithfully, so surely will God give the increase. Then with the honestly-earned success comes the consciousness of encouragement to renewed effort, and, as it were, an echo of the gracious words, 'Well done, good and faithful servant.'

Gertrude Jekyll (1843–1932), Introduction to *Wood and Garden*, 1897.

The collector's dream is to have some illustrious plant to bear his name immortal through the gardens of future generations, long after he shall have become dust of their paths. Mere beauty will not do; for the plant may fail and fade in cultivation, and his name be no more known, except to the learned, as attached to a dead dry sliver on the sheets of a herbarium. To become vividly immortal in the Valhalla of gardeners, one must own a species as vigorous as it is glorious, a thing capable of becoming and remaining a household word among English enthusiasts.

Reginald Farrer (1880–1920), *The Rainbow Bridge*, 1921.

We weed the delphinium bed. A sedentary occupation which gives us the reward of finding one or two delphiniums sprouting among the crow's foot. It is very odd. I do not like weeding in any case. I have a cold coming on. I cannot get a job and am deeply in debt. I foresee no exit from our financial worries. Yet Vita and I are as happy as larks alone together. It is a spring day. Very odd.

Sir Harold Nicolson (1886–1968), Diary, 20 March 1932, *Diaries and Letters 1939–45*, 1967. 'Vita' is, of course, Vita Sackville-West, who established the wonderful garden at Sissinghurst in Kent.

Of course, a garden can also be a source of anguish and conflict, as P.G. Wodehouse's Lord Emsworth knew only too well:

'By the way, McAllister was speaking to me again last night about that gravel path through the yew alley. He seems very keen on it.'

'Glug!' said Lord Emsworth – which, as any philologist will tell you, is the sound which peers of the realm make when stricken to the soul while drinking coffee.

Concerning Glasgow, that great commercial and manufacturing city in the county of Lanarkshire in Scotland, much has been written. So lyrically does the *Encyclopaedia Britannica* deal with the place that it covers twenty-seven pages before it can tear itself away and go on to Glass, Glastonbury, Glatz, and Glauber. The only aspect of it, however, which immediately concerns the present historian is the fact that the citizens it breeds are apt to be grim, dour, persevering, tenacious men; men with red whiskers who know what they want and mean to get it. Such a one was Angus McAllister, head-gardener at Blandings Castle.

For years Angus McAllister had set before himself as his earthly goal the construction of a gravel path through the Castle's famous yew alley. For years he had been bringing the project to the notice of his employer, though in anyone less whiskered the latter's unconcealed loathing would have caused embarrassment. And now, it seemed, he was at it again.

'Gravel path!' Lord Emsworth stiffened through the whole length of his stringy body. Nature, he had always maintained, intended a yew alley to be carpeted with a mossy growth. And, whatever Nature felt about it, he personally was dashed if was going to have men with Clydeside accents and faces like dissipated potatoes coming along and mutilating that lovely expanse of green velvet. 'Gravel path, indeed! Why not asphalt? Why not a few hoardings with advertisements of liver pills and a filling-station? That's what the man would really like.'

Lord Emsworth felt bitter, and when he felt bitter he could be terribly sarcastic.

'Well, I think it is a good idea,' said his sister. 'One could walk there in wet weather then. Damp moss is ruinous to shoes.'

Lord Emsworth rose. He could bear no more of this. He left the table, the room and the house and, reaching the yew alley some minutes later, was revolted to find it infested by Angus McAllister in person. The head-gardener was standing gazing at the moss like a high priest of some ancient religion about to stick the gaff into the human sacrifice.

'Morning, McAllister,' said Lord Emsworth coldly.

'Good morrrrning, your lorrudsheep.'

There was a pause. Angus McAllister, extending a foot that looked like a violin-case, pressed it on the moss. The meaning of the gesture was plain. It expressed contempt, dislike, a generously anti-moss spirit: and Lord Emsworth, wincing, surveyed the man unpleasantly through his pince-nez. Though not often given to theological speculation, he was wondering why Providence, if obliged to make head-gardeners, had found it necessary to make them so Scotch. In the case of Angus McAllister, why, going a step farther, have made him a human being at all? All the ingredients of a first-class mule simply thrown away. He felt that he might have liked Angus McAllister if he had been a mule.

'I was speaking to her leddyship yesterday.'

'Oh?'

'About the gravel path I was speaking to her leddyship.'

'Oh?'

'Her leddyship likes the notion fine.'

'Indeed! Well …'

Lord Emsworth's face had turned a lively pink, and he was about to release the blistering words which were forming themselves in his mind when suddenly he caught the head-gardener's eye and paused. Angus McAllister was looking at him in a peculiar manner, and he knew what that look meant. Just one crack, his eye was saying – in Scotch, of course – just one crack out of you and I tender my resignation. And with a sickening shock it came home to Lord Emsworth how completely he was in this man's clutches.

He shuffled miserably. Yes, he was helpless. Except for that kink about gravel paths, Angus McAllister was a head-gardener in a thousand, and he needed him. He could not do without him. That, unfortunately, had been proved by experiment. Once before, at the time when they were grooming for the Agricultural

Show that pumpkin which had subsequently romped home so gallant a winner, he had dared to flout Angus McAllister. And Angus had resigned, and he had been forced to plead – yes, plead – with him to come back. An employer cannot hope to do this sort of thing and still rule with an iron hand. Filled with the coward rage that dares to burn but does not dare to blaze, Lord Emsworth coughed a cough which was undisguisedly a bronchial white flag.

'I'll – er – I'll think it over, McAllister.'

'Mphm.'

'I have to go to the village now. I will see you later.'

'Mphm.'

'Meanwhile, I will – er – think it over.'

'Mphm.'

P.G. Wodehouse (1881–1975), 'Lord Emsworth and the Girl Friend', in *Blandings Castle and Elsewhere*, 1935.

Just as there are Secret Gardens, so every Garden has its Shameful Secret:

'Well, that's all there is to see, we'll go back now …'

Your hostess is lying to you. She knows perfectly well, and so do you, that there is just one more bit to see and that she doesn't want you to see it – that dreary devastated area, the skeleton in every garden-swanker's cupboard, the Glamis-monster of her domain; in a word, *The Unpleasaunce*.

Every fair-sized garden has one (it is a Law of Nature) and one Unpleasaunce is much like another: they differ only in the number and variety of Depressing Things they harbour.

Similarly, every fair-sized garden-writer has a Speciality, and since all the other opportunities for displaying erudition (including Alpine Plants, Miletian Orchidaceæ, Never-flowering Shrubs, and Absolutely Poisonous Succulents) have been done to death by other writers, we shall treat you to a fair-sized treatise on the Speciality which we have been obliged to embrace, namely, *Things which Occur in the Unpleasaunce.*

You will be glad to know that our treatise, instead of being choked up with unpronounceable and wrongly derived Latin names, is all about things which, we hope, will be full of significance for the thousands of people who can hardly speak Latin at all but can recognize an Unpleasaunce all right when they see one.

Common or garden-writers' lack of modesty compels us to let you know that in the course of our Special Researches we have investigated hundreds of gardens, right to the bitter end. We are, quite frankly, the only world experts in Unpleasauntness.

THINGS WHICH OCCUR IN THE UNPLEASAUNCE
(Our Speciality)

(i)   *Utilities.*

At its best (which it never is) the Unpleasaunce is full of things someone-forgot-he-had-plenty-of-and-ordered-more-of; virgin pea-sticks, for instance, and barren seeding boxes, besides those little heaps of clinkers, slaked-lime, leaf-mould, pot-crocks, silver-sand, and soot – all the tedious cosmetics of The Garden Beautiful.

(ii) *Futilities.*

At its worst, the Unpleasaunce presents itself as the Mecca of the Unmentionables. In it will be found that small pit for throwing things into (caused by someone's desire to throw things into a small pit) which is always half-full of disembowelled fruit-tins, senile dish-clouts, condemned mouse-traps, bald scrubbing-brushes and stricken jampots, pickle-jars and stone-ginger bottles innumerable, all doubtless aspiring to eventual manuredom and meanwhile giving rise to clouds of up-and-down midges at dusk, and places in the sun for squadrons of ink-striped blue-bottle flies and iridescent green-bottle flies.

There is usually a busted sieve somewhere in the Unpleasaunce and a devastated enamel kettle, and a rusted boot (keeping a tongueless vigil) with a docken growing out of it; and, lying in the long grass, a heavy plank with plenty of woodlice underneath where the grass … is all flattened out and anæmic, and half a symbolical ladder of success (with practically no rungs).

(iii) *Flora.*

Things grow in the Unpleasaunce, of course: young grass out of an old doormat, voluntary vegetable marrows, parvenu pumpkins, and a riot of rogue rhubarb. And in every untrampled corner strong self-made borders of *Hurtica dioica*, the hardy perennial stinging-nettle.

(iv) *Fauna.*

No doubt there are rats, (but only at night when no one would have the nerve to investigate an Unpleasaunce); which probably accounts for the inevitable Abandoned Cat, which is always very pleased to see you – but not of course for the occasional Devastated Goat, which isn't.

There is often a wasps' nest in the Unpleasaunce. For offset, there is always a bonfire (which annoys the wasps) smouldering sourly alongside the heap of dejected grass-cuttings and adding vastly to the general Unpleasauntness.

(v) *Architecture.*

Here be also Erections. A rusty grindstone without a handle, and a scarred trestle for chopping and sawing things on, now almost hacked through, and a deserted hutch for rabbits or possibly guinea-pigs, with a rent in the hexagonal wire-netting through which doubtless the beasts escaped – it is pleasing to know that they didn't starve to death.

But the architectural feature of all Unpleasaunces is the mysterious little *Shed*, grey outside and black inside, which no one has the courage to explore on account of the peculiar and distressing smell which seems to be its only inhabitant.

We can offer no explanation of this Shed or of the remarkable substance (apparently damp blotting-paper dipped in tar) with which it, and the rabbit-hutch too, is habitually cowled.

W.C. Sellar (1898–1951) and R.J. Yeatman (1898–1968), *Garden Rubbish*, 1936.

Sir John Mortimer relates how for some Englishmen the garden can assume an importance that transcends mere human relations:

The war, which had removed most of the young barristers, had done wonders for my father's practice. He rose, most days, in Court, fixed witnesses with his clear blue, sightless eyes, and lured them into confessions of adultery, cruelty or wilful refusal to consummate their marriages. As soon as he could he caught the train back from London ... to the wonders of his garden. ...

As my father could see none of these splendours he got my mother to describe them to him and in the evenings he would dictate to her a log, a diary of the garden's activities which also contained glimpses, cursorily noted, of human endeavour. Turning the thick volumes, written out in my mother's clear art-school handwriting, I can find out exactly what went wrong with the peas in 1942 and how they coped with greenfly on the roses. It is harder to discover when I was married, had children, got divorced, or called to the bar, although most of the facts are there somewhere, stuck at the far end of the herbaceous border. 'A most miserable cold and wet May,' a typical entry reads. 'Laburnums are now at their best. Mrs Anthony Waterer and Lady Waterlow are the only roses in flower. All liquidambars appear to be dead, but remaining newly planted trees and shrubs are doing well. John left for Paris after taking his Real Property exam, which he failed.' ...

I cannot discover that I did much gardening in those days. Not long after I met my first wife there is an entry which reads, 'On Christmas Eve John and I amused ourselves by digging a hole and planting the Eucryphia in it', but I think I must have been waiting anxiously for a letter or a telephone call, and turned to the entertaining hole for relief. There was one duty my father and I always shared, whenever I was available, and that was drowning the earwigs.

The ceremony of the earwigs, which became, in my father's garden, a cross between Trooping the Colour and a public execution, had its origins in my most distant childhood. My father was fond of big, highly-coloured and feathery dahlias, large as side-plates or ladies' hats, and these blooms were a prey to ear-wigs. I have no idea where my father learnt to fight these pests in the way he did, or in the macabre imagination of what tweedy gardening expert the plan was born. It suffices to say that it was a scheme of devilish cunning. Stakes were planted in the ground near the dahlias and on the top of each stake was hung an inverted flowerpot lined with straw. The gorged earwig, having feasted on the dahlia, would climb into the flowerpot for a peaceful nap in the straw, from which it was rudely awakened by my father and myself on our evening rounds. We would empty the flowerpots into a bucket of water. On a good foray we might drown up to a hundred earwigs, which my father would pronounce, with relish, to be a 'moderately satisfactory bag'.

John Mortimer (1923–), *Clinging to the Wreckage*, 1982.

As we have seen, the earwig trap sprang from the imagination of William Cobbett.

Nature is the gardener's opponent. The gardener who pretends he is in love with her, has to destroy her climaxes of vegetation and make ... an alliance with her which she will be the first to break without warning, in the most treasonable way she can. She sneaks in, she inserts her weeds, her couch-grass, her ground elder, her plantain, her greenfly and her slugs behind his back. The bitch.

Geoffrey Grigson (1905–85), *Gardenage*, 1952.

In England every man *ought* to own a garden. It's meant to be that way, you feel it immediately.

Henry Miller (1891–1980), US novelist.

What is important to the British? Not what they would call frivolity, not the quality of life, of food and drink, of socialising. It's chasing foxes on horseback, of putting your hands in the mud, of having a plot of land. That's something I have never been able to sympathise with. The English like their little house, their little back garden, they like putting their hands in the mud. They like grit behind their nails, I don't know why. All the classes – that's the one thing that binds them together: gardening. There's nothing they love more than flowerbeds, a bit of black earth that has to be weeded. What about the beautiful green grass? Wonderful, calm green grass and all they want to do is create mud, more bloody mud. I hate it. You can see it in the way that the garden suburb is extending in every direction: trickling into the countryside proper, trickling into London. This whole world of *Country Living*, magazines like that. Rustic kitchens, the Prince of Wales, the lot. It's all about softening the edges between the two, there's no concept of proper design in a city, of proper urban living, of accepting the one alongside the other. This mollification which ends in nothing. Urban life is quite different to country life and they should be able to exist in parallel. What's happening means that very soon we won't have much of either. Essentially the English don't like urban life. London isn't really a city, it's a cosmopolitan agglomeration of many villages. Look at the London map: people living in their own little villages and they love them.

Tess Wickham, quoted in Jonathon Green, *Them: Voices from the Immigrant Community in Contemporary Britain*, 1990.

Gardening is their greatest art. It is immensely widely spread, the interest in gardening and flowers. It is the most living art in this country, I think, and has been for a long time.

Ernst Gombrich (1909–), Austrian-born art historian, 1995.

H

HEROES

See also 'A People Not Used to War'.

If Arthur, the archetype of the English Hero, ever existed, it was as a Romanised Celtic clan chief, keeping some sort of diminishing civil order going in a small area of (probably) the Southwest or (possibly) Wales or (somewhat implausibly) Scotland, after the Roman withdrawal from Britain. But never mind. Each age has reinvented Arthur, and retold the stories of his Round Table, in its own image: here we see him in his High Victorian period – as a muscular English Christian, newly graduated from Dr Arnold's Rugby School.

> And holy Dubric spread his hands and spake,
> 'Reign ye, and live and love, and make the world
> Other, and may thy Queen be one with thee,
> And all this Order of thy Table Round
> Fulfil the boundless purpose of their King!'
>
> So Dubric said; but when they left the shrine
> Great Lords from Rome before the portal stood,
> In scornful stillness gazing as they past;
> Then while they paced a city all on fire
> With sun and cloth of gold, the trumpets blew,
> And Arthur's knighthood sang before the King
>
> 'Blow trumpet, for the world is white with May;
> Blow trumpet, the long night hath roll'd away!
> Blow thro' the living world – "Let the King reign."
>
> 'Shall Rome or Heathen rule in Arthur's realm?
> Flash brand and lance, fall battleaxe upon helm,
> Fall battleaxe, and flash brand! Let the King reign.
>
> 'Strike for the King and live! his knights have heard
> That God hath told the King a secret word.
> Fall battleaxe, and flash brand! Let the King reign.
>
> 'Blow trumpet! he will lift us from the dust.
> Blow trumpet! live the strength and die the lust!
> Clang battleaxe, and clash brand! Let the King reign.
>
> 'Strike for the King and die! and if thou diest,
> The King is King, and ever wills the highest.
> Clang battleaxe, and clash brand! Let the King reign.
>
> 'Blow, for our Sun is mighty in his May!
> Blow, for our Sun is mightier day by day!
> Clang battleaxe, and clash brand! Let the King reign.

'The King will follow Christ, and we the King
In whom high God hath breathed a secret thing.
Fall battleaxe, and flash brand! Let the King reign.'

So sang the knighthood, moving to their hall.
There at the banquet those great Lords from Rome,
The slowly-fading mistress of the world,
Strode in, and claim'd their tribute as of yore.
But Arthur spake, 'Behold, for these have sworn
To wage my wars, and worship me their King;
The old order changeth, yielding place to new;
And we that fight for our fair father Christ,
Seeing that ye be grown too weak and old
To drive the heathen from your Roman wall,
No tribute will we pay:' so those great lords
Drew back in wrath, and Arthur strove with Rome.

And Arthur and his knighthood for a space
Were all one will, and thro' that strength the King
Drew in the petty princedoms under him,
Fought, and in twelve great battles overcame
The heathen hordes, and made a realm and reign'd.

Alfred, Lord Tennyson (1809–92), *Idylls of the King*, 'The Coming of Arthur', 1869.

Beowulf may not have been English as we understand the term, but his poem is. The story, like many English things, came over with the Danes, but it was the English who wrote it down and made it – and its monster-wrestling hero – theirs.

Famed was this Beowulf: far flew the boast of him,
son of Scyld, in the Scandian lands.
So becomes it a youth to quit him well
with his father's friends, by fee and gift,
that to aid him, aged, in after days,
come warriors willing, should war draw nigh,
liegemen loyal: by lauded deeds
shall an earl have honour in every clan.
Forth he fared at the fated moment,
sturdy Scyld to the shelter of God.
. . .
Then from the moorland, by misty crags,
with God's wrath laden, Grendel came.
The monster was minded of mankind now
sundry to seize in the stately house.
Under welkin he walked, till the wine-palace there,
gold-hall of men, he gladly discerned,
flashing with fretwork. Not first time, this,
that he the home of Hrothgar sought, –
yet ne'er in his life-day, late or early,

such hardy heroes, such hall-thanes, found!
To the house the warrior walked apace,
parted from peace; the portal opened,
though with forged bolts fast, when his fists had struck it,
and baleful he burst in his blatant rage,
the house's mouth. All hastily, then,
o'er fair-paved floor the fiend trod on,
ireful he strode; there streamed from his eyes
fearful flashes, like flame to see.
He spied in hall the hero-band,
kin and clansmen clustered asleep,
hardy liegemen. Then laughed his heart;
for the monster was minded, ere morn should dawn,
savage, to sever the soul of each,
life from body, since lusty banquet
waited his will! But Wyrd forbade him
to seize any more of men on earth
after that evening. Eagerly watched
Hygelac's kinsman his cursed foe,
how he would fare in fell attack.
Not that the monster was minded to pause!
Straightway he seized a sleeping warrior
for the first, and tore him fiercely asunder,
the bone-frame bit, drank blood in streams,
swallowed him piecemeal: swiftly thus
the lifeless corse was clear devoured,
e'en feet and hands. Then farther he hied;
for the hardy hero with hand he grasped,
felt for the foe with fiendish claw,
for the hero reclining, – who clutched it boldly,
prompt to answer, propped on his arm.
Soon then saw that shepherd-of-evils
that never he met in this middle-world,
in the ways of earth, another wight
with heavier hand-gripe; at heart he feared,
sorrowed in soul, – none the sooner escaped!
Fain would he flee, his fastness seek,
the den of devils: no doings now
such as oft he had done in days of old!
Then bethought him the hardy Hygelac-thane
of his boast at evening: up he bounded,
grasped firm his foe, whose fingers cracked.
The fiend made off, but the earl close followed.
The monster meant – if he might at all –
to fling himself free, and far away
fly to the fens, – knew his fingers' power

in the gripe of the grim one. Gruesome march
to Heorot this monster of harm had made!
...

Then the warrior was ware of that wolf-of-the-deep,
mere-wife monstrous. For mighty stroke
he swung his blade, and the blow withheld not.
Then sang on her head that seemly blade
its war-song wild. But the warrior found
the light-of-battle was loath to bite,
to harm the heart: its hard edge failed
the noble at need, yet had known of old
strife hand to hand, and had helmets cloven,
doomed men's fighting-gear. First time, this,
for the gleaming blade that its glory fell.
Firm still stood, nor failed in valour,
heedful of high deeds, Hygelac's kinsman;
flung away fretted sword, featly jewelled,
the angry earl; on earth it lay
steel-edged and stiff. His strength he trusted,
hand-gripe of might. So man shall do
whenever in war he weens to earn him
lasting fame, nor fears for his life!

Beowulf, possibly 8th century, tr. Francis B. Gummere, 1910.

We cannot have heroes to dine with us. There are none. And were those heroes to be had, we should not like them.

Anthony Trollope (1815–82), *The Eustace Diamonds,* 1873.

Between November 1911 and January 1912 two teams of men – one British, headed by a naval officer, Robert Falcon Scott, the other Norwegian, headed by Roald Amundsen – were engaged in the last stage of a protracted race to the South Pole. Using dogs and adapting themselves skilfully to the hostile environment, the Norwegian team reached the Pole on 15 December and returned safely. Scott, leader of an ill-prepared expedition which relied on strength-sapping man-hauling, reached the Pole on 17 January. Defeated, the five-man team faced a gruelling 800-mile trudge back to safety. By 21 March, eleven miles from the nearest depot of food and fuel, the three exhausted surviving members of the expedition – Scott, Dr Edward Wilson and Henry Bowers – pitched their tent and sat out a blizzard. At some point Scott seems to have made the decision that it was better to stay put and preserve the record of their struggle rather than die in their tracks. They survived for at least nine days while Scott, in Roland Huntford's phrase, 'prepared his exit from the stage' and addressed letters to posterity: 'We are setting a good example to our countrymen, if not by getting into a tight place, by facing it like men when we get there.' Despite its failure, the expedition, wrote Scott, 'has shown that Englishmen can endure hardships, help one another and meet death with as great a fortitude as ever in the past'. The tradition of heroic death which aggrandizes his own example is also invigorated by it: 'We are showing that Englishmen can still die with a bold spirit, fighting it out to the end. ... I think this makes an example for Englishmen of the future.'

On 12 November, in the collapsed tent, the bodies and their documents were found by a rescue party and the legend of Scott of the Antarctic began to take immediate effect. 'Of their suffering, hardship and devotion to one another,' wrote a member of the rescue team, 'the world will soon know the deeds that were done were equally as great as any committed on Battlefield and won the respect and honour of every true Britisher.'

Scott's headstrong incompetence had actually meant that, from an early stage, the expedition had been riddled by tension. Captain Oates – the 'very gallant Englishman' of legend – had earlier written that 'if Scott fails to get to the Pole he jolly well deserves it'. Although clad in the guise of scientific discovery, Scott's expedition contributed nothing to the knowledge of polar travel unless it was to emphasize 'the grotesque futility of man-hauling'. But with Scott, futility ... becomes an important component of the heroic. That Scott had turned the expedition into an affair of 'heroism for heroism's sake' only enhanced the posthumous glory that greeted news of his death when it reached England on 11 February the following year.

A memorial service 'for one of the most inefficient of polar expeditions, and one of the worst of polar explorers' was held at St Paul's, and Scott's failure took its place alongside Nelson's victory at Trafalgar as a triumphant expression of the British spirit. Scott's distorting, highly rhetorical version of events was taken up enthusiastically and unquestioningly by the nation as a whole. At the naval dockyard chapel in Devonport, the sermon emphasized 'the glory of self-sacrifice, the blessing of failure'. By now the glorious failure personified by Scott had become a British ideal: a vivid example of how 'to make a virtue of calamity and dress up incompetence as heroism'.

Geoff Dyer (1958–), *The Missing of the Somme*, 1994.

I am just going outside and may be some time.

Captain Lawrence Oates (1880–1912), last words, recorded in Scott's diary, 16–17 March 1912.

Pooh sat on the floor which had once been a wall, and gazed up at the ceiling which had once been another wall, with a front door in it which had once been a front door, and tried to give his mind to it.

'Could you fly up to the letter-box with Piglet on your back?' he asked.

'No,' said Piglet quickly. 'He couldn't.'

Owl explained about the Necessary Dorsal Muscles. He had explained this to Pooh and Christopher Robin once before, and had been waiting ever since for a chance to do it again, because it is a thing which you can easily explain twice before anybody knows what you are talking about.

'Because you see, Owl, if we could get Piglet into the letter-box, he might squeeze through the place where the letters come, and climb down the tree and run for help.'

Piglet said hurriedly that he had been getting bigger lately, and couldn't *possibly*, much as he would like to, and Owl said that he had had his letter-box made bigger lately in case he got bigger letters, so perhaps Piglet might, and Piglet said, 'But you said the necessary you-know-whats wouldn't,' and Owl said, 'No, they won't, so it's no good thinking about it,' and Piglet said, 'Then we'd better think of something else,' and began to at once.

But Pooh's mind had gone back to the day when he had saved Piglet from the flood, and everybody had admired him so much; and as that didn't often happen, he thought he would like it to happen again. And suddenly, just as it had come before, an idea came to him.

'Owl,' said Pooh, 'I have thought of something.'

'Astute and Helpful Bear,' said Owl.

Pooh looked proud at being called a stout and helpful bear, and said modestly that he just happened to think of it. You tied a piece of string to Piglet, and you flew up to the letter-box, with the other end in your beak, and you pushed it through the wire and brought it down to the floor, and you and Pooh pulled hard at this end, and Piglet went slowly up at the other end. And there you were.

'And there Piglet is,' said Owl. 'If the string doesn't break.'

'Supposing it does?' asked Piglet, really wanting to know.

'Then we try another piece of string.'

This was not very comforting to Piglet, because however many pieces of string they tried pulling up with, it would always be the same him coming down; but still, it did seem the only thing to do. So with one last look back in his mind at all the happy hours he had spent in the Forest *not* being pulled up to the ceiling by a piece of string, Piglet nodded bravely at Pooh and said that it was a Very Clever pup-pup-pup Clever pup-pup Plan.

. . .

Pooh had found Piglet, and they were walking back to the Hundred Acre Wood together.

'Piglet,' said Pooh a little shyly, after they had walked for some time without saying anything.

'Yes, Pooh?'

'Do you remember when I said that a Respectful Pooh Song might be written about You Know What? . . . I wondered which you would like best: for me to hum it now, or to wait till we find the others, and then hum it to all of you?'

Piglet thought for a little.

'I think what I'd like best, Pooh, is I'd like you to hum it to me now – and – and then to hum it to all of us. Because then Everybody would hear it, but I could say "Oh, yes, Pooh's told me," and pretend not to be listening.'

So Pooh hummed it to him, all the seven verses, and Piglet said nothing, but just stood and glowed. For never before had anyone sung ho for Piglet (PIGLET) ho all by himself. When it was over, he wanted to ask for one of the verses over again, but didn't quite like to. It was the verse beginning 'O gallant Piglet,' and it seemed to him a very thoughtful way of beginning a piece of poetry.

'Did I really do all that?' he said at last.

'Well,' said Pooh, 'in poetry – in a piece of poetry – well, you did it, Piglet, because the poetry says you did. And that's how people know.'

'Oh!' said Piglet. 'Because I – I thought I did blinch a little. Just at first. And it says, "Did he blinch no no." That's why.'

'You only blinched inside,' said Pooh, 'and that's the bravest way for a Very Small Animal not to blinch that there is.'

A.A. Milne (1882–1956), *The House at Pooh Corner*, 1928.

I

INTELLECTUALS

Brains! I don't believe in brains. You haven't any, I know, sir.

The Duke of Cambridge, commander in chief of the British Army, 1854–95.

Of all nations in the world the English are perhaps least a nation of pure philosophers.

Walter Bagehot (1826–77), *The English Constitution*, 1867.

One has often wondered whether upon the whole earth there is anything so unintelligent, so unapt to perceive how the world is really going, as an ordinary young Englishman of our upper class.

Matthew Arnold (1822–88), *Culture and Anarchy*, 1869.

The clever men at Oxford
Know all that there is to be knowed.
But they none of them know one half as much
As intelligent Mr Toad!

Kenneth Grahame (1859–1932), *The Wind in the Willows*, 1908.

The English think of an opinion as something which a decent person, if he has the misfortune to have one, does all he can to hide.

Margaret Halsey (1910–97), *With Malice Toward Some*, 1938.

The intelligent are to the intelligentsia what a gentleman is to a gent.

Stanley Baldwin (1867–1947), Prime Minister 1923–24, 1924–29, 1935–37; quoted in G.M. Young, *Stanley Baldwin*, 1952.

What the upper classes think about 'highbrows' can be judged from the Honours Lists. The upper classes feel titles to be important: yet almost never is any major honour bestowed on anyone describable as an intellectual. With very few exceptions, scientists do not get beyond baronetcies, or literary men beyond knighthoods. But the attitude of the man in the street is no better. He is not troubled by the reflection that England spends hundreds of millions every year on beer and the football pools while scientific research languishes for lack of funds; or that we can afford greyhound tracks innumerable but not even one National Theatre. Between the wars England tolerated newspapers, films and radio programmes of unheard-of silliness, and these produced further stupefaction in the public, blinding their eyes to vitally important problems. This silliness of the English press is partly artificial, since it arises from the fact that newspapers live off advertisements for consumption goods. During the war the papers have grown very much more intelligent without losing their public, and millions of people read papers which they would have rejected as impossibly 'highbrow' some years ago. There is, however, not only a low general level of taste, but a widespread unawareness that aesthetic considerations can possibly have any importance. Rehousing and town planning, for instance, are normally discussed without even a mention of beauty or ugliness. The English are great lovers of flowers, gardening and 'nature', but this is merely a part of their vague aspiration towards an agricultural life. In the main they see no objection to 'ribbon development' or to the filth and chaos of the industrial towns. They see nothing wrong in scattering the woods with paper bags and filling every pool and stream with tin cans and bicycle frames. And they are all too ready to listen to any journalist who tells them to trust their instincts and despise the 'highbrow'.

One result of this has been to increase the isolation of the British intelligentsia. English intellectuals, especially the younger ones, are markedly hostile to their own country. Exceptions can, of course, be found, but it is broadly true that anyone who would prefer T.S. Eliot to Alfred Noyes despises England, or thinks that he ought to do so. In 'enlightened' circles, to express pro-British sentiments needs considerable moral courage. On the other hand, during the past dozen years there has been a strong tendency to develop a violent nationalistic loyalty to some foreign country, usually Soviet Russia. This must probably have happened in any case, because capitalism in its later phases pushes the literary and even the scientific intellectual into a position where he has security without much responsibility. But the philistinism of the English public alienates the intelligentsia still further. The loss to society is very great. It means that the people whose vision is acutest – the people, for instance, who grasped that Hitler was dangerous ten years before this was discovered by our public men – are hardly able to make contact with the masses and grow less and less interested in English problems.

The English will never develop into a nation of philosophers. They will always prefer instinct to logic, and character to intelligence. But they must get rid of their downright contempt for 'cleverness'. They cannot afford it any longer.

George Orwell (1903–50), 'The English People', written 1944, published 1947.

To the man-in-the-street who, I'm sorry to say,
Is a keen observer of life,
The word Intellectual suggests straight away
A man who's untrue to his wife.

W.H. Auden (1907–73), 'Notes on Intellectuals', 1947.

In England it is bad manners to be clever, to assert something confidently. It may be your personal view that two and two make four, but you must not state it in a self-assured way, because this is a democratic country and others may be of a different opinion.

George Mikes (1912–87), *How to be an Alien*, 1947.

Of the general inadequacy of intellect in the conduct of life Britain is the most majestic exponent.

Freya Stark (1893–1993), *Perseus in the Wind*, 1948.

Too clever by half.

The soubriquet applied by the Conservative Party 'inner circle' to Iain MacLeod (1913–70), cited in 1965 as the reason for not choosing him as leader.

Only in Britain could it be thought a defect to be 'too clever by half'. The probability is that too many people are too stupid by three-quarters.

John Major (1943–), Prime Minister 1990–97, quoted in the *Observer*, 7 July 1991.

Always in England if you had the type of brain that was capable of understanding T.S. Eliot's poetry or Kant's logic, you could be sure of finding large numbers of people who would hate you violently.

D.J. Taylor, in the *Guardian*, 14 September 1989.

J

JEWS

To be a Jew in England does not seem a bad fate, but it will bring its challenges, as being one does everywhere. A strain of antisemitism has disfigured English writing since Chaucer. Orwell, writing in 1945, detected it in Wells, Huxley, Shaw, Eliot and Thackeray (and did not even bother with the notorious antisemites like Chesterton, Belloc, Buchan and Sapper). It clearly reflected the way people thought, but never approached the systematic paranoia of central Europe (in 1909 when the notably philosemite Edward VII visited the Kaiser the conversation on world politics could not proceed till cousin Wilhelm had delivered a lengthy diatribe against the Jews). Still, it is unattractive enough.

Open the most innocuous-seeming book anywhere and the words leap from the page. In *The Fifth Form at St Dominic's*, published in 1881, we have to wait no longer than the second page before Bullinger of the Fifth calls a small boy an avaricious young Jew for whistling at the terms of a £50 scholarship. 'A Jewish boy at a public school,' noted Orwell, 'almost invariably had a bad time.'

He was looking back to the pre-Hitler world, but things were no better for English writer Frederic Raphael, at Charterhouse in the 1940s, when the preacher of an antisemitic sermon in the school chapel apologised to him later, explaining that he would never have made such remarks if he had known a Jew were present. (That shows, *inter alia*, just how numerous Jews were at Charterhouse then.) The incident was translated wellnigh unadorned to Raphael's smash-hit TV serial *The Glittering Prizes*. So were things better after the last war?

As late as the fifties candidates for jobs at the Cambridge University Appointments Board were described as Jews with clammy handshakes; there was a fuss when it came out but nobody was sacked.

Among great English writers, Orwell noted, only Dickens could be said to be positively pro-Jewish (overlooking George Eliot and *Daniel Deronda*). Since the mid-thirties and the rise of Hitler, however, it has been thought uncivilised for any serious writer to commit antisemitic sentiments to paper. Besides, Jews like Frederic Raphael, Jonathan Miller and Bernard Levin have made an increasingly attractive contribution to English life.

Jonathan Miller, for example, explained in a hilarious sketch from *Beyond The Fringe* that he was not a Jew; only Jew*ish*. What this meant, perhaps, is that Jews become accepted in England the more English they become. Thus Julius Victor in John Buchan's *The Three Hostages*, though one of the richest men in the world, is also 'the whitest Jew since Saint Paul'. He has, in effect, become an Englishman.

In a more down-to-earth context, the good done to the Jewish image by a brilliant business like Marks and Spencer, pervading every household with its bounty, is incalculable. Paul Johnson has said that intellectual life cannot flourish in any country where the Jews are even slightly uneasy. With three Jews in the 1983 Thatcher cabinet (Lawson, Brittan and Joseph) it could be said that in modern England they are easy enough: time will tell.

Godfrey Smith (1926–), *The English Companion*, 1984.

THE JONESES

Keeping up with the Joneses was a full-time job with my mother and father. It was not until many years later when I lived alone that I realised how much cheaper it was to drag the Joneses down to my level.

Quentin Crisp (1908–99), *The Naked Civil Servant*, 1968.

THE KNOWLEDGE

When you hail a London Taxicab (as you should always *do in preference to ringing for an unlicensed minicab) you may be sure that your driver will know exactly where you want to go, having done The Knowledge.*

If your cabbie doesn't know the location of your destination it is, self-evidently, because there is something dodgy about it. Thanks to The Knowledge, it is never the cabbie's fault.

And remember: in England, you have not truly 'arrived' until a cabbie says, 'I had that [insert your name here] *in the back of my cab once.' Think of the semi-apocryphal story of the London cabbie who told a fare: 'I had that Bertrand Russell in the back of my cab once, so I says to him, I says: "You're that Bertrand Russell aren't you?" So of course he has to say, "Yes". So I says, "Well, you tell me: what's it all about, then?" And do you know? – he couldn't tell me!'*

Be nice to London cabbies, and tip them with liberality. They are unique and irreplaceable.

Now sing out when I call your names ... terrific! you all know your own names, my living shall not have been in vain.

What exactly is The Knowledge?

As laid down by the London Hackney Carriage Act of 1843 all The Knowledge means is that you commit to memory every street within a six-mile radius of Charing Cross Station. Every street and what's on every street; every hotel; every club; every hospital; every department store; every shop; government building; theatre; cinema; restaurant; park; art gallery; church; synagogue; mosque; etcetera, etcetera, etcetera. Every building or amenity in public use, you name it, you got to know it.

Now this is your bible. It is called The Blue Book. Probably why it's coloured pink. Don't ask me why pink is called blue – bit like life in a way. On page number one you will find a list which we call 'page' of routes which we call 'runs'. Run number one page number one is Manor House Station to Gibson Square. Manor House is the starting point, Gibson Square is the finishing point. Not that anybody's wanted to go from Manor House to Gibson Square but you have to know how to.

So far, piece of pudding, except for one little thing. There's not one page – there's twenty-six. Not one run on each page – there's eighteen. So that's four hundred and sixty eight runs altogether. Which means that the amount of 'macaroni' that you have to 'bone up in your head', Mr Weller, is a grand total of approximately fifteen thousand eight hundred and forty two streets and the few thousand buildings on those streets, by heart.

Now don't blame me. The Knowledge goes back three hundred and fifty years, slightly before my time. It was started by decree of The Lord Protector, one Oliver Cromwell.

Now if you think you can master The Knowledge sat in your own front parlour with your blue book in one hand and your girlfriend in the other (excepting your presence Miss Stacey) watching Liverpool win one nil in the last three seconds of *Match of The Day* – thank you, goodnight and God bless – because you can't. There are Knowledge schools that can guide you but the only way to learn The Knowledge is by climbing onto your bike and doing the sod – every single street of it. There is no other way. I'll tell you a little secret – seven out of the ten of you sitting here today will never make it.

Everybody happy?

Now just in case you are all having too good a time, one last thought. On page two of your forms you answered the following two questions which are deliberately in heavy black type. 11a – Have you ever been convicted of any offence or been bound over? 11b – Are you the subject of any outstanding charge or summons? All of you answered 'no'. All of you told the truth – because we checked, as we always continue to do so right through your career as a cabbie – if you ever have one, that is. So if your hobby is mugging old ladies or driving a vehicle with a gallon of Martinis inside you and a cherry on your head – go into politics, not cab driving. Because, one conviction, ever, and you're back in the bus queue – right?

Now The Knowledge sounds impossible. It isn't. Otherwise there'd be no such phenomenon as the London Cabbie. It is true that no taxi driver in no other city in no other country in the world has to know a fraction of what you have to. Not many brain surgeons either. But there we are. That's how we built an empire and, no doubt, how we knocked the bleeder down again. We live. We learn. What we, in our ignorance, call Knowledge.

Now take these back to the young lady at the appointments window. She will book your first appointment which means your first test – so it isn't called an appointment. Come to that it isn't called a test either. It's called an Appearance. Funny old world we live in. Now that first appearance will be in fifty-six days time. Your next one fifty-six days after that and so on.

Eventually, if you are still with us it will be every twenty-eight days, finally every fourteen. How long it takes you before you get your licence and your pretty green badge is up to you and, no doubt, God. If you are a genius it might take you a year. On the other hand it might take two or seven or ten. If it looks as if it's taking you longer than that I would pack it in and take up ballet dancing.

Any questions? In that case – thank you, and good luck.

Jack Rosenthal (1931–), *The Knowledge*, Euston Films/Thames Television, 1979.

L

LANGUAGE

As George Bernard Shaw observed, the word 'fish' could be spelled 'ghoti': 'gh' as in 'trough', 'o' as in 'women', 'ti' as in 'station'. As a remedy, he founded (and, in his will, left a substantial sum of money to) a Simplified Spelling Society. But its recommendations have never quite caught on. And no wonder – spelling 'fish' as 'ghoti' would be silly.

English is not intrinsically easier to learn than French or Russian, nor is it more lyrical, more beautiful, mellifluous or more eloquent than any other language. Such judgements are almost meaningless. Lyrical for whom? English is, moreover, highly idiomatic. How does one begin to explain phrases like 'put up with' and 'get on with it'? English has some impossible characteristics. The *th* is famously difficult for foreigners who find a sentence like 'What's this?' hard to pronounce. There are some very rare and difficult vowels: the vowel sound in *bird* and *nurse* occurs in virtually no other language. There are no fewer than thirteen spellings for *sh*: *shoe, sugar, issue, mansion, mission, nation, suspicion, ocean, conscious, chaperon, schist, fuchsia,* and *pshaw.* An old bit of doggerel for foreign students advises:

Beware of heard, *a dreadful word*
That looks like beard *and sounds like* bird,
And dead: *It's said like* bed, *not* bead –
For goodness' sake, don't call it deed!

... On the other hand, the English language has three characteristics that can be counted as assets in its world state. First of all, unlike all other European languages, the gender of every noun in modern English is determined by meaning, and does not require a masculine, feminine or neuter article. In French, by contrast, the moon is *la lune* (feminine) while the sun, for no obvious reason, is *le soleil* (masculine). Worse, in the Germanic languages, is the addition of the neuter gender. In German the moon is *der Mond* (masculine), the sun is *die Sonne* (feminine), while child, girl and woman, are *das Kind, das Mädchen* and *das Weib*, all neuter. As Mark Twain put it, 'In German, a young lady has no sex, but a turnip has.'

The second practical quality of English is that it has a grammar of great simplicity and flexibility. Nouns and adjectives have highly simplified word-endings. This flexibility extends to the parts of speech themselves. Nouns can become verbs and verbs nouns in a way that is impossible in other languages. We can *dog* someone's footsteps. We can *foot* it to the bus. We can *bus* children to school and then *school* them in English. ...

Above all, the great quality of English is its teeming vocabulary, 80 per cent of which is foreign-born. Precisely because its roots are so varied – Celtic, Germanic (German, Scandinavian and Dutch) and Romance (Latin, French and Spanish) – it has words in common with virtually every language in Europe: German, Yiddish, Dutch, Flemish, Danish, Swedish, French, Italian, Portuguese, and Spanish. In addition, almost any page of the *Oxford English Dictionary* or *Webster's Third* will turn up borrowings from Hebrew and Arabic, Hindi-Urdu, Bengali, Malay, Chinese, the languages of Java, Australia, Tahiti, Polynesia, West Africa and even from one of the aboriginal languages of Brazil. It is the enormous range and varied source of this vocabulary, as much as the sheer numbers and geographical spread of its speakers, that makes English a language of such unique vitality.
Robert McCrum, William Cran, Robert MacNeil, *The Story of English*, 1986.

This book is translated into English for the love of the English people, English people of England, and for the common man to understand.
Preface to the *Cursor Mundi*, a biblical poem of the early 14th century.

Latin can no one speak, I trow,
But those who it from school do know;
And some know French, but no Latin
Who're used to Court and dwell therein,
And some use Latin, though in part,
Who if known have not the art,
And some can understand English
That neither Latin know, nor French.

> But simple or learned, old or young,
> All understand the English tongue.
>
> William of Nassyngton, 1325.

He must have been a Man of a most wonderful comprehensive Nature, because, as it has been truly observed of him, he has taken into the compass of his great *Canterbury Tales* the various Manners and Humours (as we now call them) of the whole *English* nation, in his Age. . . . The Matter and Manner of their Tales, and of their Telling, are so suited to their different Educations, Humours, and Callings, that each of them would be improper in any other mouth. . . . 'Tis sufficient to say, according to the Proverb, that *here is God's plenty.*

John Dryden (1631–1700), *Fables Ancient and Modern*, 1700.

If you cannot understand my argument, and declare 'It's Greek to me', you are quoting Shakespeare; if you claim to be more sinned against than sinning, you are quoting Shakespeare; if you recall your salad days, you are quoting Shakespeare; if you act more in sorrow than in anger, if your wish is father to the thought, if your lost property has vanished into thin air, you are quoting Shakespeare; if you have ever refused to budge an inch or suffered from green-eyed jealousy, if you have played fast and loose, if you have been tongue-tied, a tower of strength, hood-winked or in a pickle, if you have knitted your brows, made a virtue of necessity, insisted on fair play, slept not one wink, stood on ceremony, danced attendance (on your lord and master), laughed yourself into stitches, had short shrift, cold comfort or too much of a good thing, if you have seen better days or lived in a fool's paradise – why, be that as it may, the more fool you, for it is a foregone conclusion that you are (as good luck would have it) quoting Shakespeare; if you think it is early days and clear out bag and baggage, if you think it is high time and that that is the long and short of it, if you believe that the game is up and that truth will out even if it involves your own flesh and blood, if you lie low till the crack of doom because you suspect foul play, if you have your teeth set on edge (at one fell swoop) without rhyme or reason, then – to give the devil his due – if the truth were known (for surely you have a tongue in your head) you are quoting Shakespeare; even if you bid me good riddance and send me packing, if you wish I was dead as a door-nail, if you think I am an eyesore, a laughing stock, the devil incarnate, a stony-hearted villain, bloody-minded or a blinking idiot, then – by Jove! O Lord! Tut, tut! for goodness' sake! what the dickens! but me no buts – it is all one to me, for you are quoting Shakespeare.

Bernard Levin (1928–), *Enthusiasms*, 1983.

I got into my bones the essential structure of the ordinary British sentence – which is a noble thing.

Winston Churchill (1874–1965), *My Early Life*, 1930.

Prime Minister to Director of Military Intelligence
19 March 1944:

Why must you write 'intensive' here? 'Intense' is the right word. You should read Fowler's *Modern English Usage* on the use of the two words.

Winston Churchill (1874–1965), *Closing the Ring*, 1952, Appendix C.

Ballad language is English at its starkest, showing life pared to the elemental; it is keen as the black wind or the pursuer's knife; nerves can still quiver as Pretty Polly wakes in cold moonlight and sees her lover digging her grave. Hers is a world of love threatened by blood-feud, ruthlessness, immoderate passions of the nut-brown maiden, handsome seducer, avenging husband, told with brutal economy. Voltaire wrote that the secret of being boring is to omit nothing. The wild battle of Flodden in 1513 was scraped down to an anonymous sentence:

Beside Branxton is a brook; breathless they lie
Gaping against the moon; their ghosts went away.

English developed from Teutonic language which eschewed shallow decoration, stripped experience naked, yielded forthright sensation, within a multitude of dialects imposed on a Celtic sub-strata, with Latin additions. Only among the Portuguese was there a common language when Alfred translated Boethius's *Consolation of Philosophy*, once called the last independent statement of Classicism. It suited a northern temperament, Christian but not mystical, neither wholly optimistic nor pessimistic, but resolute in an age of crisis and uncertainty. God seems not all-powerful, yet provides the hope necessary for survival. Alfred's vocabulary is significant in its terseness.

Nothing is wretched save what people so think.

Who can give laws to lovers? Love itself is a law self-sufficient.

He who would have full power must first strive for power over his own mind, and not be unduly subject to his vices, and he must put away from him undue cares, and cease to bewail his misery.

The emphasis on 'undue' is already recognisably English, and Alfred foreshadows one level of English prose, plain, strong, lucid. Langland had it four centuries later, and Malory, with his robust simplicity:

And thus they fought till it was past noon, and never would stint, till at last they lacked wind both, and then they stood wagging and scattering, panting, blowing, bleeding, that all that beheld them for the most part wept for pity. So when they had rested a while they yeded to battle again, tracying, racying, foyning as two boars.

'For the most part' is a realistic touch.

Preaching to Edward VI, Hugh Latimer maintained vigorous outspokenness: 'Peers of the realm must needs be, but the poorest ploughman is in Christ equal with the greatest prince there is.' He used English to nail down truths, not to blur, soothe or extenuate the gross. Shakespeare's prose rings like a hammer:

This peace is nothing but to rust iron, increase tailors, and breed ballad-mongers.

There's no more mercy in him than milk in a male tiger.

Walter Raleigh used a laconic, hard-edged style, observing that Death is 'he who puts into man all the wisdom of the world, without speaking a word'.

Plain English can outrage tender stomachs, encourage improvers, like musical cheap-jacks recording *Gotterdammerung* for mouth-organ. The Restoration producer Sir William D'Avenant amended Shakespeare's 'The devil damn thee black, thou cream-fac'd loon: where gott'st thou that goose-look?' to 'Now, friend, what means thy change of countenance?' He also incorporated Beatrice and Benedick into *Measure for Measure*.

It would have been dangerous to amend Dr Johnson; who could express the complex and the ephemeral with equal pith:

Like sour small beer, she could never have been a good thing, and even that bad thing is spoiled.

Tomorrow is an old deceiver, and his cheat never grows stale.

This language of common sense, energetic but imaginative, was often deployed by Wellington, who wrote no masterpiece but could improvise effective comment: 'A man may be born in a stable, but that does not make him a horse.' Dickens, even in private letters, peeled off such vivid phrases as 'all the chairs upside down as if they had turned over like birds and died with their legs in the air'.

Political English was traditionally neither whining, bland nor evasive, but delivered through what Boswell called the juiciness of the English mind. A fifteenth-century tirade assailed 'that sewer of treachery, sink of greed, charioteer of treason, coffer of vice, lie-maker, vilest of informers, most supreme slanderer, traitor to fatherland, Michael de la Pole, Earl of Suffolk'. A Scots pamphleteer mentioned that Charles I's bishops were 'bunchy knobs of papist flesh'. But few modern British politicians have quickened the language. Lloyd George once complained that Ramsay MacDonald used words as if they were sounds, not weapons. 'Ah, my friends,' MacDonald once mused, 'how easy it would be to listen to the milk of human kindness.' Lloyd George himself, introducing conscription in 1916, announced that 'Compulsion is simply organised voluntary effort', straining English to the limit. The socialist John Burns remarked that the Welshman's conscience was pure and unspotted because he never used it. Neville Chamberlain cannot have been using his ears when he came out with: 'It is the opinion of my committee that a further investigation should be undertaken, taking into consideration all those matters of which, in the opinion of the new committee, consideration should be taken.' John Major confused exhortation and logic: 'When your back's to the wall, it's time to turn around and fight.'

Officialdom flourishes on debased language, like dandelions in a neglected town. In 1995 the novelist Margaret Drabble unearthed from the Department of National Heritage: 'The Hereford and Worcester County Council, which has a long and well-established tradition of providing arts and cultural service through its static service points, has been investigating the feasibility of outsourcing through facilities management, that element of service.'

One frequent comment by Victorian school inspectors was that, though fluency was increasing, understanding of words was decreasing. Sensitivity to language preceded compulsory schooling. The poor could use racy or simple individualist speech. George Lovelace, a Tolpuddle Martyr, after being sentenced to transportation in 1834, wrote a poem ending:

God is our guide! No swords we draw,
We kindle not war's battle-fires.
By reason, union, justice, law,
We claim the birth-right of our sires:
We raise the watch-word, Liberty.
We will, we will, we will be free.

Edgell Rickword wrote in *The Spectator* in 1923:

As anyone who has heard both will remember, conversation in the ranks of the wartime Army was on a much higher level than that in the officers' messes, not because there were many literate men in the ranks, but for the opposite reason. Speech, with the illiterate, is their highest form of expression, and they put their best into it, till it rings like good money flung down. Those who live more remotely, the cultured, are apt to regard it as a necessary, but sometimes wearisome, system of exchange, for which leaden counters will suffice.

Language has its enemy within – jargon – which can easily become a political weapon. The Nazis called their murder squads 'Task Forces', Stalin's KGB was 'Certain Competent Organs', Heydrich's secret police were the 'Press and Information Service'. Allied prisoners-of-war and Asian conscripts, enslaved for the atrocious Siam–Burma railway, were performing what the Japanese termed 'Logistic Imperative', and the current Burmese military dictatorship of torture, murder, beatings, censorship entitles itself 'Infrastructure of the Modern State'.

Jargon soon shades into 'political correctness', the tyranny of mediocrities over each other, which revives the concept of heresy. Designed to enforce compassion, it invites ridicule. A Sixties British publisher condemned an author as 'highly prejudiced and emotional' for having called the Moors Murderers 'iniquitous'. A girl of four was removed in 1985 from loving foster-parents to the care of her criminal father, on Council assurance that he and his mate had been 'remotivated'. Within weeks he had slaughtered her. In 1988 D.J. Enright recalled a social worker reprimanding the BBC: 'We do not call it baby-battering, we call it non-accidental injury.'

Modern English has lately been embellished with 'prospects minimised' (dismissed), 'body count' (corpses), 'vertically challenged' (short), 'household companions' (pets), 'behaviour modification' (drugs), 'domestic executive' (housewife) and 'economically inactive' (unemployed). When 'immigrant' was denounced in the House of Commons in 1996, the Home Office obsequiously substituted 'A person from abroad who comes under immigration controls'. It all recalls French revolutionaries lopping steeples, for equality.

Once the Oxford University Press claimed to be the custodian of the English Language. Its 1995 American edition of the New Testament omitted 'darkness' (as a synonym for evil or ignorance) to avoid offending blacks; 'The right hand of God', to appease left-handers; and was reluctant to mention 'The Lord', an editor explaining that '"Lord God" doesn't cut it these days because we don't have Lords.'

Peter Vansittart, *In Memory of England*, 1998.

Living here for the past 25 years has made me a cautious person. It's to do with the language. English is a beautiful language but it is also a very clever, devious language. It's like the English common law, which exists only as precedent. Other than statute, which deals with regulations, it's not simply written down. Everything is open to interpretation, it all depends on nuance. Which can be fine in the right context, but it can be used very deviously and dangerously and very often I feel totally locked out, shut out, totally by virtue of the use of language. I can hear what's being said, I can even interpret and understand the subtleties, but I know that what is said is designed to a degree. This sounds paranoiac. I think this is the reason why England became so powerful. English language is so clever. Always manipulating, never committing, always open to interpretation, all of which adds up to a very clever way of ruling. I don't think I've ever completely got to grips with it. Even with my husband I can feel that what he's saying, and what is actually happening, is completely the result of something that is so ingrained, this linguistic manipulation that is so ingrained from schooldays onwards. I'm fairly streetwise, but when it comes to dealing with members of society who are influential you really come across a degree of manipulative use of language that I can't properly handle.

Tess Wickham, quoted in Jonathon Green, *Them: Voices from the Immigrant Community in Contemporary Britain*, 1990.

LIBERALITY

I'll sing to you a good old song,
Made by a good old pate,
Of a fine old English gentleman
Who had an old estate,
And kept up his old mansion
At a bountiful old rate,
With a good old porter to relieve
The old poor at his gate,
Like a fine old English gentleman,
All of the olden time.

His hall so old was hung around
With pikes and guns and bows,
And swords, and good old bucklers
That stood against old foes;
'Twas there his worship sat in state,
In doublet and trunk hose
And quaff'd his cup of good old sack,
To warm his good old nose,
Like a fine old English gentleman,
All of the olden time.

When winter's cold brought frost and snow,
He open'd house to all;

And though three score and ten his years,
He featly led the ball;
Nor was the houseless wanderer
E'er driven from his hall,
For while he feasted all the great,
He ne'er forgot the small,
Like a fine old English gentleman,
All of the olden time.

But Time, though sweet, is strong in flight,
And years roll swiftly by;
And Autumn's falling leaves proclaimed
The old man – he must die!
He laid him down right tranquilly,
Gave up his latest sigh;
And mournful stillness reign'd around,
And tears bedew'd each eye,
For this good old English gentleman,
All of the olden time.

'The Fine Old English Gentleman', author unknown, collected and arranged by Percy C. Buck, in *The Oxford Song Book*.

The English ... think that no greater honour can be conferred or received than to invite others to eat with them, or to be invited themselves; and they would sooner give five or six ducats to provide an entertainment for a person, than a groat to assist him in any distress.

Andrea Trevisano (d. 1534), Venetian Ambassador to London, *Relation of the Island of England*, 1497.

As soon as anyone is elected mayor he may ask the City for a gift of some thousands of pounds but not more than £10,000 and the less he asks for the greater is his honour. Moreover he must daily hold open table to which natives and strangers, men or women, may go without an invitation. And as the mayor understood that we, although unknown to him, desired to eat with him, he sent us an invitation by one of the servants of the City to come to lunch on October the 13th, whither we then betook ourselves. On arrival, the sword-bearer received us and led us through the house to a handsome hall where the gentlemen received us in a very friendly manner and the women greeted us with a kiss. Then they gave us water scented with musk and other costly things to wash our hands, and when we and our interpreter were seated at the table in our cloaks he called upon his son to say grace.

Immediately all kinds of delicious dishes were served with great ceremony. And there were two servers or carvers who removed one plate after another from the table to another covered table near by, and they did nothing else but serve and carve. They put the food in small pewter bowls, placing these before each person on plates, one course after another, all most perfectly and richly prepared and served with exquisite sauces and they surrounded us with a variety of other dishes to stimulate the appetite.

The drinks consisted of the best beer and all kinds of heavy and light wines to follow, as for instance, Greek, Spanish, Malmsey, Languedoc, French and German, for in England all kinds of wine can be had for comparatively little money, because of the low freightage by sea.

After two helpings of roasts, stews and other things, dessert was served, consisting only of sweetmeats, tarts and pastries, not to be compared with the entrées for delicacy. Finally he thanked us for the honour we did him in lunching with him and asked us to accept his hospitality. . . . Mr. Button thanked him in English on our behalf for he had spoken for us often while the meal lasted, as we understood nothing of what they said to us either in Latin, French or Spanish.

And this banquet continued until towards evening, when once again we were accompanied home.

Thomas Platter (1574–1628), *Des Jüngeren Englandfahrt im Jahre 1599*.

I have seen them contribute as many shillings as they could spare, towards the maintenance of the French prisoners they made in the present war: I have seen them sorry when the news came that Damiens had stabbed the King of France: and I have heard an universal shout of joy when their parliament voted a hundred thousand pounds to the Portuguese on hearing of the tremendous earthquake. . . . Is it possible to hate people of this make?

Giuseppe Baretti (1716–89), *A Journey through London, to Genoa through England, Portugal and Spain*, 1760.

Because your husband was killed in a concentration camp,
Because your brother was beaten until he died,
Because your friends have been taken away and tortured,
Because you have lost all faith, all hope, all desire,
Because there is nothing more in the whole wide world for you to lose,
I, full of compassion, send for your comfort
Two of my husband's vests and a pair of old tennis shoes.

Virginia Graham, a member of the Women's Voluntary Service in the Second World War, 'For This Relief', in *Consider the Years*.

LISTS

Some aspects of Englishness remain constant over the centuries, others are forever changing. . . . But we could all make lists to challenge that of George Orwell. Off the top of my head, mine would include 'I know my rights', village cricket and Elgar, Do-It-Yourself, punk, street fashion, irony, vigorous politics, brass bands, Shakespeare, Cumberland sausages, double-decker buses, Vaughan Williams, Donne and Dickens, twitching net curtains, breast-obsession, quizzes and crosswords, country churches, dry-stone walls, gardening, Christopher Wren and Monty Python, easy-going Church of England vicars, the Beatles, bad hotels and good beer, church bells, Constable and Piper, finding foreigners funny, David Hare and William Cobbett, drinking to excess, Women's Institutes, fish and chips, curry, Christmas Eve at King's College, Cambridge, indifference to food, civility and crude language, fell-running, ugly caravan sites on beautiful clifftops, crumpets, Bentleys and Reliant Robins, and so on. They may not all be uniquely English, but the point about them is that unlike the touchstones of Britishness, which tend to be primped, planned and pompous, if you take any three or four of these things together, they point at once to a culture as evocatively as the smell of a bonfire in the October dusk.

Jeremy Paxman (1950–), *The English*, 1998.

> There are jewels in the crown of England's Glory – England's Glory
> And every jewel shines a thousand ways . . .
>
> Frankie Howerd, Noel Coward, garden gnomes,
> Frankie Vaughan and Kenneth Horn and Sherlock Holmes,
> Monty, Biggles and Old King Cole
> An' the people on the dole,
> Oliver Twist and Long John Silver, Captain Cook and Nellie Dean,
> Enid Blyton, Gilbert Harding, Malcolm Sargent, Graham Greene –
> Graham Greene.
>
> *Oh the jewels in the crown of England's Glory*
> *Too numerous to mention but a few,*
> *And every one could tell a different story,*
> *And show old England's Glory something new.*
>
> Last bit of kipper and Jack the Ripper, an' Upton Park,
> Maxie Miller, Gracie, Cilla, Peculiar Clark,
> Winkles, Woodbines, Walnut Whips,
> Vera Lynn and Stafford Cripps,
> Lady Chatterley buff in the mill, Winston Churchill, Robin Hood,
> Beatrix Potter, Baden Powell,
> Each as bad as Yorkshire pud –
> Yorkshire pud!
>
> With Billy Bunter, Jane Austen, Ray Ellington, George Orwell,
> Billy Fury, Little Tich, Uncle Mac, Mr Pastry and all –
> Uncle Mac, Mr Pastry an' all!
>
> *All right England, Old England, Old England, England!*
> *Oh the jewels* . . . etc.
>
> Mortimer Wheeler, Christine Keeler, and the Board of Trade –
> England's Glory!
> Somerset Maugham, Top of the Form, the Boys Brigade,
> Henry Cooper, Wakey-wakey, England's labour,
> Spag Bol an' Spotted Dick, England's workers. . .
> England's Glory!

Ian Dury (1942–2000), 'England's Glory', in *New Boots and Panties*, 1977.

M

MODESTY

It is the custom, and a very bad one, for the English never to tell their own story.

Admiral Horatio Nelson (1758–1805), quoted in Clive Aslet, *Anyone for England?*, 1997.

Be modest. An Englishman will say 'I have a little house in the country'; when he invites you to stay with him you will discover that the little house is a place with three hundred bedrooms. If you are a world tennis-champion, say 'Yes, I don't play too badly.' If you have crossed the Atlantic alone in a small boat, say 'I do a little sailing.' If you have written books, say nothing at all. They will find out for themselves, in time, this regrettable but inoffensive weakness; they will laugh and say: 'Now I know all about you,' and they will be pleased with you.

André Maurois (1885–1967), *Three Letters on the English*, 1938.

Second by second the image of the missiles on the screen grew larger. They had swung round on to a direct homing course so that all that could be seen of them now was the warheads, head on.

'As a matter of interest,' said Trillian, 'what are we going to do?'

'Just keep cool,' said Zaphod.

'Is that all?' shouted Arthur.

'No, we're also going to ... er ... take evasive action!' said Zaphod with a sudden access of panic. 'Computer, what evasive action can we take?'

'Er, none I'm afraid, guys,' said the computer.

'... or something,' said Zaphod, '... er ...' he said.

'There seems to be something jamming my guidance systems,' explained the computer brightly. 'Impact minus forty-five seconds. Please call me Eddie if it will help you to relax.' ...

'Impact minus twenty seconds, guys...' said the computer.

'Then turn the bloody engines back on!' bawled Zaphod.

'Oh, sure thing, guys,' said the computer. With a subtle roar the engines cut back in, the ship smoothly flattened out of its dive and headed back towards the missiles again.

The computer started to sing.

'*When you walk through the storm* ...' it whined nasally, '*hold your head up high...*'

Zaphod screamed at it to shut up, but his voice was lost in the din of what they quite naturally assumed was approaching destruction.

'*And don't ... be afraid ... of the dark!*' Eddie wailed.

The ship, in flattening out, had in fact flattened out upside down and lying on the ceiling as they were it was now totally impossible for any of the crew to reach the guidance systems.

'*At the end of the storm* ...' crooned Eddie.

The two missiles loomed massively on the screens as they thundered towards the ship.

'*... is a golden sky ...*'

But by an extraordinarily lucky chance they had not yet fully corrected their flight paths to that of the erratically weaving ship, and they passed right under it.

'*And the sweet silver song of the lark* ... Revised impact time fifteen seconds fellas ... *Walk on through the wind* ...'

The missiles banked round in a screeching arc and plunged back into pursuit.

'This is it,' said Arthur watching them. 'We are now quite definitely going to die aren't we?'

'I wish you'd stop saying that,' shouted Ford.

'Well we are aren't we?'

'Yes.'

'*Walk on through the rain* ...' sang Eddie.

A thought struck Arthur. He struggled to his feet.

'Why doesn't anyone turn on this Improbability Drive thing?' he said. 'We could probably reach that.'

'What are you, crazy?' said Zaphod. 'Without proper programming anything could happen.'

'Does that matter at this stage?' shouted Arthur.

'*Though your dreams be tossed and blown* ...' sang Eddie.

Arthur scrambled up on to one of the excitingly chunky pieces of moulded contouring where the curve of the wall met the ceiling.

'*Walk on, walk on, with hope in your heart* ...'

'Does anyone know why Arthur can't turn on the Improbability Drive?' shouted Trillian.

'*And you'll never walk alone* ... Impact minus five seconds, it's been great knowing you guys, God bless ... *You'll ne ... ver ... walk ... alone!*'

'I said,' yelled Trillian, 'does anyone know ...'

The next thing that happened was a mind-mangling explosion of noise and light.

And the next thing that happened after that was that the Heart of Gold continued on its way perfectly normally with a rather fetchingly redesigned interior. ...

Relaxing in a wickerwork sun chair, Zaphod Beeblebrox said, 'What the hell happened?'

'Well I was just saying,' said Arthur lounging by a small fish pool, 'there's this Improbability Drive switch over here ...' he waved at where it had been. There was a potted plant there now.

'But where are we?' said Ford who was sitting on the spiral staircase, a nicely chilled Pan Galactic Gargle Blaster in his hand.

'Exactly where we were, I think ...' said Trillian, as all about them the mirrors suddenly showed them an image of the blighted landscape of Magrathea which still scooted along beneath them.

Zaphod leapt out of his seat.

'Then what's happened to the missiles?' he said.

A new and astounding image appeared in the mirrors.

'They would appear,' said Ford doubtfully, 'to have turned into a bowl of petunias and a very surprised looking whale ...'

'At an Improbability Factor,' cut in Eddie, who hadn't changed a bit, 'of eight million seven hundred and sixty-seven thousand one hundred and twenty-eight to one against.'

Zaphod stared at Arthur.

'Did you think of that, Earthman?' he demanded.

'Well,' said Arthur, 'all I did was …'

'That's very good thinking you know. Turn on the Improbability Drive for a second without first activating the proofing screens. Hey kid you just saved our lives, you know that?'

'Oh,' said Arthur, 'well, it was nothing really …'

'Was it?' said Zaphod. 'Oh well, forget it then. OK, computer, take us in to land.'

'But …'

'I said forget it.'

Douglas Adams (1952–2001), *The Hitch Hiker's Guide to the Galaxy*, 1979.

Perhaps the habit of self-effacement stemmed from a kind of arrogance: we believed we could afford it. Traditionally we never felt the need to trumpet our strengths because they seemed to us quite obvious. … Now we seem to take our self-deprecation at face value.

Clive Aslet (1957–), *Anyone for England?*, 1997.

N

NOSTALGIA

Nostalgia is the English Condition (let us not call it a disease). Some are born with it, others acquire it in later life. Sooner or later, it affects us all.

A very large anthology could be compiled on this theme alone; when Richard Ingrams was compiling his own personal English anthology some years ago, it occurred to him that it might well be called 'Going To The Dogs'. I have solved the problem of what to include and what not by quoting, in full, only one extract (although there is more, in a similar vein, to be found in the chapter entitled 'Dear Old, Bloody Old England'). Inspired by the closure of much of our railway network in the 1960s, for me it says, or touches on, all there is to tell. The touchstone of Nostalgia is its ability to move you to tears – of affection, of love, of regret, of yearning. This does the trick for me, every time. I have been unable to locate a printed version of this piece, so it is transcribed from a recording. I have tried to check all the place name spellings but I may have got some of them wrong. I have decided this does not matter, really.

> *Millersdale for Tideswell –*
> *Kirkby Muxloe –*
> *Mal Cop and Scholar Green –*

No more will I go to Blandford Forum and Mortehoe,
On the slow train from Midsomer Norton and Mumbelow;

No churns, no porter, no cat on a seat,
At Chorlton-cum-Hardy or Chester-le-Street –
We won't be meeting again
On the slow train.

I'll travel no more from Littleton Badsey to Openshaw,
At Long Stanton I'll stand well clear of the doors no more,
No whitewashed pebbles, no Up and no Down,
From Thornby Four Crosses to Dunstable Town;
I won't be going again
On the slow train.

On the main line and the goods siding,
The grass grows high,
At Dog Dyke, Tunby Woodside, and Troublehouse Halt:
The sleepers sleep
At Audlem and Ambergate.

No passenger waits on Chittering platform or Chesney Hey;
No-one departs, no-one arrives,
From Selby to Goole, from St Erth to St Ives:
They've all passed out of our lives
On the slow train –
On the slow train –

Cockermouth for Buttermere –

On the slow train –

Armley Moor – Arun –
Pie Hill and Summercotes –

On the slow train –

Windmill End.

Michael Flanders (1922–75), 'Slow Train', from *At the Drop of Another Hat*, performed with Donald Swann, 1964.

O

OTHER BITS OF BRITAIN

To the North . . .

The noblest prospect which a Scotsman ever sees, is the high road that leads him to England! . . .

Seeing Scotland, Madam, is only seeing a worse England. . . .

A Scotsman must be a very sturdy moralist who does not love Scotland better than truth. . . .

Much may be made of a Scotchman, if he be caught young. . . .

Their learning is like bread in a besieged town: every man gets a little, but no man gets a full meal.

Samuel Johnson (1709–84), remarks on various occasions.

I have been trying all my life to like Scotchmen, and am obliged to desist from the experiment in despair.

Charles Lamb (1775–1834), *Essays of Elia*, 1823.

That knuckle-end of England – that land of Calvin, oat-cakes, and sulphur.

Rev. Sydney Smith (1771–1845), in Lady Holland, *Memoir*, 1855.

You've forgotten the grandest moral attribute of a Scotsman, Maggie, that he'll do nothing which might damage his career. . . . There are few more impressive sights in the world than a Scotsman on the make.

J.M. Barrie (1860–1937), *What Every Woman Knows*, 1908.

It is never difficult to distinguish between a Scotsman with a grievance and a ray of sunshine.

P.G. Wodehouse (1881–1975), 'The Custody of the Pumpkin', *Blandings Castle and Elsewhere*, 1935.

And to the West . . .

It strikes us as rather a pity that a civilized language should have been allowed to mar the complete Cambrianism of the proce[e]dings.

The Times, reporting the National Eisteddfod, 1866.

We can trace almost all the disasters of English history to the influence of Wales. . . .

'The Welsh,' said the Doctor, 'are the only nation in the world that has produced no graphic or plastic art, no architecture, no drama. They just sing,' he said with disgust, 'sing and blow down wind instruments of plated silver.'

Evelyn Waugh (1903–66), *Decline and Fall*, 1928.

Eddy was a tremendously tolerant person, but he wouldn't put up with the Welsh. He always said, surely there's enough English to go round.

John Mortimer (1923–), *Two Stars for Comfort*, 1962.

And a little further West . . .

The Irish are a fair people; – they never speak well of one another.

Samuel Johnson (1709–84), in James Boswell's *Life of Samuel Johnson*, 1791.

Thus you have a starving population, an absentee aristocracy, and an alien Church, and in addition the weakest executive in the world. That is the Irish Question.

Benjamin Disraeli (1804–81), speech, House of Commons, 15 February 1844.

I never met anyone in Ireland who understood the Irish question, except one Englishman who had only been there a week.

Keith Fraser MP (1867–1935), speech, House of Commons, May 1919.

Gladstone … spent his declining years trying to guess the answer to the Irish Question; unfortunately, whenever he was getting warm, the Irish secretly changed the Question …

W.C. Sellar (1898–1951) and R.J. Yeatman (1898–1968), *1066 And All That*, 1930.

A great man after pig was Lord William Beresford, at that time Military Secretary to the Viceroy. And I remember him taking a toss, which would have killed any ordinary man, when riding after a pig at the Stud Farm at Saharunpur.

Here the paddocks were divided by stout post and rail fences with wooden gates. His pig instead of jumping the fence charged through the gate, smashing the bottom bar, lifting the gate off the latch, so that as Beresford's horse rose to jump it the gate swung open under him and landing on the top of it he came a heavy crumpler on the hard roadway.

But Beresford was an Irishman and no harm resulted.

Robert Baden-Powell (1857–1941), *Pig-Sticking*.

And in general …

The rottenest bits of this island of ours,
We've left in the hands of three unfriendly powers.
Examine the Irishman, Welshman or Scot –
You'll find he's a stinker, as likely as not.

The Scotsman is mean, as we're all well aware,
And bony, and blotchy, and covered with hair,
He eats salted porridge, he works all the day,
And he hasn't got Bishops to show him the way.

The Irishman, now, our contempt is beneath –
He sleeps in his boots and he lies in his teeth.
He blows up policemen, or so I have heard,
And blames it on Cromwell and William the Third.

The Welshman's dishonest, he cheats when he can,
And little and dark – more like monkey than man.
He works underground with a lamp in his hat,
And he sings far too loud, far too often, and flat.

Michael Flanders (1922–75), 'A Song of Patriotic Prejudice',
from *At the Drop of Another Hat*, performed with Donald Swann, 1964.

P

PATRIOTISM

Patriotism is the last refuge of a scoundrel.

Samuel Johnson (1709–84), in James Boswell's *Life of Samuel Johnson,* 1791.

Be England what she will,
With all her faults, she is my country still.

Charles Churchill (1731–64), *The Farewell,* 1764.

It is therefore our business carefully to cultivate in our minds, to rear to the most perfect vigour and maturity, every sort of generous and honest feeling that belongs to our nature. To bring the dispositions that are lovely in private life into the service and conduct of the commonwealth; so to be patriots, as not to forget we are gentlemen.

Edmund Burke (1729–97), *Thoughts on the Cause of the Present Discontents,* 1770.

If I were an American, as I am an Englishman, while a foreign troop was landed in my country, I never would lay down my arms, – never – never – never!

William Pitt (the Elder, 1708–78), speech, House of Lords, 18 November 1777.

You well know how soon one of these stupendous masses, now reposing on their shadows in perfect stillness, would upon any call of patriotism or necessity, assume the likeness of an animated thing, instinct with life and motion; how soon it would ruffle, as it were, its swelling plumage, how quickly it would put forth all its beauty and its bravery, collect its scattered elements of strength and waken its dormant thunder. ... Such is England herself; while apparently passive and motionless, she silently concentrates the power to be put forth on an adequate occasion.

George Canning (1770–1827), Prime Minister 1827, speech, Plymouth, on the men-o'-war lying at anchor in Plymouth Sound, 12 December 1823.

When you've shouted 'Rule Britannia', when you've sung 'God Save the Queen' – When you've finished killing Kruger with your mouth ...

Rudyard Kipling (1865–1936), 'The Absent-Minded Beggar', 1899.

What have I done for you,
    England, my England?
What is there I would not do,
    England, my own? ...
Ever the faith endures,
    England, my England: –
'Take and break us: we are yours,
    England, my own!'

W.E. Henley (1849–1903), 'Pro Rege Nostro', in *For England's Sake,* 1900.

'My country, right or wrong' is a thing that no patriot would think of saying, except in a desperate case. It is like saying 'My mother, drunk or sober'.

G.K. Chesterton (1874–1936), *The Defendant*, 1901.

Patriotism is a lively sense of collective responsibility. Nationalism is a silly cock crowing on its own dunghill.

Richard Aldington (1892–1962), *The Colonel's Daughter*, 1931.

'That this House will in no circumstances fight for its King and country'.

Anonymous motion passed by the Oxford Union, 9 February 1933.

The night before the Russo-German pact was announced I dreamed that the war had started. It was one of those dreams which, whatever Freudian inner meaning they may have, do sometimes reveal to you the real state of your feelings. It taught me two things, first, that I should be simply relieved when the long-dreaded war started, secondly, that I was patriotic at heart, would not sabotage or act against my own side, would support the war, would fight in it if possible. ...

What I knew in my dream that night was that the long drilling in patriotism which the middle classes go through had done its work, and that once England was in a serious jam it would be impossible for me to sabotage. But let no one mistake the meaning of this. Patriotism has nothing to do with conservatism. It is devotion to something that is changing but is felt to be mystically the same, like the devotion of the ex-White Bolshevik to Russia. To be loyal both to Chamberlain's England and to the England of tomorrow might seem an impossibility, if one did not know it to be an everyday phenomenon. Only revolution can save England, that has been obvious for years, but now the revolution has started, and it may proceed quite quickly if only we can keep Hitler out. Within two years, maybe a year, if only we can hang on, we shall see changes that will surprise the idiots who have no foresight. I dare say the London gutters will have to run with blood. All right, let them, if it is necessary. But when the red militias are billeted in the Ritz I shall still feel that the England I was taught to love so long ago and for such different reasons is somehow persisting.

I grew up in an atmosphere tinged with militarism, and afterwards I spent five boring years within the sound of bugles. To this day it gives me a faint feeling of sacrilege not to stand to attention during 'God save the King'. That is childish, of course, but I would sooner have had that kind of upbringing than be like the left-wing intellectuals who are so 'enlightened' that they cannot understand the most ordinary emotions. It is exactly the people whose hearts have *never* leapt at the sight of a Union Jack who will flinch from revolution when the moment comes. Let anyone compare the poem John Cornford wrote not long before he was killed ('Before the Storming of Huesca') with Sir Henry Newbolt's 'There's a breathless hush in the Close tonight'. Put aside the technical differences, which are merely a matter of period, and it will be seen that the emotional content of the two poems is almost exactly the same. The young Communist who died heroically in the International Brigade was public school to the core. He had changed his allegiance but not his emotions. What does that prove? Merely the possibility of building a Socialist on the bones of a Blimp, the power of one kind of loyalty to transmute itself into another, the spiritual need for patriotism and the military virtues, for which, however little the boiled rabbits of the Left may like them, no substitute has yet been found.

George Orwell (1903–50), 'My Country Right or Left', 1940.

The rule is: if we've done anything good, it's 'another triumph for Great Britain', and if we haven't it's 'England loses again'. ... In the good old days we didn't bother about nationalism; nationalism was on its way out. We'd got pretty well everything *we* wanted; we didn't go around saying how marvellous we were, everybody knew that, any more than we bothered to put our name on our stamps. I mean, there are only two kinds of stamps: English stamps, in sets, at the beginning of the album, and Foreign stamps, all mixed up at the back. ...

The English, the English, the English are best,
I wouldn't give tuppence for all of the rest! ...
The English are noble, the English are nice,
And worth any other at double the price. ...
The English are moral, the English are good,
And clever, and modest, and misunderstood. ...
The English, the English, the English are best,
So up with the English and down with the rest!

Michael Flanders (1922–75), 'A Song of Patriotic Prejudice', from *At the Drop of Another Hat*, performed with Donald Swann, 1964.

THE PICNIC

'Hold hard a minute, then!' said the Rat. He looped the painter through a ring in his landing-stage, climbed up into his hole above, and after a short interval reappeared staggering under a fat, wicker luncheon-basket.

'Shove that under your feet,' he observed to the Mole, as he passed it down into the boat. Then he untied the painter and took the sculls again.

'What's inside it?' asked the Mole, wriggling with curiosity.

'There's cold chicken inside it,' replied the Rat briefly; 'coldtonguecoldham-coldbeefpickledgherkinssaladfrenchrollscresssandwidgespottedmeatgingerbeer-lemonadesodawater —'

'O stop, stop,' cried the Mole in ecstasies: 'This is too much!'

'Do you really think so?' inquired the Rat seriously. 'It's only what I always take on these little excursions ...'

The Rat brought the boat alongside the bank, made her fast, helped the still awkward Mole safely ashore, and swung out the luncheon-basket. The Mole begged as a favour to be allowed to unpack it all by himself; and the Rat was very pleased to indulge him, and to sprawl at full length on the grass and rest, while his excited friend shook out the table-cloth and spread it, took out all the mysterious packets one by one and arranged their contents in due order, still gasping, 'O my! O my!' at each fresh revelation. . . .

'Well, well,' said the Rat, 'I suppose we ought to be moving. I wonder which of us had better pack the luncheon-basket?' He did not speak as if he was frightfully eager for the treat.

'O, please let me,' said the Mole. So, of course, the Rat let him.

Packing the basket was not quite such pleasant work as unpacking the basket. It never is. But the Mole was bent on enjoying everything, and although just when he had got the basket packed and strapped up rightly he saw a plate staring up at him from the grass, and when the job had been done again the Rat pointed out a fork which anybody ought to have seen, and last of all, behold! the mustard-pot, which he had been sitting on without knowing it – still, somehow, the thing got finished at last, without much loss of temper.

Kenneth Grahame (1859–1932), *The Wind in the Willows*, 1908.

We used to picnic where the thrift
    Grew deep and tufted to the edge;
We saw the yellow foam-flakes drift
    In trembling sponges on the ledge
Below us, till the wind would lift
    Them up the cliff and o'er the hedge.

Sand in the sandwiches, wasps in the tea,
Sun on our bathing-dresses heavy with the wet,
Squelch of the bladder-wrack waiting for the sea,
Fleas round the tamarisk, an early cigarette.

John Betjeman (1906–84), 'Trebetherick', in *Old Lights for New Chancels*, 1940.

A picnic is the Englishman's grand gesture, his final defiance flung in the face of fate. No climate in the world is less propitious than the climate of England, yet with a recklessness which is almost sublime the English rush out of doors to eat a meal on every possible and impossible occasion.

Georgina Battiscombe (b.1905), *English Picnics*, 1951.

QUEUEING

An Englishman, even if he is alone, forms an orderly queue of one.

George Mikes (1912–87), *How to be an Alien*, 1946.

Need one say more?

R

RESERVE

Not only England, but every Englishman is an island.
Novalis (Friedrich von Hardenberg, 1772–1801), *Fragments*, 1799.

I was born below par to the extent of two whiskies.
C.E. Montague (1867–1928).

'Very good,' I said coldly. 'In that case, tinkerty-tonk.'
And I meant it to sting.
P.G. Wodehouse (1881–1975), *Right Ho, Jeeves*, 1934.

It is not that the Englishman can't feel – it is that he is afraid to feel. He has been taught at his public school that feeling is bad form. He must not express great joy or sorrow, or even open his mouth too wide when he talks – his pipe might fall out if he did. He must bottle up his emotions, or let them out only on a very special occasion.

Once upon a time (this is an anecdote) I went for a week's holiday on the Continent with an Indian friend. We both enjoyed ourselves and were sorry when the week was over, but on parting our behaviour was absolutely different. He was plunged in despair. He felt that because the holiday was over all happiness was over until the world ended. He could not express his sorrow too much. But in me the Englishman came out strong. I reflected that we should meet again in a month or two, and could write in the interval if we had anything to say; and under these circumstances I could not see what there was to make a fuss about. It wasn't as if we were parting forever or dying. 'Buck up,' I said, 'do buck up.' He refused to buck up, and I left him plunged in gloom.

The conclusion of the anecdote is even more instructive. For when we met the next month our conversation threw a good deal of light on the English character. I began by scolding my friend. I told him that he had been wrong to feel and display so much emotion upon so slight an occasion; that it was inappropriate. The word 'inappropriate' roused him to fury. 'What?' he cried. 'Do you measure out your emotions as if they were potatoes?' I did not like the simile of the potatoes, but after a moment's reflection I said, 'Yes, I do; and what's more, I think I ought to. A small occasion demands a little emotion, just as a large occasion demands a great one. I would like my emotions to be appropriate. This may be measuring them like potatoes, but it is better, than slopping them about like water from a pail, which is what you did.' He did not like the simile of the pail. 'If those are your opinions, they part us forever,' he cried, and left the room. Returning immediately, he added: 'No – but your whole attitude toward emotion is wrong. Emotion has nothing to do with appropriateness. It matters only that it shall be sincere. I happened to feel deeply. I showed it. It doesn't matter whether I ought to have felt deeply or not.'

This remark impressed me very much. Yet I could not agree with it, and said that I valued emotion as much as he did, but used it differently; if I poured it out on small occasions I was afraid of having none left for the great ones, and of being bankrupt at the crises of life. Note the word 'bankrupt'. I spoke as a member of a prudent middle-class nation, always, anxious to meet my liabilities. But my friend spoke as an Oriental, and the Oriental has behind him a tradition, not of middle-class prudence, but of kingly munificence and splendour. He feels his resources are endless, just as John Bull feels his are finite. . . .

In the above anecdote, I have figured as a typical Englishman. I will now descend from that dizzy and somewhat unfamiliar height, and return to my business of note-taking. A note on the *slowness* of the English character. The Englishman appears to be cold and unemotional because he is really slow. When an event happens, he may understand it quickly enough with his mind, but he takes quite a while to feel it. Once upon a time a coach, containing some Englishmen and some Frenchmen, was driving over the Alps. The horses ran away, and as they were dashing across a bridge the coach caught on the stonework, tottered, and nearly fell into the ravine below. The Frenchmen were frantic with terror: they screamed and gesticulated and flung themselves about, as Frenchmen would. The Englishmen sat quite calm. An hour later the coach drew up at an inn to change horses, and by that time the situations were exactly reversed. The Frenchmen had forgotten all about the danger, and were chattering gaily; the Englishmen had just begun to feel it, and one had a nervous breakdown and was obliged to go to bed. We have here a clear physical difference between the two races – a difference that goes deep into character. The Frenchmen responded at once; the Englishmen responded in time. They were slow and they were also practical. Their instinct forbade them to throw themselves about in the coach, because it was more likely to tip over if they did. They had this extraordinary appreciation of *fact* that we shall notice again and again. When a disaster comes, the English instinct is to do what can be done first, and to postpone the feeling as long as possible. Hence they are splendid at emergencies. No doubt they are brave – no one will deny that – but bravery is partly an affair of the nerves, and the English nervous system is well equipped for meeting a physical emergency. It acts promptly and feels slowly. Such a combination is fruitful, and anyone who possesses it has gone a long way toward being brave. And when the action is over, then the Englishman can feel.

There is one more consideration – a most important one. If the English nature is cold, how is it that it has produced a great literature and a literature that is particularly great in poetry? Judged by its prose, English literature would not stand in the first rank. It is its poetry that raises it to the level of Greek, Persian, or French. And yet the English are supposed to be so unpoetical. How is this? The nation that produced the Elizabethan drama and the Lake Poets cannot be a cold, unpoetical nation. We can't get fire out of ice. Since literature always rests upon national character, there must be in the English nature hidden springs of fire to produce the fire we see. The warm sympathy, the romance, the imagination, that we look for in Englishmen whom we meet, and too often vainly look for, must exist in the nation as a whole, or we could not have this outburst of national song. An undeveloped heart – not a cold one.

The trouble is that the English nature is not at all easy to understand. It has a great air of simplicity, it advertises itself as simple, but the more we consider it, the greater the problems we shall encounter. People talk of the mysterious East, but the West also is mysterious. It has depths that do not reveal themselves at the first gaze. We know what the sea looks like from a distance: it is of one colour, and level, and obviously cannot contain such creatures as fish. But if we look into the sea over the edge of a boat, we see a dozen colours, and depth below depth, and fish swimming in them. That sea is the English character – apparently imperturbable and even. The depths and the colours are the English romanticism and the English sensitiveness – we do not expect to find such things, but they exist. And – to continue my metaphor – the fish are the English emotions, which are always trying to get up to the surface, but don't quite know how. For the most part we see them moving far below, distorted and obscure. Now and then they succeed and we exclaim, 'Why the Englishman has emotions! He actually can feel!' And occasionally we see that beautiful creature the flying fish, which rises out of the water altogether into the air and the sunlight. English literature is a flying fish. It is a sample of the life that goes on day after day beneath the surface; it is a proof that beauty and emotion exist in the salt, inhospitable sea.

E.M. Forster (1879–1970), 'Notes on the English Character', 1920, in *Abinger Harvest*, 1936.

It's hard to make friends here, hard to meet new people. You don't hang out here, people don't introduce you to other people here. The process of getting to know people is very slow. That's very frustrating, but when you do get to know them you're much closer than in New York. A friend of mine puts it this way: he says that when you meet an English person you meet a huge mountain and you have to get over the mountain and once you've gotten over that mountain then you're friends. When you meet an American you come to a beautiful landscape and you think, Oh this is wonderful and you go through the beautiful landscape or whatever – and then you get to the mountain.

Kathy Acker, quoted in Jonathon Green, *Them: Voices from the Immigrant Community in Contemporary Britain*, 1990.

It's a myth that the English are cold. I don't think that they lack feeling, they just have a totally different way of approaching things. A few months ago a friend of ours died in Paris. The partner was French and he was English. We had to deal with both sides of the family, and I was so much better off staying with my friend's English family, because there was so much less hysteria. The French were climbing up the walls and the English were grieving quietly – it was so much nicer to be with the English. That didn't mean that anyone was grieving any the less, there was just not that extreme emotion. I go back to Mexico now and they tell me that I've become a bit British, because I no longer get easily excited, but if you ask my mother-in-law she'll tell you that I am very excitable and very highly strung. I agree, but going back to Mexico I do sometimes feel a bit odd, because I have acquired to an extent that English capacity of sitting back and just letting things happen. This tendency of not getting emotionally involved straight away, while we Latins jump into getting emotionally involved as soon as there is an opportunity. The English certainly are reserved, but that's really a way of avoiding what might be boiling away underneath. My husband is a perfect example: he seems a very calm person, but sometimes he can erupt. The sort of crime there is in English, you don't find in Latin countries. People in Mexico City will shoot each other dead because of a parking space, but those murders which feature children buried under the floorboards of an old house don't really tend to happen in Mexico. The English keep things in, until they emerge in a very refined, very sophisticated way; Mexicans are more explosive. For daily life the English way is much better.

Paloma Zozaya, quoted in Jonathon Green, *Them: Voices from the Immigrant Community in Contemporary Britain*, 1990.

RUDE RHYMES

With hey trixie terlery-whiskin
    The world it runs on wheeles
When the young man's prick's in
    Up goes the maiden's heeles.

Francis Beaumont (1584–1616), 'Merrythought's Song' in *The Knight of the Burning Pestle*, c.1607.

Little boy kneels at the foot of his bed,
Lily white hands are caressing his head,
Oh my, couldn't be worse –
Christopher Robin is screwing his nurse.

Anon., after 1924.

I know two things about the horse –
And one of them is rather coarse.

Anon.

All the little angels,
They rise up, they rise up,
Singing, All the little angels
They rise up on high.
Which end up?
Arse end up!
Which end up?
Arse end up!
All the little angels,
They rise up on high.

Anon., popular at Hampstead Hockey Club, c.1930.

The Captain's daughter Mabel
As soon as she was able,
Would fornicate with the second mate
Upon the chart-room table . . .

Anon., one of many dozen verses of 'The Good Ship Venus'.

Long-legged curates grind like goats,
Pale-faced spinsters grind like stoats,
And the whole damn world stands by and gloats
As they revel in the joys of copulation . . .

Anon., 'Cats on the Rooftops'.

Flo, Flo, I love you so,
I love you in your nightie,
When the moonlight flits
Across your tits –
Oh Jesus Christ Almighty.

Anon.

They tied her to the leg of a bed,
Parley-voo,
They tied her to the leg of a bed,
Parley-voo,
They tied her to the leg of a bed,
And fucked her till she was nearly dead –
Inky-pinky parley-voo.

They rolled her on the counterpane,
Parley-voo,
They rolled her on the counterpane,
Parley-voo,
They rolled her on the counterpane,
And fucked her back to life again –
Inky-pinky parley-voo.

Anon., though variously attributed (with variations) to Edward Rowland, and Harry
Carlton, 'Mademoiselle From Armentieres', First World War.

S

SCOUTS

Be Prepared. ... The meaning of the motto is that a scout must prepare himself by previous thinking out and practising how to act on any accident or emergency so that he is never taken by surprise; he knows exactly what to do when anything unexpected happens. ...

A scout smiles and whistles under all circumstances.

Lord Baden-Powell (1857–1941), *Scouting for Boys*, 1908.

SWEARING

OSWALD: What does thou know me for?

KENT: A knave, a rascal, an eater of broken meats; a base, proud, shallow, beggarly, three-suited, hundred-pound, filthy worsted-stocking knave; a lily-livered, action-taking, whoreson, glass-gazing, super-serviceable, finical rogue; one-trunk-inheriting slave; one that wouldst be a bawd in way of good service, and art nothing but the composition of a knave, beggar, coward, pandar, and the son and heir of a mongrel bitch; one whom I will beat into clamorous whining if thou deni'st the least syllable of thy addition. ... You whoreson cullionly barber-monger. ... Thou whoreson zed! Thou unnecessary letter!

William Shakespeare (1564–1616), *King Lear*, 1605–6.

The English (it must be owned) are rather a foul-mouthed nation.

William Hazlitt (1778–1830), *Table Talk*, 'On Criticism', 1822.

Walk! Not bloody likely. I am going in a taxi.

George Bernard Shaw (1856–1950), *Pygmalion*, 1916. The line is notable as the first utterance of its kind on the English stage.

Ma's out, Pa's out – let's talk rude:
Pee, po, belly, bum, drawers.

Michael Flanders (1922–75), 'P**, P*, B****, B**, D******', 1956.

THE SKINHEAD *HAMLET*

Shakespeare's play translated into modern English
(Our hope was to achieve something like the effect of the New English Bible – Eds)

ACT I SCENE I

The battlements of Elsinore Castle.
(*Enter* HAMLET, *followed by* GHOST.)
GHOST: Oi! Mush!
HAMLET: Yer?
GHOST: I was fucked!

(*Exit* GHOST.)
HAMLET: O fuck.
(*Exit* HAMLET.)

SCENE II

The Throne Room.
(*Enter* KING CLAUDIUS, GERTRUDE, HAMLET *and* COURT.)
CLAUDIUS: Oi! You, Hamlet, give over!
HAMLET: Fuck off, won't you?
(*Exit* CLAUDIUS, GERTRUDE, COURT.)
(*Alone*) They could have fucking waited.
(*Enter* HORATIO.)
HORATIO: Oi! Wotcher cock!
HAMLET: Weeeeey!
(*Exeunt.*)

SCENE III

Ophelia's Bedroom.
(*Enter* OPHELIA *and* LAERTES.)
LAERTES: I'm fucking off now. Watch Hamlet doesn't slip you one while I'm gone.
OPHELIA: I'll be fucked if he does.
(*Exeunt.*)

SCENE IV

The Battlements.
(*Enter* HORATIO, HAMLET *and* GHOST.)
GHOST: Oi! Mush, get on with it!
HAMLET: Who did it then?
GHOST: That wanker Claudius. He poured fucking poison in my fucking ear!
HAMLET: Fuck me!
(*Exeunt.*)

ACT II SCENE I

A corridor in the castle.
(*Enter* HAMLET *reading. Enter* POLONIUS.)
POLON: Oi! You!
HAMLET: Fuck off, grandad!
(*Exit* POLON. *Enter* ROSENCRANTZ *and* GUILDENSTERN.)
ROS & GU: Oi! Oi! Mucca!
HAMLET: Fuck off, the pair of you!
(*Exit* ROS *and* GUILD.)
HAMLET: (*Alone*) To fuck or be fucked.
(*Enter* OPHELIA.)
OPHELIA: My Lord!

HAMLET: Fuck off to a nunnery!
(*They exit in different directions.*)

ACT III SCENE I
The Throne Room.
(*Enter* PLAYERS *and all* COURT.)
I PLAYER: Full thirty times hath Phoebus cart –
CLAUDIUS: I'll be fucked if I watch any more of this crap.
(*Exeunt.*)

SCENE II
Gertrude's Bedchamber
(*Enter* HAMLET, *to* GERTRUDE.)
HAMLET: Oi! Slag!
GERTRUDE: Watch your fucking mouth, kid!
POLON: (*From behind the curtain*) Too right.
HAMLET: Who the fuck was that?
(*He stabs* POLONIUS *through the arras.*)
POLON: Fuck!
HAMLET: Fuck! I thought it was that other wanker.
(*Exeunt.*)

ACT IV SCENE I
A Court Room.
CLAUDIUS: Fuck off to England then!
HAMLET: Delighted, mush.

SCENE II
The Throne Room.
OPHELIA, GERTRUDE *and* CLAUDIUS.
OPHELIA: Here, cop a whack of this.
(*She hands* GERTRUDE *some rosemary and exits.*)
CLAUDIUS: She's fucking round the twist, isn't she?
GERTRUDE: There is a willow grows aslant the brook –
CLAUDIUS: Get on with it, slag.
GERTRUDE: Ophelia's gone and fucking drowned!
CLAUDIUS: Fuck! Laertes isn't half going to be browned off.
(*Exeunt.*)

SCENE III
A Corridor.
LAERTES: (*Alone*) I'm going to fucking do this lot.
(*Enter* CLAUDIUS.)
CLAUDIUS: I didn't fucking do it, mate. It was that wanker Hamlet.
LAERTES: Well, fuck him.

ACT V SCENE I

Hamlet's Bedchamber.

(HAMLET *and* HORATIO *seated.*)

HAMLET: I got this feeling I'm going to cop it, Horatio, and you know, I couldn't give a flying fuck.

(Exeunt.)

SCENE II

Large Hall.

(*Enter* HAMLET, LAERTES, COURT, GERTRUDE, CLAUDIUS.)

LAERTES: Oi, wanker, let's get on with it.

HAMLET: Delighted, fuckface.

(They fight and both are poisoned by the poisoned sword.)

LAERTES: Fuck!

HAMLET: Fuck!

(*The* QUEEN *drinks.*)

GERTRUDE: Fucking odd wine!

CLAUDIUS: You drunk the wrong fucking cup, you stupid cow!

HAMLET: (*Pouring the poison down* CLAUDIUS' *throat*): Well, fuck you!

CLAUDIUS: I'm fair and squarely fucked.

LAERTES: Oi, mush: no hard feelings, eh?

HAMLET: Yer.

(LAERTES *dies.*)

HAMLET: Oi! Horatio!

HORATIO: Yer? –

HAMLET: I'm fucked. The rest is fucking silence.

(HAMLET *dies.*)

HORATIO: Fuck: that was no ordinary wanker, you know.

(*Enter* FORTINBRAS.)

FORTIN: What the fuck's going on here?

HORATIO: A fucking mess, that's for sure.

FORTIN: No kidding. I see Hamlet's fucked.

HORATIO: Yer.

FORTIN: Fucking shame: fucking good bloke.

HORATIO: Too fucking right.

FORTIN: Fuck this for a lark then. Let's piss off.

(Exeunt with alarums.)

Richard Curtis (1948–), *The Skinhead Hamlet.*

T

TEA

Disturbingly, the phrase 'tea and sympathy' turns out to have been coined by the American playwright Robert Anderson. But never mind – like the Stiff Upper Lip (another American attribute, dating from around 1860) the infusion will be forever English.

Retired to their tea and scandal, according to their ancient custom.
William Congreve (1670–1729), *The Double Dealer*, 1694.

Here thou, great Anna! whom three realms obey
Doth sometimes counsel take – and sometimes tea.
Alexander Pope (1688–1744), *The Rape of the Lock*, 1714. In Pope's day, tea was a luxury commodity, and pronounced 'tay'.

A hardened and shameless tea-drinker, who has for twenty years diluted his meals with only the infusion of this fascinating plant; whose kettle has scarcely time to cool; who with tea amuses the evening, with tea solaces the midnight, and with tea welcomes the morning.
Samuel Johnson (1709–84), review in the *Literary Magazine*, 1757.

In Endymion, I leaped headlong into the sea, and thereby have become better acquainted with the soundings, the quicksands, and the rocks, than if I had stayed upon the green shore, and piped a silly pipe, and took tea and comfortable advice.
John Keats (1795–1821), letter to James Hessey, 8 October 1818.

Before I dismiss this affair of eating and drinking, let me beseech you to resolve to free yourselves from the slavery of the *tea* and *coffee* and other *slop-kettle*, if unhappily you have been bred up in such slavery. Experience has taught me, that those slops are *injurious to health*: until I left them off (having taken to them at the age of 26), even my habits of sobriety, moderate eating, early rising; even these were not, until I left off the slops, sufficient to give me that complete health which I have since had. I pretend not to be a 'doctor'; but I assert that to pour regularly, every day, a pint or two of *warm liquid matter* down the throat, whether under the name of tea, coffee, soup, grog, or whatever else, is greatly injurious to health. However, at present, what I have to represent to you is *the great deduction, which the use of these slops makes, from your power of being useful*, and also from your *power to husband your income*, whatever it may be, and from whatever source arising . . .
William Cobbett (1762–1835), *Advice to Young Men*, 1829.

There is very little art in making good tea; if the water is boiling, and there is no sparing of the fragrant *leaf*, the beverage will almost invariably be good. The old-fashioned plan of allowing a teaspoonful to each person, and one over, is still practised. Warm the teapot with boiling water; let it remain for two or three minutes for the vessel to become thoroughly hot, then pour it away. Put in the tea, pour in from ½ to ¾ pint of *boiling* water, close the lid, and let it stand for the tea to draw from 5 to 10 minutes; then fill up the pot with water. The tea will be quite spoiled unless made with water that is actually *boiling*, as the leaves will not open, and the flavour not be extracted from them; the beverage will consequently be colourless and tasteless, – in fact, nothing but tepid water. Where there is a very large party to make tea for, it is a good plan to have two teapots instead of putting a large quantity of tea into one pot; the tea, besides, will go farther. When the infusion has been once completed, the addition of fresh tea adds very little to the strength; so, when more is required, have the pot emptied of the old leaves, scalded, and fresh tea made in the usual manner. Economists say that a few grains of carbonate of soda, added before the boiling water is poured on the tea, assist to draw out the goodness: if the water is very hard, perhaps it is a good plan, as the soda softens it; but care must be taken to use this ingredient sparingly, as it is liable to give the tea a soapy taste if added in too large a quantity. For mixed tea, the usual proportion is four spoonfuls of black to one of green; more of the latter when the flavour is very much liked; but strong green tea is highly pernicious, and should never be partaken of too freely.

Time. – 2 minutes to warm the teapot, 5 to 10 minutes to draw the strength from the tea.

Sufficient. – Allow 1 teaspoonful to each person, and one over.

Isabella Beeton (1836–65), *Mrs Beeton's Book of Household Management*, 1859–61.

It is very strange, this domination of our intellect by our digestive organs. We cannot work, we cannot think, unless our stomach wills so. It dictates to us our emotions, our passions. After eggs and bacon it says, 'Work!' After beefsteak and porter, it says, 'sleep!' After a cup of tea (two spoonfuls for each cup, and don't let it stand for more than three minutes), it says to the brain, 'Now rise, and show your strength. Be eloquent, and deep, and tender; see, with a clear eye, into Nature, and into life: spread your white wings of quivering thought, and soar, a god-like spirit, over the whirling world beneath you, up through long lanes of flaming stars to the gates of eternity!'

Jerome K. Jerome (1859–1927), *Three Men in a Boat*, 1889.

E M Forster never gets any further than warming the teapot. He's a rare fine hand at that. Feel this teapot. Is it not beautifully warm? Yes, but there ain't going to be no tea.

Katherine Mansfield (1888–1923), New Zealand-born writer, *Journal*, May 1917.

After a fairly shaky start to the day, Arthur's mind was beginning to reassemble itself from the shell-shocked fragments the previous day had left him with. He had found a Nutri-Matic machine which had provided him with a plastic cup filled with a liquid that was almost, but not quite, entirely unlike tea. The way it functioned was very interesting. When the Drink button was pressed it made an instant but highly detailed examination of the subject's taste buds, a spectroscopic analysis of the subject's metabolism and then sent tiny experimental signals down the neural pathways to the taste centres of the subject's brain to see what was likely to go down well. However, no one knew quite why it did this because it invariably delivered a cupful of liquid that was almost, but not quite, entirely unlike tea.

Douglas Adams (1952–2001), *The Hitch-Hiker's Guide to the Galaxy*, 1979.

The British have an umbilical cord which has never been cut and through which tea flows constantly. It is curious to watch them in times of sudden horror, tragedy or disaster. The pulse stops apparently, and nothing can be done, and no move made, until 'a nice cup of tea' is quickly made. There is no question that it brings solace and does steady the mind. What a pity all countries are not so tea-conscious. World-peace conferences would run more smoothly if 'a nice cup of tea', or indeed, a samovar were available at the proper time.

Marlene Dietrich (c.1904–92), *Marlene Dietrich's A B C*, 1984.

U

Un-

What is it with us, that so often we shrink from expressing a negative feeling, preferring instead the lukewarm negativity of the mild denial of a positive one – as in 'unpleasant', 'unhappy' and 'unreasonable', when what we really mean is 'horrible', 'miserable' and 'outrageous'? And even worse is our snivelling affirmation of the positive by a feeble denial of the negative – as in 'not unpleasant', 'not unhappy', 'not unreasonable'. Why can't we, when writing 'proper English', say what we really mean?

Not. 2. *Not* in MEIOSIS and PERIPHRASIS. 'We say well and elegantly, not ungrateful, for very grateful' – OED quotation dated 1671. It was a favourite figure of Milton's: Eve was 'not unamazed' at finding that a snake could speak, and Comus's well-placed words were baited with 'reasons not unplausible'. It is by this time a faded or jaded elegance, this replacing of a term by the negation of its opposite; jaded by general over-use; faded by the blight of WORN-OUT HUMOUR with its *not a hundred miles from, not unconnected with, not unmindful of,* and other once fresh young phrases. ('One can cure oneself of the *not un-* formation', said Orwell, 'by memorizing this sentence: *A not unblack dog was chasing a not unsmall rabbit across a not ungreen field.*') But the very popularity of the idiom in English is proof enough that there is something in it congenial to the English temperament, and it is pleasant to believe that it owes its success with us to a stubborn national dislike of putting things too strongly. It is clear too that there are contexts to which, for example, *not inconsiderable* is more suitable than *considerable*; by using it we seem to anticipate and put aside, instead of not foreseeing or ignoring, the possible suggestion that so-and-so is inconsiderable. The right principle is to acknowledge that the idiom is allowable, and then to avoid it except when it is more than allowable. Examples occur in every day's newspapers, in which their authors would hardly claim that elegance or point was gained by the double negative, and would admit that they used it only because they saw no reason why they should not; such are: *The style of argument suitable for the election contest is, no doubt*, not infrequently *different from the style of argument suitable for use at Westminster* (often). *One may imagine that Mr. — will* not be altogether unrelieved *when his brother actor returns tomorrow* (will be much relieved).

H.W. Fowler (revised by Sir Ernest Gowers), *Modern English Usage*, 1965.

John Major, Prime Minister 1990–97, was – at least according to the many parodists of his verbal style – a past master of the rousing 'not un-' school of oratory.

V

Victoria Station

Once the home of the Golden Arrow express, and known as 'The Gateway to the Continent'....

My foreign policy is to be able to take a ticket at Victoria station and go anywhere I damn well please.

Ernest Bevin (1881–1951), Foreign Secretary, in the *Spectator*, 20 April 1951.

Weather

O wynd, O wynd, the wedder gynneth clere.

Geoffrey Chaucer (?1343–1400), *Troilus and Criseyde*.

Western wind, when will thou blow,
The small rain down can rain?
Christ, if my love were in my arms
And I in my bed again!

Anon., 16th century.

Shall I compare thee to a summer's day?
Thou art more lovely and more temperate:
Rough winds do shake the darling buds of May,
And summer's lease hath all too short a date ...

William Shakespeare (1564–1616), Sonnet 18, 1609.

When two Englishmen meet, their first talk is of the weather. ... In our island, every man goes to sleep, unable to guess whether he shall behold in the morning a bright or a cloudy atmosphere, whether his rest shall be lulled by a shower or broken by tempest.

Samuel Johnson (1709–84), in *The Idler*, No. 11, 24 June 1758.

> Though thy clime
> Be fickle, and thy ear, most part, deform'd
> With dripping rains, or wither'd by a frost,
> I would not yet exchange thy sullen skies,
> And fields without a flower, for warmer France.

William Cowper (1731–1800), *The Task*, 1785.

What dreadful hot weather we have! It keeps me in a continual state of inelegance.

Jane Austen (1775–1817), letter, 18 September 1796.

The weather was always bad. Except in May we never had two fine days together. Heavy rain fell every other day and the intervening days were cold; fog and wind made them worse than the others. What a terrible climate! It is said to be the driest in England. ... Several Englishmen told us that it does not rain here more than in France. In vain did I assert that I had never seen such horrible weather repeated day after day, that sometimes it was warm in France. They replied that there had never been such a summer in England and that we should have a better autumn. A fine consolation! Meanwhile we have had a fire nearly the whole summer and England consumed as much coal in August as France consumes wood in October.

François de la Rochefoucauld (1765–1848), *Mélanges sur l'Angleterre*, 1784.

I like the weather, when it's not too rainy,
That is, I like two months of every year.

Lord Byron (1788–1824), *Beppo*, 1818.

The massive eruption of the Indonesian volcano Tambora in April 1815 had had a global meteorological effect: in North America and Europe the year 1816 became known as 'the year without a summer'; in England snow fell in every month.

> O Wild West Wind, thou breath of Autumn's being,
> Thou, from whose unseen presence the leaves dead
> Are driven, like ghosts from an enchanter fleeing,
> Yellow, and black, and pale, and hectic red,
> Pestilence-stricken multitudes.

Percy Bysshe Shelley (1792–1822), 'Ode to the West Wind', 1819.

We are all well, and keep large fires, as it behoveth those who pass their summers in England.

The Rev. Sydney Smith (1771–1845), letter to Mrs Meynell, 1820.

My Lady Dedlock has been down at what she calls, in familiar conversation, her 'place in Lincolnshire'. The waters are out in Lincolnshire. An arch of the bridge in the park has been sapped and sopped away. The adjacent low-lying ground, for half a mile in breadth, is a stagnant river, with melancholy trees for islands in it, and a surface punctured all over, all day long, with falling rain. My Lady Dedlock's 'place' has been extremely dreary. The weather, for many a day and night, has been so wet that the trees seem wet through, and the soft loppings and prunings of the woodman's axe can make no crash or crackle as they fall. The deer, looking soaked, leave quagmires, where they pass. The shot of a rifle loses its sharpness in the moist air, and its smoke moves in a tardy little cloud towards the green rise, coppice-topped, that makes a background for the falling rain. The view from my Lady Dedlock's own windows is alternately a lead-coloured view, and a view in Indian ink. The vases on the stone terrace in the foreground catch the rain all day; and the heavy drops fall, drip, drip, drip, upon the broad flagged pavement, called, from old time, the Ghost's Walk, all night. On Sundays, the little church in the park is mouldy; the oaken pulpit breaks out into a cold sweat; and there is a general smell and taste as of the ancient Dedlocks in their graves. . . .

It is still wet weather down at the place in Lincolnshire. The rain is ever falling, drip, drip, drip, by day and night, upon the broad flagged terrace-pavement, The Ghost's Walk. The weather is so very bad down in Lincolnshire, that the liveliest imagination can scarcely apprehend its ever being fine again. . . .

Sir Leicester Dedlock has got the better, for the time being, of the family gout; and is once more, in a literal no less than in a figurative point of view, upon his legs. He is at his place in Lincolnshire; but the waters are out again on the low-lying grounds, and the cold and damp steal into Chesney Wold, though well defended, and eke into Sir Leicester's bones. The blazing fires of faggot and coal – Dedlock timber and antediluvian forest – that blaze upon the broad wide hearths, and wink in the twilight on the frowning woods, sullen to see how trees are sacrificed, do not exclude the enemy. The hot-water pipes that trail themselves all over the house, the cushioned doors and windows, and the screens and curtains, fail to supply the fires' deficiencies, and to satisfy Sir Leicester's need.

Charles Dickens (1812–70), *Bleak House*, 1853.

'Tis the hard grey weather
Breeds hard English men.

Charles Kingsley (1819–75), 'Ode to the North-East Wind', 1858.

This a London particular. . . . A fog, miss.

Charles Dickens (1812–70), *Bleak House*, 1853. In the same novel Dickens gives a very atmospheric description of a London smog; in the present work it is quoted in the London section of 'Dear Old, Bloody Old England'.

The yellow fog that rubs its back upon the window-panes,
The yellow smoke that rubs its muzzle on the window-panes,
Licked its tongue into the corners of the evening,

Lingered upon the pools that stand in drains,
Let fall upon its back the soot that falls from chimneys,
Slipped by the terrace, made a sudden leap,
And seeing that it was a soft October night,
Curled once about the house, and fell asleep.

T.S. Eliot (1888–1965), 'The Love Song of J. Alfred Prufrock', 1917.

A foggy day in London Town
Had me low and had me down.
I viewed the morning with alarm,
The British Museum had lost its charm.
How long, I wondered, could this thing last?
But the age of miracles hadn't passed,
For, suddenly, I saw you there
And through foggy London town the sun was shining everywhere.

Ira Gershwin (1896–1983), 'A Foggy Day' from *Damsel in Distress*, 1937.

This is the weather the cuckoo likes,
And so do I;
When showers betumble the chestnut spikes,
And nestlings fly:
And the little brown nightingale bills his best,
And they sit outside at 'The Travellers' Rest',
And maids come forth in sprig-muslin drest,
And citizens dream of the south and west,
And so do I.

Thomas Hardy (1840–1928), 'Weathers', 1922.

The expression 'right as rain' must have been invented by an Englishman.

William Lyon Phelps (1865–1943), US writer, *The Country or the City*.

The glass is falling hour by hour, the glass will fall for ever,
But if you break the bloody glass you won't hold up the weather.

Louis MacNeice (1907–63), 'Bagpipe Music', 1938.

Do not forget that the Englishman's soul is like the English skies: the weather is nearly always bad, but the climate is good.

André Maurois (1885–1967), *Three Letters on the English*, 1938.

Spring, I enjoyed that; missed it last year. I was in the bathroom.

Michael Flanders (1922–75), *At the Drop of a Hat*, performed with Donald Swann, 1960.

Three meteorological calendars:

Snowy, Flowy, Blowy,
Showery, Flowery, Bowery,
Hoppy, Croppy, Droppy,
Breezy, Sneezy, Freezy.

George Ellis (1753–1815), 'The Twelve Months'.

January brings the snow,
Makes your feet and fingers glow;
February's ice and sleet
Freeze the toes right off your feet.
Welcome, March, with wint'ry wind:
Would thou wert not so unkind.
April brings the sweet Spring showers –
On and on for hours and hours!
Farmers fear unkindly May –
Frost by night and hail by day.
June just rains and never stops –
Thirty days and spoils the crops.
In July the sun is hot.
Is it shining? No it's not!
August, cold and dank and wet,
Brings more rain than any yet.
Bleak September's mist and mud
Is enough to chill the blood,
Then October adds a gale.
Wind and slush and rain and hail.
Dark November brings the fog:
Should not do it to a dog.
Freezing wet December, then –
Bloody January again!

Michael Flanders (1922–75), 'A Song of the Weather',
from *At the Drop of a Hat*, performed with Donald Swann, 1960.

January's grey and slushy,
February's chill and drear,
March is wild and wet and windy,
April seldom brings much cheer.
In May, a day or two of sunshine,
Three or four in June, perhaps.
July is usually filthy,
August skies are open taps.
In September things start dying,
Then comes cold October mist.

November we make plans to spend
The best part of December pissed.

Wendy Cope (1945–), 'English Weather' in *Serious Concerns*, 1992.

The British, he thought, must be gluttons for satire: even the weather forecast seemed to be some kind of spoof, predicting every possible combination of weather for the next twenty-four hours without actually committing itself to anything specific.

David Lodge (1935–), *Changing Places*, 1975.

A woman rang to say she heard a hurricane was on the way. Well don't worry, there isn't.

Michael Fish (1944–), BBC weather forecaster, 15 October 1987. There was.

I have a small, tattered clipping that I sometimes carry with me and pull out for purposes of private amusement. It's a weather forecast from the *Western Daily Mail* and it says, in toto: 'Outlook: Dry and warm, but cooler with some rain.'

Bill Bryson (1951–), US writer, *Notes from a Small Island*, 1995.

X

XENOPHOBIA

For all that they may dislike 'Abroad', and can, from time to time, be thorough-going haters of individual nations, a generalised xenophobia – that bottomless contempt and physical loathing for all other races – has never really been evinced by the English as it has been (and often still is) by, say, the Japanese. Partly this may be because, albeit unconsciously, we are aware of our own mongrel heritage; partly, it has certainly proceeded from an assumption of effortless (hence benign) superiority.
As, for instance, in this:

It's not that they're wicked, or naturally bad –
It's knowing they're *foreign* that makes them so mad!

Michael Flanders (1922–75), 'A Song of Patriotic Prejudice', from *At the Drop of Another Hat*, performed with Donald Swann, 1964.

British xenophobia takes the form of Insularism, and the Limeys all moved to an island some time ago to 'keep themselves to themselves', which as far as I am concerned is a good thing.

National Lampoon, US magazine, 1973

Y

YAHOOS

Or, as we now call them, Yobs and Yobesses (or 'the English Underclass') ... or are they ... All of Us?

Jonathan Swift, in *Gulliver's Travels* – a book that could surely have neither been written nor published anywhere else – takes us to a land where an intelligent, cultured, civilised race of horses, the Houyhnhnms, rules a land that is also inhabited by the Yahoos. Here is Gulliver's first experience of the latter:

I fell into a beaten road, where I saw many tracts of human feet, and some of cows, but most of horses. At last, I beheld several animals in a field, and one or two of the same kind sitting in trees. Their shape was very singular, and deformed, which a little discomposed me, so that I lay down behind a thicket to observe them better. Some of them coming forward near the place where I lay, gave me an opportunity of distinctly marking their form. Their heads and breasts were covered with a thick hair, some frizzled and others lank; they had beards like goats, and a long ridge of hair down their backs, and the fore parts of their legs and feet; but the rest of their bodies were bare, so that I might see their skins, which were of a brown buff colour. They had no tails, nor any hair at all on their buttocks, except about the *anus*; which, I presume, nature had placed there to defend them as they sat on the ground, for this posture they used, as well as lying down, and often stood on their hind feet. They climbed high trees as nimbly as a squirrel, for they had strong extended claws before and behind, terminating on sharp points, hooked. They would often spring, and bound, and leap with prodigious agility. The females were not so large as the males; they had long lank hair on their heads, and only a sort of down on the rest of their bodies, except about the *anus*, and *pudenda*. Their dugs hung between their fore feet, and often reached almost to the ground as they walked. The hair of both sexes was of several colours, brown, red, black and yellow. Upon the whole, I never beheld in all my travels so disagreeable an animal, or one against which I naturally conceived so strong an antipathy. So, that thinking I had seen enough, full of contempt and aversion, I got up and pursued the beaten road, hoping it might direct me to the cabin of some Indian. I had not gone far, when I met one of these creatures full in my way, and coming up directly to me. The ugly monster, when he saw me, distorted several ways every feature of his visage, and stared, as at an object he had never seen before; then, approaching nearer, lifted up his fore paw, whether out of curiosity or mischief, I could not tell: but I drew my hanger, and gave him a good blow with the flat side of it; for I durst not strike him with the edge, fearing the inhabitants might be provoked against me, if they should come to know, that I had killed or maimed any of their cattle. When the beast felt the smart, he drew back, and roared so loud, that a herd, of at least forty, came flocking about me from the next field, howling and making odious faces; but I ran to the body of a tree, and leaning my back against it, kept them off, by waving my hanger. Several of this cursed brood getting hold of the branches behind, leaped up into the tree; from whence they began to discharge their excrements on my head: however, I escaped pretty well, by sticking close to the stem of the tree, but was almost stifled with the filth; which fell about me on every side. . . .

Gulliver is rescued from the Yahoos by the Houyhnhnms, who take him in and begin to educate him in their ways. Gulliver's attitude to the Houyhnhnms changes, from one of patronising curiosity to one of admiration, then to awed love. But, in the end, they ask him to leave: unfortunately, the Englishman is too much like a Yahoo for their taste, and they can no longer tolerate him.

My master told me, there were some qualities remarkable in the Yahoos, which he had not observed me to mention, or at least very slightly, in the accounts I had given him of human kind. He said, those animals, like other brutes, had their females in common; but in this they differed, that the she-Yahoo would admit the male, while she was pregnant; and that the hees would quarrel and fight with the females as fiercely as with each other. Both which practices were such degrees of infamous brutality, that no other sensitive creature ever arrived at.

Another thing he wondered at in the Yahoos, was their strange disposition to nastiness and dirt; whereas there appears to be a natural love of cleanliness in all other animals. As to the two former accusations, I was glad to let them pass without any reply, because I had not a word to offer upon them in defence of my species, which otherwise I certainly had done from my own inclinations. But I could have easily vindicated human kind from the imputation of singularity upon the last article, if there had been any swine in that country, (as unluckily for me there were not) which although it may be a *sweeter quadruped* than a Yahoo, cannot I humbly conceive in justice pretend to more cleanliness; and so his honour himself must have owned, if he had seen their filthy way of feeding, and their custom of wallowing and sleeping in the mud.

My master likewise mentioned another quality, which his servants had discovered in several Yahoos, and to him was wholly unaccountable. He said, a fancy would sometimes take a Yahoo, to retire into a corner, to lie down and howl, and groan, and spurn away all that came near him, although he were young and fat, and wanted neither food nor water; nor did the servants imagine what could possibly ail him. And the only remedy they found, was to set him to hard work, after which he would infallibly come to himself; To this I was silent out of partiality to my own kind; yet here I could plainly discover the true seeds of spleen, which only seizeth on the lazy, the luxurious, and the rich; who, if they were forced to undergo the same regimen, I would undertake for the cure.

His honour had farther observed, that a female-Yahoo would often stand behind a bank or a bush, to gaze on the young males passing by, and then appear, and hide, using many antick gestures and grimaces; at which time it was observed, that she had a most offensive smell; and when any of the males advanced, would slowly retire, looking often back, and with a counterfeit shew of fear, run off into some convenient place where she knew the male would follow her.

At other times, if a female stranger came among them, three or four of her own sex would get about her, and stare and chatter, and grin, and smell her all over; and then turn off with gestures that seemed to express contempt and disdain.

Perhaps my master might refine a little in these speculations, which he had drawn from what he observed himself, or had been told him by others: however, I could not reflect without some amazement, and much sorrow, that the rudiments of *lewdness, coquetry, censure*, and *scandal*, should have place by instinct in womankind.

I expected every moment, that my master would accuse the Yahoos of those unnatural appetites in both sexes, so common among us. But nature it seems hath not been so expert a school-mistress; and these politer pleasures are entirely the productions of art and reason, on our side of the globe. . . .

Being one day abroad with my protector the sorrel nag, and the weather exceeding hot, I entreated him to let me bathe in a river that was near. He consented, and I immediately stripped myself stark naked, and went down softly into the stream. It happened that a young female Yahoo standing behind a bank, saw the whole proceeding; and inflamed by desire, as the nag and I conjectured, came running with all speed, and leaped into the water within five yards of the place where I bathed. I was never in my life so terribly frighted; the nag was grazing at some distance, not suspecting any harm; she embraced me after a most fulsome manner; I roared as loud as I could, and the nag came galloping towards me, whereupon she quitted her grasp, with the utmost reluctancy, and leaped upon the opposite bank, where she stood gazing and howling all the time I was putting on my cloaths.

This was matter of diversion to my master and his family, as well as of mortification to my self. For now I could no longer deny, that I was a real Yahoo, in every limb and feature, since the females had a natural propensity to me as one of their own species: neither was the hair of this brute of a red colour (which might have been some excuse for an appetite a little irregular) but black as sloe, and her countenance did not make an appearance altogether so hideous as the rest of the kind; for, I think, she could not be above eleven years old.

Jonathan Swift (1667–1745), *Gulliver's Travels*, 'A Voyage to the Houyhnhnms', 1726.

Z

Zoöphilism

The English have long been renowned for their inordinate fondness for furry animals – a fondness that can extend to dressing up in pink coats and chasing them round the countryside for a bit; it's either a dichotomy or a synthesis, depending on your point of view. And not all *of us are afflicted with it . . .*

Of animals as companions. . .

But thousands die, without or this or that,
Die, and endow a college, or a cat.

Alexander Pope (1688–1744), *Epistles to Several Persons*, 'To Lord Bathurst', 1733.

For I will consider my Cat Jeoffrey.

For he is the servant of the Living God, duly and daily serving him.

For at the First glance of the glory of God in the East he worships in his way.

For is this done by wreathing his body seven times round with elegant quickness.

For then he leaps up to catch the musk, which is the blessing of God upon his prayer.

For he rolls upon prank to work it in.

For having done duty and received blessing he begins to consider himself.

For this he performs in ten degrees.

For first he looks upon his fore-paws to see if they are clean.

For secondly he kicks up behind to clear away there.

For thirdly he works it upon stretch with the fore-paws extended.

For fourthly he sharpens his paws by wood.

For fifthly be washes himself.

For sixthly he rolls upon wash.

For Seventhly he fleas himself, that he may not be interrupted upon the beat.

For Eighthly he rubs himself against a post.

For Ninthly he looks up for his instructions.

For Tenthly he goes in quest of food.

For having consider'd God and himself he will consider his neighbour.

For if he meets another cat he will kiss her in kindness.

For when he takes his prey he plays with it to give it a chance.

For one mouse in seven escapes by his dallying.

For when his day's work is done his business more properly begins.

For he keeps the Lord's watch in the night against the adversary.

For he counteracts the powers of darkness by his electrical skin & glaring eyes.

For he counteracts the Devil, who is death, by brisking about the life.

For in his morning orisons he loves the sun and the sun loves him.

For he is of the tribe of Tiger.

For the Cherub Cat is a term of the Angel Tiger.

For he has the subtlety and hissing of a serpent, which in goodness he suppresses.

For he will not do destruction, if he is well fed, neither will he spit without
    provocation.

For he purrs in thankfulness, when God tells him he's a good Cat.

For he is an instrument for the children to learn benevolence upon.

For every house is incomplete without him and a blessing is lacking in the spirit.

For the Lord commanded Moses concerning the cats at the departure of the
    Children of Israel from Egypt.

For every family had one cat at least in the bag.

For the English Cats are the best in Europe.

For he is the cleanest in the use of his fore-paws of any quadrupede.

For the dexterity of his defence is an instance of the love of God to him exceedingly.

For he is the quickest to his mark of any creature.

For he is tenacious of his point.

For he is a mixture of gravity and waggery.

For he knows that God is his Saviour.

For there is nothing sweeter than his peace when at rest.

For there is nothing brisker than his life when in motion.

For he is of the Lord's poor and so indeed is he called by benevolence perpetually
– Poor Jeoffrey! poor Jeoffrey! the rat has bit thy throat.

For I bless the name of the Lord Jesus that Jeoffrey is better.

For the divine spirit comes about his body to sustain it in complete cat.

For his tongue is exceedingly pure so that it has in purity what it wants in music.

For he is docile and can learn certain things.

For he can set up with gravity which is patience upon approbation.

For he can fetch and carry, which is patience in employment.

For he can jump over a stick which is patience upon proof positive.

For he can spraggle upon waggle at the word of command.

For he can jump from an eminence into his master's bosom.

For he can catch the cork and toss it again.

For he is hated by the hypocrite and miser.

For the former is affraid of detection.

For the latter refuses the charge.

For he camels his back to bear the first notion of business.

For he is good to think on, if a man would express himself neatly.

For he made a great figure in Egypt for his signal services.

For he killed the Ichneumon-rat very pernicious by land.

For his ears are so acute that they sting again.

For from this proceeds the passing quickness of his attention.

For by stroking of him I have found out electricity.

For I perceived God's light about him both wax and fire.

For the Electrical fire is the spiritual substance, which God sends from heaven to
sustain the bodies both of man and beast.

For God has blessed him in the variety of his movements.

For, tho he cannot fly, he is an excellent clamberer.

For his motions upon the face of the earth are more than any other quadrupede.

For he can tread to all the measures upon the music.

For he can swim for life.

For he can creep.

Christopher Smart (1722–71), from *Jubilate Agno* ('Rejoice in the Lamb'), written between 1756 and 1763, while Smart was incarcerated in a madhouse. It was not published until 1939.

When I observed that he was a fine cat, saying, 'Why yes, Sir, but I have had cats whom I liked better than this'; and then as if perceiving Hodge to be out of countenance, adding, 'but he is a very fine cat, a very fine cat indeed.'

Samuel Johnson (1709–84), 1783, in James Boswell's *Life of Samuel Johnson*, 1791, Vol. 4.

There is a statue of the cat Hodge outside Johnson's favourite haunt, the Wig & Pen.

> Cruel, but composed and bland,
> Dumb, inscrutable and grand,
> So Tiberius might have sat,
> Had Tiberius been a cat.

Matthew Arnold (1822–88), 'Poor Matthias', 1885.

Sir,

May I, through your columns, appeal to caricaturists and humorous writers to suspend during the present crisis the practice of making the dachshund a symbol of Nazidom or of the German nation? Absurd as it may seem, the prevalence of this idea in the popular imagination has produced a real risk of thoughtless acts of cruelty being committed against harmless little animals which are English by birth and often by generations of breeding.

I am, Sir, yours faithfully,

D.L. Murray.

Letter to *The Times*, 29 August 1939.

If a dog jumps into your lap it is because he is fond of you; but if a cat does the same thing it is because your lap is warmer.

A.N. Whitehead (1861–1947), *Dialogues*, published 1954.

> 'Tis sweet to hear the watch-dog's honest bark
> Bay deep-mouthed welcome as we draw near home;
> 'Tis sweet to know there is an eye will mark
> Our coming, and look brighter when we come.

Lord Byron (1788–1824), *Don Juan*, 1819–24.

The great pleasure of a dog is that you may make a fool of yourself with him and not only will he not scold you, he will make a fool of himself, too.

Samuel Butler (1835–1902), *Notebooks*, published 1912.

GEORGE: That flaming dog has messed our steps again. It's the one species I wouldn't mind seeing vanish from the face of the earth. I wish they were like the White Rhino – six of them left in the Serengeti National Park, and all males. Do you know what dogs are? They're those beer-sodden soccer fans piling out of coaches in a lay-by, yanking out their cocks without a blush and pissing against the wall thirty-nine in a row. I can't stand it.

POLLY: Question is whether you hate the coach party because they're like the dogs or hate the dogs because they're like the coach party.

GEORGE: I hate them all. ...

(GEORGE *enters breathless*.)

GEORGE: Where's the bucket?

POLLY: What bucket?

GEORGE: The bucket. Quick, quick, for God's sake, where's the bucket?

POLLY: What bucket?

GEORGE: The bucket. The bowl, anything. Come on. It's the dog. It's there.

POLLY: What? Oh, no, George, you can't.

GEORGE: Yes, I bloody well can.

(*He rushes out with the dripping pail. Shouts outside as he throws the water. He returns, satisfied.*) Got it. Purple in the face as it was passing some particularly recalcitrant stool. It leaped out of its skin. Sodden.

POLLY: It's not the dog's fault.

GEORGE: Maybe. Sometimes I think St Francis of Assisi was barking up the wrong tree. Of course it's the dog's fault. If it will choose our step.

(*He is about to throw another one, when there is a knocking at the door.* GEORGE *opens it, bucket in hand, sees who it is, turns round smartly and comes away from the door, followed in by* MRS BRODRIBB.)

MRS BRODRIBB: One moment, young man. Some person on these premises has just thrown a bucket of water over my dog. I have just met him running down the street soaked to the skin.

GEORGE: Your dog, Mrs Brodribb?

MRS BRODRIBB: My dog, Mr Oliver.

POLLY: What makes you think it was here?

GEORGE: Polly. If by dog, Mrs Brodribb, you mean that polka dotted sewage machine on legs, yes. It was me.

MRS BRODRIBB: So, you admit it . . . he admits it. You ought to be ashamed of yourself, a man in your position, an unprovoked assault.

GEORGE: Unprovoked? Unprovoked? Mrs Brodribb, I have lost count of the number of times that creature has fouled our doorstep. It's every time he shoves his arse outside your door.

MRS BRODRIBB: Arse! Oh!

POLLY: It does happen rather often, Mrs Brodribb. I'm sure my husband didn't mean to harm him, only to teach him a lesson.

MRS BRODRIBB: If you wanted to attack a defenceless dog why didn't you choose one your own size? They have to go somewhere.

GEORGE: Then why not on your own doorstep then?

MRS BRODRIBB: Because he needs the walk. Besides, you should be flattered.

POLLY: Flattered!

MRS BRODRIBB: When Max . . .

GEOFF: Max!

MRS BRODRIBB: (*Silencing him with a look*) . . . pauses by your doorstep he is not simply relieving himself. He is leaving a message, a sign, a note.

GEORGE: A message, is it? Then I wish he wasn't quite such a frequent correspondent. Your dog, Mrs Brodribb, is a proper little Mme de Sévigné. Besides, who is it leaving a message for, for God's sake? Not for anybody at this address. We haven't any dogs. We have a goldfish and a hamster. Surely he's not contemplating starting up a deviant relationship with them?

MRS BRODRIBB: Don't you be sarcastic with me. I don't want any of your House of Commons manners here. I know one thing. I shan't ever vote Socialist after this. Not that I ever did.

GEORGE: And another thing, Mrs Brodribb. This leaving notes business. Presumably it's to do with . . . I'm sorry to have to mention this word . . . but it has to do with sex, hasn't it?

MRS BRODRIBB: (*Who has been circling round the company, stares long and deep into* BRIAN's *face*) I've seen you on television, too. You're all the same.

GEORGE: Sex, Mrs Brodribb. But Max can go on leaving little notes for other dogs on our step until he's blue in the face, but I bet you never let him out to back them up, do you? Except once a year with some other equally spotted bitch under medical supervision at forty guineas a time in some foul kennels in Hounslow. So what's all this message leaving, Mrs Brodribb? What are all these notes? I'll tell you what Max is, Mrs Brodribb. He's all talk and no trousers. But for future reference I am not going to have my doorstep used as a poste restante by frustrated dalmatians who never come. And I mean come, Mrs Brodribb.

POLLY: We have got a bit fed up of it.

MRS BRODRIBB: It? It? What you call it, Mrs Oliver, is an extremely sensitive creature, twice champion in his class at Crufts and a thoroughbred dalmatian. That dog, as you call it, has ten times more breeding than you have.

GEORGE: Mrs Brodribb. Shit has no pedigree.

MRS BRODRIBB: Did you hear that? Did you hear that? Such ... language, and from one of our elected representatives. But I give you fair warning, if there is any repetition of this incident, if you ever interfere with Max again, I shall be forced to fetch my husband, diabetic though he be. And that's my last word.

GEOFF: Aw, piss off, you old cow.

(ENID *comes in with a jug just as* MRS BRODRIBB *is going out.*)

MRS BRODRIBB: If we had a real Conservative government I should have you horsewhipped.

Alan Bennett (1934–), *Getting On*, 1971.

A robin red breast in a cage
Puts all Heaven in a rage.

William Blake (1757–1827), 'Auguries of Innocence', c.1803.

Of animals as quarry . . .

He yaf nat of that text a pulled hen,
That seith that hunters be nat hooly men.

Geoffrey Chaucer (c.1343–1400), General Prologue to *The Canterbury Tales*, on the Monk.

A pack of hounds in full cry is one of the traditional sounds of the English countryside – here transposed by Shakespeare to Greece:

I was with Hercules and Cadmus once
When in a wood of Crete they bay'd the bear
With hounds of Sparta; never did I hear
Such gallant chiding, for, besides the groves,
The skies, the fountains, every region near,
Seem'd all one mutual cry. I never heard
So musical a discord, such sweet thunder.

William Shakespeare (1564–1616), *A Midsummer Night's Dream*, IV.i.

Better to hunt in fields, for health unbought,
Than fee the doctor for a nauseous draught.

John Dryden (1631–1700), Epistle 'To my honoured kinsman John Driden', 1700.

See! from the brake the whirring Pheasant springs,
And mounts exulting on triumphant wings:
Short is his joy; he feels the fiery wound,
Flutters in blood, and panting beats the ground.
Ah! what avail his glossy, varying dyes,
His purple crest, and scarlet-circled eyes,
The vivid green his shining plumes unfold,
His painted wings, and breast that flames with gold?
Nor yet, when moist *Arcturus* clouds the sky,
The woods and fields their pleasing toils deny.
To plains with well-breath'd beagles we repair,
And trace the mazes of the circling hare.
(Beasts, taught by us, their fellow beasts pursue,
And learn of man each other to undo.)
With slaught'ring guns th' unweary'd fowler roves,
When frosts have whiten'd all the naked groves;
Where doves in flocks the leafless trees o'ershade,
And lonely woodcocks haunt the wat'ry glade.
He lifts the tube, and levels with his eye;
Strait a short thunder breaks the frozen sky.
Oft', as in airy rings they skim the heath,
The clam'rous Plovers feel the leaden death:
Oft', as the mounting Larks their notes prepare,
They fall, and leave their little lives in air.

Alexander Pope (1688–1744), from *Windsor Forest*, 1713.

The world may be divided into people that read, people that write, people that think, and fox-hunters.

William Shenstone (1714–63), *Works in Verse and Prose*, 1764.

It is very strange, and very melancholy, that the paucity of human pleasures should persuade us ever to call hunting one of them.

Samuel Johnson (1709–84), in Hester Lynch Piozzi, *Anecdotes*, 1786.

     Detested sport,
That owes its pleasure to another's pain.

William Cowper (1731–1800), *The Task*, 1785.

There is a passion for hunting something deeply implanted in the human breast.

Charles Dickens (1812–70), *Oliver Twist*, 1838.

'Unting is all that's worth living for – all time is lost wot is not spent in 'unting – it is like the hair we breathe – if we have it not we die – it's the sport of kings, the image of war without its guilt, and only five-and-twenty per cent of its danger. . . .
    It ar'n't that I loves the fox less, but that I loves the 'ound more.

R.S. Surtees (1805–64), *Handley Cross*, 1843.

The English country gentleman galloping after a fox – the unspeakable in full pursuit of the uneatable.

Oscar Wilde (1854–1900), *A Woman of No Importance*, 1893.

Some hounds I've known were wise as half your saints,
And better hunters. That old dog of the Duke's,
Harlequin; what a dog he was to draw!
And what a note he had, and what a nose
When foxes ran down wind and scent was catchy!
And that light lemon bitch of the Squire's, old Dorcas –
She were a marvellous hunter, were old Dorcas!
Ay, oft I've thought, 'If there were hounds in Heaven,
With God as master, taking no subscription;
And all His blessed country farmed by tenants,
And a straight-necked old fox in every gorse!'
But when I came to work it out, I found
There'd be too many huntsmen wanting places,
Though some I've known might get a job with Nick!

Siegfried Sassoon (1886–1967), 'The Old Huntsman', 1917.

It isn't mere convention. Everyone can see that the people who hunt are the right people and the people who don't are the wrong ones. ... Go anywhere in England where there are natural, wholesome, contented and really nice English people; and what do you always find? That the stables are the real centre of the household.

George Bernard Shaw (1856–1950), *Heartbreak House*, 1919.

Conservatives do not believe that the political struggle is the most important thing in life. ... The simplest of them prefer fox-hunting – the wisest religion.

Quintin Hogg (afterwards Lord Hailsham, 1907–90), *The Case for Conservatism*, 1947.

There was no food for the foxes that night, and soon the children dozed off. Then Mrs Fox dozed off. But Mr Fox couldn't sleep because of the pain in the stump of his tail. 'Well,' he thought, 'I suppose I'm lucky to be alive at all. And now they've found our hole, we're going to have to move out as soon as possible. We'll never get any peace if we ... What was that?' He turned his head sharply and listened. The noise he heard now was the most frightening noise a fox can ever hear – the scrape-scrape-scraping of shovels digging into the soil.

'Wake up!' he shouted. 'They're digging us out!'

Mrs Fox was wide awake in one second. She sat up, quivering all over. 'Are you sure that's it?' she whispered.

'I'm positive! Listen!'

'They'll kill my children!' cried Mrs Fox.

'Never!' said Mr Fox.

'But darling, they will!' sobbed Mrs Fox. 'You know they will!'

Scrunch, scrunch, scrunch went the shovels above their heads. Small stones and bits of earth began falling from the roof of the tunnel.

'How will they kill us, Mummy?' asked one of the small foxes. His round black eyes were huge with fright. 'Will there be dogs?' he said.

Mrs Fox began to cry. She gathered her four children close to her and held them tight.

Suddenly there was an especially loud crunch above their heads and the sharp end of a shovel came right through the ceiling. The sight of this awful thing seemed to have an electric effect upon Mr Fox. He jumped up and shouted, 'I've got it! Come on! There's not a moment to lose! Why didn't I think of it before!'

'Think of what, Dad?'

'A fox can dig quicker than a man!' shouted Mr Fox, beginning to dig. 'Nobody in the world can dig as quick as a fox!'

The soil began to fly out furiously behind Mr Fox as he started to dig for dear life with his front feet. Mrs Fox ran forward to help him. So did the four children.

'Go downwards!' ordered Mr Fox. 'We've got to go deep! As deep as we possibly can!'

Roald Dahl (1916–90), *Fantastic Mr Fox*, 1970.

The hunt had walked round a square of ploughed field and was now moving again, the hounds following a straight line towards a copse on a hillside, the riders spreading out, the leaders galloping with mud flying, others struggling to keep up. By a hedge the protesters shouted, blew whistles and waved their banners, angered by the bright coats, the beauty of the horses and the concentrated and elaborate pursuit of death. ...

Those in the lead at the hunt remembered Dr Salter moving away from them. He left the line and galloped diagonally across a stretch of pasture, pounding the thin grass so that black earth was thrown up by his horse's hooves. He was riding at a high, an impossibly high hedge with a gate leading to a road. But he swerved from the gate and went straight for the huge hedge, faster and faster for a jump which his horse took bravely, hopelessly, into a tangle of dark wood, and below the dim light of the sky.

'Don't answer it, please!' Mrs Wickstead said when the telephone rang, but Fred got out of bed and stood naked in his living-room while Hardison told him the news. And then he was dressed and walking down a rubber-smelling corridor in the Worsfield General with a white-coated houseman. The walk seemed endless, but at last they swung open a pair of doors and were in a room where Dr Salter lay flat on his back with his eyes open.

'Sorry,' he muttered when Fred looked down at him. 'I seem to have made the most almighty cock-up!'

Some months later Simeon called on Dr Salter, whom he found in a room above the surgery, somehow diminished in size, and seated in a wheel-chair in which, from then on, he would spend his waking hours. Simeon entered the room with an expression of serious concern and was a little taken aback to be greeted by a burst of laughter, nothing like the sound made by the old Dr Salter, but all the same, the patient seemed to be enjoying a joke.

'You can laugh?'

'About all I can do. I'm still alive but unfortunately not kicking. He's got quite a sense of humour, your old practical joker.'

'Mine?' Simeon declined to be identified with whatever power had prescribed the Doctor a broken back.

'The old gentleman you claim as such a close acquaintance. The one with the beard and the irritable expression. A great prankster, apparently. No doubt time hangs heavy on his hands, waiting for you to lecture Him on the joys of the Welfare State every Sunday from Rapstone pulpit. Probably longs to get hold of a bit of fire and brimstone and smite a few backsliders for idolatry.'

Simeon waited for the Doctor's speech, which he clearly relished and had, possibly, rehearsed, to be over. It took a little longer.

'When you're next on your knees tell Him it was very funny but hardly worth His while. I mean, hasn't He got enough on His hands with wars and earthquakes and famines without spotting one ageing G.P. on the hunting-field, a fellow out with the sole purpose of getting his neck broken, and turning him into a useless sort of lump that can't even *walk* to hounds?'

Silence fell between the two men, and then Dr Salter thought to ask, 'I say. Do you think the Almighty's a member of it?'

'Of what?'

'The League Against Cruel Sports?'

'Of course not. Why should He be?'

'Well, according to you, He's a paid-up member of the Labour Party.'

Simeon smiled patiently, and asked the Doctor a question. 'Did you say you went out with the sole purpose of getting your neck broken?'

'Of course. I always told you they did you a decent death on the hunting-field.'

John Mortimer (1923–), *Paradise Postponed*, 1985.

Hunting people tend to be church-goers on a higher level than ordinary folk. One has a religious experience in the field.

Christopher Seal, churchman, in *The Times*, 30 December 1993.

My left arm ached from lifting my gun, my shoulder from the recoil, and I was deaf and stunned from the banging. ... When in the late afternoon the carnage stopped almost 4,000 pheasants had been killed. The bright limp carcasses were laid out in rows of 100; the whole place was littered with feathers and spent cartridges.

Edward VIII, then Prince of Wales, later Duke of Windsor, on a shooting party at the Beaconsfield estate of Lord Burnham in 1913. His father, George V, remarked that they had 'perhaps gone too far'.

Spirits of well-shot woodcock, partridge, snipe
    Flutter and bear him up the Norfolk sky ...

John Betjeman (1906–84), 'Death of King George V', in *Continual Dew*, 1937.

But He was never, well,
What I call
A Sportsman;
For forty days
He went out into the desert
– And never shot anything.

Osbert Sitwell (1892–1969), from *Old Fashioned Sportsmen*.

About one thing the Englishman has a particularly strict code. If a bird says *Cluk bik bik bik bik* and *caw* you may kill it, eat it, or ask Fortnums to pickle it in Napoleon brandy with wild strawberries. If it says *tweet* it is a dear and precious friend and you'd better lay off it if you want to remain a member of Boodles.

Clement Freud (1924–), *Freud on Food*, 1978

Whither England?

NOT FARE WELL,
BUT FARE FORWARD, VOYAGERS.
T.S. Eliot (1888–1965), *Four Quartets*, 'The Dry Salvages', 1941.

All attempts to answer this question begin with the question: Where are we now? And that in turn begs the questions: Where have we come from? How have we got here? and, What does this tell us about ourselves? Even if the Present may be more or less assumed to be capable of taking care of itself, the Future is very much concerned with the Past ...

It is, then, fitting that this final chapter should begin and end with the words of historians.

Thomas Babington MacAulay, the father of 'The Whig Interpretation of History' – the cause of so much embarrassment a century later – published his four-volume *History of England* in 1848, the great year of nationalist revolution in Europe. He might have taken for his text the words of Alexander Pope in the previous century: 'One truth is clear: "Whatever is, is RIGHT".' He viewed the events of the previous 150 years from a mid-19th-century eminence and, finding they had led to a very agreeable state of existence, had every confidence in the future.

I purpose to write the history of England from the accession of King James the Second down to a time which is within the memory of men still living. I shall recount the errors which, in a few months, alienated a loyal gentry and priesthood from the House of Stuart. I shall trace the course of that revolution which terminated the long struggle between our sovereigns and their parliaments, and bound up together the rights of the people and the title of the reigning dynasty. I shall relate how the new settlement was, during many troubled years, successfully defended against foreign and domestic enemies; how, under that settlement, the authority of law and the security of property were found to be compatible with a liberty of discussion and of individual action never before known; how, from the auspicious union of order and freedom, sprang a prosperity of which the annals of human affairs had furnished no example; how our country, from a state of ignominious vassalage, rapidly rose to the place of umpire among European powers; how her opulence and her martial glory grew together; how, by wise and resolute good faith, was gradually established a public credit fruitful of marvels which to the statesmen of any former age would have seemed incredible; how a gigantic commerce gave birth to a maritime power, compared with which every other maritime power, ancient or modern, sinks into insignificance; how Scotland, after ages of enmity, was at length united to England, not merely by legal bonds, but by indissoluble ties of interest and affection; how, in America, the British colonies rapidly became far mightier and wealthier than the realms which Cortes and Pizarro had added to the dominions of Charles the Fifth; how, in Asia, British adventurers founded an empire not less splendid and more durable than that of Alexander.

Nor will it be less my duty faithfully to record disasters mingled with triumphs, and great national crimes and follies far more humiliating than any disaster. It will be seen that even what we justly account our chief blessings were not without alloy. ...

Yet, unless I greatly deceive myself, the general effect of this chequered narrative will be to excite thankfulness in all religious minds, and hope in the breasts of all patriots. For the history of our country during the last hundred and sixty years is eminently the history of physical, of moral, and of intellectual improvement. Those who compare the age on which their lot has fallen with a golden age which exists only in their imagination may talk of degeneracy and decay: but no man who is correctly informed as to the past will be disposed to take a morose or desponding view of the present.

Thomas Babington MacAulay (Lord MacAulay, 1800–59), Introduction, *The History of England*, 1848.

George Orwell wrote *The Lion and the Unicorn*, an essay he had been planning to write for some years, in the dark days of 1940, when his country's very survival seemed to hang by a thread. France had fallen; Britain had withdrawn her forces from Europe; Hitler's army was massing on the French coast, and the Royal Air Force was (in every sense of the word) scrambling to meet the onslaught of the Luftwaffe. He found hope, not in jingoism, but in what he termed 'something that goes on beneath the surface, unofficially and more or less frowned on' – what the French historian Fernand Braudel termed 'an obscure history, running along under the surface, refusing to die'. The English, he was sure, would ultimately defeat Fascism simply by being English: and this gave him hope.

When the pinch comes, no one bred in the western tradition can accept the Fascist vision of life. It is important to realize that now, and to grasp what it entails. With all its sloth, hypocrisy and injustice, the English-speaking civilization is the only large obstacle in Hitler's path. It is a living contradiction of all the 'infallible' dogmas of Fascism. That is why all Fascist writers for years past have agreed that England's power must be destroyed. England must be 'exterminated', must be 'annihilated', must 'cease to exist'. Strategically it would be possible for this war to end with Hitler in secure possession of Europe, and with the British Empire intact and British sea-power barely affected. But ideologically it is not possible; were Hitler to make an offer along those lines, it could only be treacherously, with a view to conquering England indirectly or renewing the attack at some more favourable moment. England cannot possibly be allowed to remain as a sort of funnel through which deadly ideas from beyond the Atlantic flow into the police states of Europe. And turning it round to our point of view, we see the vastness of the issue before us, the all-importance of preserving our democracy more or less as we have known it. But to preserve is always to extend. The choice before us is not so much between victory and defeat as between revolution and apathy. If the thing we are fighting for is altogether destroyed, it will have been destroyed partly by our own act.

It could happen that England could introduce the beginnings of Socialism, turn this war into a revolutionary war, and still be defeated. That is at any rate thinkable. But, terrible as it would be for anyone who is now adult, it would be far less deadly than the 'compromise peace' which a few rich men and their hired liars are hoping for. The final ruin of England could only be accomplished by an English government acting under orders from Berlin. But that cannot happen if England has awakened beforehand. For in that case the defeat would be unmistakable, the struggle would continue, the idea would survive. The difference between going down fighting, and surrendering without a fight, is by no means a question of 'honour' and schoolboy heroics. Hitler said once that to accept defeat destroys the soul of a nation. This sounds like a piece of claptrap, but it is strictly true. The defeat of 1870 did not lessen the world-influence of France. The Third Republic had more influence, intellectually, than the France of Napoleon III. But the sort of peace that Pétain, Laval, and Co. have accepted can only be purchased by deliberately wiping out the national culture. The Vichy Government will enjoy a spurious independence only on condition that it destroys the distinctive marks of French culture: republicanism, secularism, respect for the intellect, absence of colour prejudice. We cannot be *utterly* defeated if we have made our revolution beforehand. We may see German troops marching down Whitehall, but another process, ultimately deadly to the German power-dream, will have been started. The Spanish people were defeated, but the things they learned during those two and a half memorable years will one day come back upon the Spanish Fascists like a boomerang.

A piece of Shakespearean bombast was much quoted at the beginning of the war. Even Mr Chamberlain quoted it once, if my memory does not deceive me:

Come the four corners of the world in arms
And we shall shock them: naught shall make us rue
If England to herself do rest but true.

It is right enough, if you interpret it rightly. But England has got to be true to herself. She is not being true to herself while the refugees who have sought our shores are penned up in concentration camps, and company directors work out subtle schemes to dodge their Excess Profits Tax. It is goodbye to the *Tatler*, and the *Bystander*, and farewell to the lady in the Rolls-Royce car. The heirs of Nelson and of Cromwell are not in the House of Lords. They are in the fields and the streets, in the factories and the armed forces, in the four-ale bar and the suburban back garden; and at present they are still kept under by a generation of ghosts. Compared with the task of bringing the real England to the surface, even the winning of the war, necessary though it is, is secondary. By revolution we become more ourselves, not less. There is no question of stopping short, striking a compromise, salvaging 'democracy', standing still. Nothing ever stands still. We must add to our heritage or lose it, we must grow greater or grow less, we must go forward or backward. I believe in England, and I believe that we shall go forward.

George Orwell (1903–50), *The Lion and the Unicorn*, 1940.

What we call the beginning is often the end
And to make an end is to make a beginning.
The end is where we start from.

. . .

    A people without history
Is not redeemed from time, for history is a pattern
Of timeless moments. So, while the light fails
On a winter's afternoon, in a secluded chapel
History is now and England.

. . .

We shall not cease from exploration
And the end of all our exploring
Will be to arrive where we started
And know the place for the first time.

T.S. Eliot (1888–1965), *Four Quartets*, 'Little Gidding', Part V, 1942.

And so we come to our own day. In 1998, the novelist and historian Peter Vansittart published *In Memory of England*. The book's narrative stops just short of the First World War but it looks forward to our own future as well as that of those who marched towards the Somme. The following extract is from his Introduction, and the last paragraph of the final chapter.

Several impulses lie behind this book. One was a sentence in John Major's speech to the 'Britain and the World' conference in March 1995: 'We are attached to our sovereignty and our national institutions.' Then there were the proposals that year to induce a sense of Britishness in schools. In some they provoked fury or contempt, but made me ponder both 'Britishness' and 'Englishness'. What would be taught? I began jotting down incidents, achievements, the trivial and the momentous, which gave me some sense of Englishness, necessarily merging into Britishness, which became this book. My first jotting was about a schoolmaster who wrote of his pupil, Winston Churchill, that he lacked ambition. I relish oddities and exceptions, like those lively or enigmatic figures in the margins of medieval books, carved on misericords, grinning from corbels. They balance the sententious, rancorous or momentous. They have place.

Again in 1995, Tony Benn replied to a *New Statesman* questionnaire: 'I don't believe in Englishness. I'm a socialist.' I then read that Brussels had granted British farmers permission to grow trees on set-aside portions of their land. Here was a minor signpost on a road barely imaginable in my youth, though in the Cuban Missile Crisis of 1962 I had realized that, for the first time in two centuries, Britain had no world role.

Britain might indeed disintegrate, England become a historical curiosity, remote as the Second Reich or the Golden Age of Spain. National sovereignty, with its moss-bound institutions and methodical selfishness, was being denounced as a pernicious obstacle to wider concepts of work, taxation, education, employment, progress. An old-timer, I had doubts whether an international society of mass-media, instant information, endlessly multiplied visual images, would much alter the regions in which many had their being, those of loneliness, fear of death and loss of beauty; private griefs, sexual and intellectual frustration, child abuse, urban gangsterism, power-hunger and irrational impulses, the unending human transience. The myths and illuminations by which we have hitherto lived can be as starved in a global studio as in a rural slum.

History, like science, fertilises the imagination, though it has often been unimaginatively taught. My own history teacher, however, has blazed within my mind since he showed me, rather ruefully, an observation by Lord Bryce: 'A clever man may teach geometry, or natural history, or Latin, to good purpose without being proficient in these subjects. But to teach history, one must have made history a study and must know something about things which are not to be found in any schoolbook.'

I was soon reading of a seamstress employed in the Tower to stitch back the heads of executed noblemen, before burial. What was her title? Was her job hereditary, like that of the Paris executioner? Had she really existed? No text book mentioned her, but if she was only imaginary, she yet remained unforgettable.

That gracious Brussels permission to grow trees seemed telling. From 1740 to 1914, Britain had felt herself supreme, issuing her own terms to Europe, usually acquisitive, sometimes ruthless. Relegation thus holds some cyclic element of retribution, and henceforward many traditions must be discarded: they are probably complacent, anti-social, or fraudulent. History, Tolstoy claimed, would be excellent matter, if only it were true! He could have added that it had been almost wholly written by men.

But none of this is an excuse for abandoning History. In 1995, Peter Prager, a Jewish teacher, described his invitation to tell Bristol pupils of his experience of Nazi persecution. 'When I asked the children, "How many of you have heard about the persecution of the Jews?", nobody had – not even the ones who had seen *Schindler's List*. It must have gone right over their heads: they saw it as a Hollywood film.' A 1995 survey among 1,600 pupils aged 11 to 14 discovered that 39 per cent identified Churchill as a song-writer. In the same year, Nina Preston wrote to *The Times*: 'I recently mentioned Samuel Johnson to two of my granddaughters, one a Cambridge graduate, the other reading Social Anthropology at London University. In both cases the reply was "Who was he?" When I tackled their mothers, they told me that modern teaching no longer includes the eighteenth century – there's no time.' In 1996, a 15-year-old boy asked an *Independent* reporter, apropos of Schubert, 'Why would we want to learn about people who are dead?', while many RAF recruits were reported to be ignorant of the Battle of Britain. ...

English history, if still taught, could benefit from new technology – graphic images, coded visual footnotes, intricate cross-references, flashpoints of revelation, co-ordinated particles of fact, multiple and far-ranging analogies. My generation was probably fed with too many unrelated facts, too few conclusions, though for me the facts were vivid enough. What of the charge that these facts of History were simply Whiggish or elitist decoration, smothering a brutal, best-forgotten past and adding further temptation to emasculate Britain, 'heritaged' into a collection of theme parks, trapped in parochial mementos and moribund, pretentious institutions sustained by tourism and Brussels grants?

I hope to demonstrate that our past is more than an inert irrelevance or a conspiracy against civilisation, and has had some share in what Luigi Barzini has called the only art worth learning but which can never be wholly mastered, the art of inhabiting the earth. ...

The twentieth century would be convulsed in crises more dangerous to Britain than the post-Reformation conflicts, the aggressions of Spain and France, the loss of America, the equivocal returns of Empire and of victory in two world wars. With the revival of Celtic demands, Englishness itself might be revoked as mere sham, the product of propaganda, credulity, misunderstanding and brute force, English History a record of exploitation, violence, opium wars, betrayals, and unequal treaties. Deploring the Empire, Dennis Potter was roundly applauded when he asserted: 'Perhaps the noblest task of the popular historian should be to make us ashamed of our forefathers.' This does not tempt me, but I agree with Eric Hobsbawm that getting History wrong is an essential part of being a nation. This of course includes Albion, the detritus of which is now left to literature, antiquarianism, Hollywood, and commercials. However, even if most of our popular history is a self-regarding tall story, I like to think that the gist of it was worth the telling.

Peter Vansittart, *In Memory of England*, 1998.

In the same year as Vansittart's book, the journalist and TV presenter Jeremy Paxman published his book *The English*. It is, for the most part, an acerbically unflattering self-portrait of a people, but the last chapter strikes an unexpectedly confident and approving note. Like so many others, Paxman seems to find hope for England's future in an evolving continuity, deeply rooted in England's past and drawing nourishment from the best of it, and us.

William and Valerie Plowden are moving out of the house their family has occupied for the last 800 years. It is a squat, half-timbered manor house squirrelled away in the blue remembered hills of A.E. Housman's *A Shropshire Lad*. There is no sign to Plowden Hall, there are no open days, no pots of National Trust jam on sale, no teas served by sturdy ladies in tweed skirts. On the drive, immature, tailless pheasants scuffle out of the way as you pass. In the drowsy fields, sheep and cattle wander aimlessly. A gardener is clipping the edges of the lawn outside the big house. Hidden away from the rest of the world, the loudest sound is the slicing of his shears. No cars, no trains, no aircraft. ...

Plowden and his wife are moving out of the ancestral home for a farm on the estate, so that their son can move in. Assuming William Plowden lives another seven years, Plowden Hall will pass to another generation of Plowdens, free of tax. He hands on a thriving business that gives the lie to the claim that time is up for all these old families who embody a traditional idea of Englishness.

These families were the core of rural English society, unemotional, practical, professedly 'non-political' but deeply conservative, quiet, kindly, unintellectual. Ask him what he thinks of the state of England now and you get terse answers about standards slipping. ... But it is when you see his car that you realize what really bothers him. He has been down to the local printers and had his own stickers printed in Day-Glo orange. They read:

SOD THE EU – HOME RULE FOR BRITAIN

'Sooner or later,' he says, 'the Common Market is going to collapse. I don't see how you can run a country with two systems of law – our own national law and then all these laws from people in Brussels which override our laws. The sooner it ends, the better.' In the rolling hills of Shropshire, the heart of England still beats. It is driving around with a sticker in the back window telling the rest of Europe to sod off.

You can see his point. What are the badges of nationality? The English lost control of their language long ago. And if the European single currency, the Euro, is a success, the British pound, symbol of nation and empire, will be consigned to history. The question that then arises is what the English would have that they could feel was uniquely their own. In their everyday lives, the English metropolitan elite now has more in common with Parisians or New Yorkers than it does with rural or suburban England. And so many of the other outward signals of Englishness, from clothing to language, are now universal property.

Dr David Starkey once ended a lamentation bemoaning the lack of celebrations for St George's Day saying that 'England itself has ceased to be a mere country and become a place of the mind … England, indeed, has become a sort of vile antithesis of a nation; we are similar to our neighbours and differ from each other.' There will doubtless be more jeremiads in similar vein. They are of a piece with the obsession with decline that has poisoned the country's idea of itself since the war. But all nations are places of the mind: the idea of a country is what informs its laws, its politics and its art. When French politicians talk about 'La France' they do not mean what they see around them but an idea of the national destiny. What is America without the American Dream? It is true that you cannot spend fifty years listening to people anatomize your decline and not be affected by it. Yet, for all claims that the country is 'finished', the attitudes of mind that made the English culture what it is – individualism, pragmatism, love of words and, above all, that glorious, fundamental cussedness – are unchanged.

The England that the rest of the world knows is the England of the British Empire. Like a pair of newly-weds in a sabotaged car, every people sets off into the future clattering behind it the tin-cans of its history. But to most of the English, their history is just that, history. The contrast is with Scotland or Ireland, where every self-respecting adult considers themselves to belong to an unbroken tradition stretching back to the wearing of woad: oppressed peoples remember their history. One-time oppressors forget it. The English now have nothing in common with the tradition they see celebrated in the red-white-and-blue. Look at the Last Night of the Proms. How many of those joyous, nerdish faces belting out 'Land of Hope and Glory' believe a word of it? 'Wider still and wider shall thy bounds be set'? Come on.

The rebels of the 1960s will soon be grandparents, their gestures of protest quietly accommodated, their places taken by wave after wave of other anarchistic inventors. The norms of the 1940s are dead and buried and they have not been replaced by new norms. No one has seen a stiff upper lip for years. Shorn of any sense of clear national purpose, each post-war generation has turned out more self-obsessed and selfish than the last. There is no longer even any consensus on questions like dress, let alone any prescriptive rules.

Yet Starkey's complaint may actually point to a strength in the English. Might it not be that individuality, firmly rooted in a sense of individual rights, is preferable to the conformity that occurred when the great boys' schools were turning out thousands of as-near-as-possible-identical young men to run an empire that no longer exists? Once such a master-class existed, everyone else knew their place in the pecking order. The stage Englishman had his elements of nobility, but to an extent, it was built on hypocrisy. The new generation are refining their own identity, an identity based not on the past but on their own needs. In a world of accelerating communications, shrinking distances, global products and ever-larger trading blocks, the most vital sense of national identity is the individual awareness of the country of the mind.

The English are simultaneously rediscovering the past that was buried when 'Britain' was created, and inventing a new future. The red-white-and-blue is no longer relevant and they are returning to the green of England. The new nationalism is less likely to be based on flags and anthems. It is modest, individualistic, ironic, solipsistic, concerned as much with cities and regions as with counties and countries. It is based on values that are so deeply embedded in the culture as to be almost unconscious. In an age of decaying nation states it might be the nationalism of the future.

Jeremy Paxman (1950–), *The English*, 1998.

In his book *In Search of England* the polymathic historian Michael Wood sets out to nourish England's medieval roots, and salvage the living sense of national identity from its many false accretions. Fifty years after the S.S. *Empire Windrush* brought the first Caribbean immigrants (by invitation) to England, he finds that 'Englishness' – as much now as in the days of Alfred and Wulfstan – is a matter of community, of shared assumptions, and owes nothing to the false identities of 'blood' or 'race'. 'After England', as he defines it, is an organic re-invention of England – just as it always has been.

The English are having a hard time of it these days, if you believe the Press. Derided abroad either as a yob culture or a heritage theme park; at home, on the verge of divorce from their partners in the United Kingdom of Great Britain and Northern Ireland. For the English, 1997 was what the medievals would have called an *annus mirabilis*. In the year in which we celebrated the 1400th anniversary of the Roman mission to our island, the New Labour Government launched an ambitious attempt to clear away the baggage of history, to untangle the relations of the English with the Welsh, Scots and Irish, the legacies of 1922, 1707, 1603, and further back still. It has all left the English feeling understandably nervous. With European union already on the horizon, along comes the break-up of Britain.

We became Britons in the eighteenth century, recast for our new imperial role in the world, and a new history was created for us. But with the pulling down of the Union flag over Hong Kong, that history has finally been put to bed. And suddenly the eighteenth-century settlement is being questioned. Older allegiances are reasserting themselves with Scottish and Welsh devolution. With shock we begin to see that Great Britain is not a solid unchanging entity at all; indeed the Act of Union of 1707 might be a temporary blip in an older continuum. And so, just as we adjust ourselves to being part of the global culture, and prepare to be good Europeans too, we have been forced to look back into our past. For the English, this is proving a strangely painful exercise. No nation, it would appear, manages self-criticism with such intensity. (What other nation so willingly accepts, and publicly expresses, imperfection and failure as a national characteristic?) Commentators as diverse as the TV anchorman Jeremy Paxman and the novelist Julian Barnes have voiced the fear that all the English have left is a heritage industry. 'England no longer has a defining identity,' said the Northern Irish poet Tom Paulin recently on the BBC. 'It has no shape: you can't define it.'

It's an extraordinary turnabout, for England was never questioned by earlier generations. After all, when Nelson ran up his signal flags at Trafalgar, it was England, not Great Britain, which expected. Queen Victoria had to lie back and think of England (or so we were told before we discovered how much she enjoyed sex!).* And in the old song from the First World War, it was in England that the Poor Bloody Infantryman at Wipers would rather be, 'to fornicate my bleeding life away'. From Edward Thomas and Stanley Baldwin to George Orwell and even John Major, in that speech about warm beer and cricket, we all thought we knew what England was about. And now, we are told, the English find themselves to be a lump whose outline can no longer be drawn, either literally or figuratively.

Part of the problem lies, perhaps, in our habit of defining England sentimentally, by moods and images: by red pillar-boxes and cricket, by Adlestrop or Baldwin's harvest home. Such things may or may not tell us about national character, but the best England watchers have always seen something altogether different. Alexis de Tocqueville, for example, that most acute of observers, has a lot to say about the funny way the English do things, but the key to what made them tick, he thought, lay deeper than that. He thought English identity was crucially to do with our regime; essentially our non-existent Constitution. The genius of the English lay first and foremost in the way we organized ourselves. And to him it was the deep past which explained the uniqueness of England. Such ideas are unfashionable now. But I wonder? Let's go back first to a politician's speech from a thousand years ago, to a time when they had no cricket, but more than likely some kind of football, and, no doubt, alehouses and warm beer.

In 1014, Archbishop Wulfstan of York gave a 'Sermon of the Wolf to the English' (his pen name was *Lupus*, 'Wolf'). After more than twenty years of war, the land had been overrun by the Vikings. By Christmas 1013, the government had collapsed and the incompetent Ethelred the Unready had gone into exile in Normandy. Wolf was a powerful figure, a lawmaker, and his sermon appears in a manuscript in the British Library with material in his own hand (including his own corrections and changes to the text). It's a catalogue of terrible stories about the breakdown of law and order, of violence, slaving, gang rape and murder. The core message is the disintegration of group feeling: the failure of the law. For Wolf, there definitely was such a thing as society:

> The devil has led this people too far astray ... the people have betrayed their own country [literally their 'earth']. And the harm will become common to this

---

* In fact it was Lady Hillingdon (see page 374).

entire people [*eallre thyse theode*]. There was a historian in the time of the Britons called Gildas, who wrote about their misdeeds; how their sins angered God so much that finally He allowed the army of the English to conquer their land. Let us take warning from this ... we all know there are worse things going on now than we have heard of among the ancients. Let us turn to the right and leave wrongdoing ... Let us love God and follow God's laws.

What is so interesting about this speech is Wolf's stress on the state of the nation: literally, 'this people', 'this nation'. (*Theod* means 'people' or 'nation'; he also uses *theodscipe*, 'nation', and *theod scathas*, 'crimes against the public good'.) Wolf seems to accept unquestioningly that through his sermon he can address the whole nation: that the English were one people, with defined customs and laws, and that allegiance to this entity was a generally recognized fact. The problem now for him was the collapse of 'group feeling'. And if we look in Wolf's speech for keywords, as modern commentators might, for example, examine a Tony Blair speech ('new', 'challenge', 'fresh', etc.), there is one word which stands out above all others: *law*.

In modern terms, Wolf was a think-tank member. No ordinary bishop, he was responsible for key policy statements, he wrote law codes, and a manifesto of rulership, the Institutes of Polity. This sermon was preached in the darkest hour of Ethelred's England to the highest in the land. And it assumes an English state under English law.

We take the state for granted today; we grumble about it, resent its 'nannyism' or whatever. But we can't live without it. Literally – for to be stateless is just about the worst fate that can befall someone today. It wasn't always so. There were times – and not so long ago, as historians measure things – when states didn't exist; when protection by a powerful lord or kin group was the only guarantee against being enslaved, robbed or coerced. The idea of organizing human society under law to make the best use of its human and natural resources, to protect people from violence and war, to codify our obligations to one another – this is not a given in history. Most of the world's 180 states today are recent – and unstable – formations, but among the stayers there is no question that one of the oldest, most effective and indeed most successful has been England. In these last days of the British state, it is interesting to ask why.

The continuity of the English and British states is one of those great myths of England: perhaps *the* great myth, much employed by conservatives and railed against by radicals. Since the 1950s, it has been somewhat unfashionable to trace English roots very far back in time. The Tudor revolution in government tends these days to be seen as the starting-point of the modern State; the Union in 1707 the formation of British identity. The idea that certain key aspects of English culture – local organization, the law, the English state itself – were firmly in place by 1200 has not been taken seriously for quite some time now. The trend in political and historical thinking during the past thirty years has been against this idea of real continuities. Post-modernist critiques of the fantasy of the British past – in polemics like those of Tom Nairn, Patrick Wright and Anthony Barnett – and also in imaginative literature – have focused on reactionary England and the triumph of the past as heritage. There are several reasons for this. Part of it is an unwillingness to engage with what is felt to be a historical anachronism, now we know so well how much of our 'tradition' has actually been invented in modern times, since the advent of mass newspapers, radio and TV. Even the 1953 Coronation so breathlessly larded with archaisms by Richard Dimbleby, actually followed an order that had been re-created from the Anglo-Saxon coronation order only in 1901! In part, too, I suspect, there has been a natural reluctance to appear to embrace what sounds like a Victorian racialist myth in multicultural modern Britain. But recently, Old English historians have begun to reformulate the idea that many of the key elements which make up Englishness – and the English State itself – go back before 1200, or indeed before the Conquest. ...

As politicians forever remind us, political consensus resides ultimately in a shared sense of history: this is at the core of allegiance (and is why, for example, revolutions must rewrite history). Bede gave the English a history which all could share, an interpretation which made sense of their past – and their future. They had been a pagan people ('out on the edge of the world, worshipping sticks and stones' as Pope Gregory famously put it); they had been given by God a beautiful island, a land of milk and honey; the Gregorian mission had given them Roman Christian civilization. From then on they were a chosen people, for whom loyalty to God's law became a condition of survival in the future. So the English became a people of the Covenant, like the Israelites, their destiny indissolubly bound up with duty to the divine law. Allegiance to that kingship and its law therefore becomes a pre-condition of being English in later times – and in a sense still is. ...

'The Making of England' is a very old-fashioned idea these days, something that seems to belong in the books of Winston Churchill and Arthur Bryant. But it is worth a fresh look, especially now that the Scots and Welsh are poised to go their own way, and the English find themselves in need of a new history, not as Britons but as English. When was England? What was distinctive about the English? The answers are not John Major's cricket and warm beer, or Orwell's red pillar-boxes. In some sense, they are surprising answers too.

The modern English state was not created in one go. It is the product of a long – and continuing – process, but its roots lie in the Anglo-Saxon period, just as the Victorians thought. But from the beginning, it was not about race, or blood, as some Victorian racial theorists liked to say. It was rather about acceptance of common language and authority, about 'group feeling', about allegiance to the state and its way of doing things. That's the core of the English story, recalling Fernand Braudel's great passage on the identity of France:

> As if prehistory and history were not one and the same process ... which still constitutes across hundreds and hundreds of years, a living feature of the present-day world ... as if our belief and languages did not come down to us from the dark ages of the more distant past ... an obscure history, running along under the surface, refusing to die.

Is that still true? Whether such ideas are still alive now, after the dramatic changes of the last half-century, I, for one, am not sure. Old institutions have out-lasted their usefulness; Europe beckons; modern Britons must take their place in that wider society which was so courted and admired by the Old English. And global culture is now rapidly breaking down those insular characteristics which once persisted, as Braudel observed, across centuries. In the twenty-first century, surely, we will finally leave that past behind, even though its residue will still persist in our ways of speech, thinking and doing things. We will be living After England.

In conclusion, what we can say is this. The Anglo-Saxons created England; the Normans and their successors attempted to create Great Britain, not succeeding half so well, despite their long attempts to dominate the cultures and societies of Ireland, Wales and Scotland. By the late tenth century, the rulers of the English had already come to a *modus vivendi* with their Celtic neighbours: marking the limits of England almost exactly as it is today – that shape of England which Tom Paulin could not visualize. It was the Normans who tried to subdue the whole island, and their failure has finally been acknowledged in the late twentieth century. England, on the other hand, is the creation of the Old English. It is something real to go back to, unlike so many modern countries whose attempts to build such allegiances have had to be fabricated. This is not to say that it doesn't need reform now: not least the system of democracy itself – for who now would claim the English are better off than, say, the Germans? But it has a long and distinguished pedigree, which, contrary to the modern critiques, is more the product of history than myth. It goes back to Gregory the Great, Bede, and the Old English and Norman lawmakers, and for a country on a small island off the shores of Europe, its practical achievements in history have been considerable. At root was a grand idea – the sense of a chosen people – but also something very practical: a workable conception of society, of order and of mutual obligations. The latter is still in place and still working; and even the former has taken a long time to fade away.

Michael Wood, *In Search of England*, 1999.

Subject Index

Index of Authors and Famous Works

Acknowledgements

The editor and publisher gratefully acknowledge permission to reprint the following copyright material in this book:

ALLAN AHLBERG: 'Please Mrs Butler', 'The Cane' and 'There's a Fish Tank' from *Please Mrs Butler* (Kestrel Books, 1983), © Allan Ahlberg, 1983. Reprinted by permission of Penguin Books Ltd.

KINGSLEY AMIS: from 'Amis Abroad' in *The Spectator* (23 November 1963), © 1963, Kingsley Amis. Reprinted by kind permission of Jonathan Clowes Ltd., London, on behalf of the Literary Estate of Sir Kingsley Amis.

NOEL ANNAN: from *The Dons* (HarperCollins, 2000). Reprinted by permission of the publisher.

W.H. AUDEN: 'To the man-in-the street who, I'm sorry to say', from *Collected Shorter Poems 1927–1957* (Faber & Faber, 1969), © W.H. Auden, 1966; from *The Dog Beneath the Skin* (Faber & Faber, 1935). Reprinted by permission of the publisher.

STANLEY BALDWIN: from 'On England and the West of England', a speech given at the Annual Dinner of the Royal Society of St George, 6 May 1924, collected in *On England* (1926). Reprinted by permission of Earl Baldwin of Bewdley.

ERNEST BARKER: from *The Character of England* (Clarendon Press, 1947). Reprinted by permission of Oxford University Press.

HILAIRE BELLOC: 'Lord Heygate had a troubled face', 'The Justice of the Peace', 'Lord Finchley', 'The Garden Party' and 'Lines to a Don' from *Complete Verse* (Pimlico, 1991). Reprinted by permission of Peters Fraser & Dunlop Group on behalf of The Estate of Hilaire Belloc.

JOHN BETJEMAN: 'A Lincolnshire Church', from 'A Subaltern's Love-song', from 'Cricket Master', from 'Death of King George V', 'Dorset', 'How to Get On in Society', 'Hymn', from 'In a Bath Teashop', from 'In Westminster Abbey', 'Slough', from 'The Town Clerk's Views' and from 'Trebetherick' from *Collected Poems* (John Murray, 1972); from *Summoned by Bells* (John Murray, 1960). Reprinted by permission of the publisher; from BBC Home Service talk (1943) and 'Time With Betjeman' interview (1983). Reprinted by permission of BBC Rights Archive.

LAURENCE BINYON: from 'For the Fallen (September, 1914)' from *The Times* (21 September 1914). Reprinted by permission of The Society of Authors on behalf of the Laurence Binyon Estate.

EDMUND BLUNDEN: from *The Face of England* (1932), © Edmund Blunden, 1932. Reprinted by permission of Peters Fraser & Dunlop Group on behalf of the Estate of Mrs Claire Blunden.

RONALD BLYTHE: from *Akenfield* (Viking, 1969), © Ronald Blythe, 1969. Reprinted by permission of Penguin Books Ltd.

MALCOLM BROWN: from *Tommy Goes to War* (Tempus Publishing, 1999). Reprinted by permission of the author and publisher.

BILL BRYSON: from *Notes From a Small Island* (Doubleday, 1995). Reprinted by permission of Greene & Heaton Ltd and the publisher.

ANTHONY BUCKERIDGE: from *The Trouble With Jennings* (Collins, 1960). Reprinted by permission of the author.

GEOFFREY CHAUCER: from *The Canterbury Tales*, translated by Nevill Coghill (Penguin Classics, 1951, Fourth revised edition, 1977), copyright Nevill Coghill 1951, 1958, 1960, 1975, 1977. Reprinted by permission of the publisher.

G.K. CHESTERTON: 'The Englishman' and 'The Rolling English Road' from *The Flying Inn* (1914); from *The Secret People* (1915). Reprinted by permission of A.P. Watt Ltd on behalf of The Royal Literary Fund.

WINSTON CHURCHILL: from *A History of the English-Speaking Peoples* (1911), *My Early Life* (1930), *The Grand Alliance* (1950) and *Their Finest Hour* (1949); from 'Don't talk to me about naval tradition', 'We must just Keep Buggering On', speech (1921), speech to the Canadian Parliament, 30 December 1941, and speech on his 80th birthday, 1954. Reprinted by permission of Curtis Brown Ltd on behalf of the Estate of Winston S. Churchill.

ALEX COMFORT: 'Letter to an American Visitor' from *Tribune* (4 June 1943). Reprinted by permission of Nicholas Comfort.

WENDY COPE: 'After the Lunch' and 'English Weather' from *Serious Concerns* (Faber & Faber, 1992). Reprinted by permission of the publisher.

NOËL COWARD: from 'The Stately Homes of England' in *Operette* (1938). Reprinted by permission of Methuen Publishing Ltd.

JULIAN CRITCHLEY: from *A Bag of Boiled Sweets: An Autobiography* (Faber & Faber, 1995). Reprinted by permission of the publisher.

ROALD DAHL: from *Fantastic Mr Fox* (George Allen & Unwin, 1970). Reprinted by permission of David Higham Associates.

W.H. DAVIES: 'Her Merriment' from *The Complete Poems of W.H. Davies* (Jonathan Cape, 1963). Reprinted by permission of Dee & Griffin (Solicitors) on behalf of Mrs H.M. Davies Will Trust.

W.F. DEEDES: 'Memories of a beer hunter' from *The Spectator* (11 November 2000). Reprinted by permission of the author and publisher.

FRANK DiGIACOMO: from an article on the 'Weakest Link' in *The New York Observer* (23 April 2001), © Frank DiGiacomo, 2001. Reprinted by permission of Intrernational Creative Management Inc.

IAN DURY (with STEPHEN NUGENT and CHAZ JANKEL): 'Billericay Dickie' and 'England's Glory' from *New Boots and Panties* (1977). Reprinted by permission of International Music Publications.

T.S. ELIOT: from 'The Love Song of J. Alfred Prufrock', 'Little Gidding V' and 'The Dry Salvages'

in *Collected Poems 1909–1962* (Faber & Faber, 1963). Reprinted by permission of the publisher.

MATTHEW ENGEL: from *Wisden* (2000). Reprinted by permission of the publisher.

GAVIN EWART: 'Not Quite Cricket?' from *Summer Days: Writers on Cricket* (Oxford University Press, 1983). Reprinted by permission of Margo Ewart.

OLIVIA FITZROY: 'Fleet Fighter' from *The Voice of War: Poems of the Second World War. The Oasis Collection* (Michael Joseph, 1995). Reprinted by permission of The Salamander Oasis Trust and Rt. Hon. A. Jessel.

E.M. FORSTER: from *Selected Letters of E.M. Forster: Volume 1: 1879–1920* and *Abinger Harvest* (Edward Arnold, 1936). Reprinted by permission of The Provost and Scholars of King's College, Cambridge and The Society of Authors as the Literary Representatives of the Estate of E.M. Forster.

H.W. FOWLER: from *Modern English Usage* (Oxford University Press, 1965), © Oxford University Press, 1965. Reprinted by permission of the publisher.

STEPHEN FRY: from *Moab is My Washpot* (Hutchinson, 1997). Reprinted by permission of David Higham Associates.

STELLA GIBBONS: from *Cold Comfort Farm* (Oxford University Press, 1932). Reprinted by permission of Curtis Brown Ltd., London.

KENNETH GRAHAME: from *The Wind in the Willows* (Methuen, 1908). Reprinted by permission of Curtis Brown Ltd., London.

ROBERT GRAVES: '1805' from *Robert Graves: Poems Selected by Himself* (The Penguin Poets, 1961),

© Robert Graves 1961. Reprinted by permission of Carcanet Press.

JONATHON GREEN: from *Them: Voices from the Immigrant Community in Contemporary Britain* (Secker & Warburg, 1990). Reprinted by permission of the author.

JOYCE GRENFELL: from *George, Don't Do That* (Macmillan, 1977), © Joyce Grenfell 1977. Reprinted by permission of Sheil Land Associates Ltd.

BARRY HINES: from *A Kestrel for a Knave* (Michael Joseph, 1968), © Barry Hines, 1968. Reprinted by permission of Penguin Books Ltd.

SASKIA HOPE: from *No Lady* (Black Lace, 1993). Reprinted by permission of Virgin Publishing.

A.E. HOUSMAN: XL. 'Into my heart an air that kills' and from LXII 'Terence, this is stupid stuff' from *Collected Poems and Selected Prose* (Penguin Twentieth-Century Classics, 1989). Reprinted by permission of The Society of Authors as the Literary Representative of the Estate of A.E. Housman.

MARY KILLEN: from 'Dear Mary…' in *The Spectator* (3 March 2001). Reprinted by permission of the author.

RUDYARD KIPLING: 'Puck's Song'; from 'Fuzzy-Wuzzy', 'Norman and Saxon (A.D. 1100)', 'The Reeds of Runnymede (Magna Charta, June 15, 1215)' and 'Tommy' in *Rudyard Kipling: The Complete Verse* (Kyle Cathie, 1996). Reprinted by permission of A.P. Watt Ltd on behalf of The National Trust for Places of Historical Interest or Natural Beauty.

OSBERT LANCASTER: from *All Done from Memory* (John Murray, 1953). Reprinted by permission of the publisher.

PHILIP LARKIN: 'An Arundel Tomb', 'Annus Mirabilis', 'Church Going', 'Going, Going', from 'A Stone Church Damaged by a Bomb', and from 'The Whitsun Weddings' in *Collected Poems*, edited by Anthony Thwaite (Faber & Faber, 1988), © the Estate of Philip Larkin, 1988; from *Selected Letters of Philip Larkin 1940–1985*, edited by Anthony Thwaite (Faber & Faber, 1992), © the Estate of Philip Larkin. Reprinted by permission of the publisher.

JOHN LATHAM: 'All Clear' from *All Clear* (Peterloo Poets, 1990), © John Latham, 1990. Reprinted by permission of the author.

LAURIE LEE: from *Cider With Rosie* (Hogarth Press, 1959). Reprinted by permission of The Random House Group Ltd.

BERNARD LEVIN: from *Enthusiasms* (1980), *The Pendulum Years* (1970) and *The Times* (1983). Reprinted by permission of the author.

DAVID LODGE: from *Changing Places* (Secker & Warburg, 1975) and *How Far Can You Go?* (Secker & Warburg, 1980). Reprinted by permission of The Random House group Ltd.

E.V. LUCAS: from *Only the Other Day* (Methuen, 1936). Reprinted by permission of the publisher.

LOUIS MACNEICE: from 'Autumn Journal' and 'Bagpipe Music' from *Collected Poems* (Faber & Faber, 1979), © The Estate of Louis MacNeice 1966 and 1979. Reprinted by permission of David Higham Associates.

ROBERT McCRUM et.al.: from *The Story of English* (Faber & Faber, 1986). Reprinted by permission of the publisher.

DENNIS McHARRIE: 'Luck' from *The Voice of War: Poems of the Second World War. The Oasis Collection* (Michael Joseph, 1995).

Reprinted by permission of The Salamander Oasis Trust and Wing Commander Dennis McHarrie, OBE.

PIERRE MAILLAUD: from *The English Way* (Oxford University Press, 1945). Reprinted by permission of the publisher.

JAN MARK: from *Thunder and Lightnings* (Kestrel, 1976), © Jan Mark, 1976. Reprinted by permission of Penguin Books Ltd.

A.A. MILNE: from *The House at Pooh Corner* (Methuen, 1928). Reprinted by permission of Egmont Children's Books.

NANCY MITFORD: from *The Pursuit of Love* (Hamish Hamilton, 1945). Reprinted by permission of Peters Fraser & Dunlop Group on behalf of The Estate of Nancy Mitford.

JOHN MOORE: from *Brensham Village* (Collins, 1946). Reprinted by permission of Peters Fraser & Dunlop Group on behalf of The Estate of John Moore.

JAN MORRIS: from *Oxford* (Oxford University Press, 1978). Reprinted by permission of the author.

JOHN MORTIMER: from *Clinging to the Wreckage* (Weidenfeld & Nicolson, 1982), © Advanpress Ltd 1982, and *Paradise Postponed* (Penguin, 1986), © Advanpress Ltd 1985. Reprinted by permission of Peters Fraser & Dunlop Group Ltd on behalf of Advanpress Ltd for the services of Sir John Mortimer.

A.N.L. MUNBY: 'Thoughts on rereading Belloc's famous lines on Dons' from *Camford Observed* by John Ziman and Jasper Rose (1964). Reprinted by permission of The Estate of A.N.L. Munby.

BILL MURPHY: from *Home Truths* (Mainstream Publishing, 2000). Reprinted by permission of the publisher.

GEORGE ORWELL: from *Collected Essays, Journalism and Letters* (1949), *Coming Up For Air* (1939), *Keep the Aspidistra Flying* (1936), *The English People* (1944), *The Lion and the Unicorn* (1940), *The Road to Wigan Pier* (1940); from 'As I Please', *Tribune* (4 February 1944; 14 April 1944; 7 July 1944), 'As One Non-Combatant to Another', *Tribune* (1943), 'Freedom of the Park', *Tribune* (1945), 'Such, Such Were the Joys' (1947); from 'A Nice Cup of Tea' (January 1946), 'Boys' Weeklies' (March 1940), 'Charles Dickens' (1939), 'Diary' (28 July 1942), 'My Country Right or Left' (1940), 'Raffles and Miss Blandish' (October 1944), 'Reviews of Churchill book' (May 1949). Reprinted by permission of A.M. Heath & Co Ltd on behalf of Bill Hamilton as the Literary Executor of the Estate of the late Sonia Brownell Orwell and Martin Secker & Warburg Ltd.

JOHN OSBORNE: from *A Better Class of Person* (Faber & Faber, 1981) and 'Damn You England' from *Tribune* (18 August 1961). Reprinted by permission of Faber & Faber Ltd.

ROSS PARKER and HUGH CHARLES: from 'There's Always Be An England' (1939). Reprinted by permission of Music Sales Ltd.

JEREMY PAXMAN: from *The English* (Michael Joseph, 2000). Reprinted by permission of David Higham Associates.

PRIVATE EYE: 'Product Recall. Britain' (22 March 2001), 'St Cake's School' (1 May 1987) and 'The Alternative Rocky Horror Service Book' (12 August 1994). Reprinted by permission of the publisher.

HENRY REED: 'Naming of Parts' from *Collected Poems*, edited by Jon Stallworthy (Oxford University Press, 1991). Reprinted by permission of the publisher.

JACK ROSENTHAL: from *The Knowledge* (Euston Films/Thames

Television, 1979). Reprinted by permission of Faber & Faber Ltd.

SIEGFRIED SASSOON: 'A Fallodon Memory', 'Glory of Women', 'The General', from 'The Old Huntsman' and 'To Any Dead Officer' from *Collected Poems 1908–1956* (Faber & Faber, 1984). Reprinted by permission of Barbara Levy Literary Agency.

W.C. SELLAR and R.J. YEATMAN: from *Garden Rubbish* (Methuen, 1936) and *1066 And All That* (Methuen, 1930). Reprinted by permission of the publisher.

GEORGE BERNARD SHAW: from *Heartbreak House* (1919), *Parents and Children* (1914) and *Pygmalion* (1916). Reprinted by permission of The Society of Authors on behalf of the Bernard Shaw Estate.

EDITH SITWELL: from 'Still Falls the Rain' in *Edith Sitwell: Selected Poems* (Penguin Poets, 1952). Reprinted by permission of David Higham Associates.

OSBERT SITWELL: 'Old Fashioned Sportsmen' from *Selected Poems, Old and New* (Gerald Duckworth, 1943). Reprinted by permission of David Higham Associates.

GODFREY SMITH: from *The English Companion* (Old House Books, 1996). Reprinted by permission of the author.

STEVIE SMITH: 'Why are the Clergy...? from *The Collected Poems of Stevie Smith* (Penguin Modern Classics, 1985). Reprinted by permission of the Estate of James MacGibbon.

STEPHEN SPENDER: 'Day Boy', quoted in *The Old School*, edited by Graham Greene (Oxford University Press, 1984). Reprinted by permission of Peters Fraser & Dunlop Group on behalf of the Estate of Stephen Spender.

JEREMY TAYLOR: 'All Along the Coast' from *Ag Pleeze Deddy!* (Jeremy Taylor Publishing, 1992). Reprinted by permission of the author. From 'Jobsworth', written and composed by Jeremy Taylor, © 1974 Peermusic (UK) Ltd, London, WC1. Reprinted by permission of the author and music publisher.

TELEGRAPH GROUP LTD: from Linus Gregordiadis and Sam O'Neill, on Oxford dons, *The Daily Telegraph* (15 January 2001), Michael Henderson, on cricket, *The Daily Telegraph* (11 September 2000), Philip Johnson, on the National Census, *The Daily Telegraph* (23 April 2001) and Sam O'Neill, 'Cheddar Man is my long-lost relative', *The Daily Telegraph* (8 March 1997); from *The Daily Telegraph Book of Obituaries: Eccentric Lives*, edited by Hugh Massingberd (1995). Reprinted by permission of the publisher.

FLORA THOMPSON: from *Lark Rise to Candleford* (Oxford University Press, 1945). Reprinted by permission of the publisher.

J.R.R. TOLKEIN: from *The Lord of the Rings. Part III* (George Allen & Unwin, 1955). Reprinted by permission of HarperCollins Publishers.

PETER VANSITTART: words from *In Memory of England: A Novelist's View of History* (John Murray, 1998). Reprinted by permission of the publisher.

AUBERON WAUGH: on 'National Service' from *New Statesman* (27 September 1974). Reprinted by permission of Peters Fraser & Dunlop Group on behalf of the Estate of Auberon Waugh.

EVELYN WAUGH: from *A Little Learning* (1964) and *Decline and Fall* (1928); from 'Diary' (1925), *Noblesse Oblige*, edited by Nancy Mitford (1956), 'Oxford Union debate' (*c.*1923) and *Paris Review* (1963), © The Estate of Laura Waugh.

Reprinted by permission of Peters Fraser & Dunlop group on behalf of the Estate of Laura Waugh.

P.G. WODEHOUSE: from 'Lord Emsworth and the Girl Friend' in *Blandings Castle and Elsewhere* (Hutchinson,1935). Reprinted by permission of The Random House Group Ltd.

MICHAEL WOOD: from *In Search of England* (Viking, 1999), © Michael Wood, 1999. Reprinted by permission of Penguin Books Ltd.

JOAN WYNDHAM: from *Love Lessons: A Wartime Diary* (Mandarin, 1995). Reprinted by permission of Little, Brown & Company and Peters Fraser & Dunlop Group on behalf of the author.

Every effort has been made to secure permission prior to publication. If notified, the publisher will be pleased to rectify any omissions at the earliest opportunity.

First published in the United Kingdom
in 2001 by Cassell & Co.

The acknowledgements on pages 528–31
constitute an extension to this copyright page.

Distributed in the United States of America by
Sterling Publishing Co., Inc.
387 Park Avenue South
New York
NY 10016–8810

A CIP catalogue record for this book is
available from the British Library

ISBN 0-304-35527-5

Designer Harry Green
Editor Ian Crofton
Indexer Hilary Bird

Printed and bound in Finland
by W.S. Bookwell

Cassell & Co.
Orion House
5 Upper Saint Martin's Lane
London
WC2H 9EA